LOUISIANA
The Land and Its People

State bird: brown pelican

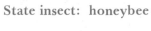

State insect: honeybee

State dog: Louisiana Catahoula
Leopard dog

State tree: bald cypress

State flag

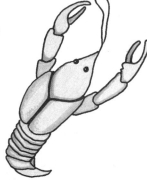

State crustacean: crawfish

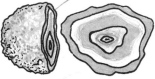

State gemstone: agate

State flower: magnolia

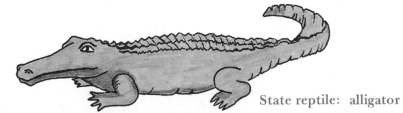

State reptile: alligator

LOUISIANA
The Land and Its People

Dr. Sue Eakin

Department of History
Louisiana State University at Alexandria

Manie Culbertson

Retired Junior High School Teacher
Louisiana Public Schools

Illustrations by James Forrest Culbertson

PELICAN PUBLISHING COMPANY
Gretna 1988

ISBN: 0-88289-486-2

First edition, January 1986
Second edition, First printing, July 1986
Second edition, Second printing, January 1987
Second edition, Third printing, October 1988

Manufactured in the United States of America

Published by Pelican Publishing Company, Inc.
1101 Monroe Street, Gretna, Louisiana 70053

TABLE OF CONTENTS

MESSAGE
TO YOUNG LOUISIANIANS

How much do you know about the state in which you live? Many of you have lived here all of your lives, and you have probably taken your surroundings for granted. This year you will have the opportunity to learn more about this wonderful state and your Louisiana heritage. This may be the only time that you will study your state.

What do you picture when you hear the name "Louisiana"? Do you think about the beautiful waterways, or the moss-covered trees, or the great fishing and hunting, or the cotton and sugarcane fields, or the first French settlement, or the exciting sports events? You may not picture any of these things. Since different people may view the same environment in different ways, it is unlikely that your picture is exactly like anyone else's.

There are some people who study Louisiana to get a particular picture from one viewpoint. These people are distinguished by different names according to the work they do. They are anthropologists, economists, geographers, historians, political scientists, and sociologists. All of them are social scientists.

It is difficult to say where one social science ends and another begins. There is much overlapping. Social scientists also use the work of people from many other fields, such as photographers, physicists, biologists, engineers, architects, climatologists, and aviators. The work of all these people is combined to give us a total picture of Louisiana.

Social scientists get their information from many sources: books; maps; articles in professional journals, magazines, or newspapers; local governmental offices; television; radio; photographs; minutes of meetings of clubs and organizations; official and personal archives; record books and scrapbooks; diaries; cemeteries; courthouse records; museums; interviews with knowledgeable persons; historical markers; almanacs; brochures; genealogical material; artifacts; and natural and man-made structures.

There are two basic sources of information from which to learn the Louisiana story. These are **primary**, or firsthand, **sources**, and **secondary**, or secondhand, **sources**. Primary sources are original works. Letters, diaries, autobiographies, and documents of a person give us a picture of what the person was like. Other examples of primary sources are historical documents and eyewitness accounts of events. We also learn from such secondary sources as a book about Huey Long by T. Harry Williams. We view secondary materials through the eyes of the author instead of having the opportunity to interpret them ourselves.

Many words are associated with Louisiana. In this book some of these terms have been used with a slightly different meaning. **Gumbo** and **jambalaya** are two of Louisiana's famous foods. Both dishes are mixtures of a variety of ingredients. **Potpourri** originally referred to a stew, but now it is the name given to a miscellaneous mixture. These terms are used in the text to cover a variety of study activities. Jambalaya activities put the facts of the chapter together. You get involved in further study with potpourri activities. Gumbo activities bring the chapter study up-to-date. **Coup d'main** is a term used to describe the custom of neighbors getting together to build a house, to shear sheep, or to do other work. This term describes the study of the entire chapter by the whole class. **En partie**, meaning "partly" in French, is used for the study of part of the chapter. **Lagniappe** means something extra. Old-time Louisiana merchants gave small gifts to their best customers. Throughout this book, many extras have been added for you.

Your study of Louisiana will include a discussion of many of the questions that troubled Louisiana's citizens during its years of growth. Some of the questions are not fully answered. Other questions that must be solved if Louisiana is to continue to move forward now face the state. Finding a solution to such problems may be in your future. Those who built and preserved this state have left it for you. In a few short years you will take your place making decisions for the welfare of Louisiana. Learning the Louisiana story is your first step in preparing to take this responsibility.

LOUISIANA
The Land and Its People

PART ONE

In the Beginning

Historic New Orleans Collection

CHAPTER 1

THE GEOGRAPHIC SETTING

You are about to enjoy the unique story of this land of Louisiana and its people. Probably no other state's history has been shaped by its geography more than that of Louisiana. Its location at the mouth of the greatest river in North America, the Mississippi, set Louisiana apart from the beginning. None of the other states has the meeting of rivers, marshes, and swamps with gulf waters and barrier islands. Louisiana has the combination of the Father of Waters, bountiful forests and wildlife, rich soils with many minerals, an abundance of water flowing through countless streams, a relatively mild climate with long growing seasons, and flowers in unbelievable varieties. All that makes a setting for a good life can be found in this land.

The Land

The first settlers who came here in 1699 had to plan their lifestyle around this special site they found at the mouth of the Mississippi. Imagine what it was like when they arrived in the New World. Let's remove all the man-made structures from our state, and try to picture this land through the eyes of the first people who saw it.

It had taken over two months for the first Europeans to cross the Atlantic Ocean. They welcomed the sight of land. The first who saw the land near the Gulf of Mexico looked at the low marshland. It was an unusual sight. Marshgrass was shoulder-high. Cane grew ten feet tall. Armies of mosquitoes buzzed overhead. Long-legged egrets pecked for food at the water's edge. Birds dipped down to catch small fish. Bullfrogs bellowed all night. Bees were apt to be in every thicket.

The newcomers found that it was almost impossible to walk in the **marshes**. Imagine their surprise to find part land and part water. The watery mud stuck to their feet. In some places they found quaking, or floating, marsh that shook when they walked on it. There were places where grass and other plants grew on soft peat or extended out onto the water. The Frenchmen must have cursed the **floating land**. Even where the footing was good enough, it was extremely difficult for them to walk through the swampgrass. They knew that the marshlands would not be a good place for their homes.

The Frenchmen found a baffling maze of **inlets, bays,** and **swamps**. The newcomers had to be careful where they walked. The marshes were filled with waterways. Muskrat holes were everywhere. Snakes slithered through the grass and across the water. Alligators could be mistaken for floating logs. Logs were sometimes mistaken for alligators. Turtles sunned on many of the logs.

When the newcomers tried to drink the water, they found that it did not taste good. This brackish water at the coast was a saltwater and freshwater mix. There were really three kinds of water in the area—**saltwater, freshwater,** and **brackish water**. The change from saltwater to freshwater was very gradual.

When they neared the southwest-

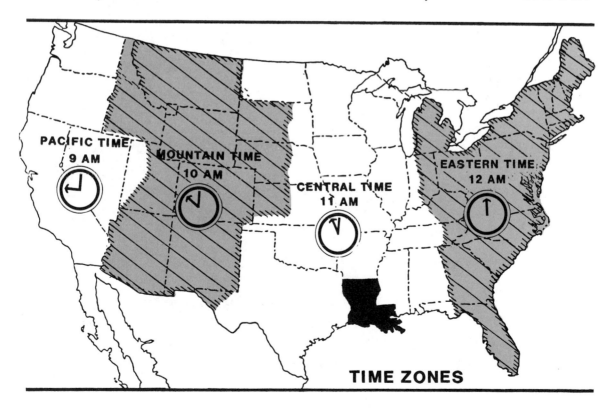

TIME ZONES

ern corner of what is now Louisiana, they saw twisted oak trees on the barrier beaches. The action of the water had built up ridges of land a little higher than the surface of the marshes. They were only a few feet above the land surface around them, but oak trees took root and grew there. The growth of the oak trees had been shaped by the force of the Gulf winds. These small ridges were called **cheniers** by the French. This is the French word for "place of oaks." The cheniers are really old beaches of the Gulf of Mexico. They show where the Gulf extended at one time.

In southwestern Louisiana they saw five distinct surface mounds. These "land islands" are really mounds above underground pillars of salt. The **Five Islands** are now called Jefferson Island, Avery Island, Weeks Island, Cote Blanche, and Belle Isle.

The opinion of the group of settlers at this point could have been the same as that of one early French explorer. He described this land as "an impossible place, fit only for the

Louisiana, the boot-shaped state, is part of the Deep South.

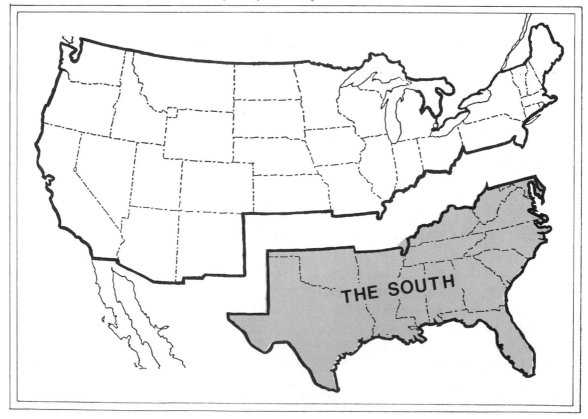

THE SOUTH

jungle savage and the prehistoric crocodile."

As they moved to the southeast, the newcomers saw the great Mississippi River. Brown pelicans were nesting on the mudlumps at the mouth. The settlers could see the soil change from Gulf marshland to higher and richer river land as they sailed up the river.

Upstream, along the **Mississippi River** and its tributaries, they found that the soil was very rich. They did not know that it is some of the richest soil in the world. The **alluvial soil** they found was transported. It had been brought from many places by the river. These first settlers must have been awed at the magnificence of it. They soon learned how fast and fine the crops grew in the soils near the Mississippi and other rivers and streams. Those who came to the Red River found a **reddish-brown soil** that was equally rich. In every direction they looked they saw evidence of luxuriant plant life. This land would grow anything! Or so they thought.

These first inhabitants sought out the **natural levees** or **frontlands** along the streams and rivers. This was choice land. During a flood these strips of land usually remained out of the water. This land stayed drier than the surrounding area. These were good places for their homes.

In some places natural levees along the Mississippi were three miles wide.

Along a small stream the levees were only a few feet wide and only a few inches high. This land was built up by the deposits of sand and silt left by the overflow of the streams. The land nearest the streams was easier to cultivate than that farther away because of these deposits of **sediment**.

Most land grants allowed each settler a portion of the frontlands near the rivers or streams. From this frontland his fields reached back to include the **backlands** all the way to the edge of the swampland where water stood all year. The backlands built up very slowly of fine clays. The land more than three miles from the stream was the lowest.

Lucky settlers found some of the old natural levees that were left when rivers changed their channels. About two thousand years ago, the Mississippi River ran along the western side of its present valley in the southern part of the state. Large natural levees were built along the old channel. Some of the best farmlands in the state are located on these old Mississippi natural levees along Bayou Teche.

The natural levees of the Red River were prized by the settlers. The Red River built its levees very high and very fast. The river brought sand and red silt in large quantities from Texas and Oklahoma. These deposits formed the river's levees.

Standing on the natural levees,

people looked out over the **flood-plains**. The early settlers knew what it meant to be in the floodplains. This area was subject to **flooding**. The floodplain of the Mississippi River is over fifty miles wide in places. Twenty-five miles is its minimum width in Louisiana. The floodplains were not places to build houses except on high spots provided, usually, by natural levees.

Adjacent to the floodplains in some places they found higher land known as **terraces** and **blufflands**. These places, now too high to be flooded, were, long ago, floodplains that had been lifted by forces inside the earth. In North Louisiana they were lifted much higher than in South Louisiana. The higher places along the coast are only a little higher than the floodplains. Those higher flat places that lay near navigable streams were good sites for farms or houses.

As the French visitors left the Mississippi and explored this land, they found **sandy clay hills** covered with trees. Both east and west of the river there were hills. They found that the farther north they went, the higher the land became. The highest point of land they found was **Driskill Mountain** in Bienville Parish. It is really not a mountain. It is only a hill. It reaches 535 feet above sea level. The hills in the north central, west central, and southeastern sections would not produce good crops,

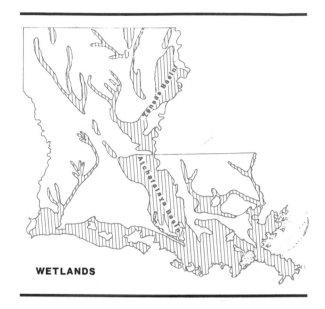

WETLANDS

although such soils were easy to plow. The soil was thin and covered with pines.

Many small streams carved valleys among the rolling hills. Some of these valleys were deep and wide. Smaller valleys met the main valleys. The Red River Valley was wide and deep. The Ouachita, Pearl, Tangipahoa, and Amite rivers also had big valleys. On the east side of the Mississippi, Thompson Creek had a deep valley. There were the valleys of Little and Boeuf rivers; and those of the Calcasieu, Sabine, and the twisting Dugedomona. There were others. The settlers cherished the valleys most of all. They usually contained the rich soils that would help them survive.

When these curious people left the hills, they saw great stretches of flatlands. They must have been utterly amazed at the flatness of this land. In years to come it would be discovered that Louisiana is one of the flattest states in the nation. Farther to the west of the river, farther than the settlers went at first to lay out farms and build houses, were stretches of flat grasslands, or **prairies**. The slightly higher land, flat-topped masses of soil set in low country, appeared like giant tables. Louisiana's lowlands flooded often but not these prairies.

The settlers roamed all over the area looking for better land. They knew that the richness, or **fertility**, of the soil varied greatly. Some soil produced much better crops than other soils. They had been very discouraged when the soil on the coast would not produce good crops.

Strange as it may sound, Louisiana is very young in measurements of **geological age**. The formation of Louisiana took millions and millions of years, but it is young in comparison to some other states. Not many of the state's deposits are more than one hundred million years old. Our land and landforms are comparatively new. Much of the state was built during the Cenozoic era. This is the youngest and shortest period of the geological time scale. The earliest geological deposits are deeply covered. Deposits down to great depths are of very recent geological age. There have been many changes in our land during these years.

Two opposing actions are responsible for forming this Louisiana land. These are the **sinking of the land** in the southern part of the state and the **rising of the land** in North Louisiana. North Louisiana moves up a little each century. This uplifting of the northern part of the state and sinking near the Gulf in South Louisiana go on very, very slowly all of the time. The movement is so slow that no one can feel or see it without special instruments.

During the past few years, Louisiana has been decreasing very slightly in size every year. Delta land is being eaten away by the Gulf. Islands are getting smaller, being eaten away by the waters. Most of Louisiana's shoreline is suffering this loss. We say the shoreline is retreating, or receding. Over the long term however, the Mississippi, Ouachita, and Red rivers are building Louisiana with layer upon layer of deposits. This action takes place primarily in the floodplains, marshes, and shallow Gulf. Many acres of new delta, marshes, and wetlands are being built every year in the Atchafalaya Bay.

The earlier settlers were only dimly aware of the geological action that never stops. The building of our state is going on and on, even under the waters of the Gulf of Mexico. The state does not stop at the water's edge but extends out to include some of the **continental shelf**. Great layers of rock particles as well as the remains of many plants and animals collect on this shelf. When waves move across it, they shuffle the deposits back and forth. This sweeping action keeps the bottom of the shelf fairly flat. The waves pick up rock particles from the bottom, especially during storms, and carry them along in the moving water. Many of these particles reach the shore to be added to the beach.

Louisiana was built by one layer of sediment forming on top of another. Naturally, the oldest layer lies on the bottom. The youngest layer lies on top. These layers have been added in several ways. Much of the state was built by streams and the ocean and is still being built by them. Streams continually leave deposits of sand, silt, and clay. Every flood adds new land to the state. After floodwaters drain off, particles of rock are left on the ground. Each time this happens, the ground rises a little higher. Storms whip debris through the air. This settles on the land. Other substances such as oyster shells, clams, and snails; the bones or teeth of animals; and the roots of trees or other plants all become part of Louisiana land.

Soil is made of sediment near the surface of the earth. Different kinds of rock layers make different kinds of soil. The rock is changed into soil by the action of wind, rain, and sunshine. This action, called **weathering**, continues during warm weather.

From the time the first European explorers came to Louisiana, they tried to describe its physical features. The early European settlers also wrote descriptions of the streams, the hills, and other features.

In 1869 **Samuel Lockett** wrote a description of Louisiana. The state was still very much like the first settlers had found it. Man had not changed it a great deal then. Lockett was hired by the legislature to make a topographical study. He surveyed the state. Lockett traveled by horseback or buggy to accomplish this task. He walked many miles studying the state's natural features. He carefully examined details of the physical features of the state. He measured distances. He identified trees and described the streams. He studied the soils. Lockett decided that the state could be divided into **natural regions**. His, like all natural regions, are cultural. In other words, they rely on a beginning idea. In Lockett's case, the beginning idea was the usefulness of each area to new settlers who might choose Louisiana as their new home. Later scholars have not been able to improve greatly on Lockett's divisions. Therefore, with little change, Lockett's divisions are in use today.

Historic New Orleans Collection

Louisiana probably looked like this when the first settlers saw it.

The Waterways

The early settlers of Louisiana saw the great Mississippi River dominating the land. They knew that it was the most important single feature of the landscape. They did not know that it is one of the largest drainage systems in North America. The Mississippi formed a great north-south highway for travelers as far away as Canada. The tremendous power of the "Big River" was felt by the Indians. They called it the Father of Waters. The Algonquin Indians named it "miss" for "big" and "sipi" for "water."

At the mouth the river waters spread out toward the Gulf of Mexico through three narrow channels. These passes form a pattern that resembles the outspread foot of a bird. Over the years geologists have called it a **bird-foot delta.** It is unlike any other in the world.

The settlers did not know how much the Mississippi had done in building this land. The Mississippi had made Louisiana rich by creating new land out of sediment. The lands near the Mississippi River are rich with mud, silt, clay, and sand deposited by overflowing waters. Huge amounts of sediment are dumped into the Gulf every day. It is estimated that this sediment would fill a freight train 150 miles long. About two million tons of sediment are deposited by the Mississippi each day. Every year 350 million cubic yards of sediment are carried into the delta.

The "Big River" appeared more than a million years ago. However, the first settlers probably did not think about that. The river is very young. The present course of the Mississippi River appeared between one thousand and five hundred years ago.

In its rush to the sea, the Mississippi has not always remained in one channel. In fact, the river has changed channels many times. You can tell where these old river channels lay. Louisiana maps show old Mississippi River channels through the state that are shaped like snakes. They writhe, twist, and form bends where the river once flowed. Even today the river is constantly at work trying to redirect its path. Other examples of rivers doing the same thing are the Teche, Tensas, and Black.

As the river changed its course, it left Louisiana veined with **bayous** and **lakes**. Sometimes the Mississippi formed great loops around parts of the land. In time some of these loops became cut off from the rest of the river. Not too long ago the length of the river was reduced by about fifty

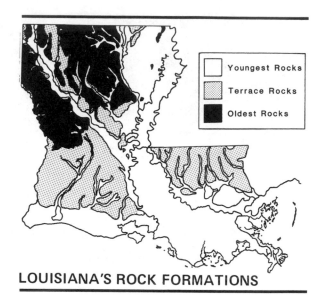

	Youngest Rocks
	Terrace Rocks
	Oldest Rocks

LOUISIANA'S ROCK FORMATIONS

miles each time it straightened its course by cutting across a big bend, leaving a loop of water to become a cutoff lake.

Early settlers could hardly believe what they saw in the Red River when they sighted the **Great Raft**. Indians explained to the early explorers and settlers that the raft had always been there. They said that even the oldest Indians had never seen the Red River clear of this giant logjam. During the floods water poured into the clogged channel. The channel became completely filled. Therefore, the floodwater poured out over the land on both sides. Water filled low places. When the flood was over, the water remained. These areas became raft lakes. They were formed because of the raft in the riverbed.

Like the Mississippi River, the Gulf of Mexico has changed its points of contact with the shore. Back and forth, the Gulf waters have chewed away at our shores and then built up deposits. Sometimes the water has overrun the land. Then, when it fell back to its own seabed, some of the water stayed in low spots. These formed lagoonal and deltaic lakes.

The waterways held a very important place for these first settlers. They were the settlers' highways. Louisiana's many other water resources were extremely important, too. It did not take the newcomers long to learn that there was ample rainfall for agricultural production. Countless springs in the hills provided cool drinking water. They could always find a good water supply for their homes.

The land and water in Louisiana have been measured. There are 48,114 square miles in the area of the state. Of this, 3,593 square miles are water. Louisiana has more water surface than any other state. Louisiana has approximately 8,000 miles of waterways. According to available sources, one-fourth of all the **wetlands** of the United States are in Louisiana. The state has about forty percent of all the coastal wetlands of the United

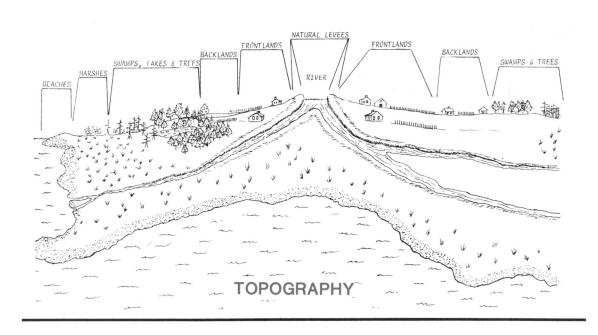

TOPOGRAPHY

States. The daily flow of the state's rivers is over 450 billion gallons. The state's water resources are more abundant than in most other states.

The early settlers were not aware of some of the problems they would encounter in their new location. The state has the lowest potential **waterpower** of any of the states. Waterpower was needed to turn the wheels of early grist mills and, later, for cotton gins and sawmills. Waterpower requires flow from heights not present in Louisiana. It was necessary to dam streams to provide enough water force to turn the wheels.

En Partie 2 (Studying a Part). 1. Why did the early settlers live along waterways? 2. What makes this state water-rich? 3. Name some of the kinds of lakes in the state. 4. What are the state's main rivers? 5. What is the birdfoot delta?

The Forests

Vast virgin forests existed when the early settlers came from France. The forests had rich resources beyond anything they had dreamed. When these people came to Louisiana, the forests covered eighty-five percent of the land. If they had measured, they would have found that almost twenty-six million of the thirty-one million acres in this land were covered with trees. These newcomers found almost 150 species of native trees. From **hardwoods**, like oaks, to the **softwoods**, like pine, the settler had his choice.

These almost endless trees presented both a burden and a bounty. The pioneers were confronted with the immediate need for houses and food. They had to grow much of their food. The land had to be cleared for planting, and lumber had to be made for building. With their crude tools, the settlers had to meet the challenge.

The forests yielded lumber for every possible need. Tall pine trees seemed to reach the sky. The hills were covered with these pines. Loblolly pines were felled for making lumber and other wood products. The trees included cypress, which the new settlers put to use in their first homes. Cypress grew in the deep swamps. The cypress tree could be identified by its feathery green leaves. The settlers probably marveled at the way the cypress flares at its base. Its many strange knees, or roots, come out of the water for air.

The riches of available lumber must have made their eyes open wide in wonder. Here was wealth. They hoped to make tar, pitch, and other products from the forests. They believed that they could sell the huge timbers to the motherland for use in

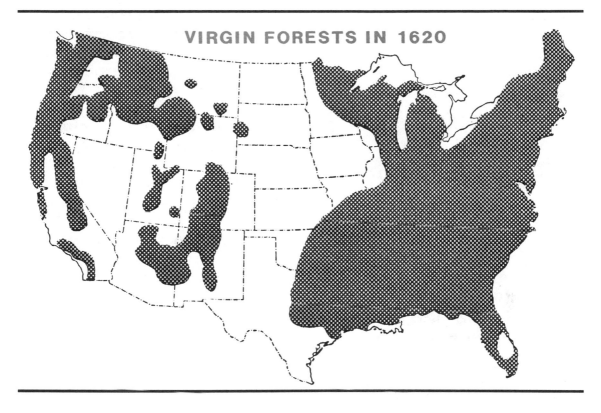

VIRGIN FORESTS IN 1620

building ships.

Beautiful live oak and cypress trees were hung with "iti shumo," or "tree hair," according to the Choctaws. The Frenchmen called it "barbe à l'espagnole," or "Spanish beard." Later, the Americans labeled it **Spanish moss**. There was much of it draped on the trees near the coast. As the settlers moved north, they found less of it. Newcomers found the moss useful in various ways. They used it in horse collars, ropes, mattresses, and pillows. It was also used with mud to form insulation for their homes. The resulting product was called **bousillage**.

In the forests the settlers found many kinds of **wild berries, roots,** and **nuts**. They gathered **pecans, walnuts,** and **hickory nuts. Grapes, plums, persimmons, acorns, sunflowers,** and **lamb's-quarter** were all gifts of nature. **Muscadines, blackberries, dewberries,** and **wild strawberries** added to their diet. They gathered the roots of **sassafras** trees to make tea. They powdered the dry leaves to make **filé**. Leaves and nuts provided **dyes**. They even gathered **honey** from the forests.

No doubt the newcomers realized

that the advantages of the abundant forests far outweighed the disadvantages.

En Partie 3 (Studying a Part). 1. What kinds of trees did the settlers find in Louisiana? 2. How did the forests present problems? 3. How did the first settlers use the forests? 4. What else did they find in the forests?

Wildlife and Fish

The gift of wildlife the settlers found was nothing short of fantastic. Louisiana's location on the Mississip-

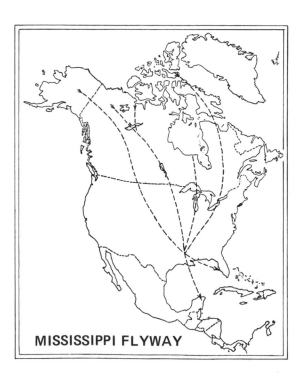

MISSISSIPPI FLYWAY

pi Flyway provided many dividends. Each year, the pioneers saw seventy-seven percent of all the species of birds known on the North American continent. In the summer they saw the **catbird, orchard oriole, purple martin, kingfisher,** and **chimney swift.** In the winter the **coot, crane, song sparrow,** and **woodcock** were just a few of the visitors. One-half of the continent's **ducks** and **geese** passed overhead on the route of the Mississippi Flyway. The **rose-breasted grosbeak** and **scarlet tanager** were transitory visitors. Then there were many permanent residents such as the **brown pelican, bald eagle, barn owl, bluebird, red-winged blackbird,** and **crow.**

The woods were filled with wild creatures. **Wild turkeys, wolves,** and **deer** found food and shelter in the underbrush. **Wild horses, hogs,** and even **cattle** roamed the woods. They had been brought to this land by European explorers. Their offspring had multiplied over a century or more. **Quail, squirrels, doves, rabbits,** and similar game offered the settlers tasty food. **Bears** provided fat.

Many saw in the New World an opportunity to earn money from the sale of furs. Furbearing animals such as the **raccoon, bobcat, mink, opossum, muskrat, skunk, beaver,** and **red fox** were abundant.

Lizards and **snakes,** useful in the control of insects, were numerous. The most common lizard, the little American chameleon, blended into its environment. Of the state's thirty-nine species of snakes, thirty-three were not the least bit harmful. The six poisonous snakes in Louisiana that the settlers found were the **copperhead, coral, cottonmouth moccasin, pygmy rattlesnake, canebrake rattlesnake,** and **eastern diamondback rattlesnake.** The swamp-forest was a great hiding place for these snakes and lizards as well as **alligators.**

The marshlands were home to many wild creatures. The Louisiana marshes serve as nurseries for a large percent of the fish in the northern Gulf of Mexico. Imagine the amazement to find the state's saltwater fish—the **redfish, sheepshead, croaker, mackerel, mullet, drum, tuna, amberjack,** and **tarpon**—so plentiful. The state's riches from coastal waters included **shrimp, oysters, crabs,** and **sea turtles. Frogs** were everywhere. **Loggerhead snapping turtles,** the largest freshwater species in the state, weighed as much as fifty pounds. They provided much food for the early settlers.

The settler found that he could catch a variety of freshwater fish in the many waterways. **Bass, catfish, perch,** and **trout** abounded. He could have whatever he liked best just for the catching. Fish was one of the most valuable and most enjoyable resources found.

Only royalty could hunt and fish in Europe. Here the early settlers enjoyed the sport. Even more important, game provided food for their families.

En Partie 4 (Studying a Part). 1. What types of wildlife and fish did the settlers find? 2. Which poisonous snakes are found here? 3. How did they use nature's gift of wildlife and fisheries? 4. What is the Mississippi Flyway?

Climate and Weather

It took some time for the newcomers to learn about the climate. The French tried to raise grapes, citrus trees, and silkworms on mulberry trees before they learned about the growing seasons.

Scientists describe the climate as **humid and subtropical.** These settlers found that Louisiana had plenty of moisture; long, hot summers; and relatively short, mild winters. They also found that there were no dry seasons, even if it did not rain for a few weeks. They did not know that the state's climate is chiefly determined by three factors. These are the state's location on the Gulf of Mexico, its subtropical latitude, and the huge land mass to the north. The lack of

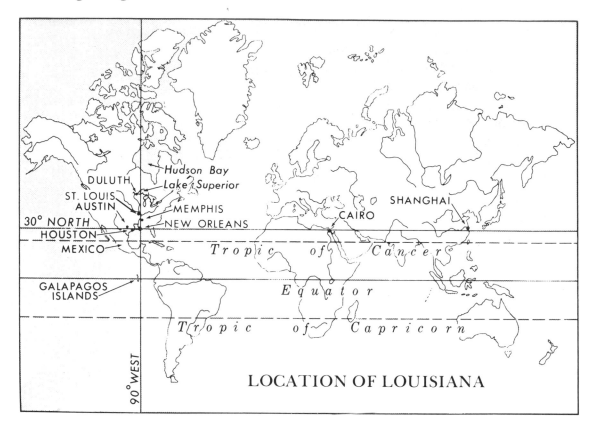

DULUTH
ST. LOUIS
AUSTIN
Hudson Bay
Lake Superior
MEMPHIS
NEW ORLEANS
30° NORTH
HOUSTON
MEXICO
CAIRO
SHANGHAI
Tropic of Cancer
GALAPAGOS
ISLANDS
Equator
Tropic of Capricorn
90° WEST

LOCATION OF LOUISIANA

mountain barriers allows the cold arctic air to enter the state.

The newcomers found that there are really **two seasons** in Louisiana—summer and winter. Fall and spring are too brief to notice. They knew that August with an average of eighty-two degrees is the warmest month. January, the coldest month, averages about fifty-three degrees. In the winter there are "cold spells." Each cold spell usually lasts only one to three days. Often, the newcomers found, they bring rain. During most winters they did not have to worry about the problems of snow. Snow was rare

even in the northern part of the state. The problem was that the settlers were not prepared for snow when it did fall.

The settlers learned that if they stayed near the Gulf coast, the weather was milder. The state average temperature is about sixty-seven degrees. In the northern part of the state the average is sixty-four degrees. It is nearly seventy-one degrees near the coast. South Louisiana has fewer extremes in temperature. North Louisiana, they found, has hotter summers and colder winters. The farther away from the Gulf settlers went, the greater the extremes in climate they encountered.

Early farmers found that the mild climate allowed a long **growing season**. They could grow two crops of vegetables every year. It was very important to grow as much food as possible between the last killing frost in the spring and the first killing frost in the fall. They learned that there is little danger of a killing frost in North Louisiana after March 31. They expected the first killing frost in North Louisiana around November 1. Near the coast they planned for a growing season from February 1 to December 15.

They looked forward to the abundant rainfall to help produce their food. They could count on about fifty-six inches of **precipitation** each year. Sometimes they must have thought that the rains would never end. Still, there were droughts occasionally. These usually occurred in the northern part of the state.

Our early settlers found that the heaviest rains fell along the Gulf coast. There were fewer such rains as they ventured away from the coast. The periods of rainfall became fewer as they moved toward Northwest Louisiana. Most rainfall, they learned, falls in March and December and the least amount in September and October.

They became familiar with the cycle. On a beautiful day the weather suddenly changed. Dark clouds appeared. The temperature dropped, and the rains started. After the storm passed, the skies cleared quickly.

Thunderstorms were part of the pattern. They brought lightning, thunder, strong winds up to fifty miles per hour, and a downpour of rain. At times there was a great deal of hail. The thunderstorms sometimes brought welcome relief from dry spells.

Moisture was an everyday occurrence. Heavy dews over the land provided small amounts of moisture. The high **humidity**, or mugginess, was very uncomfortable. It was impossible to see through dense fog that often covered the coast. Dealing with fog was part of life for the first settlers. The mildew attacking their supplies was a problem, too.

Louisiana weather can be violent. The new settlers were harassed by winds strong enough to sweep away their hard-built houses. These newcomers soon realized that they were in one of the stormiest places in the world. Most of all they feared the two deadly storms—**hurricanes** and **tornadoes**.

Hurricanes come out of the Gulf between June and November. The settlers learned to dread September most of all. The hurricane winds blew across a wide expanse of land tearing down trees and buildings. Rarely did the storms extend far inland. The heavy rains following hurricanes were sometimes as destructive as the high winds. Another problem was created by the high waters from the Gulf washing onto the shore. The low-lying coastal areas suffered most from the storm's fury when the sea waters covered the ground, sometimes to depths of fifteen feet. At least hurricanes did not come often. Usually, they averaged about one every four years.

Tornadoes sometimes seemed to come out of nowhere. The settler could recognize a tornado when it came through. The dark funnel clouds with whirling winds were terrifying to see. The tornado's destructive path was narrow, usually about one-fourth of a mile wide. In the spring and fall the settlers were on the lookout for these deadly funnels in the sky. If they were in the northern part of the state, they had even more reason to watch for them, especially in March, April, and May.

All in all, the first who braved the Louisiana climate suffered vast miseries. However, they could be thankful for the long summer. They learned that Louisiana could have spells of intense cold in winter. Usually, though, winters were brief and mild. Their shabby housing caused no problems most of the time. The weather was milder near the Gulf than farther north so they hovered near the Gulf waters.

They stayed near the Gulf for other reasons, too. The Gulf of Mexico offered a way to Europe, if life became too hard to bear. Supplies came by ship through the Gulf.

En Partie 5 (Studying a Part). 1. Describe Louisiana's weather. 2. How many seasons do we have? 3. Give important facts about tornadoes and hurricanes. 4. What is the growing season?

So our first settlers found a country rich in natural resources. They slowly learned to make use of these resources. They had so much to work with—the soils, the waterways, the forests, the wildlife and fisheries, the rain, and the sunshine. But there was more. Early French and Spanish records contain frequent mention of the many **salt licks** found at different points throughout the state. Salt springs flow out of the land. When the water evaporates, the salt is left. These salty places were quickly found by wild animals and cattle. The earlier settlers made good use of the salt.

Then there was the natural beauty. Early settlers must have stopped to enjoy the sight of Louisiana **wildflowers.** Some woods became beautiful with dogwood blossoms in the spring. Wild azaleas, rare orchids,

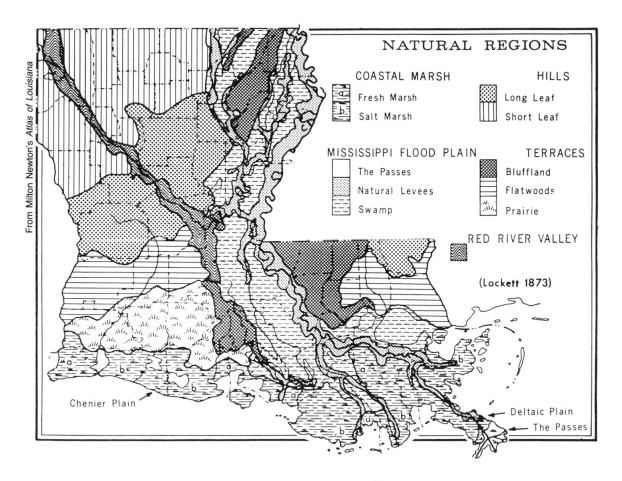

From Milton Newton's Atlas of Louisiana

NATURAL REGIONS

COASTAL MARSH

a. Fresh Marsh
b. Salt Marsh

HILLS

Long Leaf
Short Leaf

MISSISSIPPI FLOOD PLAIN

The Passes
Natural Levees
Swamp

TERRACES

Bluffland
Flatwoods
Prairie

RED RIVER VALLEY

(Lockett 1873)

Chenier Plain

Deltaic Plain
The Passes

irises, spider plants, and many other plants bloomed in this land. In fall bright berries and changing leaves provided color.

This was the natural setting in which the history of Louisiana unfolded.

Lagniappe—*State Divisions*. Louisiana has sixty-four parishes. This is the only state with parishes instead of counties. The use of the word *parish* instead of *county* remains from the French colonial period. The original divisions of the state fitted in with the divisions of the Roman Catholic church. The Catholic church calls its church divisions *parishes*. The names of parishes indicate French, Spanish, American, and Indian influence.

Coup d'Main
(Completing the Story)

Jambalaya (Putting It All Together)

1. In what ways is the geography of our state linked to its history? How does geography influence daily living—food, clothing, shelter, health, occupations, and recreation?

2. (a) What did this land now known as Louisiana have to offer the first settlers? (b) What are the state's natural resources? (c) What were the disadvantages in the natural surroundings?

3. (a) In what ways has the appearance of this land changed since the first settlers arrived? (b) How has technology changed our environment?

4. What are some of the geographic characteristics of the part of Louisiana where you live?

5. (a) Compare North and South Louisiana in these areas: elevation, rainfall, soils, climate, vegetation, special or unusual characteristics, waterways, and growing seasons. (b) Why do statements about an area usually have exceptions?

6. Define these key words:

a. backland
b. bottomland
c. brackish
d. chenier
e. coastline
f. delta
g. elevation
h. floating land
i. floodplain
j. frontland
k. geologic age
l. humid
m. latitude
n. longitude
o. marsh
p. natural levee
q. natural region
r. relief
s. shoreline
t. swamp
u. time zone
v. watershed
w. weathering
x. wetland

7. Map work: (a) Label Louisiana's border states. (b) Label waterways that serve as boundaries. (c) Mark the latitude and longitude of the state. Show (d) the coastline, (e) the shoreline, and (f) the longest distance across the state. Give the measurements for (d), (e), and (f). Label (g) the Five Islands, (h) the highest point, and (i) the major cities.

8. Complete this chart about Louisiana:

a. _____ planet
b. _____ hemisphere
c. _____ continent
d. _____ country
e. _____ section of U.S.
f. _____ time zone
g. _____ plain
h. _____ shape of state
i. _____ percent water
j. _____ rank in size
k. _____ area in square miles

Potpourri (Getting Involved)

1. Find examples of architecture, economic activity, or any other examples that show adaptations to the environment.

2. Locate pictures that show the

advantages and disadvantages of living in different parts of Louisiana.

3. Associate the influence of climate, location, and natural resources with the social and economic activities in the state.

4. Research: What does Louisiana need that it does not have? What does the state not have in the right amount or the right kind?

Gumbo (Bringing It Up-to-Date)

1. Identify specific ways of living that would be affected if modern ways of controlling our environment were removed. Identify some of the things over which we have no control or practically no control.

2. Plan a trip to some spot in Louisiana. Describe the people, vegetation, land surface, crops, livestock, waterways, and any other important points.

3. Find pictures that look most like Louisiana.

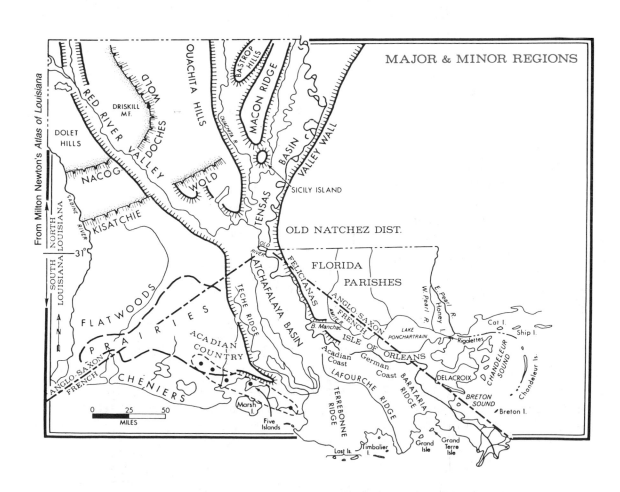

CHAPTER 2

LOUISIANA'S FIRST INHABITANTS: THE INDIANS
(10,000 B.C.– Present)

When the first Europeans came to this land that became Louisiana, there were people living here. These were Indians. Their lifestyle was so different from the Spanish, the French, and the English that each group of newcomers called them "uncivilized." To be civilized was to be like themselves, European. The Indians spoke different languages, worshipped different gods, and wore fewer clothes than the Europeans of that day. The Europeans measured everything by what was familiar to them. On this basis they labeled the red men "savages."

Since the Indians had no written language, there is no way of knowing what they thought of the white men who came into their land from overseas. The white man's violence, deceptions, and greed must have appeared equally savage and uncivilized to the Indians.

Scholars studying the Louisiana Indians have provided us with some interesting facts. According to these scholars, it was probably as far back as 10,000 B.C. that the first Indians came to Louisiana. Indians have been in the state for about 12,000 years, if this date is correct.

Scholars name two periods of Indian residence:

(1) **The prehistoric period.** The prehistoric Indians lived in the state from about 10,000 B.C. to 1699 A.D. The coming of the white man to Louisiana ended this period. This time is called pre-historic, since there were no written records.

(2) **The historic period.** For Louisiana, this period started around 1700. From the beginning of this period, we have written accounts by the Europeans. This

historic part is the study of Indians since Iberville and other white men began to settle the state.

Indians in General

Description. Many different Indian tribes lived in Louisiana. It is impossible to identify all of these Indian groups. It is not even possible to give the names of the tribes who belonged together. The exact location of the various tribes in Louisiana is unknown.

Various names were used for the same tribe. Some of the confusion has arisen because Europeans did not spell the names of the tribes the same. Some tribes had nicknames that the Europeans used in referring to them. Later, it was not clear if these names represented different groups. Many mistakes have been made. Some of these mistakes are now recorded as facts.

Not all of the Indians identified as once living in the area lived here at the same time. A group of Indians arrived in Louisiana, disappeared, another arrived and disappeared, and so on through many thousands of years.

Not all of the Indians who came to Louisiana came from the same place. The exact migration patterns cannot be traced. Some came when the entire tribe decided to move into the area. Others left their large groups and came in small groups.

The first Indians lived in groups of four or five families. These groups were called **bands**. The bands grew into larger groups called **tribes**. In turn the large tribes joined together to form loose **confederacies**. The list of tribes included in a confederacy was not always the same.

How would you describe what these Indians looked like? How would you describe what an American looks like today? The same problem exists in both cases. The skin color of Indians living in Louisiana varied from light yellow to olive to dark brown. Not all Indians had coarse black hair. Many had soft brown hair. Indians wore their hair different lengths and styles. Indians varied in physical appearance as much as any other group of people. Only sunburned or painted Indians were red. The Europeans gave them the name red man because of the red oxide they used to decorate themselves. Louisiana Indians probably did not look like the fierce warlike men wearing colorful war bonnets as seen in movies. Neither did they all look like the bronze warrior with bow and arrow in hand nor like the Indian on the Indian-head nickel.

Their **lifestyles** also differed from one group to another, as the lifestyles of Americans today differ from one group to another. The Chinatowns, the Germantowns, and the French settlements in America all have some-

ESKIMOS

ESKIMOS

NORTHERN

HUNTERS

NORTHWESTERN
FISHERMEN

SEED
GATHERERS
&

PLAINS

INDIANS

SOUTHWESTERN
INDIANS

EASTERN
WOODLAND
INDIANS

CULTURAL AREAS
OF THE
NORTH AMERICAN INDIANS

what different lifestyles. The same was true of these early Americans. Also, just as with Americans today, each succeeding generation had a different lifestyle from the generation before it. Their customs differed from European customs. Even though they were very much alike in many ways, certain characteristics allowed other Indians and whites to identify each group.

Scholars, studying the Indians of the entire North American continent, have divided Indians into groups. One classification is based on how the Indians lived. There are ten of these culture groups. Louisiana Indians are classified as Southeastern Indians.

Each Indian group had its own special characteristics. There were similar characteristics among groups, too. For instance, many Indian tribes spoke similar languages. In the United States, there were forty-eight language families with different dialects. At one time scholars divided Louisiana Indians into six language groups with certain tribes assigned to each group. This division has been studied and new groupings have been proposed. Linguists disagree as to exactly how these groupings should be made.

One thing that all Indians had in common was their dependence on nature. Indians in early Louisiana obtained the necessities of life from the environment. Therefore, they had to know the environment in every possible detail. Their food, shelter, and clothing came from the wilderness. It was necessary to kill, gather, or grow all of their food. They had to distinguish between animals and plants that were harmful and those that would help them survive.

What the Indians used for **food** depended heavily on what was available in their living area. Louisiana Indians had roots, herbs, berries, seeds, and nuts of many kinds. Wild game and fish were plentiful. South Louisiana Indians had saltwater fish as well. Indians in northwestern Louisiana hunted buffalo. The buffalo later disappeared from the area.

Indian **homes** differed, too. Not all Indians lived in the same kind of house, just as all modern people do not live in the same kind of house. There cannot be just one description of a Louisiana Indian home. Indian homes in Louisiana changed according to the period of time and the culture. Some of the houses were round and some were rectangular.

The **tribal organizations** varied little. There was a chief in most family or kinship groups. These groups lived and traveled together. Some tribes had both a war chief and a peace chief. All tribes had a shaman, or medicine man. Usually the shaman was an old Indian man thought to have magical powers in curing the sick. He often "drove off evil spirits" to make the patient well. The sha-

Medicine Man

man served at religious and other solemn ceremonies of the tribe.

Indians could be distinguished by the way they adorned themselves. Many Indians **tattooed** their faces and bodies. Tattoos were symbols for sex, age, and marital status. Indian women thought tattoos made them more beautiful. While the idea seems strange to peoples of other cultures, we are so accustomed to seeing Americans today with tattoos, lipstick, hair dyes, and eye makeup that we do not think it odd. Yet generations from now people of another day and another culture may think our customs strange, also.

The Indians' practice of scalping enemies sounds shocking. Indians felt it essential to prove one's ability as a warrior. Some thought that the head of the enemy must be cut from the body or the person would be reborn and could fight again. These "trophies" were displayed in very much the same way a sportsman collects trophies today.

Contributions of the Indians. There are few things left to remind us that all of Louisiana once belonged to the Indians. None of the Indians who lived here was famous. No single individual among the Indians was distinguished as a leader. At least European and American writers recorded none.

Yet, these people passed on to the white man their knowledge of **how to survive in this land**. They made life much easier for the early settlers. Their help enabled the Europeans to avoid the risks of learning the hard way. **Where to secure foodstuff, what and when to plant** in Louisiana soil, **how to deal with insects**, and **how to handle the many problems of everyday living** were learned from the Indians. They showed the Europeans **new foods**. Indians taught them how to make use of the wild game of the forests and the abundance of fish in Louisiana waters. They taught their **skills in hunting, fishing, and trapping** to the white man. Indians taught the Europeans **how to live with the**

Archaeologists focus their attention on digs, or excavations.

"floating land" on the coast. The Indians pointed out **dyes** to be found in the forests. They showed the Europeans **herbs** and other seasonings— bay leaf, cayenne, and wild cherry. They recommended **teas** for medicine such as that made from sassafras roots. They made **filé** from the sassafras leaves. Indians showed the Europeans the way to travel on the bayous in a light boat—the **pirogue**. Newcomers learned about **mud baths** from the Indians, too.

Many Indian words have become names for places in Louisiana. These include Natchitoches, Caddo, Atchafalaya, Istrouma, Opelousas, and Ouachita.

Sources of Indian History. We are largely indebted to the **archaeologists** for what we know about prehistoric Indians. The archaeologists have used their scientific methods to unlock the secrets of the past. With their knowledge the archaeologists have pieced together much of the history of the early Indians. Archaeologists have documented the many changes in Indian culture during historic times as well. These scientists have excavated the sites of Indian villages, burial grounds, and fortifications. Louisiana is rich in such findings.

Until very recently Indian sites were not protected by Louisiana law. As a result, much of the evidence left

This is a mound of the Marksville Indians.

by Indians has been lost forever. Countless sites have been destroyed. It is now unlawful to dig into, alter, or take anything from a site of Indian artifacts on state or federal land without a permit. Other laws seek to protect the remaining sites.

Lagniappe. People who have archaeological sites on their property may place them on the Registry of State Cultural Resource Landmarks. Once the site is placed on the registry, the owner and the state agree on a protection plan.

Louisiana's archaeological sites have been divided into three classes: **midden, mound,** and **village.** A midden is often called a dump. It com-

pares with the city dumps of today. Middens are deposits of refuse that accumulated near residences. They are seldom more than eight feet deep. They have no particular shape. Within the middens broken pieces of pottery are found. These are called **potsherds.** They reflect something about the cooking done by Indians, the type of pottery they made, and other details about their lifestyles. Sometimes a broken arrowhead or spearpoint may be found in these trash heaps.

A mound is something different. It is a structure built by the Indians. It was planned for a definite purpose by the builders. Some mounds are round at the bottom and rise to a peak. Others suggest a dome. Some are square or rectangular at the bottom. They have flat sides and flat tops.

All Indian mounds found in North

Louisiana were made of dirt. In South Louisiana there were different types of mounds. One mound that was located at Grand Lake in Cameron Parish was made of clamshells and was shaped like an alligator.

Burial mounds are common. All kinds of possessions owned by the person buried at the site have been found. Among the items are beads and necklaces, stone tools, weapons, clay pots, bones of animals and humans, mats of split switch canes, and both whole and broken pots.

Sites of entire Indian villages reveal that a small group of people lived there in a permanent settlement. The arrangement of the houses, the plan by which they were built, and many facts about the lives of the people in the village may be learned by archaeological studies. Scientists study the designs and methods used by these prehistoric peoples in manufacturing articles. Pottery and projectile points tell the scientists much about the identity of particular groups of Indians. By classifying the articles produced by prehistoric Indians, the life of these people may be carefully reconstructed. Skeletons of Indians reveal something about the first people who lived in Louisiana. Through the information thus accumulated, scientists have acquired mental images of entire villages.

Scientists have found a way to date the findings of archaelogists.

This is known as the **carbon-14** test. Using this method, which includes analyzing the radioactivity of some of the carbon isotopes, the scientists can compute the age of plant and animal remains.

Adding to the information on historic Indians furnished by archaeologists are the **writings** of Europeans. The Europeans who wrote about the Indians included the adventurers, explorers, traders, and priests. Many left records. Most told more about the character and background of the writer than that of the Indians. Sometimes Europeans did not understand what they saw. Seldom are the records accurate. The accounts leave many gaps. There are many conflicting statements given. None of them seem to have agreed.

Indians themselves depended upon **oral history**. The Indians passed on stories of the past from one generation to another by one person telling it to another. Therefore, the story taken from the spoken words of Indians themselves was entangled with **legend** as the story was passed down to them. Many of the legends were shared by different Indian groups.

The scientists continue to build a more complete picture of the Louisiana Indians. There are a number of sites of Louisiana Indian settlements that you may visit to learn more about the early Louisianians. Scientists have created museums displaying artifacts from Indian life at these sites.

The Arrival of Indians in Louisiana. Most authorities believe that the first Indians crossed the narrow Bering Strait from Siberia into Alaska. At the time the Indians crossed from Asia into North America, the world was in the midst of the Ice Age. These Indians crossed on an extensive land bridge that connected Siberia and Alaska. These first people might have come over forty thousand years ago. However, some evidence dates their arrival between twenty-three thousand and eight thousand years ago.

The first Indians were probably hunters. For thousands of years after reaching the American continent, they spread southward, very likely in pursuit of game. In this manner, they made their way into present-day Louisiana.

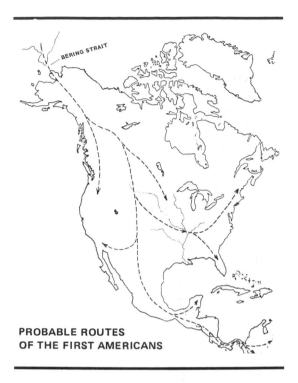

PROBABLE ROUTES OF THE FIRST AMERICANS

En Partie 1 (Studying a Part). 1. (a) What are the two periods in the story of the native people of the state? (b) What event marks the end of one and the beginning of the other? 2. Explain: Not all Louisiana Indians lived in Louisiana at the same time. 3. (a) How did the ancestors of the first Louisianians probably come to the New World? (b) From where? (c) When? (d) When did they probably arrive in Louisiana? (e) Why did they come here? 4. Why can't you describe the typical Louisiana Indian or the typical Louisiana Indian house? 5. To which general United States Indian group do Louisiana Indians belong? 6. (a) Why did Indians live in tribes? (b) What is a tribe? (c) A confederacy? 7. What are contributions made by the Indians? 8. (a) How have we obtained information regarding prehistoric Indians? (b) How complete is this information? (c) How do these people work? (d) Where are Indian artifacts found? 9. How is our Indian heritage protected by the government? 10. (a) How have we obtained information about historic Indians? (b) How accurate is this information? 11. Describe Louisiana Indians in general.

Prehistoric Indians

The way of life, or **culture**, of prehistoric man in Louisiana passed through three major periods. Each lasted thousands of years.

Paleo-Indians. The first culture to develop in Louisiana came in the **Paleo-Indian era.** Scientists have found sites dating back to the earliest Indian cultures. One is located on Avery Island in Iberia Parish. Another was discovered in May 1970 near the Vermilion River. Most similar remains have been found in the hill country and around the salt domes of Louisiana. Both early and late Paleo-Indian period materials were found at the John Pearce site in Caddo Parish.

The Paleo-Indians moving into this land of Louisiana did not find the same plant and animal life that we know today. The western half of the Louisiana area was probably one vast prairie. Large **buffaloes, mammoths, mastodons, horses, sloths,** and **peccaries** roamed over the rich land. The only coastal areas where the Indians could live were slightly high places like beach ridges, natural levees, and river terraces. The presence of water, salt, chert, and an abundance of animal and plant life

LOUISIANA'S PAST

A.D. 1542 to Present	Historic	
A.D. 400 to A.D. 1542	Coles Creek - Plaquemine - Mississippian - Caddo	
500 B.C. to A.D. 400	Tchefuncte - Marksville	
2000 B.C. to 500 B.C.	Poverty Point	
6000 B.C. to 2000 B.C.	Meso-Indian	
10000 B.C. to 6000 B.C.	Paleo-Indian	

Jon Gibson

for food made it possible for the Indians to live in Louisiana.

Louisiana's Paleo-Indians had the simplest of social organizations. They were **nomads**—people who migrated with the seasons—who needed only temporary shelter. They made these shelters with tree branches, grass, and hides. They camped near streams. They were hunters and gatherers who moved in small groups as the animal herds moved. Four or five families probably formed such a group. Then the group joined with others on certain occasions when larger numbers were needed. Men and older boys probably hunted. Women and children collected foods that grew wild.

Big-game hunting was an important part of the lives of the Paleo-Indians. They developed weapons and fine spearpoints according to their needs. They also developed other stone tools and implements.

The Meso-Indians, or Archaic Indians. After thousands of years, the way of life of prehistoric man in Louisiana changed. Nobody is sure why this change occurred. Perhaps the large game animals that had furnished a food supply became extinct. Possibly new groups of people arrived in Louisiana. For whatever the reason, around 5000 B.C., a new cultural period called the **Archaic era** replaced the old Paleo-Indian era.

Archaic man was a **hunter**, but he depended more on gathered foods than the people who came before him. Archaic man also had more **tools**. He fashioned scrapers, knives, axes, choppers, picks, and drills from stone, or sometimes from bone. He also made flint points that were put on darts and hurled by using a spear thrower or atlatl. He produced stone beads, stone pipes, and stone mortars and pestles with which to grind seeds and nuts. It was Archaic man who tamed the **dog**.

Life for Archaic man was almost as difficult and dangerous as it was for the Paleo-Indian. At best he had only crude shelters to protect him from the hot sun in summer and the cold in winter. It was necessary to be constantly on the move each season, searching for food for himself and his family. He was still **nomadic**. However, he stayed longer than before at one place before moving on. He did not go as far from home as his ancestors had done. The Indians enjoyed the elevations of beach ridges and natural levees with an abundance of food, water, and other natural resources available for the taking.

The climate was warmer during the Archaic Age, which followed the Ice Age. Indians found some of the same plants and animals that we know today. There were **different animals** than Paleo-Indians had known. Rivers and smaller streams were filled with fish, mussels, and clams. Louisiana had more lush **grasslands** than today. Large deltas and coastal marshes were developing along the Gulf coast. Natural levees developed higher and higher as the streams flooded their banks with sediments brought from the north.

There were many choices to replace the big-game diet of the Paleo-Indians. These Indians enjoyed Louisiana shellfish. Large quantities of oysters, clams, and many other kinds of seafood were available from the coast. Indians ate large numbers of deer and wild turkey. The alligator was also used for food.

Jon Gibson

Spear throwers, called atlatls, were hooked onto darts to improve the hurling distance and power.

The Neo-Indians. The final cultural era of the prehistoric period in Louisiana was called **Neo-Indian**. It lasted from 2000 B.C. to 1600 A.D. During this era, the Indians learned to make **pottery**. They regularly built shell and earthen mounds. They began to use the **bow and arrow** for hunting. The development of **farming** was the most important event that occurred in the Neo-Indian era. Some Indians learned how to plant crops for food, allowing them to settle down in one place. Corn, beans, and squash were important crops.

The **Poverty Point** Indian culture belonged to the Neo-Indian period. The political and religious center for the entire culture was located in Louisiana. These Indians were located at Poverty Point on the west bank of Bayou Macon in West Carroll Parish at Epps. Macon Plateau is a stretch of ground fifteen to twenty feet higher than the surrounding Mississippi Valley.

It was here that these people chose to lay out their city. The Indians built earthen ridges shaped like half-moons. There were six of these. They also built a series of six dirt terraces about one hundred feet wide. This was where they lived. Their palmetto-covered homes were round. They measured about fifteen feet in diameter and looked something like warm-weather igloos. It is estimated that as many as five or six thousand people lived in the village at Poverty Point.

On the west side of the village, the Poverty Point Indians built an amazing **mound**. It was about six hundred feet long and seventy feet tall. It was joined to a terrace by a long, flat platform twenty feet high. A ramp or stairway led from the platform to the top of this mound. All this the Indians built by hand. Imagine carrying the dirt required to build these ridges and mounds. The Indians loosened the dirt with shells or stones. Then they filled baskets and animal hides with the loose dirt. The unbelievable fact is that 530,000 cubic yards of earth were moved in those baskets! The Indians constructed 11.2 miles of ridges in a geometrical design. It probably took several generations to complete the site.

These Indians used stone choppers and knives for cutting meat. They cleaned the hides of deer and other animals with stone scrapers. These scrapers were used for digging, also. Poverty Point residents did not use the bow and arrow but had spears and darts. Bolas were made with five or six heavy weights or plummets. The weights were tied to leather thongs or animal fibre and used for catching large birds like ducks, geese, turkeys, and other small animals. The Indians held the leather strings, whirled the weight around the head,

Construction of earthworks at the Poverty Point site required well-organized leadership.

Jon Gibson

and hurled it at the bird or animal. The weights wrapped the cords around the head or legs of the living target.

The Poverty Point culture lasted from about **2000 B.C. to 700 B.C.** Archaeologists have estimated that this village was built nearly three thousand years ago. The Poverty Point culture flourished for over one thousand years at this site. By 700 B.C. it had virtually disappeared. This was probably the last time that Louisiana Indians built such massive earthworks or traded over such a large area. At its peak the Poverty Point village may have been the largest community in the entire area now covered by the United States. Louisiana contained the largest center for the Poverty Point people.

The Poverty Point residents lived a thousand years before the cliff dwellers in Colorado, New Mexico, and Arizona. Their territory spread over Louisiana, Mississippi, and Arkansas. Even the Mayan and Toltec Indian cultures in Mexico and Central America either had not begun to develop or were only in the beginning stages. The culture of Greece was just beginning to develop. Old Testament prophets like Elijah, Isaiah, and Solomon were alive. Yet the Poverty Point people planned in a way we think of as modern. Their **earthwork construction, planned village, clay figurines, stone beads,** and **pendants** were very advanced. Many

of the things done by the Indians at Poverty Point have been compared with those of the Indians of Mexico and Central America.

Artifacts recovered from the site are on display at the Poverty Point Museum. They are also shown in the Masur Museum of Art in Monroe, the Louisiana State Exhibit Museum in Shreveport, and the Smithsonian Institute in Washington, D.C.

The next Indian culture built in Louisiana was the Tchefuncte culture. These people lived from 500 B.C. until 200 A.D. The Tchefuncte Indians lived in family groups with a simple lifestyle. This group of Indians was the first to make large amounts of pottery. Most of these Indians lived in the coastal areas and in the lowlands. Clams made up a big portion of their diet.

The **Marksville** Indians represented another tribal group. They built larger, more permanent settlements than the state's earlier Indians. The Marksville Indians were influenced by the Hopewell culture, which was centered in Ohio and Illinois. They built dome-shaped mounds in which they buried their dead.

The Prehistoric Indian Museum at Marksville is located on the Avoyel prairie. The museum displays specimens of articles found in the many mounds left by these Indians. This museum visually tells the story of these Indians of the lower Mississippi

Valley from about 400 B.C. until modern times.

Before the historic period, other Indian cultures developed. The Indians lived much like the Indians who had been here before them. The people lived peacefully—hunting, fishing, and gardening.

En Partie 2 (Studying a Part). 1. Make a time line of the prehistoric Indian cultures found in Louisiana. 2. Give some of the outstanding characteristics of each of the prehistoric groups. 3. (a) Locate Poverty Point on a map. (b) Describe Poverty Point culture. (c) What amazing job did the Poverty Point Indians accomplish? 4. How did life change for prehistoric Indians?

Historic Indians

When the Europeans arrived, the prehistoric era of the Indians ended. The historic period began around 1700. This means that there were now written records about the Indians. The first explorers found many tribes and bands of native people already living here. It has been estimated that **twelve to fifteen thousand** Indians made the area their home when the first explorers set foot in Louisiana.

Scholars in the past have assigned historic Louisiana Indians to various groups. Usually these groupings were based on language. Modern Louisiana Indians have traced their ancestry and made their own groupings. The Inter-Tribal Council of Louisiana has written the history of the major tribes and the groups that merged with them. The council's groups include the Atakapa, Caddo (Kadohadacho), Chitimacha, Choctaw, Coushatta (Koasati), Houma, and Tunica.

Each Indian group included several tribes. The territory claimed by each group had no specific boundaries. However, the territory claimed by each was recognized by the others. Within such territories one basic language was spoken. All the people felt a sort of kinship, which exerted an influence against fighting within their group. Groups speaking the same language often banded together to form a confederacy. They stood together against outside tribes with different languages and different customs.

By 1700 most of the Indians no longer built mounds. They lived in small villages along the rivers and streams. They mostly farmed. However, they continued to hunt, fish, and gather.

The coming of the Europeans brought quick changes in the Indian culture. Most, if not all, Indians developed a trade system with the Europeans. The Indians furnished salt, horses, furs, and other goods for them.

The white men gave the Indians glass beads, bottles, guns, ammunition, knives, ceramics, bells, and bracelets. Whiskey was traded to the Indians for their furs. The white man's diseases, such as measles and smallpox, killed many Indians. The Indians no longer were the only humans here. The Europeans took more and more of the land. Thus, Indians lost their freedom to live as they chose. They could no longer move as they wished in the vast wilderness. Since Louisiana Indians were located between the French and the Spanish, both groups attempted to control Indian trade and secure the Indians as allies in conflicts with each other.

Finally, the United States government tried to protect the Indians to some extent. Mistreatment of the Indians by some whites, trespassing by whiskey traders and unlawful hunters, and other offenses finally brought

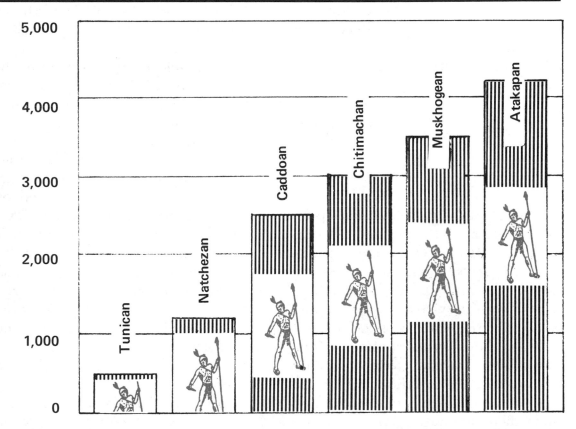

LOUISIANA INDIAN POPULATION IN 1700

action. Indian agencies were established. Dr. John Sibley was appointed United States Indian agent for Louisiana in 1805. He lived at Natchitoches.

After the Louisiana Purchase in 1803, more white settlers began pushing into the Indian territory. The ancient domain of the Indians began to slip completely from their grasp. Gradually they lost most of their lands. The story for each tribe differs slightly, but the pattern was much the same. Most of them migrated from one place to another looking for a location for a peaceful home. Tribes combined to survive the advance of the Europeans.

Each tribe has its own special story as told by the Inter-Tribal Council.

Major Louisiana Tribes

Atakapa. This large group of Indians occupied the prairies of southwestern Louisiana. Their area extended from Bayou Teche to the Sabine river and from Opelousas to the coastal marshes. They were a semisettled, partially agricultural people. They established their villages along waterways. The Atakapas were culturally less advanced than their neighbors. However, they were more advanced than their reputation as wandering cannibals suggests. They had several semipermanent villages and are known to have traded with other Indians along the Texas coast. They traded fish to the Opelousas for flints. The Atakapas also traded for other items that they did not manufacture.

In 1885 a considerable vocabulary of Atakapa was gathered from two women living in Lake Charles. They belonged to the last Atakapa village. It was on Indian Lake (later called Prien Lake). A later survey disclosed a few former residents of the old town were still living in 1907 and 1908. By 1942 all known villagers of the last Atakapa village were dead.

The **Opelousa** group lived in the vicinity of the present city of Opelousas. They acted as middlemen in trade between other Indians in the South. They bought fish from the Chitimachas and Atakapas, which they exchanged for flints from the Avoyels. Some of these flints were passed on to the Karankawas from the Texas coast. The Opelousas traded for globular or conical oil jugs. They traded such items as Caddo pottery, Texas pots, stone beads, arrowpoints, and salt. Their trade routes extended from the interior of Texas to the coast and inland through Caddo country in northern Louisiana and onward through Arkansas.

Caddo (Kadohadacho). The name Caddo is applied collectively to an important group of approximately twenty-five tribes. These tribes formed three or more confederated groups of Kadohadacho. Their area covered the present states of Arkansas, Louisiana, and Oklahoma.

Their culture was considerably different from those of other Louisiana tribes. They allied themselves with the plains cultures. Unlike the other tribes of the state, who were afraid of horses, the Caddos readily accepted them. They used them for hunting buffalo and other game.

The Caddo tribe was very large and powerful before the arrival of the Europeans. They had highly developed social and ceremonial organizations with surrounding tribes. They were excellent farmers. They were also noted for their outstanding pottery. Their importance in history, however, quickly diminished with the arrival of the white man.

The Caddo name comes from their own word Kadohadacho. The name was later shortened to Caddo by the white man. They seem to have always lived on the Red River. There they planted corn, pumpkins, and various vegetables. They did not tolerate idleness, and those who did not work were punished. They worked their fields in good weather. They attended to their handiwork, made bows and arrows, clothing, and tools during cold rainy weather. The women kept busy making mats out of reed and leaves. They made pots and bowls from clay.

Building was usually a community project.

When it was time to till the fields, all of the men assembled. They worked first one field and then another until every field of all the households was ready for planting. The planting was never done by the men. Women planted the fields. To supplement their crops, the men hunted and fished.

Each tribe had a chief called a *caddi*. He ruled within the section of country occupied by his tribe. The larger tribes also had subchiefs. The number of subchiefs depended on the size of the tribe.

The Caddos lived in a communal arrangement. Eight to ten families lived in a single conical-shaped grass house. Some of their houses were made of thatch supported by a pole frame. Mat couches lined the walls and served for seating during the day and for beds at night. A fire burned in the house night and day.

Their houses were arranged around an open town square. The square was used for social and ceremonial functions. The members of each household were responsible for farming the fields adjacent to their house.

The Caddos played the role of ambassadors of peace under the rule of the French, Spanish, and United States governments. For this, the Caddos were promised that they would never be driven from their land. However, the purchase of the Louisiana territory resulted in increased immigration of whites into Caddo country. Even with military assistance it soon became an impossible situation for the Caddos. The United States government could not restrain the white settlers from inhabiting the Caddo lands. Finally the Indian agent was authorized to purchase the Caddo land. The Caddos moved westward into Texas.

After their migration, their relations with the whites were no better. Finally, on August 1, 1859, the Caddos migrated to the Indian territory of the Washita River in what is now Caddo County, Oklahoma. The remnants of the tribe reside there today in or around Anadarko.

By the early nineteenth century, the importance of the Caddos as a distinct tribe was at an end. Survivors merged with other tribes.

The **Adai** tribe lived near the present site of Robeline. One portion of their villages was under French control. The other part was under the Spanish. An ancient trail between their villages became the noted "contraband trail." This was the trail along which traders and travelers journeyed between the French and Spanish provinces. War between France and Spain almost exterminated the Adais. It is probable that they combined with the Kadohadachos. By the close of the eighteenth century all of the Adais had disappeared.

Small tribes of Caddos included the **Doustoni**, the **Nasoni (Nissohone or Nisione)**, the **Natasi**, the

INDIAN GAME

Navatsoho, the **Soacatino (Xacatin)**, the **Washita (Ouachita)**, and the **Yatasi**. These tribes united with the Kadahadacho or disappeared as a distinct tribe by the early eighteenth century.

When first discovered in the 1690s, the main tribe of Natchitoches Indians lived near the present city that bears their name. (They pronounced their name "Nashitosh.") They were primarily farmers in 1702. When their crops were ruined, they requested permission from the French to relocate. St. Denis moved them to the north side of Lake Pontchartrain near the Acolapissas. Twelve years later he took them back to their country and established a French post close to their village. As long as he remained the commandant of this post, his influence over the Natchitoches and other tribes living nearby was great. Even after his retirement, relations between the settlers and Indians continued to be harmonious. The Indians remained in their old villages until the first of the nineteenth century. Then they joined the rest of the Caddo tribes and accompanied them to Texas and Oklahoma.

Chitimacha. The Chitimachas are the only Louisiana Indians known to currently live in the vicinity of their ancestral homelands. It is evident that

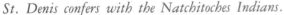

St. Denis confers with the Natchitoches Indians.

Louisiana Office of Tourism

44

In the Beginning

they were one of the largest tribes in Louisiana. Their large population was probably the result of a favorable environment. Their surroundings provided an abundant food supply of plants, animals, and marine life without the necessity of extensive hunting or fishing expeditions. It was not necessary to periodically abandon their village sites for lack of food. The men did the hunting and fishing.

The Chitimachas inhabited two groups of villages. One group was located along the upper reaches of Bayou Lafourche near the Mississippi River. The other group was located on Grand Lake and the Bayou Teche area. These areas consist of many bayous and swamps. They were easy to protect because they were difficult to reach.

Women exerted strong influence in the tribe's affairs because important political positions were available to them. Usually the men controlled the governmental offices. If a chief died, his widow could assume his responsibilities if she were a capable leader. Women could also work as medicine "men." Only the leadership of religious affairs was denied them.

The political system was run by a group of powerful men. One head chief controlled the affairs of an entire confederation. Subchiefs governed the outlying villages. These leaders inherited their offices. They lived in large homes. They carried heavily

decorated peace pipes to all ceremonies and social affairs as reminders of their importance. They ruled by personal orders. Their proclamations were enforced by subadministrators appointed especially for that purpose. They maintained groups of warriors to protect them and to defend their villages against raids by neighboring tribes.

The Chitimachas had a true caste system. The leaders and their respective families composed the noble class. All others belonged to the commoner class. Noblemen addressed commoners in popular languages. However, commoners spoke to noblemen only in terms that were used solely for that purpose. Noblemen almost always married into the families of other noblemen. In the case of the exceptions, the husband joined the clan of the wife. Therefore, he would become a commoner. A nobleman was inclined to remain unwed if no women of his class were free to marry.

Religious affairs were controlled by holy men and their assistants. Holy men were in charge of the sacred ceremonies of their respective clans. They had the responsibility of passing down the ancient parables and stories of miraculous events. Their moral code contained beliefs concerning man's kinship to nature and to nature's creatures.

The Chitimacha men wore long hair weighted with pieces of lead to hold their heads erect. They wore necklaces, bracelets, and rings made of copper, gold, and silver. Women wore their hair in braids, used make-up of red and white dyes, and wore bracelets, earrings, and finger rings.

They appreciated beauty. This quality was shown in their manufacture of objects from shells and stones and their excellent baskets. Basketmakers gathered swamp cane and split it into strands. Then they dyed it either black, yellow, or red and let it dry. When the strands were completely dry, they wove them into baskets in two layers. They wove in such a way as to produce symbolic designs on the exterior.

Their first contact with Europeans was in 1699. This was the year of the first French settlement. Between 1701 and 1705 war broke out. A party of French soldiers reinforced by Acolapissa and Natchitoches Indians took twenty Chitimacha women and children prisoner. In response, Chitamacha warriors killed a French missionary, St. Cosme, and his three companions in a battle near the Mississippi River. When the news of the incident reached New Orleans, the governor of the French colony declared war.

When peace finally came thirteen years later, many Chitimachas had been killed, displaced, or enslaved. This mighty Chitimacha nation was reduced in population. It had lost its power and political importance among the southern Louisiana tribes.

In 1762 another important milestone in Chitimacha history occurred. The Acadians from Nova Scotia began arriving at New Orleans and moving out along the bayous. These Cajun French people often married Chitimachas. Within a century full bloods became scarce. The Chitimachas began speaking Cajun French instead of their own language. Many converted to the Roman Catholic religion.

By 1880 the remaining Chitimacha people were struggling for survival. They were too poor to own any of the large sugar plantations. They worked on them during the summer and harvest time for wages. Some of them cut timber, manufactured baskets, or raised small quantities of vegetables and sugarcane the rest of the year to supplement their wages.

In 1905 the Chitimachas fought a court battle to retain the last 505 acres of their once vast territory. An out-of-court settlement was made. They were given title to 280.6 acres of the disputed tract. This, too, was almost lost. The attorney in the litigation presented them a bill plus interest almost a decade later. However, Sarah Avery McIlhenney, a wealthy and charitable woman, intervened. She purchased the judgment on the land for $1,450. She agreed to assign ownership to the United States government on behalf of the Chitimachas.

This action prevented the loss of the last of their land.

In response to McIlhenney's efforts, government officials took an interest in the Chitimacha affairs for the first time. On May 8, 1916, Congress placed the land in trust for the benefit of the tribe. A roll of all known living members was established. Only sixty members were named. However, they did not receive any actual government assistance until a reservation school was established in 1934.

Until the 1940s they still relied upon traditional occupations. There were few job opportunities near the reservations. Many Chitimachas shuttled back and forth between the reservation and area lakes, where fishing was good. It took all day to get to the outlying lakes from the reservation in their "push-skiffs" or pirogues.

World War II marked a general turning point in tribal history. Returning war veterans infused the tribe with new ideas, enthusiasm, and a desire to ensure tribal identity for the future. On November 28, 1946, Chief Earnest Darden resigned as chief. He urged the tribe to appoint someone to engineer the formation of a constitutional form of government. This ended the traditional chief-type rule that had existed since prehistoric times.

The **Chawasha** was a small tribe allied to the Chitimachas. In 1713 British slave traders formed a party of Natchez, Chickasaws, and Yazoos to attack the Chawashas under the guise of a peace embassy. They killed the head chief and took eleven prisoners including the chief's wife. Then in 1730 Governor Périer allowed a band of slaves to destroy the Chawasha town. He described it as a total massacre. It is more likely that the adult men were absent from the village on a hunting trip. Possibly only seven or eight of the Indians were murdered. In 1758 Governor Kerlerec stated that they had formed a little village three or four leagues from New Orleans. Afterward the population steadily

Louisiana Indians have preserved the art of basket-weaving.

Louisiana Office of Tourism

declined. They seemed to have disappeared toward the close of the eighteenth century.

The **Tensas** occupied seven or eight villages near Lake St. Joseph, on the west bank of the Mississippi River in northeastern Louisiana. In March 1700 the temple near Newellton was destroyed by lightning and was never rebuilt. Fearing raiding parties from the Yazoos and Chickasaws, the tribe abandoned their villages in 1706. They moved down the Mississippi River to the Bayougoula village. The Bayougoula treated them well. Soon after their arrival the Tensas turned on the Bayougoula. They killed many and drove the rest away.

The Tensas were still at Bayou Manchac in 1715. They also had a village on the south side of the Mississippi above New Orleans. From 1744 to 1763 they lived on the Tensas River. Next they moved to the Red River, then to Bayou Lafourche, later to Bayou Boeuf, and finally to Grand Lake (Tensas Bayou). Gradually, they intermarried and were lost as a distinct people.

The **Washa** was a small Chitimacha tribe. The Washas lived on Bayou Lafourche west of the present city of New Orleans in 1699. By 1805 there were only five individuals. They lived with French settlers.

Choctaw. The Choctaw was the second largest tribe in the southeastern United States. They were excellent farmers who lived in permanent towns in the territory that is now southern Mississippi and southeastern Alabama. Although they were not nomadic, they developed and maintained extensive trade routes. They traded with other tribes as far away as Canada. Some of our modern road and highway routes follow those established by this tribe.

The women did most of the farm work, fetched the water, and cut the firewood. They spun cloth for long skirts from buffalo wool and strong herb fibers, silk grass, or mulberry bark. It was a thick canvaslike material. It could be worn with either side out.

Their society was divided into different classes or castes. At the top were the chiefs. One presided over war ceremonies and another over peace ceremonies. Next was the upper class (the tribe's "own people" or "friends"). Then there were five classes of slaves.

The Choctaw women had their babies alone. It was not until later times that they accepted the practice of mid-wives. When the mother was about to give birth the father retreated to another house. He would not eat until after sunset. Also, he would not eat pork and salt until the baby was born. When the baby was born the mother washed him and placed him in a cradle. A bag of sand was tied over his forehead to flatten it. This is the reason the Choctaws were called "flat heads" by neighboring tribes.

Mothers were not allowed to discipline their sons. This was the duty of the maternal uncle who acted as the boy's teacher. All the boys were schooled morning and afternoon in tribal legends, hunting with bows and arrows, and other manly tasks.

In 1540 the Spanish explorer de Soto began trading with them. The Choctaws were intrigued by Spanish goods, especially metal. They also established trade with the French. By the 1700s they had adopted many French ideas, lifestyles, and cultural attitudes. They had adopted French words into their language. Unlike their Indian neighbors, the men continued to wear their hair in full-length styles.

The Choctaws served as guides for the European expeditions across Louisiana. This relationship resulted in many Choctaw words being used as place names throughout our state.

As colonization increased, there was pressure to choose alliances among the white men. They could join the French to keep the English and their powerful allies, the Chickasaw and Creek nations, from closing trade routes to the north and Canada. Or they could become allies of the English.

From 1754 to 1763 the Choctaws were in almost constant warfare. In 1763 the French and Indian War ended with France ceding all of its lands east of the Mississippi River to the English. About half of the Choctaw towns allied with the French. The other half went to the English. War pressures in the Choctaw Nation eventually led to civil war.

Prior to 1778 Choctaw communities moved from North-central Louisiana to LaSalle, Rapides, Jackson, and Grant parishes. Choctaws lived in the vicinity of two sawmill towns—Jena and Eden. Other Choctaw communities were scattered throughout the Florida parishes north of Lake Pontchartrain.

The Choctaws migrated to the west of the Mississippi in search of farmland and peace. Between 1801 and 1830 they were methodically negotiated off their tribal homelands. A considerable number remained in Mississippi. Smaller bands migrated to northern and central Louisiana.

The **Jena band of Choctaws** incorporated in 1974. The basically rural people live northeast of Alexandria.

Coushatta (Koasati). The Coushatta occupied many villages in their Alabama homeland. They lived in towns and farmed the surrounding lands. The tribe was divided into clans. Each clan was allotted specific fields. A portion of their crops were collected for the public grainery. This reserve supply was used in years of poor harvests and during wars. It was used to feed hungry travelers and the needy.

Courtesy of Rose Kelly

Excavation of a one-thousand-year-old canoe in northwestern Louisiana.

The clans elected their best orator as chief. He appointed a town chief and a war chief for each town. In the center of the town was a square where tribal leaders met to discuss religious, political, and economic affairs.

The Coushattas were primarily farmers. They supplemented their crops by hunting, fishing, and trading with other tribes. They were skilled archers and were reluctant to accept guns. They also used their bows and arrows for fishing. They used blowguns, hook and lines, spears, traps, and hand nets.

In 1540 a Spanish exploration party led by de Soto robbed an outlying Coushatta village. The chief and other leaders were kidnapped. They threatened to burn their hostages alive unless the tribe agreed to give future explorers whatever they wanted.

The Coushattas lived rather peacefully among the French and Spanish until the end of the American Revolution. Settlers pushed farther and farther into Coushatta territory. The years were marked by a continuing struggle over land, with warfare, broken treaties, migration away from white settlements, and a dwindling

Coushatta population. The final blow came when three thousand warriors were killed and twenty-two million acres of Indian land were lost in the Creek War of 1813–1814.

The Coushattas migrated through Georgia, Alabama, Mississippi, Louisiana, and Texas in search for unclaimed land. They looked for a place to reestablish their peaceful agricultural way of life.

By the beginning of the Civil War in 1861, some 250 Coushattas had settled along the Calcasieu River near Kinder. Here the tribe continued its traditions. It enjoyed friendly relations with its neighbors. Their peaceful and prosperous existence was again lost when American settlers became interested in Coushatta lands. In 1884 most of the Coushattas remaining in Louisiana moved to a site fifteen miles east of the Calcasieu River and three miles north of Elton

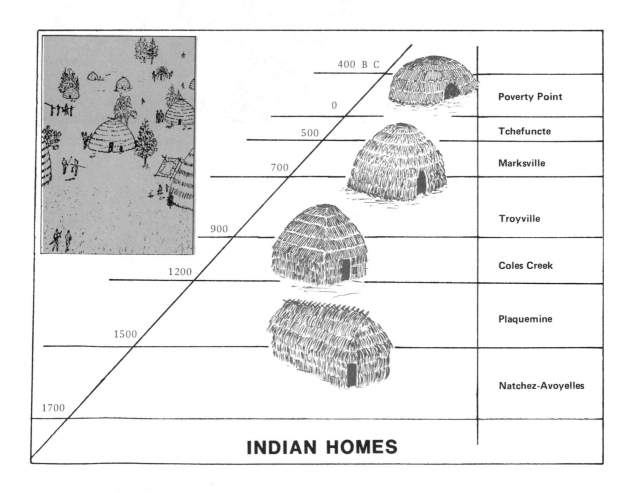

INDIAN HOMES

in Allen Parish. Life was hard for the Coushattas. By 1920 individual tribes of people had carved out an Indian community that occupied more than 1,000 acres of farmland, forest, and lush, green swamps.

In 1898 the United States government placed 160 acres in trust for the tribe. The government assumed partial responsibility for educating the children. Later a federally sponsored elementary school for grades one through five was established. Medical services were added for the tribal members. In 1958, the United States government ended its trusteeship of tribal lands. The government discontinued its meager services. Legally this meant that the Coushatta tribe no longer existed.

In 1973 the newly formed Coushatta Alliance finally succeeded in getting the United States government to legally reestablish recognition of the Coushatta tribe. With the development of a strong tribal government came the revival of a culture almost lost, a heritage almost forgotten.

Houmas. The Houmas were accomplished farmers. They lived in towns or villages and farmed the surrounding lands. Certain unique cultural traits indicate that they may have migrated to Louisiana centuries ago from a homeland somewhere in South America. It is evident that they had some contacts with other Indian cultures in Mexico and South America. One indication of these ties is their grooved blowgun. It is quite different from the can blowgun used by other tribes of the southeastern United States. Several varieties of squash and pumpkin native to the Indians south of the equator were part of the Houma agriculture.

A red crawfish was recognized as their war symbol. War parties were led by women as well as men. One woman was so fierce and respected that she occupied first place on the council of Houma villages. Women could also serve as chiefs.

The French explorer La Salle first encountered the Houma in 1682. The meeting was in the area now known as Wilkinson County, Mississippi, and West Feliciana Parish, Louisiana, near Angola. This was the first known contact with Europeans. When the French returned to the area in 1700, half of the Houma tribe had died of abdominal flu.

In 1706 the Houmas and Tunicas formed an alliance to strengthen their defense against the Chickasaws and their British allies. Three years later the Tunicans turned on their allies. Many Houmas were massacred in the ensuing battle. Those who survived fled southward. They settled briefly on the Mississippi River near Donaldsonville.

During much of the 1700s they migrated from place to place searching for a suitable location for resuming their agricultural economy. As their tribe decreased in size they united with other tribes and pursued hunting, fishing, and trapping. With other tribes joining and merging with the Houmas, their cultures and customs were interchanged. This continued until the tribes were indistinguishable from one another. Only

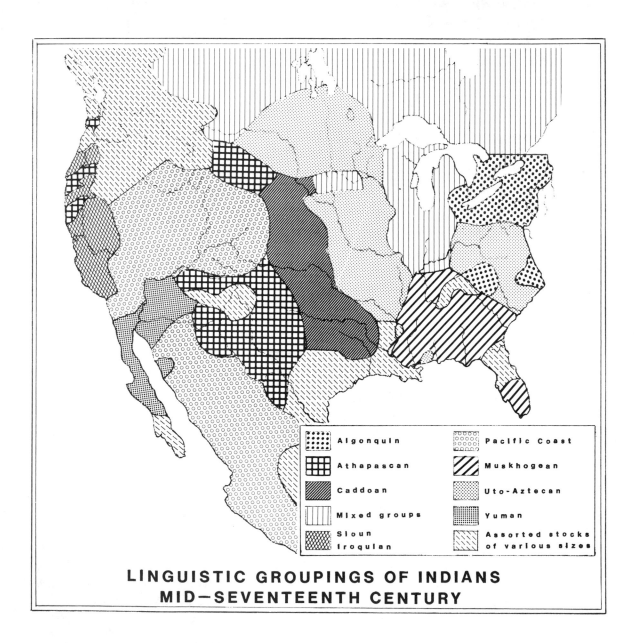

Algonquin

Athapascan

Caddoan

Mixed groups

Sioun Iroquian

Pacific Coast

Muskhogean

Uto-Aztecan

Yuman

Assorted stocks of various sizes

LINGUISTIC GROUPINGS OF INDIANS
MID–SEVENTEENTH CENTURY

the various chiefs attempted to maintain their tribal identities.

From 1820 to 1840 the Houmas migrated farther south until they reached the Gulf of Mexico. They settled along the bayous and swamps in Terrebonne and Lafourche parishes. They shared this territory with the French Acadians and gradually adopted the French language and Catholic religion.

Their skill in weaving finely decorated cane baskets was lost. It was replaced with palmetto, cypress, and plain cane weaving. They were also skilled at moss mat-making. Many of the men are skilled wood carvers.

By 1940 they supported themselves almost exclusively by trapping muskrats and raccoons in the coastal marshes, by fishing with nets for shrimp and other fish in season, and by gathering oysters. Some hired out to cane and rice growers in the lower parishes. Thus, their traditional agricultural economy evolved into a hunting and fishing one on the coastal fringes.

Two distinctively separate tribal governments currently exist. The Houma Tribe, domiciled in Golden Meadow in Lafourche Parish, serves Lafourche, St. Bernard, St. Tammany, Orleans, Plaquemines, Jefferson, and Terrebonne parishes. The Houma Alliance is domiciled in Dulac in Terrebonne Parish.

In 1699 the **Acolapissas** lived on the Pearl River. The **Bayougoulas** lived below Plaquemine. The **Mugulasha** tribe lived with them. Gradually the three groups united with the Houmas.

In 1541 the Spaniards described the **Okelousas** as a tribe "of more than ninety villagers not subject to anyone, with a very warlike people and much dreaded," occupying a fertile land. In 1682 they appear as allies of the Houma. The two tribes destroyed a Tangipahoa village on the east bank of the Mississippi River. They were a wandering people living west of the river on two little lakes to the west of, and above, Pointe Coupee. By the eighteenth century they were a small tribe living west of the lower course of the Mississippi River. They evidently joined the Houma tribe and ceased to exist as a distinct group.

The **Quinapissa** tribe was found by La Salle in 1682. It was located a few miles above the present site of New Orleans. They lived on the opposite side of the river from the Okelousas. The people received La Salle with flights of arrows. On his return they used peacemaking overtures as a mask for a treacherous but futile attack on his force. Four years later, La Salle's friend Tonti, made peace with this tribe. In 1699 Iberville, the founder of Louisiana, hunted for them in vain. He later learned that they were identical to the Mugulashas. The tribe lived with the Bayougoulas about twenty leagues above their former settlement. However, according to Sauvole, Iberville's second in command, the Quinipissas were not identical to the Mugulashas. He said that they had united with them. In any case, there can be no doubt that the chief of the Quinipissas in 1682 and 1686 was the same man who was the chief of the Mugulashas in 1699.

In May 1700, shortly after Iberville had visited them for the second time, the Mugulashas were attacked. They were almost destroyed by their fellow townspeople, the Bayougoulas. The destruction was probably not as complete as the French writers would have us believe. We do not hear of either Mugulashas or Quinipissas afterward. The remnant must have united with the Bayougoulas or Houmas.

The **Tangipahoa** tribe was probably related to the Acolapissa. It was originally a part of that group. Eventually the Tangipahoa merged with the Houmas.

Tunica. Tradition and early records indicate that the **Tunica** tribe lived in northwestern Mississippi and neighboring parts of Arkansas. By 1682 they had concentrated on the Yazoo River. Parties were scattered throughout northeastern Louisiana to boil salt that they traded. They had a village on the Ouachita as late as 1687. In 1706 they feared attacks by the Chickasaws and other Indians al-

lied to the English. The Tunicas abandoned their villages and moved to the Houma townsite opposite the mouth of the Red River. They were well received by the Houmas. However, they soon rose against their hosts, killed more than half, and drove the rest away.

Sometime between 1784 and 1803 they again abandoned their villages. They moved up the Red River to the Marksville prairie. There they settled on a strip of land formerly owned by the Avoyel Indians. This land was recognized as the Indians' Reserve. Their mixed-blood descendants have continued to occupy the land. A part of them went farther west and joined the Atakapas, and another part moved to the Chickasaw Nation in Oklahoma. They settled there along the Red River.

The **Avoyels'** main village was near the rapids of the Red River near Alexandria. Another village was established near the city of Marksville.

Their name signifies "Stone People," or "Flint People." They were active in the manufacture or trade of arrowpoints and raw flint materials. It was not until 1700 that Iberville met some members from this tribe. At that time they acted as middlemen in providing a market for horses and cattle plundered from the Spaniards.

In 1767 they were still occupying a village near the rapids. Although they spoke a Natchezan lan-

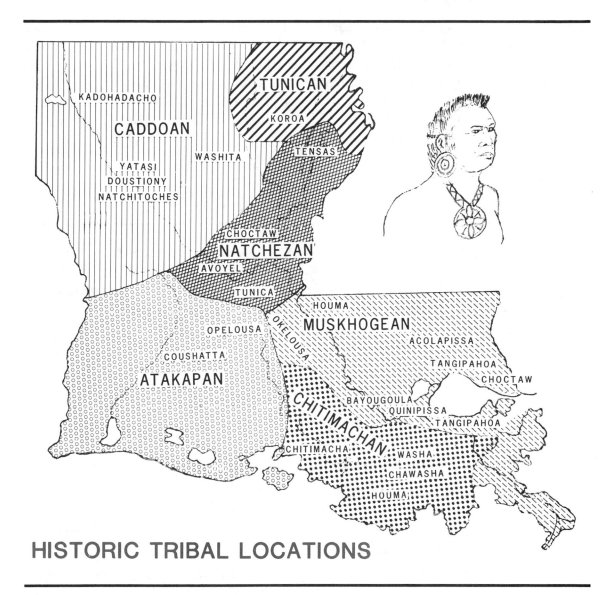

HISTORIC TRIBAL LOCATIONS

guage, the tribe merged with the Tunicas. They lived south of Marksville by 1805, except for two or three women. They made their homes with French families on the Ouachita. It was not until 1932 that the last known person of Avoyel blood passed away.

The **Biloxi** was a Siouan tribe. The group located on the Pascagoula River and Biloxi Bay in the 1690s. They were probably formerly residents of the Ohio Valley. In the early 1700s (1700–1703) they settled on Pearl River at the site formerly occupied by Acolapissas. Later, they drifted back to the Pascagoula River near the Pascagoula tribe.

They lived near the same tribe in that general region until 1763 when both tribes moved across the Mississippi. The Biloxis settled first near the mouth of the Red River. They must have soon moved to the neighborhood of Marksville. They established two villages. One was a half-

Before 1970 the census takers classified the people. Most Indians were grouped as nonwhite. Now each person counted classifies himself.

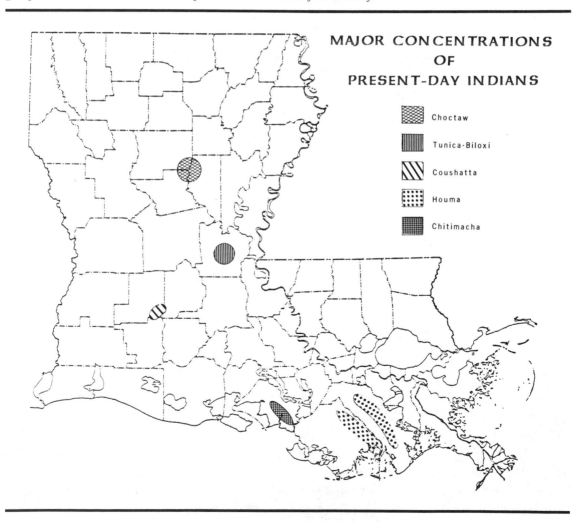

MAJOR CONCENTRATIONS
OF
PRESENT-DAY INDIANS

Choctaw

Tunica-Biloxi

Coushatta

Houma

Chitimacha

This Coushatta Indian, ninety years old, from Elton, was photographed in 1945.

In 1886 a few Biloxis living on Indian Creek five or six miles west of Lecompte were discovered by the Bureau of American Ethnology.

En Partie 3 (Studying a Part). 1. Make a time line of the historic Indian cultures. 2. Map work. Color the areas occupied by the historic Indians: Atakapan-yellow; Caddoan-red; Chitimachan-purple; Muskhogean-green; Natchezan-orange; and Tunican-blue. Label the tribes included in each family. 3. Give some of the outstanding characteristics of each of the historic tribes. 4. Approximately how many Indians were in each group in Number 2 above?

section adjoining the Tunicas. Soon afterward they sold or abandoned this site. They moved to Bayou Rapides. From there they moved to the mouth of the Rigolet de Bon Dieu. Finally, they crossed to the south side to Bayou Boeuf between 1794 and 1796 below a band of Choctaws.

Soon after 1800 they sold their lands to William Miller and Alexander Fulton. The sale was confirmed by the United States government on May 5, 1805. However, the Biloxis remained in the immediate neighborhood. They gradually died out or fused with the Tunicas at Marksville and Choctaws where they still reside. A large group moved to Texas.

Lagniappe. An Indian reservation is land held in trust by the United States government. The federal government is responsible for giving assistance and protection to the Indians. The Bureau of Indian Affairs works with the Indians to make decisions important to the tribe. Indians make the final decisions.

Present-Day Indians

Many Louisianians are of partial Indian descent. However, very few full-blooded Indians live in the state now. Thirteen Louisiana Indian groups have been identified in the state today. Of these, only three receive federal recognition and benefits given such recognized tribes. These are the Chitimachas, Coushattas, and Tunica-Biloxis. Until the 1980s the Chitimacha reservation was the only one in the state. About 250 Chitimachas live on the reservation at Charendon near Baldwin in St. Mary Parish. This reservation has existed since 1935. In the early 1900s the Coushatta reservation was established at Elton. In 1981 it received federal recognition. The Tunica-Biloxi's 150-acre reservation near Marksville was established in 1982. About 150 Indians live there.

Since 1974 the state has officially recognized the Jena-Choctaws, Houmas, Clifton Choctaws, Choctaw-Apaches of Ebarb, and the East Baton Rouge Choctaws. There are a few other small Indian groups scattered throughout the state. The largest group of Indians in the state are the Houmas.

Many Indians in Louisiana have lost their old ways of life. After World War II they entered the labor forces and merged with American life. They live like their white neighbors. Many Louisiana Indians are bilingual. Most Houmas speak French. Many Indians speak at least four languages. These languages include various Indian languages as well as French and English. Interest has been shown in preserving the Indian languages, tribal songs, dances, and crafts such as basket-weaving.

Several Indian tribes have taken steps toward regaining ownership of much of Louisiana's state-owned, as well as privately owned lands, in a legal fight. The Caddos have filed lawsuits. They sued for the difference in what they were paid for their land and what it was worth at the time they gave it up. They have won one suit and lost one.

In 1977 the Chitimacha Tribe of Louisiana filed a suit against eighty-two defendants. The tribe wanted to recover damages for the occupancy of what is allegedly the property of the Chitimachas. The suit asked for oil, gas, and mineral leases and titles to lands in St. Mary Parish. According to their claims, this land is their original territory. The suit claimed that the land is subject to the protection of acts between the Chitimacha tribe and the French crown in 1767 and the Spanish crown in 1777. The acts were carried forward by the Louisiana Purchase, according to the suit filed. The lands include the center of the ancient Chitimacha tribal territory. The Chitimachas lost this suit.

Lagniappe. In 1934 an Indian elementary school was established for the Chitimachas. It was federally funded. A state-supported elementary school was established for the Choctaws about the same time. If an Indian wanted to attend an Indian high school, he had to go to one in Kansas or one in Mississippi. Few Indians could afford to send their children away to school. Until the late 1960s, Indians did not attend public schools in Louisiana except in a few cases. A few parishes had three school systems—one for whites, one for blacks, and one for Indians. Other parishes had two systems. Indians were not permitted to attend white schools. They did not choose to attend black schools. After the integration movement in the 1960s, Indians started attending public schools. A cycle of low education and low-paying jobs resulted from their poor educational backgrounds.

Louisiana established an office of Indian affairs in 1972 to help meet the needs of the Indian communities. The office is also responsible for working with the federal, state, and local governments on matters pertaining to Indians. Since May 1975 the Inter-Tribal Council of Louisiana has provided the leadership to meet the needs of the state's Indians.

En Partie 4 (Studying a Part). 1. Where are Louisiana's Indian reservations? 2. Which groups of Indians reside on them? 3. How large is each reservation? 4. How many Indians live in Louisiana today? 5. Why are the pre-1970 population figures for Indians not accurate?

Present-day Louisiana Indians are still questioning the rights of the white man to this land. In 1774 the French writer and explorer **Le Page du Pratz** recorded the feelings of a Natchez Indian chief, Tattooed Serpent, about the same subject.

Why...did the French come into our country? We did not go to seek them: they asked for land of us because their country was too little for all the men that were in it. We told them they might take land where they pleased, there was enough for them and for us: that it was good the same sun should enlighten us both, and that we would walk as friends in the same path; and that we would give them our provisions, assist them to build and to labor in the fields. We have done so; is not this true? What occasion then had we for Frenchmen? Before they came, did we not live better than we do, seeing we deprived ourselves of a part of our corn, our game, and fish, to give a part to them? In what respect, then, had we occasion for them? Was it for their white, blue, and red blankets? We can do well enough with buffalo skins which are warmer—our women wrought feather blankets for the winter, and mulberry-mantles for the summer; which indeed were not so beautiful; but our women were more laborious and less vain than they are now. In time, before the arrival of the French, we lived like men who can be satisfied with what they have; whereas at this day we are like slaves, who are suffered to do as they please.

Coup d'Main (Completing the Story)

Jambalaya (Putting It All Together)

1. Approximately how many Indians were in Louisiana when the explorers set foot on Louisiana soil?

2. What were the means of transportation common to the early Indians?

3. How did the white man affect the Indian's life?

4. Explain how geographical factors affected the way Indians lived and where they settled.

5. Which animals were probably in Louisiana when the first Indians were here but are not here now?

6. (a) What did the Indians gather to eat? (b) What else did they eat in Louisiana?

7. Key words and phrases:

a. Archaic era
b. artifacts
c. atlatl
d. Bureau of Indian Affairs
e. carbon 14
f. filé
g. herbs
h. historic
i. Inter-Tribal Council
j. maize
k. midden
l. mound
m. oral history
n. Paleo-Indians
o. potsherds
p. Poverty Point
q. prehistoric
r. refuse
s. sassafras
t. seminomadic
u. shaman
v. spearpoint

Potpourri (Getting Involved)

1. Prepare a map of Louisiana showing (a) location of prehistoric Indian sites, or (b) location of historic sites.

2. Make a model of (a) an Indian village, (b) an Indian house, (c) an Indian tool, (d) an animal trap used by the Indians, or (e) one or more Indian weapons.

3. Demonstrate how Louisiana Indians (a) farmed, (b) secured food, (c) made arrowheads, (d) played games, (e) dressed, (f) danced, (g) talked, (h) cooked, or (i) made pottery.

4. Research (a) carbon-14 dating, (b) Indian warfare, (c) the practices of medicine men, (d) Indian legends, (e) forms of amusement, (f) Indian music, or (g) the history of any tribe.

5. On a map trace the migration of an Indian tribe.

6. Produce a mural, film, or play on (a) the history of Louisiana Indians from their origin to present or (b) the struggles between the Indian and the white man.

7. Compare and contrast the Indians in Louisiana with Indians from other areas.

8. Pretend that you are (a) an Indian boy or girl in Louisiana before the first Europeans arrived, (b) the first European to visit Louisiana, or (c) an Indian being driven westward by the white man. Write a letter or diary entry describing your feelings.

Gumbo (Bringing It Up-to-Date)

1. Research (a) Louisiana's present Indians, telling how and where they live, (b) a Louisiana Indian tribe from the time it left the state until today, (c) lawsuits involving Louisiana Indians, (d) Louisiana's Indian reservations, or (e) the role of federal and state governments in present-day Indian affairs.

2. Prepare an exhibit or bulletin board entitled "Indians—Then and Now."

CHAPTER 3

LOUISIANA'S EXPLORERS
(1519–1687)

When Christopher Columbus discovered the New World in 1492, he began an explosion of adventurers and explorers from Europe. They were out to discover what the rest of the world was like. That period is called the Age of Exploration. Columbus himself had set out to find a new water route to the Orient. He thought that if he were to sail far enough to the west, he would come to Asia. He failed to reach that goal. Other explorers would find what Columbus did not as they sailed from all the nations of Europe to explore the New World.

There were sound economic reasons for finding a new route to Asia. In the latter half of the 1400s, Europeans needed new and better ways of trading with the Orient. For several hundred years Europeans had learned to want many products from Asia. Sugar, glass, steel, cutlery, rugs, pepper, cloves, cinnamon, nutmeg, porcelain, and silk were some of the products they sought. They did not produce these items for themselves. Because Europeans wanted these things so badly, a lot of money could be made from buying and selling these luxuries. This one fact had a great deal to do not only with the discovery of the New World but also with its later development.

Two hundred years after Columbus set foot in the Western Hemisphere, the Louisiana colony was settled. During these two centuries, many European countries sent men to find out more about the land across the sea. Only two countries—Spain and France—sent men to explore what is now Louisiana.

The Spanish Explorations

Columbus's voyages gave Spain claim to the islands of the Caribbean and changed the course of Spanish

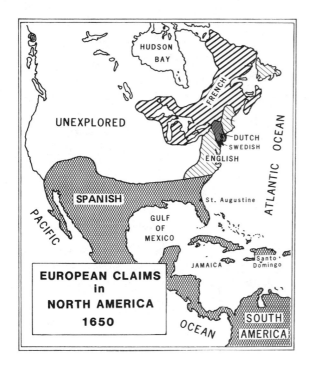

EUROPEAN CLAIMS
in
NORTH AMERICA
1650

Other Spaniards came to escape the harsh rules of both the church and government. Others sought adventure and fame. The Spanish, then, have been described as coming to the New World for the "three *G*s"—gold, God, and glory.

By 1500 the colonies that had been started in the West Indies by Spain became the bases from which numerous explorers sailed. Spaniards went to the mainland of both North and South America in search of wealth in the form of gold, silver, and precious stones. Several of the many exploring journeys or expeditions of the early 1500s had a direct impact on the history of Louisiana.

It is not certain who was the first white man to set foot on the soil that is now Louisiana. It was probably

history. Gold was found in Mexico and Peru, and there were promises of even more. **Hernando Cortés** captured the vast treasures of Montezuma in Mexico. **Francisco Pizarro** conquered the Incas in Peru and gained tremendous stores of gold and silver. The loot was sent to the treasure house of the king of Spain. The hope of great wealth brought other explorers.

Tales of the rich lands spread so that others wanted to seek their fortunes. The desire for riches was not the only reason people came to the New World, however. Friars and priests also came because they wanted to spread Christianity and baptize and save the souls of the Indians.

Christianizing the Indians

one of the many Spanish adventurers. The Spanish crown's approval of funds for explorations required that records be kept by the explorers. We are indebted to them for the original accounts of Spanish travels. These accounts offer a fascinating glimpse of what went on. An explorer—or some explorers—visited the land around the Gulf of Mexico and learned enough to draw maps. Maps dating from 1520 document this fact.

Piñeda's Journey. In 1519 the governor of Jamaica sent **Alonzo Alvaréz de Piñeda** to explore the Gulf of Mexico from Florida to Vera Cruz, Mexico. As his fleet sailed along the coast, he made maps of the area and showed the rivers he had discovered. Piñeda went ashore in several spots along the way, but it is not known exactly where. Piñeda reported that the entire coast from Florida to Vera Cruz was part of the mainland. He described the Indians as peaceful. He wrote that he saw dwarfs, men of medium size, and giants. (The giants were probably the Karankawa Indians who lived on the Gulf coast near present-day Galveston, Texas.) Piñeda's map showed that the all-water route to the riches of the East was not anywhere in the Gulf area. The voyage was also important because it gave the first account of the landmass of the New World.

Narváez's Expedition. In 1527 the king of Spain gave **Pánfilo de Narváez** a grant to explore and settle all land between the Cape of Florida and Rio de las Palmas (probably the Rio Grande). Early the next year, the expedition of four hundred men, eighty-two horses, and four ships left Cuba and landed on the west coast of Florida to search for gold.

Alvar Nuñez Cabeza de Vaca was the treasurer of Narváez's trip. He was to look after the king's interest and collect the king's share of gold and silver. Narváez and de Vaca disagreed about the best route to follow. Narváez did it his way. He chose to march his troops overland to the Rio de las Palmas. He and his men suffered many hardships during the next few weeks. They lost their way in the swamps and forests of Florida. Narváez's men robbed the Indians for food. They fought and killed hostile Indians and almost died of starvation.

The Indians were already angry because of the cruel treatment they had received from earlier explorers. The Spaniards had become enemies of the Indians because they had attempted to destroy the symbols of the red man's religion. They felt that they must make Christians out of the Indians. The Indians attacked the Spaniards and forced them back to the seacoast where they were without food. The Spaniards were forced to kill and eat their horses.

Narváez had sent the fleet to

the Rio Grande. The men who went ashore were to meet the ships at a point farther up the coast. When the explorers arrived there, no ships were to be found. Finally, the Spaniards, who found themselves stranded, decided to try to go to Mexico by sea.

They built five crude horsehide boats. Sails were made from the men's clothing. Ropes and rigging were devised from the manes and tails of the horses. They used tools that they had brought from Europe to make saws and hatchets. They made nails from melted swords, stirrups, crossbows, and armor. They cut trees to make planks.

About 250 brave seamen set out along the Gulf coast in their pitifully inadequate sailing vessels. Upon setting sail, two of the craft quickly capsized, and the occupants drowned. As the days passed, the food supply was exhausted, and the horsehide water bags rotted. Many of the men died of hunger and thirst. Those who lived became so weak that they could hardly hold the oars in the Gulf, which was often rough and stormy. Narváez and 80 weary and sick Spaniards were about halfway to their destination in November 1528 when a storm drove them to land. The coast where they found themselves was probably what is now the state of Texas. They landed about where Galveston now stands.

While most of his men slept ashore that night, Narváez stayed aboard ship. During the night, he was blown to sea. He was never seen again.

By the time the winter of 1528–1529 was over, severe weather and lack of food and shelter had reduced the 80 men to 16. Hostile Indians had enslaved some of them. Soon the survivors resembled their primitive Indian masters. They ate fish, snakes, and lizards. They labored for long hours. At times the Spaniards were cruelly beaten.

After five years of living under these circumstances, there were only a few survivors. One of these men was Cabeza de Vaca. Other survivors were Castillo, Dorantes, and Estevan, a skillful Negro slave. By chance, the living conditions of the survivors improved. By giving the sign of the cross and praying, they appeared to have cured several Indians who were thought to be very ill. For that, they came to be looked upon as medicine men. Because of their new position, they received the best their captives had to offer. They were also free to travel.

The Spaniards used their freedom to leave their captors and walk from the site of their shipwreck to Mexico City. It took eight to ten years to make the trip. In July 1536 Cabeza de Vaca, Estevan, and the other survivors finally reached their destination. Once in Mexico City, they told the head of the government, Viceroy Antonio de Mendoza, about their adventures.

De Vaca then went to Spain. He was anxious to tell the king about his experiences. He told stories about the Indians who claimed that there were valuable metals and precious stones that could be found in the interior of North America. De Vaca asked the king if he could lead an expedition to the New World to look for those riches. His wish was not granted. The king had given that task to one of his friends, **Hernando de Soto**, only a short time before.

Hernando de Soto's Travels. De

DE SOTO'S TRAVELS THROUGH LOUISIANA

Travel through the marshes was difficult.

Soto was a veteran of the Spanish expeditions. He had been a lieutenant of Pizarro's when they robbed the Incas of Peru. He was soon getting ships, men, and supplies ready to sail for Florida. It was done largely at his own expense. It took a year for him to get ready for the journey.

On April 6, 1537, de Soto began his trip with one of the largest and best-equipped outfits that ever set sail for the New World. He had seven large ships called galleons, each with three or four decks. He had a smaller ship called a caravel with one deck. There were two brigantines used to service the other ships. They were also used as lookouts. There were about six hundred men, including twelve priests, in the party. The assemblage made a spectacular sight.

De Soto planned for everything. Such things as steel, iron for saddlebows, spades, pickaxes, crates, ropes, and baskets, as well as many other tools, were aboard ship. The cargoes included about one hundred horses and some hogs to supply meat for the explorers. De Soto took bloodhounds for running down escaped Indian slaves. So much was aboard that double rations were allowed for everyone.

At their stop in Santiago, Cuba, the Spanish explorers were met by a parade. The soldiers participated in races and tournaments. Games and great celebrations were held. After visiting Havana, they finally left on

May 12, 1539. On the last day of May they reached Florida.

Three days after they arrived in Florida, de Soto sent some of his men to claim the land for the king of Spain. For the next few days, the ships were unloaded. Then de Soto ordered the ships to return to Cuba so that the men would not be able to use the ships to desert.

Early in the journey de Soto found a young Spaniard from the Narváez expedition. His name was Juan Ortiz. Ortiz had been captured by the Indians and kept as a slave for about ten years. He told de Soto all he knew about the Indians and their methods of warfare. Ortiz served as interpreter and helped de Soto make friends with some of the Indian chiefs.

The Spaniards had to fight their way through the country because most of the Indians were hostile. The Spaniards treated the Indians very harshly. Frequently the Spaniards used their fierce dogs to frighten or kill the Indians. They also took food from the Indians. The Spaniards usually won the battles, but they lost both men and horses. When the Indians learned that the Spanish soldiers had a big advantage with their horses, they used the tactics of shooting the horses from beneath the riders. By the time de Soto reached the Mississippi River, more than half of his men and horses had been lost.

After two years of wandering, on May 8, 1541, the men looked through an opening in the pine forest and saw before them a mighty river. They had discovered the Mississippi River. They did not realize that they had found something more important than gold. Instead, they saw it as a problem; it would be difficult to cross the broad expanse of water in their search for gold.

De Soto had his men build rafts with which to cross the river. On the western side of the river, they marched through what is now Arkansas. After spending the winter in the area, they continued their journey to reach the Gulf.

This trip took them into present-day Louisiana. Researchers believe that de Soto and his men stopped at places in Louisiana now known as Jonesville, near Lake Bistineau; the town of Columbia; and Drake's Salt Lick near Winnfield.

Just three years after the journey started, forty-two-year-old de Soto died of a fever at an Indian village called Guachoya. This was near the present town of Ferriday, Louisiana. His body was first buried inside the walls of their little fort at the mouth of the Arkansas River. Then, when it was feared that the Indians would find the newly made grave and realize that the Spanish leader was dead, his body was dug up. It was placed in the trunk of a hollow tree, weighted down, and buried in the Mississippi River.

DE SOTO'S SECOND BURIAL

Luis de Moscoso, who had been with de Soto in Peru and was the commander of one of the galleons of the expedition, became the leader. Moscoso and the other officers first attempted to go to Mexico instead of returning by the Mississippi River and sailing for Cuba as de Soto had planned. Eventually they returned to Guachoya. After spending the winter there, they started down the river on July 2, 1543. About 350 soldiers and 25 Indian servants with thirty horses and eighteen hogs spent twenty days getting to the Gulf coast. By staying close to the coastline, they reached the Spanish colony located where the city of Tampico, Mexico, is today. Sixty-one of the party had died on the way. Approximately 312 men reached Mexico City.

De Soto and his men found no gold, but de Soto is acknowledged as the discoverer of the Mississippi River. Knowledge of the great river spread throughout the European world. Firsthand accounts helped spread information about the trip. At least four original accounts of de Soto's travels exist.

The Spanish explorations revealed that the great lands that had been traveled were not rich in gold or other precious metals like those found in Mexico and South America. The Spaniards failed to see the great value in the land they explored. Henceforth, they lost interest in the land that they might have claimed. For a century and a half, the Indians continued to live undisturbed by Europeans. It remained for another nation—France—to claim and settle the land that was to become the state of Louisiana.

En Partie 1 (Studying a Part). 1. Why did the explorers travel in a westward direction? 2. What were the goals of the Spanish? 3. Why were the explorations of Piñeda, de Vaca, and de Soto important? 4. Why were the Indians hostile toward the Spanish? 5. Why was de Soto's discovery of the Mississippi River far more important than the finding of gold would have been?

French Explorations

The history of Louisiana really began with the French expeditions.

These explorations spread from Canadian settlements to the Mississippi Valley in the latter part of the seventeenth century. The story of Louisiana had its origins in the ambitions of Louis XIV and the French settlers in Canada.

New France was the land now known as Canada. The French started settling it only a year after the English planted their first settlement at Jamestown, Virginia. The English lived close together as protection against Indian attacks. The Frenchmen strung their settlements out along streams far into the wilderness. The French established trading posts here and there. They came down the St. Lawrence River and into the Great Lakes. That gave them an easy way to travel to other sections of the continent.

The French were concentrating on the fur-trading business. Rich Europeans clamored for furs to adorn themselves. The price was high enough for the fur business to compete with gold mining as a sure road to wealth. Fur traders kept pushing farther westward and southward. They made trade agreements with Indians covering areas of the vast wilderness where rich furs could be obtained.

Fur trading did not encourage large groups of settlers. A number of Frenchmen became **coureurs de bois**, or woods runners. These lived with the Indians or lived like the Indians. They trapped animals and sold furs.

Their enterprises naturally led them into every stream, and they heard about the "Great Water" from the Indians. Curiosity about where the river went stirred the explorers into searching for the answer.

Marquette and Joliet's Trip. In 1673 Governor Louis Frontenac of Canada ordered **Father Jacques Marquette**, a Jesuit priest, to go with **Louis Joliet**, a fur trader, on an exploration of the Mississippi River.

FRENCH EXPLORERS

French and Indian trade was important to the colony.

(The French always took priests along to Christianize the Indians.) They followed the Mississippi to the mouth of the Arkansas River, but they were afraid to go farther because of possible trouble with the Spaniards. They returned by way of the Illinois River after a four-month journey. Their trip had shown that the Mississippi flowed southward.

The Journeys of René-Robert Cavelier, sieur de La Salle. La Salle, a rich fur trader, heard tales about the Mississippi River. He decided to try to do what no other white man had done; he would follow the great river to its mouth. He hoped to set up a string of forts and to find a passage across the continent to the Pacific Ocean and the Far East. He also hoped to attract the fur trade of the Great Lakes region to Louisiana. La Salle had made an agreement to help finance the trip himself in exchange for trade rights. He was to have the sole right to trade in buffalo hides in the region.

There was another reason for La Salle's trip. The king of France, Louis XIV, wanted a harbor for French ships on the Gulf of Mexico. Spain, France's enemy, had gold and silver mines in Mexico that the king wanted to reach. In 1679 he became very angry when Spanish warships on the Gulf of Mexico captured a French ship. The king, therefore, wanted La Salle to find a harbor so French ships could harass the Spanish.

On February 6, 1682, La Salle, at the age of thirty-nine, with his friend **Henri de Tonti** and a priest, **Father Anastase Douay**, began the historic journey. With a small band of fifty-six people, they started at the Great Lakes and journeyed toward the Mississippi. The party included ten Indian women and three children. Upon reaching the Mississippi, they started their canoe caravan down its long and twisting path toward the Gulf of Mexico. As they went along, they selected locations for forts and gave names to the places where they stopped. It took them more than two months to make the journey. Finally they reached the mouth of the river and landed.

With great ceremony, on April 9, 1682, La Salle set up a cross bearing the coat of arms of France. It was inscribed "Louis the Great Reigns." It was erected amid shouts and the solemn chants of the priest leading the mass. Then standing near the cross, La Salle read his speech. He announced the naming of the new land "Louisiane" for Louis XIV, king of France. The party chanted the "Te Deum," a song of praise to God, and they sang the song of France. Then they fired their muskets into

Frenchmen explore the Mississippi

the air. With suitable words in honor of the king, La Salle claimed for King Louis XIV of France the Mississippi River and all the land drained by the river and all its tributaries. He buried a metal plaque marking the spot. In this manner, he set up a claim to territory already explored by Spain.

La Salle was pleased with the results of his trip. He was eager to tell the king of his discoveries. As rapidly as possible, he returned to Canada and then crossed the ocean to France. He told King Louis about the Mississippi. He explained that if

Historic New Orleans Collection

La Salle took possession of Louisiana and the Mississippi River in the name of Louis XIV in April 1682.

a French colony were established at the mouth, it would be easy to attack the Spaniards and take their wealth.

King Louis was so pleased that he approved La Salle's plan to build a fort near the mouth of the Mississippi River. He named La Salle governor of all the lands that he had claimed for France. The king outfitted four ships, gave La Salle four hundred colonists, and sent him to make a settlement where he had set up the cross. It was 1684. It had taken La Salle two years to get back to France and make preparations to return to the New World.

The four ships bearing La Salle's colonists sailed from France July 24, 1684. They took a course toward the West Indies. La Salle quarreled constantly with Beaujeu, the naval commander who was in charge of the ships. On the way the supply ship *St. Francis* was lost to Spanish pirates. La Salle blamed Beaujeu for this. At Santo Domingo La Salle became ill, and the trip to Louisiana was delayed six weeks. Some of the colonists probably felt that the project was off to such a bad start that they stayed in Santo Domingo.

The expedition missed the mouth of the Mississippi. Perhaps it was due to the quarreling of La Salle and Beaujeu. There may have been other reasons. The river waters pour into the Gulf of Mexico through three narrow passages that were not so well defined in 1684 as today. Some historians say that La Salle may have wanted to go closer to Mexico and its silver mines. Whatever the causes, La Salle and Beaujeu missed the Mississippi River entirely.

La Salle's party, in the three remaining ships, sailed four hundred miles farther to the west. They landed at Matagorda Bay in what is now Texas on February 15, 1685. A storm came up suddenly and sank one ship. Another was grounded. That left only one ship. Beaujeu lost no time in returning to France in it. Beaujeu took about forty settlers with him. They took items badly needed by those left behind—priceless guns and ammunition, food, supplies, and clothing. La Salle and about two hundred settlers were left stranded in an area of hostile Indians.

In 1685 La Salle directed the construction of a fort at Garcitas Creek. He named it Fort St. Louis. With scant supplies, La Salle and the little colony, which had dwindled to about forty-five people, survived for two years. La Salle hoped to get to Canada and seek help for the colony. Canada was fifteen hundred miles away. Twice, La Salle and a party started out but finally had to return to Matagorda Bay. It was March 1687 when a third and final attempt was made.

On March 18, 1687, La Salle was assassinated. Many stories exist about the assassination. At least one reason given for his assassination is strange indeed. According to that version, La Salle's men were sitting around a campfire eating wild game that they had roasted. La Salle's nephew was in the group. A quarrel arose over who was to have the privilege of eating the marrow from the bones of the animal. In the fight that followed, the nephew was killed. Nobody wanted to tell La Salle. They knew that they would pay with their own lives. Therefore, they killed La Salle when he returned to the camp.

Another version has it that La Salle's murder was planned by angry followers. According to this story, the assassin had slashed the heads of La Salle's nephew, his servant, and an Indian guide while they were sleeping. When La Salle came upon the scene, he was murdered.

The Spanish sent out expeditions to search for La Salle's colony. In 1689 a party found the ruins of the doomed settlement on Matagorda Bay. It is known that many of the handful left at Fort St. Louis had died of disease long before La Salle was killed.

It is believed that the Indians killed all except a young man and some young children. According to the story, the survivors lived with a kind old Indian woman.

Much of the information learned about La Salle's trip has been learned from firsthand sources. One of the four survivors of La Salle's second expedition kept a diary. His name was Joutel.

One of the stories written about the explorers concerns La Salle's friend Tonti. "Iron Hand" was the name given him by the Indians. Tonti was an Italian who had served in the

French army. He had lost his hand in battle. According to some, he amputated it himself. He received his nickname because of a metal device that he wore attached to the stump of his arm. La Salle met Tonti in France in 1677. Tonti became his lieutenant and devoted friend. He was with La Salle during his exploring and trading operations around the Great Lakes and on the Illinois River. He and La Salle were partners in a fur-trading business. They operated from a post on the Great Lakes. All fur traders were constantly exploring the new continent in search of more furs for trade. La Salle and Tonti were often involved in such expeditions. Tonti was second in command when La Salle made his voyage down the Mississippi. Tonti was in Canada when La Salle was in trouble with his new settlement, Fort St. Louis in Texas. Tonti became alarmed about La Salle's failure to report and took an expedition down the Mississippi River to find him. For two years, Tonti searched and was unable to find any trace of La Salle. He left a note written on bark with an Indian chief somewhere near the mouth of the Mississippi River.

La Salle made a place for himself in Louisiana history as well as in the history of the world. He was the first man to fully appreciate the size and importance of the Mississippi Valley. La Salle was the first white man to

EUROPEAN CLAIMS IN 1689

explore the Mississippi from its upper waters to its mouth. It was because of his efforts that the French eventually became interested in colonizing the great Mississippi Basin.

En Partie 2 (Studying a Part). 1. What were the purposes of La Salle's expedition? 2. Describe the ceremony at the mouth of the Mississippi River when the land was claimed for France. 3. What was the name given the land? 4. What area did he claim? 5. Why did the French king assist La Salle in his plans to settle Louisiana? 6. Who was Tonti? 7. Why did La Salle fail to find the Mississippi? 8. Describe La Salle's second expedition. 9. What happened to La Salle?

Coup d'Main
(Completing the Story)

Jambalaya (Putting It All Together)

1. Make a chart using the following headings. In chronological order, fill in the information. Explorer; Country; Date; Purpose; Area Explored; Results.

2. On a map, trace the routes of the Louisiana explorers and show the territory claimed by La Salle.

3. Which European country had the first claim to Louisiana?

4. Which European country next explored Louisiana?

5. Which country had the best claim?

6. What is the relationship between the following?

  a. de Vaca's journey
     Narváez's journey
  b. Coronado's expedition
     Louisiana explorations
  c. Tonti
     La Salle
  d. de Soto
     Moscoso
  e. de Soto
     trouble with the Indians
  f. Explorers
     poor means of travel
     and communication
  g. Explorers
     westward travel
  h. Purpose of explorations
     success

Potpourri (Getting Involved)

1. Imagine that you made one of the trips with a Louisiana explorer. Give reasons why you were selected. Tell about your experiences. Include the preparations for the trip.

2. Pretend that you were an Indian boy or girl who watched the landing of a ship loaded with an exploring

expedition. Tell what you saw, how you felt, and how you greeted the visitors. Tell how you were treated by them.

3. Describe the lifestyle of the *coureurs de bois*.

4. Make a model of (a) the type ships used by the explorers or (b) Fort St. Louis.

5. Make a timeline showing various expeditions, settlements, and wars during the period of exploration of Louisiana. Show what was happening in the rest of North America and/or the world.

Gumbo (Bringing It Up-to-Date)

1. Report on any part Louisiana has in current explorations.

2. Compare: (a) La Salle's trip with a trip in space, (b) the support given to the early explorers by people from their home countries with the support given the space programs in the United States and Russia, (c) the reasons for interest in the New World with the reasons for interest in space, or (d) the preparation for a trip by an early explorer with preparations for a space trip.

FRENCHMEN ARRIVE IN LOUISIANA

PART TWO

During the Colonial Period

Louisiana Office of Tourism

Chapter 4   *French Colonial Louisiana*
Chapter 5   *Spanish Colonial Louisiana*

CHAPTER 4

FRENCH COLONIAL LOUISIANA
(1699–1762)

By 1690 France was at war in Europe. That was three years after La Salle died. The peace treaty was signed in 1697. Because of the war and the spending of Louis XIV, France had no money for foreign investments. King Louis XIV had constructed a palace at Versailles. It had been furnished at great cost. France could not afford to settle its Louisiana colony. To plant a colony required vast sums of money. Yet, without any sign that France had possession of the land, other nations could claim Louisiana.

Many thought that a colony should be established. Books published in France and in England kept the idea of colonization alive. Two early explorers published books about Louisiana. These books had great influence on the decision to send another expedition to settle Louisiana.

One book was written by La Salle's friend Henri de Tonti. The book *La Salle's Last Discoveries in America* was published in 1697. It stimulated the French people's interest in the Mississippi Valley. Tonti gave reasons why France should hasten to cinch its claim to Louisiana by planting a colony there. The colony would be located at the mouth of the Mississippi River. It would be close to the silver mines of Mexico. From the colony, France could seek to capture these mines. Along the coast Louisiana had a wealth of fur-bearing animals. Louisiana, at the mouth of the Mississippi, formed a pathway to Canada, which the French owned. The colony would prevent the English from settling in the area.

The other enthusiastic explorer was Father **Louis Hennepin**. He had been on one of La Salle's expeditions. Later he became a subject of Great Britain. He wrote two books, which were published in England. In his books Hennepin urged England to place a colony at the mouth of the

Louisiana Office of Tourism

Louisiana was named for Louis XIV.

Mississippi River.

Already there were signs that the English were preparing to settle Louisiana. They were finding settlers to send. There were signs that they were outfitting ships. Other nations were also interested. Among them was the Netherlands.

The Count de Pontchartrain, the minister of the marine in France, supported the establishment of a colony. He knew that whoever controlled the lower Mississippi River Valley would control the "back door" to the entire continent. He was able to convince King Louis XIV that France had to send colonists to Louisiana as quickly as possible.

French Colonization

Iberville's Expedition. There had already been requests from men who wanted to lead an expedition to Louisiana. Among these was Henri de Tonti. These offers were rejected. Instead, the minister started the search for the most suitable leader available. Finally, he selected a young Canadian. The twenty-seven-year-old man was **Pierre Le Moyne, sieur d'Iberville**.

Iberville was a lieutenant in the Royal Navy. He was the first Canadian to receive such a commission. Iberville was already a hero in Canada. He had shown his skill and courage in King William's War when he defeated the English at Hudson Bay and Newfoundland. He was also a skilled woodsman. Iberville seemed well qualified to command the colonizing expedition.

Iberville was from a family of at least eleven children. Four of the sons of Charles Le Moyne and Catherine Primot became famous. The two most famous contributed to the development of Louisiana. They were Iberville and Jean Baptiste, known as Bienville. Records show that eight of the sons won honors in the French navy. The father and three of his sons died fighting for France.

Charles Le Moyne was born in France. When he was a youth, he went to Canada and settled on an estate. He started as a *coureur de bois*. Later, he earned a fortune in fur trading and was granted a title of nobility.

Lagniappe. In Canada, landowners followed a custom of the nobility of Europe. They added the names of their estates to their Christian names. In this way Pierre Le Moyne became known as Iberville. Jean Baptiste became known as Bienville.

Pontchartrain asked Iberville what he needed for his task. The list included the ships, people, and supplies for accomplishing the mission. The lieutenant asked for an eight-month supply of provisions for the ship. He required goods for six months for the fort that he planned to build in Louisiana.

The ships included two frigates, the **Badine** and the **Marin**. In addition, Iberville had four small pre-fabricated boats. These were made in parts to be assembled in Louisiana. Iberville stored them in the hold of the *Badine*. Some thought that Iberville used too much space for the boats. They felt that space was needed for food and other supplies.

About three hundred men began the voyage. The group included Iberville's eighteen-year-old brother, Bienville. As was the custom on all French expeditions, a priest went along. With Iberville and his party was Father Anastase Douay. The priest had been with La Salle on his first expedition down the Mississippi River to claim the territory. Father Douay could speak several Indian dialects. It was a very useful skill for one traveling in the New World.

In September 1698 Iberville was finally able to leave the port of La Rochelle. There had been a month's delay. Workmen had been slow in repairing the *Badine*. Once out to sea, they found that water was seeping into the *Marin*. It was causing the hardtack, a tough biscuit, to spoil. There was nothing to do but return to a French port. The expedition depended on this very important part of the food supply.

The flotilla anchored in the harbor at Brest, France, on October 24, 1698. It remained there for seventeen days. At last they were once more ready to sail. After forty-one days at sea, on the morning of December 4, they arrived at Santo Domingo, an island in the West Indies. One of the ships had been blown off course by a great storm. Ten days later it arrived at Santo Domingo. Damaged by the storm, the ship had to be repaired. The other boats were in need of supplies, which they were able to secure on the island.

At Santo Domingo the *François* was added to Iberville's convoy. The ship would lend extra protection in case it proved necessary to battle another country for the land at the mouth of the Mississippi River. Ten crewmen had either died on the voyage from France or were seriously ill with yellow fever. Iberville replaced them with some tough pirates. He hired a guide, Laurent de Graaf, who had explored the northern Gulf coast earlier. Then he asked de Graaf and the former pirates what they knew about this new land.

Iberville, trained as a naval officer, kept careful records of the voyage. He took notes day by day. It is from his journal that we learn about this first settlement.

Iberville had the benefit of reports and maps from members of the La Salle expedition. His reference materials included valuable books. He used a copy of Joutel's *Journal Historique*, the works of Hennepin, and the stories collected by Father Leclerc from members of La Salle's first expedition. He was depending on the description of the mouth of the river given to him years before by La Salle himself. Above all things, he did not want to make the same mistake as La Salle and miss the Mississippi River.

As soon as Iberville sighted the Gulf coast he carefully watched for English ships. It was said that the English were also planning to set up a colony on the Mississippi. He sailed as close to the shore as he dared.

The French convoy went into the harbor at Pensacola on January 26, 1699. The fog lay heavy over the coast. The French were surprised to find that a large number of Spanish boats filled the harbor. Iberville dropped anchor out of range of cannons that might be fired from the shore. To his surprise the Spaniards caused no problems. They were half-starved and sick. Iberville pretended to be searching for some lost Canadians. He was glad to learn about the surrounding country from the Spanish settlers. A few days later the Frenchmen sailed on along the coast to the west. The ship that had guided them from the islands returned to Santo Domingo.

On January 31, 1699, Iberville wrote that he had anchored at Mobile Bay. In the area he slept on an island, which he christened Massacre Island. He and his men found the bones of sixty people who had been killed there a few years before. Later, the name of the island was changed to Dauphin. It was named for the dauphin, the oldest son of the king of France and the person next in line for the throne.

Iberville's expedition island-hopped as it continued along the Gulf coast. Once the winds blew so hard that Iberville and his men could not return to their flagship. On another occasion the men went hunting. Iberville wrote that they killed eighteen buzzards, several ducks, and a raccoon.

Iberville wrote about Dauphin Island and the other islands that the sailors found near Mobile Bay. "I found all sort of timber, oak, elm, ash, pine and other wood unknown to me; numerous vines; sweet-scented violets and yellow-flowers; horse-beans similar to those of Santo Domingo; walnut [pecan] trees with a very delicate bark; birch trees; high ground which does not flood, Indian footprints and huts, which they abandoned not more than six days ago. I fired several shots in order to be heard, and I made marks on the trees." At one island he brought hay for the cattle and wood aboard the ships. The weather, he wrote, was beautiful.

They sailed slowly along the Gulf coast. They made soundings and took notes. At last, on February 10, 1699, they arrived at Ship Island. It was so named because it had a natural harbor.

The next day, Iberville wrote that he had gone through the shallow water to shore. "The woods there are very pretty—mixed vegetation. There were numerous blooming plum trees, turkey tracks, partridges which are only as large as quail, hares comparable to those in France, and fairly good oysters."

Iberville's expedition went farther west following a string of barrier

Bienville was governor four times under the French.

islands. He named Horn and Cat islands. The "cats" were probably raccoons or opossums.

One day Iberville saw a campfire along the shore of an island. Another day he found Indian tracks. He followed them until darkness fell. The next day, he "continued to follow the Indian tracks, having left two hatchets, four knives, two packages of porcelain beads, and a little vermillion [red dye] at my campsite, not doubting that the two Indians, who had come at daybreak to observe me at three hundred paces, would go there when we would depart."

On February 13, 1699, Iberville and Bienville visited the Biloxi Indians on the mainland. There were three men and two women in the group. They chanted words of peace. Iberville gave them gifts and walked with them to their canoes. The Indians made a bread called sagamite from maize for Iberville and his men. The next day the Indians came in their canoes. By this time Iberville was able to persuade three of them to come aboard the ship. To do so, he left his brother Bienville and two other men as hostages with the Indians on shore. They smoked the calumet, or peace pipe. Then Iberville shot the cannon for them. The Indians told him about a great river to the west. They said that it could be reached by a short land journey. They called the river Malbanchia. They agreed to guide him to it. On the appointed day they failed to appear.

Some of the Indians Iberville saw wore only loincloths. Others wore breechcloth leggings, moccasins, and feather headresses. Some wore necklaces of bone and the bills of flamingos. Others wore nose rings and earrings. These were the Biloxi Indians, a peaceful, friendly people.

The Frenchmen knew that finding the Mississippi would be difficult. The land was low and flat. There were many small islands covered with grass and tall reeds. Locating the river could be a problem.

About the middle of February 1699 Iberville decided on a plan to find the river. One of the officers would remain at Ship Island with the fleet. Iberville and Bienville would go in one boat. Sauvole, who was an officer, and Father Douay would go in another. The search party was to return within six weeks. If it did not, Surgeres would return to France in the *Marin* if provisions ran short.

On February 27, 1699, Iberville set out with two large boats and two canoes. About forty-eight men started the trip. They took provisions for twenty days. They sailed along the coast to the west. They very carefully watched for a sign that they were approaching the great river. The fog, heavy rains, lightning, and winds made the job very tedious.

They approached the river by sailing from the Gulf into what is now known as the North Pass. After four days, on March 2, 1699, Iberville discovered fresh water. The stream became much wider. It had a swift current. As he reached the widest part, Iberville knew that this had to be the Mississippi.

The next day Iberville continued upstream. After four days, he met some Houma Indians. Indian guides joined the party of Frenchmen. The Indians showed them a short path leading to a small bayou.

Iberville's Indian friends had sent the word to the Bayougoulas and

Mongoulachas. These Indians lived not far from Bayou Plaquemine. They knew that the Frenchmen were on their way. Therefore, Iberville's expedition received a very warm welcome. They were even invited to smoke the peace pipe at a nearby village. The Bayougoulas pointed out the crescent in the river to Iberville. They thought that this would be a good spot for a settlement. (The spot that the Indians pointed out is the site of present-day New Orleans.)

A description of the French and Indians' meeting is given in the *Journal of Paul du Ru*:

Everybody dresses up to meet the Bayougoulas. Beards are trimmed and fresh linen put on. Here is the landing place. Our vessels assemble to enter the port in order. The landing begins. The whole bank is black with savages who sing the Calumet to us. M. de Bienville is in the escorting canoe; M. de la Ronde is in the wooden canoe which he calls *Hardy* and M. Chateauguy in another wooden canoe, all with flags at the stern and all firing shots. We arrive in good form.

Iberville was still not sure that he had found the Mississippi. When he saw the Mongoulacha chief wearing a blue coat, his doubts were erased. Father Douay had told Iberville that Tonti had left his Montreal blue coat with the Indian chief. He also told him that Tonti had left a letter with the Indian chief. It was to be given to the first white men who came by. The chief did not give the letter to Iberville. He thought Iberville was a Spaniard.

The Frenchmen moved up the river. They came to a spot on which a red pole about thirty feet tall stood. It marked the boundary between the Bayougoulas and the Houma Indians. The Indians called the red stick "istrouma" in their language. The French called it "baton rouge" (red stick) in theirs.

The next day the Indians took the French through a sharp turn in the river. This place was called Pointe Coupee. The Frenchmen traveled for two more days. They reached the Houmas' village. There they feasted. In turn they gave presents to the Indians. The chief of the Houmas told Iberville that Tonti had been to their village twice. Once he was on the way to the mouth of the river. Again, he came when he returned to the north.

Iberville and Bienville did not return together to Ship Island. Instead, Iberville chose to take the shortest route home. He went through Bayou Manchac. It connects the Mississippi with a lake. Iberville named it Lake Maurepas for the son of the minister of the marine of France. From Lake Maurepas, he sailed into a

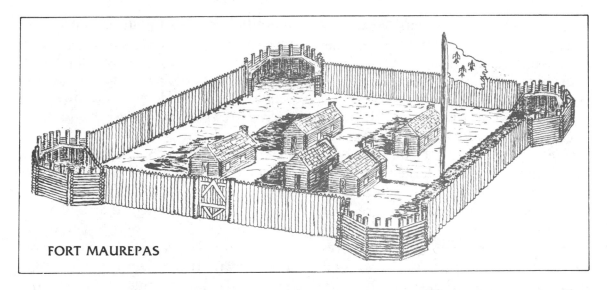

FORT MAUREPAS

larger lake. Iberville named it Lake Pontchartrain for the minister of the marine. Iberville found that waterways connected Lake Pontchartrain with the Gulf of Mexico. He sailed through them. Then he went through the Gulf waters back to Ship Island in Biloxi Bay.

Bienville, Sauvole, and the others returned the same way they had come. They went down the Mississippi River. Then they sailed out into the Gulf of Mexico and sailed east to Ship Island. Bienville's crew stopped at the Mongoulacha village to get Tonti's letter to La Salle. The Indians had hidden it in a hollow tree thirteen years before. For that reason, they called it "the speaking bark." The letter was final proof that the Frenchmen had found the Mississippi River. Iberville recorded a copy of Tonti's letter in his journal. "Al-

though we have neither heard news concerning you nor seen signs of your presence, I do not doubt God will crown your affairs and your enterprise with success. I desire it with all my heart, for you do not have a more loyal servant than myself, who sacrifices everything to find you."

The two brothers arrived back at the starting point within a few hours of each other. It was just one month after starting the trip to find the Mississippi.

Fort Maurepas. Iberville selected a site on Biloxi Bay for building a fort. The French had planned to set up a colony on the Mississippi River. However, Iberville decided to place the settlement on Biloxi Bay instead. He was not sure that the ships could go through the passes at the mouth of the river. The fort was needed to secure supplies from the ships. The area was low and marshy on the coast, so he carefully selected the highest ground. It was a quiet bay. He thought there would be shelter from the winds.

Plans were drawn for the fort. Iberville directed the crew as they cleared the site. There was an abundance of very large hardwood trees. Iberville wrote that he had no experienced lumberjacks to fell the trees. Still the men managed. Iberville had a forge set up to repair the axes, which broke often in the hardwood. Carpenters and other craftsmen had been brought along for such work.

Construction began on April 8. By May 1, 1699, the fort was completed. The small square fort had four bastions. On these were mounted twelve guns. A ditch was dug around the fort for protection. Iberville named it Fort Maurepas.

The settlers started preparing their homesites. Cabins for ninety colonists were built outside the fort. The colony was named Biloxi for the friendly Indians who lived nearby.

Many activities helped to get the colony started. Priests ministered to the newcomers, who worked to construct their fort. Twenty-five men were ordered to clear land. Then they planted peas and beans so they would have food. Livestock were unloaded from the ships. There were bulls, cows, hogs, and fowl, including turkeys. When the ships were unloaded,

Iberville recorded the inventory. There were "eight casks of completely rotten peas, two kegs of spoiled bacon which had not been salted, two barrels of flour which was like dust and had soured." The olive oil and wine had leaked out of their containers.

Friendly Indians. Several Bayougoula braves came to the fort. Later, they returned with the chiefs of five nations. They presented Iberville with the calumet of peace and honored the French officers in their own way. There were three days of ceremony. The Indians sang and danced three times each day. As part of the ritual, an Indian raised Iberville to his shoulders. Another held his feet. They carried him to a clearing where they had driven a stake. There the Indians danced around the stake. As the Indians danced, they made sharp sounds with calabashes filled with pebbles.

At the fort there was a warehouse. It held trinkets and other items to be used as gifts to the Indians. Iberville and his men gave the Indians mirrors, combs, glass beads, guns, hats, rings, and other things. Iberville's presents to the Indians also included shirts, stockings, hatchets, knives, and blankets.

The French gave the Indians picks and shovels. They showed them how to make ax handles. The Indians taught the French how best to plant seeds. They also taught them how to care for plants. They showed the Frenchmen many foods that they could find in the forests. Another important thing the Indians taught the French was the art of making "dug-out" canoes. These were canoes dug out of a single log. The Indians gave the French bearskins. The French built a good relationship with almost all of the Indians. They were not successful with the Natchez and the Chickasaws, however.

Bienville started learning about the Indians as soon as he set foot in the New World. He traveled in canoes with Indian guides. He carefully studied the Indian languages and dialects. By the time he had made a trip with the Mongoulacha guide up the river, he was able to understand the language. He could speak it with some ease.

Iberville's First Return Trip. After Iberville was sure he had arrived at the Mississippi, he was relieved. Once he planted a settlement, he decided to return to France. It was necessary to get supplies and enlist new colonists. He was eager to report to the king. He had accomplished his mission "to find the Mississippi River and chart it and to establish a fort." Iberville left Sauvole in charge. Bienville was made second in command. Iberville selected seventy-five of the best men and six cabin boys to remain at Fort Maurepas. He took the other men with him to man the ship. He sent a ship to Santo Domingo to secure supplies for those left at the fort. He left enough provisions with them to last six months. On May 4, 1699, he departed for France. He reached France on July 2, 1699.

Difficulties at Fort Maurepas. As leader while Iberville was gone, Sauvole had a terrible time. Keeping the men working and the fort in order were his biggest problems. Coping with deserters and threats of desertion were a constant burden. He was to look for a better location for building a permanent fort. Keeping friendly with the Indians was highly important. Moreover, it was necessary to improve the area around the fort.

Many of the colonists did not like to farm. That first year few crops were planted. Their gardening efforts did provide some food. The colonists were surprised at their success with lettuce seeds. Eighteen days after planting, they were amazed to find the lettuce ready to eat. Later the hot sun burned the crops. The land around the fort was sandy and infertile. It would not grow much even if the settlers had worked hard at farming. They preferred to hunt, trap, or search for gold and other precious metals. They wanted wives to make homes for them. In other words, most were not very happy about being in the New World. They certainly did not like the hard work of growing food.

The marshy area became so dried out that there was not even good drinking water available. There was no rain at all during that first July, and men became ill due to lack of good drinking water. The suffocating heat was almost unbearable. There were alligators, which frightened the settlers, and there were many snakes. Fungus grew on furniture and clothes in the hot, humid climate. Worms and insects plagued the Frenchmen. The vicious mosquitoes and hostile animals added to their discomfort. Sudden tropical gales, uncertain water currents, and uneasy footing in the marshes presented untold problems. The colonists became bored and discouraged. They drank liquor excessively.

Bienville's Explorations. Bienville went on an exploring trip to the mouth of the Mississippi River. He went by way of the lakes and Bayou Manchac.

In May 1699, while Bienville was exploring, he learned from some Indians near Lake Pontchartrain that a group of Indians had been attacked by some Englishmen. The threat of attacks by the Indians or the English was always present. Bienville worked at winning the friendship of the Indians.

The English Turn. On September 15, 1699, Bienville had an interesting experience. About eighteen miles below the present site of New Orleans, he saw a big ship. It was flying an English flag. Bienville recognized Captain Lewis Banks as a person he had known in Canada. Banks was looking for a place to start a settlement. He inquired of Bienville about the river and his location on it. The quick-thinking Frenchman informed Captain Banks that he was trespassing on French soil. Bienville told him to turn back without delay. He also told him that there were many Frenchmen at the settlement just around the bend of the river. Captain Banks turned his boat around and left. Because of the incident, that point on the river is called *Détour des Anglais*, or English Turn. Today there is a historical marker at the spot. Historians have wondered what would have happened if the English had not turned back.

Iberville's Return. In France Iberville was given much encouragement. He was supplied with full equipment for a second voyage. His brother Chauteuguay, age seventeen, joined Iberville for his return trip. He was also joined by two other kinsmen—Louis Juchereau de St. Denis and Pierre de Boisbriant.

Upon Iberville's departure for the colony, King Louis XIV had instructed him to keep peace with the Spaniards. He cautioned Iberville not to have any contact with Spain.

As soon as Iberville reached the settlement at Fort Maurepas on January 8, 1700, he heard bad news. In fact, he received the news even before he left his boat anchored in Biloxi Bay. Sauvole came aboard Iberville's ship to report. Sauvole told what had gone on in the colony during Iberville's absence. Four men had died, he said. He had heard also that two priests had been killed by the Natchez Indians. This brought concern that the colonists at the mouth of the Mississippi might be cut off from the north country by hostile Indians.

Iberville listened to Sauvole tell about how Bienville had met the English and turned them back. The English presence alarmed Iberville. He thought that the powerful English might well return to challenge the French claim to Louisiana.

Fort de la Boulaye. Iberville left Sauvole in charge of Fort Maurepas and made another trip to the Mississippi River. With him were Bienville, St. Denis, and sixty men on two barges.

They planted sugarcane near Bayou St. John. Their most important business on this expedition, however, was the building of a fort. The fort was intended to protect France's claim to the Mississippi River.

Iberville selected the site. It was about fifty miles above the mouth of the river. Workers built a small blockhouse and powder magazines of red cypress. The house was twenty-eight square feet. Five or six cabins remained to be constructed according to the plans. They were to have roofs of palm leaves. A Frenchman who saw the place kept a journal. He said that the fort was "only an idea here in the midst of the Mississippi woods."

The little fort was equipped with four four-pound guns and two eighteen-pound guns. A moat twelve feet wide was dug around the fort. The fort was named Fort de la Boulaye. It was the first European settlement in what is now the state of Louisiana. It was completed in February 1700. It was not a permanent fort since it was abandoned several years later.

While this work was going on, Iberville made other plans. One was to meet with Boisbriant. Boisbriant was coming to the river with men from Fort Maurepas. Their goal was to look for mines. After these men arrived, Iberville decided to ascend the Mississippi River again.

While the fort was being built, some Frenchmen from Canada arrived. Tonti had heard that the French were settling the territory. He decided to find out for himself what was being done. With him were fifty men, ten canoes, and a cargo of furs. Tonti had visited the Natchez Indians on the way. He told Iberville that it was not true that the Natchez had killed two French priests. He remained at the fort for three days before he, Bienville, and Iberville left together. Iberville and Bienville left Tonti at the present site of Natchez, Mississippi, among the Chickasaws. Iberville thought that this spot would make a good place for a settlement. Tonti understood the mission of going among the powerful tribe of the Chickasaws. It was necessary to try to build better relationships for the French.

After Iberville returned to Fort de la Boulaye, he became ill with a fever. For a while he rested at the fort before returning to Fort Maurepas. Bienville was left in command of the new fort.

Iberville's Second Departure. Sauvole remained in charge at Fort Maurepas. There were 123 men left at the fort. The ailing Iberville sailed for France at the end of May 1700.

Exploration of the Red River. Because King Louis XIV had ordered Iberville to locate mines in the colony, Sauvole sent twenty-five men to search in the area near the Spanish territory. Bienville and St. Denis went through Old River to reach the Red River. Bienville and his party came upon the Indians called Natchitoches, or "Chinkapin-eaters."

Life at Fort Maurepas. Things did not go well while Iberville was away. There were threatening signs from Indians stirred up by the English. Canadians were coming into the territory with their furs to trade. The settlers did not need any competition from the French in Canada. The settlers in Louisiana needed all the fur-trade business of the lower Mississippi Valley.

Supplies at Fort Maurepas were getting low. Shipments from France came now and then. The settlers could not depend on these shipments. It was not possible to predict when shipments would arrive. Also, the Frenchmen at the fort had little success with their game-hunting or their farming. As a result, food was scarce. The peas, beans, maize, and other vegetables did not grow well in the coastal soils at Biloxi. The colonists were often ill, and there was no medicine. Once a ship that was to bring medicine left with the medical supplies rotting in the warehouse in France. The crew forgot to load them on the ship. Nearly a third of the fort's settlers died within the first two years.

Sauvole's Death. On August 22, 1701, Sauvole died of yellow fever. Bienville, then twenty years old, was left to run the colony. Bienville had been living at Fort de la Boulaye. After Sauvole died, Bienville left there. He returned to Fort Maurepas and took charge. Only 150 persons remained in the colony. St. Denis took Bienville's place at Fort de la Boulaye.

Iberville's Arrival. In December 1701 Iberville returned from France. A carpenter named Pénicaut came to Louisiana with Iberville on this third trip. He remained in the colony twenty years. Pénicaut wrote an account of his life in the colony. When he returned to France, he published a book, *Fleur de Lys and Calumet*. Historians today question the truth of Pénicaut's account. His accounts do not agree with others writing at the same period.

Fort St. Louis de la Mobile. While in France Iberville had gained permission from the king to move the fort to a more suitable site. He first moved most of the settlers to Dauphin Island (Massacre Island) in early 1702. Iberville later selected a higher and healthier site for the new fort. Bienville began construction of a new fort at Mobile Bay. That site had a good harbor and better farmlands.

The new fort was named Fort St. Louis de la Mobile. Within the fort walls were quarters for the commandant, a house for the officers, a guardhouse, a chapel, and a storehouse for supplies. Barracks for soldiers and homes for the settlers were built outside the fort. The new fort was much larger than Fort Maurepas. Fort St. Louis de la Mobile became the capital of the Louisiana colony.

A group of soldiers were left at Fort Maurepas and another post was established on Dauphin Island. Iberville, founder of Louisiana, had now completed four settlements—Fort Maurepas, Fort de la Boulaye, Fort St. Louis de la Mobile, and Fort Dauphin Island. A few plantations and farms had been established along the banks of the Mississippi River.

Spanish Warnings. The Spanish governor of Pensacola, Arriola, demanded that the French leave Fort Maurepas. The peppery governor had earlier tried to get Mexican officials to help him get rid of the French on the Gulf coast. The Mexicans refused. At that time Sauvole was acting governor of Louisiana. Sauvole had flown an English flag over Fort Maurepas to deceive the Spanish leader. The Mexicans then promptly sent help to the Spanish governor, Arriola, to attack the "English" settlement at Biloxi and destroy it.

Governor Arriola reached Biloxi with four ships and four hundred men. He captured a boat that was flying an English flag and found that all aboard were Frenchmen. They told him about the strength of the French colony. Arriola decided not to attack. He sent a letter to Sauvole instead. In the letter, he wrote that the French were in violation "of the treaties," which gave Spain claim to the land. Arriola claimed that the treaties applied not only to Biloxi but to all the land bordering the Gulf of Mexico. Arriola threatened several more times. Then he sailed away.

A storm wrecked Arriola's ships. One wreck drifted toward Biloxi. When the French from the fort sailed out to see what was floating in the water, they found Arriola clinging to his wrecked ship. He was half-naked and ill from his ordeal. Some of his men were left marooned on the islands in Biloxi Bay.

Bust of Louis XIV.

Louisiana Office of Tourism

Sauvole sent a rescue party to take the governor and his surviving men to Fort Maurepas. There they provided a feast, wine, and fresh clothes. Then the French escorted the Spanish back to Pensacola. The French were amused by this incident.

Iberville's Final Trip. The colony was badly in need of supplies by the spring of 1702. Iberville decided to return to France. He left on April 27. With him was the Jesuit priest Father Paul Du Ru. A new war, Queen Anne's War, had broken out in 1701. Iberville was needed in France to serve in the French navy. He tried to get more soldiers and settlers to send to Louisiana. However, the mother country was too busy fighting to send help.

Iberville was still weak from his six-year fight with what some historians have called yellow fever. When he became well enough, he was placed in command of a fleet belonging to France and Spain. The two countries were allied in the war against England. He was expected to capture the English colony Carolina. Iberville reached Havana in 1706 and was to complete plans to attack Carolina. Before he could do so, he died.

Problems. There were many serious problems in the colony. There was much illness and a lack of medicine. The deadly fevers often killed settlers. After 1702 the settlements in the Louisiana colony grew very slowly.

Most of the colonists were soldiers. Many of the men deserted and joined the English in Carolina. A number of the men took Indian women as mates during the first years at Fort Maurepas. Neither the French leaders nor the Indians approved of the situation. Iberville had pleaded with France to send families who would till the soil. Most of the people who came, however, were adventurers and fortune-seekers. They expected to get rich easily. They were not willing to put forth the effort or make the sacrifices necessary for survival in the colony. They had not dreamed of the hardships they would have to endure.

Lagniappe. "Creole" became a very popular word in the colony. It was used to apply to people and things native to the colony. Descendants of early French or Spanish settlers were Creoles. Originally, the term applied to a native, especially of the West Indies, Central America, South America, or the Gulf states. The word comes from the Spanish *criollo*—a child born in the colony. Usage of the term has changed over the years. In modern usage, the term pertains to anything characteristic of, or related to, Creole people. It is even used to describe a special outlook on life. It would be difficult to find two Creoles who would agree on the exact meaning of the word.

Until the arrival of the "*Pelican* girls" in 1704, there had been no French mates for the colonists. The bishop of Quebec sent twenty-three young women to the Mobile colony on the *Pelican*. They were chaperoned by Mlle. Boisrenaud. They were to become wives of some of the men. The women soon threatened to leave. They did not like the food, especially the Indian maize. They wanted French bread. Bienville's housekeeper taught them how to use maize. She taught the women to grind the corn into meal for cornbread. They also learned to make hominy, grits, and succotash.

Arriving with the Pelican girls were two nuns and a curate (religious leader). Seventy-five soldiers and four families of artisans also arrived on the *Pelican*. There was another addition to the population in 1704. The first Creole, Jean François LeCamp, was born in the colony.

Almost all of the settlers were extremely unhappy with their living conditions. The homes of the colonists were crude and poorly built. They resembled Indian huts with thatch roofs. The shipments of supplies from France did not arrive regularly. Too much time elapsed between shipments of much-needed goods. Once the situation became so desperate that the Spanish in Pensacola came to the rescue with provisions.

France was in serious financial trouble. It had no money to spend on the Louisiana territory, which had not brought the riches the French officials had expected. King Louis XIV and his officials had ordered the soldiers to search for pearls and for gold and silver mines. The French

INDIAN AND FRENCH TRADERS

The economic development of France was based on the fur trade.

government tried to promote such schemes as having the settlers tame buffalo or raise silkworms.

There was no relief for the settlers. In 1705 thirty-five persons, including Tonti, died of yellow fever. Malaria and dysentery were common.

Complaints About Bienville. The settlers were generally dissatisfied. They constantly quarreled among themselves. They also complained about Bienville. Iberville's death seemed to encourage them to attack Bienville fiercely. Even the priests joined the attackers. They bitterly protested to authorities back in France about their young governor.

There were so many charges against Bienville that the king sent a man named **Diron d'Artaguette** to investigate Bienville's performance as governor. Bienville was ordered to return to France for questioning. Before Bienville was to leave, d'Artaguette cleared him of all blame. A dishonest official in France had been stealing money that Bienville had been accused of taking.

De Muy was named governor as the replacement for Bienville. He had been the commander of French troops in Canada. However, he died before he could assume the position. Bienville remained as governor.

Fort St. Louis de la Louisiane. It was decided to relocate Fort St. Louis de la Mobile. There was always the danger of Indian attacks on the fort. The site was also subject to flooding. The flood of 1709 was the immediate cause of the move. About 1710 the fort was moved closer to Dauphin Island and Biloxi. The name was changed to Fort St. Louis de la Louisiane. It became the capital of the colony.

Bienville. Bienville remained as governor until 1713. At that time a new governor was appointed. Bienville, although cleared by the investigator, had been retained in the position only until a new governor could arrive at Mobile.

Bienville was still in his teens when he arrived in Louisiana in 1699. He had no experience in governing. The soldiers and settlers at the fort had only the barest necessities for survival in a wilderness. Yet the colonists did not want to work at such chores as planting potatoes and peas. The soil on the coast was not the best for planting. The heat was oppressive, and mosquitoes swarmed around them. Many died from fevers. Yet with all these problems the youthful

Bienville was able to keep the colony in existence for a decade.

En Partie 1 (Studying a Part). 1. Why were the French interested in the Mississippi Valley? 2. Why did France wait many years after La Salle's death before sending colonists to Louisiana? 3. Why were the Le Moyne brothers especially well prepared to begin a settlement in Louisiana? 4. Who headed the expedition? 5. (a) Where did they settle? (b) When? (c) Why? 6. After landing, what expedition did Iberville and Bienville undertake? 7. What was the story of the English Turn? 8. Why did Iberville earn the title "Founder of Louisiana"?

Louisiana under Crozat, the Proprietor (1712–1717)

Louis XIV and his officials were greatly upset over the Louisiana colony. Gold and silver mines had been the dearest dreams of the king. So far, none had been discovered. The colony was a great problem for France. It added to the nation's critical need for money. France was in a depression and burdened with debts. The people were heavily taxed. The prestige of the military was shrinking. The War of the Spanish Succession

(Queen Anne's War, 1701–1713) continued. There were constant problems with the Indians in the colony. The English in Carolina had plans to settle the land at the mouth of the Mississippi. It was true that France and Spain were allies against England. Yet, the Spanish resented the French settlement in Louisiana. Canadians thought that the governors of the Louisiana colony were trying to divert the great fur trade of the upper Mississipi Valley down to the settlement on the coast. They wanted to keep the center of the fur business of the New World in Canada. France had had enough of Louisiana. A wealthy merchant, Antoine Crozat, offered to take Louisiana as a commercial venture. France gladly accepted. According to some historians, there is evidence that Crozat was even pressured by officials to make his offer.

Crozat's Commercial Monopoly. Crozat was a peasant's son. At fifteen he was a clerk in a commercial firm. After being there twenty years, he was made a partner. He married his partner's daughter. At the death of his father-in-law, he became owner of the business, which furnished slaves to the New World. He also dealt in other trade with Africa. He became very wealthy and was interested primarily in making more money.

Crozat received a royal charter on September 14, 1712. It granted him the sole right to carry on trade in the Louisiana territory for fifteen years. For his part Crozat agreed to send two shiploads of colonists and supplies to Louisiana each year. For nine years France was to allow him a sum of money to pay the soldiers and colonial officers. After that the expenses were to be borne by Crozat. The king was to get the "royal fifth" from the proceeds from mining and from any precious stones found. Crozat also had to follow the laws of France in Louisiana. In addition, he was to own all factories started by him. He was also given all the land he could cultivate. He was the only one who could import slaves from Africa. Crozat held exclusive right to trade in all hides and furs except beaver skins. Beavers were protected in Canada because they were used in the place of money.

Appointment of Cadillac. Antoine de la Mothe Cadillac had been appointed as governor May 5, 1710. He did not arrive in Mobile until March 17, 1713, however. He had personal affairs to settle before he could leave Canada. The governor of Canada refused to furnish Cadillac an escort from Detroit to Canada. Cadillac went from Canada to France and from there to Louisiana. Cadillac's wife chaperoned twelve girls who made the trip from Paris.

Cadillac was sixty-seven years old when he came to Louisiana. As a boy in Canada, he had trained for a career in the French army. He became a lieutenant when he was twenty-one. For over twenty years he was in the service of the king. During this period he made a glorious reputation for himself. He had founded Detroit, the chief fur-trading center in all the Western world. He had expected to live the rest of his life in the place he had founded. Then came his selection as governor of Louisiana. He was

French Colonial Government

King

Governor

Superior Council

bitter about the appointment. Detroit was much more advanced than Mobile at that time. Living there was much more comfortable than on the raw frontier.

The settlers first learned about the removal of Bienville as governor when Cadillac arrived. It took several weeks for news from New Orleans to reach the distant posts. Sometimes direct communications were entirely cut off for months. Most of the settlers did not object when they did hear the news of Bienville's removal.

In 1712 there were only about three hundred people in Louisiana. These settlers lived along the Gulf coast and along the Mississippi River. Probably fewer than fifty persons were in the present state of Louisiana. There were two companies of soldiers with about fifty men in each. Between seventy and eighty Canadians employed by the king completed the makeup of the colony.

From the moment he saw the colony, Cadillac criticized it. He seems to have planned to compensate for his misery by getting rich off treasures in Louisiana. He traveled to the Illinois country hoping to find silver mines. All he found were lead mines. Crozat grew angry at Cadillac's lack of leadership in developing Louisiana's trade. He filed complaints against the governor with French authorities.

A new set of officials were sent to Louisiana with Cadillac. The **Superi-**

or **Council**, appointed for three years, was established as an advisory body. The council consisted of the governor, the intendant, and two agents who were to represent Crozat's interests. The attorney general used the Custom of Paris laws. These were the written laws and legal customs of Paris and the surrounding area.

Crozat's Plans. Crozat started his new business venture by sending over two shiploads of new settlers. They were mostly people expecting to get rich quickly. Most of them made poor settlers. Volunteers had stopped coming to the colony. Criminals, debtors, and orphans were almost the only ones coming. Crozat offered free passage to settlers. Soldiers were allowed to bring their families. In 1716

FORT ST. JEAN BAPTISTE

a royal decree returned all land grants to the royal domain so that the land could be given to new settlers.

Crozat planned to make money in many ways. He sent a large quantity of goods, which he hoped would be sold at a profit. Crozat's dream of obtaining riches from Louisiana commerce depended heavily on the sale of Louisiana furs. This included selling all supplies to the settlers and buying their pelts for the European market. To drive better bargains, he obtained monopolies.

St. Denis's Trip. Once Crozat undertook the Louisiana project, he moved quickly. He shipped tons of merchandise for trade to the capital at Mobile. He finally succeeded in getting Cadillac to appoint a representative to go to Mexico. Crozat had plans to start trade with Mexico. For this job Cadillac chose St. Denis, the veteran explorer. St. Denis was then in charge of Fort de la Boulaye.

Cadillac could not have made a better choice than Louis Juchereau de St. Denis. He was a heroic figure to the Indians living in western Louisiana. St. Denis already knew the vast stretch of land to the west very well. He spoke several Indian languages as well as Spanish and French. He respected the Indians and helped them in times of need. Rarely has there been such a gifted salesman as St. Denis. He had the polish and skill needed by a diplomat.

Cadillac had received a letter from Father Hidalgo, a Spanish priest. Father Hidalgo had once worked with the Tejas Indians. Father Hidalgo asked the French to send missionaries to minister to the Tejas because his own government would not allow Spanish priests to cross the Rio Grande into the land of the Tejas Indians. The letter provided an excuse for St. Denis's presence in Spanish Texas. St. Denis was ordered to locate Father Hidalgo. He was to establish trade relations with the Indians along the way and obtain a trade agreement with the Spanish.

Natchitoches in 1714. St. Denis's first stop was with the Natchitoches Indians on the Red River. He signed a treaty with them. Then he built a storehouse for his goods. After that he left some of his men at the village. They were to form a garrison on the Red River against the Spanish. They were to guard the goods left in the warehouse. A fort, **Fort St. Jean Baptiste de Natchitoches**, was later established at the garrison. The storehouse became a trading post, and an important settlement grew around it. This was Natchitoches, the first permanent settlement in all the Louisiana territory and the oldest settlement in Louisiana.

After a short while St. Denis started for Mexico with a pack train. He and twenty-five men took a load of goods with them. He sold goods

Louisiana Office of Tourism

These primitive huts are within Fort St. Jean Baptiste, a state museum.

to Indians all the way to the Rio Grande. Some Tejas Indians agreed to guide St. Denis and his party to San Juan Bautista.

After months he was ready to cross the river into Mexico. It was a very daring thing to do. The Spanish were ready to shoot any stranger who dared to cross the boundary. A presidio, or Spanish fort, guarded the boundary. St. Denis was not fazed, however.

On July 18, 1714, St. Denis arrived at the mission of San Juan Bautista. He became the guest of the commandant of the presidio. He discussed trade with the commandant. Perhaps St. Denis offered him a share of their profits from a trade agreement. Supplies from France and Spain were never enough for early settlers. They were so far away from rulers that perhaps they felt that they had a right to secure goods wherever they could.

St. Denis fell in love with Manuela, the granddaughter of the commandant. The lovely lady was only seventeen years old. St. Denis was thirty-seven.

While at the presidio in Mexico, St. Denis was placed under arrest. His presence had caused a former suitor of Manuela's to report that a foreigner was at the presidio. No foreigner or foreign goods were allowed legally in Spanish territory. Both St. Denis and his valet, a dwarf, were sent to Mexico City for questioning by authorities there. St. Denis was jailed. Somehow the glib-tongued Frenchman convinced the authorities of his innocence. It helped that Father Hidalgo himself was in Mexico City. St. Denis was released in a few weeks.

The viceroy (Spanish authority) chose Captain Domingo Ramon to lead an expedition to reestablish Spanish occupation of the land of the Tejas Indians. St. Denis was chosen as second in command. On February 17, 1716, they left with a group of sixty-five. The party included about a dozen priests, twenty-five soldiers, and the families of the soldiers. By late 1716 they were in the land of the Tejas. They established four missions in a line leading toward the Red River.

Captain Ramon and St. Denis traveled into Louisiana for talks with French officials. They were told that the French had no desire to interfere with Spanish control of Texas. Nevertheless, the Spanish built two more missions close to French territory. One was at the present site of San Augustine, Texas. The other was at what is now Robeline, Louisiana. The mission San Miguel de Linares de los Adaes was erected only fifteen miles west of the French settlement of Natchitoches.

In January 1719 war broke out in Europe between France and Spain. The king of France directed his forces in the colony to move against Spanish holdings. The governor of Louisiana sent out scouting parties to determine the strength of Spanish defenses for the missions in Texas. When the French scouts arrived at the mission San Miguel in June 1719, one priest and one soldier stationed there surrendered.

The Frenchmen began to gather booty at the mission. Chickens escaped from a pen and ran under the Frenchmen's horses. The horses threw their riders. The trouble with the chickens was the only trouble the

Frenchmen had. Seven scouts had driven the Spanish out of East Texas. This is sometimes called the "Chicken War."

Los Adais or Los Adaes (both spellings appear in historical records). In the spring of 1721, the Spanish returned to reoccupy East Texas. The Spanish claimed the Red River as their eastern boundary. Near the mission San Miguel, the Spanish built a new presidio or fort. They named it Nuestra Senora del Pilar de los Adaes. They left more than one hundred well-supplied soldiers there. The fort and the settlement that grew around it were called Los Adaes. It became the official capital of Texas and remained so for fifty years.

The person in charge of the western area of French Louisiana was St. Denis. St. Denis became commandant of Fort St. Jean Baptiste in 1722. St. Denis agreed to keep his traders east of the Red River. He protested the location of a Spanish fort on French soil.

St. Denis and Manuela had married at her home in Mexico in 1716. When they came to Natchitoches, they lived on a plantation and reared a family. Records of the St. Denis family are preserved at a Catholic church and the courthouse at Natchitoches.

Child King. Louis XIV died September 1, 1715. During the last months before the king died, little was done for Louisiana. **Louis XV** had been named by the old king to take his place. He was the five-year-old grandson of Louis XIV. To actually carry on the government until Louis XV was thirteen, France was ruled by three **regents**. One of these was the duke of Orléans, the child-king's uncle.

Fort Rosalie. The Natchez resented the coming of the white man to their lands. From time to time, this resentment resulted in Indian violence against the European settlements. The Natchez were especially irritated by the French presence. Still, Bienville was usually successful in maintaining a friendship with them. It was Bienville who established Fort Rosalie at the present Natchez in 1716. It was named Rosalie for the wife of the Count de Pontchartrain.

A series of wars broke out after the founding of Fort Rosalie. The first Natchez attack against the French at Fort Rosalie occurred in 1716. In the background, the English were pushing the Indians to take action.

Cadillac's Departure. Cadillac was a notably poor governor of the Louisiana colony. He offered no leadership for the struggling colony. The settlers blamed him for their hardships. Crozat blamed Cadillac's inefficiency for his failure to secure profits from Louisiana. Cadillac carried on a feud with Bienville. There was a story that Bienville had refused to marry Cadillac's daughter. Cadillac

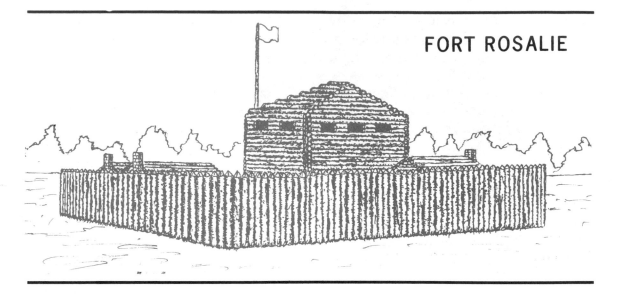

FORT ROSALIE

himself hated the colony. In 1716 he was transferred to another post. Thus, the situation was relieved. In Canada and Detroit Cadillac had been successful. As governor of Louisiana he was a failure. Bienville was appointed temporary head of the colony again.

Governor Lepinay. The new governor was **Jean Michiele, Seigneur de Lepinay.** He arrived in less than a year with fifty colonists and more soldiers. He decorated Bienville with the Cross of St. Louis, awarded him by the king of France. As additional recognition for his service to France, he was presented with the title to Horn Island, an island in Biloxi Bay.

Lepinay was also a failure. Almost immediately his conflicts with Bienville divided the colonists into two opposing factions. One faction included those on the side of Bienville.

The others were on Lepinay's side. When the English heard that the French were quarreling, they took advantage of the conflict. They found ways to make inroads in the Indian trade.

Crozat's Failure. When Crozat heard about Lepinay's problems, he wanted to give up his plans. He asked the king to release him from his agreement. That was done in August 1717, five years after Crozat started his venture. Crozat was bankrupt.

Why did Crozat fail in his Louisiana venture? The monopolies did not work. The settlers had no money with which to buy. Besides, Crozat's goods were overpriced. Nobody else was free to generate trade. This caused commerce to grind to a halt. The small vegetable trade with the Spanish ceased because the colonists were not allowed to own seagoing vessels. Crozat expected to make large profits from trade with Mexico and the Spanish islands. This trade was closed to him. The slave trade did not prove profitable, either. Few colonists had the money required to buy slaves.

It did not occur to Crozat to cultivate friendships with Indians. He did not realize that this was extremely important. He stopped giving trinkets, which the Indians had learned to expect.

English traders from Carolina consistently paid the Indians higher prices for furs. It was only natural that the Indians chose to trade with the English. The Spanish at Pensacola also offered the Indians more for their furs. That wasn't all. Both the English and Spanish sold European goods more cheaply to the Indians.

Crozat also neglected agriculture in his search for quick riches. He had expected to develop mining in the northern reaches of the Louisiana colony. This, too, was unsuccessful.

There was another investor waiting to take over the Louisiana colony. Perhaps he would learn from Crozat's mistakes.

En Partie 2 (Studying a Part). 1. Why did King Louis XIV wish to get rid of the Louisiana colony? 2. Describe Crozat's efforts to get rich from Louisiana. 3. What type of people came? 4. Describe government under Crozat. 5. Why was a post established at Natchitoches? 6. (a) Who was St. Denis? (b) What was his mission in Spanish territory? 7. Describe the settlements of Los Adaes and Fort Rosalie. 8. Why was Crozat's venture a failure?

John Law's Mississippi Bubble

John Law's Plan. Red-headed John Law was no ordinary man. By the time he was twenty, he had already gambled away a fortune. He was a playboy in Scotland. After he killed a man in a duel, he fled to France.

John Law was always on the lookout for an opportunity to make a profit. He took pains to cultivate the rich and powerful. Among those he charmed was the duke of Orléans. As regent for young King Louis XV, the duke was the most powerful man in France. He made decisions at the highest level of government. With France in financial chaos, the duke of Orléans was looking for a solution. Law sold to the duke a scheme to make money off the Louisiana colony. He vowed that he could turn Louisiana into a source of wealth for France. The duke gave him a monopoly in the colony for twenty-five years.

In 1716 John Law established the Bank of France. Large quantities of paper money were printed. It was a year later that he got the idea of obtaining riches from Louisiana. In 1717 the paper money of the Bank of France was accepted throughout France. John Law was at the peak of power in 1718. He became the director general of his Royal Bank of France.

Company of the West. John Law organized the Company of the West in 1717. The new company took over the Louisiana colony. Law had much the same arrangement as Crozat's, as well as the right to select a governor. His territory included the Illinois country, which had not been included in Crozat's charter.

Law sold stock in his Company of the West. Frenchmen excitedly bought it. A buyer made a down payment of only twenty-five percent. Shares could be bought for five hundred livres each. Law could hardly keep up with the demand for his stock. Not only everybody in France who had any money to invest, but also some outside its boundaries, bought shares in the company.

Settlers for John Law's Louisiana. John Law was a great promoter. He advertised the Company of the West in Germany, Switzerland, Italy, and Holland. He told the people that Louisiana was a "land of milk and honey." All over France, people were told of the wonderful venture.

The Company of the West was required to send six thousand whites to the Louisiana colony every year. Also, they were to send three thousand slaves yearly. John Law tried many ways to get settlers. He started a big advertising campaign. He put out giant handbills, posters, circulars, and broadsides. All described the wonderful opportunities in the colony. Such an inviting picture of Louisiana was painted that many poor people were convinced. Many French people mortgaged or sold their homes to seek their fortunes in Louisiana. They left France to become pioneers, homesteaders, prospectors, or miners.

In August 1718 eight hundred colonists arrived in three ships. Among them was Le Page du Pratz, one of Louisiana's first historians. So many came to the colony that the population increased from seven hundred to five thousand by 1721. The advertising led these people to expect too much. When they found that they could not produce four crops a year, they felt cheated. They knew that John Law had lied to them. Friendly Indians did not do most of the work as John Law had promised. The new settlers sent gloomy reports to France. People no longer chose to move to Louisiana.

Thereafter, the main sources for the Louisiana population were the prisons and houses of correction in

France. Petty criminals were brought to the colony. They had been given the choice of Louisiana or prison. Some who chose prison were forced to come anyway. Some of these criminals were women. The wives and children of convicts were allowed to come to Louisiana with their husbands and fathers. Girls from orphans' homes were sent to become wives of the settlers. Officials were ordered to kidnap people to send to the colony. The streets were searched for prospective settlers. Grace King, a Louisiana writer, described it as "dog-catcher's work." She said that servants and children were taken from the streets. Beggars and idle persons were forced to go. These actions caused so much hatred in France that even the word "Louisiana" became distasteful. This did not help in attempts to recruit volunteers.

A law was passed in 1720 prohibiting vagabonds and criminals from going to Louisiana. The experiment in emptying prisons for settlers had not worked. The ones already in the colony proved that they did not change their habits by coming to the New World. They had begun to settle in the frontier towns to gamble, drink, and fight.

The company tried several other methods to get colonists. Wealthy noblemen received large grants of land called concessions. Individuals of lesser wealth were given smaller grants

This Indenture made the 13th day of July in the year of 1757 between John Ezelle of the one party and Isaac Colbert of the other party. The said Isaac Colbert doth hereby promise to serve the said John Ezelle from the date above; for the term of seven years. In Return, the said John Ezelle doth promise the said Isaac Colbert to pay for his passing, and to find him meat, drink, clothing, and lodging, with other necessaries during the said term; and at the end of the said term, to give him one whole year's provisions of corn and fifty acres of land, according to the laws of the country. In witness whereof, the said John Ezelle and Isaac Colbert have put their seals on the date above written.

called habitations. Concessionaires (grantees) were expected to bring over many settlers to develop their grants. Some did develop their grants. Few grantees came themselves. Diron d'Artaguette was granted the land where Baton Rouge now stands. Bernard de La Harpe received land in the Natchitoches area. Other offers were made to attract settlers. Free passage, food, equipment, and supplies were sometimes furnished.

Some indentured servants were brought into the colony. These were persons whose passages were paid by prospective employers. The servants worked for a specified number of years to pay for their passages.

Being an indentured servant was

not much different from being a slave. Yet the New World's promise of a better life caused some hard-pressed people to accept indenture. Seven years of hard labor were usually necessary to repay the cost of passage. Yet the master could add years for such offenses as running away. Meantime most of the indentured servants arrived on crowded ships under the watchful eye of the ship's captain. These ship captains created a lively business for themselves. They crowded as many indentures as possible to bring on the ships. Once here, they sold the labor contract for a price to a settler. Often housed in a barn and set to work at menial tasks, the servant found that he or she had paid a high price for the Louisiana journey.

New settlers found life in the colony vastly different from that pictured by the Company of the West. After the miseries of the month-long trip, they needed time to restore their energies. Yet they were faced with cutting down trees and building their own shelters. Supplies from France were scant, and they were forced to fish, hunt game, and search for edibles in the forests.

Probably the most successful settlers were those who came from outside France. The French who could have been successful colonists did not come. Most French peasants did not believe that they would be better off in the new country. Most Germans

wanting to come to the New World chose the new colony of Pennsylvania instead of Louisiana. However, some German peasants did accept John Law's offer. So did some Swiss. Some Germans arrived in 1721. Nine hundred sixty-five left France. Two hundred arrived in Louisiana. They became some of the colony's most valuable settlers. John Law selected the German settlers for his laborers on his concession on the Arkansas River. The hard-working Germans greatly helped the colony.

Bienville Governor Again. The government remained very much the way it was under Crozat. During the first two years, the management of colonial affairs was entrusted to a board of directors appointed by the king. One of John Law's first actions was to replace Governor Lepinay. In 1718 Bienville once more became governor.

Capture of Pensacola. The task of fulfilling the pledges that the company itself had not made good fell upon Bienville. In the midst of all the problems he was having as a result of Law's scheme, war broke out in 1719. This was a war between France and Spain. Bienville seized the opportunity to make a surprise attack on Pensacola and burn the fort. He took prisoners. There were no supplies with which to care for them in the colony. Therefore, the prisoners were sent to Havana in French vessels. The Spanish in Havana seized the vessels and used them to recapture Pensacola. Later, Bienville took Pensacola a second time. Spain regained Pensacola when a peace treaty was signed between France and Spain in 1721. The post at Pensacola was a constant threat, however.

⭑ **Founding of New Orleans, 1718.** Another goal of the company was to establish a port to handle the fur commerce on the Mississippi. La Salle, Iberville, and Bienville all had thought that if France were to control the entire Mississippi Valley, the chief settlement should be on the Mississippi River. For a long time Bienville had wanted to establish a settlement at a certain point. The site was on Lake Pontchartrain. Bienville wanted New Orleans to overlook that "beautiful crescent of the river." The chief engineer, Le Blond de la Tour, did not approve of the place that Bienville had selected. Other engineers were consulted and agreed with de la Tour that it was a poor site. Bienville's choice was a low, marshy strip of land.

In spite of the engineers, Bienville had his way. In February 1718 Bienville had eighty men—slaves, prisoners, and a few carpenters—clearing the site, digging drainage ditches, and making the place ready for new settlers. He named the new city *Nouvelle-Orléans* (New Orleans) for the duke of Orléans.

The first building that finally took shape was a hut covered with palmetto palms. It became Bienville's headquarters. Other crude huts similar to those of the Choctaws were built. The huts could not stand the damp heat and winds. Flooding was a regular event. Storms ripped roofs off of the huts. They were rebuilt. Then fire destroyed them. Hurricanes swept them off. But the little village was rebuilt every time. New Orleans survived.

Snakes, mosquitoes, and water seeping up through the marsh soil made New Orleans something less than appealing. The muddy streets often looked like canals. For three years the little village was almost deserted. City engineers recommended that a new site be found. Bienville persisted in making New Orleans the capital. He finally convinced French officials.

Bienville set about constructing a new city with a master plan in 1721. **Adrien de Pauger**, the royal engineer, worked with Bienville in laying out the city. With a gridiron pattern, the large blocks were laid out along the banks of the river. The plan was shaped like a parallelogram. The settlement was 4,000 feet long by 1,800 feet wide. A public square beside the river was to be used as a parade ground and for ceremonial occasions. The square was called the Place d'Armes. The space around the public square was to be occupied by barracks for the soldiers, a church, a residence for the priest, and a prison. This eleven-by-seven-block rectangle is known today as the **Vieux Carré**, or **French Quarter**.

In 1721 there were 470 people living in New Orleans. Of these 145 were free Frenchmen, 65 were French women, and 38 were children. There were 29 indentured servants, 172 black slaves, and 21 Indian slaves. Most of the people in the area lived just outside the city. Indigo plantations were worked by nearly 1,800 slaves. There were Acolapissa and Choctaw Indian settlements on and around the land occupied by present-day New Orleans. About 350 families of Houma Indians lived there until 1720.

Company of the Indies. By 1719 the Company of the West was expanded to include five other companies. The company received a new name: Company of the Indies. It purchased the trading rights of the East India, China, Africa, Senegal, and West Indies companies. This gave the company control of practically all foreign trade of France, including the slave trade. Again shares of stock sold rapidly.

In 1719 the company bought the sole right to coin money for France for a period of nine years. It also bought the right to collect all French taxes. Directors of the company were given large land grants in the Louisiana colony. They were supposed to settle that land. Very few of the directors came across the sea to the New World colony. However, some sent settlers to their lands.

Plans were made to bring many more settlers. The company also planned to establish new settlements, to promote agriculture, to extend trade, and to send currency to the colony.

German Settlement. In time, the German settlers on Law's land in Arkansas became disgusted. There had been a lot of promises and little else. Food supplies from France rarely reached them. Most of the French

JOHN LAW, PROMOTER

Land of milk and Honey Louisia Colony

settlers were living near the capital. French troops were located all around the mouth of the river. Shipments of goods from France were unloaded at the port. The German settlers thought that they would be better off to move down the river. They located just north of the new settlement of New Orleans. There the Germans established their small farms. They were a hard-working thrifty people. Their farms produced a great deal of food. They actually saved New Orleans with food from their farms. The settlement they formed above New Orleans became known as *Côte Les Allemands* (the German Coast). This German settlement among the French and Indians has retained its identity as the German Coast.

Bursting of the Mississippi Bubble: 1720. John Law was made comptroller general of France in 1720. The Company of the Indies was teetering at the verge of collapse. In France, paper money was everywhere. Even the government refused to accept it. Stockholders began to withdraw their deposits. The bank could not allow withdrawals by depositors. John Law was frantic. He combined the Bank of France with the Company of the Indies in hopes of saving both. The bank was abolished by the French government. The company was broke. Its stock became worthless. John Law fled France in women's clothing to escape death from angry mobs of people. All had lost their investments.

There was no sound basis for John Law's claims that large profits could be made from Louisiana at that time. There was no reason that his money-making scheme should work. The people did not realize that mere paper with no real wealth or value behind it was not good money. Gold and silver had not been found. There would never be any precious metals from the colony. Tar, pitch, and forestry products produced in Louisiana did not compare with those produced in France. There were few laborers skilled in preparing lumber products. The lumber industry that Law planned would someday exist in Louisiana. However, that was more than a century away.

Louisiana Under the Company of the Indies: 1721–31. The Company of the Indies was left in control of Louisiana. The French government did not wish to take on the company's debts and expenses. They did not want to be responsible for the colony, either.

A new policy was established for managing the colony. This was done in cooperation with the French government. In 1722 the French government granted an annual subsidy of 300,000 livres to the company. It was to pay the four directors of the colony. It was also to cover the cost of military fortifications.

With this assistance from France, Bienville, as governor, tried to place the colony on a sound footing. He went to France to confer with officials on how this could be done. The king wanted a successful colony. During Bienville's absence in 1723, Boisbriant was acting governor.

Black Code, or *Code Noir*. Accurate figures for the number of slaves in the colony during the first two decades are not available. Exact dates of arrival for that period are not known. It is clear that enough slaves arrived during the time of Crozat and Law that it was necessary to have written laws concerning them.

Slavery caused problems in the colony. Bienville attempted to solve some of them. He formulated the Black Code, or *Code Noir*. The provisions of this code were collected from rules and customs governing slaves under France and Spain. It was put into law by Bienville in 1724 to govern relations between the slaves and their masters. The code dealt with other problems as well.

The first article expelled Jews from the colony. Other articles prescribed religious instruction in the Roman Catholic faith. The code ordered that Sundays and all holidays be given to the slaves as days off. Masters were made responsible for moral instruction of slaves.

The code forbade mingling of the two races. Masters were absolutely forbidden to force marriage between slaves. The children of slaves were to belong to the master of the mother. If the father were a slave and the mother a free woman of color, the children were to follow the condition of the mother and be free. Slaves who were husband and wife could not be seized or sold separately when belonging to the same master. Children under the age of fourteen could not be taken from their parents. Other provisions were included in an effort to protect slaves from cruel masters.

Four articles of the Black Code dealt with provisions for the feeding and clothing of slaves. The code stated that old and sick slaves must be cared for by their masters. "In case they should have been abandoned by said masters, said slaves shall be adjudged to the nearest hospital, to which said masters shall be obliged to pay eight cents a day for the food and maintenance of each one of these slaves; and for payment of this sum said hospital shall have a lien on the plantation of said master."

Slaves could not own property. They were forbidden to carry weapons except for hunting. Slaves of different masters could not assemble in crowds. Branding with the fleur-de-lis was the severe penalty for those who violated the code. If a slave struck his master or mistress or their children so as to make a bruise or draw blood, they were to suffer capital punishment. All acts of violence on the part of slaves against free persons were to result in severe punishment to the offenders. This could mean death. Theft of horses, cows, or other valuable property could also result in the death penalty. A runaway slave who was gone for as much as one month had his ears cut off. He was also branded on the shoulder with the fleur-de-lis. If he tried to run away a second time, he was hamstrung and branded on the other shoulder. The third offense meant death.

The Louisiana slave laws seem cruel by today's standards. They were very lenient for that time. The code was signed by Bienville during March 1724 in the name of the king. It was the last important act of Bienville under the administration of the Company of the Indies.

Lagniappe. Cattle and stock were very scarce and valuable at this time. The laws about cattle and stock applied to slaves as well as to freeborn whites. No man was permitted to kill his own female stock even for food without permission from the authorities. The senseless killing or maiming of a horned animal by anyone not its owner was punishable by death.

Bienville's Troubles. Disaster struck the struggling little town of New Orleans on September 11, 1722. The first recorded hurricane destroyed thirty-four huts and the makeshift church and rectory. A small fleet of vessels sank in the Mississippi. One ship loaded with grain, fowl, and produce ran aground. There was a shortage of food and a quickness of tempers. The people were very angry, and Bienville again became their target.

The citizens were unhappy with Bienville for many reasons. One concerned the land that he had ceded himself. He chose some choice river property about eight miles long on the east side of the Mississippi. He also got a large tract on the west side. After the French government told him that this act was unethical, he gave up part of his land. The part he kept was about the size of today's downtown section of New Orleans.

Another source of trouble was the jealousy existing between different factions in the colony. Two different political groups grew in the colony— the pro-Bienvilles and the anti-Bienvilles. Those against him blamed him for all of the colony's problems. The Company of the Indies blamed him because the colony had brought no profit. The king and those around him seethed with anger at the same question. Why had France so little for such huge investments?

Part of the political trouble in the colony was due to the custom of sending officials to French colonies with overlapping duties. The offices of governor and *ordonnateur* represented such a problem. The duties of each official were neither clearly defined nor clearly separated. It was a constant source of trouble. There was so much trouble that it took stronger police protection to maintain order.

In 1723 a band of Natchez attacked and murdered a French traveler and kidnapped two children. After that Bienville attempted to meet with the chiefs and settle the problems. Since only three villages of the tribe were involved, Bienville marched against these villages. He used a small force of seven hundred Indians and white men. Nothing was accomplished by Bienville's challenge. In fact, the colonists laughed at the "war." It only served to further anger the Indians. The only plunder brought back were chickens captured by the soldiers.

Finally, a secret committee of investigators headed by Jacques de La Chaise arrived in the colony. The mission of the committee was to investigate the actions of Bienville. On February 16, 1724, Bienville was recalled to France in disgrace to answer charges against him. Boisbriant acted as governor while he was gone. Not only was Bienville removed from office, but every kinsman and partisan of his was likewise removed from office. Bienville was banished from the city that he had founded. He was awarded an annual pension of 750 livres.

For the first time since the colony had been founded, not a single member of the Le Moyne family had any part in the governing of the colony. The officials hoped that the changes would bring peace to the colony. Bienville's policies were no longer in use.

The New Governor: Périer. Etienne Périer replaced Bienville in 1726. He found that he could not satisfy the complainers any more than Bienville had. The new governor worked to improve the economy. He succeeded in bringing in new settlers. However, some of them did not make good colonists. Périer stressed agriculture and urged the settlers to produce indigo and tobacco. He brought in specialists to advise planters on these crops. However, for plantations to produce these crops, more labor was needed than a family could supply. The only answer they had was to purchase slaves. Most of the colonists were too poor to invest in slaves.

Périer tried to bring profits from forest products to the company and to the settlers. Unlimited resources of virgin forests were at hand. The settlers could produce such products as tar, pitch, masts, and lumber needed in France and the West Indies. Many forest products were needed for ship-building in France. However, there were so few craftsmen experienced in preparing these products for market that this industry did not succeed. Shipbuilding itself was encouraged in the colony. Very skilled carpenters were needed, but there were few in the colony. So not much was accomplished by Périer in his attempts to improve the economy.

Périer sought to increase commerce. He felt that that could be done between the French-owned islands of the West Indies and Louisiana. The Louisiana settlers needed to buy coffee and sugar from the islands. The islanders badly needed lumber and food produced in Louisiana. Ships to carry goods and money for investment did not exist in the colony. Therefore, Périer had no success with those plans either.

Périer tried to improve transportation and communication. Both were very difficult during the French period. Waterways in these years were the arteries of the colony. Travel for any distance had to be by water. Settlers were responsible for keeping the waterfront to their property clear of obstructions. A variety of watercraft was used on inland bayous and creeks. Interior posts were linked to New Orleans by waterways. There were no bridges. Cattle or horses moved overland. They were made to swim bayous and rivers. Fear of Indians caused settlers to travel in convoys.

Horseback was a major mode of overland transportation. Usually this was only for short distances. Those families able to afford them bought carriages. Two-wheeled carts were used for short overland hauls. These vehicles were of little use unless there were good roads. Only buffalo and Indian trails existed. These paths ran mostly alongside streams. Périer required all landowners along the Mississippi to build roads in front of their property.

Mail came from France irregularly. It was simply placed aboard ships carrying supplies. The same was true of mail from colonists to their homeland. So valued were these early communications from the colony that an interesting custom started in France. One sheet of each letter from Louisiana was given to each related family to preserve.

The Ursuline Nuns and the Casket Girls. In 1726 the Jesuits were granted permission to establish headquarters in New Orleans. They were to secure the service of the Ursuline nuns. In September 1726 the Company of the Indies made a contract with the Ursuline sisters to furnish twelve nuns for the colony. The following February 1727 the nuns sailed from France.

The nuns were given eight arpents of land, a house, and eight Negroes to till their land. While

URSULINE NUNS AND CONVENT

they waited for their house to be built, they were temporarily housed at Bienville's residence. The permanent convent was completed in 1734.

The nuns served in the hospital and gave religious instruction to the girls of the colony. They also taught the girls to raise silkworms and make the silk into cloth. The nuns taught them how to make dresses with the cloth. Most importantly, the nuns and the girls provided a refining influence on the frontier population. It was the nuns who sheltered the girls of good character and gave them useful training to become wives of the colonists.

In the fall of 1727 the first of the *filles à la cassette* arrived in New Orleans. They were the famous "Casket Girls." The girls were volunteers who came to become wives of the settlers. They were not, of course, the first women to come to the colony. They simply received more publicity because of the small pieces of luggage that they brought with them. They carried small portable trunks, or *cassettes*, which were given to them by the company. Each girl brought two dresses, two petticoats, six headdresses, and underwear. The carefully selected girls were placed in the care of the nuns. The girls remained in the convent until they were married. They were locked up at night. During the day they walked through the streets if the weather permitted. That way the men could meet the girls. The actual choice of a husband was left to each girl. Still, she had to choose from the suitors approved by the nuns. Within a few weeks, all were married.

Soldiers who married the casket girls were rewarded. Each one received his discharge from military service, a plot of land, a cow, provisions, and a rifle.

The French and Indian Troubles. The Indians of Louisiana came to bitterly resent the French. The Natchez were particularly hostile. The hostility of the Indians toward the French was encouraged by the English on one side and the Spanish on the other. The Indians saw the French overrunning lands that they had always considered their own. The Indians felt that the Frenchmen were driving away the wild game from the forests. Moreover, the French had sometimes outraged the Indians with acts of ruthlessness. Another reason for trouble was the lack of a steady supply of trinkets and gifts expected by the Indians. The English were always in a better position to trade with the Indians. The English studied the Indians to find out what they wanted. They tried to supply these wants. The English made the best deals for the Indians. The French did not give them enough for their furs, and they charged too much for their goods.

For several years, the Natchez

CASKET GIRLS

had been at peace with the French. By 1729 three hundred French settlers made their homes in Natchez territory. That year the Natchez massacre occurred. It was started by the high-handed act of Captain Chepart, the commander of Fort Rosalie. Chepart had already been scolded by the French officials for his conduct toward those under him. He made impossible demands on the Natchez Indians, ordering them to abandon White Apple, their most important village.

Chepart wanted to build his own plantation on a choice Indian plot. This land was the site of the Indians' burial ground and temple. To make matters worse, Chepart demanded a portion of their harvest.

The Natchez held a council and sent word to other Indians to join them in an effort to destroy the French. The Natchez struck in late November 1729. The Frenchmen at Fort Rosalie were massacred. Women, children, and Negro slaves were taken as prisoners. About 250 Frenchmen and a dozen Indians were killed. Around 300 women and children were captured. The Indians burned Fort Rosalie and all buildings belonging to the French.

News of the Natchez massacre reached New Orleans on December 2. An exhausted refugee who had been in the woods when the massacre took place had made his way to New Orleans. The details of the massacre increased the panic and horror of the colonists. Within a few days the report of the massacre was confirmed by several other people who had escaped. Only three of the white men at the fort had survived. It was rumored that this was only the beginning of a general Indian war against the French. New Orleans was believed to be in danger. A moat was dug around the city. Guards were posted at its four corners. Word was sent to France for help. Messages were sent to outlying settlements. Emergency refuges were planned for the women and children.

Governor Périer sent a detachment of regular French troops and militia under the engineer Broutin. These were joined by a force from the French post at Pointe Coupee. They were ordered to made a bold, sudden strike against the Natchez to rescue the French women and children. Ammunition was sent from the Illinois post. Seven hundred Choctaw warriors joined the French against the Natchez. The Avoyels, Tunicas, and other small tribes joined the French, also. After days of battle, on March 1, 1730, the French found that the Natchez had deserted Fort Rosalie.

Périer's attacks on the Natchez did not subdue them. Instead, it drove them into desperate, widely scattered groups. These continued to harass the French.

After the Natchez massacre, there

was rumor that the Negroes and Indians were planning an uprising. Blacks were given a choice—hanging or attacking Indians. Eight Negroes armed with knives, hatchets, and bayonets ambushed a small settlement of peaceful Indian farmers. The blacks killed seven or eight innocent Indians. After this incident there were strained relationships among the whites, Negroes, and Indians. Each group was suspicious of the others.

The Tunica Indians caught four Natchez braves and took them to New Orleans. They publicly burned them alive in an elaborate ceremony. Other Natchez Indians murdered the Tunica chief and destroyed the rest of the Tunica nation.

It was August 10, 1730, before French soldiers arrived in New Orleans. They brought French military strength up to between 1,000 and 1,200 regular troops and militia. On January 28, 1731, Périer secured the surrender of the small fort of the Natchez located at Sicily Island. The Natchez had taken refuge at Sicily Island after the Natchez massacre.

The French king sent delegates to Louisiana to investigate the Indian policies of Périer. They reported that the evils growing out of Périer's policies were without remedy. Most of the Indians were now hostile to the French due to Périer's cruelty to the Indians. The only way to improve the situation, the delegates reported,

was to return Bienville as head of the colony.

Last Year of the Company of the Indies: 1731. The Company of the Indies finally gave up its charter on July 1, 1731. It would not have expired for another eleven years. The Natchez massacre caused the company to request permission to surrender control over the Louisiana colony. The directors had learned the same lesson that Crozat had learned. Colonies were too expensive for private investors. Colonies, to be successful, required the vast resources of a nation. The directors had done all they could to generate profits from the Louisiana colony. They felt that Louisiana would develop slowly. It would take a long time before Louisiana could even be self-supporting.

Contributions of John Law. Even though the investors in the Company of the Indies lost money, John Law's scheme did some lasting good for the colony. If it had not been for Law's efforts, Louisiana as a French colony probably would not have survived.

To begin with, the population increased. The colony had grown considerably under the Company of the West. There were about 700 persons (500 whites and 200 Negroes) when John Law took control. The Company of the Indies left 7,500 persons in the colony, including about 2,500 slaves and 5,000 whites. The population figures were probably not accurate. It was difficult to determine the number of white inhabitants absent on trading and other missions. The count could have included only those in permanent homes.

The potential for agriculture was revealed. Plantations were established along the Mississippi River. The land was rich, and the production of crops like indigo and vegetables was promising. Staple crops for export were needed. Cattle and poultry were also badly needed.

Many lessons were learned. France learned that it must provide enough troops to keep the Indians from killing settlers during raids. Settlers also needed protection from the English and Spaniards. Since France could not afford the expense, the settlers would have to pay for their own protection. Only settlers of good character who were willing to work must come to the colony. No more criminals would be allowed. Louisiana needed money from the mother country to construct public buildings. The colony must grow its own food. The colony also learned not to depend on shipments from France. It was clear that large numbers of slaves were needed to develop agriculture.

Trading posts were established at New Orleans and at some inland ports in the colony. New Orleans had grown into a bustling trading center. In 1719 a fort had been built on the present site of Baton Rouge.

Further explorations of the colony were made during mining expeditions.

John Law and his companies had done great things for Louisiana. However, the commercial life and prosperity of the colony were on the verge of ruin in 1731 when the Company of the Indies withdrew.

En Partie 3 (Studying a Part). 1. Why was the Company of the West organized? 2. Tell the John Law story. 3. How were settlers obtained? 4. Describe the settlement of New Orleans. 5. What was the Black Code? 6. What was the Company of the Indies? 7. Why did Law's bubble burst? 8. What contributions did Law make to the colony? 9. Why did the Company of the Indies give up its charter? 10. Who were the Ursuline Nuns? 11. Who were the Casket Girls?

Louisiana: A Royal Colony

For the next thirty-one years, Louisiana was a royal colony. This meant that it was once again under the direct control of the king. Périer served as governor for two years after the Company of the Indies returned the colony to the king. Then he lost interest in Louisiana and resigned.

Bienville's Last Term as Governor. By this time the colonists—

even some of those who had opposed him—wanted Bienville back as governor. Perhaps it was the Natchez massacre that caused some of them to want the old Indian fighter back at the head of the colony. His influence over the Indians had been greatly needed.

In September 1732 Bienville was appointed governor for the fourth and last time. He did not arrive in New Orleans from France until March 3, 1733. There was great rejoicing at his return. Nobody seemed to remember his mistakes. Only good things were recalled.

Bienville, like Périer, realized that the Louisiana colony must become self-supporting. The settlers must have ways to make their living. Also, Bienville knew that agriculture was the place to begin.

An experimental farm had been in existence for a long time near New Orleans. A staple crop had to be found. Tobacco and indigo were being tried. Bienville added experiments with cotton, hemp, flax, and silk to see if one of these would be right for Louisiana. It had long since been proven that rice, corn, and vegetables could be produced readily. These were essential for the use of the settlers. There was not enough produced with which to build an export business, however.

Agriculture was a critical matter. The colony had to have a crop to sell for cash. Without cash they had no way of obtaining badly needed products from foreign countries. To find a marketable crop for the Louisiana settlers to produce was difficult. There was a scarcity of seed in the colony. There was never enough labor. The lack of sufficient numbers of farm animals and improved farm implements was an obstacle. To farm the land for the first time, virgin forests had to be cleared. The soil had to be broken up and prepared in rows for planting. Horses, mules, and oxen were in short supply. Under such conditions, progress beyond simple subsistence was very slow indeed.

It was possible to sell forestry products to France and the islands of the French West Indies. The quality of these products was below standard due to the lack of experienced craftsmen to handle the production. Therefore, the prices obtained for these products were low. Shipping costs, on the other hand, were high.

Bricks were made in Louisiana, but they were too soft and crumbly for marketing overseas. They were also too bulky to make exporting them profitable. They were useful only for colonial buildings. Sometimes they were used aboard ships as ballast.

With the unending financial troubles in France itself, there was no way for the colony to be unaffected. Only a few metal coins circulated in the colony; these came mostly from the Spaniards. In 1733 France printed card money to be used in Canada. The king then ordered 200,000 livres of card money to be used for circulation within the Louisiana colony. Card money was really worthless and solved nothing. Inflation followed. The colonists were left to trade mostly without money. They resorted to the barter system. Trade with the Indians was a matter of barter. Certain goods such as bear oil, tobacco, or corn were used as a standard of measurement.

Health Care. The King's Hospital had been established in 1722 in New Orleans. It took care of the military. Male nurses were used there until the Ursuline nuns took charge. The Ursulines provided nursing services from 1727 until the end of the French period.

In 1736 Jean Louis, a former sailor, left a fund for the establishment of a hospital for the poor. Dr. Prat, who had been in charge of the King's Hospital for years, was placed in charge. In 1759 a new building was built. It was named *Maison de Charité*, or **Charity Hospital**.

The king had provided a physician for the colony. The physician was responsible for all of the sick. There were never enough doctors in the colony. Midwives were sent, too. They attended births. Each settlement was supposed to have a midwife.

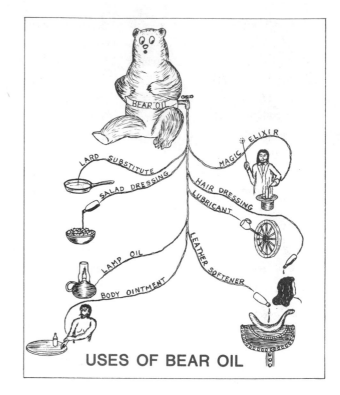

USES OF BEAR OIL

There was a problem of contagious diseases in Louisiana. Apparently a separate hospital was established for smallpox cases. It was thought that the diseases were brought in from Santo Domingo. A crude system of quarantine was used. People with contagious diseases were separated from patients without such diseases.

Treatment was hindered by the limited knowledge of medicine. Medicines were compounded on the spot. Native medicinal herbs and plants were used. Dr. Prat established a garden of medicinal plants. One of the Ursuline nuns, **Sister Xavier**, compounded medicines from a variety of plants and homegrown herbs. She is believed to have been the first female pharmacist in America.

More Indian Troubles. Indian troubles continued to plague Louisiana. The bitterness following the Natchez massacre lived on for years. A few Natchez warriors survived to cause trouble for the French. In one of the continuing acts of revenge against the French, a band of Natchez Indians attacked Fort St. Jean Baptiste at Natchitoches in 1732. St. Denis, the commandant, did not respond to their assault. As a result the band of Natchez Indians burned alive a French woman they had captured just outside the gates. A bitter fight followed. The French pursued the attackers to a lake just west of Cloutierville. The battle was continued on the shores of the lake. The French and their Indian allies killed every Natchez warrior. After this battle, the lake and the hill rising above it were called *"Sang pour Sang,"* or "Blood for Blood."

There were other Indian groups who harassed the colonists. The Choctaws divided their loyalties between the French and the English. All Indians expected a flow of gifts from the European nations. With France's lack of funds, the supply of trinkets was too small to keep the Indians satisfied.

The Chickasaw War. The Chickasaws disliked the French. They enjoyed a close relationship with the English settlers to the east. When French traders went among the Chickasaws and obtained some of their trade, the English were angry. They insisted that the Indians tell the French traders to stay out of Chickasaw territory. Perhaps it was for that reason that the Chickasaws murdered several French traders.

Bienville wanted to punish the Chickasaws for helping the Natchez. He ordered the Chickasaws to give up the Natchez refugees who lived with them. The Chickasaws refused. Bienville planned an attack.

In May 1736 Bienville assembled a force of over five hundred whites and forty-five free Negroes. He ordered Pierre d'Artaguette, a commandant in Illinois, to meet him with an army in the Chickasaw country. Bienville left from New Orleans with his forces, which had been joined by six hundred Choctaw Indians. When d'Artaguette reached the rendezvous point, Bienville had not arrived. D'Artaguette looked for him for ten days. Unable to find Bienville, d'Artaguette decided to attack the Chickasaws without him. His forces overran one village. However, the commandant and some of his men were captured at the second village they attacked. Meanwhile, Bienville had been delayed by stormy weather. When he and his men finally arrived, Bienville decided to attack. He was soundly defeated. The Indians had not harmed their prisoners prior to Bienville's attack. Afterward, d'Artaguette and fifteen of his men were slowly burned to death.

France could not endure this defeat. The French had lost over one hundred of its soldiers to the Chickasaws. Its defeat at the hands of the Indians was a critical blow in the nation's struggle for survival on the continent. French prestige demanded revenge. Therefore another campaign against the Chickasaws was planned.

Bienville asked France to send more troops to Louisiana. There had to be military supplies and equipment assembled for a march in force against the Chickasaws. Not to do so would mean eventually the end of the French colony. In order to secure the necessary supplies from France, Bienville was forced to delay the campaign against the Chickasaws for two years.

Troops were sent from France, and French troops already in the New World were alerted. Some were from Canada. Others were from the Illinois country. Bienville moved his troops northward from New Orleans.

The campaign lasted until 1739. The French built a fort where Memphis, Tennessee stands today. About 3,500 men assembled and prepared for battle. Their preparations lasted so long that soldiers died and provisions ran short. When all was ready, Bienville was relieved of command.

The French government sent the Sieur de Novilles to take his place. The war of the French against the Chickasaws finally ended in a stalemate. Neither side could claim victory. Instead, the French and Indians signed a peace treaty. The Chickasaws continued to harass the French colony even after the treaty was signed.

Bienville's Last Years. During the war there was no chance for progress on the home front. Louisiana settlers were drafted into the army. This required leaving their farms for months. Affairs at home were neglected. The normal commerce that brought supplies from the Illinois country to Louisiana was destroyed. Hostile Indians made trade down the river a risky business. Inflation in the colony brought problems.

It was as though nature herself were out to destroy Louisiana during this period. Storms and hurricanes in semitropical Louisiana came as predicted during certain seasons. Once on October 11, 1739, and twice in September 1740, the colony was swept with the disastrous winds that took everything in their paths. There were always the periods of flooding after the winter rains. Weather problems, along with the war, the lack of money, inflation, and the poor state of the economy, caused great discontent among the colonists. Again the blame was centered on Governor Bienville.

Bienville, too, must have grown

weary of so much criticism over so many years. He never recovered from the grief and humiliation of the Chickasaw defeat. He was very disappointed. The king was especially frustrated about the failure of Bienville's Indian policy. As a result of all this, Bienville was discouraged and hopeless. He wrote to the minister of the marine, begging to be recalled. After nearly forty years of service in Louisiana, the **Father of Louisiana** retired. He handed over the authority to the Marquis de Vaudreuil on May 10, 1743, and left Louisiana forever. He died in Paris in 1767 at the age of eighty-seven.

Vaudreuil, A Most Unusual Governor. Pierre François de Rigaud, Marquis de Vaudreuil, was appointed governor April 27, 1742. Vaudreuil was the third son of a governor of Canada. He was reared in all the luxury that New France could provide. After joining the army as a young man, he received the rank of major at the age of twenty-two. He led an expedition against Indians in Canada and became a hero. He was awarded the highest honor in the French army, the Cross of St. Louis, at age twenty-six. Before he was thirty, he was appointed governor of one of the largest settlements in Canada. He remained there for nearly a decade. At thirty-nine years of age he was named governor of Louisiana.

Vaudreuil's outlook on being governor of Louisiana was different from the previous governors. His years in the colony were known for the governor's lavish entertainment, elegant ceremonies, and military display. He imitated the court at Versailles as much as possible. He succeeded rather well. Vaudreuil formed a miniature court around the governor's office. His distinction of manner, his generosity, and his personal grace seemed to cast a direct reflection of the glory of Versailles. There was more entertainment and display during Vaudreuil's service in Louisiana than the colony had ever known. Some people resented this display of wealth.

There was a variety of entertainment for those who were not wealthy. People played cards and billiards. Their *fais-do-dos* were enjoyed by young and old. The settlers also hunted and fished.

Vaudreuil at first tried to be friendly with the Indians. He did what he could, but he was too handicapped by lack of money. He could not afford the required gifts, and he could not sell for cheaper prices. The European wars cut off contact with France for much-needed supplies. He did not receive enough trade items. Other problems with the Indians existed. The continual prodding of the Indians by the English resulted in harassment of the French colony off and on during Vaudreuil's administration. A group of Choctaws favorable to the English attacked the German settlements on the Mississippi River above New Orleans. Settlers were driven from their homes. Some were murdered. In 1748 Vaudreuil led an unsuccessful expedition against the Chickasaws. He did destroy some villages. In 1752 the Chickasaws attacked French settlements again. Vaudreuil with his seven hundred men burned villages. Finally the Indians sued for peace.

The new governor tried to bring financial order to the colony. He removed the old paper money at a value much less than its face value. The colonists who held this money lost a great deal in the change to a new series of money.

Like all of the earlier governors, Vaudreuil tried to improve agriculture. Farming was the mainstay of the colony. Agriculture was aided by the immigration of planters from Santo Domingo. Indigo and tobacco were staples there. The new governor experimented with sugarcane. An unsuccessful effort was made to manufacture syrup and sugar. The wax of the myrtleberry was still an important article of trade. The Jesuit fathers had a flourishing and beautiful plantation of crepe myrtles. The wax was produced for candles and other purposes. Vaudreuil wanted to try cotton as a staple crop. This was done, but removing the seed from the cotton required many slaves working for many hours.

The colony was still small and struggling. A census taken in 1744 showed three thousand white inhabitants, eight hundred soldiers, and over two thousand slaves in the colony. On September 3, 1749, there was another setback. A hurricane destroyed crops, domestic animals, and buildings in the lower Mississippi area.

During his last years as governor, Vaudreuil was preparing for the next war against the English. This war was the **French and Indian War**. The French knew that it would be a showdown between France and England. The victor would dominate the North American continent. Vaudreuil worked to improve defenses. Defense of the Mississippi Valley would play a large part in the war.

The forts and military defenses of the colony had long been neglected. The neglect was at least partly due to the lack of funds with which to maintain and supply them. There were never enough troops to protect the settlers on the frontier in inland Louisiana. It was necessary to be ready to defend Louisiana against attack. Vaudreuil thus received enough scarce money to improve the defenses of the colony.

Vaudreuil made worthwhile contributions to colony. He started Louisiana's first flood-control efforts.

Watson Library, Northwestern State University of Louisiana

This picture was widely used to advertise the Louisiana colony.

He required all owners of property along the Mississippi River to maintain a levee and a public road along the levee. Louisiana also started its first formal police regulations under Vaudreuil.

Vaudreuil had his problems, too. He was accused of engaging in an elaborate system of kickbacks and other forms of corruption. Although it was not proven, he was under attack for hiring members of his family for government jobs and for profiting from the sale of army supplies. Even his wife was said to be involved in illegal business. He prevented an investigation by conducting his own inquiry. Then he wrote reform laws.

When the governor's office in Canada became vacant, Vaudreuil requested that he be considered. He was appointed governor of Canada on June 8, 1752. However, he remained in New Orleans until February 3, 1753. The vessel on which Vaudreuil sailed for France was stuck on a sandbar at the mouth of the Mississippi. His trip was delayed for six weeks.

Vaudreuil could be pleased with his years as governor of Louisiana. In spite of the war in Europe and Indian troubles, the colony at last seemed to be prospering. With his social background, Vaudreuil brought an elegance to New Orleans that had never been there before. Louisiana—and New Orleans before he came—had an image of mud, heat, and mosquitoes. Vaudreuil gave the little port and the colony a boost with the social life he led. He provided a more inviting image. There were merchants in the port who were becoming wealthy. They responded joyfully to the social circle. Vaudreuil's appointment as governor general of Canada proved that the king was impressed with his tenure in Louisiana.

It was Vaudreuil's misfortune to arrive in Canada at the beginning of the French and Indian War. General Montcalm appealed to him for support in preparing Quebec for an attack by the English. Montcalm was defeated and killed at Quebec. Vaudreuil was forced to surrender

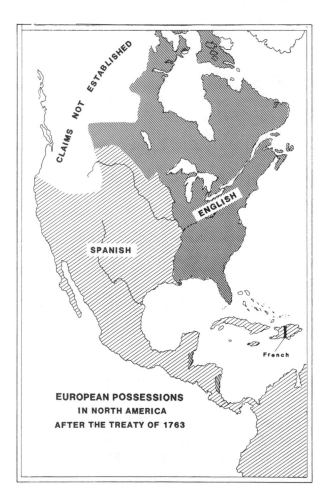

EUROPEAN POSSESSIONS
IN NORTH AMERICA
AFTER THE TREATY OF 1763

Montreal to the British on September 8, 1760. It was his last official act as governor of Canada. He was recalled to France and thrown into the Bastille (prison). Vaudreuil had been honored as few Frenchmen had. Now he was blamed for the loss of Canada to the English. It was a sad man who was tried in 1761 in France. He was acquitted and awarded a pension. A few years later his wife died. Vaudreuil lived fourteen more years in Paris. He was a lonely man without honor.

Governor Kerlerec. Louis Billouart, Chevalier de Kerlerec was appointed governor. The date was April 1, 1752. As usual the new governor did not arrive in Louisiana until months later. It was February 3, 1753, when he arrived in New Orleans. Vaudreuil was in charge until Kerlerec arrived.

Even before he came to Louisiana, Kerlerec complained of his low salary. He said that it was not enough to live in the style that the position demanded. He had reason to complain. Vaudreuil had introduced lavish entertainment by the governor. This meant leading a social whirl of top officials, rich merchants, and planters in New Orleans. Kerlerec complained for six years about his salary and continually asked for more money. He received no higher salary, so he began asking for a bonus. He also asked for a grant of land. He finally did get a bonus. There is no evidence that he received a land grant. Certainly, the constant social activities drained whatever funds he possessed.

On the other hand, Kerlerec was a military man. He had served in the French navy twenty-five years. As governor, he was concerned about defense of the colony and built a palisade around New Orleans.

Kerlerec and another French official in the colony feuded. This kept the colonial government in turmoil for several years. Rochemore was *ordonnateur*. The office was of almost equal rank with the governor. Their duties sometimes overlapped. The office of *ordonnateur* was designed so the officer became a watchdog over the governor. Both men were blamed for the quarrel. Neither would concede. This situation did not help Kerlerec's position with the officials in France.

A religious "war" between the Jesuits and the Capuchins, two groups of Catholic religious orders, went on during Kerlerec's administration. The war concerned spiritual supremacy in Louisiana. In 1717 the Capuchins had arrived in Louisiana. Nine years later, the Jesuits arrived. There was a struggle for power. Each claimed authority over all religious orders in the colony. The colony divided itself into religious factions. The Capuchins ultimately prevailed, and, in 1764, the Jesuits were forced to leave Louisiana. They disbanded in 1773, only to reorganize in 1814 and return to

the colony. The Jesuits remain in Louisiana today.

In all fairness to Kerlerec, it is likely that no governor could have succeeded in the position at the time. He became governor at one of the most critical points in the colony's history. France was fighting for its colonies in America. Battles were not fought in Louisiana, but Louisiana was greatly affected by the French and Indian War. Louisiana was practically a "lost colony" from 1754 to 1763. France sent no settlers, money, or supplies. The colony was neglected and abandoned by the French government. By the end of Kerlerec's years in the colony, France had entirely lost interest in Louisiana.

On November 3, 1762, **France ceded all the colony west of the Mississippi River and the Isle of Orleans to Spain**. The secret treaty was signed at Fontainebleau, France. The king of France gave Louisiana to his cousin, the king of Spain, to keep Louisiana from being taken by England. For the record it was to repay Spain for helping France during its war against England.

After Louisiana had been ceded to Spain, Kerlerec continued to act as governor. Kerlerec was notified a year later that Jean Jacques d'Abbadie had been appointed to replace him.

Kerlerec returned to France in late 1763 and was thrown into the Bastille. This was for debts contracted while in Louisiana. He died in prison. His descendants later brought suit to change this insult against Kerlerec. He was officially restored to his former reputation.

En Partie 4 (Studying a Part). 1. How was Vaudreuil an unusual governor? 2. Why was the colony neglected by France? 3. (a) What was the Treaty of Fontainebleau? (b) In what year was it made? 4. Why was Louisiana given to Spain?

France had lost the war. Therefore, it was being forced to give up the colony that it had founded in Louisiana. France was completely expelled from the mainland of North America. For these reasons, French prestige declined all over the world.

Coup d'Main
(Completing the Story)

Jambalaya (Putting It All Together)

1. Why was it difficult for the people of Europe to obtain reliable information about Louisiana?

2. (a) Describe Bienville's governorship. (b) Why was he called the Father of Louisiana?

3. What mistakes did the French make in settling Louisiana?

4. Describe French-Indian relations.

5. What was life like for the colonists? Shelter? Food? Education? Recreation? Health care? Religion?

6. (a) Why were slaves brought to Louisiana? (b) When? (c) How many?

7. Why were the rivers the main routes of transportation?

8. On a map, locate all settlements made by the French. Put the date of settlement by each. Circle the capitals.

9. Compare Louisiana under Crozat, under John Law, and under the king.

10. Trace the growth of the Louisiana colony.

Potpourri (Getting Involved)

1. Prepare an illustrated time line of the French colonial period.

2. Construct an authentic model of (a) an early French fort, (b) a French colonial home, (c) a pirogue, or (d) a flatboat.

3. Prepare a map showing place names given by the French.

4. Dramatize (a) Iberville's journey, (b) the importation of slaves to Louisiana, (c) the treatment of Indians, (d) a fur-trading trip, (e) the Natchez massacre, (f) the arrival of Casket Girls, (g) a voyage of unwilling settlers, or (h) life in the colony.

5. Interview La Salle, Iberville, Crozat, Bienville, and John Law con-

cerning the failure of the French in Louisiana.

Gumbo (Bringing It Up-to-Date)

1. Relate present-day Louisiana to the French colonial period. How is Louisiana's present social and cultural background a reflection of its French heritage of the colonial period?

2. Report on what is being done to preserve Louisiana's French heritage.

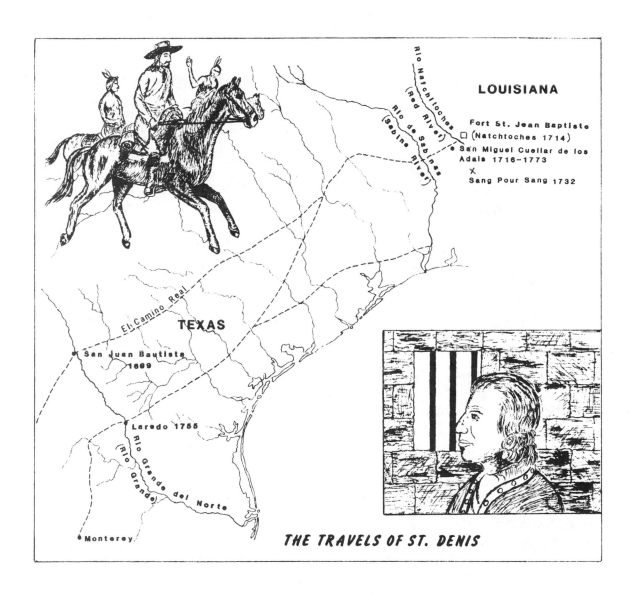

THE TRAVELS OF ST. DENIS

CHAPTER 5

SPANISH COLONIAL LOUISIANA
(1762–1800)

The French and Indian War ended in 1763 with the Treaty of Paris. France was completely expelled from the mainland of North America. The British got Canada and all of the French territory east of the Mississippi except the Isle of Orleans. Spain officially received the French territory west of the Mississippi and the city of New Orleans. Louisiana now belonged to Spain. The colony had been secretly given to Spain in 1762 in the Treaty of Fontainebleau.

The Colony in Limbo

The change of ownership caused much confusion and bitterness. Neither country—France nor Spain—felt responsible for the colony. From the beginning Spain blundered in taking control. Spain did not take over Louisiana immediately. The Spanish had a policy of *mañana* (Spanish for tomorrow), meaning that they were in no hurry to take over the colony. France continued to act as trustee of the colony. French officials complained about spending more money on the lost colony. France no longer sent supplies. Louisiana was of no value.

D'Abbadie: French Governor. Kerlerec remained as governor until late 1763. D'Abbadie replaced him. The king intended that d'Abbadie remain in the position until Spain took possession of the colony.

D'Abbadie found the colony in a terrible condition. He complained of the disorder "long existing in the colony." He referred to the "license" of too much freedom. There was a shortage of all kinds of supplies. He did what he could to restore trade and strengthen defenses. He tried to relieve the distressed French colonists. He asked Spanish officials to reform the Superior Council.

In the fall of 1764 d'Abbadie

received official word from France that the colony belonged to Spain. French officials in Paris ordered him to transfer the Louisiana colony to Spain. It was not until d'Abbadie posted an announcement that the Louisiana people learned that Spain owned the colony. (The custom was to post such notices on the door of the church.) It was almost two years after the secret treaty ceded the colony to Spain.

The people reacted strongly to the news. They were filled with grief, anger, and fear. It saddened them to lose their mother country that they loved so dearly. They were angry that the king had given them to a foreign ruler without considering their wishes. For a long time stories had circulated about the cruelty and tyranny of Spanish officers in Mexico, Florida, and the West Indies. Louisianians were afraid. They did not want to change their flag, laws, language, and customs.

Critical Times in the Louisiana Colony. The colony was in a sad state. France was no longer concerned. Even though Spain owned the colony, there was no sign of the Spanish. The settlers had to manage for themselves. Louisiana colonists were bitter over their abandonment.

A mass meeting was held in New Orleans. The excited people were there to discuss what action they might take. Every district of the colony was represented.

To protest the transfer, a petition was drawn up to send to King Louis XV of France. A leading merchant of New Orleans named **Jean Milhet** was sent to France. He was to present the petition to the king. For two years Milhet tried to get an audience with the king but never succeeded. Bienville tried to help. However, even the elderly former governor was not granted his request. Together he and Milhet called on the prime minister.

Aubry In Control. The order to d'Abbadie to transfer Louisiana to Spain came to him in New Orleans on September 30, 1764. He was ready to deliver the colony to an official bearing credentials from Spain. However, d'Abbadie died suddenly of a stroke on February 4, 1765. An officer from Spain had not yet arrived to accept possession of the colony.

France did not appoint a successor to d'Abbadie. Spain was expected to take control of the colony at any moment. The next highest ranking official in the colony was **Captain Charles Philippe Aubry**, commander of French troops in the colony. He was now in charge of Louisiana. He had no official authority except as an army officer. Aubry had no instructions from France.

Things had gone from bad to worse in Louisiana. The only money in use, French paper money, had gone down in value. Many citizens were financially ruined because of this.

The French government would not redeem the money at face value. Rumors in the colony were that the money would be completely worthless under Spain. It was well known that Spain kept rigid control of the commerce of its colonies. Without such controls French merchants had been able to develop a brisk and thriving trade at the port of New Orleans. This trade appeared to be doomed under Spain.

Almost every Frenchman wanted the colony to remain under France. They were discontented and distressed. It was easy to stir the people to rebel against Spain. French officials knew that they would soon be replaced. They wondered where they would find jobs.

Month after month went by with no sign that Spain was planning to take possession of Louisiana. The people began to think that Milhet's trip to Europe had been successful. They were getting used to the news of Spain's ownership. Business went on as usual.

Ulloa's Announcement. Five months after d'Abbadie's death, **Antonio de Ulloa** wrote a letter to the Superior Council. In it he stated that he was the new Spanish governor of Louisiana. The letter, dated July 10, 1765, was from Havana, Cuba. He wrote that he would be arriving soon to assume his duties.

Weeks and then months went by. Still the Spanish did not take control. The French flag had not been removed from the government buildings in New Orleans. French troops had not been withdrawn from New Orleans. A Frenchman, Aubry, was still in authority. It was over three years after Louisiana was given to Spain when the Spanish governor finally arrived in New Orleans.

En Partie 1 (Studying a Part). 1. What were the results of the French and Indian War? 2. (a) Who took d'Abbadie's place as governor? (b) What was his official role? 3. (a) How long was it before the colonists knew that Louisiana belonged to Spain? (b) How did they learn the news? (c) What was the reaction of the colonists? (d) What action did they take? 4. (a) Why did Spain delay in taking over control? (b) What did France think about the delay? 5. Why were conditions in the colony critical? 6. What did Jean Milhet and Bienville do? 7. What news was received about the change in authority?

The Acadians' Migration to Louisiana

Arrival of the Acadians. In the midst of the gloom and depression, a

Louisiana Office of Tourism

Acadiana is a twenty-two-parish area in South Louisiana. The culture there is that of the French-Acadians, or Cajuns.

party of strangers arrived in the colony. Twenty Acadians landed in New Orleans. They had been exiled from their homes in Canada for almost ten years. They came from the peninsula of Acadia. Many more Acadians followed in the 1760s. They, too, felt that they had been abandoned by France.

About fifty years before Louisiana was transferred to Spain, Acadia, a large peninsula on the east coast of Canada, had been ceded by France to Great Britain. The transfer was made at the end of Queen Anne's War. The British then changed the name of the province to **Nova Scotia** (New Scotland).

It was over four decades later when the French and Indian War started. The British were afraid that the Acadians would not fight against their fellow Frenchmen and that they might even give aid to them. The English governor of Acadia asked the French settlers to swear their loyalty to England. They were also told that they must leave the Catholic church. They might have been willing to sign their allegiance to England had they not been asked to leave their church. When the Acadians refused to meet the governor's orders, the English drove about six thousand persons from their homes. The English took over the small farms of the Acadians. They burned their houses and fields and sent the Acadians out to sea in crowded boats.

In 1755 the Acadians were deported from their homeland. Families and friends were separated. The Acadians went in different directions seeking new homes. Some went to Canada. Others headed for France. Some stopped at the British colonies along the Atlantic coast. Others went farther south to the West Indies. Many made their way to Louisiana.

Some of the Acadians arrived in Louisiana in 1765. In the first five months 650 of them arrived. Most of them were poverty stricken. D'Abbadie requested funds with which to assist them in settling in Louisiana. They were supplied with tools, livestock, and food from government stores in New Orleans. The Acadians received grants of land along Bayou Teche and in the prairie section farther west. Later others settled along the river below New Orleans. Some chose to settle above the city as far as Baton Rouge and Pointe Coupee. Others settled along Bayou Lafourche. In time the Mississippi River settlements became known as the Upper and Lower Acadian coasts.

More Acadians arrived in Louisi-

Louisiana Office of Tourism

ana. Aubry had a difficult time finding supplies for them. He went to the royal storehouse in New Orleans and got what he could. Each family was given food, clothing, a gun, and gun powder. Aubry sent them to settle on the lower Bayou Teche.

Longfellow's Evangeline. Henry Wadsworth Longfellow wrote the epic poem *Evangeline* about the expulsion and wanderings of the Acadians. He described the Acadian country of Louisiana. Today the land remains much as he described it. According to legend, the poem is based on the story of a real couple, Louis Arceneaux and Emmeline LaBiche. Others say that there were many couples separated in the tragic situation encountered by Evangeline and Gabriel in the poem.

"Evangeline's" grave and statue can be found in the old Atakapas Cemetery. The statue was presented by a movie star who played the part of Evangeline in an early film. The movie star, Dolores Del Rio, had modeled for the statue. The home of "Gabriel" is now the Acadian Museum in Evangeline State Park at St. Martinville. The Evangeline Oak, the meeting place of Evangeline and Gabriel, is also located in the park.

Louisiana named a parish Evangeline and another one was named Acadia for these people who added so much to Louisiana.

En Partie 2 (Studying a Part). 1. Describe the migration of the Acadians to Louisiana. 2. What story is told in the poem *Evangeline?*

The Establishment of Spanish Rule

Arrival of Ulloa. The first Spanish governor was Antonio de Ulloa. He arrived on March 5, 1766, in a drenching rain to take possession of Louisiana. He was given an unfriendly but polite reception when he arrived in New Orleans. Captain Aubry formed his few troops in the public square to receive the new governor. Ulloa had only ninety soldiers with him. This was hardly enough to impress the colonists with his position as head of state. The forty-eight-year-old former officer of the Spanish navy did not impress the French settlers in any way. His small stature did not help his image. He had a reputation throughout Europe as being one of the outstanding scholars of his generation. Ulloa was a mathematician, scientist, and writer. This was not known nor appreciated in the colony.

Ulloa did not take control immediately. Instead, Aubry continued to be in charge. Ulloa left New Orleans without lowering the French flag and raising the red and yellow colors of Charles III. French citizens, already confused, were more than puzzled at his failure to do so.

Ulloa sensed the distaste of the colonists for a Spanish governor. He was a practical man. He had expected the French troops under Aubry to serve for Spain. They refused. With so few troops Ulloa felt it unwise to assume complete control of the colony. Orders were issued in Aubry's name, but they were under Ulloa's direction. The arrangement proved to be very awkward and confusing.

Historians note that Ulloa was simply obeying orders from Spain. The Spanish government planned to allow the French a period of adjustment to the new Spanish government. Ulloa was told that Louisiana would be governed differently from other Spanish colonies. He was also advised to leave things as they existed under the French as much as possible.

Ulloa did not report to the Superior Council. Nor did he respond when the governing body asked for his commission or credentials. Since he ignored the body, it refused to accept Ulloa's authority. Members of the Superior Council were unhappy over this show of disrespect to their position. Worse, it increased the colonists' fears about Spanish rule.

Ulloa visited the interior posts and settlements. He was accompanied by Aubry. He stayed longer at Natchitoches than any other place. There he studied how he could establish communication with Mexico.

He ordered a census taken. There was a total of 5,552 white people and about the same number of Negroes. The many Indians living in Spanish Louisiana were not counted. Some Indians had crossed the Mississippi into Spanish Louisiana after Pontiac's War in 1766. Later, a few other tribes came from the region south of the Tennessee River.

Ulloa left New Orleans in September 1766 without explanation. He went to the **Balize**. The pilot port city at the mouth of the Mississippi was a lonely, marshy place. Ulloa raised the Spanish flag and established residence there. In late spring he was still at the Balize. Ulloa did not explain to the Superior Council nor anybody else why he did this. Had he done so, he might have found the people more tolerant. Aubry and other officers made trips to the Balize to report to Ulloa. Aubry issued orders from New Orleans. Ulloa conducted scientific experiments while he waited. He completed some unique plans for the colony.

Trade Regulations. On September 6, 1766, Ulloa received new orders from Spain. Under these he issued trade regulations that caused a great disturbance in the colony. No French ship was permitted to enter the port without first obtaining a permit from a Spanish official. The agents of foreign vessels were required to furnish lists of the goods aboard the ships. This list had to include the prices for which the goods were to be offered for sale. If the prices were too high, the agent was not allowed to unload. Also, the Spanish were not allowed to accept the French paper money in payment. When the agent left port, he was required to take at least one-third of his cargo in products of the colony. In the spring of 1768, more regulations were issued. Only Spanish ships could be used in commerce. Trade was restricted to Spanish ports.

French ships had continued coming in and out of the port of New

Orleans. They brought goods from Europe that the colonists needed. Spain's new regulations meant that henceforth Louisiana would only trade with the mother country. Spanish colonists were not allowed to trade with other Spanish colonists. Supplies desired by the colonists could not be obtained from Spain. These people were, after all, Frenchmen. They wanted goods from France. Even worse, the regulations confirmed the worst fears of French businessmen. They thought that the new orders were an indication that more restrictions on trade would follow.

New Orleans was a prospering small port by the 1760s. A group of the city's businessmen had taken advantage of opportunities to build a lively commerce. Some had become quite wealthy. The economy of the little capital was largely dependent upon this trade. Now it seemed that it was going to be destroyed. Spanish trade regulations were too strict. The merchants were alarmed. They were afraid that their businesses would be ruined by these regulations.

Formal Possession. Ulloa planned to officially take over Louisiana from the French at the Balize. When Aubry protested, he decided to wait until more Spanish troops arrived. At the Balize Ulloa and Aubry signed a document called the *Toma de Posesion* on January 20, 1767. This was nearly ten months after his arrival. It was an agreement to divide control of Louisiana between France and Spain. Both Ulloa and Aubry would govern. This joint rule would last until more soldiers arrived from Spain. The dual arrangement was known to both French and Spanish officials. They made no protests.

On December 4, 1767, Ulloa was still living at the Balize. By then he felt called upon to make an announcement. He said that he was still waiting for Spanish troops to arrive. He announced that Juan Joseph de Loyola would become minister of finance on January 1, 1768. This meant that Spain was finally relieving France of the financial burden of the colony. This was five years after the colony became the property of Spain.

Ulloa's Wedding. Another reason for Ulloa's delay in officially taking over New Orleans was his forthcoming wedding ceremony. He had been waiting for his bride, Dona Francisca Ramirez de Laredo y Encalada from Peru. She and Ulloa had been married by proxy, a privilege of royalty alone. She was a wealthy young woman. Ulloa waited seven months for her to arrive. Although they were officially married, a marriage ceremony was performed by Ulloa's chaplain at the Balize when she arrived.

Nothing could have done more harm to Ulloa's acceptance by the French people. The idea of the governor of Louisiana being married in such a simple way upset them. The social elite in New Orleans were insulted. They felt that there should have been feasting, dancing, and celebrating. Even the religious leaders criticized Ulloa's marriage. They felt that it should have been performed in a church in New Orleans. Since Vaudreuil's term as governor, New Orleans society had rarely been without a celebration of some sort. A big wedding would have offered the opportunity for another celebration.

To make matters worse, Ulloa and his wife never joined the New Orleans social circle. The wives of the leading citizens would not call on her. They thought Ulloa's new wife was even more cold, haughty, and exclusive than her husband. Even after the couple went to New Orleans, they remained apart from the French society. The bride had brought attendants and friends with her from Peru. She seemed to prefer their company. She did not even attend mass with the New Orleans people. Ulloa's bride only spoke Spanish. Her inability to speak French may have caused her to remain with her own group. In any event Ulloa and his wife used poor judgment indeed in their social lives. He may have thought that participation in New Orleans's social functions was unimportant. If so, he was not prepared to be governor of Louisiana.

Problems. Ulloa used some of the gold and silver he brought with him to pay the soldiers of France under Aubry. Even that attempt to help the colony met with disappointment. The French were distressed that the French paper money was worth only one-fourth its face value under the Spanish. They wanted more for their paper money. It seemed that nothing Ulloa did pleased the French. He had tried to improve the economic conditions of the colony.

The financial situation had worsened. Commerce in New Orleans was paralyzed. Ulloa forbade illegal trade. Spain's new commercial regulations increased the problems. One regula-

The site upon which the Cabildo stands was set aside for government use in 1721.

tion that made the Frenchmen furious concerned their wine. Only Spanish wines could be imported.

Underneath all of their honest, legitimate complaints against Spain was the unalterable fact that the colonists were French. Being French, they dreaded being the subjects of the Spanish king. Their hopes faded when they got the news about their petition. Jean Milhet returned to New Orleans in late 1767. After an absence of two years, he announced the failure of his mission. He had not been granted an audience with the king.

Plot of Revolutionists. Finally, French leaders, officials, officers of the armed forces, merchants, and planters met. At this meeting they made secret plans to get rid of Ulloa. The acknowledged leader was Nicolas Chauvin de Lafreniere, attorney general of the province. Nicolas Denis Foucault, first judge of the Superior Council, was one of the principal leaders. Others were Lafreniere's brother-in-law Joseph Villeré and Jean Milhet and his brother Joseph.

A day was set for the colonists to gather in New Orleans. The date was October 28, 1768, at eight o'clock in the morning. Noyan, a nephew of Bienville, led a band of armed men from the Acadian coast. Villere was the leader of another group from the German Coast. Colonists came from below New Orleans. About four hundred people assembled. The leaders

of the revolution had prearranged the entire protest. French soldiers under Aubry refused to fight the rebels. Aubry advised Ulloa and his wife to leave their official residence and go to a Spanish warship in the harbor.

Expulsion of Ulloa. Leaders of the angry people presented a **petition** against Spanish rule to the Superior Council on October 29, 1768. It was signed by 560 of the leading men of the colony. The next day, the Superior Council voted in favor of the petition. The council had no authority under Spain. Nevertheless, it ordered Ulloa to leave the colony within three days. Aubry protested. It did no good because he did not have sufficient troops to suppress the rebellion. Ulloa had sent the few Spanish soldiers he had to various inland ports over the colony. The troops he had been promised had not arrived. Plans had been made to abolish the Superior Council when more troops arrived for support.

Aubry was caught in a bad position. He had written back to France before this incident, "My position is most extraordinary. I command for the King of France and at the same time I govern the colony as if it belonged to the King of Spain."

The Spanish warship was not able to leave the port of New Orleans immediately. Ulloa left it and boarded a French ship instead. Before the ship was to leave, a curious incident was said to have occurred. Some historians say that the ship was set adrift by young Frenchmen before daylight on November 1, 1768. The young men were returning from a party late at night. They cut the rope that moored Ulloa's ship to the wharf. Afterward, Ulloa angrily ordered the captain to sail for Havana, Cuba. Another version simply states that Ulloa left New Orleans in a French sailing vessel headed for Havana. Historians state that threats to cut the ropes had been received.

When Ulloa arrived at Havana, he sent to Spain a report of the Louisiana mob action against him. It brought quick response. Spanish officials, furious at the insult, were determined that Spain would be avenged. The French leaders would be punished. The Spanish flag would be respected by the Louisiana French.

Meanwhile, the Superior Council again ruled Louisiana. The council sent a petition to the king of France asking him to take control of Louisiana. Although he refused, rebel leaders and their friends felt that they had succeeded. Ulloa was gone from the colony. The leaders rejoiced, sang patriotic songs, and cheered King Louis.

The revolution had happened without the Louisiana leaders foreseeing the position in which they would find themselves. The colony belonged to Spain. That they knew. However justified they felt in their anger, they were now at the mercy of Spain. They had insulted Spain by expelling Ulloa. However much at fault Ulloa had been, he represented Spanish authority in a Spanish colony. France had turned a deaf ear to their pleas. What should they do now?

Second Petition to France. Another meeting of French leaders was held in New Orleans. The group drew up a second petition to King Louis XV. It was called "Memorial to the Planters and Merchants of Louisiana on the Events of October 29, 1768." The Louisiana French asked France not to give the colony to Spain. The petition recited the story of the colony under France. It repeated the loyalty of the people to France.

Three men took the document to France. King Louis paid no more attention to the second petition than he had paid to the first. All France wanted was to wash its hands of the expensive colony. France did not wish to anger its ally Spain, either.

Revolution of 1768: Aubry. While the revolutionists were taking their petition, Captain Aubry sent his report of these events. The series of acts against Spain were now called the Revolution of 1768. Aubry had no sympathy for his fellow French. He felt entirely different about the Spanish government in Louisiana. He called leaders of the revolution "twelve fire-brands." Aubry's role was never entirely clear. In Aubry's report to

France he said Ulloa was responsible for the revolution. He added, "It is no pleasant mission to govern a colony which undergoes so many revolutions."

Last Appeal. The leaders of the rebellion were spurned by France. The revolutionists sought other solutions. Now they realized that their very lives were at stake. In desperation they appealed to the English, who now owned Pensacola. The English would have nothing to do with the situation. They refused to offend Spain over Louisiana.

Finally, the leaders considered independence. They could establish a republic in Louisiana. However, they were practical. They knew that an independent republic could not survive without the support of a powerful nation. France, England, and Spain would be against the independent republic. This being so, the leaders realized that it could not last.

Some of the people involved in the revolution left New Orleans. They moved across the Mississippi River to live in English West Florida. Some remained there permanently. Others later returned.

Alejandro O'Reilly's Arrival. Lieutenant General Alejandro O'Reilly was an impressive military man. He was born in Ireland but moved with his parents to Spain when he was ten years old. O'Reilly had saved King Charles's life in 1765 during a raid

Alejandro O'Reilly.

in Madrid. He received the king's commission appointing him governor and captain general of the province of Louisiana on April 16, 1769.

On August 17, 1769, O'Reilly arrived at the Balize with more than two thousand men and twenty-four ships. This was a show of power to support his authority. It had been eight months since Ulloa had left. The colonists were amazed that the king of Spain had sent one of his highest officers and one of the greatest generals of Europe to Louisiana. They were anxious then to see the next step to be taken.

O'Reilly brought with him a man named **Don Luis de Unzaga**. He was to become governor of Louisiana when O'Reilly left the colony.

O'Reilly had orders to put down the Louisiana rebellion. The leaders of the revolution tried to get people to resist the new Spanish governor. The colonists paid no attention. In such a crisis, three of the leaders of the revolution met O'Reilly at the Balize. These were Lafreniere, Pierre Marquis, and one of the Milhets. They wanted to make known their willingness to live under Spain. O'Reilly entertained the visitors at dinner. He treated them so courteously that they admired him. The rebel leaders thought that O'Reilly was not going to hold their past actions against them.

O'Reilly's Entry into New Orleans. O'Reilly's dramatic entry with his display of military force was a big contrast to Ulloa's arrival. This display was meant to impress Louisianians with the power of Spain. On August 18, 1769, a great colorful ceremony was held at the Plaza de Armas, or French Place d'Armes. The colony was formally transferred by Aubry to O'Reilly. Aubry's troops were lined up at the square. Amid the roll of drums and the flare of trumpets, O'Reilly's two thousand soldiers, in full uniform, watched the flag ceremony. The French flag was lowered, and the Spanish flag was raised high on the staff.

Arrest of Conspirators. O'Reilly lost no time in arresting the twelve leaders of the revolution. For his information about them, he called on Aubry. The French people bitterly resented Aubry's part in the actions against his fellow Frenchmen. Some critics of Aubry think that he wanted to impress O'Reilly. They think he went too far in denouncing his fellow citizens. Some historians believe that he followed orders received from France.

O'Reilly quickly took measures to secure justice against the revolutionists. He invited ten ringleaders of the revolution to his house. He gave various reasons for doing so. As they arrived, one at a time, he had them arrested. They were taken to different places of confinement. They were not allowed to communicate with one another. The French considered this to be treachery on O'Reilly's part. One of the rebels, Joseph Villeré, did not accept the governor's invitation. There are different stories about his fate. One states that soldiers were sent to get him and to place him under arrest. He was killed. The Spanish soldiers said that he resisted arrest.

The People's Reaction. The people of New Orleans were in a state of frenzy. Each thought that he would be next. They closed themselves up in their homes. Many prepared to leave the colony and seek refuge with the British. O'Reilly finally realized the extent of their fears. He issued a statement pardoning all persons except those arrested. Three days later a meeting was held so that citizens could pledge allegiance to Spain. If they refused, they were required to leave the colony. O'Reilly sent officers to the military posts in the interior. This was so that citizens there could take the oath of allegiance to Spain. Most took the oath.

Punishment of Rebels. Spanish law defined a traitor as anyone "who labors by deed or word to induce any people or any provinces under the domination of the king, to rise against his majesty." The law stated that traitors were to be put to death.

The trial of the rebel leaders was carried out according to Spanish law. It lasted for several weeks. There was no trial by jury. Each of the accused was examined separately. So were the witnesses. Judges made the decisions. No one questioned the fact that the rebels were attempting to get rid of Spanish rule. One defense used by the rebels was that Spain had not taken legal possession of the colony. Therefore, they argued, they had not broken any Spanish laws. The judges ruled that the revolution was carried out on Spanish soil. They were, therefore, under Spanish law.

O'Reilly pronounced the sentences. Joseph Petit was sentenced to prison for life. Balthasar de Mason and Julien Doucet got ten years. Jean Milhet and Pierre Poupet got six. Hardy de

Boisblanc also got a prison sentence. Villeré was declared "infamous" (disgraced). Five were sentenced to be hanged. They were Lafreniere, de Noyan, Caresse, Marquis, and Joseph Milhet. They were to be led to the gallows with ropes around their necks. They were to be mounted on donkeys and hanged. The public hangman was instructed to destroy any revolutionary documents belonging to the group.

The town criers of New Orleans read the death sentences. No Frenchman would act as hangman, in spite of the large reward that had been offered for anyone who would serve. The leaders sentenced to be hanged were executed by a firing squad of Spanish soldiers. Those sentenced to jail were sent to a huge prison called Morro Castle at Havana, Cuba. Later, they were pardoned by Charles III of Spain at the request of the French ambassador.

Not only were the leaders executed or imprisoned, but also their property was seized by the Spanish government. These men were the wealthiest business and political men of Louisiana. Most of them were related. Their wives and children were left with nothing.

Aubry's Fate. Aubry left for France. He had a large amount of money with him. At least that is what was said in the colony. His ship wrecked off the coast of France on

February 17, 1770. Aubry drowned. Many colonists felt that he got what he deserved. They felt that he had testified against his own people.

"Bloody O'Reilly"? O'Reilly was soundly hated by the French in Louisiana. He was called "Bloody O'Reilly." Yet, as tragic as the revolution was for its leaders, O'Reilly was sent to Louisiana for one purpose. He was to punish these leaders. How else could the French people of Louisiana be taught that it was not safe to insult Spain? Spanish honor had to be upheld and respected.

Rebellion was in the air—and not merely in the Spanish colonies.

O'REILLY DEFENDS THE HONOR OF SPAIN

The English colonies on the east coast were seething with rebellion.

Spain was having trouble with two other colonies. It felt the need to get Louisiana colonists under control. It also wanted the treatment of the revolutionists in Louisiana to serve as a warning to all others who might be thinking of rebelling against Spanish authority.

Contributions of O'Reilly. O'Reilly changed the government from French to Spanish. His reorganization cut the expenses to half of what they had been under the French. O'Reilly employed attorneys to write a set of laws under which Louisiana would be governed. This set of laws came to be known as the **O'Reilly Code.** All laws, orders, and decrees were published in Spanish after December 1, 1769. The form of government established by O'Reilly was used throughout the Spanish period.

General O'Reilly abolished the Superior Council. In its place he formed another group, the **Cabildo.** It was composed of ten members. The governor presided. Most of the members were from New Orleans. O'Reilly ordered that a suitable building be constructed for the new government. Then the general appointed **commandants** for each district in the colony. These were selected from among the French residents. They were in charge of most minor official matters involving persons living at their posts. The commandant was responsible for the preservation of order; the upkeep of levees, highways, and bridges; and the policing of slaves. He also enforced locally the royal decrees and ordinances passed by the Cabildo.

O'Reilly visited interior forts. The Spanish general knew that the colonists had given him the unflattering nickname "Bloody O'Reilly." He said that he was going to the distant forts to show the colonists that he did not have "horns, hoofs, and spiked tail."

O'Reilly appointed a surveyor for each district. The French had not made **surveys** to determine exact boundaries of property. This led to many disputes. The Spanish recorded property boundaries. The surveys aided farmers by establishing land titles. The surveying of land was one of the most important contributions made by the Spanish.

On February 18, 1770, O'Reilly's **land ordinance** was issued. It remained unchanged until the 1790s. It was O'Reilly's system of homesteading. The attractive offer is believed to have been the reason for the large increase in population during the Spanish period. The ordinance provided that each newly arrived family was given a tract of six to eight arpents of frontland on a river or bayou. The tract was forty arpents in depth. The grantee had three years to build a levee and drainage ditches. A road behind the levee with bridges

over ditches also had to be constructed. Within three years the grantee had to clear the entire front to a depth of two arpents. A fence had to enclose the cleared land and all improvements had to be maintained.

The grant could not be sold for three years. Some grants in Opelousas, Atakapas, and Natchitoches were limited to one league front by one league depth (42-by-42 arpents). These large grants were made to encourage cattle-raising. An applicant for such a grant had to have one hundred head of tame cattle, some horses and sheep, and two slaves to look after the livestock. There were smaller grants in the same region for applicants with fewer cattle.

All tame cattle had to be branded before they were eighteen months old. If they were not branded, the owner could not claim them. All wild cattle were to be destroyed July 1, 1771. These were very small animals with no value for meat or milk.

A census was taken under O'Reilly's orders. New Orleans had 3,190 persons. Of these, 1,225 were slaves, and 100 were free people of color. In the whole colony there were 13,538 people. At least half were slaves.

O'Reilly continued the trade policies issued by Ulloa. However, he did urge Spain to allow the colony to trade with Cuba. Spain could not use lumber from the colony, but Cuba was in need of it. It was not until

Spanish Colonial Government

King

Governor

Cabildo

1777 that Spain allowed the colony to trade with Cuba.

O'Reilly vowed to break up the practice of "going to Manchac." This was a common expression in Louisiana. It referred to the trade between the colonists and the English located on Bayou Manchac. This unlawful trade commenced after the English gained possession of the land east of the Mississippi in 1763. Here the English traders sold supplies needed by planters and merchants of New Orleans. Such trade became even more important when the Spanish banned French ships from the port of New Orleans. Goods from Europe had to be secured if the Louisiana business was to prosper. There had to be a way to obtain such supplies. Under these conditions much smuggling developed.

O'Reilly forbade the importation of West Indies slaves. He required that slaves imported be those from Africa. This way they would not have adopted voodoo. Slaves transported to the islands practiced this strange cult. Fresh from their homeland, slaves could be trained to better suit the needs of settlers. They would not absorb any ideas of freedom that might exist among the island slaves.

During the seven months O'Reilly was in Louisiana, he made other changes. Shortly after he arrived, he started sending the military troops that he had brought with him back to Spain. He organized about one thousand men in the colony into a military unit for defense. These actions proved to be very smart moves on O'Reilly's part. It made the people feel more in control of their own fate rather than being under the heel of "foreign" troops. Another step he made was to divide Louisiana into twenty-one parishes. O'Reilly's parishes were strictly religious divisions. O'Reilly changed the jurisdiction of the Catholic church in Louisiana from Canada to the bishop of Santiago de Cuba.

The first meeting of the Cabildo was held on December 1, 1769. At this meeting O'Reilly transferred the office of governor to Unzaga. He had brought the well-trained Unzaga with him for the purpose of making him governor. O'Reilly stayed a while after Unzaga took the position to be sure that the colony was on sound footing. After O'Reilly completed the work that he was assigned to do, he left Louisiana. He sailed back to Spain on October 29, 1770.

En Partie 3 (Studying a Part). 1. (a) Who was the first Spanish governor? (b) When did he arrive? (c) How many troops did he have? (d) Why did he stay at the Balize? 2. (a) What did the colonists do to protest Spanish rule? (b) Who were the leaders? (c) Did Milhet succeed in his mission? 3. What was Ulloa's relationship with the Superior Council? 4. How did the new trade regulations affect the colonists? 5. What were some of the problems Ulloa faced? 6. Under what circumstances did Ulloa leave? 7. What other plans did the revolutionists have? 8. Describe the arrival of O'Reilly. 9. How was O'Reilly's takeover different from that of Ulloa? 10. (a) What did some of the leaders of the revolution do when O'Reilly arrived? (b) What were the results? 11. (a) What part did Aubry play? (b) How did the French feel about him? 12. What happened to the leaders of the revolution? 13. Describe the government set up by O'Reilly. 14. What else did he do?

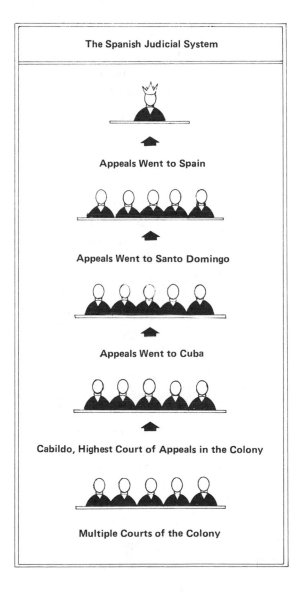

The Spanish Judicial System

Appeals Went to Spain

Appeals Went to Santo Domingo

Appeals Went to Cuba

Cabildo, Highest Court of Appeals in the Colony

Multiple Courts of the Colony

Spanish Rule until 1800

Unzaga's Rule. Unzaga was an elderly man when he came to the colony with O'Reilly. He had been a colonel in the troops at Havana, Cuba. He was a mild-mannered Spaniard for whom O'Reilly had prepared the way. Unzaga won the goodwill of the colonists. Unzaga's marriage to a French woman helped him become a part of the population. He was well liked. He also continued to appoint Creoles to important positions in the government.

The governor did not go out of his way to find violations of Spanish law. He ignored the illegal trade situation with the English. That is, he made no attempt to stop anyone from "going to the Manchac." Unzaga knew that he must gain the friendship of the French citizens of Louisiana. Stopping the trade would ruin his chances of doing so. Unzaga allowed English merchants to establish stores in New Orleans as well.

Louisiana became prosperous under Spain. That helped the people accept Spanish rule. Silver from Mexico was used to pay the cost of officials and other costs borne by Spain. This brought **hard money** into the colony instead of the old French paper money. Trade improved. The Spanish fixed the trading value of the French paper money at one-fourth of its face value. It was not long before paper money disappeared. Hard money maintained its value much better than the paper money.

In 1771 the king of Spain made plans for a **public school** in the colony. He sent Manuel Andres Lopez de Armesto and three assistants to New Orleans as schoolmasters. They were to introduce the Spanish language and instill loyalty to Spain. The school failed because the French parents would not send their children. Most of the children who attended were those of Spanish officials.

There had been only the Roman Catholic church in the colony under the French. The Spanish were even more dedicated to the Catholic church than the French. No other religion was allowed in the colony. There was one problem, however. The people spoke French, so they wanted French-speaking priests. None of the Spanish priests spoke French well. The Spanish Capuchins arrived and tried to secure the dismissal of the French priest, Father Dagobert. Unzaga agreed with the French. Father Dagobert was not removed.

The American Revolution was brewing in the years that Unzaga was governor. The thirteen English colonies on the Atlantic coast were rebelling against the English. Unzaga was concerned that Louisiana did not have sufficient military supplies and troops to defend itself against attack. He strengthened the militia when it was

Elaborate wrought-iron and cast-iron balconies from the Spanish grace the front of many French Quarter buildings.

rumored that the British were planning to attack.

Eventually Spain put Unzaga's military plans into effect. In 1776, a forceful young militarist, **Don Bernardo de Gálvez**, became commander of Spanish troops in Louisiana. He quietly aided the American colonists by sending them the supplies that he could spare.

In 1776 Unzaga was promoted to captain general of Caracas, Venezuela. This was the same year the English colonies declared their independence. Unzaga left the colony in March 1777.

He had seen the bad feelings against the Spanish gradually disappearing. When he left, there was much regret.

Military Governor: Gálvez. Gálvez became governor in 1777. A brilliant young military officer of the age of twenty-nine, Gálvez came from a line of prominent military men in Spain. He had already gained military experience in Portugal and Mexico. His father was viceroy of Mexico. His uncle became president of the Council of the Indies.

The military operations of Gálvez dominated life in Louisiana during much of his administration. The American Revolution was going on in the Atlantic seacoast region. France was allied with the revolutionists. Most French Louisiana residents were sympathetic with the rebelling Americans, also. As for Gálvez, he was an ambitious young military officer. He could see possibilities of capturing English possessions across the Mississippi River. He would thereby gain recognition and promotions. The Spanish officials favored the American colonists because they considered England a powerful rival.

As long as Spain remained neutral, Gálvez secretly aided the American revolutionists. So did other Spanish officials in Louisiana. They lent money to the colonists. They allowed American agents to make New Orleans their headquarters. The agents helped the colonists obtain guns and ammunition for use against the British. Military supplies were shipped to New Orleans. Then these supplies were shipped up the river to George Rogers Clark, a hero of the American Revolution who saved the western land for the United States. **Oliver Pollock** was one of the most active of these American agents in New Orleans. He was the fourth largest financier of the Revolution. Pollock also helped Clark by securing credit to buy supplies locally. Pollock's signature was all that was needed for Clark to be allowed to buy with drafts on the state of Virginia.

Lagniappe. Oliver Pollock lost his entire fortune by helping to finance the Revolution. After the war he was thrown into debtor's prison. He paid a lawyer $1,760 to serve his prison term so that he could get out. He then made enough money to pay his debts. He also built up another fortune.

Even though his sympathies were with the Americans, Gálvez offered homes to the British refugees from West Florida in early 1778. These people were left homeless because of **Willing's raid**. James Willing, a rebelling colonist, made a raiding expedition down the Mississippi and into British territory. Apparently he was on an errand for the Continental Congress. He attempted to persuade the people of West Florida to support the colonists. Those who did not agree to take an oath to support the United States suffered. Willing looted the plantations in West Florida and destroyed or took much of their belongings. Later he tried to dispose of his stolen goods in New Orleans. Gálvez was placed in an awkward situation when Willing arrived in New Orleans. He was greatly relieved when Willing left. Many of the people who fled to New Orleans were able to return to their homes.

Spain joined France as an ally of the colonists three years after the Declaration of Independence. This was May 8, 1779. The decision was very important to Louisiana. Gálvez then had reason to attack the English across the river. War tended to disrupt the normal development of the colony.

When Spain joined the rebelling colonists, Gálvez saw his opportunity. He placed Don Martin Navarro, the intendant, in charge of civil affairs in Louisiana. Then he marched on the nearest English forts. He had planned to attack before he did, but a hurricane sank all of his vessels. He replaced them in a very short time. In 1779 he quickly captured **Fort Bute** at Manchac.

A week later he captured Fort New Richmond at **Baton Rouge**. He did this by deceiving the British. Some of his men hid in the woods during the night and pretended to be ready to attack. The British wasted their ammunition during the night. Meanwhile Gálvez moved some of his men to the other side of the fort. At daylight on September 21, 1779, he started the attack. It ended in the afternoon. The British commander surrendered. He gave up the fort at Baton Rouge and **Fort Panmure** at Natchez to Gálvez. This Spanish vic-

tory prevented the British from getting a stronghold on the lower Mississippi. For this achievement the young Gálvez was promoted to brigadier general.

Spanish vessels captured several English gunboats on the lakes and on the Mississippi. One incident was between a British ship with a crew of seventy and a Spanish ship with fourteen Creoles. The French Creoles fired on the British ship. The British crew went below deck. The Creoles boarded the ship, fastened the hatches, and captured the ship.

Next, Gálvez headed for **Mobile**. Again he had problems. This time a tropical storm struck. Several ships went aground, and many men and guns were lost. It took a month to regroup. Gálvez captured Fort Charlotte at Mobile from the English in 1780. For this achievement he was rewarded with a promotion to major general.

On May 10, 1781, Gálvez captured Fort George at **Pensacola**. It was then the strongest fort in the Floridas. This victory established Spanish control over East Florida. Luck played a part in this victory. The battle had gone on for more than a month. The Spanish appeared to be losing. A lucky shot from a Spanish cannonball caused the powder magazine inside Fort George to explode. With part of the fort walls destroyed, the Spanish were able to storm the fort. The English surrendered. Gálvez was then given new titles that were even more imposing than the old ones: Knight Pensioner of the Order of Charles III, lieutenant general, and finally, captain general of Louisiana and Florida.

A few months after the fall of Pensacola, fighting in America ended. As a consequence of Gálvez's victories, Spain received the Floridas when peace was made in 1783. This marked the end of the American Revolution. His campaign had other results. The military genius of Gálvez was recognized and rewarded. The fighting spirit and ability of Louisianians were demonstrated.

Civil Affairs. During these years of accomplishment for Gálvez, the Louisiana colony had survived. However, the war had overshadowed routine civil affairs. Louisiana was now important enough that, for the first time, Spain separated the Louisiana colony from Cuba.

Spanish citizens were encouraged to come to the colony. However, not very many of them came. Some Spaniards—the **Isleños** ("Islanders")—migrated to the colony. They came from the Canary Islands. As they settled, they found homesites around St. Bernard and Bayou Lafourche. One group settled on the Amite River. A total of 1,582 Canary Islanders had arrived by 1779. **Spaniards** from Malaga, Spain, settled at New Iberia on the Teche. Five hundred settled at New Iberia. Acadians continued to come into Louisiana. The 1784 census showed a total of 32,114 whites and blacks (slave and free) in the colony. This total probably included Louisiana and the Floridas.

A royal decree in 1778 encouraged settlers to come to Louisiana. The head of each family was given a land grant of five arpents fronting a stream. He could own as far back as he could clear. The allotment also included one bushel of corn for each adult and half a bushel for each child for the first year. Each family received a hoe, an axe, a scythe or sickle, a spade, ten hens and a cock, and a two-month-old pig.

During Gálvez's years as governor Spain allowed more freedom of trade to the French businessmen in New Orleans. They were allowed to trade with the French West Indies. Then Spain went even further in freedom of trade. Trade was allowed with France for a period of ten years. Gálvez encouraged trade by reducing the export and import duty. For two years ships were duty-free. Plans were made for a customhouse, too. The Spanish, then, learned to favor trading with the French to "going to the Manchac."

Louisianians hated to see the brilliant young military man and his Creole wife, Felicie de St. Maxent d'Estréhan, leave the colony. He was given the highest prize the Spanish king could give him in colonial administration; he was named viceroy of Mexico. He was allowed to use *Yo solo* (I alone) on his coat of arms as well. Gálvez has been called Louisiana's first Creole folk hero. Galveztown was named for him. The colonists grieved to hear that he did not live to enjoy his honors. He died in Mexico in 1786 of a fever. He was only thirty-eight years old.

Governor Miro: 1784. The next governor of Louisiana was one of the mildest mannered and most progressive the colony ever had. He was **Don Estevan Miro.** Miro had been on the military expeditions with Gálvez. He was acting governor when Gálvez organized his expedition against Mobile in 1780. His rank was brigadier general. He had been appointed temporary governor in 1784, while Gálvez was absent on leave. He was a well-educated man who spoke both French and Spanish. Miro also married a Creole, Marie Celeste Elenore de Macarty. His marriage helped him win the goodwill of the people. Miro had difficulty supporting the lifestyle expected among his wife's class, though.

Miro's administration was outstanding. Miro was more flexible than other Spanish governors. He relaxed restrictions against the colonists' trade with Americans up the Mississippi River. During his administration a hospital for the treatment of leprosy (Hansen's disease) was established in Iberville Parish. It was a forerunner of the present United States Marine Hospital No. 66 at Carville.

Louisiana prospered, and the population increased. Miro encouraged Americans to settle in the area now called the Florida parishes. Most of these settlers were **Protestants.** They did not have to become Catholics. The same rules still applied to other settlers, however. In the rest of Louisiana settlers had to pledge allegiance to Spain and practice Catholicism. In 1785 the **Post of Ouachita** (Fort Miro, Monroe) was established by Don Juan Filhiol. In the 1790s Colonel Abraham Morehouse of Kentucky

FORT MIRO
... ...
Original stockade built on this site in 1790 by Commandant Jean Filhiol and Lieut. Joseph de la Baume of Ouachita District. Half of timbers furnished by officers; half by garrison and settlers.

took settlers to the Ouachita River Valley. They settled on the land grants of Bastrop and Maison Rouge.

A census was taken in 1788 by Miro's administration. The Spanish colony had 43,111 residents. Negroes numbered 19,945. Within the limits of present-day Louisiana there were 34,000 persons. The population of the entire colony had more than doubled since the Spanish took over.

Most of the residents of the colony lived in and around New Orleans. New Orleans was a busy port town. About forty boats at a time could be seen anchored at the docks. It was still a dirty town. When it rained, sewage floated into the narrow streets. The town was infested with insects and reptiles. But life went on with zest despite the problems.

New Orleans Fire. One of the most significant events of Miro's administration was a great fire. The fire destroyed much of New Orleans. On Good Friday, March 21, 1788, 856 buildings valued at 2.6 million dollars went up in flames. Over a thousand people were left without homes. The fire started in a private chapel in the home of the treasurer of the colony, Vicente José Nuñez. It was caused by a lighted candle falling against lace draperies. In five hours almost all residences and government buildings had been destroyed.

The story has been told that the Capuchins would not ring the church bell because it was Good Friday. The bells would have called the city's volunteer firefighters.

In this disaster, Miro became a hero. With admirable speed he supplied tents for the homeless people. He dispatched ships to the United States to obtain food. All restrictions on American trade on the Mississippi River were removed so that the homeless could be helped.

The richest man in the colony, **Don Andres Almonester**, helped pay to replace the buildings destroyed by fire. The Cabildo, the St. Louis Cathedral, the Presbytere, Charity Hospital, a new governor's house, the public school, the church of the Ursuline convent, and sheds for an outdoor market were built. The new structures featured Spanish architecture. There were courtyards, ironwork, high ceilings, balconies, and arched windows and doors.

Spanish Plot Against the United States. The fire temporarily took Miro's attention away from a plot against the United States. He was ambitious for the mother country. He saw the possibility of Spain's securing the land between the Allegheny Mountains and the Mississippi River. American settlers had poured across these mountains after the Revolution. The new nation was young and struggling to survive. It was so beset by the many problems in building a nation and becoming accepted

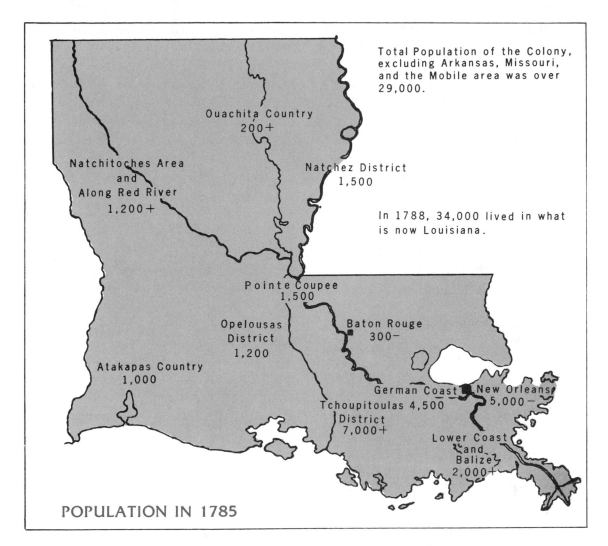

Total Population of the Colony, excluding Arkansas, Missouri, and the Mobile area was over 29,000.

In 1788, 34,000 lived in what is now Louisiana.

Ouachita Country
200+

Natchez District
1,500

Natchitoches Area and Along Red River
1,200+

Pointe Coupee
1,500

Opelousas District
1,200

Baton Rouge
300—

Atakapas Country
1,000

German Coast 4,500
Tchoupitoulas District 7,000+

New Orleans
5,000—

Lower Coast and Balize
2,000+

POPULATION IN 1785

among older nations that there was little time for giving attention to anything else. Settlers who crossed the mountains into the frontier of Tennessee, Kentucky, and other areas felt neglected.

Miro contacted well-known Americans to interest these resentful settlers in starting a movement to ob-tain Spanish annexation of this United States territory. Miro's most active agent was **General James Wilkinson** of the United States Army. Thus, Wilkinson received pay from both the United States Army and Spain at the same time. Historians disagree over Wilkinson's motives. Some think that he was a traitor to the United

States. Others think that he was trying to get trade advantages in New Orleans for the Kentucky settlers.

Inquisition Crisis. Miro also became a hero to the people of Louisiana in a religious crisis. There was a new king of Spain, Charles IV, who was very strict in religious matters. In Spain, there was an Inquisition—a type of church court—to search out heretics and punish them. The Inquisition seized and tried people who had opinions contrary to those of the Catholic church. Father Antonio de Sedella was sent to Louisiana to carry out such a mission. Miro forced him to return to Spain. Because of Miro's action, there was no Inquisition in Louisiana.

Other Efforts of Miro. Miro did as much as he dared to relax the strict Spanish trade regulations. Many of the regulations started under Gálvez were still in effect while Miro was governor. Miro taxed imports and exports at a lower rate than previously used. Spain had placed obstacles in the way of western traffic on the Mississippi River. They were meant to encourage westerners to leave the United States and join Spain. Miro pleased Louisianians by permitting limited trade with Americans.

Miro made every effort to secure the goodwill of the **Indians**. The Indians were able to play the Spanish against the Americans to the east. The latter wanted to bargain for the

Indians' furs and sell to them. Miro ignored Spanish rules so that he could get along with the Indians. He allowed agents to bring in some American goods from Georgia and the Carolinas to trade with the Indians. The American traders gave the Spaniards many worries. They made better deals with the Indians. Miro met with the Choctaws, Chickasaws, and Alabamas at Mobile and signed treaties with them. He promised to help protect their land.

Miro's Departure. Miro was old and tired and ready to return to Spain. After many requests fell on deaf ears, finally he was granted permission to go home. The people over whom he had ruled for seven years regretted his leaving.

When Miro retired, another able governor headed the Louisiana government. His full name was Francisco Luis Hector, Baron de Carondelet.

Governor Carondelet: December 30, 1791. Carondelet was a veteran in government service when he came to Louisiana to begin his work as governor. Like Miro, he became a very efficient governor. He had already served as governor of the Spanish province of Guatemala in Central America. He was serving as governor of San Salvador when he received his Louisiana assignment. It is probable that Carondelet's high position came to him from his marriage into the Las Casas family. They had been involved in the settlement of the New World since the time of Columbus three centuries earlier.

Carondelet did not speak English. Neither did he have any knowledge of the Mississippi Valley. Carondelet did have a lot of ability and energy. He quickly won the friendship and respect of the Creoles.

Effect of French Revolution. Carondelet was governor during a period of crisis. George Washington had been inaugurated as president of the United States in 1789. That same year, France broke into revolution. Louisiana was much affected by the revolution. The French people in Louisiana were in sympathy with the efforts of their kindred across the seas. Most of the colonists were openly sympathetic. The king of Spain did not want the new French ideas about liberty extended to the colonies. He forbade his subjects from having in their possession any coin, clock, or other article that showed the figure of Liberty.

After Louis XVI was beheaded, Spain declared war on France. Carondelet's troubles increased. The ideas of "liberty, equality, and fraternity" of revolutionary France caused problems in the colony in spite of the king's warnings. Frenchmen in the New Orleans theater had the orchestra play the national anthem of France. They sang the "Marseillaise," the "Ca

Ira," and other songs of the French rebels. Rebellion seemed to be in the air. The expressions of sympathy reached such a state that Carondelet had to interfere. He issued a proclamation to silence the sympathizers. They were not allowed to discuss or read aloud any printed matter about the French Revolution. Those who did so were fined or sent to the prison of Morro Castle. Carondelet forced about seventy persons to leave the colony. He sent six of the leaders of the French rebels in Louisiana to prison to silence them.

The governor took further measures to meet the dangerous situation. He reorganized the military and repaired fortifications around the city. These had been allowed to deteriorate and were useless as they were. He even had a few boats made to patrol the Mississippi River. This, he wrote to Paris officials, was to impress the citizens with the power of the government. These precautions were necessary to check any inhabitants whose sympathies with the French revolutionists might be too strong.

A long message from the revolutionaries in France was received in Louisiana. It was printed in Philadelphia and sent to the colony. It was circulated by secret agents. It was addressed "The Freemen of France to their brothers in Louisiana; 2nd year of the French Republic." It urged Louisiana people to rebel against Spain.

The moment has arrived when despotism must disappear from the earth. France, having obtained her freedom, and constituted herself into a republic, after having made known to mankind their rights... is not satisfied with successes by which she alone would profit.... Frenchmen of Louisiana, you still love your mother country; such a feeling is . . . in your hearts.... Compare your situation with that of your friends—the free Americans.... Therefore, inhabitants of Louisiana, show who you are; prove that you have not been stupefied by despotism . . . demonstrate that you are worthy of being free and independent.

Many French royalist refugees came to Louisiana to escape the Reign of Terror in France. Carondelet encouraged them to come. He hoped that their tales of horror would discourage the sympathizers in the colony. Large land grants on the Ouachita River

The Presbytere was designed as a companion building to the Cabildo.

were made to two of these royalists. The Baron de Bastrop received more than thirty square miles of land. The Marquis de Maison Rouge received a vast stretch of land on the river. Newcomers were granted land in West Florida and other parts of the colony. They had to take the oath of allegiance to Spain. If Protestant, they could not erect churches or worship publicly.

Genêt Affair. Governor Carondelet was upset. He learned that Genêt, the first minister of the new French Republic to the United States, was trying to organize an expedition to take Louisiana. Carondelet made plans to defend the colony against invasion. No invasion came. George Washington requested that the French government recall Genêt. Part of the reason for the request was his action against the Spanish in Louisiana and Florida. Genêt returned to France.

Trade. With the Genêt threat gone, Carondelet restricted navigation of the Mississipi River. One reason for doing so was the hope that residents along the river would ask that their area belong to Spain. The use of the river was very important to them. The navigation of the Mississippi was the bait Carondelet offered.

Navigation on the Mississippi River was important to many groups of people. Merchants from the Atlantic states had become an important part of the commercial life of the port of New Orleans. Western produce came down the Mississippi to seek outside markets. Imports went up the river to the westerners. Spanish authorities were unable to prevent the sale of American goods to planters on the lower Mississippi. The problem continued for many years.

Carondelet was liberal in interpreting and enforcing Spanish law. Despite existing Spanish laws, he allowed Louisiana residents to trade with Americans. He also allowed foreign ships to enter the port as Spanish. Spain was not in a position to supply the colony. The people were grateful for the governor's policy allowing some **free trade**. It helped to improve the welfare of the colony.

Agricultural Development. Meanwhile, the planters along the lower Mississippi were desperate to make a living. Agriculture was the basic industry. In the early 1790s a new insect attacked the **indigo** crop, the chief staple. In three years these insects almost destroyed that crop. During the crisis the idea of planting **sugarcane** was revived. A great deal of extra effort went into the problem of producing sugar. Until this time Spain had not allowed the sugar industry to thrive. This was probably because sugar was a staple of Spanish islands. Spain did not want Louisiana to compete against them.

Sugar planters had migrated from Santo Domingo to Louisiana. They were accustomed to raising cane as a staple. Now they lent their help to the Louisiana effort. The refugees taught local planters how to plant and cultivate the cane. They also taught them how to construct sugar mills and manufacture high-quality sugar.

In 1794 **Etienne de Boré** planted sugarcane on his plantation (now Audubon Park in New Orleans). In 1795 de Boré started the profitable sugarcane industry when he succeeded in granulating sugar. In that year he produced a sugar crop worth twelve thousand dollars. Sugarcane rapidly became a major crop. After sugar was granulated, more land and slaves were acquired. Sugar mills were built. Sugar-producing plantations increased in number.

Once Spain had agreed to buy all of the **tobacco** the colony could produce. In 1790 the Pointe Coupee District produced nearly seventy-five thousand pounds of tobacco. During this period Spain reduced considerably the number of pounds of tobacco it would buy from Louisiana. Now there was no market for the tobacco in Europe. Prices fell, and the growers were forced to find a new crop that could be sold at a profit. It was at this time that **cotton** began to take the place of tobacco as one of the staple crops of Louisiana.

Unrest. In spite of all the problems, the population of the colony steadily increased. Secret societies that aimed at returning Louisiana to France still existed in New Orleans. The city gates were closed at an early hour to prevent outsiders from coming into town. A system of syndics was established. The syndics were men living no more than nine miles apart serving as citizen-guards. A commandant was in charge. Any signs of rebellion, such as gossip or talk about plans against the government, were to be reported. Travelers were questioned. Any knowledge that they might have was to be written down and reported.

The Pointe Coupee Slave Rebellion. On the island of Santo Domingo there had been a rebellion of slaves. A series of terrible massacres followed. Tales of these happenings reached the slaves in the Pointe Coupee District. Their hopes for freedom came alive. Slaves on the plantation of Julien Poydras, one of the most humane slave masters in the colony, began to plot. It quickly spread across the district. Three white men aided the slaves in their plot. April 15, 1795, was set as the day on which blacks were to rise and slay their masters. Before that date the slave leaders quarreled. The wife of one told the parish officials about the plot. The ringleaders, including the three whites, were seized and thrown into prison. Some slaves tried to rescue the prisoners. Fighting broke out. Twenty-five people were killed. About sixty were captured. Twenty-three blacks were tried and hanged at various points along the river. Their bodies were left on public display for several days as a warning to others. Thirty-one slaves were whipped. The three white men were simply banished from the colony.

Slave Problems. White people of the colony were so fearful of slave revolts that they asked Carondelet to stop the entry of slaves into Louisiana. The governor ordered that this be done. Slaves were not permitted to come into the colony from Santo Domingo after 1792. However, the import ban was temporary.

The French Black Code of 1724 regulated slavery during the early part of the Spanish period. In 1784 more stringent regulations were adopted.

Kent House was built during the last years of the Spanish period.

Louisiana Office of Tourism

Louisiana Office of Tourism

St. Louis Cathedral was erected from 1788 to 1794, but two fires partially destroyed it. The structure as it stands today dates from 1850.

Slaves were not permitted to carry dangerous weapons. They could not sell anything without written permission from the master. They were not allowed to purchase intoxicating liquor. They could not assemble except in small groups under white supervision. Spanish regulations required that slaves have instruction in religion. But this regulation was not enforced. Marriages of slaves were encouraged, but the slaves were not enthusiastic about marriage. They felt that marriage was another type of bondage.

In 1790 the Spanish government called for better treatment of slaves. Colonial officials did not comply. They argued that lenient treatment would lead to insubordination and insurrection. On the whole, self-interest of masters dictated the care of the slaves. The food, clothing, and shelter provided depended upon the master.

In 1790 the richest man in the colony, Benjamin Farrar, owned 290 slaves. Some other masters owned 28, 42, 60, and 169. Prices of slaves in Spanish Louisiana depended upon the age and special skills of the slave. In 1785 a skilled slave workman brought 1,200 pesos. In 1787 such skilled slaves sold for 2,000 pesos each.

At times bands of runaway slaves were a cause of fear to settlers. Slaves organized under capable leaders. The forests and swamps made it rather easy for a slave to run away. Some ran away when they were faced with a task that they did not wish to perform. Often they were looking for family members located on other plantations. Most were seeking freedom. Hunger and loneliness usually caused most of them to return. Runaway slaves lived by stealing from storehouses on plantations and in New Orleans. They did not hesitate to commit murder to avoid being caught. Planters used several different methods to catch them. Squads of soldiers, or militia, were sometimes sent out to trace runaways. Sometimes the masters themselves looked for the slaves. In 1784 a military expedition was used to capture an armed band of runaways. Over fifty were caught. The four ringleaders were hanged and the rest imprisoned.

The Second Fire. A second fire destroyed much of New Orleans on December 8, 1794. The fire was caused by some boys playing with fire. A high wind helped the fire spread rapidly. In about three hours forty city blocks were destroyed. There were two hundred buildings leveled. Only two stores escaped destruction. Many people were left homeless. A smaller portion of the city burned than six years before. However, the money value of the losses was greater than in the first fire. The loss of foodstuff was so great that there was again danger of famine. Carondelet won the praises of the inhabitants by his efforts to relieve the distress.

One public building that was not destroyed by the fire was the **St. Louis Cathedral**. It was under construction. The earlier cathedral had been destroyed by the fire of 1788. The new structure was completed in 1794. It was dedicated on Christmas Day.

After these two fires almost wiped New Orleans out of existence, little of French architectural influence remained. The buildings erected after the fires were of Spanish architecture. They were mostly made of brick with roofs of tile. The only surviving French building in the Vieux Carré, or French Quarter, was the **Ursuline convent**. This ancient building survives today.

First Newspaper. The first paper in Louisiana was published in 1794. It was called *Le Moniteur de la Louisiane* (*Louisiana Monitor*). It was a weekly written in French. The Spanish government sponsored it as the official journal of the colony. This means that government documents were printed in the paper. The journal included royal decrees and ordinances. At that time official documents were written in both Spanish and French.

Indians. Carondelet did not work simply to maintain peace with the Indians. He signed military protection treaties with the Chickasaws, Creeks, Cherokees, Talapouchas, and the Alabamas. The Spanish policy was to use Indians as allies in wars against Spain's rival nations.

Carondelet's Canal. One outstanding project of Carondelet's was the digging of an immense canal leading into New Orleans from Bayou St. John. This waterway, Carondelet wrote to Spanish officials, would drain the city of stagnant waters. Since New Orleans was on such low ground, flooding was always a great problem. The canal would also allow navigation to the seas. Small vessels could reach the heart of the city from the Gulf of Mexico by sailing through Lake Pontchartrain. Local planters contributed their slaves for a period of time to help dig the canal. It was widened later to fifteen feet. The canal was named for Carondelet.

Life in Spanish Louisiana. A Catholic bishop wrote that only about one-fourth of the people of New Orleans attended church. All churches were Catholic. There were rarely enough priests. The bishop wrote to the king explaining that these people were ripe for rebellion.

There were few schools. The Ursulines maintained a school for girls. The bishop complained that the French language was used there. There were private schools for both boys and girls. Most parents could not afford private schools or tutors. Consequently, most children received no education at all. At the time of the great fire in 1788, four hundred boys and girls were being taught "reading, writing, and ciphering" in eight private French schools. Spanish officials tried to introduce public schools to teach the Spanish language in order to instill loyalty to Spain. French parents did not send their children to the public school. With so few students, the school was turned over to the Catholic Church in 1789. There were no colleges in Louisiana. French fathers who could afford to do so sometimes sent their sons to college in France.

Spain opened a small **library** in New Orleans with several hundred books. Wealthy residents often owned fine personal libraries.

Life in Spanish Louisiana was more comfortable than it had been in the early years under the French. Farming, crafts, and trade had developed to provide colonists with more home furnishings. Still, medical practice was crude, and modern sanitation was unknown. The population had grown. Commerce at the port continued to increase, attracting more and more attention from Europe.

Entertainment was simple. There were theatrical performances in New Orleans. Cafés or coffeehouses were favorite meeting places of the men. There were card games, billiard tables, and drinks in the cafés. Business deals were often arranged at these places. Dances and parties were held in private homes. Hunting and fishing were favorite sports for men. Both men and women played cards.

Possession Problems. Americans had tried to secure Louisiana for the United States for a long time. Some wanted to start a revolution in Louisiana. Others wanted to organize an expedition on the upper Ohio River to invade and capture the Spanish colony. Problems between the Americans and Spanish officials over this effort continued until the end of the Spanish period.

Like Miro, Carondelet continued to try to obtain the area between the Allegheny Mountains and the Mississippi River for Spain. His efforts were unsuccessful.

With Kentucky applying for statehood, a new approach was used by the Spaniards. Spanish agents tried to influence delegates from Kentucky to make a constitution so radical that Congress would reject it. Then the West would fall into the hands of Spain. The same tactics were attempted in the case of Tennessee. These Spanish schemes came to an end with the admission of Kentucky as a state in 1792 and the Pinckney Treaty in 1795. The westerners had what they wanted then. They were no longer interested in Spanish promises.

The Pinckney Treaty. Spain was losing power among the nations during these years. When the news reached Spain that John Jay of the United States had gone to England to discuss

Destrehan Manor, near Destrehan, was built from 1787 to 1790.

a treaty, Spanish officials were worried. They thought the two nations were plotting against Spain. Spain wanted the friendship of the United States. The American meeting with England made Spain more receptive to discussions with the United States about such matters as navigation on the Mississippi River. This problem had existed for a long time.

In 1795 Thomas Pinckney, the American minister in Spain, was able to conclude a very favorable treaty with Spain for the United States.

This famous document was known as the Pinckney Treaty. It opened the Mississippi River to free navigation by Americans. Americans acquired the valuable **right-of-deposit** for a three-year period. At the end of that period Spain was to decide whether to renew it. American businessmen could use warehouses at New Orleans for goods awaiting later shipment to markets elsewhere. There was no charge for this service. Spain also agreed to keep in check the Indians under its control who had been attacking Americans. The treaty set the northern boundary of West Florida at thirty-one degrees north latitude.

The time came to carry out the provisions of the Pinckney Treaty. Carondelet and Don Manuel Gayoso de Lemos, the commandant at Fort Panmure at Natchez, had no intention of doing so. Spain had held onto the Natchez area, which had been ceded to the United States by the Pinckney Treaty. Gayoso claimed he was at Fort Panmure to defend against an attack by the British from Canada. A United States commissioner, Andrew Ellicott, was to survey and mark out the boundary between the United States and Spanish West Florida. Ellicott found only excuses—and more excuses—from Carondelet and Gayoso. An uprising of the Americans resulted in 1797. Carondelet and Gayoso resisted to the point of war. Gayoso was once forced to take refuge in Fort Panmure. The American commissioner declared that he would repel by force any attempts to imprison American citizens in Natchez. The anger of the people was such that no matter what Gayoso tried, there could be no peace. He and Carondelet had stirred up a resistance because they refused to honor the Pinckney Treaty. Gayoso appealed to the American commissioner to quiet the people, but Ellicott had no sympathy for him.

Finally Gayoso granted the requests of the Americans to honor the treaty. The American commissioner did not trust some members of the committee to negotiate a settlement. He prevailed upon Gayoso to have another permanent committee elected. Once this was done, there was peace. The Spanish surrendered the post at Natchez. The West Florida boundary at the thirty-first parallel was finally surveyed. It was marked as the international boundary between American and Spanish possessions.

Carondelet's Last Years in Office. European conditions prevented Spain from devoting much time or attention to the development of Louisiana. Agriculture remained the principal industry. Cattle-raising continued in the southwestern part of the colony. The Spanish government could not find a market for all the tobacco produced. In spite of Spanish neglect, the colony prospered to a degree.

Before Carondelet ended his career as governor, there had been one crisis after another. In 1795 a French crew had captured the Balize. Naturally, that frightened the colonists. Within a few months the Spanish regained control. Commerce was also a problem. Robberies were so frequent on the unlighted streets of New Orleans prior to 1796 that something had to be done. Also, Carondelet feared that the many friends of the

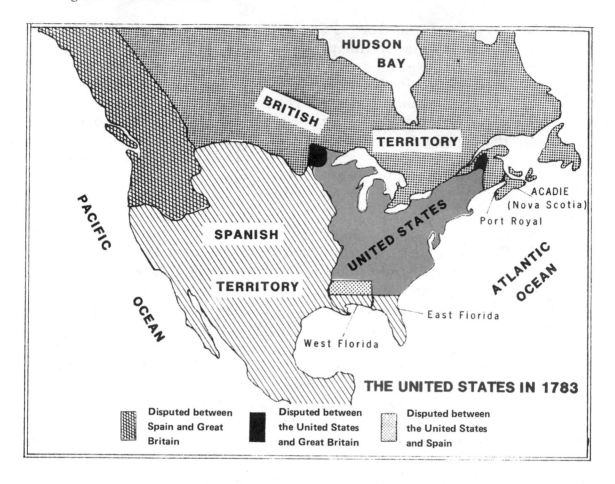

HUDSON BAY

BRITISH

TERRITORY

PACIFIC OCEAN

SPANISH

TERRITORY

UNITED STATES

ACADIE (Nova Scotia)

Port Royal

ATLANTIC OCEAN

East Florida

West Florida

THE UNITED STATES IN 1783

Disputed between Spain and Great Britain

Disputed between the United States and Great Britain

Disputed between the United States and Spain

French Revolution in Louisiana might cause trouble. For those reasons he put lights and watchmen on the streets of New Orleans for the first time. Oil lamps were hung by chains at the corners. In 1796 he organized a regular twenty-four hour police force for New Orleans. There were thirteen *serenos* (watchmen). They called out the hour and the state of the weather. This was the practice in Europe. Police were called at night only in case of alarm. Carondelet placed a tax

of nine reales (12 1/2 cents) on every chimney to provide funds for improvements. He ordered the people of Baton Rouge to rebuild their levees.

Carondelet carried out the laws and punished violators. He removed officials who did not perform their duties well and replaced them with others who would.

What was described as the first epidemic of yellow fever visited New Orleans in 1796. Morales, the intendant, wrote back to Spain that it was a disease known in America as "black vomit." Others called it yellow fever, the same disease that had caused so many deaths in Philadelphia two years before.

French General Victor Collet visited New Orleans in late 1796. He was studying the value of Louisiana. France had plans to repossess the colony. General Collet visited Etienne de Boré while in the city. The governor sent sixty soldiers to arrest the general. Although Carondelet placed the guest in prison at first, he later allowed him to remain at a house with a Spanish soldier as guard. The governor took maps, drawings, and writings away from him. On November 1, 1796, Collet was sent to the Balize. He was retained there nearly two months. After that, he left on a barge for Philadelphia.

Louisiana, in spite of many problems, prospered under Carondelet. He was given a promotion and sent to Quito (early name of Equador) in 1797.

Short-term Governors. There were three other governors before the end of the century. They were Gayoso, Casa Calvo, and Salcedo. These last three governors shared a common problem. Navigation of the Mississippi River dominated the administration of each of them. Americans upstream evaded the Pinckney Treaty's provision for right-of-deposit in New Orleans. The use of the river and the

need of the facilities at the port for free trade heightened the interest of the United States in securing New Orleans for itself.

Don Manuel Gayoso de Lemos became Carondelet's successor on July 30, 1797. Born in Spain, Gayoso was forty-five years old when he became governor of Louisiana. Ten years earlier, the army lieutenant colonel had been assigned to Natchez as commandant.

A year after he arrived in Louisiana, Gayoso published the policies he planned to pursue in the colony. He felt some order had to be introduced in making grants of land and in admitting immigrants. He sent such instruction out to commandants at the various posts. "Commandants are forbidden to grant land to a new settler coming from another spot where he has already obtained a grant. Such a one must either buy land or obtain a grant from the Governor himself."

Gayoso demanded that settlers who were single remain at least four years and work "in some honest and useful occupation" before they could receive a land grant. An exception could be made if the individual "should marry the daughter of an honest farmer with his consent, and be recommended by him." Only married people could receive land grants at once. No Protestants were to receive land grants. The limit of these grants was eight hundred arpents. The size of the land grant varied according to the number of productive household workers. Religious freedom for Protestants was granted to the first generation only. Their children had to become Catholics.

Trouble over navigation of the Mississippi continued in 1798. Spain refused to renew the right-of-deposit for another three years. That caused renewed agitation in the West. Americans were in favor of the seizure of New Orleans. They were determined to continue free navigation of the Mississippi.

Royal princes from France visited New Orleans in 1798. They were refugees and great-grandsons of the duke of Orléans. Their father had been executed during the French Revolution. Two of these brothers were the duke of Montpensier and the count of Beaujolais. The eldest of the three visitors, the duke of Orléans, later became King Louis Philippe. He ruled France from 1830 to 1848.

Governor Gayoso and Morales, the intendant of Louisiana, had a dispute over their respective areas of authority. Their disagreement was similar to the one that had existed between French governors and ordonnateurs. The conflict was ended by the death of Gayoso.

Gayoso, at the age of forty-eight, died of yellow fever on July 18, 1799, during an epidemic. He had done a satisfactory job during a very troubled time for the colony.

Don Francisco Bouligny served as acting governor after Gayoso's sudden death. He was commander of Spanish troops in the colony. He had come over with O'Reilly and was primarily a military man. He had fought with Gálvez. Bouligny served from July 18 to September 13, 1799. Nothing of importance happened during his short term.

Sebastian Calvo de la Puerta y O'Farril, Marquis de Casa Calvo was sent from Havana as the newly appointed governor. Casa Calvo had come to Louisiana with O'Reilly when he was eighteen. He had not remained in the colony, however. His appointment was only temporary. He was to serve until the Spanish king named a permanent governor.

Carondelet had temporarily stopped the entry of slaves from foreign countries. In 1799 planters of lower Louisiana requested that Governor Casa Calvo allow the free trade of slaves. The cabinet in Spain allowed five thousand slaves to be sent to the colony duty free. The cabinet resolved "not to go farther" in extending the privilege. This action satisfied the planters.

During Casa Calvo's term, negotiations were underway for Spain to return the colony to France. With Napoleon rising to power at the same time, a new factor was affecting the destiny of Louisiana. This factor was the yearning of the French people for their former American empire. Napoleon wanted the Louisiana colony back for France.

On October 1, 1800, the secret **Treaty of San Ildefonso** was signed. Spain ceded Louisiana to France. The treaty was kept secret for some time. France made no immediate preparations to take over the colony.

Casa Calvo left for Cuba when the next governor, Salcedo, arrived. **Juan Manuel de Salcedo** was appointed governor October 24, 1799, but he did not arrive until the middle of June 1801.

Salcedo was an old military man. His son was a Spanish officer in Louisiana. It was said that this son dictated most of Salcedo's policies as governor. During Salcedo's entire term of office, France owned the colony. Salcedo had one important duty to perform. He was to assist in the formal transfer of Louisiana from Spain to France.

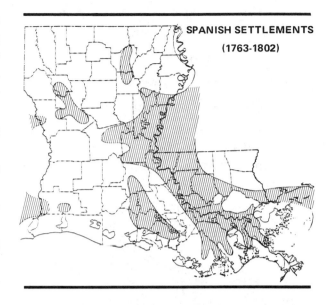

SPANISH SETTLEMENTS
(1763-1802)

En Partie 4 (Studying a Part). 1. Who became governor after O'Reilly? 2. What was Unzaga's attitude toward trade with the English? 3. What part did Louisiana play in the revolt of the American colonists? 4. Trace the action of Gálvez during the American Revolution. 5. What part did Miro play in trying to get United States territory for Spain? 6. Describe the first New Orleans fire. 7. What did Miro do when Spain attempted to prosecute non-Catholics? 8. What European revolution was going on during Carondelet's administration? 9. What effects of the revolution were felt in Louisiana? 10. What measures did Carondelet take to improve life in New Orleans? 11. What was the right-of-deposit? 12. How did the slave revolt in Santo Domingo affect Louisiana? 13. (a) What treaty did the United States sign with Spain? (b) How did it affect the colony? 14. Who were the last three Spanish governors? 15. (a) What were the provisions of the Treaty of San Ildefonso? (b) When was it signed?

Coup d'Main
(Completing the Story)

Jambalaya (Putting It All Together)

1. Summarize the Spanish period by naming the main events in chronological order. Make a topic sentence with each main event.

2. Describe the conditions of the following under Spanish rule: (a) slaves, (b) agriculture, (c) trade, (d) religion, (e) standard of living, (f) money exchange, (g) education, and (h) health care.

3. Map work: (a) show the territory in dispute between Spain and the United States from 1783 to 1795; (b) label Spanish settlements in Louisiana; (c) show boundaries of Spanish Louisiana; and (d) label the Floridas.

Potpourri (Getting Involved)

1. Compare Longfellow's poem with the true story of the Acadians.

2. Trace the route of the Acadians.

3. Research to find out the reasons Longfellow happened to write *Evangeline.*

4. Make a model of an Acadian house, or dress a doll in typical Acadian dress.

5. Prepare a time line of events for the years 1762 to 1803.

6. Conduct a forum to contrast O'Reilly with Gálvez—their personalities, their administrations, and their reputations. Show how events in history altered their careers.

7. Write a series of letters to someone in France from a well-to-do Creole, tracing the feelings of the French toward the Spanish.

8. Debate: "The Spanish contributed more to the development of Louisiana than did the French," or "The right-of-deposit should not have been given."

9. Stage a council between Indian chiefs and Spanish officials. Include all aspects of Spain's Indian policy.

Gumbo (Bringing It Up-to-Date)

1. Report on ways the Acadians are preserving their heritage.

2. Show the influence of the Acadians on modern Louisiana.

3. Conduct an imaginary tour of Acadian country.

4. How have the Spanish buildings in New Orleans been preserved? What is the present status of preservation?

5. Compare (a) the Spanish hard specie with present-day United States money, or (b) Spain's control over the right-of-deposit with present shipping arrangements at the port of New Orleans.

6. Show the Spanish influence in present-day Louisiana.

PART THREE

From 1803 until 1860

CHAPTER 6

LOUISIANA: TERRITORY TO STATE
(1800–1812)
New Owner: France

Plans of Napoleon. The French Revolution brought many years of chaos to France. Finally, Napoleon Bonaparte, one of the most remarkable men in history, became ruler of France. He attempted to resolve the problems of the nation. It was his goal to reestablish an orderly government within the country. Then he settled differences with the enemies of France by military conquest. That strategy resulted in treaties favorable to France.

A famous statesman, Talleyrand, was one of Napoleon's ministers. He had lived in the United States while he was exiled during the French Revolution. He realized that Spain had a very weak hold on most of its possessions in North America. He encouraged Napoleon to get a foothold on the North American continent for France again.

For a long time Napoleon had dreamed of rebuilding the French empire. The people of France had always regretted losing the Louisiana colony. Some of the French in Louisiana still hoped that they would belong to France again.

Spain had held the colony for almost forty years. During most of this time, the power of Spain had been declining. Even though the colony had been prosperous during the 1790s, Spain still could not afford Louisiana. Spain was not a wealthy country. It was costing about $337,000 a year to keep Louisiana.

Napoleon tried to persuade Charles IV of Spain to make a deal. He wanted to give Spain property in Italy in exchange for the Louisiana territory. He argued that Charles IV could look to France to police the Spanish-American frontier. The Pinckney Treaty had seriously weakened Spain's position on the lower Mississippi. French Louisiana would hold a position between Spanish Texas and the United States. A strong France could hold back American expansion. The United States had been threatening to seize Louisiana in its disagreement with Spain over the right-of-deposit.

Napoleon had a study made of the Louisiana colony. In September 1800 he received the results of the study. It gave a full description of Louisiana. It listed the colony's resources. There was a review of the history of the colony. The document included a remarkably clear statement of the colony's relations with its American neighbors.

Treaty of San Ildefonso. Less than a month after Napoleon received this report, he closed a deal with Spain. France, with the Treaty of San Ildefonso, received a bargain. On October 1, 1800, the treaty was signed giving Louisiana and the Floridas to France. In return, Napoleon promised to create a kingdom in Italy for the son-in-law of the Spanish king, Charles IV. The kingdom of Tuscany was to be given to the son-in-law, the duke of Parma. This agreement was kept secret for almost two years.

The treaty was not ratified by the king. Charles IV balked until it was agreed that France would never give up Louisiana to any other country. This, too, was kept secret. On March 21, 1801, a second treaty was negotiated at San Ildefonso.

Meanwhile, someone leaked information about the treaty to United States Secretary of State **James Madison**. He, in turn, informed President **Thomas Jefferson**. **Robert Livingston**, United States minister to France, remained in doubt about what he regarded as a rumor. He asked Talleyrand. The French minister assured him that no final settlement had been made concerning Louisiana. The Americans were afraid to have someone as powerful as Napoleon take possession of such a large part of North America.

Delay in Occupation of Louisiana. When the secret Treaty of San Ildefonso was worked out between Spain and France, France agreed to wait six months before claiming Louisiana.

By the time Napoleon was ready to take charge of the colony, it was 1802. Then it was necessary for him to send military troops to Santo Domingo. Napoleon thought that this island was the key to the new French empire. Slaves led by Toussaint L'Ouverture were in revolt on the island. Napoleon's first task was to get the Santo Domingo slave rebellion under control. For this operation, he chose his brother-in-law General Charles Victor Emmanuel Leclerc.

A series of events kept Napoleon from following his plans. Yellow fever attacked the soldiers, including General Leclerc. Leclerc and 20,000 troops had landed at Santo Domingo in January 1802. Most of the soldiers died. General Leclerc died on November 2, 1802. The blacks resorted to guerrilla warfare and revolted more violently than ever. The French could not secure the island. Napoleon had second thoughts about taking possession of Louisiana. War with England seemed certain. He could not risk another expedition to Santo Domingo under the circumstances. Even though France owned the Louisiana colony, Spain continued to control it. The need for more troops and ships for transporting them caused further delay in carrying out French plans to take over Louisiana.

En Partie 1 (Studying a Part). 1. (a) Why did France want Louisiana back? (b) Who was the leader of France? 2. Why did Spain consider giving up Louisiana? 3. How did France obtain Louisiana? 4. What were two agreements made by Napoleon in his deal with Spain? 5. Why was ratification of the treaty delayed? 6. Relate the revolution in Santo Domingo to the occupation of Louisiana by France.

The Purchase of Louisiana

The Right-of-Deposit. Meanwhile, the right-of-deposit was withdrawn and renewed again by the Spanish. The Spanish threat of withdrawal continued. United States officials felt something had to be done.

The right-of-deposit had been granted by Spain to the Americans for three years. The right was renewed. Business in New Orleans had doubled in the five-year period ending in 1798, because of the use of the city's facilities. On October 16, 1802, Morales, Spanish intendant at New Orleans, caused a crisis. He issued a proclamation withdrawing the right-of-deposit at New Orleans. Farmers were no longer allowed to store their products in New Orleans without paying duty. Furthermore, all United States commerce with Spanish possessions on the river was prohibited.

One of the probable reasons for Morales taking such action had to do with traders from the upper district of Louisiana. Legally, they were required to take their produce to one place in New Orleans for deposit in a Spanish warehouse. The freewheeling peddlers ignored this order. Instead, they stopped at plantations along the river. There they unloaded produce for whoever would buy. The planters liked it that way. Many flatboats unloaded their goods before reaching New Orleans. This was an open violation of the letter and spirit of the right-of-deposit. Morales resented this. The only way he could break it up was to withdraw the right-of-deposit.

Whatever reason Morales had for

his actions, he could not foresee the chain of events his action would set in motion. He could not predict the final outcome: the purchase of Louisiana by the United States.

People living west of the Mississippi River and in the upper valley of the river were intensely angry at Spain. President Jefferson wrote to the United States minister to Spain instructing him to impress upon Spanish officials the serious crisis provoked by Morales. The withdrawal of the right-of-deposit and navigation rights on the river gave them no outlet for marketing their crops.

The entire trade of the American West passed through New Orleans. In 1802, the city accommodated 158 outgoing American vessels carrying 21,383 tons, 104 Spanish vessels with 9,573 tons, and 3 French ships carrying 105 tons. The total value of exports leaving New Orleans in 1803 was over $2 million.

New Plans. Radicals in Congress proposed measures that could lead to war. President Jefferson and others preferred to try diplomacy. It was Robert Livingston whom Jefferson instructed to buy the Isle of Orleans for a maximum price of ten million dollars. Livingston was also told of offers to make if Napoleon would not sell the Isle of Orleans. Jefferson and other United States leaders thought that this country must acquire New Orleans. The president sent **James Monroe** as a special diplomat to assist Livingston in dealing with Napoleon and French officials.

Meanwhile, England was reportedly planning to seize Louisiana rather than allow France to occupy it.

Napoleon was reconsidering his earlier plans. He knew that war with England lay ahead. He feared that England would seize Louisiana when the conflict started. He also feared that the United States would form an alliance with England if he did not satisfy them regarding navigation on the Mississippi River. Wars had drained the French treasury. Napoleon needed money for the impending war. He did not wish to extend himself with this overseas empire and risk losing control in Europe. Despite heated opposition from his inner circle, Napoleon decided to sell.

United States–France Negotiations. On Sunday, April 10, 1803, Napoleon decided he would sell the entire colony to the United States. He put the sale of Louisiana in the hands of his minister of finance, Barbé-Marbois. On the eventful day that Napoleon made his decision, his prime minister contacted Livingston. That same day James Monroe arrived in Paris after traveling for three months.

Livingston and Monroe were startled to find that not only the Isle of Orleans but all of the Louisiana colony could be purchased. Livingston had been negotiating with France for

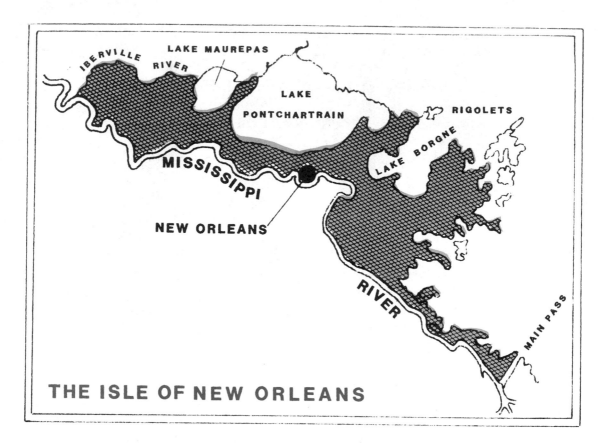

THE ISLE OF NEW ORLEANS

months to try to purchase the Isle of Orleans. The United States representatives explained that they were authorized to negotiate only for the Isle of Orleans and the Floridas. At that time, transportation between Washington and France was by sailing vessel, which took many weeks. It would take too long to reach Jefferson for approval. Therefore, without consulting their government, Livingston and Monroe proceeded.

Negotiations continued. Napoleon set the selling price at a minimum of 50 million francs (10 million dol-

lars). He was expecting to get more. Barbé-Marbois first offered Louisiana for 100 million francs (20 million dollars). The American representatives said that this amount was far more than the United States could pay. Livingston reported every detail to President Jefferson. He wrote, "We shall do all we can to cheapen the purchase; but my present sentiment is that we shall buy." The wrangling over the price went on for about two weeks. Finally, the arrangements were made for the United States to purchase the Louisiana colony for 15

million dollars. That amounted to about four cents per acre. It included 11.25 million dollars for the land and 20 million francs (4 million dollars) for claims of French citizens against the United States.

Historians have argued whether it was the elder Livingston or the youthful Monroe who made the deal with the French. It doesn't really matter. It was Napoleon who had made up his mind to dispose of the Louisiana colony. Napoleon sold Louisiana without having taken formal possession of it. Finally, the Louisiana Purchase Treaty was signed on **April 30, 1803.** News reached the United States July 3, 1803.

In the United States there was the problem of getting Congress to approve the purchase of the territory. The purchase would nearly double the land area of the nation. President Jefferson had all along believed in sticking closely to the words of the Constitution. Of course, the Constitution said nothing about the nation buying Louisiana.

New England politicians strongly opposed it. They said that it violated the Constitution. They argued that the price was too high. They were also sure that adding so many "foreigners" would destroy the Union. Even so, Congress approved the purchase. However, the nation had to secure the great amount of money required. The United States finally borrowed the money from Holland and England to pay France for Louisiana. With the interest added, the total cost ran around $27 million. The United States was to pay the principal amount of the debt in three payments. The agreement called for the first payment to be made in 1819. The remaining balance was to be paid during the next two years.

Spain protested the sale of Louisiana. The king demanded that Napoleon revoke the sale. Spanish officials pointed out that it violated the agreement made earlier with Napoleon. Napoleon had agreed to never give up Louisiana to any other country. Spain, they wrote, would never acknowledge this sale! "The sale of this province to the United States is founded in the violation of a promise so absolute that it ought to be respected," a Spanish minister wrote to Secretary of State James Madison in September. The differences between the two countries were eventually resolved, however. Finally Spain approved the sale. This came a month after the formal transfer of the colony to the United States.

In the meantime Napoleon had trouble convincing fellow Frenchmen that this was best. The French very reluctantly gave up their dreams of restoring their American empire. Nobody had been more furious over the sale than Napoleon's two brothers.

The dispute over whether France

had a legal title to Louisiana was debated among the three countries involved. The dispute became the weapon of New Englanders in Congress opposing the Louisiana Purchase.

En Partie 2 (Studying a Part). 1. Why was Louisiana important to the United States? 2. Why did Spanish officials withdraw the right-of-deposit? 3. What drastic action were some radicals in Congress considering to take about the right-of-deposit problem? 4. (a) Identify Robert Livingston. (b) What was his assignment? 5. Why did Napoleon change his mind about selling Louisiana? 6. Explain the complications that arose because of lack of communication. 7. Give the details of the Louisiana Purchase. 8. What was the reaction to the purchase?

French Possession

Occupation by France. Napoleon planned for France to occupy Louisiana as though the nation would own it forever. He sent a group of

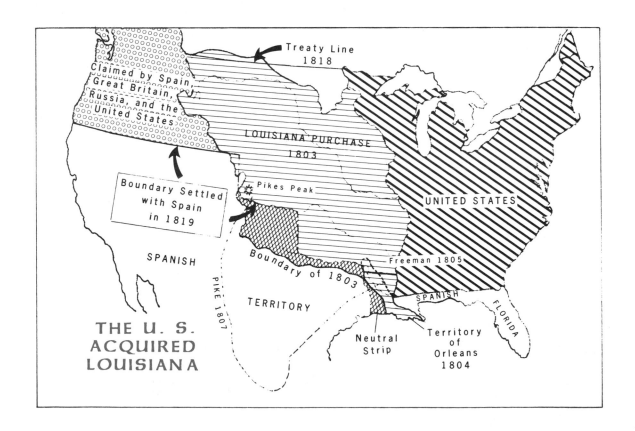

THE U. S. ACQUIRED LOUISIANA

Napoleon (center) shakes hands with Livingston after selling Louisiana.

experts to gather all possible information about the colony. General Victor was to be in charge of the military. **Pierre Clement de Laussat,** a young career colonial official, became governor. He and his young family arrived in the colony before he had learned of the sale of the Louisiana Territory. General Victor and the French troops were to be sent at a later time. Later it was learned that the troops were sent to Santo Domingo.

Laussat represented France as the key figure on the occasions of both transfers of ownership. Laussat left a firsthand account of this great milestone in the history of Louisiana and the United States. It was years after Laussat's death in 1835 that one of his descendants discovered Laussat's

account of these events. In his own handwriting Laussat told his story. He wrote about the events that occurred during the years that he, his wife, and three daughters lived in Louisiana.

The ambitious young Laussat arrived in the colony March 26, 1803. This was just two weeks before Napoleon made his decision to sell Louisiana. He thought that he would play an important role in rebuilding the French empire. He immediately issued a proclamation to the French people of Louisiana stating his intentions.

Laussat was not informed of events relating to Louisiana that were going on behind the scene. There were months after his arrival that he heard nothing from France. Laussat did not know the reason that General Victor and the soldiers had not arrived. Laussat had prepared for Victor's arrival. He built barracks and purchased supplies. He had a report on the military needs of the colony ready for Victor. He heard only indirectly that France had sold the colony to the United States. On July 28, 1803, Laussat wrote to the French government that a rumor that the colony had been sold was going around New Orleans. He had branded the rumor a lie and was trying to do what he could to stop it. Shortly afterward, a French ship came with the official news that the colony had been sold to the United States.

The Spanish in Louisiana were informed of the impending change in ownership. Steps were taken to ensure order. Intendant Morales issued an order forbidding export of foods. The Spanish king revoked Morales's withdrawal of the right-of-deposit from the United States.

Laussat became ill with yellow fever. He gradually recovered. While he was ill, he received official word that war had been declared between France and England on May 18, 1803. He finally received a letter from Napoleon giving his reasons for the sale. Laussat was ordered to deliver the colony to the United States on the same day that he received it for France from Spain. The colony was to be turned over immediately because Napoleon did not have any French troops to support Laussat. It proved impossible to observe this order.

Casa Calvo was governor of Louisiana when it was purchased by the United States. At this time Casa Calvo returned from Cuba to assist in the formal ceremonies transferring the colony to France. He caused trouble from the time he arrived in the colony on May 10, 1803. In order to get rid of him, Laussat decided to accept the colony from Spain as soon as possible. Spain and France were ready, but the United States was not. There would be a delay in the acceptance by the United States because no plans were yet made for the transfer.

The remaining months of 1803 brought sometimes bitter exchanges among: Laussat, the Frenchman; the Spanish both in New Orleans and in Madrid, the capital of Spain; and English-speaking Americans. Laussat and Salcedo, the Spanish governor, who had been in office since 1801, had disagreements over the division of authority. Salcedo broke off official relations with Laussat. Their parting resulted from a disagreement concerning the recruiting of sailors for a French ship at New Orleans.

Transfer Ceremonies. In June 1803 Laussat received his appointment as French commissioner to take possession of Louisiana. At last the time came for the transfer of the colony from Spain and France. On **November 30, 1803**, formal ceremonies took place at the public square, or Plaza de Armas, transferring Louisiana to France. Thus ended almost four decades of Spanish rule.

The transfer of Louisiana was conducted with all the pomp possible. French and Spanish soldiers stood at attention in the square while officials exchanged documents in the Cabildo. Salcedo and Casa Calvo delivered the colony to Laussat. They then walked together to the balcony. As they stood, the Spanish flag, flying high on the staff, was lowered. The Spanish regiment accepted it. The Spanish troops marched off in double time. Then the flag of France was raised. This flag was quite different from the flag lowered in the same spot when O'Reilly took over. Cheers came up from the crowd. The cold stormy weather did not dampen the spirit of the crowd.

Days of partying, dancing, and dining followed. Laussat described one of the events:

Seventy-five people came for dinner. There were as many Spanish and Americans as Frenchmen. They began gambling before dinner. . . . There was all sorts of tomfoolery. They continued until eight o'clock the next morning. Two big servings were interrupted by three toasts. [The toasts were made to the French Republic and Napoleon, then to Spain and Charles IV, and, finally, to the United States and Jefferson.] With each of these toasts, there were three salvos of twenty-one guns fired. . . .

French Government. Laussat then went about his business of governing the colony as though he had no knowledge of the imminent transfer to the United States. Such reforms were effected that historians have wondered what would have happened if Louisiana had remained longer under the able Laussat.

Laussat abolished the Cabildo and set up a French government. He looked to the preservation of colonial archives. He improved the city's police force. He created two adjutants and a municipal court for New Orleans. He published a new code of French law based on the **Napoleonic Code**. For the first mayor of New Orleans, he chose Etienne de Boré. He named the son of Joseph Villeré to the council. Members of the council included such well-known names as Derbigny, Fortier, and Destrehan. Laussat explained his actions.

I wanted some merchants, some Americans, and some experienced businessmen. I intended . . . to honor the memory of the Frenchmen who had been sacrificed under O'Reilly . . . I wanted a municipality . . . that would do me honor and hold its own with dignity before the Americans. This being the dominant act of my short-lived reign and the one to which I attached the greatest importance... for the future of Louisiana.

En Partie 3 (Studying a Part). 1. Describe the general confusion in the government of Louisiana from 1800 to 1803. 2. Who was Laussat? 3. Describe the transfer of Louisiana from Spain to France. 4. When did the transfer take place? 5. Give reasons for the delay in the transfer. 6. What were some official actions of Laussat after the transfer?

Transfer to the United States

France's dream of a colony in the Mississippi Valley was forever ended. On December 20, 1803, Louisiana was transferred to the United States. The procès-verbal of transfer, the official document, was read aloud. General James Wilkinson and W. C. C. Claiborne accepted the territory for the United States from France. Laussat recalled the ceremony:

I handed over the keys to the city, tied together with the tricolor [the colors of the French flag] to Monsieur Wilkinson. Immediately afterwards, I [excused] from their oath of allegiance to France the inhabitants who chose to remain under the [rule] of the United States.

Various marching groups camped outside the city. At a designated time they moved in parade formation to the public

The American flag was raised in the transfer ceremonies December 20, 1803.

square. Militiamen from Ohio, Kentucky, and Tennessee received a twenty-one gun salute when they arrived. The military forces of both France and the United States participated in the ceremonies. The dignitaries appeared on the balcony to watch the flag ceremony. The French lowered their flag as the American flag ascended the flagpole. When the two flags met, a gun sounded. Every cannon in the vicinity answered.

More parties, dances, and state dinners marked the second transfer of Louisiana. At one dinner, twenty-four kinds of gumbo were served. Several incidents occurred over the choice of dances. Arrangements were made to dance an English quadrille after every third French dance. However, attempts were made to interrupt this sequence, and confrontations resulted. Laussat recounted the events of January 8:

Two quadrilles, one French, the other English, formed at the same time. An American took offense at something and raised his walking stick at one of the fiddlers. [A fight] ensued. Claiborne remained quiet until Clark roused him. Unable to explain himself in French, Claiborne appeared embarrassed. He yielded at first. Then he [tried] to assert his authority. In the end, he [tried] to

persuade rather than to [take] stern measures in order to silence the American. The French quadrille resumed. The American interrupted it again with an English quadrille and took his place to dance. Someone cried, "If the women have a drop of French blood in their veins, they will not dance." Within minutes, the hall was completely deserted by the women. The Marquis de Casa Calvo...continued to play cards, laughing up his sleeve.

Laussat remained in New Orleans for a few months. He needed to finish some business for France. Laussat left on April 21, 1804. Some Spanish officials lingered in New Orleans. Many had French Creole wives. They had made their homes in the colony. Some kept up a series of intrigues that worried Claiborne and the authorities in Washington. The Spanish claimed to be boundary adjustment agents or church officials. Finally, over two years after the transfer of the colony, Casa Calvo departed. He had received a passport from Claiborne with a note hinting that he leave. Others were asked to leave. Thus, some were forced out.

Louisiana now belonged to the United States.

That memorable period when Louisiana was changing hands so rapidly did not arouse strong feelings in the majority of the people. The Spaniards had not developed deep feelings for the colony mainly because only a few Spanish settlers had come. The French people did not have the deep loyalty to France that had existed when Spain first received the colony. There were rumors that Napoleon planned to get the colony back. There were still some French who hoped that France would regain the colony. The colonists did not know the Americans. They would need many years before they would appreciate their new country. One fact was evident. Changing ownership did not change the people. Their customs and language remained the same.

En Partie 4 (Studying a Part). 1. Give details about the transfer of Louisiana to the United States. 2. What was the attitude of most Louisianians toward the change in ownership?

Contributions of the French and the Spanish

In twenty days three flags flew over Louisiana. The country was still French in language and spirit. Spanish customs also had become a part of the life of Louisiana.

Contributions of the French. To begin with, the French achieved a permanent settlement. It was done with great hardship. Sailing across the Atlantic in ships of that day was enough to discourage all but the most

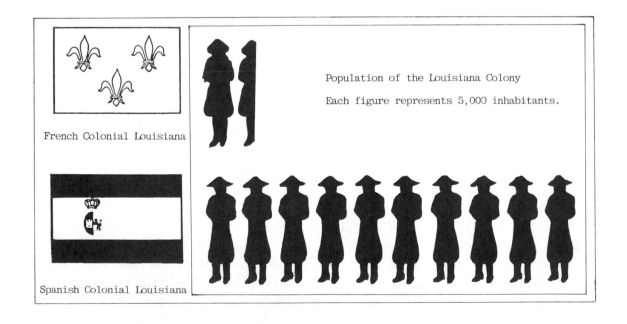

French Colonial Louisiana

Spanish Colonial Louisiana

Population of the Louisiana Colony

Each figure represents 5,000 inhabitants.

hardy. Water was scarce and bad. Food stored for the long journey was spoiled. People were crowded so that there was barely room for sleeping on the floor. Storms of such power tossed the ships that there was a constant danger. Laussat wrote in his story:

The weather became foul; and the seas very high. There was rain, strong winds, squalls, roaring waves, and water 38 to 48 fathoms deep. The brig rolled and pitched. No bottom at 100 fathoms. The prolonged and deafening noise of the sea; the impact of the waves as they broke against the side of the frail vessel; their sudden and furious eruptions as high as the tops of the sails, from which they fell back in torrents that flooded the deck; and the distant whistling of the wind—this was our most distressing situation.

The mosquitoes, fevers that plagued the people living in the lowlands, Indians who came out of nowhere and attacked the Frenchmen— these hardships came with the wilderness. Hard manual work in the struggle to clear woods and construct shelters was not for the lazy. France itself was in deep financial trouble. It could hardly do justice to the colony overseas. Yet, with all those problems, France founded Louisiana.

One of the gifts of the French

was their outlook on life that helped them endure. This was the *joie de vivre* or "joy of living." To work hard and well was of first importance, yet to be cheerful and happy was essential. Louisiana inherited from the French a habit of laughter, dancing, high spirits, and love of being together with friends and family. The French manner of turning drudgery into a festive event has become a way of life in Louisiana.

The Catholic religion was the only religion legally permitted under both the French and Spanish. The French approach to religion is still a part of Louisiana.

The customs of the French people —the folkways—became a part of Louisiana forever. *Boucheries* (hog-killings), *cochons de lait* (roasting suckling pigs over a slow fire), and Mardi Gras are only a few of the best known. Not so well known but even more important, perhaps, are skills of craftsmen passed down through generations. These include skills from carpentry to sewing. French cooking has remained a part of Louisiana. The French gave us their patterns of inheritance and of settling the land. Their music and art left their marks. Acadian houses with outdoor stairs belong to the French. Most obvious is the French language. Place names are often in French. *Choupique* ("shoe pick"), courtbouillon, and countless other French words remain in the language of Louisianians. For nearly three hundred years the rollicking spirit of our French ancestors has influenced Louisianians, whatever their roots.

Contributions of the Spanish. The major contribution of the Spanish was in administration, which established a badly needed stable economy. A sound financial base was laid. Gold and silver coins were brought by the Spanish to the colony. The Spanish piece of eight (*real*) became the model for the United States silver dollar. The efficient governors provided a dependable framework of government for settlers. The population increased. New Orleans developed into a sizable city and important port. Spanish architecture is still evident in New Orleans, Natchitoches, and elsewhere in the state. The beautiful ironwork of the Vieux Carré has been appreciated since Spanish colonial days. The Spaniards made a most valuable contribution in surveying property lines and establishing firm boundaries. The Spanish also left their place names. Their peppery cuisine is one of the reasons Louisiana is noted for its delicious foods.

Louisiana's French and Spanish inheritance makes our state unique. No other state in the United States has the same background.

En Partie 5 (Studying a Part). 1. List the contributions of the French.

2. List the contributions of the Spanish.

Territory of Louisiana

Territorial Government. The territory was left without a government. William Charles Cole Claiborne was instructed to take charge until Congress could provide for a government. He directed the civil affairs of the colony. During that time General **James Wilkinson** commanded the army. He spent weeks assembling a military force. Both men had held similar positions in the Mississippi Territory. They had represented the United States in the transfer from France. President Jefferson appointed these two men to take over all of the duties of the government.

Claiborne was a native of Virginia. He moved to Tennessee when he was a young man. At age twenty-one he helped draw up Tennessee's constitution. Later he represented Tennessee in Congress. He worked to secure the election of Thomas Jefferson, but he was not Jefferson's first choice to head the government of Louisiana. Claiborne was appointed on a temporary basis while Jefferson tried to make a permanent appointment of a more prestigious or well-known person.

Jefferson hoped to appoint officers who could speak French, but he was unable to do so. The ability to

William C. C. Claiborne.

speak French was a rare accomplishment among people in the United States at that time. Jefferson first tried to persuade General Lafayette to come from France to serve as governor of the territory. When Lafayette declined, he next tried James Monroe. Monroe declined also. He then appointed Claiborne, who knew no French.

The Territory of Orleans. On March 26, 1804, Congress passed a law that divided Louisiana into two parts. Below the thirty-third parallel was the Territory of Orleans. This was the land that now constitutes most of the state of Louisiana. North of that line was the District of Louisiana. The Territory of Orleans contained most of the population. It was a very small part of the land area known as Louisiana under French and Spanish control.

The status of Louisiana was that of an **unorganized territory** of the United States. A territory with more than five thousand white males was eligible to become an organized territory. The difference between organized and unorganized territories was in the participation of citizens in the government. The people in an unorganized territory had no voice in the government. Local leaders bitterly resented Louisiana's unorganized status. They felt that the territory met the population requirement. Perhaps Congress did not think that Louisianians could govern themselves.

The government for the Territory of Orleans included a governor, secretary, and legislative council. A superior court of three judges was also included. All were appointed by the president. The governor was appointed to serve three years. He was given all executive powers. The secretary and judges had four-year terms. The secretary kept the territorial records. The thirteen members of the legislative council were given one-year appointments. The legislative council assisted the governor in making laws.

The laws had to be submitted to Congress for approval. In reality, Claiborne made nominations and the president approved them. Claiborne had difficulty finding people to accept the appointments.

Dissatisfaction of the People. The people were greatly displeased about the government. The people complained that the governor had too much power. Claiborne was almost a dictator. There was no appeal from his decisions. Even in Spanish Louisiana they were allowed to appeal to the captain general in Havana. The Creoles particularly resented that they were unable to govern themselves. They had heard about the rights of citizens in the United States. They expected these rights also. They were indignant when they did not receive the rights enjoyed by the people of the Mississippi Territory. The treaty provided that the people living in the former colony should have all the rights and privileges enjoyed by the citizens of the rest of the country. The people of Louisiana did not get these rights in 1804.

Other American actions aroused the ire of residents. The Louisiana Purchase Treaty forbade the bringing of slaves into the territory from foreign countries. Smuggling of foreign slaves into the territory resulted from this restriction. Only citizens moving into the territory could bring slaves from older sections of the United States. Elsewhere, slaves were still imported from Africa. According to the United States Constitution, Congress could not forbid the importing of slaves from foreign countries or obtaining them from other states until 1808.

The people of the Orleans territory did not like to see their great province divided geographically. Residents of the territory were dissatisfied with the naming of their land. They felt that the name Louisiana belonged to the southern portion of the former colony. They wanted that section to become a state immediately.

The Creoles were also angry because English was the official language. Governor Claiborne's inability to speak French was considered an

CREOLES

Creoles were the American-born descendants of the French and Spanish.

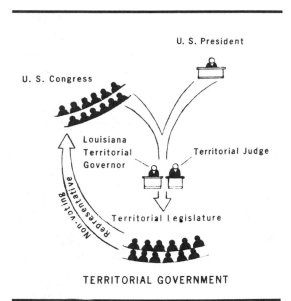

U. S. President

U. S. Congress

Louisiana Territorial Governor

Territorial Judge

Non-voting Representative

Territorial Legislature

TERRITORIAL GOVERNMENT

insult to Louisiana's French population. They said that the use of English made them feel like foreigners in their native land. The people accused Claiborne of showing a preference for the English-speaking Americans. Some pointedly refused to cooperate with him or even serve in the new government. Etienne de Boré resigned as mayor of New Orleans to show his opposition. The attitude of the most influential citizens made it difficult to find people to serve in the government.

The actions of Congress reflected most United States citizens' fear of foreigners. The Louisiana citizens were considered foreigners. They were of French and Spanish heritage. To the English-speaking people, Louisianians had a foreign language and strange customs. Congress felt there was a danger in allowing too much freedom to people in Louisiana. Louisianians resented being regarded as foreigners.

Another factor that added to the discontent was the scarcity of money. The Spanish had brought large amounts of silver coins from Mexico. These were used to pay the expenses of government. When the flow of coins ceased, money became scarce. Claiborne established the Bank of Louisiana. Its purpose was to furnish the currency and credit needed by the planters and merchants. The bank was of limited value at first because people did not trust it.

The discontent led to several mass meetings in New Orleans. The group petitioned Congress for a larger measure of self-government. Edward Livingston, brother of Robert, wrote the memorial. A group went to Washington to lay the case before Congress. The spokesmen of the group were Pierre Derbigny, Jean Noel Destrehan, and Pierre Sauve. They asked that the territory be admitted as a state. The request was not granted. Provisions were made, however, for its admission when the population amounted to sixty thousand. The group made a very favorable impression. The Orleans territory enjoyed a more representative government after the memorial was presented.

Organized Territory. A new act

relating to Louisiana was passed on March 2, 1805. It named Louisiana an **organized territory**. It gave the people the same rights as those enjoyed by the inhabitants of the Mississippi Territory. This form of government lasted until Louisiana became a state.

No changes were made in the executive and judicial branches of the government. Claiborne remained as governor. The most important change was in the legislative branch. The new government had both a legislative council and a house of representatives. Membership in the legislative council was reduced to five. Congress was to appoint the five from a list of ten names. The names were to be submitted by the territorial house of representatives. Claiborne did not nominate them. He did send his recommendations. Councilmen were to serve five-year terms. The house of representatives was to be composed of twenty-five members. They were to be elected by qualified voters for two-year terms. A voter had to own fifty acres of land. Voters had to be residents for two years. A representative had to own two hundred acres of land. They had to have been residents for three years.

The legislative council divided the Territory of Orleans into twelve **counties** for purposes of local government. These were Orleans, German Coast, Acadia, Lafourche, Iberville, Pointe Coupee, Atakapas, Opelousas,

Natchitoches, Rapides, Ouachita, and Concordia. A system of local government was provided for each county. This system did not meet with popular approval.

The second session of the legislature created nineteen **parishes** in 1807. The first parishes were Orleans, St. Bernard, Plaquemines, St. Charles, St. John the Baptist, St. James, Ascension, Assumption, Lafourche Interior, Iberville and Galveztown, Baton Rouge, Pointe Coupee, Concordia, Ouachita, Rapides, Avoyelles, Natchitoches, St. Landry, and St. Martin. The original twelve counties of 1804 were preserved. Counties continued to exist for certain purposes. They were abandoned by the state's second constitution in 1845.

Claiborne had great difficulty in putting the system of local government into effect. Many prominent citizens refused appointments. By 1805 country judges replaced civil commandants. Justices of the peace replaced syndics. Eventually the police jury system became the parish governing body.

The city of New Orleans presented totally different problems from the rest of Louisiana. New Orleans required a different structure for its government. It had a port dealing in world commerce. New Orleans was incorporated on February 17, 1805. A complete plan of government was provided.

Claiborne made changes only gradually. He continued to use those Spanish laws that conformed to the laws of the United States. He was careful to retain what had worked in the past.

In 1805 the English common law was used in criminal cases. Claiborne had a new civil code drawn up and put into effect in 1808. It was based on the **Napoleonic Code** of France. In 1825 it was rewritten. It remains the basis of Louisiana's civil law. A new slave code based on Bienville's 1724 *Code Noir* (Black Code) was prepared. Provisions from Carondelet's code were also added.

All laws had to be written in both French and English. Legal papers were prepared in both languages. When cases came before the courts, both languages were used. The evidence of witnesses and the judge's charge were interpreted in both languages for the jury. The membership of the juries had to be composed equally of English-speaking and French-speaking men. The speeches of the lawyers, however, were not translated from one language to another.

It became the custom for the members of the jury who could not understand the language of the lawyer to dismiss themselves. They went out in the hall to take a recess during his speech. It was often necessary for two lawyers—one French and one English—to be hired. That way, each side could be presented to the jury.

Claiborne's Accomplishments. Claiborne realized that his first job was to gain acceptance of himself. He was openly resented because he was not French. Since he could not speak French, some considered him inadequate as governor.

The young governor achieved amazing success in spite of the language handicap and other problems. He was very unpopular during the early years, however. The legislature and Claiborne were in conflict constantly. The French faction controlled the legislature. All legislation was a compromise between American and Creole views. During the entire territorial period, the leaders of the colony criticized Claiborne. Daniel Clark and Edward Livingston were two of his opponents. The twenty-eight-year-old governor displayed unusual ability in handling people with such different backgrounds.

Claiborne established confidence in American government at a difficult time in his personal life. In 1804 he lost his twenty-one-year-old wife and his daughter to yellow fever. His secretary and many of his close friends also died during the epidemic. Then five years later his second wife, only twenty-one years old, died of yellow fever.

Claiborne took action in much-needed areas. He organized a local militia. He started inoculation against smallpox. In 1806 fees of doctors were fixed by law. There were severe penalties for overcharging. Physicians, surgeons, and apothecaries all had to be licensed.

During this period the seed for a free public school system was planted. Claiborne was a strong supporter of public education. The colonists believed in their church schools. Louisiana education was in a sad state at the time of the Louisiana Purchase. It was estimated that only a few hundred people could read and write well. The Ursulines had seventy boarding students. There were about one hundred day-pupils at the convent.

As many American ideas as possible were introduced. The first Protestant church—Christ Church of New Orleans—was organized. Protestant Claiborne, as well as many others in Louisiana, enjoyed freedom of worship under the United States government. This privilege was very important to the happiness of the citizens. The natives had not anticipated that the new American government would work so well. Claiborne's work must have pleased the officials in Washington. He received numerous appointments from Presidents Jefferson and Madison. In fact, there are some historians who think that Claiborne should be given a better place in history because of his contributions in Louisiana.

En Partie 6 (Studying a Part). 1. Trace the development of the government of Louisiana as a territory. 2. List problems in obtaining statehood. 3. Why did the people want statehood? 4. Who was appointed to govern the territory? 5. Why were the people dissatisfied? 6. What were some of the problems that resulted from Creole-American differences? 7. What did Claiborne accomplish?

Boundary of the Louisiana Purchase

Exploration of the Louisiana Purchase Territory. The people of the United States knew very little about the newly purchased land. President Jefferson sent expeditions to find out what the territory was like. Lewis and Clark in 1804 and Zebulon Pike in 1805 began expeditions. In 1807 Pike was arrested by Spanish authorities for taking military possession of some of their territory. The Spanish escorted Pike to the United States boundary near Natchitoches and released him. Members of the Freeman and Hunter expedition explored the Ouachita and Red rivers. These explorers described the land, animals, plants, and Indian tribes in the new territory. They gathered information about the inhabitants. When the report was sent to Washington, the president and Congress had a better understanding of local conditions. This information was combined with reports received from local officials in New Orleans. The exchange of information worked to better relationships between the American government and the inhabitants of the Territory of Orleans.

Boundary Disputes. The boundary of the Louisiana Purchase was in dispute. When the territory was purchased, nobody knew exactly what its boundaries were. The papers drawn up at the Louisiana Purchase were not clear. Its boundaries to the north, west, and south were vague and undetermined. The French ministers told Monroe and Livingston that they were selling what France had gotten from Spain. They were unable to say exactly what that was. Questions were

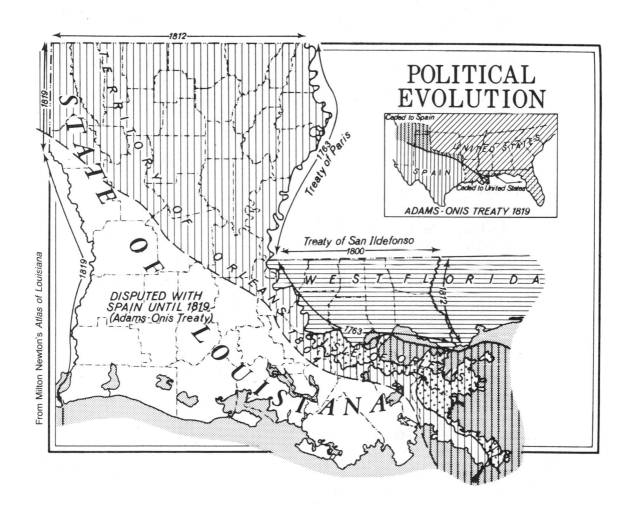

From Milton Newton's Atlas of Louisiana

asked. Had Spain given back to France all that had been called Louisiana in the days of Bienville? Did the United States purchase what was called Louisiana in the time of Napoleon? Spain insisted that the United States owned only the Isle of Orleans east of the Mississippi River and land extending to the Calcasieu River to the west.

There was a suspicion that Napoleon caused the confusion on purpose. In other words, he left the boundaries vague to provide future trouble between the United States and Spain. For two decades they had a strained relationship because of undetermined boundaries. Napoleon sided with Spain in the boundary disputes. He did so to try to make up for the transfer of Louisiana to the United States.

The first of what the French considered the boundaries was dated January 15, 1714. The missionary priest Lemaire wrote: "The province of Louisiana ends on the north at a place called Detroit, between Lake Erie and Lake Huron. On the south, it is bounded by the Gulf of Mexico and runs east and west about two hundred leagues; to wit: from the Madeline River. There are as yet no definite boundaries fixed in the distant lands lying on the east and west."

Trouble in the Felicianas. The American government claimed that West Florida was part of the Louisiana Purchase. Spanish officials still held this region. It had belonged to Spain since Gálvez captured the area from the English in 1779. Spain kept a military post at Baton Rouge. The district above Baton Rouge was called New Feliciana ("Happy Land") by the Spaniards. It had been settled since 1763 by English-speaking Americans, or Anglo-Saxons. After the purchase more Americans poured into the area. They lived across the Mississippi River from the Territory of Orleans and communicated frequently with the English in the Natchez area. Anglo-Saxons, especially those from Natchez, Mississippi, moved down the Mississippi River and settled on the fertile land in the Felicianas. They formed a strong wedge of English culture in the Spanish colony. They settled on plantations a mile or so apart and formed plantation settlements very much like those around Natchez. Then they constructed an Anglican church. The planters in this area became leaders in agriculture. They emphasized education and the arts. Such interest was rarely found outside an elite group in New Orleans. Statues were found in their formal gardens. Fine libraries were not uncommon around Bayou Sara and St. Francisville. These refinements only developed through the years.

When Louisiana was purchased by the United States, these English-speaking Americans were still in Spanish territory. They wanted to join their own kind. They wanted to become United States citizens. Some leading planters were not satisfied with life under the Spanish government.

Kemper Insurrection. When some citizens learned that Congress had not included West Florida in the Territory of Orleans, they took action. About two hundred men tried to drive out the Spanish authorities. This attempt was the Kemper Insurrection in West Florida in 1804. Three Kemper brothers—Nathan, Samuel, and Reuben—headed the movement to seize the fort at Baton Rouge from the Spanish. Their plans failed. The three Kemper brothers were captured by General Wilkinson of the United States Army. Afterward, the intense feeling against Spanish authority continued in West Florida.

Rebellion of 1810. Finally, a rebellion began in West Florida. The people demanded more voice in the government. This uprising was called the West Florida Rebellion.

Men from plantations near St. Francisville gathered to discuss their quarrels with the Spanish officials. They decided to set up a convention. It was to levy taxes and to do whatever else was needed for the general welfare and safety of the people. The convention, consisting of fourteen members, held its first meeting on July 26, 1810, and acted as if it were the regular government.

At the meeting, a sheriff, three judges, and militia officers were elected. Another item of business was the organization of their complaints. The planters wrote their demands for government reform and presented them to the Spanish governor. Something of the spirit of these men may be gleaned from reading minutes of meetings held in the summer of 1810.

Thursday, July 26, 1810—On motion of J. U. Leonard, pledged allegiance to Ferdinand VII. Then took up list of grievances:

(1) Fugitives from justice allowed to reside in West Florida, while desirable citizens are excluded.
(2) Want of and neglect of laws respecting roads, slaves, and livestock in the country.
(3) No fee bills exhibited by officers of government, and citizens charged exorbitant fees for services.
(4) No uniform standard of weights and measures in use.
(5) Exiled French from Cuba allowed to settle in West Florida.

Committee of five elected to draft plan for redress of existing grievances and safety of the country, and John Mills elected to said committee.

Friday, July 27, 1810 . . . More grievances presented;
(1) Inability of inhabitants to obtain titles to lands.

(2) No penalty prescribed for assault and battery, both of which crimes pass unnoticed.

Spanish officials did not have enough troops to put an end to the rebellion. The governor pretended to cooperate with the reformers. At the same time he contacted his Spanish superiors to send him more troops to put down the movement. The people were pretending to go along with the Spanish governor, too. They even proposed to raise taxes to pay his salary so that he would not have to wait to get it from Spain.

The people felt that the Spaniards opposed their actions. They were just pretending to approve. In September 1810 the Feliciana planters heard that the captain general of the Floridas was coming with an armed force. He planned to put an end to the uprising and punish its leaders.

When the leaders learned of the deception, they made plans. Colonel Philemon Thomas was appointed commander of the militia. He was ordered to raise a force of volunteers and capture the fort at Baton Rouge. This was done. One Spanish soldier was killed and two were wounded. The Americans had no casualties. They took down the Spanish flag and replaced it with the Lone Star flag. They proclaimed West Florida to be a free and independent state.

Leaders wanted the United States to annex the area promptly. (Annexation came later without mention of the rebels.) In the meantime the rebel leaders proclaimed a new nation called the **Republic of West Florida**. They organized a government. They drew up a constitution and held an election. The legislature of the little republic met in St. Francisville in November 1810. Fulwar Skipwith was elected president of the Republic of West Florida.

Plans were then made to organize a large force under Philemon Thomas to drive the Spaniards from Mobile and Pensacola. A force of four hundred was raised before the federal government put a stop to their activities.

Annexation of the Republic of West Florida. On December 10, 1810, President James Madison ordered Governor Claiborne to occupy West Florida and govern it. Madison completely ignored the existence of the Republic of West Florida. The area became a part of the Territory of Orleans as the County of Feliciana. The Orleans territory and the Mississippi Territory both wanted to annex West Florida. Governor Claiborne offered a compromise. The Mississippi Territory got the land east of the Pearl River. The land west of Pearl River became a part of the Orleans territory. On December 22, 1810, four parishes were made out of this territory. They were Feliciana, East Baton Rouge, St. Helena, and St.

Tammany. The area is still referred to as the **Florida parishes.** Even though the United States took over the territory, Spain did not give up its claims until 1819.

"No Man's Land." A definite western boundary of Louisiana had not been determined. The Spaniards in Texas considered it to be the Red River. The Americans claimed it to be the Trinity River, or at least the Sabine. Finally, a neutral strip was created in 1806 when no decision was forthcoming. This area between the Territory of Orleans and the Spanish to the west was known as the **Neutral Ground.** It was also known as the Sabine Strip and "No Man's Land." General James Wilkinson, representing the United States, met with the Spanish commander at Los Adais to make this agreement. Neither country would claim the land between the Sabine River to the west and the Calcasieu River to the east. The boundary line was not finally determined until the United States bought Florida in 1819.

Neither the laws of the United States nor Spain applied to this forty-mile-wide region. There were five thousand miles of ungoverned territory. It attracted all kinds of people. Outlaws of both nations settled in the area. It was also used as a place for slaves to hide. Outlaws enticed slaves to the area with the promise of freedom. Then the outlaws sold them.

The building that surrounds this courtyard was built in 1816 by a New Orleans wine merchant.

Lafitte, the pirate, took stolen slaves up the Sabine River and into the strip. Judges sometimes sentenced criminals to the Neutral Ground. Holdups were frequent for migrants heading west through the strip. There were people other than outlaws in the area. Some were former outlaws trying to start a new life. Others were simply Americans or Spaniards desiring to live within the area.

When the agreement for the territory was made, someone said, "This area will be the stepping off place of all kinds of smuggling and outlawry known to mankind." It proved to be so. Even after it was no longer a lawless area, the tradition of violence remained.

En Partie 7 (Studying a Part). 1. How was information about the new territory obtained? 2. Why was there confusion about the boundaries? 3. (a) Describe the formation of the Republic of West Florida. (b) When did that section become part of the United States? (c) How? 4. (a) Why was "No Man's Land" created? (b) Why did that area develop into a land of lawlessness? (c) How did it become a part of the United States?

Aaron Burr's Conspiracy

The American union was young and weak when the Louisiana Purchase was made. The people in the territories did not have respect for the authority of the United States government. They did not appreciate its value. Neither did the Creoles in Louisiana. In other parts of the Mississippi Valley, there were many restless people who were plotting reckless ventures.

One of these persons was Aaron Burr. He was the former vice president of the United States who had killed Alexander Hamilton in a duel. At the time of the duel Burr was running for governor of New York. Burr believed that there was a chance for him to reestablish his influence. He planned to take advantage of unsettled conditions and discontent in the West and Southwest. Burr might have made his plans because he thought the United States was going to war with Spain over the Louisiana Purchase boundary dispute. It was said that Burr and his followers planned to capture Mexico from the Spanish. Just which territory Burr had in mind was never clear. That a conspiracy was planned appears certain. There was reason enough to believe that he wished to grab land and set himself up as ruler.

Aaron Burr went to New Orleans in 1805. He was entertained, and he conferred with General Wilkinson and other New Orleans leaders. After ten or twelve days in New Orleans, Burr left for St. Louis. He had planned to return to New Orleans in the fall. However, he changed his mind and went back east.

By then Burr had developed his schemes. He would split the discontented Southwest from the Union and make it an independent nation. He would head this new nation. He would drive the Spaniards from Texas and the Floridas. Burr took his ideas to the British minister in Washington. The minister was interested. His government did not get involved, however. Burr then tried the Spanish minister. Burr made promises regarding this new nation he planned. He promised to protect the Spanish colonies from seizure by the United States. The Spanish minister lent him money. He even tried unsuccessfully to get more funds from his government for Burr.

Burr later claimed that he had purchased land on the Ouachita River. He was simply planning to take settlers there. The land had been granted to Baron de Bastrop by Carondelet. In 1806 Burr collected provisions, tools, and arms. He had a number of flatboats to take his men and supplies down the river. There were many wild rumors concerning his plans.

It was believed that Burr intended to seize the Spanish fort at Baton Rouge. The Spanish captain general of the Floridas quickly went to Baton Rouge to stop Burr. Burr did not go to Baton Rouge. Instead, he and his troops stopped in New Orleans. Governor Claiborne would not allow them to enter the city. Claiborne's actions in the Burr case won the approval of Jefferson.

Burr wrote to his former friend, General Wilkinson. He tried to explain his reason for coming down the river with a force of armed men. Wilkinson immediately sent the message to President Jefferson.

General Wilkinson reported to President Jefferson that Burr was scheming to separate the western states from the United States. There is no way to know if the general's testimony was accurate. It is known that General Wilkinson had once worked with Governor Miro to secure the West for Spain. "The West" at that time was the area of Kentucky and Tennessee. Wilkinson had accepted pay from the Spanish to assist them in securing other United States territory. At that time he was an officer in the United States Army. Because his present interests were not known, Wilkinson was not considered to be a dependable source for accurate information. He had been accused of planning to work with Burr if there were any hope of success for Burr's schemes.

Wilkinson strictly looked out for himself. He took the position of a United States law officer attending to duty and ordered Burr's arrest. This action was taken in spite of whatever dealings with Aaron Burr he may have had earlier.

Wilkinson's men were sent to capture Burr as he came down the Mississippi with a boatload of well-armed men. Burr was arrested by Mississippi authorities at Bayou Pierre, about thirty miles above Natchez. Later he was released on bail. The governor of the Mississippi Territory again ordered his arrest. Burr fled into the woods with a companion.

In New Orleans Wilkinson's men arrested several of Burr's agents. Wilkinson took other steps to prevent an invasion of the territory.

When Burr heard that he was being sought by United States officials, he tried to reach Spanish West Florida. A reward was offered for his capture. He was arrested at Fort Stoddard, Alabama. He was tried for treason in Richmond, Virginia. He was acquitted. There was no proof that he was guilty of any treacherous acts against the United States.

The conspiracy caused much excitement in the Territory of Orleans for many months. It showed the Spanish in Texas and the Floridas that the western country would not be separated from the eastern states. The results of the conspiracy helped Claiborne, too. Some of the same prominent citizens who were suspected of supporting Burr also opposed Claiborne. After the incident, Claiborne's opposition in New Orleans subsided.

En Partie 8 (Studying a Part). 1. Describe Aaron Burr's involvement with the Territory of Orleans. 2. What were the results of this conspiracy?

Settlement in the Territory

In 1804 there were about fifty thousand people living in the present state of Louisiana. These people were settled mostly in the southeastern quarter of the state. The majority were clustered around New Orleans, the only city. There were ten thousand in the city. Baton Rouge, Opelousas, St. Martinville, Natchitoches, and Monroe were small villages. In the rural areas along the Mississippi there were planters and farmers. Many settlements had developed along the important bayous. There were scattered isolated homes on the Red and Ouachita rivers and in the wilderness.

New Orleans had developed into a trade center. It was little more than the Vieux Carré. Ships and boats with their cargoes were sometimes two or three deep. A stockade enclosed the city. Four gates were used to enter and leave the city. At night they were guarded. Five forts provided protection. Present-day Canal Street was a ditch, or moat. Wooden gallows and public pillories stood in the public square. New Orleans had a naval yard and a customhouse. Branches of eastern stores were among the wholesale and retail establishments.

Commerce and agriculture were fairly well established. Rice, sugar, indigo, tobacco, and cotton were the main crops. Sawmills produced shingles and cypress, cedar, and maple

Historic New Orleans Collection

This view of New Orleans was taken from the Marigny plantation in 1803.

boards. These were shipped to the West Indies.

Early settlements were made along the waterways. In the colonial period French and Spanish settlers located on the biggest river of them all, the Mississippi. Choice land was that facing the stream on either side. Land holdings were laid out stretching from the river. Each settler held a share along the stream so he could ship his crop out to market. This location was also necessary to receive needed goods. During the French period the settlers formed **line villages**. Each family built its house facing the stream. The houses of the settlers were close and made for a close-knit community.

After 1763 the English settled on their plantations on the east side of the Mississippi. The English had a different settlement pattern from the French and Spanish. The English homesites were scattered and apt to be an average of a mile-and-a-half apart. The English worked at building their plantations to be as self-sufficient as possible. The distances between homes did not encourage the warm neighborliness of the French and Spanish. When the English joined the territory, they offset the French majority. Many members of Congress felt better about the territory becoming a state because of the English people in West Florida.

Settlers constantly searched for inland bayous where they could settle. Soon most of the richest land in Louisiana was claimed. That land was the alluvial soil along the rivers and largest bayous. Creek bottoms were also desirable locations.

The problem of **land claims** immediately arose. Congress undertook to adjust all land claims fairly and legally. Those actually settling the land had little difficulty in establishing their titles. The absentees who claimed vast tracts of unsettled land had greater difficulties. Squatters who had settled illegally also had trouble. They were later granted relief under the preemption laws. They were allowed to keep the land because they had occupied it before the Louisiana Purchase. Not all land claims were settled in Louisiana during the territorial period. Some had trouble determining the exact boundaries of their property.

The first to join settlers already on the streams were the speculators and traders. Frequently they traded the Indians out of their land for a few dollars worth of groceries, tobacco, and other supplies. The speculators secured the land from the Indians in order to sell it to incoming pioneers.

Many French colonists from Cuba joined the settlers in the Orleans territory. These people had gone to Spanish Cuba during the great slave rebellion in Santo Domingo. There they grew sugarcane. When the war broke out between Spain and France, they had to flee again. This time they chose to come to Louisiana. Near-

ly six thousand persons arrived by the middle of 1809. About one-third were slaves. New arrivals to Louisiana could not bring in slaves legally, but they were allowed to do so nevertheless. About ten thousand refugees filtered into Louisiana. A large number of free Negroes were among them.

United States citizens ordinarily continued to think of Louisiana as populated by foreigners. These "foreigners," they thought, would not prove loyal to the United States. When Louisiana was purchased, most white residents were either French or Spanish. However, English-Americans poured into the area. Migration rose after Louisiana became a state. Large family groups left Virginia, South Carolina, Alabama, and Georgia. Others poured into the state from North Carolina, Tennessee, Kentucky, Ohio, Pennsylvania, and New York. Some were waiting across the Mississippi River in the Mississippi Territory for Louisiana to become a state. It was the beginning of a period when the lure of cheap lands to the west kept many people on the move.

Covered wagons strung out across trails through the wilderness. A group from South Carolina first reached the banks of the Tennessee River to camp before the year 1800. They found Nickajack Cave there and lived in it for months. The men among the party of about a hundred people cut down trees and built flatboats. The boats provided living space. A fenced-in area on the boat held farm animals. At night these flatboats were pulled to the banks of the river. The men had time to hunt game to add to the food supply of the pioneers.

The South Carolina migrants floated into the Ohio River and then the Mississippi River. Once there the pioneers were on the last lap of their voyage. They floated for days, going about their routine housekeeping on primitive houseboats.

When the group reached Natchez around 1800, they stopped to look around. This was where they had planned to stop. The men rode horseback around the area and decided that it was not the place for them. They decided that it was already too crowded. The choice farmland had already been taken. They returned to their flatboats and continued down the river.

Farther down along the river they stopped again. Again they rode horseback through the wilderness. Finally, they decided to settle at this point. Robert Tanner, the leader of the group, surveyed and laid out a town. This was Woodville, Mississippi. The people bought land, cleared the trees, and began farming. In about a decade, Tanner and others began riding their horses into the Louisiana Territory. They were searching for a new place to settle. They wanted to move to a new location when Louisiana became a state.

The surveyor, Robert Tanner, and a group of men rode deep into Louisiana in search of a new homesite. They found land on Bayou Boeuf in Central Louisiana. It was already in the hands of speculators. It had remained unsettled because the little bayou was not dependable for shipments of supplies and transportation of crops to market in New Orleans. Nevertheless, the South Carolina migrants decided to move to the Boeuf. There they expected to establish cotton plantations. There was one drawback, according to an old letter that survives. They thought bears in the woods might eat their hogs.

Some of the original settlers remained on their farms at Woodville. Others left with Tanner for the new location in Louisiana. These sold their farms and bought land along Bayou Boeuf for around $1.25 to $1.50 an acre. Tanner surveyed and laid out Cheneyville on the banks of the bayou. He surveyed land for plantations. Many of these plantations belonged to the twelve children of Robert and Providence Tanner. For a dozen miles, the people of this single migration began plantations. In the course of settlement they founded a crossroads village. In such a manner did thousands of groups arrive in Louisiana after it became a state. Most were cotton planters.

En Partie 9 (Studying a Part). 1. Where was the population of Louisiana centered in 1804? 2. Which towns existed? 3. Describe New Orleans in 1804. 4. How did the French and Spanish settlements differ from the English settlements? 5. Why were there problems with land claims? 6. Why were Louisianians considered foreigners?

Statehood: 1812

Eighteenth State. The United States census was taken every ten years beginning in 1790. It was taken for the first time in Louisiana in 1810. At that time there were 76,556 people in the Louisiana Territory. Of these, 34,660 were slaves. There were 7,585 free persons of color. The census showed that 77.5 percent of the population was rural.

The census showed that the territory had more than the sixty thousand residents required to become a state. Julien Poydras called attention to this fact in Congress. He asked for statehood. Claiborne had sent a letter giving his reasons for opposing statehood. The first attempt to gain statehood failed in Congress in 1810. In early January 1811 debate began on a bill for admitting the Territory of Orleans into the Union as a state. Some members of Congress opposed the measure—some on constitutional

grounds. It was argued that Congress had no right to make new states from a territory that was not a part of the United States when the Constitution was adopted. Some feared that new states would outnumber old ones. Then the new states would gain control of the government.

In spite of the opposition, the bill for statehood passed in February 1811. It provided that all qualified free white male voters could elect the members for a convention. The convention was to write a constitution. The constitution had to be consistent with the United States Constitution. It had to guarantee citizens civil and religious liberty and the right of trial by jury. Congress also required that all laws and other important official documents be in English.

The convention met in New Orleans at Tremoulet's Coffee House in November 1811. Julien Poydras was president of the convention. Only twenty-eight of the forty-five delegates were present. The convention immediately adjourned for two weeks. The time allowed for a yellow fever epidemic to subside. The work was finished in January 1812. The convention gave the new state its name—**Louisiana**—and drafted the **constitution**. It was modeled after Kentucky's.

The state's first constitution stated that no citizen could become governor unless he owned five thousand dollars worth of property. The people would vote for the governor. The legislature would then choose from the two who received the highest number of votes.

On April 8, 1812, President James Madison approved a bill passed by Congress admitting Louisiana to the Union. On April 14, 1812, West Florida was made a part of the state. The effective date of the act was **April 30, 1812.** That was the day Louisiana officially became the eighteenth state admitted to the Union.

The Capital of Louisiana: 1812. Almost a century old, **New Orleans** was a French and Spanish city. It was the capital of Louisiana in 1812 and the only city in the state of any important size. The population of New Orleans was eighteen thousand. It was not the busy metropolis familiar to us today.

In the city the most important public buildings were made of brick and were at least partially fireproof. These buildings were erected after the great fires that swept the city in 1788 and 1794. The finest houses of the well-to-do were often made of brick. Because the native bricks were soft, posts were placed between them for support. There were many more modest dwellings of ordinary citizens and the rude huts of the poorest people. The poorer class had frame houses raised off the ground eight to fifteen feet. This was done because of high water and snakes. **Bousillage,** mud mixed with deer hair or Spanish moss, was still common. It was plastered between the logs and kept the inside of the houses snug and dry. Some roofs were tile or slate. Most were cypress shingles.

Architecture was predominantly Spanish, with houses built flush with the sidewalks, or **banquettes.** An enclosed outdoor living space, or courtyard, was the center around which the rooms were built.

Street lights brightened the intersections with pools of soft oil light in the darkness. A few streets were carefully laid with adobe bricks (handmade and dried in the sun). These were the short city streets. Most streets, like the country roads, were dirt trails. They were dusty in summer and muddy in winter.

Garbage disposal presented a street problem as well. New Orleans had no system for waste disposal. The people allowed garbage and sewage to get into the ditches. When flooding occurred, the waste matter washed out into the narrow streets. The river and streams were also used for dumping.

Fire protection consisted of a supply of sturdy buckets to be used in a bucket brigade. In 1807 New Orleans passed a bucket ordinance. Each householder was required to keep two buckets on hand. A watchman on the roof of the city hall was to ring a bell at the cry of "fire." The city kept increasing the numbers of buckets available for use when there was a fire. No doubt the men of New Orleans knew to race to the fire when the warning bell sounded. There every man was needed to pick up the buckets and form a line beginning at the water supply. The buckets of water could be passed rapidly from one man to the next down the line toward the location of the fire. The men nearest the fire kept dashing the water on the flames.

New Orleans in 1812 was a cozy little city. It was made up of two rival groups: the Creoles and the Americans. In this setting the first state government was assembled.

First Governor. Claiborne was elected as the first governor of the state of Louisiana. He took the oath of office July 30, 1812. The first business he conducted with the general assembly was to annex the West Florida parishes. Among other business were plans for a system of public education. There were plans for organization of the court system and for a more efficient organization of the militia. There was yet a more urgent matter. The United States Congress had declared war on England on June 18, 1812.

En Partie 10 (Studying a Part). 1. Why was there opposition to statehood for Louisiana? 2. When did Louisiana become a state? 3. What star represents Louisiana on the American flag? 4. Describe Louisiana's first state capital. 5. Who was the first elected governor? 6. What were some of the first items of business for the government?

The War of 1812

Invasion of Louisiana. In June 1812, six weeks after Louisiana entered the Union, the United States was at war. The purposes of the war were to defend American rights on the high seas and to put an end to the Indian troubles in the West promoted by the English. This war has been called the "Second American Revolution." Many Americans felt that England had never given up the idea of getting back its lost colonies.

Trouble had been brewing for some time. Congress had adopted the Embargo Act in December 1807. It was designed to prevent seizure of American ships by keeping them off the high seas. It was supposed to punish England and France. They were going to be deprived of American goods. Instead, it injured the United States most of all. The people of the Orleans territory were greatly affected. New Orleans commerce was dead. All foreign trade was stopped except that carried on illegally. There

Louisiana Office of Tourism

This shop is said to have been Lafitte's headquarters in New Orleans.

was so much protest that the act was repealed in 1809. England continued to be the main obstacle to neutral commerce. By 1812 controversies with England led to war.

For two years of the war, all the fighting was done on the high seas and in the far north near the borders of Canada. During that time, the war had not touched the daily lives of Louisianians. However, Governor Claiborne had organized the state militia as soon as statehood was declared.

The Baratarians. During the War of 1812, **Jean Lafitte** and his older brother **Pierre** became famous. They were known for their smuggling operations centered at Barataria Bay. Beginning in 1806 in New Orleans, a blacksmith shop served as a front for their main business—smuggling. Pierre had served in the French navy.

He directed the capture of vessels. Jean was the leader. Pierre and Dominique You were his lieutenants. About five hundred men were in the organization. At one time, there were reported to be a thousand.

The smugglers' hideout was on the island of Grand Terre. There they built storehouses for the goods from their plunder. Cafés and gambling houses were a part of the establishment. A fort at the entrance of the bay defended their quarters. Their light, swift sailing vessels could go into the shallow waters of the bay area. Heavy ships in pursuit could not follow them.

The Baratarians got their goods by overpowering Spanish and British merchant vessels. They carried papers called **letters of marque**. These let-

THE BARATARIANS

ters were obtained from countries at war with Spain or England. The documents gave them authority to attack ships as an ally of the warring nation that issued the letters. Without the letters of marque, they would have been considered pirates. With them, they were not. The vessels sailing in this manner were called privateers.

The Baratarians violated the law when they brought the captured goods into the country. The smugglers avoided payment of import duty on the goods. They secretly brought their goods into New Orleans and sold them at very low prices. The stolen goods, under heavy guard, were sent to New Orleans almost every day. A fleet of barges shuttled to and from Barataria. Much of the stolen goods was sold to merchants and planters along the route. Local merchants could not compete with Lafitte on any item. Some of the well-known people in New Orleans were Lafitte's best customers. By 1813 Jean Lafitte's loot could be seen in almost every store in New Orleans. Public officials received a portion of the profit to keep them quiet about Lafitte's operations. Members of the band received shares, too. Lafitte's activities involved so many officials and merchants that it was not easy to prosecute him.

Since some of the Spanish governors had allowed breaking trade laws, it had become a pattern. Many people of Louisiana did not consider the actions of the pirates to be a serious offense. Instead of condemning Lafitte, many saw him as a most glamorous man. He built himself a mansion of brick and stone with money he accumulated.

Reward for Lafitte's Arrest. Governor Claiborne attempted to put an end to the capture of vessels under the flag of Spain. Spain was friendly with the United States. The governor ordered the bandits to disband. They simply ignored his orders and threats.

The Lafitte brothers were eventually arrested, but they were not punished. Some of their smuggled goods were seized by government officials. The smugglers fought a battle with the officers in broad daylight and recovered the goods.

Governor Claiborne offered a re-

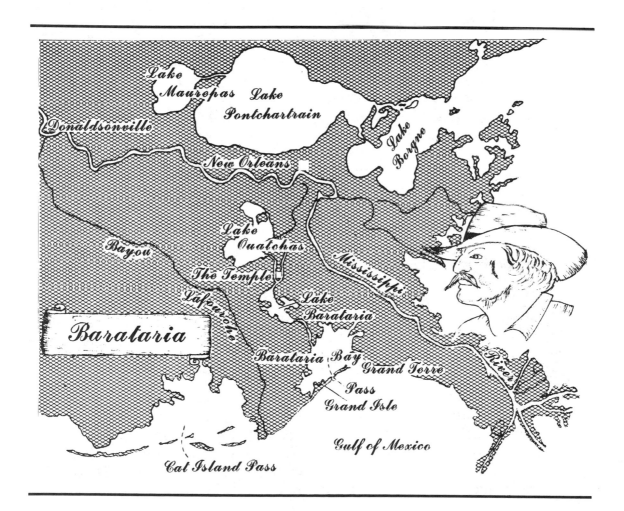

ward. Five hundred dollars would be given for the arrest of Jean Lafitte. Jean Lafitte countered with his own offer of fifteen hundred dollars for Claiborne. The governor asked the legislature to help destroy Lafitte's organization. The legislature would not provide the required funds. Claiborne attempted to break up the smuggler's settlement at Barataria. Pierre Lafitte was arrested and sent to jail in New Orleans.

British Offers. While the Lafitte struggle continued, the British were planning to capture New Orleans. Colonel Edward Nicholls was sent with two warships to find guides and pilots for the British ships. They hoped to maneuver a big fleet of warships into Lake Borgne.

Nicholls heard about the Baratarians and their troubles. He sent a written offer to Jean Lafitte, proposing to make him a captain in the British navy if he would help the British in the coming battle to take New Orleans. Five thousand dollars was offered as additional bait. In another document, Nicholls had an order to destroy the Baratarians' hideout. This was intended to punish the Baratarians for damage done to British ships during their piracy at sea. Nicholls would give Jean Lafitte a choice of documents. In other words, Lafitte could either help the British or be attacked by them.

Lafitte requested two weeks to make his decision. He informed his friend in the legislature, Jean Blanque, about the British offer. As his reward for the information, Lafitte requested that Pierre be freed from prison. Blanque then told Governor Claiborne what he had learned.

Shortly afterward Pierre "escaped" from prison. Lafitte offered Claiborne the services of his Baratarian pirates. Claiborne was ready to accept his offer. Leaders of a United States expedition against the pirates were not. Instead, the expeditionary force destroyed the Baratarian settlement. The brothers escaped and joined friends on the German Coast.

By 1814 the war was not going very well for the Americans. The British officer, Nicholls, made an offer to the people of the state. He would free Louisiana from the United States. Perhaps the British thought that the people of the new state did not really have any feeling of belonging to the new country. Most Louisiana citizens had lived in the colony when it belonged to Spain or France. The people rejected Nicholls's offer.

1814. Meanwhile, General **Andrew Jackson** was in charge of the defense of the Gulf. He had been fighting with Indians on the Florida borderlands when he heard of a possible invasion. He received a message from Governor Claiborne about the crisis at New Orleans. With this news Jackson moved west along the

Gulf coast arriving in New Orleans in December.

A week after Jackson arrived, British troops anchored off the coast of Louisiana. Over fifty ships carrying ten thousand of Great Britain's finest troops had left Jamaica in November 1814. The fleet was commanded by Vice Admiral Sir Alexander Cochrane. The soldiers were led by General Sir Edward Pakenham. The British came in through Lake Borgne and reached the Mississippi River a few miles below New Orleans.

The first clash between American and British forces took place on December 14, 1814. The British won the Battle of Lake Borgne and controlled the lake. They lost more men than the Americans.

The available American troops were many days' march from New Orleans. Jackson had to gather troops to defend the city. Frenchmen in Louisiana complained that they were not really Americans and, therefore, had no intention of getting into the fight. The town officials simply did not trust Andrew Jackson. The rugged Jackson paid no attention.

Jackson went below New Orleans —almost to the Gulf of Mexico. He inspected Fort St. Philip and such troops as Governor Claiborne had assembled. Jackson then set to work training them. He posted them along the river below New Orleans. He planned fortifications and placed guns

to greet the British invaders at two points. These were at the Rigolets and at Bayou St. John.

There are many stories about the British invasion of New Orleans. There was, for instance, the British scheme to secure information about the terrain. They needed to know about traveling through the strange flat country that broke into water frequently. British officers disguised themselves as fishermen to test the trip. They found men who told them the best way to get to New Orleans. They met others who told them more about the country. The British decided that there would be no problem in invading.

On December 22 six hundred British soldiers started moving toward New Orleans. They traveled along a canal to General Villeré's plantation. On the way they captured a few Americans who had been out to secure information about the invading army. The prisoners told the British that Andrew Jackson had six thousand troops in New Orleans. They had been instructed to tell this to the enemy.

The story is told of one of the many heroes of the New Orleans defense, Major **Villeré**. He was the son of General Villeré. The two Villeré brothers were sitting on the gallery of the plantation home when the British invaders were suddenly upon them. Major Villeré managed to free himself and jumped out of a window. He escaped through the thick woods, which he knew well. In this way he was able to avoid the gunfire of the guards who ran after him. He climbed up a big oak tree to hide. His dog had followed him and stood barking at the foot of the tree. In order to keep the dog's bark from revealing his hiding place, Villeré had to kill the animal. He quickly buried the dog and hid in the tree again. The British rushed past him. Major Villeré got down quickly and continued his trip to let Andrew Jackson know the location of the enemy. Young Villeré stopped at a neighbor's house. The neighbor joined him. They rode horses at full speed into New Orleans to find Andrew Jackson.

When Jackson got the news of the British invaders, he assembled troops at Fort St. Charles. The Louisiana militia was "called to the colors." Frontiersmen all over Louisiana came to defend New Orleans. A battalion of free men of color was among the troops. Jackson had assembled there one of the strangest armies that any general had ever faced. There were Indians in war paint and backwoodsmen in coonskin caps, as well as trained and polished soldiers.

When Jackson learned that the British were near the city, he quickly called two thousand of his troops into action. They marched down the Mississippi River. Commodore Patterson, on the armed schooner *Carolina*,

moved down the river, also, and anchored in the darkness opposite the British. Campfires clearly marked the enemy's position.

In the cover of darkness, the *Carolina* opened fire. General Coffee's Tennessee sharpshooters and General Jackson's troops of assorted origins arrived soon afterward. They quickly and forcefully fell upon the British. Both sides fought savagely in the darkness with muskets, tomahawks, knives, and bare hands. It was difficult to distinguish friend from foe. When a heavy fog descended on the battleground, both sides withdrew. The Americans had lost two hundred men—the British three hundred. Neither side could claim a decisive victory.

Jackson moved his troops two miles toward New Orleans. He selected a place where a canal separated the Chalmette and Rodriguez plantations to set up his defense. This place was about fifteen hundred yards wide between the Mississippi River and the swamp. The remains of a corn crop from fall harvest still lay in the field. Jackson ordered his men to establish earthworks on the New Orleans side of the canal. (These earthworks, between the river and the swamp, stand today.) The defenders took their stations behind the wall of dirt. Fifteen cannons were pulled into place by the defenders. The barricade was pierced at intervals to provide space for them. Their muzzles were ready to belch a torrent of cannon-balls into the British soldiers as they marched toward Jackson's men.

Jackson had quickly blockaded the passage of the British through all the approaches to the city as best he could. He cut the levee just below the line of earthworks. With luck, the river would flood the area between the British position and his own. However, this did not happen. The bayous did rise, but this was to the advantage of the British. The British used the bayous to move up their troops and heavy guns.

The Americans received reinforce-ments. The pirates from Barataria sent word that they were ready to join in the fight against the enemy. If some leaders hesitated, General Andrew Jackson did not. Among Lafitte's men were many who were trained to handle heavy cannons. They were all used to fighting and danger. Jackson received others who were raw recruits who had never seen fighting. His total forces now reached four thousand.

Christmas came, and both sides paused to celebrate. Neither side knew that the war in which they were fighting had actually already ended.

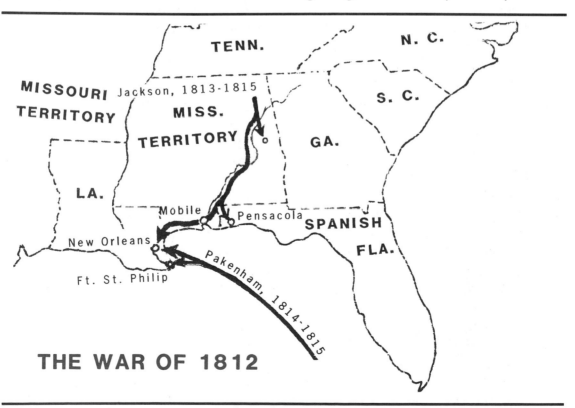

THE WAR OF 1812

A peace treaty was signed on Christmas Eve in Ghent, Belgium, by the Americans and the British. But travel was slow. News came so slowly across the sea that it was weeks before most Americans knew about the signing of the peace treaty.

The British were strengthening their position. Their forces reached eight thousand. On December 28, the British attacked. The American riflemen and artillerists were so accurate that the advance of the British toward New Orleans was stopped. Dominique You was one of the excellent marksmen. He had been a cannoneer for Napoleon.

1815. A major clash occurred on January 1, 1815. The British shelled Jackson's earthworks. Again, the British gained nothing.

For a week the British were busy with preparations for battle. They cut the Villeré Canal through to the Mississippi River. This was a distance of about two miles. The canal was to serve as a waterway over which they moved soldiers and guns. Jackson decided the best protection for his defenders would be an embankment of earth. When completed, the earthworks were nearly twenty feet thick in some places. Jackson also flooded the canal in front of the earthworks. Jackson placed troops at various other points around New Orleans lest the British attack from another direction. Just before the beginning of the

battle, Kentucky and Tennessee sharpshooters arrived. It could not have been more timely.

The big battle—known in history as the **Battle of New Orleans**—was fought on January 8, 1815. British General Pakenham ordered a full-scale attack on the American line.

There was a heavy fog over the flat, marshy battlefield. The British knew that the Americans were lined up behind the earthen wall to block their march into New Orleans. The attackers' plans to move their troops through their canal to the battle area had failed. The banks of the canal caved in. Only about half of the soldiers were transported over it. The strong current took the troops farther downstream than they had planned to go. Pakenham decided that they would make a frontal attack on the Americans. That is, they would march straight into the fire of the Americans.

As they marched toward the American defenders, the British soldiers were ordered to pick up dried cornstalks from the plantation field. These were used as braces for jumping across the shallow little canal and the earthworks just beyond it. The British planned to face the Americans eye-to-eye.

The battle began about six o'clock in the morning as the British moved a solid mass of soldiers toward the American lines. The Americans opened fire with artillery and muskets. The

British responded. British soldiers who survived the artillery fire were cut down by the sharpshooters firing from behind the earthworks.

After little more than an hour, the slaughter ended. General Pakenham was among the more than two thousand British who lay dead on the battlefield. Behind their barrier the Americans counted only six dead and seventy-one wounded.

After the Big Battle. The British would not give up after the Battle of New Orleans. Maybe they could not believe that their highly trained veteran troops could not defeat a group of American irregulars. The British continued to attack. After a few weeks, they finally admitted defeat and left.

Henry Miller Shreve steamed up the Red River in his boat, the *Enterprise*, returning veterans of the Battle of New Orleans to their homes. Earlier he had used his boat to haul supplies for the war. He took women and children away from the war zone. The use of steamboats for routine transportation on the Red River was still a few years away.

Andrew Jackson kept New Orleans under martial law another two months after the battle. He received biting criticism from some of the people for this action. Jackson felt that martial law was needed until it was certain that the British were not planning another attack.

A man named Louis Louaillier was so insistent that martial law be ended that Jackson ordered his arrest. A judge of the federal district court ordered his release. The feisty Jackson then ordered the arrest of the judge and the attorney general. On March 13, 1815, Jackson declared the end of martial law. News had come at last from Belgium that a peace treaty had been signed. The attorney general, released from jail, sued Jackson. This was in the court of Judge Dominick Hall, whom Jackson had also ordered arrested. Hall fined Jackson one thousand dollars. Years later Congress returned Jackson's money with interest.

Results of the Battle of New Orleans. Although the war was officially over before the battle began, it served important purposes. First, Jackson's call for troops brought response from all over Louisiana. The French, Spanish, Indians, pirates, Negroes, and big planters—they were there together fighting to defend their country. There would never again be a question of their loyalty to the United States. And the people of Louisiana themselves had a new feeling of belonging. The people in and around New Orleans had only been in the new nation a short while and felt no real kinship with the United States. Fighting together to defend their home against an enemy made them realize that they were a part of the United States of America. They were proud that they were citizens. Secondly, the battle also united the nation and broke the bonds that Americans had with Europe. It was the final defeat for Britain's colonial ambitions in the New World.

Thirdly, the victory at the Battle of New Orleans was needed by the United States. It bolstered the country's claims at the peace table. The truth was that the United States had won too few victories during the War of 1812. In the negotiations that followed the peace treaty, this victory gave United States representatives more influence. The battle has been described as "the most conclusive battle in American history."

Finally, the Battle of New Orleans resulted in Andrew Jackson's becoming president of the United States. Jackson became an instant hero and collected a variety of colorful nicknames, including "Old Hickory." His frontier image and fighting spirit inspired followers. He was elected to the presidency in 1828.

Jackson, leaving New Orleans with his troops, took a route leading through the Florida parishes. According to legend in that area, he camped near Bodcaw. The little village felt itself honored. The village was renamed Jackson.

The public square in front of St. Louis Cathedral had its name changed again. When the block was laid out under the French it was christened **Place d'Armes**. The Spanish changed its name to **Plaza de Armas**. Now, under the Americans, it became known as **Jackson Square**.

Jackson's monument was placed in position in the square with appropriate ceremony in 1856. The Baroness Pontalba, who had constructed the apartment houses on the sides of the square, had furnished most of the money for the statue. She had a request. She wanted Jackson placed so that he seemed to be looking up at her window. Later, someone observed that both front feet of Jackson's horse are lifted off the ground. This is a posture reserved for the horses of heroes who died in battle. Nobody seemed to mind this mistake. Few monuments in Louisiana are more deserved.

Later, Fort Jackson was built on the Mississippi River below New Orleans. The star-shaped masonry fort was built between 1822 and 1832. It was constructed to keep invaders from threatening New Orleans again.

En Partie 11 (Studying a Part). 1. Describe the Lafitte brothers. 2. Identify the causes of the War of 1812. 3. What was unusual about the Battle of New Orleans? 4. What part did the Lafitte brothers play in the war? 5. Why was New Orleans important to British strategy? 6. Why

Jackson Square has been the center of the city since New Orleans was first laid out in 1720.

were the Americans able to win even though they were outnumbered? 7. What were the results of the battle? 8. Explain how the role of Louisiana in the war helped to unite the people of the state.

Coup d'Main
(Completing the Story)

Jambalaya (Putting It All Together)

1. Summarize the conditions existing in Spain, France, England, and the United States at the time of the Louisiana Purchase.

2. How did the Louisiana Purchase affect the United States in (a) size, (b) wealth, and (c) population?

3. Map work. Outline (a) the boundaries of the Louisiana Purchase territory, (b) the part the United States was originally interested in buying, (c) the part of present-day Louisiana obtained by the purchase, (d) the two rivers that formed most of the boundaries of the Louisiana Purchase territory, (e) the part of the United States controlled by the Americans before 1803, and (f) the present states that were part of the purchase.

4. Identify (a) Andrew Jackson, (b) Casa Calvo, (c) Claiborne, (d) Jefferson, (e) Laussat, (f) Monroe, (g) Morales, (h) Napoleon, and (i) Wilkinson.

5. Compare the two transfer ceremonies.

6. Compare the contributions of France with those of Spain to the Louisiana colony.

7. Discuss the political career of W. C. C. Claiborne.

8. What factors contributed to Louisiana's Americanization?

9. Map work. On a Louisiana map show (a) the Territory of Orleans, (b) "No Man's Land," and (c) the Florida parishes. Show the part included in the state in 1812.

Potpourri (Getting Involved)

1. Get a cross-section of opinions and reactions to the Louisiana Purchase. "Interview" the people in 1803: (a) Creoles, (b) government officials of the United States, France, Spain, and England, and (c) the American settlers.

2. Reenact (a) the Louisiana Purchase from the time of the negotiations to its financing or (b) the transfer ceremonies. Do research to bring out facts not previously mentioned.

3. According to some historians, the Louisiana Purchase is rated second to the winning of American independence and formation of the Union as the most important event in

the history of the United States. Support this position.

4. Summarize Jefferson's actions to explore the territory after the purchase. Give reports on information obtained.

5. Prepare a chart showing the various nationalities represented in Louisiana.

6. Write an entry in the diary of a young American who has moved to Louisiana. Relate how you are treated by the native Louisianians. Express your opinions about your strange new surroundings.

7. Make a diorama illustrating (a) line villages, (b) the battle plan for the Battle of New Orleans, or (c) Lafitte's smuggling operations.

Gumbo (Bringing It Up-to-Date)

1. Compare (a) the price of the Louisiana Purchase with the present value of the land that was purchased, and (b) the interest rate paid for the loan with the interest rate on such a loan today.

2. Pretend that the United States were purchasing Louisiana today. If the same circumstances existed except that modern methods of transportation and communication were available, what changes would be made in the activities surrounding the purchase?

3. Compare life in Louisiana in 1803 with today.

4. Compare Louisiana in 1812 with Louisiana today in size, population, cities and towns, means of making a living, transportation, communication, government, and the ways of producing goods.

5. Contrast smuggling in Lafitte's day with smuggling today.

CHAPTER 7

ANTEBELLUM LOUISIANA
(1812–1860)

Settlements

New Orleans. The port, which was so important to the United States, was the **largest city in the South** by 1840. It was the **third largest city in America**. From 1835 to 1852 New Orleans was at the peak of its prosperity and growth. The commercial prosperity of New Orleans was due to the role it played. The port served as the outlet for the goods of most of the Mississippi Valley. This river traffic on the Mississippi was at its peak from 1840 to 1861. The port received goods from Europe, Mexico, and the Caribbean Islands. It led the nation in exports and tonnage on the wharves. In a short period New Orleans doubled the tonnage of New York. The city gained the nickname "Queen City of the South." The population of New Orleans grew rapidly.

The prosperity of New Orleans could best be seen along the bustling levee and wharves. Along a three-mile stretch of the levee at the river's crescent was an unbroken line of businesses. There were storehouses, cotton presses, and shops. Slave gangs loaded and unloaded merchandise of every description. Furs, sugar, molasses, rice, mules and horses, tobacco, corn, pork, barrel staves, wheat, oats, and flour were some of the products. Cotton far outweighed the other products. New Orleans was the largest cotton market in the world. The levee and the streets were piled high with cotton. In the 1830s steamboats arrived and departed every hour. As many as fifty lined the docks at one time. Fifty thousand bales of cotton waited for shipment almost every day.

The New Orleans banks were the largest among those of the fifteen slave-holding states. They financed cotton crops for Louisiana and other areas in the South. They were first in capital stock, deposits, and hard money.

The wide commercial connections caused New Orleans to be a **cosmopolitan city**. The population of the city consisted of many nationalities from all over the world. In fact, almost forty percent of the city's population was foreign-born.

New Orleans was the place to which the most affluent planters and professional men in rural Louisiana took their families for the social season and during the winter months. Some planters lived in New Orleans and provided homes for their overseers on their plantations. Many people came from other states to visit New Orleans.

The city became divided between the Americans and the Creoles. Creole supremacy had been a major problem since the Louisiana Purchase. For years the issue in all elections was Creole versus American. The competition between the two groups extended into every area of life. The feelings grew steadily worse. Canal Street became the dividing line between the factions. The wide median strip became known as the Neutral Ground. The Creoles built up the French Quarter. American businessmen constructed their own city on the other side of Canal Street. The more Americans came the more the supremacy of the Creoles was threatened.

The Americans kept arriving in great numbers. They changed many things about the city. A more elegant style of architecture was used. They even divided the city's government. Three separate cities were formed. From 1835 until 1852 New Orleans had a Common Council for the three districts. For seventeen years the three municipalities shared little except Canal Street. Each had its own government.

Commercial prosperity led to economic and social improvements on a large scale. By 1835 the city spent nearly five million dollars improving streets, drains, and banquettes. Even after the improvements were made, only twenty-five percent of the city was paved. Paving stones from Europe and the North were used for the project. A building boom in the 1830s produced many new hotels and other residences. Public buildings rivaled those of any other city in the nation.

Some enterprising individuals contributed to the character of New Orleans. One of these was James Caldwell. He lighted the city with gas lanterns. They were suspended on ropes or chains above the middle of the city's main streets. He built the American Theater. The theater became the destination of the wealthy ladies in their fine silks and satins. His next addition was the St. Charles Theater. Then in 1837 he completed

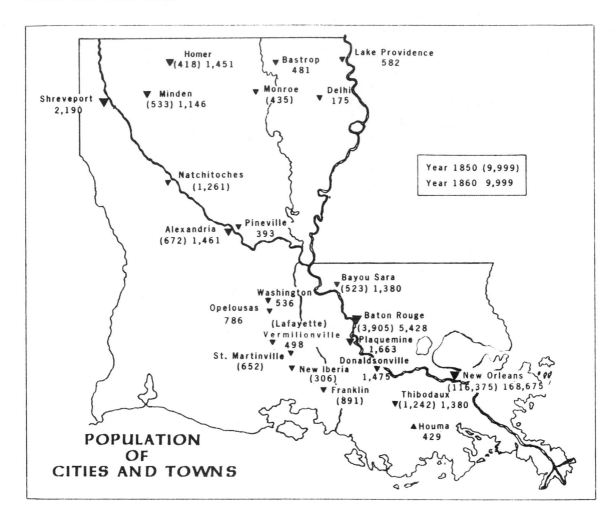

POPULATION
OF
CITIES AND TOWNS

the majestic St. Charles Hotel. He had employed James Dakin and James Gallier to build the six-storied building. The St. Charles became world famous. Its gleaming white dome could be seen for miles up and down the river.

The Creoles built their St. Louis Hotel at the same time the St. Charles was being built. The St. Louis Hotel became famous for its slave auctions, which were conducted daily. Free lunch was served around the auction block. Slaves were often costumed to make them sell better. Auctioneers also sold paintings, bales and barrels of goods, and even plantations.

Another builder of New Orleans was John Davis. His buildings included the Davis Hotel, the Orleans Ballroom, and the Theater d'Orleans. Davis also introduced big-time gambling to America. In his gambling house he offered free meals and drinks for those who played. Profits from his gambling business were used to finance his cultural offerings. He introduced grand opera and the first regular ballet troupe to New Orleans. Davis supported opera for about thirty years.

Creole millionaire Bernard de Marigny subdivided his plantation located downstream from the French Quarter. He started his own city and gave his streets fancy names. Eventually, Marigny's steet names were changed. This same man also introduced "galloping dominoes," or dice, to America.

Some of the buildings constructed during the boom had problems because of the unstable floating land. The Planters Hotel collapsed on May 20, 1835, killing twenty people. The St. Charles Hotel had settled 28 inches before it burned in 1851.

In 1850 and 1851 two apartment buildings were built flanking Jackson Square in the French Quarter. There were shops on the ground floor. The buildings were erected by Micaela Leonard Almonester, Baroness de Pontalba. They became known as the Pontalbas. These two buildings and the three built by her father—the St. Louis Cathedral, the Cabildo, and the Presbytere—are historical landmarks.

Louisiana's booming city developed quite a reputation. New Orleans was described as having the worst sanitation in America. The city was known for being an unhealthy city. The only sewers were open drains. They were frequently stopped up with waste products. When it rained, the city's streets flooded. The debris was scattered everywhere. In the dirty city, the life span of its residents was said to be the shortest in the country. The proud people of New Orleans resented any criticism of their city. They denied that it was less healthy than other places.

The people were described as being obsessed with having fun and making money. There were more alcoholics and gamblers there than in any other city in America, according to reports. Some of the best food in the world could be found in New Orleans. The city was supposed to have had the longest social calendar in the nation. Balls, ballets, and operas were regular features on the calendar of the elite.

New Orleans was the host to many important visitors. In 1825 the Marquis de Lafayette, hero of the American Revolution, came from France and toured the United States. New Orleans entertained him lavishly. Vermilionville was renamed Lafayette in his honor. Andrew Jackson visited the state in 1840.

New Capitals. New Orleans was the capital of Louisiana until 1830.

From its beginning in the French colonial period, the city had been the center of Louisiana's population. However, some people felt that New Orleans represented the French and the urban capital population too much. Most people also thought that New Orleans offered legislators too many things to do. The legislature wanted to move the capital to a rural area. It chose **Donaldsonville**. If New Orleans had provided too much entertainment for the legislators, Donaldsonville was too small and provided too little. The legislators were not happy with the area. Finally, in 1850, the capital was moved to **Baton Rouge**.

The people of Baton Rouge had given the land for the new capitol. They planned a big celebration after the first meeting of the legislature. Just before the event was to take place, Baton Rouge was swept by fire. Twenty percent of the city's buildings were destroyed. The citizens gave the money for the celebration to the disaster's victims.

Other Settlements. Most of the towns developed on the rivers and bayous as trading centers for the surrounding area. The country towns grew gradually as their neighboring trade territory developed. Baton Rouge developed after the capital was moved there. It took unusual occurrences to speed up the development of any antebellum Louisiana town. Rural population was concentrated on the plantations until late in the antebellum period.

Lagniappe. A German settlement was made in 1834 near Grand Ecore in Natchitoches Parish. A group of German immigrants, under the leadership of Count Von Leon, established a small colony. The goal was to achieve a "heaven on earth." This was one of many such colonies established at different sites in the nation. The colony was based on a plan of communal living in which all that was produced was shared by members. Tragedy struck when swamp fever hit the small settlement. Among the colony members who died was Count Von Leon.

In 1835, his widow, Countess Von Leon, took the small group to a new

SETTLEMENT BY 1840

site near Minden. The group carried on their colony until 1871. It is said that funds of the colony were lost in cotton speculations.

Twentieth-century Governor Robert Kennon is a descendant of one of the original German settlers, John Bopp.

Germantown is now an historical area where visitors may see some of the buildings and artifacts of the pre–Civil War colony. The well-kept cemetery with German names on the simple tombstones is a monument itself to those who lived there.

Towns and settlements of Louisiana in the 1840s were quite different in appearance from our cities today. Many were merely collections of scattered cabins and shacks. Streets were unlighted and unpaved. The streets became mudholes when it rained. The parish seats often had only a courthouse, a jail, a few stores, and a few private buildings. Churches, courthouses, schools, and other public buildings advanced in architectural appearance as the years went by.

Crossroad villages developed mostly around the numerous small bayou and river ports. They met the needs not met on the plantations. Although almost every plantation had its own dock where barges stopped, usually a larger point for depositing freight was necessary. From these places, wagons were used to distribute supplies to other points. The area doctor, a schoolmaster, a church, and a general store often formed a center around which community living revolved. The church became a central gathering place for people. The general store was also a favorite gathering place, and usually there was a post office in the store.

Plantations did not stimulate the growth of towns. Each large plantation was a small village within itself. Planters were merchants with plantation commissaries or general stores on their places. Even post offices were often located in plantation stores or in commissaries of the largest plantations.

Outside the New Orleans area, Louisiana was part of the western frontier of the United States. The northern part of the state was sparsely settled until after the Civil War. Great virgin forests still covered thousands of acres of land.

Lagniappe. What was "the West"? This term has meant different things to different people at different times in our history. To the first immigrants at Jamestown, it was just a short distance into the woods. To Daniel Boone and pioneers of Kentucky and Tennessee, it was beyond the Appalachian Mountains. Around 1812 it was across the Mississippi

River. The Oregon pioneers and the Forty-niners pushed it to the Pacific Ocean. From about 1830 to 1860, men thought of the West as being across the Great Plains and across the Rocky Mountains to the Pacific Ocean.

Westward Movement. Moving west was always a thought in the minds of the people of Louisiana, as elsewhere. The West, with free land (or almost free), lay across a stretch of land that anybody could reach if he wanted to badly enough. No soon-er did some of the immigrants get to Louisiana than they decided that things sounded better a little farther on. This was the mysterious appeal of the westward movement. Louisiana lost some settlers to other states after 1840. Mississippi, Arkansas, Texas, and California were the choices of most of the people who left this state. Although many thousands moved through Louisiana, many others be-came permanent Louisiana settlers. Thus, the population rapidly increased as the people moved westward.

Louisiana's population increased greatly after the Louisiana Purchase. The population of 1820 was almost double what it had been in 1812. Most of Louisiana's population at that time was French and Spanish. Many foreigners came to the state after 1830. Ireland and Germany contributed the largest numbers. Most of these for-eigners settled in New Orleans. The Irish became very active in politics. Their participation gave rise to the American movement that opposed the Creoles.

Americans came into Louisiana before 1860 mostly from these states: Alabama, Georgia, Mississippi, North Carolina, South Carolina, Tennessee, Virginia, Kentucky, New York, Penn-sylvania, Ohio, and Texas. The greatest influx from the other southern states came after 1840. This was the time when the region north of the Red River was settled.

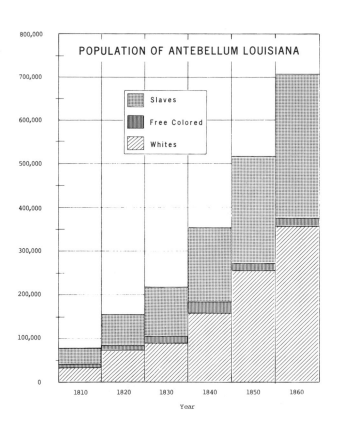

POPULATION OF ANTEBELLUM LOUISIANA

Slaves
Free Colored
Whites

Year

The free colored population in antebellum Louisiana increased until 1840. After that it remained almost stationary. Most of these people lived in the old French sections. Some were scattered over the state.

The Great Raft. The presence of the Great Raft delayed the exploration and settlement of North Louisiana. The raft was a logjam about 165 miles long that filled the bed of the Red River. The raft obstructed navigation above Natchitoches to the Arkansas border. The westward movement in the early 1830s led to an increasing demand to clear the raft. The development of the steamboat influenced the decision to try to clear the waterway.

Funds were provided by Congress to remove the logjam. The work was not progressing when an extraordinary pioneer in the development of water commerce, **Captain Henry Miller Shreve**, made suggestions. He knew how it could be done. Shreve showed how to use his snag boat *Archimedes* to loosen the logs so that they could be removed. He started his work April 11, 1833, at Campti. By June 27, 1833, he reached Coates' Bluff, located in present-day Shreveport. The worst part of the jam was above the site of Shreveport. He continued to work until 1841. Though there was great improvement, the logjam began to re-form in later years. United States engineers finally cleared the channel in 1873. They used nitroglycerine, which had not been available to Shreve.

Founding of Shreveport. Shreve and seven other men formed the Shreve Town Company on May 27, 1836. They obtained the land given to Larkin Edwards by the Caddo Indians. Then they laid out eight streets. On March 20, 1839, the legislature granted a charter to the town of Shreveport. Thus, a river settlement developed to serve North Louisiana and East Texas. The presence of the raft had delayed the development of a port at this location.

The frontier town developed into a Texas port of entry. The settlers of Texas looked to Shreveport for their

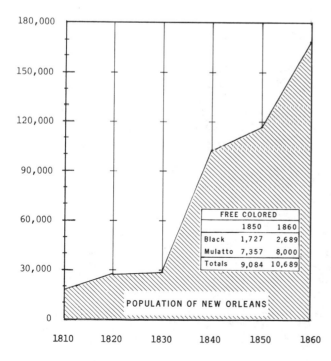

FREE COLORED		
	1850	1860
Black	1,727	2,689
Mulatto	7,357	8,000
Totals	9,084	10,689

POPULATION OF NEW ORLEANS

supplies. It was a market for their cotton, hides, and furs. Caravans of oxteams, bringing the produce, traveled the Texas Trail to the riverfront. Later, the New Orleans commission merchants built warehouses on the riverfront to store cotton until the season of high water. That was when steamboats made their trips to and from New Orleans.

There was a period when Jefferson, Texas, took much of the Texas trade from Shreveport. This was when the raft re-formed above Shreveport. After it was cleared by the use of nitroglycerine, trade again returned.

Many American immigrants finding their way to Texas came to Shreveport. The town became the point toward which this migration moved. People traveled by stagecoach from Alexandria through Natchitoches to Shreveport. Others came by stagecoach from Monroe through Mount Lebanon and Minden. Some came by covered wagon with an oxteam or by horseback or muleback. Others came up the river from New Orleans.

Henry Miller Shreve cleared the Red River of the 160-mile-long Great Raft.

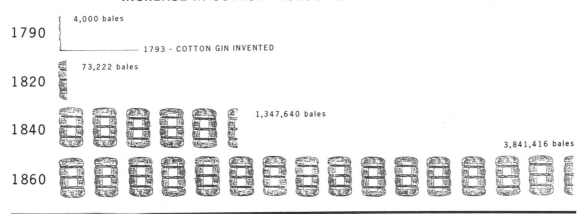

INCREASE IN COTTON PRODUCTION IN THE UNITED STATES

1790 — 4,000 bales

1793 - COTTON GIN INVENTED

1820 — 73,222 bales

1840 — 1,347,640 bales

1860 — 3,841,416 bales

Shreveport grew steadily during the twenty-four years before the Civil War. The war checked the city's growth and prosperity.

1820 . . . 1830 . . . 1840 . . . 1850 . . . 1860. During these decades, for the most part the state was being settled. Agriculture was still the leading industry. In the rich delta soil along rivers and bayous there were many plantations that were producing large cotton and sugarcane crops. North Louisiana hill country lands were still sparsely settled.

Plantations were expanded backward into the swamps. New areas of virgin soil were constantly being brought into cultivation. The small farmers along the Mississippi sold out to the planters and moved to the prairie west of the hills of North Louisiana. The number and size of plantations increased. There was an unbroken chain along the Mississippi.

As wave after wave of land-hungry cotton planters and farmers moved into Louisiana from the eastern United States, the production of cotton increased. By the middle of the 1830s more than a half million bales of cotton were produced every year. Louisiana was becoming dependent upon the cotton economy. This was true not only for the planters but also the farmers. Some farmers cultivated only a few acres. Other farms were much larger. They all raised cotton. New types of cotton were introduced. Methods of cultivation improved. Louisiana became one of the five leading cotton-producing states. It was largely from these states that the image of the plantation South emerged.

Lagniappe. *Homesteading in North Louisiana*. In 1814, twenty miles north of Plymouth, England, George

Cole was born. He was one of the youngest members of a family of twelve children. As was the custom of the lower middle class at that time, George was put out to work when he was eight years old. Few children attended school, but George's wife taught him to read in later life. He never learned to write. George's situation was not unusual. For instance, the English novelist Charles Dickens was the same age as George and went to work at age nine. The dreary, harsh, long hours of work indoors was exposed in Dickens's writings. People longed for a better life with advantages for their children.

Relatives of George Cole's wife who had settled at Minden wrote urging the couple to come to Louisiana. George Cole did not want his five children to work long, hard hours as he had done as a child. The decision was made to go with another couple of kinfolks to Louisiana.

Therefore, on October 20, 1853, George and Sarah Cole sailed from Liverpool. They landed in New Orleans and went by boat up the Mississippi River into the Red River. They arrived at Campti. In January 1854 they went overland to Minden. Sarah Grace Cole died, and one year later her husband, George, homesteaded 160 acres three miles north of Cotton Valley. In November 1856 he added 120 acres south of the land he had

homesteaded. Trees were felled and a one-room cabin with a fireplace was built on the land for George and his second wife, Mary Ann Staton.

The log cabin built by George Cole was still standing in 1973. Since then it has fallen. Shingles were hand hewn, and square nails were used. Logs were hand-pegged to fit snugly into walls. The one room had a large window and a door. Meals were cooked in another fireplace in a smaller cabin and were eaten away from the original cabin. A brick walk connected the two buildings. A well furnished water.

As the children grew up, they in turn homesteaded lands offered by the government, and so farming became a prosperous way of life in Cotton Valley. Stephen Life Cole, Sr., the youngest child of George Cole, acquired six hundred acres about one mile from the cabin of his father. Following the dream of a school for the children, a log building was built with the help of a neighbor, Kelly. On Sundays church services were held in the building. On other days school was held with one teacher for all the children. Standards and requirements set by the state were followed. There were ten pupils enrolled at all times. Each pupil proceeded through the first reader to the second and so on. The same thing was done in arithmetic. The Cole and the Kelly families furnished the teacher with room and board. The school operated from 1888 until 1904.

As the children of Stephen Life Cole, Sr., finished grammar school at the Cole-Kelly School, the first classes of Cotton Valley High School were forming. Some of the Cole children were in the first graduating classes. These graduates then attended Louisiana Polytechnic Institute at Ruston, Louisiana State Normal College at Natchitoches, and Mansfield Female College at Mansfield. Male members of the Cole family mainly continued in farming. Most of the women were schoolteachers.

Recent generations have increased the number of Cole descendants to hundreds, and the activities and work of present-day family members is varied. The land, which was patented by the government, is still held by members of this Cole family. It has never been sold. At this time, it is mostly planted with pine trees.

En Partie 1 (Studying a Part). 1. Describe New Orleans during the antebellum period. 2. Trace the change of the location of the capital. 3. Describe settlement outside of New Orleans during this period. 4. How did the westward movement affect Louisiana? 5. What was the West in 1812? From 1830 to 1860? 6. What was the Great Raft? 7. Who was Henry Miller Shreve? 8. How did the settlements of Louisiana change between 1820 and 1860?

Life in Antebellum Louisiana

Most immigrants who came to Louisiana before 1860 were farmers. These families had often moved from place to place before they finally decided on the land they wanted. Their lives were hard and simple, if we measure them by today's standards.

They were skilled in many tasks and worked long hours. They had to produce almost all of life's necessities with their own hands. There was very little money for store-bought goods even if such goods were available. Sometimes they traded their animals or farm produce with merchants, craftsmen, and millers for necessary goods or services.

They had **large families**. It was not unusual to have ten or more members. Everyone was expected to do his part of the work. The men cleared the land, built the houses and furniture, grew the crops, tended the livestock, and hunted. Women cooked, made most of the clothing, and reared the children. They washed, ironed, made soap, and performed many other household chores. The more ambitious ones even found time for a flower garden. The children did their part, too. Boys plowed, milked, hunted, fished, and gathered produce from the garden. They worked alongside their fathers. Girls cooked, sewed, and tended to the younger children. By helping their mothers, they learned the art of housekeeping. Some fortunate girls learned to play the piano or organ. Boys and girls were expected to be able to manage a farm or household by the time they were fourteen. Marriages occurred at early ages. Often, children left home at a young age.

Houses. Building a house was one of the first tasks when a family moved to a new location. The husband often set up a tent or pole shelter for temporary use by the family. Then he cleared the land and cut the timber. If he were a good woodsman, he could cut fifteen to twenty trees a day. The average man cut about eight.

Some of the houses had dirt floors while others had puncheon floors. Puncheon floors were made from short sections of heavy squared logs set on end in a bed of sand or soft dirt. The end forming the floor's surface was made as flat and smooth as possible. The logs were held together with pegs.

Plain wooden shutters covered the windows. Sometimes greased paper or thin rawhide was used in the windows to keep out mosquitoes and flies. Rarely was glass used. Even if obtainable, it was too expensive.

Furnishings in the homes varied according to the financial means of the families. Only a very few wealthy people imported furniture, draperies, and luxuries from Europe. After 1835 a few mansions were equipped with gaslights. Only rare families were able to build fine houses and furnish them with expensive furniture. Almost all Louisiana people depended

Interior of the Caspiana House, Shreveport.

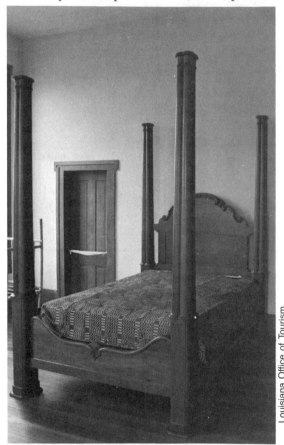

Louisiana Office of Tourism

Cooking was done on fireplaces until a decade or so before the Civil War.

upon what they could make from the materials found around them. There was plenty of hardwood in the swampland, and men skilled as carpenters built solid furniture for their houses. In fact, for the people who could not afford to purchase furniture, it was the skill of the men in the family that determined the type furnishings they had. Ordinary furniture was constructed locally. Pioneers built their beds, tables, and armoires to last. Homemade tables, stools, and wooden chairs with deerskin or cowhide seats furnished most homes. Some of their homemade furniture remains today as treasures from frontier days. Spinning wheels and looms for making homespun cloth were necessary. Wall pegs and shelves were used instead of closets. This was true even in the most elaborate homes.

There were only a few cabinetmakers. Most of them lived in New Orleans. Mallard and other skilled craftsmen who concentrated on the art of cabinetmaking left a legacy of the finest furniture. Only the wealthiest families could afford such furnishings.

Guns were usually placed over the mantel and over the front door. Guns were essential household articles for protection and hunting. Hunting and fishing provided food to supplement that produced on the land.

Ordinarily **mattresses** were stuffed with moss or corn shucks. Moss was hanging from the trees, available along the bayous for picking. Those who could afford it preferred other materials for stuffing their mattresses such as cotton and duck feathers. They considered the moss unsightly and dirty.

Rugs, if used at all, were homemade. They were sometimes woven of grass or rags or were simply cured hides of animals.

Fireplaces were the center of homelife. They were essential for cooking, heating, and lighting. Cranes and hooks made the open fireplace useful for cooking. Families and friends gathered around the fireplaces to keep warm during cold weather. Firewood was plentiful from the forests nearby. It could be obtained freely. Most families had only two or three pots and utensils that they used for cooking at the fireplace. A frying pan, a three-legged skillet, and a Dutch oven were considered essential. Blacksmiths contributed to household needs as well as the needs of the farmers. Skilled men made coffee mills, corn grinders, and sausage grinders. Such equipment was not available to everyone.

Candles lit the houses, and almost all families made their own. Before molds were available, candles were made by dipping a string into hot wax over and over again. Hot melted wax was poured into candle molds into which wicks had been placed. Some of the candles were made of tallow, a product of animal fat. Some families had lamps that burned lard.

Plumbing facilities were not available in the country. Indoor plumbing was not introduced in the cities until very late in this period. Even then, only a handful of wealthy people could afford it.

Clothing. Mostly, clothing was homemade until late in the period. The farmers grew the cotton, and the women and girls spun it into thread on a spinning wheel. They then made the threads into cloth on a loom. They cut out and sewed the clothes for the family. A few decades before the Civil War, cloth could be bought along with other supplies shipped from New Orleans to rural stores. Linsey-woolsey, a combination of flax and wool, was a favorite kind of cloth. "Jeans," a cotton-wool blend, was also popular.

The few people who could afford lace and silks from abroad had skilled dressmakers copy the latest fashions. Some imported their clothing from France and England. Tailors in New Orleans made clothing copied from fashions in Paris and London. There was an interest in fashions being worn in the cities and in the Old Country (Europe). The pioneers became clever at copying these styles in their clothes.

For dress-up occasions the gentlemen wore black frock coats with fancy vests, ruffled shirts, and string ties. Often with these went expensive leather boots and wide-brimmed hats. The planters' wives frequently had kid walking shoes. Shoes for those who could afford them were almost always made to order. Milliners made hats for sale in the city. All such luxuries came through New Orleans and were shipped out to rural Louisiana. Ready-made clothing for men and women was available in the stores of the larger towns shortly before the Civil War. Yet most clothing was still homemade.

In rural villages talented women set up hat shops. The hats sold were often made by themselves. Ordinarily shoes were sold in large lots. There was no distinction between shoes to be worn on the left or right foot. Many people made their own shoes. Leather was made from animal hides. The shoemaker was a familiar figure.

Everyday clothes were usually made from one simple pattern. Clothes were meant to be serviceable and last a long time. They took a long time to make. Most people possessed only two or three changes of clothes. There was little money to buy things that could not be made at home. The Sunday dress of silk or calico might be bought from a peddler.

Women knitted socks, braided straw hats, and embroidered pieces. They made sheets, pillowcases, towels, blankets, and quilts from their homespun cloth. In addition, it was necessary to mend everything.

Food. Providing food for the family was a major task. Quantity was important because these hardworking people used so much energy. As soon as the weather permitted, most families started a garden. Some plantation owners did not plant gardens so that they could concentrate their efforts on cash crops. It was very ex-pensive to buy vegetables, though. Four turnips cost as much as two pounds of meat. Fruit trees—plums, peaches, figs, pomegranates, and pears —were planted. Gathering vegetables from a garden, cleaning them, shelling peas and beans, and peeling cushaw or Irish potatoes were a few of the many tasks in preparing food. Preserving food for winter was a necessity. All dairy products had to be prepared at home. Milking cows, churning butter, and making cheese were jobs that had to be done. Storing butter and milk in a semitropical climate where there was no ice was a problem. It was secured in tight jars or crocks and lowered into the cool water of a well or underground cistern or the cool waters of creeks and springs. Cheese was made by the more ambitious homemakers who could find the necessary time.

Ice was not available to most rural people. It was sometimes available in the larger towns. However, it was very expensive. Huge chunks of ice were cut from the Great Lakes. It was brought down the Mississippi or by sea from New England to New Orleans. It was stored in dark, cool cellar-like structures in Louisiana ice houses. After 1850 ice was manufactured in Louisiana. Rarely was it used for preserving meats. Instead, it was used for cooling drinks. Ice was prized as an aid in lowering fevers of the very ill.

This well is similar to those used in the antebellum period.

The diet of most of the rural people was simple and monotonous. Sweet potatoes, strong coffee, and cornbread were basic parts of the diet. Other foods were added in season. Wheat bread cost as much as meat so it was not a part of the diet of rural people.

From the beginning food in Louisiana was of extraordinarily fine quality. The French, Indians, Spanish, Negroes, English, Germans, and others had contributed to an unbeatable blend of seasonings and food mixtures. There was plentiful game in the woods, and there was a wealth of fish and seafood. Bear oil, the colonial shortening, was available for frying. Pecans and other nuts were also plentiful. These were all available to those making the effort to obtain them. While the few rich people served food in fine homes with imported linen tablecloths, china, and silverware, people at all financial levels could usually eat as well even if it were not served so elegantly.

Cattle and hogs were raised for a meat supply. Some meat was prepared for family use in a variety of ways. Some was ground and made into sausage. Sometimes meat patties were fried and stored between layers of grease in a crock. A smokehouse constructed near the house was used for curing ham and other meat. Salt meat and bacon were mainstays. Poultry was raised for home use and for sale in the town markets.

Obtaining **water** for the household required considerable effort. Some families had wells. Water had to be pulled by a rope from a shallow well or pumped from the depths of an underground cistern into buckets. If a drought came, the cistern might dry up. Gutters, or shallow troughs that ran around the eaves of the house, had to be kept clean to let rainwater into the cistern. In times of water scarcity, cistern-owners hauled water in barrels or buckets from the nearest stream or creek. In some wooded areas icy spring water was available the year round. Water was transported by bucketfuls to the kitchen or bathtub. If hot water were needed, it was heated on the wood stove.

The water that could be obtained was often unfit to drink. Youngsters spent hours filtering it through porous stone or cleaning it with lime, alum, or charcoal. In New Orleans drinking water was carted from the river. It was sold for two cents a bucket.

Country Stores. All over the state men gathered at crossroads stores. They were located close enough to be reached by horseback or wagon. Men sat around the potbellied stove, chewing tobacco and talking. All the news of the countryside came up for discussion. There they exchanged news with neighbors, talked about their crops, and heard the latest cotton prices from New Orleans.

These rural stores, wherever located, became a focal point for a large area. The merchandise included a variety of items. Medicines, plows, Christmas toys, seed, horse collars, laces and ribbons, the materials needed for burials, wagons, buggies, pants, flour, coffee, sugar, fruit, shoes— everything came from the general store. All of these supplies arrived by boat from New Orleans.

Mail. Mail service was slow and uncertain. After the Louisiana Purchase there was supposed to be regular mail service. This was impossible for decades. Roads had to be improved, if not made. Ferries and bridges had to be provided.

As the migrants moved west, letters became extremely important in keeping in touch with people back home. Distances that could be traveled in less than an hour by automobile today presented problems for families wanting to visit each other. Letters then were often the only means of communication. Most had to be hand-delivered from settlement to settlement by chance meetings with migrants headed west and willing to deliver a letter.

Mail riders on horseback, stagecoaches, and boats delivered mail. Many communities in the state were totally dependent on regular steamboat lines for mail. In the early antebellum days steamboats did not make trips regularly. Mail service was irregular throughout the antebellum period.

Transportation. Horses or wagons and carts drawn slowly across the wilderness by animals provided overland transportation. A horseback trip of twenty miles took a whole day and sometimes longer. In 1817 William Darby, the first American-born naturalist, wrote that it commonly took between thirty and forty days to go overland from Natchitoches to New

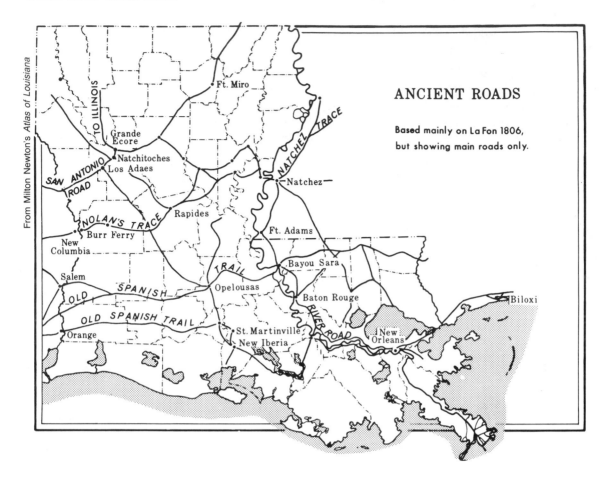

From Milton Newton's Atlas of Louisiana

ANCIENT ROADS

Based mainly on La Fon 1806,
but showing main roads only.

Orleans. There were no state high-ways during this time. There were some trails that followed Indian trails. All road construction was the responsibility of the parishes or individuals. Each landowner along a river or bayou was required to maintain a public road in front of his property. Most of these roads were impassable except when it was dry. In some places where land was swampy and timber was cheap and abundant, plank roads were built.

Land routes were less important in the transportation of mail, freight, and passengers after the steamboats became active. More regular ship connections with the Atlantic seaboard also reduced the demand for land transportation.

Most long distance travel was by boat. Canoes, pirogues, and dugouts were used for transportation by water. Rafts, arks, and broadhorns carried larger cargoes than the smaller craft. Keelboats came later and were faster.

All types of boats—flatboats, brigs, clippers, sloops, and schooners—went in and out of New Orleans. Many of these kinds of boats could also be seen on inland streams.

The first **steamboat** to arrive in New Orleans came down the Mississippi River in 1812, the same year that Louisiana became a state. Nicholas I. Roosevelt and his wife took the first steamboat, *New Orleans*, from Pittsburgh to New Orleans. People all along the way lined the river bank to see the curious craft. Many could not believe what they saw. Some doubted that it could make the return trip.

The doubters were partly right. The first steamboats did not have enough power to make the return trip. They had to stay in the lower Mississippi. Henry Miller Shreve solved the problem. He designed a boat that could go anywhere it could float. In his boat, the *Enterprise*, he made the first return trip up the Mississippi. He went to Louisville. He also made the first trip by steam up the Red River. Captain Shreve designed a boat that needed only three feet of water to keep it afloat.

The *Enterprise* was seized by agents of Robert Fulton and Robert Livingston. Fulton and Livingston had sponsored Roosevelt's trip. The Louisiana Legislature had given Fulton and Livingston a monopoly to steam navigation on Louisiana streams. Shreve challenged this grant. He said that the river was free to all. Shreve took his case to the United States Supreme Court and won. This was a very important decision. The progress of the state would have been greatly hindered if only one firm had been allowed to operate steamboats. It was still nearly a decade before steamboats came into common use, particularly on inland streams.

Steamboat navigation began on the Red River about 1820. By 1826 they were going as far up as Natchitoches. By 1840 steamboats were in use either as regular packets or for occasional trips on all the important waterways of the state. Steamboating reached its peak about 1850. By 1860 steamboat travel could be had on all rivers in the state on regular lines, except when bad conditions temporarily stopped it. By 1870 steamboating was competing with the newly laid railroad lines which gradually replaced them.

These steamboats were of two types: sternwheelers with the paddlewheel in the rear and sidewheelers with the paddlewheels mounted on both sides. Sternwheelers were more common in narrow, shallow channels. These steamboats were also specially built for a certain purpose. Cotton riverboats were built to hold that particular merchandise. The size of the cotton vessel was expressed in the load it could carry: a one-thousand-bale boat or a two-thousand-bale boat.

The heyday of river traffic on the Mississippi was between 1840 and 1861.

It took skill to load the cotton boats to capacity by fitting and balancing huge bales just so. Rates for shipping cotton varied according to the conditions of the river and the amount of freight on board. Charges also varied with prices charged by competitors. The charges were one to two dollars per bale at the lowest, and the highest charges were ten dollars per bale.

Cattle boats were common sights on the rivers of the state. Texas longhorns were driven to Shreveport and held in stock pens on Cross Bayou until shipped down the Red River on cattle boats. At the town of Washington a common sight before the Civil War were pens of cattle brought from Texas over the Texas Road winding through the wilderness to Courtableau Bayou at the inland port of Washington. There were similar arrangements along the Ouachita and other rivers for holding cattle for shipment on the rough cattle boats to New Orleans.

Some of these steamboats—packets —were operated as big businesses. Towboats moved many yards of barges transporting several hundred carloads of freight.

The boats designed for travel by the elite were floating palaces. These steamboats were really waterborne hotels with bars and barbershops. Orchestras, food prepared by skilled chefs, elegant furnishings, and entertainment made such boats vehicles for fantastic trips. Gamblers enjoyed a heyday on steamboats.

Refinements came in the steamboat as man depended on it regularly for transportation. Each year steamboats were built larger, faster, and more luxurious. However, some problems remained the same. Passengers had to contend with the heat, mosquitoes, sandbars, and ever-present dangers of fire and explosions. A steamboat blew up almost every week on some river. In 1833 Senator J. S. Johnston died in an explosion of a Mississippi steamboat. On occasion these steamboats were also the instruments for the spread of the dreaded yellow fever. Even with all the problems, though, steamboat travel was much better than the other methods available. Before steamboats it could take many months to travel from St. Louis to New Orleans. It took only eleven days for the first steamboats to make the same trip.

Steamboating gradually disappeared as the chief means of transportation. Railroad transportation took over by 1900.

There was a constant demand for clearing waterways and cutting canals to connect them with each other. The **railroad** boom came when the canal-building era in Louisiana had just started. Louisiana had only thirty-six miles of canals by 1860.

Railroad development in Louisiana began in the early 1830s. The early lines were short. They were not united in a great system as today. The first railroads in the state were built at New Orleans. They linked different waterways. The Pontchartrain Railroad connected New Orleans to Lake Pontchartrain. Other short lines linked inland towns with rivers. The Panic of 1837 put an end to the first railroad-building boom in the state. The panic caused many of the railroad companies to go into bankruptcy. The federal government finally made land grants to several railroads in the 1850s. After 1850 the second era of railroad-building got underway. Railroads gradually became the chief type of land transportation. The Civil War ended this initial building of railroads.

Education. The Constitution of 1812 made no mention of public education. That tells us the value the public and their representatives placed on education. The French and Spanish Catholics were accustomed to religious schooling. This lack of emphasis on public education remained in Louisiana until the twentieth century.

The contrast in interest in education in the state with that of New England has been made repeatedly. The lifestyles of the two sections are reflected in their different views of education. Louisiana—except for New Orleans—depended upon agriculture and its woodlands for income. The

Ralph Smith Smith, an engineer, built the first railroad west of the Mississippi River. It was built in Louisiana in 1837.

skills needed were not the same as those needed in Massachusetts or Connecticut or in other New England states. Learning the knack of planting different crops in soils that varied was part of the education received by Louisiana's boys and girls from their parents. Handling a saw, hammer, plow, or team of horses was no small thing. How to care for a sick cow or watch over a litter of newborn pigs was learned on the job. The children of farmers participated in all the phases of farm life. Some children found it interesting to learn the work of the cooper who made barrels. Or they learned from a blacksmith who sharpened plow points and made tools needed for the farm. Boys became apprentices to such craftsmen at an early age. Girls not only learned household chores but worked with poultry, gardens, and flowers—all part of Louisiana rural life.

Children of planters, merchants, and professional people had different lifestyles. The governing planter class felt that it was the responsibility of every man to take care of the education of his own children. Many of these children were taught in their homes by **private tutors**. Parents able to afford it educated their children in this manner throughout the period. **Private academies** were also established by the elite.

From 1803 to 1845 the policy of **beneficiarism** was practiced in the funding of schools. The practice of beneficiarism went along side by side with the academy movement. The legislature provided funding for two or three academies in each parish. Groups of private citizens organized to form an academy. The money with which to construct the first buildings was contributed by the legislature. For five years thereafter state funds were provided for these academies. Since the planter-merchant class dominated the government, they could vote such funding. Parents paid fees to the school as well as boarding fees. The payment of state funds to what were actually private schools was explained by the fact that each was expected to enroll a specified number of indigents, or needy persons.

The reputation of public schools caused proud people in Louisiana and the rest of the South to reject them. Early public schools were called "**paupers' schools.**" In the society of that day to be a pauper, or a poor person, was a disgrace. The people outside the planter class refused to send their children to public schools for that reason. It would have meant that they accepted the fact that they were of the lower class. The idea of paupers' schools came to Louisiana with those migrating here to make new homes. (Some have called this and many other ideas brought from older sections of the country the "**cultural baggage**" of migrants.)

In the Constitution of 1845 there was a plan for a public school system. It remained on paper. The Constitution of 1852 also affirmed the interest in public education. Little or nothing was done to convert the interest into schools. One historian wrote that Louisiana had the best public school system in the South, but it was only on paper. Little progress was made in the development of free public schools before 1860.

In short, only those who had the money to afford private schools or tutors received a formal education before the Civil War. Some private schools had high standards for their studies. Many did not.

During the antebellum period higher education was almost entirely for men. Some sons of Louisianians were sent abroad to be educated. Some of the French who were able to afford it sent their sons to France. Some were sent to northern and eastern colleges for advanced work. As hostilities increased between the two sections, this pattern stopped. There were very few doing work of today's college level in antebellum Louisiana colleges. Much of the higher education was vocational. The colleges in Louisiana compared favorably with those in other states, however.

Two schools for free people of color existed in New Orleans. Funds for them were provided by the great philanthropist, John McDonogh.

Libraries. The state library was founded in 1838. By the end of the antebellum period the larger towns had some sort of library facility. In 1842 in New Orleans B. F. French opened his extensive private library to public use. In 1846 it contained 7,500 volumes. Many private citizens had large collections. French's was no doubt the largest in the state. Some of them were willing to allow others to use their books. Many of them advertised in the papers for return of missing books that had been borrowed.

Recreation and Amusement. The variety and character of recreational activities depended upon the population and the locality. New Orleans had theatrical performances, opera, and musical concerts. Other towns had quite a variety of amusements as well. Only when the rural population could get to town did they enjoy these offerings.

The rural population usually depended upon homemade amusements. Since people in Louisiana lived mostly on farms, the amusements fitted in with their way of living. Fishing, hunting, and swimming were important forms of recreation. Fish fries and gatherings after a hunt were joyous occasions. Small boys learned to fish and hunt as they learned to walk and talk.

Having sugarcane "chews," popping corn, and pulling taffy at syrup mills were things boys and girls enjoyed. Some men and boys liked to carve wood. Some types of work were social occasions. Neighbors got together for a house or barn raising or a quilting bee. The hostess often served a meal. Telling tales was a big part of the fun. Weddings, christenings, rail splittings, wood choppings, and election days were festive occasions.

The people enjoyed other activities. Billiards was a favorite indoor sport for both men and women. This pastime was usually confined to the upper classes. Cardplaying was a popular pastime for both sexes. Bull-

and bearbaiting were sports that faded out by the 1820s. Cockfights and boxing were popular, too.

While the affluent hosted balls, the less well-to-do danced to the music of a fiddler. Musical instruments were made by skilled whittlers. The Virginia reel was danced by old and young. Minstrel shows and plays by amateur theater groups added some variety to the entertainment.

Horse racing was one of the routine pleasures of the people. The planters and farmers, as well as people in New Orleans and the villages around the state, spent much leisure time at the horse races. Famous animals ran races before fashionable crowds. There were small racetracks in both farm and plantation communities. Some of the largest racetracks were located in New Orleans. Other racetracks were located in Baton Rouge, Alexandria, St. Francisville, Natchitoches, Opelousas, Franklin, and New Iberia. Enthusiastic groups met on Sunday afternoons to watch local horses prove their abilities to outrun competitors.

Jockey clubs were organized at most of these racetracks. They held regular meetings.

Lagniappe. In the 1840s a planter from Natchitoches named Ambrose Lecomte gave a small colt to another planter named Thomas Jefferson Wells.

Wells was very proud of the little colt and named it Lecomte for the man who gave it to him. Wells owned a plantation on the Texas Road in central Louisiana. He did not grow cotton, corn, or sugarcane, but he raised fine animals. Wells and his brothers had gone to college in the Bluegrass area of Kentucky. They visited South Carolina, also noted for fine horses at that time. There they learned to appreciate horses and cattle.

The outlines of the old track used for training Lecomte can still be seen in

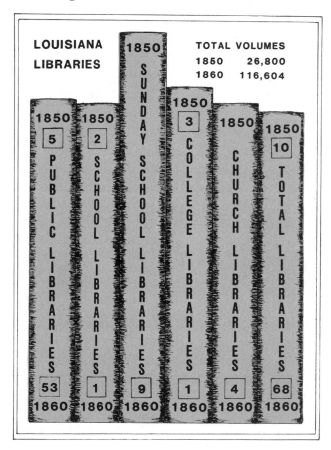

LOUISIANA LIBRARIES

TOTAL VOLUMES
1850   26,800
1860   116,604

PUBLIC LIBRARIES 1850 — 5 1860 — 53

SCHOOL LIBRARIES 1850 — 2 1860 — 1

SUNDAY SCHOOL LIBRARIES 1850 1860 — 9

COLLEGE LIBRARIES 1850 — 3 1860 — 1

CHURCH LIBRARIES 1850 1860 — 4

TOTAL LIBRARIES 1850 — 10 1860 — 68

a circle of crepe myrtle trees. A slave named Harkness became famous as the man who trained Lecomte. His fame grew as the horse became a sensation wherever people admired race horses. Lecomte achieved such a reputation that other owners of famous horses wanted to enter their horses in races against the colt.

Finally, the biggest race of all was held at Metairie Race Track in New Orleans in 1854. Lecomte was scheduled to race Lexington. Lexington was the half-brother of Lecomte and a world champion. They were to race in three heats. There was feverish excitement as people gathered in New Orleans to be on hand for the race. There were supporters for both horses ready to see the event. The St. Charles Hotel was overflowing with enthusiastic racetrack fans. Approximately ten thousand people watched the big event. Lecomte won the race, beating Lexington in two heats.

The little village near Wells's plantation where Lecomte was trained was renamed Lecomte in honor of the racehorse. The village, still bearing the name, stands today a few miles south of Alexandria. The spelling was changed by a sign painter who put a *p* where it did not belong.

Another widespread activity was Mardi Gras. This was a celebration among the South Louisiana French left over from the days when Louisiana belonged to France. New Orleans had been celebrating Mardi Gras in various ways for many years. In 1838 the first formal parade was held. Maskings and balls were a big part of the Mardi Gras season.

Rural Mardi Gras was not celebrated the way it was in New Orleans. The men of rural communities gathered the night before Shrove Tuesday, a day of celebration before the forty days of Lent in which Roman Catholics fasted. The men made plans that night to "run the Mardi Gras." They decided which roads the group would follow the next day.

By daylight the next day, the men met again. This time they were all on horseback. They wore colorful costumes and homemade masks made by their wives or sweethearts. They wore tall pointed hats. Their plan was to ride through the countryside and collect materials to make gumbo, a heavy soup. All morning the Mardi Gras riders traveled. Their leader remained unmasked. He carried a cow horn he blew to lead his followers. The men followed an old ritual. The leader knocked at the door and asked the farmer and his wife if his men could "run the Mardi Gras" on their farm. If they said yes, the leader of the riders blew his horn.

Then the riders dismounted and did a merry little dance for the farmer and his family to see. It was sort of a "thank you" for giving them something for the "big gumbo." The riders invited them to come that night and eat gumbo with them.

Sometimes the farmer and his wife gave the men sausage or rice or sweet potatoes for the night's feast. Sometimes they laughed and told them that maybe they could catch a chicken or pig. The men raced to catch the squawking hen or rooster, a duck, or whatever they were given to put in the gumbo. As they mounted their horses to ride away, they sang a French song that has been sung since Louisiana was settled. Their song asked for a little fat hen, then for a little bit of lard, and a little bit of rice, and so on.

The night's entertainment began with eating gumbo and drinking and ended with a *fais-do-do*, a dance for everybody.

Organized folklore groups have renewed public interest in running the Mardi Gras—*le courir*. The most prominent one is run at Mamou. Modern celebrations are on a larger scale than the spontaneous earlier ones.

North Louisiana residents were much more strict than people of South Louisiana in their attitude toward amusements. For many Protestants, drinking, dancing, and other amusements were forbidden. Therefore, other sports and festivities entertained many North Louisianians. Commu-

nity sings were organized for groups to sing gospel songs. Ability to sing or play the piano or organ was much prized. Quartets, duets, and soloists performed for the songfests, also. Camp meetings, as well as religious events, were social.

Honor and Violence. The South had no publishing houses of any size. Those were in the North. Books, therefore, came mostly from the North. Books from the North were looked on with suspicion. These books dealt with slavery and shed an unfavorable light on the South. It was for this reason that the planters before the Civil War looked to England for reading matter. The writer Sir Walter Scott wrote stories about Old England with knights and fair ladies. These books were very popular not only in Louisiana but all over the South. Plantations were named Waverly, Melrose, and other names used by Scott.

The picture of the knights and their ladies fitted the image planters had of their society. Women were to be placed on pedestals, like saints. They were to be treated as delicate creatures. That idea trapped the women of the plantations. Their role was spelled out. They were never considered men's equals. The woman was to be protected by the man.

The planter was much concerned with honor. This too had knightly associations. English knights had a code of honor. This code was adapted to suit the Southern planter. It became part of the planter lifestyle. Honor was spelled with a capital *H*. Men had to defend their Honor. If someone suggested that a planter was not telling the truth, he felt that he had reason to kill his detractor. If there were a rumor started about a woman by a man, a male member of her family felt that he had to defend the family Honor. He did not usually pull out his pistol and shoot the offender but was more likely to challenge him to a duel. Creoles called it "an affair of honor." Americans called it **dueling**. Arguments over politics were a common cause for duels. Friends sometimes killed one another in these exercises in the name of Honor. The least thing could provoke a challenge.

Bienville had outlawed dueling in 1722. Both the Spanish and French governments enacted strict laws but never enforced them. Duels were not legal when Louisiana became a state. This did not seem to matter. Duels continued. There were very firm rules laid down for duelists. Only the planter class fought duels. No planter would lower himself fighting a duel with a man of lower status. Until the Civil War there were very few men in public life who had not fought a duel. Governor Claiborne fought Daniel Clark. Micajah Lewis, the governor's secretary and brother-in-law, was killed in a duel. The victor had protested Claiborne's policies.

Dueling in New Orleans was widespread and difficult to control. There were probably more duels in New Orleans than in any other place in the United States. There were thousands of duels fought under the Dueling Oaks in what is now City Park. Duels were fought in that location for almost eighty years.

There were many young men trained by experts in the use of weapons. At one time New Orleans had academies for sword, rapier, and pistol training. A mulatto, who was not allowed to duel because of his race, taught dueling to the top Creoles.

New Orleans had a dueling "master of masters," Don José Pépé Llulla. The greatest swordsman in Louisiana, he fought forty-one duels. He advertised for a challenge by putting up posters in three languages. He could not get another match.

One of the state's most famous duels was fought in 1827. It was called the **Sandbar Duel**. It was fought by a group of planters from Rapides Parish. Jim Bowie, later one of the heroes of the Alamo, took part in it. The duelists had their friends with them as support. The two groups had longstanding hostilities toward each other. Some of the anger came from gossip about a woman related to several men of the party. The largest part of the friction stemmed from differences over politics. The chief argument was over the political race for the presidency of the United States. Some of the planters supported Henry Clay. Others supported Andrew Jackson.

The two groups left Alexandria in their horsedrawn carriages for the dueling site on neutral ground. It was to be held on a sandbar in the Mississippi River. The sandbar was located in neither Louisiana nor Mississippi. It was not subject to the laws of either state. The duel was held as planned. Neither of the duelists was a very good marksman. Neither was so much as grazed. Instead, their supporters got into a shooting spree. Two were killed.

War and Courage. Men, especially in the planter class, felt that men proved their courage in war. It was part of a boy's training in the early days of the state to become a fine marksman. Too, a boy was expected to become an excellent horseman. In those days when wars were fought by men on horseback in face-to-face combat, those skills were important.

Stories about the Battle of New Orleans and the men who fought there were told over and over. General Jackson, Dominique You, Lafitte, and the smartly dressed British were known to every boy growing up in Louisiana in the years after the famous battle. Stories of Jim Bowie and his famous knife were told and retold. The gallant defense of the Alamo was a favorite story. Many Louisianians had joined the fight for Texas independence.

When Texas came into the Union, there was talk about a war with Mexico. That war came in 1846, and many volunteers left their homes in Louisiana to fight the Mexicans. General Zachary Taylor, stationed at Fort Jesup, recruited men for the Mexican War. Patriots held barbecues and "speakings." Frank Bennett, age eleven, wrote to his uncle in New York in 1847: "I attended a Barbeque last week. Us had a fine dinner and two speeches and delivered by V. P. Thudly and the other by Mr. Taylar. War is all the talk. A good many went from this place to fight, I think if I was old enough I should be off like a brave fellor to help to give them jesse. Pa is contented to Stay at home and fight grass for he has plenty of it."

The sheriff of Bennett's parish and a number of others left for the Mexican War. The sheriff, Leroy Stafford, later became a general in the Civil War. The entire state sent about six thousand volunteers to the Mexican War. They were equipped by the state. The Louisiana Legion was organized. Some Louisianians gained fame in the Mexican War. Major P. G. T. Beauregard, Captain Braxton Bragg, and Colonel Jefferson Davis, Taylor's son-in-law, were the best known.

Lagniappe. Zachary Taylor is the only United States President in whom Louisiana has had any claim as a son of the state. In fact, the "Taylor for president" movement started in Louisiana during the last half of 1847. There were rallies, barbecues, dinners, and mass meetings held in various parts of the state.

General Zachary Taylor was in com-

mand of the United States troops of the Southwest. His headquarters were in Baton Rouge during 1827 and 1828. In 1840 he was sent to Baton Rouge again.

In 1840 he did not live at the army post. Instead, he bought a small cottage on the banks of the Mississippi. The cottage had been the residence of a Spanish commandant. He returned to his home after the Mexican campaign. He also owned a plantation with three hundred slaves. Louisiana was his home until he went to the White House in 1848.

The Mount Lebanon Baptist Church was built in 1837. The Louisiana Baptist Association was organized here.

Louisiana Office of Tourism

Religion. Catholicism was the only religion legally present in Louisiana at the time of the Louisiana Purchase. The church grew steadily during the antebellum period. Many Protestant churches became a part of Louisiana as Americans moved in. Baptists and Methodists gained a strong position by 1830 and continued their development. They became particularly strong in North Louisiana. The Episcopal, Presbyterian, Lutheran, and Disciples of Christ churches were fewer in number. There were Jewish synagogues as well. Before 1850 there was one in New Orleans. By 1860 there were five Jewish synagogues in the state.

Protestant churches were built wherever enough people settled to support them. Louisiana was considered a missionary field throughout the antebellum period. Camp meetings held in the open air were common as the hill country became settled by small farmers from the seaboard states. Church suppers, bazaars, and socials brought people out in their Sunday best. Churches played social, religious, and even political roles.

Slaves usually attended the churches of their owners. Some of these churches were built with special balconies for the slaves, or else segregated space was set aside on the same floor. There was so much fear of blacks plotting to obtain their freedom that the planters did not dare risk their gathering together even for religious worship.

It was considered sinful not to belong to a church, but this did not mean that all people attended church regularly. In New Orleans the priests complained that the people did not attend church regularly. The priests said that the women usually went to mass every day, but the men did not attend. The church occupied a very important place in the community, but transportation outside New Orleans was slow and distances from churches often long. Roads were mostly muddy trails, and church members often lived far apart on farms. The circuit-rider preachers served many communities. The children and young people got much of their religious training at home. Matters relating to the Bible were debated frequently. The family Bible was the one book that almost every family owned.

Health Care. Illnesses were frequent during the antebellum period. There were many fearsome epidemics. The death rate in New Orleans was twice that of most large urban areas. The rate for Americans was higher than for blacks and Creoles.

New Orleans suffered from epidemics of **yellow fever, malaria,** and **typhoid fever** from time to time. During these epidemics boats were prohibited from going to and from New Orleans to keep the fever from spreading into other parts of the state. Despite this precaution, the fevers seemed to spread. Bedding and clothes were burned. Sulphuric acid was used to try to keep the disease from spreading. New Orleanians refused to drink river water. They drank their cistern water instead. They did not know that cistern water was a good breeding ground for the *Aedes aegypti* mosquito, the unknown carrier of yellow fever.

Yellow fever was the unsolved mystery of the nineteenth century. From 1817 to 1860, there were twenty-three yellow fever epidemics in Louisiana. During these forty-three years there were 28,292 deaths. After the 1822 epidemic an ordinance forbade the tolling of church bells and chanting of priests during funerals. The ringing of bells was very depressing. In 1853 one of the worst, if not the worst, epidemics struck. It had been six years since New Orleans had had an epidemic. That year about half of the population was stricken. More than 40,000 cases were recorded. At least 50,000 people left the city that summer. About 10,000 of those who remained died. From 12 to 15 died every hour. In the little inland port of Washington one-third of its population of around 300 persons died.

During one day, August 20, 1853, or "the Black Day," 269 people died in New Orleans. The city businesses, banks, and stores closed. After most of the patients died and the rest left, one hospital was abandoned. In the

next six years about 12,000 more died of yellow fever in New Orleans.

Besides yellow fever, there were other epidemics. In 1832 there was a cholera epidemic. Malaria plagued Louisiana residents. It broke out every summer. Deadly fevers spread through communities killing many people. Typhus and typhoid fever took their toll. Yellow fever and cholera were the diseases that people dreaded most. People died by the dozen in a day's time when these epidemics came. Infantile paralysis (poliomyelitis)—which was not yet identified—was common.

There were few **doctors**. Trained doctors could be found in New Orleans and some of the other towns. Some of these were educated in the best medical schools in the United States and abroad. Many rural doctors were simply men who felt that they had the knack of healing. Would-be doctors served as apprentices to doctors until the twentieth century. A doctor's education up to that point was often no more than grade school. It was said that doctors who had been to college charged more. All doctors did a large amount of charity work. Charity Hospital rendered a great service to the poor of New Orleans. Charity services also took care of people who became ill while traveling in the state. The parish police juries took care of the poor who could not afford to pay.

An effort was made to start a

board of health for the city of New Orleans. The board lasted only a few years. Other organizations helped with health care. In 1837 a volunteer group to aid the sick was formed in New Orleans. It was called the Howard Association. In 1842 it was chartered by the legislature. The group cared for the sick and tried to provide for the children left orphans after each epidemic. Similar groups were founded in other towns of the state for similar purposes. Religious societies and other similar organizations gave valuable voluntary aid in cases of epidemics.

The life expectancy in antebellum Louisiana was short in comparison to that of modern times. People died at an early age. Many did not live to be thirty or forty years old. The infant mortality rate was unbelievably high. Many things contributed to this short life expectancy. Superstitions, poor sanitation, polluted water, and lack of trained doctors all had an effect.

Most sick people were treated with **home remedies**. Laxatives, like castor oil; quinine; other medicines that caused vomiting; and medicinal tea, such as sassafras, were favorite treatments. Hot cane juice, tar, honey, egg whites, spices, mineral oils, and alcohol were used by housewives as medicines for their families. Herbs were often used for medicine and were mostly from prescriptions of Indians. Housewives used cobwebs to stop bleeding and prickly-ash bark for toothaches. Occasionally, the housewife had to set a broken bone or perform simple surgery.

The planter was responsible for the health of his slaves. Slaves who were ill were sometimes cared for in plantation hospitals on the larger plantations. Most slaves probably remained at their own cabins, and medicine was taken to them there.

Burials. Women made shrouds while men made coffins of wood to bury the dead. The services were conducted at home. In the rural areas burial was in a family graveyard near the house or cabin.

In New Orleans people were buried above the ground. The ground was soggy. Water was about eighteen inches below the surface. Graves filled with water shortly after they were dug. New Orleanians, therefore, adopted the Spanish custom of above-ground burials. These "cities of the dead" soon became filled with magnificent granite and marble structures designed by funerary architects. Dominique You, Marie Laveau, and the two brides of Governor Claiborne are among those buried in these "ovens" (the name used by the local residents).

Lagniappe. All Saints Day is set aside as the day to clean and decorate

THE PLANTATION CASTE SYSTEM

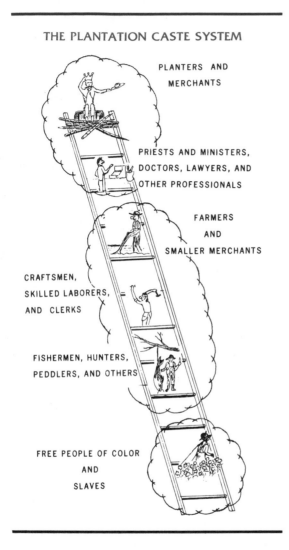

PLANTERS AND MERCHANTS

PRIESTS AND MINISTERS, DOCTORS, LAWYERS, AND OTHER PROFESSIONALS

FARMERS AND SMALLER MERCHANTS

CRAFTSMEN, SKILLED LABORERS, AND CLERKS

FISHERMEN, HUNTERS, PEDDLERS, AND OTHERS

FREE PEOPLE OF COLOR AND SLAVES

the cemetery. Families whitewash the houses of the dead, cut grass, and place flowers on the graves. The traditional flower is the chrysanthemum.

Care of Criminals. Louisiana had a penitentiary system that was above average for all the states. The state jail was located in New Orleans until 1832. Then it was moved to Baton Rouge. Each parish maintained a jail for prisoners who were awaiting trial for serious offenses.

In the early years in New Orleans, convicts were employed on the streets. In Baton Rouge convicts worked in industries located in the prison. After 1842 Negro convicts were assigned to the state board of public works. They built levees, cleared bayous, and built highways. After 1844 the state penitentiary was leased to private individuals. The convicts then worked in the industries within the prison walls for these individuals. The practice was criticized throughout the state. It was felt that the use of the penitentiary was unfair competition since the convict labor was free.

En Partie 2 (Studying a Part). 1. Summarize what life in Louisiana was like during this time. 2. Describe a yellow fever epidemic. 3. How did the fight for Texas independence and the Mexican War affect Louisianians? 4. What gave a great boom to transportation in 1812? 5. Why did education make so little progress?

The Caste System

Louisiana had a caste system, or a rigid arrangement of social classes.

At the top were the planters, who considered themselves aristocrats. At the bottom of the social ladder were the slaves, who numbered as many as all others who lived in the state. Besides the planters, the aristocracy included merchants, bankers, lawyers, and doctors, as well as other well-to-do businessmen. Between the aristocracy and the slaves were the remainder of the white people living in the

state. This class included farmers, small businessmen, craftsmen, and others. Somewhere, sandwiched just above the slaves, were the free people of color.

Status was directly related to the way people made a living. The only white employees on plantations were often overseers and storekeepers. Most plantations had a skilled blacksmith, who welded broken plow parts, sharpened plow points, and the like. A cooper, who made barrels and other wooden containers, and carpenters were often on the planter's payroll. Others were hired as sugarmakers. On many plantations skilled slaves performed these different crafts. Extra skilled labor was hired during the sugarcane grinding season. Planters sometimes relied on Irish laborers for clearing land, ditching, and other types of plantation work.

Some redemptioners, or indentured servants, were used on plantations in Louisiana. Indentured servants had come to Louisiana in colonial days. After statehood they continued to come. The Germans proved to be the most dependable of the group. Many served their terms and became independent farmers or joined the planter class.

Status was an invisible fact of life in plantation country. It was not something that could be abandoned. The master class kept a social distance not only from the slaves who

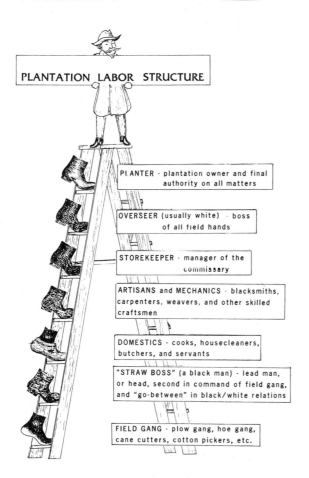

PLANTATION LABOR STRUCTURE

PLANTER - plantation owner and final authority on all matters

OVERSEER (usually white) - boss of all field hands

STOREKEEPER - manager of the commissary

ARTISANS and MECHANICS - blacksmiths, carpenters, weavers, and other skilled craftsmen

DOMESTICS - cooks, housecleaners, butchers, and servants

"STRAW BOSS" (a black man) - lead man, or head, second in command of field gang, and "go-between" in black/white relations

FIELD GANG - plow gang, hoe gang, cane cutters, cotton pickers, etc.

worked their fields but also from all others not of their class. The caste system grew with the necessity of controlling the slave population. The idea of a superior people who had a right to command those beneath them was essential in a slave society. The first rule for controlling slaves was to use the idea that people who were slaves were born inferior. This had to do with the prime goal in any plantation society: to maintain its labor supply.

Since there were as many blacks as whites in Louisiana, the problem was a very real one. The ratio of blacks to whites in the lowlands was far greater than that. In a community of plantations two-thirds or more of the population were black. In the hill country there were usually either no blacks at all or very few. If there were any, it was usually a family of free people of color. Almost all blacks in the state were slaves. At least ninety percent of all Louisiana blacks lived on plantations. Many free people of color lived in Natchitoches and New Orleans. Others were scattered all over the state.

Members of the planter elite felt superior to other whites as well as blacks. The planter class could allow no challenge to its authority. Planters were forced into a pattern of interlocking controls. Since the days of the first plantation on the east coast, the planter did what he felt he

must. The planters made themselves leading figures in every walk of life. In politics, in the churches, and in society, the authority of the planter prevailed. He and his fellow planters took over the government. Above all, the domination of government was essential in controlling the slave labor force.

Farmers began locating in the hills of North Louisiana about 1840. A few had come in much earlier. Usually they worked small tracts of land. In the uplands families cut down trees, cleared the land, and made small farms. The farmer depended upon himself and his family for the work needed. The small farm afforded enough land for the family to raise necessary foodstuffs. Space to raise pigs for a winter meat supply was included. Pasture for a milk cow was required.

The idea that all farmers dreamed of becoming planters has little to do with reality. These people and the planter represented quite different lifestyles. Farmers more often despised the lowland dweller who owned slaves. Generally, he felt that the planter represented an immoral society. The stories of planters having slaves as mistresses were heard in the highlands. The Protestant from the hills was horrified at what he considered a sin. He believed in relying on himself. He honored work, and he had no respect for people who depended

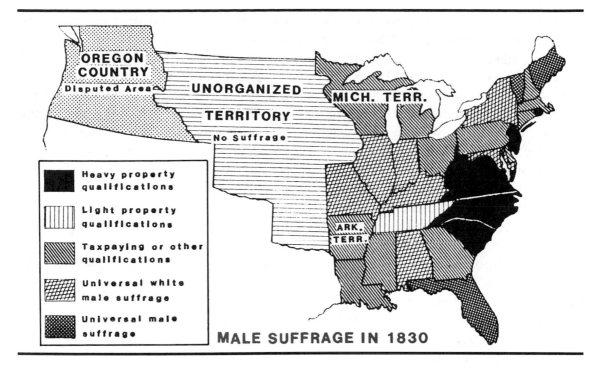

MALE SUFFRAGE IN 1830

Legend:
- Heavy property qualifications
- Light property qualifications
- Taxpaying or other qualifications
- Universal white male suffrage
- Universal male suffrage

upon others to "wait on them."

Not all nonplanter whites were farmers. Since Louisiana was predominantly rural, most were farmers. But others might be designated as "plain people." They included townspeople, clerks, tanners, coopers, and persons in a variety of trades.

It is necessary to understand the lifestyle of these basic groups—the planters, the slaves, the farmers, and plain people—in order to get the setting before the Civil War. There were, of course, merchants and others in the society. Merchants were closely tied to the planter class.

The Planters. There was a special reason for this great inpouring of

people into Louisiana after it was bought by the United States. The states bordering on the Gulf of Mexico were found ideal for growing short staple cotton. Many planters or their sons from the Carolinas and Virginia were looking for new land. They joined thousands of planters and farmers growing cotton for a living in Louisiana. Certainly, Louisiana was a land of plantations, mostly cotton plantations. Cotton was grown all over the state. It was a part of the Southern plantation system.

Plantations, based on slavery, were similar to old feudal institutions of early England and European nations. The idea of a lordly owner employing large numbers of people to work his lands was little different. Plantations used the black slaves. The owners of such enterprises in the Old World were pledged to provide soldiers for their king. This situation was of course absent in the New World. However, even the notion of the soldiers of the Old World had its parallel in New World plantations. Knights and chivalry, dueling, and admiration of the soldier were a part of the plantation lifestyle. Because of the military association, almost every leading planter acquired a military title. Few of these titles were earned on a battlefield.

Plantations were first settled in Virginia when the colony was owned by a private company. Plantations were used by many nations to transport labor and settle large tracts of land. The planters were given complete control of their plantations. As long as they did not violate the laws of Virginia and England, the planters made whatever decisions they wished on their own plantations.

The English-speaking people who came into Louisiana from older plantation sections continued this pattern. It was very little different from the plantations of the French or Spanish pioneers, which they found when they arrived. Planters of the colonial period had claimed the rich lands along the Mississippi River. They had also laid out plantations along the bayous and rivers nearest New Orleans. There

were some plantations on the Red River and a few on the Ouachita River.

Almost every person in Louisiana made his living in agriculture. Most of the agricultural holdings were small or large farms rather than plantations. Between twenty and twenty-five percent of the white people lived on plantations in antebellum Louisiana. Lawyers were mostly concerned with the business of planters. This was true of bookkeepers and other white-collar workers. The planter himself was involved not only in agriculture but in related businesses as well. These enterprises involved a number of people. In some way everyone in Louisiana was involved in the plantation system. Since the planter class dominated the government and set the standards, everyone was directly or indirectly under their control. The entire financial system was directly related to agriculture.

In the first years of settlement families of planters, like those of farmers, were usually very large. Not all of a man's sons could make a living on their father's plantation. Traditionally, French planters divided their land equally among their heirs. Among the English, the oldest son received the plantation and all that went with it upon the death of the father. He became responsible for his father's place in the family and in the community. It was his duty to care for the widow and his father's younger children. Since life expectancy was short, the planter often left a number of small children in the care of the eldest son. There were no systems like today's social security or public welfare to provide help. At this period in history only rare women took over the management of a plantation.

Planters found that they not only had to produce crops but they also had to market, or sell, them. Financing a huge plantation took a large amount of money. The planter ordinarily did not have the funds. He had to borrow the money. In the colonial days there was not enough money in Virginia and other colonies to finance the plantations. There were no banks in the early history of the colonies. Planters in the East and Southeast borrowed the money from England.

Communication with England was very slow. A letter from the colonies to England was carried on a sailing ship. The trip across the ocean took more than a month. The planter, therefore, had to have a contact in England to tend to his business there. The financial agents in England were called factors.

Factors borrowed money from banks in England for the planter. The unplanted crop was part of the security required by the factor. In other words, the planter promised that when the crop was harvested, it would be shipped to the factor in England. The factor sold the crop, paid the debts of the planter, including the factor's own fees, and sent any money left over to the planter. The amount he paid himself ordinarily included about two percent of the money received for the crop. It represented his earnings for handling the planter's banking business. This pattern of financing the growing of crops on plantations came to Louisiana with the westward migration of planters. It has had a big impact on the development of the state's economy.

New Orleans served the developing state of Louisiana in the same way that England had served the eastern planters. In fact, New Orleans developed as the leading financial center of the South. It served planters in a large area, down the Gulf to the east. New Orleans was the financial center for Mississippi planters as well as those in Louisiana. Factors were in business in New Orleans. They lent money against unplanted crops. The factors did both purchasing and marketing for the planter. There was a settlement at the end of each crop year.

The early plantations, mostly French, developed close to New Orleans. There are several reasons why these plantations were so located. The planters needed the river for transportation of their products. Also, the soil in that region was very rich. There was rich soil along all the rivers and bayous in the state, however. The main reason for locating near New Orleans was the role played by the city.

The business of planters was not limited to agriculture. The planter had to feed and clothe his slaves. He had to secure large quantities of supplies. Therefore, he found it convenient to have a commissary, or store, on the plantation. His factor purchased what the planter ordered. Items for the planter, his family, his slaves, the farm animals, equipment, and the like were kept at the commissary. Some commissaries became country stores serving a number of people living within its area.

Each plantation was its own little world. Most of the work was done by hand. There were few machines of any kind. The plantation produced grain for making meal for bread. Most had gristmills to grind corn into meal. Smaller planters took grain to the mill. A small portion of the cornmeal was left at the mill in payment for milling. There were almost always blacksmiths and coopers on the plantations. The blacksmith made plows and kept the hoes and plow points sharp. The cooper manufactured products of wood such as barrels, buckets, hoe handles, spokes for wheels, "dough" bowls, and many other items. There were often saw-

mills to make planks from the trees cut off the back woodlands. If the plantation raised sugarcane, there was sure to be a sugar mill or a syrup mill. Many plantations had cotton gins for separating the seed from the cotton fibers. In such a way the planter operated other businesses. He was a merchant and small manufacturer as well.

The workday on a plantation for both whites and blacks usually began just before sunrise. The plantation bell sounded to call the workers to the fields. Negro slaves, living in the "quarters," reported to work in the fields at daylight and worked all day long. The day ended when the sun set. There was always work to do. When it rained, work was done indoors. On most plantations slaves had Saturday afternoon and Sunday off.

The plantation needed to produce a crop for which there was a demand on the world market. In the East it had been tobacco. In Louisiana it was cotton. The story of Louisiana in the entire nineteenth century is closely connected with cotton. Sugarcane also was a major crop in South Louisiana.

Sugarcane had become an important staple on the lower Mississippi before the Louisiana Purchase. Several advancements caused the growing of sugarcane to spread. In 1817 Jean Coiron, a Louisiana planter, introduced the state to ribbon cane, a hardier type than the Creole cane. In 1822 Coiron was the first to use steam engine power instead of horsepower to grind his cane. In 1830 a free person of color, Norbert Rillieux, introduced the vacuum pan process of making sugar. It revolutionized the sugar industry. These improvements speeded up the making of sugar and increased the profits. At the same time it meant that planters had a great expense erecting the sugarhouses and supplying the necessary equipment. In 1833 Louisiana produced 75,000 hogsheads of sugar. In 1853 there were 449,000 hogsheads produced.

Tobacco was produced as a staple crop in some sections of the state. Large amounts were raised north of the Red River. Perique tobacco was grown in St. James Parish. Around Opelousas and Natchitoches other varieties were grown. Frequently, cotton and tobacco were raised on the same plantation. These crops were harvested at alternating periods.

No matter what part of the state one settled, there was the problem of getting the crop to market in New Orleans. For this reason plantations were usually located close to the banks of the river in reach of steamboats. Transportation was an expensive and

Built in 1799, Oakley plantation served as a residence and study for naturalist and artist John James Audubon.

Louisiana Office of Tourism

time-consuming operation. For instance, a cotton planter on the Ouachita River had to ship his cotton crop to New Orleans through a route that involved the Old River, the Red River, and finally, the Mississippi River. Robert Tanner, the planter on Bayou Boeuf in central Louisiana, sent his cotton by flatboat downstream many miles to the inland port of Washington. The cotton was unloaded from the flatboat to be stored in a warehouse along the bayou. The planter paid to have the flatboat captain take the cotton to Washington. He paid Irish laborers or the owner of slaves to unload the cotton and place it in the warehouse. He bought insurance against loss of the cotton both on the flatboat and at the warehouse.

The cotton was then shipped to New Orleans by steamboat—if the shipment were made in the year after steamboats came into Courtableau Bayou. (Courtableau was deep enough for steamboats to come to the port.) There was, again, the cost of moving the cotton. This time it was removed from the warehouse and placed aboard ship for the New Orleans journey.

It is hard to imagine the extent of the problems that came at this point. The movement of boats depended entirely on the water level. The water level was low in the small inland streams much of the time. The boat loaded with cotton at Washington moved along the Courtableau eastward until it reached the Atchafalaya. At the juncture of the Courtableau and the Atchafalaya a sandbar obstructed the waterway. The steamboat captains gave it the name "Little Devil." The water level had to be extremely high before a boat heavily loaded with cotton could get through the narrow opening.

Once in the Atchafalaya the boat had to go north to a smaller inland port, Simmesport. The route from Simmesport to the Mississippi was Old River, a connecting link. Once in the Mississippi, the ship moved south to New Orleans.

The amount of cotton produced depended upon an adequate rainfall, but there could be too much. There were years when rain fell all year and floods came. No crops were made. There was no money to pay creditors. On the other hand, there were years of drought with little or no rain. Results were the same. The storms of Louisiana could play havoc with a crop that had taken a year to grow. As if the weather were not enough to worry about, there were insects. Caterpillars ate entire crops for two succeeding years in the mid-1840s.

Most planters lived in big unpainted farmhouses made from the lumber brought from the woods near the plantations. Many of the planters built better houses during the 1850s when cotton production reached its peak. Only a few built the type of plantation homes shown in movies and described in books. Some planters lived in luxury and their homes were imposing. Those just above New Orleans were very large and fine. Farther upstream they were not so large or well built. A few were of brick. Most were made of rough squared timbers. Spaces between boards were filled with mortar, and the house was whitewashed.

Women of the planter class did not plow, chop cotton, make gardens, or tend to livestock as did the women in the families of most farmers. Most plantation women, however, were equal to their hill country sisters in the amount of work performed. The difference was in the kind of work. Both bore many children and cared for them. The planter's wife may have had a slave to help with the children or cooking or both. She usually had the task of seeing to the necessary sewing for her family. This included shirts, undergarments, and nightshirts for men. It included clothes for herself and the children. She had the task of making quilts, linens, mattresses, and pillows for the beds. Clothing for the slaves may have required her attention, also. Contrary to the myth, most planters did not purchase high-priced slave women to serve at the "big house." Grand

mansions with many servants could not have accounted for more than a small percent of the total number of planters.

Among farmers the relationship between husband and wife was likely to be that of partners. This was never the case with the planter and his wife. The planter was the master of his wife and children. This was as true as in his role of master of his slaves. His wife and children were his possessions. It was the planter who made decisions. He felt that a properly submissive wife was a man's due.

The planter was ordinarily more educated than the average farmer. He set himself apart from the farmer. His French and English were that of the educated class. He dressed better. He knew and respected the proper manners of the time. These qualities, he felt, showed that he was different from the farmer. One of the main duties he assumed was his responsibility to hold political office. It was necessary to be the kind of man the planter was to be governor or to be in the legislature. The planter class filled political offices of most power during the years before the Civil War.

The Large Farmers. There were farmers who cultivated as many acres as planters. The difference lay in their respective lifestyles. A farmer finan-

SLAVEHOLDERS					
The U. S. in 1860			**Louisiana in 1850**		
1	slaveholder owned	1,000 – over	0	slaveholders owned	1,000 – over
13	slaveholder owned	500 – 999	4	slaveholders owned	500 – 999
2,278	slaveholders owned	100 – 499	316	slaveholders owned	100 – 499
8,366	slaveholders owned	50 – 99	728	slaveholders owned	50 – 99
35,616	slaveholders owned	20 – 49	1,774	slaveholders owned	20 – 49
61,682	slaveholders owned	10 – 19	2,652	slaveholders owned	10 – 19
89,423	slaveholders owned	5 – 9	4,327	slaveholders owned	5 – 9
109,588	slaveholders owned	2 – 4	6,072	slaveholders owned	2 – 4
76,670	slaveholders owned	1	4,797	slaveholders owned	1
			These figures had changed little by 1860		

cially able to operate such a farm usually had sons working with him. His attitude toward work was in contrast to the planter in the lowlands who regarded manual labor as a sign of lower class. The farmer himself did as much of the work as he could. If need be, he hired help, often during harvest. He and his neighbors exchanged work. Occasionally he owned a slave who worked beside him in the fields.

His lifestyle was simple, and he and his family lived much like the small farmers. He prided himself on multiple skills from carpentry to blacksmithing. He was likely to scorn the pattern of going in debt for each year's crop. Instead, he was apt to spend as little as possible. The large farmer lived in almost stark simplicity in his unpainted dogtrot house. He did not lay claim to being a member of an aristocratic class. He therefore had no concern about his clothes, house, or other possessions as status symbols. His pride was more than likely in the amount and quality of his work.

The Small Farmers. Most Louisiana farmers cultivated small acreages of land compared to the planters. This was not true of all farmers, however. They raised most of the food they needed. The farm was a self-sufficient unit. Usually, there were only a few acres in cultivation. In the state's mild climate, they were able to raise two crops of vegetables—one in the spring and one in the fall. Wild game was available from the woods. Fish were easily secured from Louisiana's many streams. Berries and fruits grew wild in the surrounding woods. The small farmer often herded livestock over open or timbered land.

Once a year the farmer took his cotton to the gin. His wagon was filled with the cotton picked by himself and his family. He sold the cotton to a buyer at the gin. Or he might have sold to the store owner who bought cotton. The store owner often "furnished" him. That is, the merchant extended credit until the crop was gathered if the farmer requested credit. After paying what he owed against the crop, the farmer might trade whatever cotton he had left for items at the store. Thus, the farmer provided for some of the needs for himself and his family. His grocery needs might include a barrel of flour for biscuits, a barrel of sugar, and a barrel of coffee beans. He bought or traded for a bolt or two of cloth to be made into dresses and shirts for the family.

Most farmers were skilled in many crafts. They were carpenters, bricklayers, blacksmiths, and more. They sometimes "hired out" to planters on contract jobs as carpenters or bricklayers. Planters avoided manual work as a sign of lower class, but the ordinary farmer prided himself on his skills at many crafts.

The wives and daughters of farmers were self-sufficient women. Perhaps they were the first liberated women. They were far more equal partners with their husbands than the planters' wives. They were not trapped in the plantation lifestyle with the idea of women's dependency on men for their existence. There was no place for anyone—male or female—who shunned work in the do-it-yourself hill country society. These women often plowed. They took their places chopping the grass out of the cotton.

They made gardens. They tended stock. They worked at making quilts, caring for children, and doing household chores as well. Their houses were simple affairs that they tended.

Slaves. The South, in 1860, was not filled with vast plantations and many, many slaves. A false image has been created by writers and moviemakers. Most southerners were not slaveholders. One family out of four owned slaves. In 1860 there were 1,600,000 families in the South. Only about 400,000 owned slaves. Thirty percent of these families owned only one slave. The large slaveholder was the exception rather than the rule in this state.

At the time of the Louisiana Purchase there were nearly as many slaves in the state of New York as in all of Louisiana. By 1810 Louisiana had more than twice as many slaves as New York. In the next ten years the number of slaves in Louisiana had almost doubled. In the half-century ending in the 1850s, slaves in Louisiana increased from 40,000 to 330,000.

Slaves had been in Louisiana since French colonial days. Relatively few slaves came to Louisiana directly from Africa. Most of the slaves came from plantations established earlier on islands in the Caribbean. The slaves had been brought from Africa to these islands. There they had worked on great sugar plantations. They became

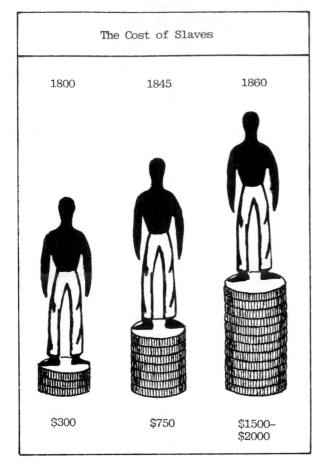

The Cost of Slaves

1800	1845	1860
$300	$750	$1500–$2000

Louisiana or Texas to raise cotton usually brought their slaves with them.

used to doing the work required on the plantations. They learned the routine of plantation life. They learned the language of the owners. This replaced their African language. The slaves were said to be "seasoned," or experienced. These slaves formed the labor force for early French and Spanish plantations in Louisiana.

Other slaves came from Virginia, the Carolinas, or the older states that began the practice of slavery in the United States. Planters migrating to

Slavery grew as new plantations were carved out of the wilderness. Eli Whitney invented the cotton gin about twenty years before Louisiana became a state. Since it speeded up the business of getting the seed disentangled from the fluffy cotton, planters grew more and more cotton. They then needed more and more slaves to work in the cotton fields. New Louisiana planters cut plantations out of the wilderness and brought slaves to work in the cotton and sugarcane.

The Louisiana Purchase Treaty prohibited the importation of slaves from foreign countries as of January 1, 1804. A United States law forbade the importation of slaves from overseas, that is, from Africa, after January 1808. The new slaves in this country had to come from the offspring of those already slaves. Since none could be brought into the country legally, those who were here increased much in value. Smuggling slaves was a common practice. Lafitte was one who engaged in this practice. As the demands grew, so did smuggling.

The price of slaves doubled and tripled as the years passed. So did the price of land. The kidnapping of free blacks from northern states became fairly common. These people were sold into slavery. It seems likely that owners of slave auction barns had an understanding about handling these kidnapped victims.

Solomon Northup was a free person of color. He was born free. Both of his parents were free. He was kidnapped in New York by two men in 1841. He left behind a wife and three children.

Northup was sold to a slave dealer and shipped to New Orleans, the center for the slave market for the whole South. He was sold to Theophilus Freeman, owner of the auction barn there. William Prince Ford, a Baptist minister from Rapides Parish, then bought him. Ford also purchased a woman who had been sold into slavery. One of her children was sold and taken away. Freeman kept the second child himself. Like this family, others were sometimes tragically separated.

Northup was first taken to Rapides Parish. This was the "jumping off place of civilization." It was at the outer edge of the inhabited area. In 1843 Ford sold Northup to Edwin Epps of Avoyelles Parish. Northup's life changed after someone from Avoyelles helped him get a message back to New York. A New York lawyer came to central Louisiana to rescue the citizen of New York. Solomon Northup was freed in January 1853 through the legal process and returned to New York.

Northup told a writer the story of his twelve years as a slave. Careful checks have been made to verify all of the facts given in his book. Northup's story is a true one. Northup said that slaves were beaten, and stocks were used for punishment. Children were sometimes separated from their parents. The experience of slavery varied according to masters. There were such annual occasions as slave festivals during the Christmas season.

Some people would not refer to slavery by name. Instead, they talked of the "**peculiar institution.**" The slaveowner spoke of "my hands," "my servants," "my people," or "my force," rather than "my slaves." If a slave were a craftsman, the owner usually referred to him as "my blacksmith" or "my ginner." Words did not hide the nature of slavery, however.

One description will cover neither the master nor the slave nor the institution. Slavery was as humane in Louisiana as it was in any other state. The treatment of slaves depended upon the character and attitude of masters and overseers. Owners were different, and therefore they did not all treat their slaves alike. Some slaveowners were cruel people. On the other hand, many masters were kind and generous. Natural ties of affection developed among many of these people who were dependent upon one another as slaveowners and slaves.

Slaves themselves were like the rest of the human race. Some were smart. Some were not as gifted. Some were strong. Some were weak. Some worked hard. Others did not. Each, in his own way, adapted to slavery. Each worked out his own way to be the master's slave and to reserve of his life whatever he could for himself.

Although the slaves were treated differently according to their owners, there were certain general patterns used in the handling of slaves. If a planter owned only a few slaves, he usually supervised their work in the field himself. In this close relationship, the slaves were likely to be treated well. If a man owned several hundred slaves, he probably used an overseer for supervision of the field work. He likely did not know the slaves. Some slaves required almost constant supervision. Others seldom saw their owners. In some cases slaves lived almost as if they were freemen. As a general rule, slaves were not allowed to leave the plantation without permission. The master or overseer had to know where they were and what they were doing at all times. Unauthorized white persons were forbidden to visit the slaves for fear that they would cause trouble. Strangers in plantation country were always suspected of being abolitionists.

Most slaves lived on the plantations in cabins lined up close together and called "**the quarters.**" Usually they were near a bayou, for the slaves' water supply came from the streams. Housing of slaves normally consisted of cabins. Some were doubled to contain more people. There were only slight variations in the structure of cabins. They were often unpainted frame houses with fireplaces around which life in the cabins centered. There were few comforts in the cabins.

Although there were exceptions, there were many **family units** among the slaves who enjoyed a life together. Plantation legal records often listed slaves and their spouses and children. Slaves were sometimes sold away from their families, but this was not usually true. Instead, many slaves, their children, and their children's children lived and died on the same plantation. On some plantations slaves did not live together in families. The father of the slave child often did not live with the mother. The slave women were expected to have many children. The slave child, according to custom and law, belonged to the owner of the mother. It was the mother who cared for the slave child.

It was up to the owners to furnish **food** and **clothing** The mother often cooked the food in a big pot in the fireplace. A pan and spoon served as plate and flatware. There were usually no dining tables, plates, forks, or knives. Water was brought to the house in buckets from the bayou or creek, and gourd dippers could be used to enjoy a drink.

On some plantations food for all the slaves was cooked at one central place in great black pots. In such arrangements, slaves ate together, serving themselves from the pots.

A cheap, apparently standard, diet included pork and cornbread. This was supplemented with sweet potatoes, which grew plentifully in the fields. This diet sounds strange to us today, but corn, rather than wheat, was the main ingredient for bread for all rural Southerners. Cornbread was

Harper's Weekly

The overseer was a part of the plantation system.

eaten almost every day, and pork seemed to have been more frequently used than beef or mutton. Slaves had a tendency to steal poultry and pork to add to their diets. Most slaves enjoyed fish, which were easily taken from Louisiana's many streams. Being farm people, the Louisianians—black and white—had the opportunity to raise vegetables. A great variety of vegetables was included in the diet of many of these people. Much depended on the attitude of the planter and the chance to grow food. Likewise, game, such as the opossum and coon, was fun to hunt and a fine source of food. Slaves were allowed to hunt with permission from their masters. Coon and 'possum were hunted at night after the work in the fields was done. Solomon Northup wrote of arrangements by which he was allowed to hunt.

Moss was used by slaves to make pads or **mattresses** on which to sleep. Sometimes corn shucks or cotton, scrapped from the fields, were used as well.

Slaves usually enjoyed their own type of **amusement**. Boys and girls played in the open areas of the quarters. There were many children to join the singing and dancing games. The black children enjoyed the same types of homemade games as the white children. However, as soon as black children were old enough, they worked in the fields with their parents.

A fact difficult for us to understand today is that people—the slaves —were **property** just as cattle and barns were property. Slaves represented money to their owners. Many planters were indebted for slaves. Slaves represented most of the investment in the farm or plantation. Since a slave cost hundreds, or even several thousand dollars, it was to the owner's advantage to take care of this property. His slaves had to be fed well. He needed to house them comfortably and to clothe them adequately. It meant he had to care for them when they were sick.

The **health** of the labor force was very important to the planter. The larger plantations provided hospitals and regular medical attention for the slaves. Slaves in the swampy regions were somewhat more sickly than those in the upland regions. Working in sugarcane was particularly hard on slaves. Sugarcane was harvested during cold, and often wet, weather. The cold sticky cane juice and the sharp flags of the cane added to the discomfort of the workers.

Slaves had lives within their own slave society. Among other slaves, the slave played another role. Actually, slaveowners knew little about what went on in the slave cabins at night. When the slaves were away from the white planter and his family, they were free to talk among themselves without fear of being overheard. They laughed and spoke of their own ideas about their lives, including their work and their white owners. They often talked of freedom. Sometimes they made plans to escape. William O'Neal, for example, was not satisfied to be a slave boy. He tried to get one of the men to escaped with him to a free land. He planned to pose as the son of the older slave, but he was never able to convince the man that the scheme would be safe.

The **education** of slaves depended upon the attitude of the master. After 1830 teaching Negroes to read and write was generally prohibited under severe penalties. It was feared that they might read abolition literature and cause trouble. There were always some slaves who could read and write in spite of the laws.

Owners usually looked after the **spiritual welfare** and **recreation** of their slaves. Most slaves enjoyed regular rest days and vacations. Some were given extra vacation time as reward for faithful work. These vacations came after the crop was harvested. Some plantations even provided places for holiday dancing. Usually, such organized recreational activities took place in the plantation ginhouse, the sugarhouse, or a barn. Slaves were usually given religious instruction. After 1830 this was mostly done by white preachers. Negro preachers were seldom used because it was feared they might organize the slaves for an escape to freedom. However, some slaves began to preach and formed "invisible" churches on the plantations. They were called invisible because they were secret.

Music was used by the slaves to express their sorrow at being slaves. Nobody could reprimand them for music, which was a way of saying what they really felt about the loss of their freedom. There was a distinctive "moanin'" that told, without a word, the slave's feelings. There were happy songs and dances also that told of the joys they still found in living. Our American heritage of the great Negro spirituals came out of the black slave experience.

It was hard to **escape** to freedom. Fugitive, or runaway, slaves were common in Louisiana. In 1850 Louisiana had ninety fugitive slaves. In 1860 there were forty-six. Once in a while a slave would hide for a time in a nearby swamp or forest. Usually he would be successfully hunted down or would surrender as a result of hunger. Newspapers of the period carried many advertisements of runaway slaves. Regular periodic drives for rounding up fugitives were organized by planters.

In order to prevent trouble among the slaves and to catch runaways, the antebellum white planters formed patrols. All black gatherings and encampments were patrolled. In keeping with the law, men on horseback patrolled the areas around their plantations at night. Yelping bloodhounds were used in the search for runaway slaves. If an escapee were caught, he was taken to his master. The police juries of every parish appointed the patrols for each area. Special night patrols were organized during times of insurrection or rumors of trouble. During the territorial period the government paid for slaves killed, property destroyed, and the cost of putting down an insurrection. Rewards were made to slaves who were loyal during insurrections. Much more care was maintained with the advent of the Underground Railroad movement of the 1830s. A better patrol system was provided. Unauthorized white persons were not allowed to visit the quarters.

Slaveowners apparently lived in constant fear of attack on the slavery system. Rumors of planned uprisings were frequent. There were also slave conspiracies. Naturally, these were not publicized. We have no way of knowing how often they happened. Still, some were recorded in the newspapers of the time. Therefore we know that they occurred. Those caught encouraging slaves to revolt were severely punished.

Some slaves used various ways to show their resentment to the harshness of slavery. Many put rocks, bricks, or wood in the bottom of a cotton sack. The added weight helped to hide a day of loafing. Others damaged crops, injured livestock, destroyed tools and machinery, and stole from the planters. This day-by-day resistance was practiced frequently. Some slaves participated in open revolts, which had little chance of success.

There had to be a workable relationship established between planters or overseers and the slave work force. The production of the laborers depended upon morale and motivation, and hostile slaves did not get the work done.

The Black Code was still in effect in antebellum times. The enforcement of the slave code varied with the planter. Usually as the number of slaves increased the more rigidly the code was carried out. The laws regulating slaves became stricter after the abolition movement began.

Usually the **punishment** for something serious was a whipping. Sometimes a slave was put in jail on the plantation. Clapping chains and irons on a slave was an extreme form of correction. Forcing the slave to wear an iron collar was also used. The iron collar fit tightly around the neck and sometimes had a bell attached. The collar was about an inch wide. Sometimes the collar was left on for weeks. Some wore them for life. Shaming a slave was another form of punishment. A male slave, for instance, might be made to do a woman's work, thus injuring his pride. Other types of ridicule were used as well. Severe penalties were given slaves involved in insurrections or in plotting uprisings. Fugitives were severely punished when caught. Some of these punishments were used to set examples for the others.

Manumission, or freeing slaves, was relatively common in Louisiana. In 1850 Louisiana freed more slaves than all states except three. In 1860 only one state freed more. Louisiana had 159 manumitted slaves in 1850. In 1860 there were 517 manumitted slaves.

Manumission was often given for devoted service. Often it was given to the slaveowner's kinsmen among the slaves. Many of those slaves were freed after the death of the owner. Heirs were left to deal with any problems. Many times the presence of a second family was unknown to the white family until the death of the slaveowner. The descendants had to deal with the problems of the two families—one white and one black. Masters were responsible for the conduct of freed slaves. They were responsible for seeing that they did not become public charges.

Lagniappe. A man known for his unusual treatment of his slaves was John McDonogh, one of the richest men and largest landowners in Louisiana. McDonogh apparently never sold a slave. In fact, he helped slaves. He usually kept them fourteen years before he freed them. In 1842 he sent eighty slaves he had freed back to Africa. Some remained in the area and worked in a variety of jobs. Some stayed to work on his sugar plantation or to work at other jobs for McDonogh. McDonogh continued to send slaves back to Africa at a more or less regular rate until his death. He freed all of his three hundred slaves. Not only were the slaves freed, but they were also given money, clothes, household implements, and agricultural tools.

When McDonogh died in 1850, he

RICH LAND
+
CHEAP LABOR
+
COTTON GIN
=
PLANTATION ECONOMY

was worth over three million dollars and owned 610,000 acres of land. He left New Orleans and Baltimore each about $1.5 million for free public schools. The fund financed thirty-

A New Orleans voodoo ceremony.

Historic New Orleans Collection

five schools. All of these schools bore his name.

Voodoo

Voodoo had been a part of life in the West Indies since the 1500s. The original name of the Afro-Caribbean rite, religion, or cult, was *vodu*. Later it was called other names including *hoodoo*. The people were also called voodoos.

The first slaves who came to the Louisiana colony brought their voodoo with them. During the time Spain owned Louisiana, Governor Gálvez prohibited the importation of slaves from Martinique. The white settlers were scared of voodoo. They felt that more voodoo worshipers would make the colony unsafe. In 1788 slaves from Santo Domingo were banned for the same reason.

Refugees fleeing the revolution in Haiti brought their voodoo to New Orleans with them in 1791. It had existed in Louisiana from the time the slaves came to the state, but it was not organized. Between 1790 and 1840, the black magic was organized for the first time in New Orleans. A newspaper reported on June 25, 1873, that New Orleans had three hundred voodoos in the city. About eighty percent of them were females. For a century it was a powerful force in the lives of many blacks and whites.

Voodoo was first mentioned in legal records in the *gris-gris* case of 1773. A *gris-gris*, or a voodoo powder, was made of alligator innards and herbs. It was supposed to have been used by three blacks to poison their overseer. The leader of the group was never released from prison. The other two were freed.

In the New Orleans area people congregated at the Wishing Well, a place on Bayou St. John. Frenzied voodoo worshippers, drunk on tafia (rum), worshiped Zombi the snake. They took chickens apart. These people were described as shaking, quivering, leaping, and screaming until they collapsed around bonfires.

Newspapers reported the voodoo happenings. The New Orleans City Council in 1817 passed an ordinance to try to keep groups from meeting. Slaves could not gather for dancing or for any other purpose except on Sunday. Then the places had to be designated by the mayor. Congo Square, the place selected by the mayor, was the site of voodoo rites for twenty years. These rites attracted curious crowds. White people watched in amazement.

King Voodoo, or **Doctor John** Montaigne, presided over the cult for three decades in New Orleans. Wearing a cape and dressed all in black except for a frilly white shirt, the bearded Dr. John performed his rituals. His power supposedly included faith healing and patent medicine. His specialties were vexes (*gris-gris*) and fortune-telling. For a fee he would place a curse on someone, or he would remove the curse. White people disguised themselves to seek Dr. John's services.

Dr. John created a spy system, which helped him gain power. He paid blacks to spy on their masters. He blackmailed blacks and whites from every level of society. It was said that he knew more about the private lives of New Orleans white society than anyone else in the 1840s. When he died at eighty-two, his student Marie Laveau became the Voodoo Queen.

Marie Laveau was a free woman of color. In 1809 at age fifteen she moved to New Orleans from Santo Domingo. She married Jacques Paris, a freeman. They had fifteen children. One was a daughter, Marie, who looked like her mother. Her mother used her to pretend to be two places at one time.

Marie's voodoo ceremonials included Zombi snake worship, black cats, and blood drinking. She was supposed to have a twenty-foot snake. Later she borrowed incense, statues, and holy water from the Catholic religion and added them to her ceremonies. Marie sought the friendship of many public officials in the city. She conducted the annual rites of St. John's Eve on Bayou St. John.

Her spy system was even more elaborate than her teacher's had been. She paid domestic servants, as well as many other household employees of the wealthy, to feed her information. She knew something about everyone—even her spies. Her clients included blacks and whites. They included the rich and the poor.

The Voodoo Queen placed curses, removed them, told fortunes, and distributed *gris-gris*. For a price she could get someone a lover, hold the lover, or get rid of the lover. While common people paid ten dollars for a visit, the rich were charged much more for her advice.

Marie became so powerful that she gained the title "The Boss Woman of New Orleans." She was described as an angel of mercy and a she-witch.

Marie gave up voodoo in her last years. She was supposed to have practiced Catholicism after that. She died in 1881.

Louisiana voodoo is usually associated with New Orleans. Associations of magic and casting spells came naturally in the big port city. Yet, voodoo or hoodoo has been just as much a part of the lifestyle of rural Louisiana people as it has been with the people of New Orleans. In fact voodoo existed all over the state. In Shreveport in 1937 there was a Negro voodoo murder.

Robert Murray, a man dealing with magic, "read cards" at his comfortable home on the edge of Cheneyville, an old cotton plantation town. Both whites and blacks frequented his place, seeking information he claimed to read from his cards. Joe Louis, the great prize fighter, once visited him. Many well-known state personages did as well.

Drugstores throughout rural areas sold love potions, good luck powders, and the like. Special candles were thought to give luck at cards.

Practices involving magic and the supernatural are not discussed readily with outsiders. There is no way to know to what extent these practices still exist. Superstitions and beliefs in magic may have dimmed with modern communication and education. However, they have not altogether disappeared.

En Partie 3 (Studying a Part). 1. Explain Louisiana's social caste sys-

tem. Describe life for each of the groups. 2. Describe voodoo.

It was clear as the years of the nineteenth century passed that the two sections of our nation represented two different cultures—two very different ways of living. The plantation system set Louisiana and the rest of the South in conflict with the North. This system, based on the feudal institutions of the Old World, could not exist in the United States. War was inevitable.

Coup d'Main
(Completing the Story)

Jambalaya (Putting It All Together)

1. Identify these key words, phrases, and people.

a. Creoles	h. manumission
b. dueling	i. Mardi Gras
c. factors	k. planters
d. *fais-do-do*	j. packets
e. Fort Jesup	l. plantations
f. free persons	system
of color	m. plantation
g. John	n. slaves
McDonogh	o. Zachary Taylor

2. Explain the reason for the steady and rapid growth of the state in antebellum times.

3. What type of immigrants came to the state?

4. Trace the population growth of whites and blacks.

5. Describe the plantation system.

6. Why did the plantation system in some way affect everyone in the state?

Potpourri (Getting Involved)

1. Role-play the escape of a slave. Show the reaction of the slave, owner, sympathizers, and law-enforcement officers.

2. Research one of the following topics and present the results in a mural, diorama, chart, or other visual form: mail service, clothing, housing, food, transportation, recreation, social life, health care, farm tools and implements, country stores, the Bank of Louisiana, westward migration, voodoo, steamboat trip from New Orleans to some other Louisiana location, or settlement of a town.

3. Draw a cartoon to depict the movement of Louisiana's capitals up until 1850.

4. Compare (a) life on the farm with life in the city, (b) life on a small farm with life on a plantation, (c) the life of a Louisiana boy or girl with that of a cousin from the North,

(d) the life of a slave with that of a free person of color, or (e) education of Negroes with that of children of small farmers or children of planters.

5. Dramatize (a) a cotton farmer who has just seen the new cotton gin at work, (b) a slave auction, (c) a private tutor conducting a class, or (d) a yellow fever epidemic.

6. Make a model of (a) a plantation, (b) the first cotton gin, (c) a steamboat, or (d) pioneer tools, utensils, or furnishings.

7. Make a chart showing how everyone was affected by and depended on agriculture.

Gumbo (Bringing It Up-to-Date)

1. Give an account of an imaginary trip from St. Louis to New Orleans in 1810. Then take the same trip in 1840, 1850, and 1980.

2. Compare Louisiana's position in the nation in the antebellum period to its position today.

3. Compare (a) the number, size, and appearances of Louisiana cities today with cities of 1850 and 1860, (b) life for blacks during the antebellum period with life today, or (c) antebellum agricultural practices with modern agricultural practices.

4. Show how Louisiana's social class system of today compares with the social class system of the antebellum period. Include status symbols of each period.

5. Relate the bilingual conditions of that day with present bilingual Louisiana.

PART FOUR

During the War and Reconstruction

CHAPTER 8

THE CIVIL WAR IN LOUISIANA
(1861–1865)

Sectional Strife

Causes of Conflict. The tensions caused by the conflict between the North and the South were felt in Louisiana. People in the agricultural South and the industrial North had many differences. The people held radically different views about such issues as internal improvements at federal expense, tariffs, banking and currency, public lands, and the question of slavery.

Many issues, such as **transportation**, played a part in developing this conflict. From the beginning of the 1850s the effects of railroads could be seen. Railroads were becoming a vital part of the nation's economy. Surplus products were being shipped rapidly from one part of the country to another. Railroads stimulated the building of factories in the North. As factories increased, people from Europe were attracted to the North.

These developments were making a new way of life in the North. The North prospered with new factories and the growing demand for manufactured products.

The South followed a different path. Fewer railroads and factories were built in the South than in the North. The South gambled everything on the growing of cotton. **Cotton was "king."** The South prospered as the price of cotton rose, and the annual production more than doubled. The South was almost entirely dependent on the North for its grain and manufactured goods. On the other hand, England and New England needed the South's cotton for their factories.

Plantations dominated the South. They dominated Louisiana. Planters held tight control of the government. They were leaders in all aspects of life. They were tied to the "peculiar institution" of slavery. The cotton they grew was the product the South sent to market. With the profits, goods were imported from elsewhere. The entire state was tied to the arrangement.

Slavery, then, shaped the outlook of Southerners the way that the factory shaped the outlook of Northerners. The protests against slavery from the North angered Louisiana's planter-leaders. Any criticism of slavery came to be regarded by planters as an attack on their right to grow cotton and earn a living. The planters argued that slaves lived more healthfully and happily than Irish workingmen and others in the Northern factories. People who wanted to do away with slavery were considered troublemakers. The South reminded the North about its part in the slave trade that brought slaves to America. The North had not found slavery practical on their farms and in their factories.

In 1820 the conflict flared out into the open. New states were being formed to the west. Those protesting slavery did not want slavery allowed in new states. In 1820 when Maine and Missouri applied for statehood, the fight began. The famous **Missouri Compromise** was made. Missouri would have slavery. Maine would not. This satisfied both North and South. Each time the question arose about whether a state should be slave or free, the tension mounted. When California applied for statehood, the

conflict reached another crisis. There was a nightmare of trouble over slavery in Kansas. The dispute over slavery became increasingly bitter. It affected every action of the United States Congress.

While the number of free states in the Union was getting larger than the number of slave states in the 1850s, a plan was made. Louisiana men secretly joined the Knights of the Golden Circle. They planned military expeditions. These expeditions would march on certain Latin American countries. Such expeditions were called **filibusters**. The men hoped that filibusters could capture Mexico, Cuba, or Nicaragua. These countries would become a part of the United States. They would be slave states. Most of these filibusters originated in New Orleans. Recruits were signed up at the St. Charles Hotel for the projected private invasions of foreign countries.

In 1854 William Walker of New Orleans signed a contract to lead a filibuster to Nicaragua. He was a doctor from Pennsylvania who had come to New Orleans to operate a newspaper. Men from all over Louisiana and the rest of the South as well as the North followed Walker to Nicaragua. Walker led four expeditions between 1855 and 1860. They invaded and captured Nicaragua. Walker's rule lasted very briefly. The natives took their country back. Then

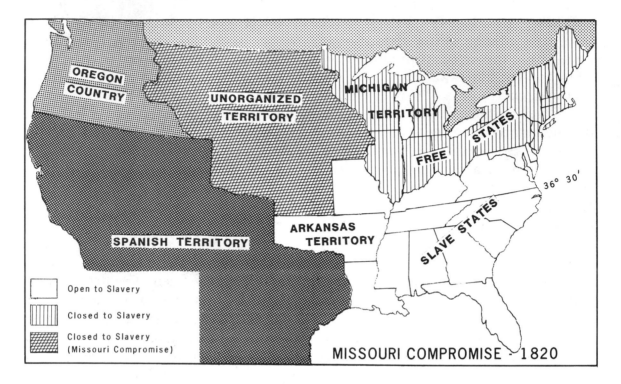

Open to Slavery

Closed to Slavery

Closed to Slavery
(Missouri Compromise)

MISSOURI COMPROMISE — 1820

they executed Walker.

Another filibuster was planned to take Cuba. It never left Louisiana.

There was a lot of talk about **states' rights** in Washington and in Louisiana. This was the right of states to control their own society. The Southerner's way of life included a strong belief in states' rights. This term meant the rights of planters. Planters had such control in Louisiana that they were a very privileged group. The males of the planter class represented not more than one-fourth of all white males in the state. Yet the nonplanter group did not have as much of a part in the government as the planters. Women in Louisiana had no part in government at all. They could not vote, much less hold office.

Louisiana was not democratic. This state was, nevertheless, part of the United States founded on the idea of democracy. There was the promise of freedom and equality. Some nonplanter whites talked among themselves about what could be done. So did slaves talk among themselves.

In 1827 there was a **plot** by slaves to kill the planters along Bayou Boeuf and flee to Mexico. The slaves collected food and hid it for months. When the time came, Lew Cheney, a slave, revealed the plot to the planters. Slaves were hanged on the courthouse lawn in Alexandria. Nobody knows how many. This action was meant to be a lesson to any slaves thinking of rebelling. Lew Cheney was given his freedom and allowed to leave the state. He was given a five-hundred-dollar bonus for revealing the plot. The money given Cheney came from a fund that Louisiana planters provided. It was a tax to provide financial relief for planters who lost slaves in such a manner. It provided bonuses for information regarding slave plots.

Many local incidents occurred about which nobody knew except those residing on the affected plantations. The situation was handled on the plantation since it was self-governing. The planter was still the final authority.

The slaves got support from some people who wanted to free them. These people, called abolitionists, urged Negroes to revolt or escape. Abolitionists made speeches. They wrote books and pamphlets. They also published newspapers. The abolitionists urged that slavery be abolished. A series of escape routes, called the **Underground Railroad**, was devised to help slaves escape. By 1850 the antislavery movement had become a strong force. There were only a few abolitionists, but their influence was felt in the North and South. In the North they were widely regarded as radicals. In Louisiana they were strongly opposed by the majority.

There was great opposition in Louisiana to other things. *Uncle Tom's Cabin*, a book published in the North in 1852, was written by a New England woman. There has been much controversy about whether the real Uncle Tom's cabin was at Natchitoches. Harriet Beecher Stowe wrote the story drawn from images of slavery as seen by abolitionists. This book sold more copies than any other book except the Bible up to that time. Louisiana planters reacted with fury. Louisianians felt that the book was unfair to planters.

In 1859 **John Brown's raid** against Harper's Ferry in Virginia alarmed Louisianians. Brown and eighteen followers made an armed attack to free slaves. Brown's name joined that of Harriet Beecher Stowe as an enemy of Louisiana. Finally, there came word that the Republicans had nominated **Abraham Lincoln** for President. In Louisiana there was quick reaction. If Lincoln were elected, there would be war. That seemed clear. Louisianians strongly disliked the **Republican party**, which nominated him. It had been organized in 1854 to prevent slavery from becoming legal in the territories.

Added to the other problems was a **power struggle** going on in Washington, D.C., between North and South. Four of the first five presidents of the United States were from Virginia. All were planters. The planter lifestyle allowed time to develop leaders, and the plantation itself was excellent training ground. Northerners spoke of a "slavocracy" planning to dominate the United States government. Northern political leaders wanted to direct the course of the nation, also. The two groups represented two separate lifestyles. Both wanted power. The South was shrinking geographically in relation to the rest of the United States. The North wanted to claim as much of the West as possible. Slavery was an issue, but it was not the only issue.

Time of Decision. It was as though all that Louisiana had feared was suddenly coming to pass. Leading planters like Sheriff Leroy Stafford of Rapides Parish favored the Union at this stage. He later became a Confederate general in the Civil War. Others, like Thomas Overton Moore, saw no way to satisfy the North and were ready to confront opponents of slavery. Moore was governor of Louisiana. He owned three plantations near Alexandria. He represented the slaveowner's view absolutely. He and his party worked for secession.

Abraham Lincoln was elected. Lincoln's election united Southern planters in an almost solid opposition. Lincoln had not received one vote in Louisiana. Public opinion in Louisiana was sharply divided about what the next course of action should be. The planters felt that there had to be

a showdown. One group of Louisianians wanted to wait until after Lincoln's inauguration to take a stand. Another group favored secession immediately. Still another proposed a convention of the Southern states. Probably the majority of people who voted in Louisiana in November 1860 opposed secession. These were almost all nonplanters.

The news of Lincoln's election caused Governor Moore to call a special session of the legislature for December 10, 1860. A bill was passed that called for an election of delegates to a state convention on January 7. The act appropriated $500,000 for military defense.

News came in December 1860 that South Carolina had seceded from the Union. The people were divided. Those who favored immediate secession opposed the cooperationists. Many of the state's leaders showed immediate support for secession. The cooperationists believed that Louisiana should cooperate with the other Southern states. This group believed that the Southern states should act together after they decided on a course of action.

The days were tense. The crisis had come.

An election for convention delegates was held in January 1861. Many qualified voters did not vote. In New Orleans only about half voted. Twenty-nine parishes were for secession. Nine-

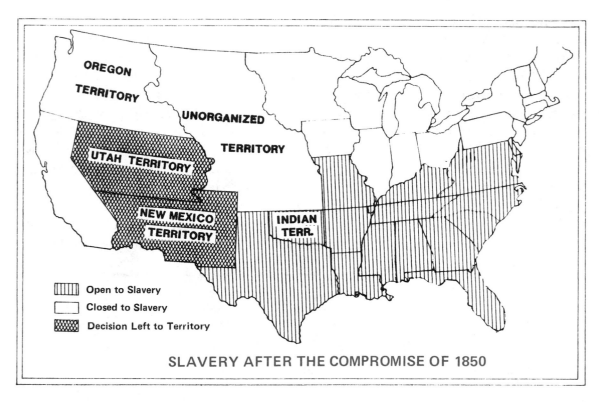

SLAVERY AFTER THE COMPROMISE OF 1850

teen were not. The details of the vote were not known until the convention, however. Only the names of the successful candidates to the convention were announced.

The crisis sent an electric shock through the nonplanters. They felt that the state was rushing toward war. The planters were speaking for the state. Most people who did not own slaves felt that the state was going to war to save slavery. All the years of feelings against slavery and against planter control were now released. Public opinion in Louisiana was generally in favor of going along with the other Southern states. Businessmen in New Orleans were stunned and confused.

Some people spoke out against secession. Judge James G. Taliaferro of Catahoula Parish asked Louisiana people and the leaders to look ahead and see what war would do to the state. He published a newspaper in Jonesville in which he printed his views. It was quickly closed. He was elected to the Secession Convention. There he made an eloquent speech against secession. A Natchitoches Parish leader and others worked hard to secure votes against secession. They reaped strong disapproval from those in favor of secession.

The Secession Convention. The Secession Convention was held at the capitol in Baton Rouge on January 23, 1861. Enthusiasm for secession was running high. Former Governor Mouton presided over the excited gathering. In a speech Governor Moore reported that after the January 7 election he had seized some United States government military property. After much debate, the Ordinance of Secession was adopted by a vote of 113 to 17.

Four days after the convention started, Governor Moore declared that Louisiana was out of the Union. Louisiana now stood alone. It was a republic. A delegation was elected to attend the convention of Southern states called to assemble at Montgomery on February 4. The purpose of the convention was to form a Southern confederacy.

After the voting, the supporters of secession marched to the flagpole on the lawn of the capitol for a

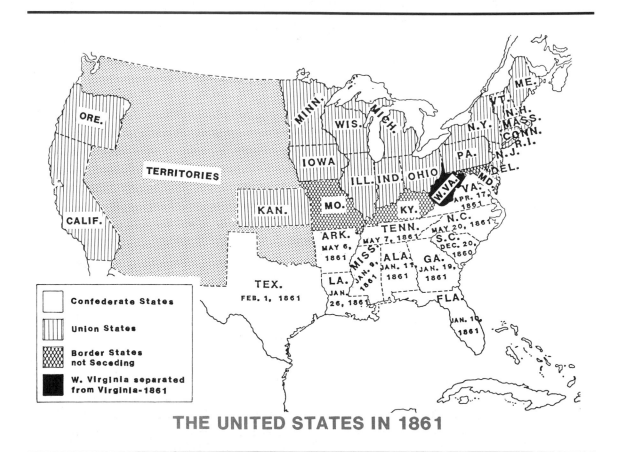

THE UNITED STATES IN 1861

victorious celebration. They were led by Governor Moore. The Stars and Stripes of the United States came down. The Louisiana state flag took its place. There were cheers from those who had wanted to secede from the United States. Those celebrating did not think of war in the triumph of the moment.

Reactions in the newspapers were mixed. Most of the planter-merchant voters were enthusiastic. Throughout Louisiana many people celebrated the move with great joy.

The Republic of Louisiana. The Louisiana republic existed for fifty-four days. Louisiana was an independent nation from January 26 until March 21, 1861. Governor Moore served as president. The state legislature and the Secession Convention, meeting in New Orleans, continued to function. These bodies handled most of the republic's business. Louisiana's senators and representatives in Congress withdrew in February 1861. The old state flag was replaced with the newly adopted national flag of Louisiana. The flag of the Republic of Louisiana was unfurled on February 21 in Lafayette Square in New Orleans to a twenty-one gun salute.

In January and February 1861, Governor Moore took over all the remaining property of the United States in Louisiana. This included over $600,000 in the United States Mint in New Orleans.

The Confederacy. Louisiana was not independent long. The Southern states voted to bind themselves into the **Confederate States of America**. On March 21, 1861, the Secession Convention ratified the state constitution. Only one change had to be made in the 1852 constitution. "United States" was changed to "Confederate States."

The Southern states wanted to form a new nation that would allow them to live as they wished. They would be bound to each other very loosely. They felt that the North might let them leave the Union without any fuss. After all, the Southerners reasoned, the citizens in the Northern states did not like the Southern way of life anyway. Some Northerners did favor letting the Confederacy go in peace. Many others did not.

In the North Louisiana hill country there was often anger at the move. Many residents were determined not to take part in a war to oppose the abolition of slavery. They pointed out that they had no slaves. In other parts of the state there were joyous celebrations. In New Orleans each home that shared the hopes of the Confederacy was to burn a light to show its loyalty to the cause. There were Louisiana citizens who disagreed with the secession, but that no longer mattered. All living in Louisiana were committed to the route taken by planter governments of the Southern states.

En Partie 1 (Studying a Part).
1. What were some of the events leading to the war? 2. What were the political issues of the period? 3. Identify reasons for Louisiana's position. 4. Why did the Republican party develop? 5. What was the purpose of the filibusters? 6. What were the two opposing views about the action the state should take? 7. Give the details of the Secession Convention. 8. What was the Republic of Louisiana? 9. When did Louisiana join the Confederacy?

The Civil War

General Pierre Gustave Toutant **Beauregard**, handsome French-Louisiana West Point graduate, was in charge of troops at Charleston, South Carolina, in April 1861. It was General Beauregard who demanded the surrender of Fort Sumter on April 12, 1861. Nobody was killed as Fort Sumter was turned over to the Confederacy. Yet the seizure of the fort was far from being a minor event. It began four years of war between North and South.

There was nervous excitement over the war in the planter society. After years of mounting tension, there was something of relief that at last a decision had been made. Right or wrong, the waiting was over. Now there was direction. Louisiana planter society was among its own kind in the Confederate States of America. The people were excited about their new "nation," as they called the Confederacy.

"In Defense of My Country." Louisiana contributed more than its share of fighting men. Within three months, by June 1861, sixteen thousand Louisianians volunteered for military service in a great burst of enthusiasm. In the first six months of the war, twenty-four thousand troops left Louisiana for Virginia. Others were sent as fast as they could muster in and get equipped. The Louisiana Tigers made themselves famous at the first battle, Manassas, or Bull Run. Altogether about sixty thousand men joined the military service. So many able-bodied men of the state were sent elsewhere to fight that Louisiana suffered serious defense problems.

Before the men left, there were parties, balls, picnics, and barbecues given in their honor. The first troops were often outfitted by local groups. Women quickly made gray Confederate uniforms for the men because the Confederate government was not prepared to outfit all of them. A Confederate flag made by local women was presented to each local company. A flag presentation ceremony was usually held, and it sometimes included a dress parade of the soldiers.

Louisiana crowds watched their men loaded into steamboats that took them to Virginia to fight under General Robert E. Lee. Bands played, and women wept as the young soldiers said goodbye.

Many of the soldiers went to Camp Moore in Tangipahoa Parish for training. Red measles spread through the camp, and a number of the men died.

Planters quickly showed their power during the war. The Confederate government allowed those with influence to get out of the fighting in all manner of ways. The Confederacy instituted a military draft in 1862. A despised law of the Confederate government provided exemption from military service for owners of twenty or more slaves. Planters often entered the war as officers. Many left for Texas with their slaves. There were contracts to collect cotton bales over the countryside. There were contracts to deliver cotton to Mexico to be used to pay foreign countries for war supplies. There were contracts for hauling salt from salt mines in Louisiana to Confederate camps. Moreover, the Confederacy rented armies of slaves to dig trenches, throw up breastworks, and do other work. Mules and wagons were rented from planters by the Confederacy. A man who had money to do so could even hire a substitute to take his place in the army.

Planters who went to war as officers often had trusted slaves along to serve as valets and take care of the horses. Other planter influence was shown in assignments that took men away from the fighting. A phrase used to describe the war would later prove poisonous for planter rule over the masses after the war. That phrase was "a rich man's war and a poor man's fight."

As events developed, war between North and South ended the waiting for other Louisiana whites as well. These were the white people outside the planter society. Some men in Winn Parish left to go north and join the Union forces. Others simply vowed that they would never fight for the slaveowners. Some, like the young Boltons from Shiloh in Union Parish, felt differently. They felt that they were defending the South against "another section telling the South what to do."

The Boltons were independent farmers. They were very patriotic. George and his two brothers volunteered for the Confederacy. Practically every able young man at Shiloh joined the Confederate forces. Few, if any, owned slaves. George wrote back from Camp Moore to his homefolks in Union Parish. George wrote what was perhaps in the hearts of most of these young men: " . . . the morning when I bid farewell to you all to volunteer in defense of my country. I think of it often, but never with a feeling of regret that I left you all to join in a cause so glorious. Of course,

I would like to see you all very much but where duty leads there must the true heart go without feeling."

Many free blacks and slaves joined the Union forces. Over four thousand blacks enlisted in the Union army at New Orleans. By the end of the war nearly twenty-one thousand more Louisiana blacks had joined them.

Leaders. During the course of the war, Louisiana supplied the Confederacy with some of its most prominent leaders. Outstanding generals of the state, other than Beauregard, included Braxton Bragg; Leonidas Polk; and Richard ("Dick") Taylor, son of Zachary Taylor and brother-in-law of Jefferson Davis. Taylor distinguished himself at the Battle of Mansfield. Leonidas Polk, although not a native, was closely associated with Louisiana. He was the cousin of a former United States President, James K. Polk. He had been an Episcopal bishop for twenty years and was called "The Fighting Bishop." He gave up his position to join the army. During the war, he received the rank of major general. He was killed in battle in 1864.

Other Confederate leaders from Louisiana included Judah P. Benjamin, John Slidell, Duncan F. Kenner, Pierce A. Rost, and former Governor A. B. Roman. Benjamin served as attorney general, secretary of war, and then as secretary of state in the cabinet of Jefferson Davis. He was

called the brains of the Confederacy. Slidell worked desperately to get support of France for the Confederacy. When it was clear that the Confederacy could not win, Slidell's mission was hopeless. Kenner and Rost worked to gain recognition for the Confederacy in Europe. Roman served on a commission to work with Lincoln's administration.

False Optimism. Outside of New Orleans, Louisiana was primarily a rural society. Little boys on plantations had their own horses at about age three. Their first guns arrived not much later. Horses were the very symbol of the elite society. Horsemanship was one of the top values the people admired. Horse races were the gentleman's sport. Marksmanship might have been even more prized than horsemanship. Almost every planter and planter's son hunted wild game. A reputation for being a good shot brought beams of pride.

With this background Louisianians felt that the North did not have a chance. They believed that Northern men and boys lived in cities. They would not know how to shoot a gun or handle a horse. There were boasts that it would take two Yankees to equal one Southern soldier. The general feeling was that the war would be over soon. The South would be victorious, and the men would return for fall harvest. Many of these young Confederates considered this under-

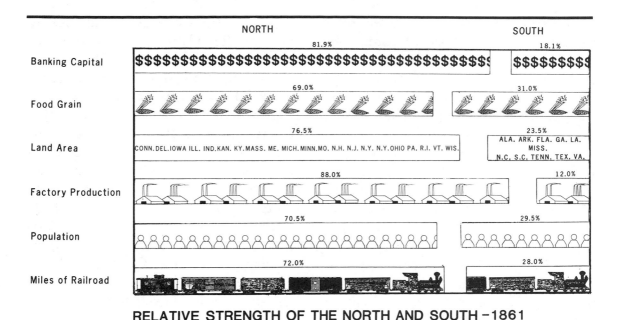

RELATIVE STRENGTH OF THE NORTH AND SOUTH – 1861

	NORTH	SOUTH
Banking Capital	81.9%	18.1%
Food Grain	69.0%	31.0%
Land Area	76.5% CONN. DEL. IOWA ILL. IND. KAN. KY. MASS. ME. MICH. MINN. MO. N.H. N.J. N.Y. N.Y. OHIO PA. R.I. VT. WIS.	23.5% ALA. ARK. FLA. GA. LA. MISS. N.C. S.C. TENN. TEX. VA.
Factory Production	88.0%	12.0%
Population	70.5%	29.5%
Miles of Railroad	72.0%	28.0%

taking to be a kind of holiday adventure. Early victories added to the false optimism.

The mood of the people changed after the war began in earnest. When they received news that sons or brothers or husbands had been killed or wounded, people grew more serious about the war. News was usually received about a battle. Then sometimes weeks passed before anxious families learned about the fate of their loved ones. Nearly every letter brought bad news about some friend or relative. Sometimes the letters were delivered by couriers. Couriers, who were often men too old to go to war, delivered letters to and from the soldiers.

Preparations for War. Governor Thomas O. Moore seized the United States arsenals in Baton Rouge, Forts Jackson and St. Philip, and other federal properties. The Louisiana Legislature appropriated approximately $1.5 million during 1861 for military equipment and supplies. The Confederate government was supposed to reimburse the state for these funds. Steamboats were sent into the rivers and bayous of the state to collect scrap iron to be used for making "the tools of war." Much of this iron was sent to foundries in New Orleans. Below New Orleans men were put to work building barricades to keep Union ships out of the mouth of the Mississippi River. The two forts, Fort Jackson on the west side and Fort St. Philip on the east side, were reinforced to prohibit the use of the river by Union forces. Fort Macomb and Fort Pike protected Lake Pontchartrain. Fort Berwick guarded Berwick Bay. Sharpshooter lookouts guarded the Mississippi River for signs of Union boats. Heavy iron cables with rafts attached were placed between Fort Jackson and Fort St. Philip. Breastworks were constructed all the way around the city of New Orleans. Bayous were blocked. An underwater log boom was laid across the Mississippi River. Gunboats were fitted out on the Mississippi River to aid in resisting attack.

Women went to work making bandages, supplies, and clothing. The women of each family tried to take care of the clothing of the male members who had gone to war. They knitted socks and mittens and made flannel shirts and blankets. Women organized sewing societies in most towns to see that all soldiers from that area were outfitted. Boxes of clothing were sent to the men. Sometimes food was added.

By the end of 1861 Governor Moore was worried about the defense of Louisiana. Before General Beauregard left for Charleston, he cautioned the military to take care of the defense of New Orleans. He told them to arm Forts Jackson and St. Philip with the heaviest guns possible because he feared an attack on the city. Confederate leaders in Richmond ordered Louisiana to supply more troops and supplies for the Confederate armies to the east. They ordered two ironclads being readied in New Orleans to proceed up the Mississippi. General **Mansfield Lovell** was in charge of Department I of the Confederacy, which was Louisiana. He was convinced that the Federals would attempt to capture New Orleans. Even though he warned the Confederate leaders, plans were not changed. It was unbelievable how casual the Confederacy was about defending its largest city. Lovell and Governor Moore attempted to defend New Orleans as best they could. Lovell had only three thousand troops.

After some months, Louisiana defenders were left with neither guns nor ammunition. Governor Moore wrote repeatedly to President Davis asking for war supplies. Some small factories were built to make war supplies. Supply depots were set up. Most Louisiana soldiers left to guard the state had only wooden sticks with which to drill. Privateers were outfitted at the Algiers shipyard so they could help.

Union Plans. The Union plan to win the war fitted somewhat the idea of one of Lincoln's generals. It was the **Anaconda plan**. Like a great snake, the Union forces would wrap themselves around the Confederacy. Yankee troops would capture the Mississippi River and cut the Confederacy in two. Union armies would march south through the border states. The Union would **blockade** the coasts of Southern states and stop commerce. The blockade was ordered one month after the war started. No vessel could enter or leave any harbor in the Confederacy without risk of being captured by a Union vessel. The blockade greatly crippled the Confederacy.

Louisiana was a key target in Union plans. The great port of New Orleans was the largest city in the South, and its commerce was one of the main targets of the blockade. By the summer of 1861 effects of the blockade were being felt. Common commodities became scarce. Prices on ordinary necessities soared. Foreign commerce had been destroyed. This created financial problems in New Orleans.

"Running the blockade" was the Southern response to the Northern blockade. On dark nights fast-sailing Confederate vessels that could navigate in shallow bays and inlets would slip out. They were loaded with cargoes of cotton for the West Indies. On return trips they brought such things as cannons, rifles, lead, blankets, shoes, coffee, and medicines. Some took their cotton to Mexico and returned with badly needed goods.

1862: Capture of New Orleans. A year after the war began, the Union was ready to capture New Orleans. Louisiana residents were grieving over the death of the Confederate commander at Shiloh, General Albert Sidney Johnston, on April 7, 1862. The general's body arrived in New Orleans for burial as frightening reports reached the city of a Union invasion. A federal expedition of fifteen thousand troops under General **Benjamin F. Butler** and forty ships under Flag Officer **David G. Farragut** were headquartered at Ship Island. It took three weeks to get the gunships over the bar at the river's mouth.

On April 18 Farragut began bombardment of Forts Jackson and St. Philip. The Union had seventeen warships and twenty mortar schooners commanded by Captain David Dixon Porter. There was a fierce battle as men on the ships tried to bombard the forts into submission. The Union had twice the firepower of the two forts. Over thirteen thousand shells rained on the Confederate bastions, but there were only four casualties.

After five days Farragut changed his plans. The Confederates were not surrendering as he had thought they would. He camouflaged the ships. Some were painted black. Then branches and brush were placed against the sides to disguise them. During the night of April 24 a heavy fog concealed the Union fleet. The ships appeared as "black shapeless masses." In the wee hours of the morning the Union fleet slipped by the forts and was on its way to New Orleans.

Farragut encountered only a token Confederate naval force. In two hours six Confederate ships were sunk, run aground, or abandoned. The Union lost one ship and three gunboats. Most of the ships on the river belonged to the state. They were virtually defenseless. Richmond had commissioned two battleships, the *Mississippi* and the *Louisiana*, but they were unfinished when the Union attacked.

The next day Farragut demanded of Mayor John T. Monroe that he surrender New Orleans. Lovell had turned the affairs of the city over to Monroe and the city council. Lovell, with too few men to defend the city, had already taken his troops northward. They had destroyed valuable war supplies before leaving. Lovell had burned immense quantities of timber, cotton, coal, and other provisions. Mayor Monroe spoke for the desperate residents. He could not surrender the city.

On May 1, 1862, the army troops brought by Farragut to **occupy New Orleans** did just that. General Benjamin F. Butler was in command. The Confederacy lost its largest city and its much-needed factories.

Butler in Command. New Orleans began seven months under Butler's rule. He established his headquarters at the St. Charles Hotel. During the time Butler was in command, he became bitterly hated by the people of New Orleans. He gained the title "Beast Butler." Probably Butler's Order No. 28 received the most criticism. It started when women spat at the Union troops and tried to harass them all they could. In response, Butler issued a stern order (Order No. 28) for his troops to treat the women with the same discourtesy. This boomeranged. Because of the Southern idea of "knights and ladies," Butler's Order No. 28 served to spur Confederate soldiers to fight harder than ever. General Beauregard read it to the troops to inspire them. The order caused a storm of protest not only in New Orleans but in the rest of the United States and abroad. Butler arrested and imprisoned Mayor Monroe for his opposition to the order. Later the mayor received an apology and was restored to office.

New Orleans papers refused to publish Butler's orders. He then seized the office of the *True Delta* and had his orders printed in the May 2 issue. Butler's troops printed the paper. He prohibited the further circulation of Confederate money. He confiscated the property of prominent secessionists. On June 7, 1862, Butler had William B. Mumford hanged for tearing down the American flag from the United States Mint on April 26. All inhabitants were disarmed by order of Butler. On September 24, 1862, Butler ordered all Americans in his department to renew their allegiance to the United States. At the same time they had to register all their real and personal property. Failure to follow these orders resulted in severe penalties. Soon thereafter sixty thousand had met the provisions of the order.

Not all of Butler's actions were bad. The feelings were so strong against him that any good he did was overlooked. He did bring some order to the city. Butler attempted to relieve the destitution of the residents by supplying provisions. He levied taxes on disloyal persons to feed the poor. He reopened the port to commerce of all friendly nations. Butler issued very strict quarantine orders to control the yellow fever threat. He did this to protect the Union troops, but it helped clean up the city. Strict orders against drunkenness were issued as well.

Other Activities. After the capture of New Orleans General Shepley occupied strategic points of approach to the city to prevent Confederates from reoccupying it.

Farragut sailed on from New Orleans to Baton Rouge and took that city. He left Commander Porter in charge of two ships at Baton Rouge. Guerrillas fired from the riverbanks as his boats proceeded to Vicksburg and Natchez. General Butler ordered the evacuation of Baton Rouge. The reasons for his doing so are not clear. Commander Porter abandoned the city on August 23, 1862.

Governor Moore had moved the capital to Opelousas before the Union took control of Baton Rouge on May 7, 1862. It was later moved to Alexandria where it remained for a very short time. From there the capital was moved to Shreveport.

On August 5, 1862, Confederate General John Breckinridge and about three thousand men were encamped on the Amite River. He planned to recapture Baton Rouge. The ironclad *Arkansas* was to disperse the federal gunboats while Breckinridge took the garrison. Plans were made so that Breckinridge would march on Baton

General Butler defying the rebels at New Orleans.

The Banks expedition at Baton Rouge.

Rouge when he received word that the *Arkansas* had passed Bayou Sara. Breckenridge entered Baton Rouge from the east and drove out the federal troops. General Thomas Williams, who was in command in federally occupied Baton Rouge, was killed. The *Arkansas* did not arrive. Five miles before it reached its destination, its engines failed. To keep it from becoming the property of the Union, the crew destroyed it. Breckinridge was unable to hold Baton Rouge, so he withdrew about thirty miles north. His new location was Port Hudson. Port Hudson then became the Confederate defense port and the point for receiving supplies.

On December 17, 1862, **General Nathaniel Banks**, commander of the Union army in Louisiana, reoccupied Baton Rouge. Eleven days later Union troops burned the state capitol. The fire destroyed most of the state's official records. The capitol had been used as a federal hospital.

In October 1862 Union General Godfrey Weitzel led an expedition in the Bayou Lafourche area. The federal troops succeeded in capturing Napoleonville, Labadieville, and Thibodaux. Weitzel continued on to the Bayou Teche country to attack troops under General Alfred Mouton, son of former Louisiana Governor Mouton.

General Butler, on November 9, 1862, declared all property of disloyal citizens in Lafourche Parish to be confiscated or taken over by the Union. The plantations owned by loyal men were to be worked by Negroes for the benefit of the United States. The next month General Butler was replaced by General Nathaniel P. Banks in Occupied New Orleans.

1863: Invasion of the Red River Valley. In the spring of 1863, while **General Ulysses Grant** was working on his attack of Vicksburg, Banks led an invasion of the Red River Valley. This movement was perhaps designed to cause the withdrawal of Confederate forces that would oppose Grant's troops attacking Vicksburg. Banks took his men to Brashear City (Morgan City) on the Gulf coast. From there he marched up Bayou Teche. He captured **Opelousas**. Then he marched his troops six miles northwest to the little inland port of Washington. From there his soldiers marched along the narrow, winding Bayou Boeuf to **Alexandria**. Alexandria was captured on May 7, 1863.

The Rebels later recaptured Alexandria, Opelousas, and the towns along the Teche.

Soldiers from Connecticut, Vermont, Maine, and other New England states were with Banks in the Red River invasion. Some jotted down notes on what they saw. Many kept diaries. Their march up the Teche and then up the Boeuf was obviously a miserable undertaking. One wrote: "The heat was intense and the roads dusty. Our marches were long and fatiguing. On one occasion we marched nearly ten miles without rest, and destitute of water. Finally, in the heat of the day we halted at the dooryard of the Widow Webb. Arms were stacked, blankets thrown down, and one grand rush made for the cistern...[Mrs. Webb]...wished the water would poison all of us miserable, meddling Yankees. There were dead cats in the cistern, she said ..."

Banks's march was lined with cotton and sugarcane plantations. When

Baton Rouge during the Civil War.

Harper's Weekly

his men passed through the area, they tore down fences, burned houses, and destroyed crops. He reported that he had taken twenty thousand horses, mules and cattle, and five thousand bales of cotton. Besides these he had taken all the hogsheads of sugar he could carry away. Historians have tried to determine whether Banks was selling cotton for the benefit of the Union or for himself.

A Yankee soldier wrote that "the Regiment put up at the nearest plantation to permit the officers to rewrite their rolls. The house was turned topsy-turvy to find tables and chairs, and the rooms were filled with busy scribblers, to the horror of the female members of the family."

When Banks wired Washington, D.C., about the capture of Alexandria, he received orders to move his men to help Grant take Vicksburg. Orders were given to the soldiers on this first invasion of the Red River Valley to turn around and retrace their steps back to the Gulf of Mexico. The troops did not face the prospect of the return trip with pleasure. "A weary road of 150 miles had to be traversed again. No wonder that the men were discouraged when it was known that they were short of rations, and their shoes were nearly worn, and that rebel bands were concentrating in their rear."

Banks ordered his soldiers to go into all plantation quarters and get every able-bodied Negro to follow the army back to the Gulf coast. No preparations were made for the freedmen's reception at the coast. Some soldiers wrote in their diaries various descriptions of this long parade of black people. Some say it was six miles; some estimate nine miles long. When the Negroes reached the coast, they were left in sugarhouse shelters, barns, and the like. Some of the able-bodied men were taken into the Union army. Others were left to drift back to their former locations or find places on other plantations.

Meanwhile Banks took some of the soldiers through Simmesport and Bayou Sara to lay siege to Port Hudson. Port Hudson was located in rolling hill country between Baton Rouge and St. Francisville on a river bluff. Port Hudson and Vicksburg were the last Confederate strongholds on the Mississippi River. At that time the Union controlled all of the great river north of Vicksburg and all of it south of Port Hudson. Grant laid siege to Vicksburg from May 22 to July 4. Confederates had strongly fortified Port Hudson against attack by river or land. Port Hudson was needed to protect transportation of supplies from the Red River Valley to Confederate forces east of the Mississippi.

Other War Activities. In March 1863 the federal forces occupied a large portion of the Florida parishes.

Confederate General Richard Taylor went to Berwick Bay. There he captured seven hundred men, guns, ammunition, medicine, and other supplies. He proceeded to Donaldsonville. Taylor prevented federal troops from reaching Banks and Grant to reinforce them. His troops captured Kenner.

Invasion of Northeastern Louisiana. A number of men from Union Parish were in the Twelfth Regiment of Louisiana Volunteers. They were among the Confederate soldiers sent to Cairo, Illinois, on the Mississippi River in 1861. Their job was to stop Grant. No matter how hard they fought, Grant captured one important Confederate fortification after another as he marched down the Mississippi.

Grant had not been able to capture Vicksburg in 1862. Union plans called for control of the Mississippi River. By the end of this second year of the war, United States forces controlled the river from occupied Baton Rouge to the Gulf of Mexico. General Ulysses S. Grant, who had been in charge of troops coming down the river from the north, reached as far as Vicksburg, Mississippi. He was determined to capture Vicksburg and push on down to Baton Rouge. This would close the river completely.

During the winter of 1862–1863, Grant and his lieutenant, **William Tecumseh Sherman**, laid the ground-

Officer Parker of the gunboat Essex *raising the Union flag at the state capitol.*

Harper's Weekly

work for the capture of Vicksburg. The determined general decided on a totally different approach for attacking Vicksburg than the one he had used earlier.

He landed his men on the Louisiana side of the river at Lake Providence opposite Vicksburg. His ships, traveling from north of Vicksburg to the south, were subjected to the murderous fire from Confederate batteries on the high bluffs rising above the river on the east. To avoid this, Grant planned to dig a canal to run across De Soto Point. He could then safely move his troops to points below Vicksburg. Grant's plan was to make a crescent-shaped waterway on the Louisiana side of the river. The new route would allow the Union troops passage around the city. The canal would connect waters that would lead to the river below Vicksburg. The ships could then approach the Confederate stronghold from the south.

Grant had his men begin digging a canal a mile-and-a-half long and sixty feet wide. After months of working on the canal, Grant decided that it was impractical and abandoned the idea.

Grant had allowed the troops to add to their rations by plundering. Much property was destroyed in northeastern Louisiana that winter.

Summer of 1863: The Turning Point. That summer of 1863 was a grim time for the people of Louisi-ana, as well as the rest of the Confederacy. **Vicksburg**, just across the Mississippi from the state, fell after a month-long siege, on July 4, 1863. As the bad news drifted back to Louisiana, it was known that Lee, in his deepest penetration of enemy territory, had also been turned back on that same day at **Gettysburg**. It was hard to believe that so much bad news came at one time.

Capture of Port Hudson: Last Confederate Stronghold on the Mis-

The Battle family home in Shreveport was used as the Confederate state capitol.

sissippi. One of the most dogged battles of the war took place at Port Hudson. About five thousand Confederates under the command of General Frank Gardner guarded the fort at Port Hudson. Banks had over twenty-five thousand troops for the attack. At last, stalwart defenders had nothing left to eat but their horses. There is a story about this incident:

> Fifteen days before the surrender of the fort the men worn out with dry corn, asked the officers to issue horse or mule beef. This was done, and the killing of the fattest of these animals was ordained.
>
> The next morning, while I was seated on a log with a tin plate holding a fat, juicy steak of mule, I observed Griff coming towards me with an expression of grief and anger . . . on his face. They had killed 'Old Jack,' his saddle mule . . . Here I was with difficulty succeeding in swallowing my first morsel of the sacrificial mule. . . .

After the 145 days of battle with 21 days of hard fighting, the defenders were exhausted. They heard that Vicksburg had surrendered. These Confederates, "digging in" on the bluff above the river, finally had to surrender, too. On July 9, 1863, just five days after the fall of Vicksburg, Port Hudson fell.

With the surrender of Vicksburg and Port Hudson the very last segment of the Mississippi River remaining in Confederate hands came under the control of Union forces. After the fall of Port Hudson, Lincoln said, "The Father of Waters goes unvexed to the sea." Much of Louisiana was occupied by the United States soldiers. The Blues held the Mississippi River and a strip of territory from New Orleans westward to Berwick Bay.

Louisiana men had long been fighting—and dying—in battles wherever the Confederate army fought. Louisiana did not see much activity in the last half of 1863. The reason was that Banks spent the latter part of 1863 on an expedition from New Orleans against Texas by sea. Confederate General Richard Taylor now held all the region of Louisiana west of the Mississippi River. In 1864 the federal troops planned complete occupation of Louisiana.

Government. In January 1863 the capital of Confederate Louisiana was moved to **Shreveport.** In that part of Louisiana that remained under the Confederacy, a new governor was elected in the fall of 1863. He was **Henry Watkins Allen,** a disabled veteran who was on crutches when he took office.

Allen had been in charge of the Fourth Regiment of Louisiana. He was badly wounded at the Battle of Baton Rouge. Like Moore, Allen was a planter. His plantation was Allendale in West Baton Rouge Parish. Governor Moore left to establish a plantation in Texas. Allen added life to the war effort when he started new programs.

Many sections of Louisiana were occupied off and on. New Orleans was occupied from April 1862 until the end of the war. Two governments existed during the war.

On December 15, 1862, officers for the United States Provisional Court for the state of Louisiana arrived in New Orleans from New York. The court went into operation early in 1863. It lasted throughout the remainder of the war. Under General Banks, a movement started in February 1863 for the reorganization of a loyal government in Louisiana. Many Union Associations were organized as part of this movement.

Emancipation Proclamation. President Abraham Lincoln issued his Emancipation Proclamation on January 1, 1863, as a propaganda device. He knew that England and France would like to help the Confederacy but knew that the proclamation could influence them to lean toward the Union. Besides, the North had lost battles, and the people needed something to spark new spirit. The proclamation was worded so that not a single slave was freed by it. The Emancipation Proclamation declared free all slaves held in parts of the United States not in the possession of the Union armies. In other words, Lincoln proclaimed that on January 1, 1863, all slaves within the Confederate lines were free. Lincoln had no jurisdiction over Confederate territory. He could not free slaves in the Confederacy. It was the Thirteenth Amendment to the United States Constitution that really ended slavery. That amendment was passed many months later.

Lagniappe. "Juneteenth" was called Emancipation Day in Texas and Louisiana for years. This date was not, of course, the anniversary of the Emancipation Proclamation. It was the date—June 19, 1865—that a proclamation was read to former slaves who had been in Texas during the war. Only then were they told that they were free. Many Louisiana slaves had been taken to Texas by their owners for the duration of the war. Therefore they were in Texas when they got the news.

Juneteenth was celebrated as a holiday. Often there were gifts of food, such as ice cream or watermelon, from the planter on whose place the workers were living. This was the day for all-day picnics, fishing trips, and the like. The planter usually provided the vehicles for transportation. In the 1960s these old-style celebrations ceased.

The Home Front. The people of Louisiana never imagined that the state itself would be a battlefield. Whether soldiers or homefolks, everybody was in the battle zone. Louisianians were greatly affected from the beginning to the end of the war.

Fortunes were lost, families ruined, homes burned, and land left idle for lack of anyone to work it. Fields left unattended grew up in cane or brush. The blockade prevented the sale of cotton and the purchase of clothing, tools, and household necessities. Trains ceased to run due to lack of repairs. In some cases the tracks provided iron for the war effort. Several miles of track near Shreveport were used for construction of the Confederate ironclad *Missouri*. No new railroad lines were added. There was no way to repair old ones. Steamboats rotted. Roads were not repaired. Bridges were destroyed or rotted.

Life behind the Confederate lines was very grim. It was not glamorous the way it often appears in movies and novels. At the outset of the war the South was pitifully short of everything except good fighting men. Nearly all able-bodied men went into the army. The homefront provided the fighting men with food and arms.

There were times when the soldiers ran out of food, however. The South managed to keep the men in weapons. Many of their weapons were taken from the enemy.

Louisianians were urged to economize. Louisiana citizens were proud of the sacrifices they made. They even joked about some of these sacrifices. They called tin spoons and cups "Confederate silver," cornmeal "Confederate flour," and pine torches "Confederate candles." Many items that once had been easily obtained became very scarce. Matches, nails, writing paper, soap, needles, cutlery, glassware, and starch were among the scarce items.

Families grieved over the death of a beloved father, brother, son, or husband. Approximately one-fifth of the Louisiana men who had gone to war died in battle or hospitals.

Women and children were often alone on the plantations. Slaves were restless with talk of armies coming to free them from slavery. The people at home feared slave uprisings or military invasion. Many slaves left. The war wreaked incalculable damage to Louisiana plantations. The contents of plantation houses were often taken by the Union soldiers, guerrilla fighters, or the slaves.

The Union soldiers and their leaders believed that destroying Southern property would help win the war. Besides, both armies lived off the land. Chickens, horses, corn, and anything else edible were taken. Many families saw the foodstuff needed for the winter swept away in an hour. Sometimes more was taken than could have been used. Looters took watches, jewels, and silverware. After Banks and his men confiscated property, the practice was continued by other Union men.

The year 1863 educated all of Louisiana that had not yet learned about the tragedy of war. Horses walked across fields and gardens. The cavalry and the infantry of both armies had crisscrossed plantation fields and torn down fences for firewood. Union soldiers took grim delight in holding hands in a tight line and rushing against a fence to destroy it. If a planter were off fighting for the Confederacy, there was no mercy. Food was scarce. Both sides took food when they found it.

The worst suffering from lack of food was in the Florida parishes. Flour and coffee were rarely found except in the federally occupied areas. Parched corn, peanuts, and thinly sliced sweet potato toasted brown and crisp were substituted for coffee. Salt was very scarce until 1862 when a mine was found. Great quantities were mined at Avery Island and distributed in the state. In the regions that escaped the federal invasion, hominy, cornmeal, and pork were usually available. Rice, sugar, and syrup were available in southern parishes.

Louisiana's economy stagnated during the war. The federal blockade along the Gulf of Mexico practically

LOUISIANA GOVERNORS DURING THE WAR

CONFEDERATE LOUISIANA	OCCUPIED LOUISIANA
Thomas Overton Moore (1860-1864)	George F. Shepley (1862-1864)
Henry Watkins Allen (1864-1865)	Michael Hahn (resigned) (1864-1865)
	James Madison Wells (succeeded as lt. governor) (1865-1867)

stopped commerce in New Orleans. Shipping to inland Louisiana by waterway ceased with the war. There was no money to buy anything. Confederate currency was worth less and less as time passed. Banks were in unsound conditions. Most were at the point of bankruptcy. To help the situation, Governor Moore stopped the banks from making payments in gold and silver. Confederate money had to be accepted at face value. By the end of 1864 Confederate money was worth nothing. Eventually, this worthless money ruined many banks in New Orleans. They had no money to lend. Merchants could not provide credit. Louisianians lost millions in Confederate currency. Approximately $170 million invested in slaves had vanished. The labor supply was gone. Crop production dropped drastically. The crops that were raised could not be sold. Goods were scarce. Prices soared.

After the Union captured New Orleans, aroused citizens in the state above New Orleans went into action to plan against further invasion of the state. It was a frightening time. In Rapides Parish, as in other places over the state, men met to form **Committees of Public Safety**. This plan was patterned after a Revolutionary War organization by the same name. They had to decide what was to be done should the enemy invade inland communities.

In the crisis, with troops occupying New Orleans and Baton Rouge, the committee met frequently to make plans. Their work included such projects as authorizing collections of food and clothing for the needs of suffering people in the occupied city of New Orleans. They also planned to punish persons ridiculing or reflecting adversely on Confederate currency. The members discussed setting up a system of warning lights to indicate the approach of invading Union troops. Moreover, there was the problem of working out ways to hide cotton and livestock from invaders.

The people went back to the American Revolution for plans used during that war. Couriers were placed at points along possible invasion routes, much like the plan used when Paul Revere made his famous ride. By a series of light signals and by couriers racing ahead of the invaders, people were to be warned of the location of the enemy and the action he was taking.

The Committee of Public Safety allowed a man to appear before an Alexandria group to ask for food for the people of Occupied New Orleans. After the Union troops took over the city, New Orleans was under martial law. All commerce ceased. All work disappeared. Confederate money was useless. There was no United States money. People were starving. Would Rapides Parish residents help fill two ships waiting in the harbor with supplies to help the suffering people of New Orleans? They would help. But the committee voted for safeguards to be sure that the supplies were for the New Orleans residents. Every article on the ships was carefully checked before leaving Alexandria.

A letter written by a Louisiana housewife in 1865 gives an indication of what was going on inside Occupied Baton Rouge:

I have made my home spun dress and actually worn it several times, it is very comfortible . . . I like the stile of sleeve very much, it does not take much cloth and is very becoming. I got the fashion from a lady who lives in the Yankee lines. She said that they were very much worn. That lady bought us several articles. She went to Batten Roughe [Baton Rouge] and smuggled them out for us. She brought out three Hats, one for your Pa and one a piece for the boys; they cost $6 a piece in good money, they are very fine, one pr. of large size sisors, Splendid articles four dollars. a set of shoe tools for George, two paper nedles, three paper tacks, pencils, etc. She could not bring anything large as she had to bring them under a hoop.

Clothing was a problem. When leather became scarce, shoes were made of heavy canvas with soles of wood. When buttons were not available, substitutes were made. Persimmon seed or circular pieces of gourd had holes punched through them. Women made canvas and other kinds of cloth in their homes. Old spinning wheels were brought out. Women learned the art of spinning and weaving. They made dyes at home. When old garments showed wear, they were ripped apart and turned inside out. Then they were made into another garment.

Escape to Texas: 1862–64. From the fall of New Orleans to the second invasion of the Red River Valley, residents of Louisiana fled to Texas. Texas was a haven for young men avoiding the draft. Many gathered all of their possessions—livestock, farm tools, poultry, and slaves—and moved to Texas. In some parts of Texas the landscape and the soil looked much like that of Louisiana. Once they located a site, they threw up a log house. Some found abandoned farm houses. They cleared land or purchased land already cleared and went about their farming operations.

Many of the displaced Louisiana citizens remained in Texas after the war was over. Some refugees got no farther than the banks of the Sabine River. There they camped.

Union officers took charge of abandoned houses to use as headquarters for the troops. Sometimes the houses were burned to the ground when the troops left.

At least one particular group of refugees went to Texas with a unique idea. They established a company for mining bat guano (bat droppings) for saltpeter in southwestern Texas caves. Many of these caves had remained unvisited by man since their formation. Bats had roosted in their dark depths for centuries. The odor in the caves was overwhelming. Hundreds of bats beat their wings in the darkness.

The guano could be filtered to obtain saltpeter, which was used for making **gunpowder**. The Confederacy was desperate for gunpowder. Men working on such projects were exempt from the Confederate draft. Slaves, rented to the company by their masters, were involved in the undertaking also.

Cotton Sales. Refugees from Louisiana with wagons and mules found that they could rent out their equipment to the Confederacy for hauling cotton across the border to Mexico.

Cotton was used as a medium of exchange with foreign countries in place of Confederate money. Therefore, the Confederacy had trains of wagons streaming in and out of Mexico. There the cotton could be shipped aboard Mexican ships. These ships could evade the blockade of the enemy. In this way the South secured desperately needed war supplies from such countries as France and England.

Guerrilla Fighters and Jayhawkers. Not only was the Union to be feared, but equally frightening for the home folks were the sporadic night attacks of bold Jayhawkers. These bands of men, of the age to be drafted, operated from the piney woods in both northern and western Louisiana. They were not willing to serve in the Confederate army. They did not want to go to war to fight for slavery. They owned no slaves, nor wanted any. They did not like the planters who thought themselves to be of a higher class. Most of the accounts about the Civil War in which the Jayhawkers were described were writ-

YEAR-BY-YEAR PROGRESS OF UNION FORCES IN LOUISIANA

Confederate Louisiana   Occupied Louisiana

ten from the viewpoint of this planter class. The Jayhawkers were always described as villains.

During the day they stayed hidden deep in virgin forests of the hill country, and they roamed the plantation areas at night. Near Glenmora one identified Jayhawker hideout survives. It is called Jayhawker's Island. There were others north of Jonesville.

At night Jayhawkers on horseback rode into plantation lowlands. There they stole anything handy. They wrecked, destroyed, and harassed. They robbed civilians. By daylight they were back at the hideouts.

People of the woodlands saddled fresh horses and left them waiting for the Jayhawkers. The tired horse used that night for a foray into the lowlands was left to get food. Hunting and fishing in virgin country yielded bountiful wild game and fish for food for the Jayhawkers. Sympathizers supplied the rest.

There were undoubtedly outlaws among the Jayhawkers. On the other hand, there were many who were guerrilla fighters for the Union. So important did they become that, later in the war, men from the Confederate army were detailed to come to western Louisiana to search for these men. They were told to offer them the opportunity to join the Confederate army with no questions asked. Bands of local citizens searched for them. The stealing of livestock, burn-

ing, and destroying of Confederate property went on throughout the war.

1864: Second Invasion of the Red River Valley. In 1864 **Banks** executed his second and largest invasion of the Red River Valley. It was the last major campaign of the Civil War in Louisiana.

Banks took the same route from Brashear City that he had taken in 1863. Union soldiers marched up the Teche. From Washington they went north up the winding Bayou Boeuf to Alexandria. This time they were aided by ten thousand soldiers released from Vicksburg. These came into central Louisiana at Simmesport on transports under General A. J. Smith. General Banks had twenty-six thousand troops. Another fifteen thousand troops were expected to come from Arkansas to attack Shreveport. In a fleet of nineteen warships, Admiral **David Porter** headed up the Red River. Union naval gunboats and transports entered the Red River through Simmesport.

Major General **Richard Taylor** was in command of Confederate troops south of the Red River. With him was Brigadier General **Alfred Mouton**, member of a well-known family from Lafayette. As Banks advanced toward Alexandria, Taylor's troops were also headed north, advancing to meet him. Taylor had only 8,800 men commandeered from all the area. Union forces were more than three times greater.

Near Marksville a fort had been constructed. It had been built by slaves. This was **Fort de Russy**, an earthworks barricade. Confederates hoped that it would stop any invasion up the Red River. Fort de Russy lasted only a couple of hours or so before the big guns from the Union ships brought its surrender on March 14. After that the Union's fleet of ships had clear passage up the river to Alexandria.

Banks captured Alexandria and set up controls. About five hundred Jayhawkers came to Banks's headquarters and joined the Union army. Porter proceeded upstream. Banks led his army on toward Shreveport. Taylor's and Mouton's troops moved at the same time in the same direction. There were skirmishes along the way between the small groups of the two armies. There was wholesale destruction of houses, fences, crops, and other possessions. All the land over which the invaders traveled was a battleground. Everything in the path of the invaders was in the war zone.

Natchitoches was captured. Since Porter was increasingly concerned about the low-water stages of the Red River, it was decided that the fleet would go no farther than about six miles beyond Natchitoches. This was at Grand Ecore.

Banks's route did not follow the river closely. Banks followed the beaten trails which ran through the pine-covered hill country to Shreveport. Banks arrived at Mansfield. The village was located on a stretch of flat land among gently rolling hills. Taylor decided to challenge the invaders at this point. On April 8, 1864, the **Battle of Mansfield** was fought. The Union was soundly defeated.

Banks moved his tired soldiers eight miles south to **Pleasant Hill**. On April 9, 1864, a second major battle was fought. The Union won as decisively as the Confederates had won at Mansfield the day before. There were heavy losses on both sides. To the complete surprise of the Confederates, Banks then retreated. Banks was apparently discouraged from going on to Shreveport. His weary troops were driven in disorder back toward Alexandria with Taylor close behind.

It was the third effort at great expense that Banks had mounted to invade Texas. Why did he change his mind at this point?

The defenses were so weak at Shreveport that "**Fort Humbug**" was arranged atop a bluff. Union boats on the Red River were expected to believe that there were huge cannons aimed toward the river below. Actually, the only "big guns" were large logs painted to resemble cannons. Shreveport and the surrounding area were never invaded, however.

Porter began to return south to Alexandria. The Red River was very shallow at some places. Getting to Alexandria was an enormous job. The water level was falling every day.

General Sherman had taught at Louisiana State Seminary at Alexandria. He knew the problems of navigating the Red River. He had cautioned Admiral Porter about the rapids in the river a little above the city. These rapids had posed hazards to navigation since man had known the river. They had presented a problem to the invasion all along, as Sherman saw it. Sherman warned Porter that the river waters might fall dangerously low for the big boats. That is exactly what happened.

Now, when Admiral Porter attempted to navigate the Red River back toward Alexandria, he ran into a critical problem. When Porter had steamed up the river, he had gone past the rapids with ease due to the high water. However, when he reached this point in returning, he could not get the fleet over the rapids. General Banks, with the army stationed at Alexandria, was available to help the navy avoid a disaster, but how?

Bailey's Dam. There was near-panic. The fleet could not possibly get by the rapids. Colonel Thomas Bailey, a Wisconsin lumberman, presented his plan for a wing dam to General Banks.

The dam would force the water into a narrow but deeper channel through which the fleet could escape.

The idea sounded fantastic. Almost no one believed it could be done. Since all else had failed, Bailey was finally told to build his dam.

Bailey was assigned three thousand soldiers to assist him. Union men scoured the country for what remained of old buildings, iron kettles, the tracks of the old Red River railroad—whatever! All of the material was placed into the river along with trees cut from Pineville hills. It was done in a manner that restricted the flow of water and caused the surface level to rise. The incredible feat was accomplished in record time.

The moment came to see if the dam would work. The first attempt to get a boat through the new channel failed. The banks of the river were lined with Union soldiers and sailors laughing at the effort. This changed to cheers quickly when the entire fleet of sixteen boats, boat by boat, crossed to safety.

The Burnt District. General Banks's steamboat was waiting for him to give the signal to leave. Nobody knows who gave the order—or if one was given. Some historians even say that it was the Jayhawkers who caused the holocaust that followed. Each side blamed the other. **Alexandria** was burned to the ground. Eyewitness accounts taken later by Louisiana Governor Allen told something of the story: "The Court House was the only building on the square.

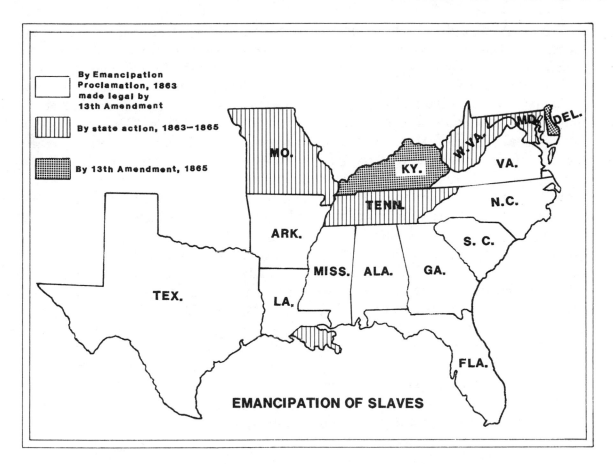

By Emancipation Proclamation, 1863 made legal by 13th Amendment

By state action, 1863—1865

By 13th Amendment, 1865

EMANCIPATION OF SLAVES

It fronted the river, the three other sides facing blocks of buildings, all of which had been consumed, and had fallen down in smoldering ruins, and yet the Court House stood uninjured. It was fired in the interior and was consumed with every record of the Parish."

There were now no records of who owned the land. There were no defined boundaries of property. There were no marriage records. These and more turned to ashes. The area became known as the "burnt district."

Buildings were burned along the river all the way to Natchitoches. A person who saw the wrecked countryside described it: "His [Banks's] march from five miles outside of Natchitoches, had been illumined by the glare of burning homesteads."

After this second invasion of the Red River Valley, disheartened people began to make plans to defend themselves against a third. Plans were made for forts to be constructed at Alexandria. These included two forts on the Pineville side, Fort Buhlow and Fort Randolph. A third, much larger fort was planned on the Alexandria side. The first two were earthworks. The third was never built.

1865. The collapse of government in Confederate Louisiana began during the spring of 1865. Actually, law and order had not prevailed for some time. There was no enforcement of the civil law in the state. There was very little military enforcement. As soon as the Rebels knew that they were defeated, many deserted. Since the fall of Vicksburg and Port Hudson, desertion had increased. Deserters were shot if they were caught. At one time five or ten from Kirby Smith's army were executed every Friday.

Wild disorder prevailed as lawless groups robbed and took what they wanted. Storehouses were pillaged by both civilians and soldiers. Supplies were taken. Deserters roamed everywhere. Maintaining order became impossible.

There was practically no military activity in the state in 1865. On May 26, 1865, the Department of Trans-Mississippi under **General Kirby Smith** was the last Confederate command to surrender. Smith had moved the headquarters of the department from Shreveport to Houston. General Simon Buckner, acting for Smith, signed the surrender papers in New Orleans. Smith signed the official documents for surrender

of his army at Houston, but the final phase of the surrender took place on June 11, 1865, in Shreveport.

Governor Allen delivered a farewell address to the people at Shreveport on June 2, 1865. Then he went across Texas into voluntary exile in Mexico. He died there in 1866.

Long before then, many a Louisiana soldier, defeated and near exhaustion, was making his weary way home after the surrender at Appomattox on April 9, 1865.

About six hundred military engagements had taken place in Louisiana. Most of these were just skirmishes. Louisiana had suffered more destruction and casualties than any of the other Confederate states except Georgia, Virginia, and South Carolina. The fighting was over, but the war continued.

En Partie 2 (Studying a Part). 1. What was this war called? 2. When was it fought? 3. What was done to prepare Louisiana for the war? 4. Why was 1862 a fateful year for Louisianians? 5. How did the blockade affect Louisiana? 6. Describe the major battles in Louisiana. 7. Why was the location of the capital changed? 8. How did Louisiana contribute to the war effort? 9. How did fighting on Louisiana soil affect the state? 10. Why did the Union want to capture the Mississippi River? 11. (a) Which department of the Confederacy was the last to surrender? (b) When? (c) Who was the commander of the department? (d) Where did the last phase of the surrender of the Confederacy take place? (e) When? 12. Describe the ending of the war.

Coup d'Main
(Completing the Story)

Jambalaya (Putting It All Together)

1. Identify:
   (1) abolitionists
   (2) Abraham Lincoln
   (3) Alfred Mouton
   (4) Bailey's Dam
   (5) Benjamin Butler
   (6) Blue
   (7) Camp Moore
   (8) Committee of Public Safety
   (9) Confederate States of America
   (10) David Farragut
   (11) Emancipation Proclamation
   (12) Gray
   (13) Henry W. Allen
   (14) Jayhawkers
   (15) Judah P. Benjamin
   (16) Kirby Smith
   (17) Leonidas Polk
   (18) Mansfield Lovell
   (19) Nathaniel Banks
   (20) Occupied Louisiana
   (21) Order No. 28
   (22) P. G. T. Beauregard
   (23) Rebels
   (24) Richard "Dick" Taylor
   (25) Robert E. Lee
   (26) Thomas O. Moore
   (27) Ulysses Grant
   (28) Union
   (29) William Mumford
   (30) Yankees

2. Map work. On a United States map, color the Confederate states gray, the United States blue, and the border states red. Outline the cotton states. On a Louisiana map, label the capitals of Louisiana during the Civil War. Give the date for each capitol in parentheses. Label major Louisiana battles. Underline Union victories in blue and Confederate victories in gray.

3. How did the war affect the following: slaves, free people of color, planters, small farmers, housewives, merchants, teenagers, manufacturers, planters, and bankers?

4. Describe the economic conditions in the state before and during the war.

5. Chart the course of the war in Louisiana and relate it to the rest of the war.

6. Compare life before the war with life during the war.

7. Trace the development of Louisiana government from the time of secession until the war ended.

Potpourri (Getting Involved)

1. Research the background of *Uncle Tom's Cabin*. Relate the book to Louisiana. Give an oral review. Read excerpts.

2. Conduct a panel discussion on the causes of the war. Include political, social, and economic factors.

3. Dramatize a scene involving a discussion of Louisiana's secession.

4. Describe the procedures followed and dangers encountered in your work on the Underground Railroad. Plan an escape route for a runaway slave.

5. Make an illustrated timeline of events from 1861 to 1865.

6. Write a series of letters as a Confederate teenager in Louisiana to a friend describing hardships endured during the war. Relate not only physical sufferings but also injuries to pride and reaction to unjust treatment by Union soldiers.

7. Construct a mural to depict (a) homelife during the war, (b) activities of the Jayhawkers, (c) a certain battle, or (d) any of the happenings leading to the war.

8. Tell Civil War stories to the class. Read aloud a selection of diary accounts of the war in Louisiana.

9. Research the role of (a) the Negro, (b) cotton, (c) Louisiana troops, or (d) Louisiana leaders in the war.

10. Contrast (a) the life of Billy Yanks with Johnny Rebs or (b) the homemaker in the North with the homemaker in the South.

Gumbo (Bringing It Up-to-Date)

1. Pretend that you were a Northern sympathizer in Louisiana opposed to slavery. Imagine what life would have been like during the war if your neighbors had known your feelings. Compare your life then with life today for someone who does not go along with the popular thinking on integration.

2. Relate the geography of the United States to the lives of the people. Show how the thinking of the people then and now is influenced by geography.

3. Compare (a) the states' rights issues of the period with the modern states' rights issues, (b) Northern and Southern advantages and disadvantages of the Civil War period with those of today, or (c) abolitionists' actions with civil rights activists' methods.

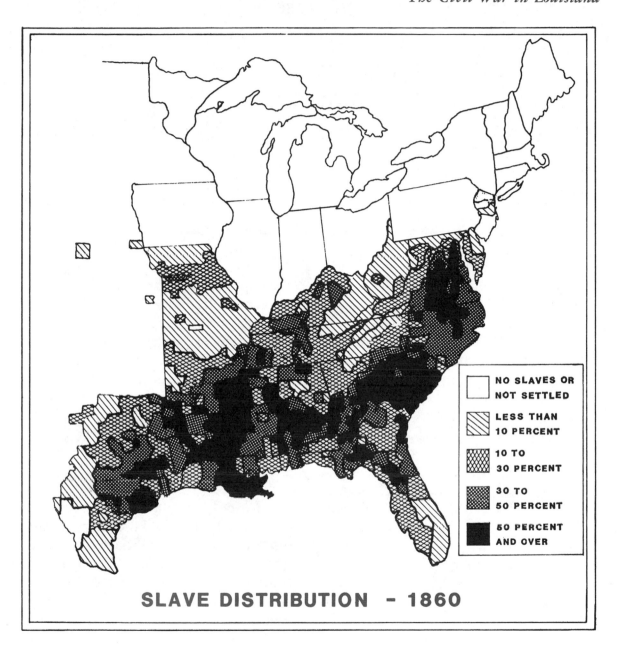

SLAVE DISTRIBUTION – 1860

NO SLAVES OR NOT SETTLED

LESS THAN 10 PERCENT

10 TO 30 PERCENT

30 TO 50 PERCENT

50 PERCENT AND OVER

CHAPTER 9

RECONSTRUCTION
(1865–1877)

The war was over. The men headed home. Louisianians, still in their gray uniforms, trudged along dusty roads toward their loved ones. Many were limping. All were sick at heart. For four years they had been away from their families. They had fought and endured much hardship. They had seen friends die. Now, despite their hardships and suffering, the Yankees occupied and controlled the South. The way of life the Confederacy had fought to save was ended. The men were not returning to a hero's welcome. Most Louisianians returned to badly run-down farms and plantations. They were overgrown with weeds, and the workers were gone. In the regions where Banks's army had been, and that included most of Louisiana, the men came home to ruins. Cotton gins and sugar mills had been burned. Horses and other livestock were gone. Steamboats were not running. Railroad lines were destroyed. Louisiana was a sad sight. The spirits of many of the people were broken. Some did not have the heart to start life again. Others chose to go to Mexico, South America, or Europe. Most Louisianians—both returning soldiers and those who remained at home—waited anxiously to find out what their fate would be under the Union conquerors.

Political Readjustment

Lincoln's Plan. On December 8, 1863, President Lincoln presented his idea of how the South should be restored to the Union. Some conditions had to be met. First, full pardon would be granted to all Southerners except some Confederate civil and military leaders. Southerners had to promise to accept the federal laws and proclamations dealing with slavery. When at least ten percent of the people voting in the election of 1860 took the oath of allegiance to the Union, then a state could draw up a new constitution, elect new officials, and return to the Union on a basis of full equality.

Andrew Johnson, President. When President Lincoln was assassinated on April 14, 1865, Andrew Johnson became president. Johnson was a Southerner from Tennessee. He had not worked for the Confederacy, but he sympathized with the South's problems after the war. He led the planters to believe that there would be no penalty for being defeated in the war. He followed Lincoln's policy with few exceptions. Property seized by federal troops was restored to those taking the loyalty oath. He promised the former Confederate states that they would be readmitted into the Union and granted full self-government. Before the citizens of the state could elect their own officials, they had to elect delegates to a state convention to write a new constitution. In turn, these constitutions had to provide for the end of slavery, acknowledge that a state had no right to secede, and declare that the money borrowed by the state from its citizens to fight the war would not be repaid.

Johnson was aware of the opposition to this plan in Congress. He tried to get all the Confederate states to meet the conditions immediately. Louisiana did so. The people of the state were able to run the government for two years before the Radical Republicans again took control.

The Radical Republicans. Not all leaders of the Republican party agreed with the President's plan for reconstruction. One group called the Radical Republicans wanted to punish the South. The South had lost the war, and the Northern victors had won the right to impose penalties on the South. That is, the Radical Republicans thought so. The Radicals in Congress bitterly opposed what they considered as being too easy on the South. They thought it the right of Congress, not the president, to plan reconstruction.

The Freedmen's Bureau. The Freedmen's Bureau was set up by President Lincoln in 1865 strictly to provide welfare services to the needy of both races after the war. A hostile Congress under President Johnson extended the bureau a year later but shaped it into a radically different organization. It was an arm of the Republican party. Its functions now included supervision of labor contracts between the freedmen and the planters, assistance with voter registration, and the education of the freedmen.

In important ways the Freedmen's Bureau represented radical thinking regarding the role of the federal government. Never before had the United States government interfered with business operations. Northern industrialists feared that this new power of the central government might extend to the Northern factories as well. Most of the Northern leaders and the other people did not want such control.

The Freedmen's Bureau was not immune from the corruption that dominated the goverment in both the North and South during this period.

Carpetbaggers and Scalawags. After the war many people from other sections moved into the South, including Louisiana. The newcomers were Republicans. These people, called carpetbaggers, came for many reasons. Some were trying to make money in the war-torn section. Others were missionaries who wanted to educate the former slaves. Some thought they would teach the South how to live in the modern world of industrial expansion. Others came for political advantages. Some came simply to live in a milder climate. They had discovered the advantages of the warmer climate when they were soldiers here during the war. Some men had met Louisiana women and wanted to marry them and settle in the state.

Louisiana had a carpetbag government throughout the period of Military Reconstruction ordered by Congress. That is, the state government was controlled by these newcomers from other parts of the country.

COMING HOME

Scalawags were native Louisianians who joined the Republican party. Most were sugar planters. These planters supported the industrial North's position on the protective tariff. The protective tariff included sugar. The importing of cheap foreign sugar would hinder the sales of Louisiana sugarcane crops.

Scalawag Governor James Madison Wells. When the Union won the war, it took over the government of the Southern states, including Louisiana. The old Confederate government was out of business. The United States government in New Orleans, supported by the United States military, was Louisiana's only government. Michael Hahn, a New Orleans lawyer, and James Madison Wells, a Rapides planter, were elected governor and lieutenant governor of Occupied Louisiana on February 22, 1864. Hahn resigned on March 4, 1865, when elected to the United States Senate. President Johnson then recognized Wells as governor.

Wells was a member of a family of early settlers in Rapides Parish. He was a big planter and slaveowner. He had strongly opposed secession and had taken no part in the Civil War. His fellow planters resented this. Wells had opposed the Confederate government of Louisiana during the war. He followed Banks's retreating army at the end of the Red River Valley campaign. He was a scalawag.

He was a native who sided with the Union and joined the Republican party. Perhaps in favoring the Union, Wells's position is best explained by his feeling that the South was committing a tragic mistake in seceding from the Union and fighting against the North. Wells had spent much of his early life in Kentucky and attended college in Washington, D.C. He knew the great advantages in the North's large population, railroad lines, and factories that could turn out war materials. He had felt from the beginning that the South could never win a war against the North.

Governor Wells altered his views enough to gain support from Confederate sympathizers. In May 1865 Governor Wells ordered a new registration of voters. Only men could vote, and they had to be white men over twenty-one years of age. They had to have lived in the state a year and had to have taken the oath of allegiance to the Union. The Louisiana Constitution of 1864, written for Occupied Louisiana, empowered the governor to extend the suffrage, or voting rights, to some Negroes. Governor Wells refused to do so.

President Johnson allowed Southerners to think that they could return to the way life was before the war. That is exactly what Louisiana planters proceeded to do.

Louisiana Democrats. The Democratic party met in New Orleans the fall after the Civil War ended. Representatives to the Democratic Convention were from the planter-merchant class, which had always controlled Louisiana government. They accepted the 1864 constitution until another could be fashioned. The Democrats claimed the right to ask the government for compensation for the slaves freed by the war. Before the war this proposition had been advanced by abolitionists. However, nothing came of it. Now that the war was over there was small chance that anything would be done about the planters' losses. Over the South the value of slaves amounted to two billion dollars. Louisiana's slave losses amounted to one-third of its total wealth.

The Black Code. When the legislature met in 1865 after the war ended, the planters proceeded to pass legislation "to put the Negro back to work." Like in all Southern states, this set of laws was called the Black Code. Louisiana's Black Code gave the freedmen only slightly higher status than they had had as slaves before the war. Freedmen were not allowed to serve on police juries or bear arms. A freedman could not testify against a white man in court. If not working, the freedmen could be charged with vagrancy. In that case a fine was levied, which he likely could not pay. If not, he was placed under the authority of a planter or assigned to public work.

Louisiana and the Fourteenth Amendment. In June 1866 the Fourteenth Amendment was sent to the states for ratification. It granted citizenship to all persons born or naturalized in the United States. This constitutional amendment was passed by Congress after Johnson vetoed their Civil Rights Bill. President Johnson advised the South that it did not have to ratify the Fourteenth Amendment. President Johnson kept assuring the officials that people sympathetic toward the South would be elected in the fall of 1866. That was not true. As it turned out, even more Radical Republicans were elected to Congress. Louisiana did not ratify the Fourteenth Amendment. Of the Southern states, only Tennessee ratified it. That was due to the efforts of President Johnson's political enemy, "Parson" Brownlow, in his home state. Tennessee did not have to endure Military Reconstruction because the state ratified the Fourteenth Amendment.

New Orleans Riot. Governor Wells decided that a new constitution was needed to replace the 1864 constitution. He called for a constitutional convention, but the former Confederates voted it down. He then decided to reconvene the Constitutional Convention of 1864. The group included black leaders.

The convention met at the Mechanics Institute in New Orleans on July 30, 1866. The mayor of New Orleans, John T. Moore, called upon the police and citizens to stop the convention. Federal police had been scheduled to help protect those attending the convention, but they arrived too late. A riot broke out, and the Metropolitan Police sided with Moore and the protesting whites. In the riot 34 Negroes were killed and 119 wounded. Among those killed was one of the most outstanding black leaders in the state, Dr. A. P. Dostie. Three white Unionists were killed and about seventeen were wounded. Among the wounded was Michael Hahn, former Republican governor of Occupied Louisiana and senator-elect.

A riot also occurred in Memphis, Tennessee, during the summer of 1866. These two riots in major Southern cities and the Black Codes passed by all the Southern legislatures under the Johnson administration brought angry protest from Northern people. This added to the determination of the Radical Republicans to place the South under Congressional control.

Military Reconstruction. When

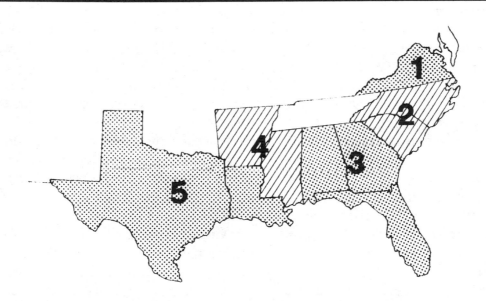

MILITARY DISTRICTS DURING RECONSTRUCTION

the first Southern congressmen elected after the war went to take their seats in December 1865, they were not accepted. Instead, Congress took matters into its own hands regarding the defeated South. A joint committee from the Senate and House of Representatives was appointed to visit the South to find out if the South had accepted defeat. The status of the freedmen was to be examined. Finally, the committee was told to come back with a Congressional plan for Reconstruction. This they did.

In 1867—two years later—Congress passed its own Reconstruction Acts. This was Military Reconstruction. The South was treated as conquered territory and divided into five military districts. Each district was placed under the rule of an army general backed with federal troops. Under the new laws Louisiana would have to write a new constitution to give Negroes the right to vote and hold office. The ruling generals would then register voters, including Negroes. The right to vote was taken away from high-ranking Confederate military men and officials. Certain other provisions were laid down under which Louisiana might reenter the Union.

General Philip H. Sheridan, famous Union cavalryman, was briefly in command of District 5, which included Louisiana and Texas. Sheridan removed Governor Wells and appointed a former schoolteacher, Benjamin F. Flanders, as governor. Sheridan was also involved in racial troubles in New Orleans. In the city there were about twenty thousand black people who were free before the Civil War. They were willing to fight for equal rights. The first civil rights demonstrations took place in New Orleans in 1867. A black man, William Nichols, tried to ride an all-white streetcar. He was removed. This incident encouraged other demonstrations. About five hundred blacks hurled stones at "star cars" (so called because a star designated them all-white cars). One demonstrator took over an empty streetcar and drove it through the city. His supporters shouted. General Sheridan ended the situation. He met with the mayor and officials of the transit company. Sheridan announced that the streetcars would be desegregated immediately.

Sheridan was replaced by Winfield S. Hancock in command of the state. Hancock appointed Joshua Baker governor. Baker governed for only a short period.

Constitution of 1868. The constitutional convention met at the Mechanics Institute in New Orleans on November 23, 1867. Forty-nine blacks and forty-nine whites wrote the new constitution. It incorporated the principles of the Thirteenth and Fourteenth amendments to the United

States Constitution. It contained a bill of rights. Negro males over the age of twenty-one were given the right to vote. The constitution required that public places and public conveyances be open to all people, regardless of race. Public education was also open to all. This constitution was unenforceable without federal troops.

Election of 1868. After the constitution was written, people elected officials and ratified the constitution by a large vote in 1868. For the first time blacks voted. Henry Clay Warmoth, a twenty-six-year-old carpetbagger, was elected governor. A black, Oscar J. Dunn, was elected lieutenant governor. Other blacks were elected to offices. Two carpetbaggers, William Pitt Kellogg and John H. Harris, were elected to the United States Senate. The elections increased the anger of the planters toward the Republicans. Nothing so irritated the planters as allowing their former "properties" to vote.

General Ulysses S. Grant, hero of the Union army, became president in 1868. He served a term that was remarkable for its scandals.

Governor Henry C. Warmoth. Warmoth was the first governor elected by the voters under the Reconstruction Acts. Therefore, he actually began Radical Reconstruction in Louisiana. He was the first elected after the Constitution of 1868 was written.

At eighteen, Henry C. Warmoth had opened a law office in Springfield, Missouri. When the Civil War broke out, he joined the Union army and became a lieutenant colonel. He remained in New Orleans after the war. There he opened a law practice and appeared in military courts.

Warmoth was one of those rare individuals who possessed so much charm that even his political enemies saluted him. He was as much a racist as it was possible to be. He believed as much as any Southerner in white supremacy. He was an artist at wielding political power. Through the offices of sheriffs throughout the state, he gained a hold on the state's power structure. In time Warmoth became practically a dictator. He controlled the legislature.

For the first time in history, ordinary people held office. They sought public services—education, levees, roads, and the like. Earlier Louisiana governments had never supplied these services. Partly because of these extras the expense of government rose much higher. Dishonesty in public spending was another cause. Under Warmoth and Military Reconstruction, the state debt increased. In less than three years Warmoth's administration added three million dollars to the state's debt.

More blacks than whites voted in Louisiana during this period of radical Reconstruction. Under the laws

82,907 blacks and 44,732 whites registered to vote. There were about an equal number of blacks and whites in the state. Even with the heavy casualties of the war, the numbers of white and black males over twenty-one should have been about equal. The registrars eliminated many whites. The registrars had the right to deny them the right to vote. They did this on the grounds that the white men were not sincere in their loyalty oaths. A large number of white men did not try to register. They felt it an indignity to submit to the black registrars, or they wanted no part of the new government, or there were other reasons. The fact that black voters were in the majority enraged the planters and merchants.

After black males were voting in the South, a movement began to secure passage of an amendment allowing all adult males to vote. Blacks were not allowed to vote in all Northern states. This movement resulted in the Fifteenth Amendment to the United States Constitution. The Fifteenth Amendment granted the right to vote to all citizens, regardless of race or color.

Metropolitan Police. Warmoth's legislature declared the area that comprised Orleans, St. Bernard, and Jefferson parishes a Metropolitan Police district. Warmoth got the legislature to expand the work of the Metropolitan Police. The city police

of New Orleans formed the nucleus of this enlarged force. The Metropolitan Brigade acted as the state militia. They received orders from a five-man commission under the governor's control. The Brigade was subject to the call of the governor.

Changes in Louisiana Government. Reconstruction brought radical change. Universal male suffrage (the right of all male adults to vote) was only one of the ways that Louisiana government had changed. Former slaves could not only vote, but, as officeholders, could cast votes to tax the property of their former masters. A "propertyless" class in control of the state government chilled the hearts of men who had long felt that their ownership of property gave them the right to govern.

For the first time in history, the state government included nonplanters. People with little or no property had a voice in the government. The ideas of democratic government were introduced. The ordinary people now in positions of power in Louisiana government felt that they were in the state's politics to stay.

The planter-merchant class was not included in the government of 1868. These were the men who had dominated, even monopolized, Louisiana government up to this time. In 1868 there were, according to Warmoth, sixty-five Republicans and thirty-six Democrats in the legislature. Thirty-five of the Republicans were black. None of the Democrats was black. The House of Representatives was nearly fifty percent black in its membership. Of twenty-three Republicans in the Senate, seven were black and all thirteen Democrats were white. The new situation presented a totally different government. This group ratified the Fourteenth and Fifteenth amendments to the United States Constitution.

The former ruling class scoffed at the officials who had taken their places in government. They pointed to their lack of education and ridiculed their manners and their language. Their own point of reference was of course what they considered proper. Manners of the Victorian period were very precise. The way one dressed, held his fork, crossed his legs, or blew his nose were critical signs of proper deportment to the ruling class of society. They were people with time to devote to learning the refinements of the Victorian age. The people in the government from 1868 to 1877 had little concern for, or even knowledge of, such niceties. In the minds of the old ruling class of that day, such matters defined a gentleman. Opponents of the government at this time found that there were no gentlemen in the legislature. The fact horrified them.

The Redeemers. The former Confederate leaders deeply resented the

Louisiana's 1868 Legislature

Senate — 23 Republicans — 7 Blacks, 16 Whites; 13 Democrats — 13 Whites

House of Representatives — 65 Republicans — 35 Blacks, 30 Whites; 36 Democrats — 36 Whites

Reconstruction government forced upon them. They were determined to do something about it. They began a movement to undermine the government imposed by the North. The leaders of the movement were called the "Redeemers." The Redeemers were passionately dedicated to their goal. They planned to redeem, or restore, the South as they thought it had been before the Civil War. Sadly, the Redeemers saw the pre-war society through rose-colored glasses. What they wanted to redeem had never existed. It was merely a dream. Yet, the Redeemers felt that the prosperous cotton kingdom with a planter aristocracy and armies of happy slaves was real. The planters did not know or care to find out how the blacks really felt.

The Redeemers made a practice of wrecking elections. Freedmen were threatened. The threats were often carried out. Blacks and whites opposing the Redeemers were too often found among the missing. Weights were placed on the bodies of the murdered. Then the bodies were thrown into the rivers to sink from sight. A number of blacks working with the Republicans were killed. White men whose political beliefs were not agreeable to the Redeemers were often tarred and feathered, or worse. The Republicans responded to election frauds with the Returning Board and with tricks and violence of their own.

In order to accomplish their goals, the Redeemers went "underground." That is, things were done in secret. Many joined groups like the Ku Klux Klan. The identity of members was known only to other members. The most popular underground group in Louisiana was not the Ku Klux Klan, however. It was the Knights of the White Camellia. This group began on the Louisiana Gulf coast. The Bulldozers were another such underground group. Bulldozers operated in the Felicianas.

The Returning Board. The Republicans reacted to the stealing of elections by the Democrats by creat-

ing the Returning Board. The board, in effect, monitored elections. If the Returning Board decided that there had been fraud or intimidation of voters, the election could be cast out. This, in effect, gave Republicans control of elections. The Returning Board was Warmoth's idea.

The Union League. The Republicans had organized the Negroes into the Union League during the war. It was organized to enlist the freedmen into the Republican party. The League used a ritual that was later copied by the Ku Klux Klan.

The Louisiana Lottery. The planter legislators of 1866 had established a state lottery. When Military Reconstruction was imposed, this lottery was no longer in effect. In 1868 a second lottery called the Louisiana Lottery was chartered to last for twenty-five years. This lottery was the brainchild of the Republicans. Lottery tickets were sold all over the United States. The sales amounted to a figure somewhere under $30 million a year. About half of these funds were paid in prizes to holders of the lucky tickets. Every month there was a drawing for a prize of $30,000. Twice a year the prize was $100,000. The owners of this monopoly paid Louisiana $40,000 a year. They paid no taxes. Thousands of poor people who hoped to get something for practically nothing spent their hard-earned money for lottery tickets. They bought

This lithographed broadside hung in thousands of black homes.

The Ku Klux Klan was used by the Redeemers to restore home rule.

tickets again and again. Antilottery societies sprang up shortly after 1868 to rid the state of the menace. The company that operated the lottery had become nearly as powerful as the legislature. The lottery added to the terrible corruption of the state. A man named E. A. Burke was in charge of political deals for the lottery. In effect, Burke was the state's political boss for the years of the existence of the lottery.

Republican Factions. About 1872 a group of leading Republicans had broken away from the party on the national level. The scandals of the Grant administration repelled this splinter group of Republicans. They opposed Grant as a candidate for reelection. Henry Warmoth joined this group.

The split was evident in Louisiana. The Republican group in the state favoring Grant was led by United States Marshal Stephen B. Packard. The center for the Packard Republicans was the customhouse in New Orleans. For this reason, followers of Warmoth ridiculed the Packard group as the "Customhouse Ring." Lieutenant Governor Dunn left Warmoth to join the Customhouse Ring. His reason for this move was disgust over Warmoth's racism. Warmoth had much the same attitude as the Redeemers toward freedmen.

An important member of the Customhouse Ring was a man named Casey. He was a relative of President Grant's wife. Casey and Packard controlled federal patronage for the state. That is, they were allowed to make appointments to federal jobs. That assured them considerable power.

Election of 1872. Warmoth did not get the nomination for governor for a second term. William Pitt Kellogg, a carpetbagger, was nominated. C. C. Antoine, a Negro from Caddo Parish, was nominated for lieutenant governor.

Warmoth shifted his support to the Redeemer-Democrats. This group nominated John McEnery from Ouachita Parish for governor and Davidson Penn for lieutenant governor.

The Republicans claimed their candidate, William Pitt Kellogg, won the election. McEnery supporters proclaimed his victory. Warmoth, as "lame-duck" governor, was a major influence in the election. He was in control of the Returning Board. This board itself was a creation of Military Reconstruction. Now its use was as wild and corrupt as the election itself. It supported McEnery.

Kellogg turned to the federal courts to support him as winner of the election. There was no way to know who won. This was true of every election of the Reconstruction period. Both sides claimed victory. The 1872 election reached a new low in fraud, corruption, and trickery.

Warmoth's Administration. Warmoth was impeached by the Kellogg legislature. He was impeached on charges of fraud in counting votes in the presidential election of 1872. The House of Representatives brought him to trial.

Under the Constitution of 1868, the governor, if impeached, was removed from office until after his trial. Warmoth did not recognize his suspension from office. He was never convicted.

According to most historians, Warmoth used his office to become very wealthy. He earned $8,000 his first year in office. He admitted that he accumulated $100,000 that same year. Warmoth made his money by manipulating state treasury notes and securities. He also had majority ownership in the New Orleans *Republican*, a newspaper. The newspaper did the official printing for the state. Apparently Warmoth did what many others of his time were doing. Men in and out of public office were using the government for private profit. Scandals like Warmoth's did not exist only in Louisiana.

Warmoth remained in Louisiana for the rest of his life. He served as a delegate to the state Constitutional Convention of 1879. In 1888 he was a candidate for governor. In 1896 he served as a delegate to the National Republican Convention.

P. B. S. Pinchback: Governor. In accordance with the Louisiana constitution, the lieutenant governor became governor until the trial took place. Pinchback, therefore, became governor. He had become lieutenant governor after the death of Dunn in 1871. Pinchback, the son of a white Mississippi planter and one of his slaves, served only one month as Louisiana's only black governor.

Two Governors: Two Legislatures. Both Kellogg, the Republican, and McEnery, the Redeemer-Democrat, claimed election in 1872. The two governors proceeded to organize separate governments. Each side elected members of the legislature.

The Kellogg government had the legal backing of President Grant and the federal courts. Kellogg was inaugurated on January 13, 1873, at the Mechanics Institute in New Orleans. John McEnery was inaugurated on the same day at about the same time at New Orleans's Lafayette Square. Two governors and two legislatures operating a block apart in New Orleans were the climax of Reconstruction turmoil.

Most of the people of Louisiana, being Democrats, recognized McEnery as governor. With the strength of popular support, McEnery formed a militia under General Fred N. Ogden. Using the militia, McEnery attempted to take control of the New Orleans police. This resulted in the Battle of the Cabildo on March 5, 1873. General Longstreet was in control of the Metropolitan Police (actually the state militia) and arrested sixty-five of the McEnery militia.

White League. The White League was organized in June 1874 to rid the state of carpetbag government. The group, dedicated to returning control to Louisiana white men, grew rapidly. Because of the support of the Radicals by federal troops, the White League was convinced that it was necessary to fight to regain control. Its members were organized into military companies. The group was not a secret organization, but its members drilled regularly at night in secret. They did not hide their identities with robes or other disguises.

Violence. This period of constant lawlessness and political turmoil resulted in many riots and conflicts. There were far too many acts of violence to recount. Some were gruesome. New Orleans was hit harder than the rural areas. Planters enforced their own authority on their plantations.

The state was peppered with fresh outbreaks every day, and the tension mounted steadily. Kellogg sent troops to St. Martin Parish to collect taxes. They were defeated there by a citizens' army. Federal troops had to be called out to restore order. In such political tension explosions were sure to come. One of the worst was the battle at Colfax in 1873 in newly created Grant Parish.

One of the largest former slaveowners in the South lived at Colfax. His name was Meredith Calhoun. Calhoun secured the creation of a new parish, Grant Parish. It was cut from Rapides and Winn parishes. The new parish was named for President Ulysses Grant. Its parish seat was located on one of Calhoun's three plantations. The new parish courthouse was a vacated plantation structure belonging to Calhoun. It was located in the new village named Colfax. It was named after the vice president under Grant, Schuyler Colfax.

It was at Colfax in Grant Parish that a clash between opposing political groups erupted. Each faction claimed that its candidates for election as judge and sheriff of Grant Parish had been elected. Both sets of officers were given commissions by Kellogg. Both thought the positions were theirs. One pair, supported by McEnery, was white. The other set was black. They were supported by Kellogg. Black leaders later claimed that Kellogg had deliberately set the stage for the riot. He did this by giving commissions to both sets of officers. Such a riot would cause Grant to send him more troops. This would keep him in power. As the tension mounted before Easter Sunday, the black postmaster took the mail to Alexandria for safekeeping.

Whites and blacks gathered from a wide area of Louisiana. Troops of both sides were drilled for the forthcoming battle. On Easter Sunday, 1873, a pitched battle occurred at Colfax. The black men had taken over the offices in the courthouse. A trench was dug by the defenders. The white men, supported by McEnery, moved a small cannon from a steamship to the site. It was aimed at the courthouse. The black forces were trapped inside the courthouse when the building was set on fire.

This was no riot but a planned battle. Once the conflict began over seating the officials, both sides gathered support. No records were kept of the number of blacks killed. Local tradition has it that hundreds were killed.

Survivors from the burning courthouse were taken to a Calhoun sugar warehouse, and that night they were shot. Three white men died during the battle. Nine white leaders were captured and taken to federal prison in New Orleans. One of those listed as dying in the riot actually died in prison. Some time later, the survivors were released. They were welcomed as heroes when they returned to Grant Parish.

A year after the Colfax Riot, there was the Coushatta Massacre. Red River Parish, in which Coushatta is located, was tense with rumors of con-

Under the carpetbag rule blacks were taken to the polls to vote the radical Republican ticket.

flict. In August 1874 the rumor was spread that the blacks were going to attack the white Democrats. The White League arrived. White Republican leaders had ruled the parish during Reconstruction. They agreed to leave the state if they were protected. Five officeholders and one of their friends with an escort left for Texas on August 30. A mob soon killed all six Republicans. Apparently the mob attack was prearranged. The clash that occurred there and others across Louisiana kept the people on edge.

Two weeks after the Coushatta Massacre, the Battle of Liberty Place, or Canal Street, occurred in New Orleans. This battle has been referred to as the Revolution of 1874. It involved the securing of arms from the North by the White League. The Metropolitan Police made a stand to prevent a shipment of supplies from reaching the volunteer army of the Redeemers. A battle was fought between the two groups on September 14, 1874.

Few battles have ever taken place under such circumstances. Notices appeared in New Orleans newspapers on September 13, 1874, about the meeting on Canal Street. The following day, people closed their businesses, and large numbers assembled. The steamboat *Mississippi* had arrived in New Orleans with weapons and ammunition for the Leaguers. Kellogg's Metropolitan Police, mostly blacks, were ordered to stop the Leaguers from getting the shipment. Streetcars were overturned and used for breastworks. Camp Street was blocked off with logs and barrels. Thousands watched and cheered. The Metropolitan Police blocked the levee. The Leaguers used a moving freight train to shield their maneuvers. The Metropolitan troops withdrew. Kellogg fled to the customhouse under the protection of federal troops. Many of the guns brought in aboard the *Mississippi* were seized by the White Leaguers. Eleven of the policemen were killed and sixty of them were wounded. From the White League sixteen were killed and forty-five wounded.

The White League took possession of state government for the McEnery administration. For two days McEnery was governor. The White League celebrated with a victory parade. The federal government stepped in to support Kellogg. President Grant restored the Radical Republicans to office. The Leaguers did not confront the federal troops.

On September 17, 1874, McEnery retired from the contest. For almost two years the two rival administrations had functioned. Kellogg held power only with the backing of federal troops.

Louisiana was no nearer submission to the military-supported government than it had been in 1868. Only the United States Army could maintain the Republicans in power.

Force and violence were used against Military Reconstruction not only in Colfax, Coushatta, and New Orleans, but also in Opelousas and St. Martinville. In Winn Parish, the overthrow of the Republicans was accomplished without bloodshed. In Natchitoches, the main city officials and parish officials for Military Reconstruction left the scene. Threats prompted their flight.

Home Control. The goal of the Redeemers to regain local control of Louisiana government was in sight by the fall of 1876. More and more resistance to Military Reconstruction had been felt during Kellogg's administration. The overthrow of Radical Republican rule in local government was accomplished parish by parish. The Democrats had regained control of most of the parishes along the Mississippi River by 1872. By 1876 the Democrats were in control in all North Louisiana parishes. By then they controlled enough parishes in the state to be a threat to the Republicans.

Cost of Carpetbag Government. The state owed around fourteen million dollars after the war. Debts made by the state of Louisiana under the Confederacy during the war were cancelled by the victorious United States. This included payment of war bonds and money printed by the Confederate government. Materials of war had been bought on credit. So the fourteen million dollars was an obligation assumed before the Civil War.

There is no way to get an accurate figure on the cost of government during the Reconstruction period. Records were destroyed. The expenses of the legislature in 1872 were $958,956 or $113.50 per member each day of the session. It is known that the state bonded debt rose to $53 million. Taxes increased five hundred percent. In 1874 the state was bankrupt. Kellogg investigated the state debt. During his administration the state debt and taxes were reduced.

1876 Election. It was election time. The leader of the Republicans in Louisiana was Stephen B. Packard. He was candidate for governor on the Republican ticket. The Redeemers nominated a Confederate war veteran who had been so shot up in battle that he was a physical wreck. An arm and leg had been amputated, and his eyesight was impaired. He was Francis T. Nicholls.

The 1876 election was conducted according to the grim pattern which had been maintained throughout Military Reconstruction. "The end justifies the means" was the battle cry on both sides. Stuffing ballot boxes and casting dead persons' ballots were tricks used by both political parties to steal elections. Dishonesty was commonplace.

Again both candidates claimed victory. Strangely enough, it turned out that the Confederate veteran, Nicholls, had been aided by funds from the Louisiana Lottery. Its owners wanted to be on the side they knew would be winning control of the state. Nicholls accepted their money and thereby committed himself to support the corrupt lottery.

Both men were inaugurated in

A statue commemorating the Confederate soldier stands in front of the Claiborne Parish Courthouse.

Louisiana Office of Tourism

New Orleans in separate ceremonies on January 8, 1877. The state again had two governors, indeed, two entire rosters of officers. Nicholls had the support of the native whites. About ten thousand of his enthusiastic supporters watched the swearing in. Packard claimed support of the white Radical Republicans, many of them carpetbaggers.

The Weary North. By now, however, the Northern population was weary of what appeared a hopeless task. That task was to reconstruct the South according to ideas developed in the North. Many Northerners believed that the South needed to work out its own problems of government and race relations. Moreover, they were tired of worrying about the South. When several thousand men from the White League, now called Continental Guards, marched into New Orleans and took over police stations, the arsenal, and the Cabildo, there were no federal troops to support Packard. President Grant, at last, gave up. If the Republican government had to be supported by military troops in Louisiana to stay in power, then it would have to resign. There would be no more federal troops. Packard offered no resistance.

The Republican legislature, which had been holding its sessions within a short distance from the Democratic legislature, disbanded. Governor Packard resigned. Francis Tillon

Nicholls was unchallenged in his position as head of the state government. The situation remained tense, however, until the March 4, 1877, presidential inauguration.

A Compromise. There had not been an honest election in Louisiana— nor probably in the South—since Military Reconstruction began. In early 1877 there was still no way of knowing which candidate for president of the United States had received winning votes in three Southern states. Either a Republican, Rutherford B. Hayes, or a Democrat, Samuel J. Tilden, would become president of the United States. Louisiana's electoral vote would help decide the winner. Louisiana sent two different sets of results for the presidential election. South Carolina and Florida returns were in doubt. Louisiana agreed to go with Hayes if certain conditions were met. A compromise was reached to give the presidency to Hayes, although Tilden probably won the election. One condition was that military troops be withdrawn from the South.

Hayes also agreed to give federal support to Southern Democrats and the Nicholls government. After President Hayes was inaugurated, on March 4, 1877, Louisiana governmental affairs, tangled as they were, changed swiftly.

Packard had thought that President Rutherford Hayes would send the federal troops, which former President Grant had refused to send. Instead, the new president sent an investigating committee to New Orleans on April 2, less than a month after he became president.

Two months after Hayes's inauguration, all federal troops were at last withdrawn from the state on April 24, 1877. Military Reconstruction was over. Nicholls was finally established in power. He was the first native of Louisiana to serve since the Civil War. Louisiana had lived under military government longer than any other Southern state. New Orleans had been under federal domination for fifteen years.

Louisiana: Part of the Solid South. Since the Republican party was formed to keep slaves out of the territories, the South rejected the party. Planters felt that the Republicans brought on the war to free slaves. The people of Louisiana, like the rest of the South, hated the Republican party. The Republicans were responsible for Military Reconstruction. Voters were determined to rid the state of the Republicans. This is the reason Louisiana became a part of the Solid South. The Solid South voted the Democratic ticket. It took nearly a hundred years to overcome the bitterness resulting from the war and Reconstruction. The first Republican elected governor of Louisiana since Reconstruction was elected in 1980.

En Partie 1 (Studying a Part). 1. Describe conditions at the end of the war. 2. How did Lincoln plan to treat the South? 3. What was Johnson's viewpoint? 4. What political groups were competing for leadership? 5. What was the original purpose of the Freedmen's Bureau? 6. Why did the carpetbaggers come to the state? 7. What happened to Louisiana representatives sent to Congress in 1865? 8. Who was charged with vagrancy? 9. What was the conflict between Congress and Johnson? 10. When did Military Reconstruction begin and end in Louisiana? 11. Describe Military Reconstruction. 12. Which groups arose to challenge Military Reconstruction? 13. How did the cost of state government change? 14. Describe the elections that resulted in two sets of officials. 15. What was the compromise made in 1877? 16. (a) Who organized the Louisiana Lottery? (b) Why? (c) How did it work? 17. Describe the changes in government and voting during Reconstruction. 18. Identify: Abraham Lincoln, Andrew Johnson, Black Code, C. C. Antoine, Carpetbaggers, Colfax Riot, Democratic party, 1868 constitution, Fifteenth Amendment, Fourteenth Amendment, Francis T. Nicholls, Freedmen's Bureau, General Philip Sheridan, Henry Clay Warmoth, home control, impeachment, James Madison Wells, Knights of the White Camellia, Ku Klux Klan, Metropolitan Police, New Orleans Riot, P. B. S. Pinchback, Radical Republicans, Reconstruction Acts, Redeemers, Republican party, Returning Board, scalawags, Solid South, Stephen Packard, Union League, and White League.

Social and Economic Readjustment

The political changes in Louisiana were not the only changes to follow the Civil War. Louisiana faced social and economic adjustments as well. These were equally difficult for Louisianians. The people of the plantation lowlands in the state, along with the New Orleans commercial interests, were hardest hit. The end of slavery and the impact of the war meant that there could be no complete return to the pre-war ways of life. New ways of living were necessary. The state and its citizens had to make these adjustments with desperately limited financial resources.

There was one clear fact that emerged in Louisiana from the defeat in the Civil War. The society was in chaos. Slaves were freed. How were they to make a living? Where did this leave planters whose plantations depended entirely on the army of black workers?

Planters. Ezra Bennett, one of the most outstanding planters in

Rapides Parish, had remained at "Bennettville" throughout the Civil War. He was born in New York of Connecticut forebears, and he had settled in the Bayou Boeuf community as a young man. That was in the 1820s. He had used his New York education in the three Rs in a teaching job at Cheneyville. Such young people as Bennett had been in demand as private tutors for children of planters. Later he took a job working at a store at Eldred's Bend and found that he liked that much better. He married Sarah Eldred, daughter of the planter who owned the plantation on which the store was located. He eventually bought the store and his father-in-law's plantation. He became a valued agent for New Orleans factors, or financial agents, who financed all the crops grown on neighboring plantations on both sides of Bayou Boeuf.

In 1865 everything was gone. The store had closed early during the war. The Union blockade of the port of New Orleans quickly stopped the flow of goods to such inland stores. With the capture of New Orleans and Baton Rouge in 1862, the complete collapse of the plantation economy was in sight. Factors, who supplied the all-important money, were out of business. Bennett and his neighbors planted only what they could use. The waterways connecting inland Louisiana with New Orleans mon-

ey and the New Orleans market were given over to the war. Union and Confederate soldiers and sailors lived off the land, taking goats, cattle, poultry, and crops. In short, they took whatever they needed. Soldiers of both armies moved over his land in 1863 and 1864. All of his neighbors fled to Texas. Sarah Bennett wrote in 1865: "this is a very lonesom country now. so many have left. Old Mrs. Ford and me has to do our visiting among our selves. . . ."

Bennett's oldest son, a hopeless asthmatic, had gone to Texas to mine saltpeter for the Confederacy. Maunsel and Hebert, the second and third sons, had been at the Battle of Port Hudson. They survived that holocaust, but Hebert was killed at an Alexandria fort near the end of the war. A Confederate cannon exploded when he fired it in April 1865 at Fort Randolph.

So much was gone that Ezra, at the age of fifty-seven, had no thought of rebuilding. Back taxes owed to the United States government were due on his property as soon as the war was over. There was no money with which to pay them. The old Confederate money and the war bonds issued by the Confederate States of America were worthless. In addition the victorious United States had imposed a cotton tax as a penalty. Planters and farmers were required to pay a tax of fifteen dollars on every bale

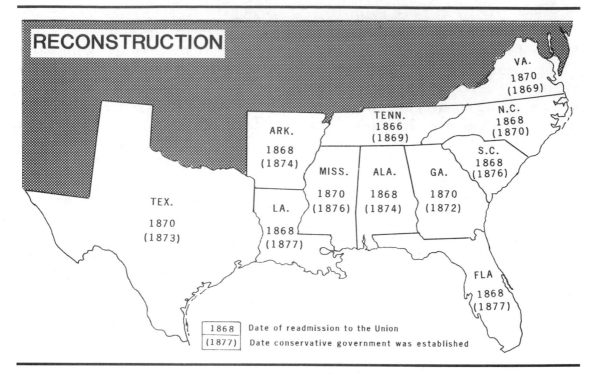

RECONSTRUCTION

VA.
1870
(1869)

N.C.
1868
(1870)

TENN.
1866
(1869)

ARK.
1868
(1874)

S.C.
1868
(1876)

MISS.
1870
(1876)

ALA.
1868
(1874)

GA.
1870
(1872)

LA.
1868
(1877)

TEX.
1870
(1873)

FLA
1868
(1877)

| 1868 | Date of readmission to the Union |
| (1877) | Date conservative government was established |

of the new cotton crop that they grew. Ordinarily the amount would have seemed small. With no money at all to pay obligations, Ezra Bennett was sick from worrying about how he would pay the cotton tax and back taxes. The federal government demanded that all taxes owed since the state left the Union be paid promptly. Sarah wrote: "... the Yankees have called on the planters for three years taxes to be paid by the first of Oct. there are a very few that can get the money. if they don't pay, their land will be sold. ..."

The eight slaves he had owned were free. Sarah Bennett wrote about the situation to their son, Frank, still in Texas and adrift.

Riney cooks for us. she also gets a portion of corn for her and *Carlens* work. *Louisiana* gets $4 per month. She does not work Saturdays. that comes out of her wages. she looses her sick days too. we feed and clothe them. *Sily* did not make any bargain, she works as usual. *Louisa* is an expense. she is nearly blind. she does not do much of anything. Old *Jake* came in after he found he was free. he went to Alex and worked there a while. he is working in the neighborhood now. I expect your Pa will hire him soon. ... I would like very much to get a good white woman to do my work. I suppose that will be impossible. . .

Planters like Ezra Bennett at least had a roof over their heads. Many planters' homes had been burned. Their farm animals and farm equipment were gone. Wagons and plows had to be replaced. Fences were down. Their places were grown up in weeds. Planters generally found nothing left but their land. It was of little value. There was no money. Many planters and farmers were bankrupt. They could not secure working capital or credit. The slaves were gone. Often debts incurred before the war now had to be paid. Nobody could have been prepared for the many problems planters faced. Planters, who had lived well compared to most people and who had claimed to be superior people, were now broke and powerless.

Under such circumstances many plantations were seized and sold for debts at sheriffs' sales. A large number changed hands. Planters, who had little if any cash to hire farm laborers, began to sell portions of their plantations. As a result of the breakup of some of the large plantations and the opening of new lands, the number of small farms increased. But within a decade or so plantations were usually larger than ever. Some planters changed to subsistence farming. They provided for their families from their own land.

There was an ever-present fear that the words of military officers, sounding off on policies, were true. They threatened that the United States government would seize all plantation land and redistribute it as small family farms to the freedmen. Actually, a Freedmen's Bureau act of March 3, 1865, provided for allotting confiscated property to former slaves. However, during 1865 most of 65,528 acres of farmland the Freedmen's Bureau had seized and leased to freedmen were restored to original owners. Eighty-six buildings confiscated by the Freedmen's Bureau in New Orleans had been restored to their former owners.

Somehow, Ezra and others managed to pay the delinquent taxes owed to the United States. Somehow, too, they managed to pay the cotton tax. Some gradually rebuilt their homes and outbuildings.

Crop-Lien System. The crop-lien system developed. Land was no longer good security for a loan. Land value had depreciated greatly. The creditor chose instead to lend money on the unplanted crop, usually cotton. The creditor took a lien, or mortgage, on the producer's crop. Because farming is so risky, interest rates were extremely high. Cotton was so much in demand after the war that cotton farmers could get credit. Sugar planters had a much harder time securing loans. Sugar plantations required much more capital than cotton plantations.

Planters went in debt for not only one but often two and three years of making crops. Once a planter began to borrow, it was very difficult to break the chain of indebtedness. This year's profit was used to pay last year's debts. It was necessary to borrow again to make the next year's crop and pay living expenses. This was nothing new. The credit system had always been part of the plantation system. The debt cycle went on and on. Living was always on credit—with interest. The interest cost was extremely high.

Small farmers were less often in debt and in debt for less. They did not own sufficient collateral to borrow money in the amounts the planter did. They were more likely to seek advances at a planter's store against the small crops they expected to harvest in the fall. Then, too, the farmer's lifestyle was much simpler and less demanding of cash outlays.

Working Arrangements. The freedmen found themselves in a desperate situation after the war. A few found solutions to provide themselves with a living off the plantations. A small percentage of freedmen found work as day laborers. Some jobs were in villages, but most were on plantations or farms. Work was scarce in impoverished Louisiana. Money was even more scarce.

The freedman had his work to offer. The planter had nothing but his land and such buildings as remained. He had no money. The only solution for him and the freedman was to pool their resources and make a crop. This was how **sharecropping** developed. The freedman received a share of the crop. How much he received depended upon the particular arrangements between each cropper and planter.

Every year more and more Negroes became sharecroppers. Ninety percent of the freedmen in the state eventually became sharecroppers. Life on the plantations after the war was little changed from life on plantations before the war.

People outside the South did not seem to understand how little things had changed. Or perhaps they were too busy getting back to normal life after the war to care much about the way things were on Louisiana plantations and other plantations in the South. The sharecropper reported to work in the same way he had before the war. On the plantations he furnished nothing but his labor. He received a weekly quota of rations from the plantation commissary or store. He received wages for his work, and he and his family had the use of a small strip of land to farm as their own. He also got a cabin, seed, tools, and a mule. The sharecropper plowed his land. He and his family planted, chopped grass out of the cotton, and picked it at harvest. The planter sold it, and the sharecropper received one-fourth to one-half of the value of the cotton produced on his acre or two.

"Settlin' up time" in the fall was when the sharecroppers and planter figured what was due. If the planter were an honest man, he followed a simple procedure. This was a matter of adding up purchases at the store and credits for the sharecropper's labor on behalf of the planter. The sharecropper was given credit for his part of the income from the sale of the cotton. If the planter were not honest, there might not be any settlement at all. In other words, the planter's word was the last word in any disagreement. The sharecropper could not move without the creditor's permission. The laws of the state had been quickly changed to protect the planter or merchant to whom the sharecropper owed money. Informal rules among planters were even stronger controls.

The average cash income of the sharecropper was less than two hundred dollars a year. That of the average white independent farmer was no more. This amount of money cannot be judged by late twentieth-century standards. The world in which the sharecropper and other plain folks lived used very little money. Outside New Orleans most people lived on the farms and made their income from what the farm produced. This was true of the small independent farmer and the sharecropper. They were subsistence farmers who lived off their farms. They produced little, if anything, to sell.

The planter did not, however, have things altogether his way. For his plantation labor, like other workers, had to be satisfied within reason. The sharecropper had to have an incentive to work. Sharecroppers had at least, in theory, the freedom to change plantations. They could move off the plantation if they were not reasonably satisfied. They did have to be free of debt before they could move.

Right after the war the fears of not having labor to produce the cotton crops influenced the treatment that the black sharecropper received. The more desirable blacks received better treatment and working agreements. Those blacks who were politically active or particularly outspoken about their civil rights were not able to find a planter willing to employ them. Those who voiced their displeasure could not find land to rent. Without land there was little hope for gaining even the bare living sharecropping provided. In other words, sharecropping became both a social and economic factor in the lives of black Louisianians.

Some planters felt that the problems of dealing with the freedmen were so great that they searched for other sources of labor. Efforts were

Glencoe dates from 1870 to 1903.

made to replace blacks with Chinese, Italians, and other peoples. Agents were sent to locate white families in other states to become sharecroppers on the plantations. None of these tactics worked. By the end of the century, the plantation labor was little different from that of plantations before the war.

Many blacks and whites entered into a **tenant** relationship with a large landowner. A planter usually rented portions of his land to several tenants. The tenants supplied their own seed, mules, and provisions. They were charged yearly rent without a percentage of the crop being involved. Usually only small acreage was involved in the tenant arrangement. Most tenant farmers rented only the amount of land that their families could work.

Some workers were hired. Sugar plantation workers were paid from fifteen to eighteen dollars per month. These wages went to prime men. If they fed themselves, they made twenty-five to thirty dollars per month. Women, children, and older men were paid wages according to the contribution the planter thought they could make. The planter always furnished a cabin. He usually provided credit at the commissary or store. Of course, the goods were usually highly priced.

Freemen and Freedmen. Two groups of black people still existed in the state after the war. The people who had been called "free persons of color" before the war were freemen. They were free before the war. Others were freedmen. These were freed by the war. Both groups faced social and economic adjustment problems, but the freedmen were the hardest hit.

When freedom came to the black Louisianians, it is doubtful that many people realized the problems created by the end of slavery. Many Negroes could not believe that they were free. To them freedom meant that they did not have to work on the plantations any more. They wandered from parish to parish. They depended on the Freedmen's Bureau to provide them with food, shelter, and medical care. Many wanted to leave the places where they had been slaves. Few wanted to remain as hired hands for their former masters. Some left Louisiana.

Emancipation aroused dreams of moving north or west. Many blacks migrated to Louisiana from the southeastern states. For some it meant leaving the plantations for good. They crowded into New Orleans or relocated in the villages. There they believed that they might be both safer and more likely to find employment. Thus, for a short time there was a great movement among the freedmen. One thing was certain: the North did not want the freedmen. The Northerners felt that former slaves should remain in the South.

Many freedmen waited for promised land allotments. Despite denials by the Freedmen's Bureau agents, many Negroes believed in a false rumor. The rumor was that on New Year's Day, 1866, each former slave was to receive forty acres and a mule from the United States government. Instead of working, many waited around the Bureau offices hoping that the rumor was true.

General Banks was quoted as urging the distribution of free land to blacks. He was not alone in demanding confiscation of the plantations. It was during this period that planters hustled off to the legislature to pass Black Codes. These were said to be for the purpose of "putting the Negro back to work." These laws clearly pointed out the manner in which

THE FREEDMEN'S BUREAU BROUGHT MANY CHANGES

planters expected to deal with the former slaves.

Federal officials, especially those of the Freedmen's Bureau, made it clear that former slaves would have to find jobs. The Bureau tried to arrange for jobs. It was the Bureau's responsibility to see that blacks received fair treatment. All but a handful of the freedmen had no skills except those related to farming.

Most of the freedmen, sooner or later, found themselves back on the plantations. Many never left. After all, there were few choices. Many of the former plantation slaves went back to the same plantation routine working for planters—with little different arrangements. They were working for a small wage. In reality this was credited against the charges for necessities bought at a plantation store. The store might be a commissary used for a single plantation. It could be a larger store serving people on many plantations. The planter or overseer issued work orders the same as he had under slavery. For work on his sharecrop the freedman and his family received no wages. Later he would have a share, perhaps one-fourth, of the crop produced on this land.

Some did change plantations. This movement from one plantation to another was part of the newly found freedom. However, freedmen had no money, no land, and no way to finance a move off the plantation. Slaves who had lived on a prosperous, well-run plantation before the war probably had better living conditions than they did after the war. Where were they going to move? Not all desired to undertake the hardships of those beginning life anew in shacks thrown up in the woods. Jobs in the cross-road villages were few. New Orleans held promise of jobs loading and unloading ships and various other jobs. The truth was that the Louisiana economy was based on cotton. The cotton plantations at least offered food and shelter in a familiar setting. The skills learned on the plantations could be used to secure a living.

Black planters were few in number, but there were some with large landholdings. Some of these imitated the aristocrats. They held themselves aloof from other blacks. Some designated black by the legal definition of blacks in Louisiana had more white blood than black.

Some freedmen left the plantations and found poor land at the edge of forests where they began a new life. They worked to save money for land of their own. The women took in washing and ironing for white families. The men found jobs such as cutting wood. Many of mixed black and white heritage received land from their white planter parents. However the land was acquired, a number of independent black farm communities developed. These were often on marginal (unfertile) or uncleared land.

The public was hardly aware of the large number of black men and women on their own small farms. These communities were scattered throughout the state. North Louisiana seems to have had more than other areas. The Black Lake community near Shreveport and one near Grambling were two such communities. Perhaps the number of northern settlements was due to the vast unsettled pine-covered hills. Land was cheap. Some could be homesteaded. Men and women worked under circumstances in which they had to subsist on minimum food in order to pay for their small plots of land. The entire family provided the labor needed on these farms.

Like the white pioneers, they built sturdy log houses. In the mild Louisiana climate, simple log or wood frame homes were comfortable. Mud chimneys were used for the fireplaces, which furnished heat in the winter and served as the place for cooking meals. Furnishings were primitive but adequate. Anything clever hands could fashion out of wood could be made from the plentiful supply growing in virgin forests.

Vegetables and fruits could be grown in season. There were chickens in the backyards of the cabin. Eggs for the family came from the chicken house. There was always a hog fattening for the day it would be ready to add to the family meat supply. When they could manage, settlers had cows to furnish milk. Cash was needed for flour and sugar. Molasses came from the local syrup mill. Water was free. It came from springs and streams, and underground cisterns were dug. Candles and oil lamps gave light. Wood as fuel for heating and cooking required a yearly trip to the forests at the backs of the farmlands. Almost all men regularly fished and hunted game.

Sports were enjoyed in pastures and stretches of cleared land. Blacks invented games and improvised equipment. Sometime a ball was donated or bought with donated cash. Other times they used rag balls, made with rags wound around a rock core. Tin-can shinny became popular. A tin can was kicked from one player on the team to another as opposing players tried to intercept it.

These independent communities were cradles of outstanding black leaders. Almost hidden in isolated areas, these blacks meant to avoid white interference in their affairs. Many growing up in the black world had little contact with "the other race," as they referred to the white man.

Although most Negroes of this era worked on farms, some did find other employment in the cities and towns. Cities like New Orleans had sections where freedmen gathered. Plantation villages were filled with craftsmen, railroad workers, janitors, and the like. The few who had learned crafts as slaves now used them as freedmen. They worked as brickmasons, carpenters, wagonmakers, blacksmiths, and tanners. Barber shops, funeral homes, general stores, and countless other small black businesses developed within black urban communities. The largest group of Negroes working in industry were found in lumbering. Blacks crossed daily into the white community where most were employed. Blacks sometimes did manual work in the "Main Street" stores, banks, post offices, and the like, which were owned and run by white people. Handymen, draymen, and drivers of teams were able to find a livelihood in the towns. Women were almost always assured employment as domestics in the homes of white people on the "other side of the track."

When railroad tracks were laid across the state around 1880, the urban black communities almost invariably expanded on one side of the tracks. A parallel white community grew on the other side. "On the other side of the track" took on different meanings according to whether you were black or white.

The black man, woman, and child learned to play two opposing roles. One was that of a servile black indicating respect for the superiority of whites by body language, speech and actions. This behavior was displayed on the "white side of town." Blacks shared experiences, shared their own views of "Whitey," and were involved in the affairs of their own community. In rural areas, among themselves, blacks referred to white planters as "Mister Cholly," and plantation mistresses as "Miss Ann."

Before the war free Negroes were scattered throughout the state. Some had their own farms. Some were planters. The largest group of freemen were in New Orleans. According to some historians, before the war this cultured free Negro group had reached a higher level of living than any other Negro group anywhere in the world. Some were highly educated and well-traveled. Approximately twenty thousand were in New Orleans before the war started. Many of them owned their own businesses. A good portion of their trade was with the Union military occupation forces. Many of the wealthy freemen received political recognition during the occupa-

tion period. Two brothers in the group, Dr. Louis Roudanez and Joseph B. Roudanez, published the Republican *La Tribune de la Nouvelle-Orléans*, the first black daily newspaper in the United States.

The Role of the Church. Blacks and whites turned to the churches. Membership in white churches grew steadily. The small Protestant churches of North Louisiana were community centers for whites. The Catholic church was still the dominant church in South Louisiana. The Protestant churches were, first of all, places for religious worship. After that, they were schools. By a decade after the Civil War primary schools were established at almost every church. The churches also served as welfare centers. Fellow church members provided sources of help and relief in emergency situations, and the church was the place where beginning political organizations were formed. The first organizations of white farmers were get-togethers at the church buildings where mutual problems were discussed. The church was a social center as well. Revivals, or protracted meetings, were important in the white Protestant churches of North Louisiana.

Whether in New Orleans, on plantations, in villages, or in communities of independent farmers, blacks all had one center in their lives: the church. Since so many other avenues were closed to Negroes, the church played an especially important role in everyday life.

As soon as Negroes were free, they set up churches whenever they could. "Invisible" churches that had operated under cover on some plantations sprang to life. Under the strict controls of slavery, the right of assembly of slaves had been denied. Gatherings of blacks had been held secretly. These gatherings were mostly in plantation quarters in the homes of members or in a vacant cabin. At least one relic of an invisible church survives. This is the communion cup used during antebellum times by the black congregation from Edgefield Plantation. (This plantation was owned by Confederate General Leroy Stafford.) The freedmen formed Edgefield Baptist Church.

The black freedmen's church became the headquarters of benevolent associations that handled inexpensive burial insurance for members. It was also a welfare agency where the orphans and elderly could find help. The church was the political center for sharing black problems. Negroes discussed among themselves conditions on different plantations. It was also the educational center. The black church gave the members an opportunity to work together in a formal organization. Very importantly, the church developed leaders. Here with their own kind they had identities as respected human beings. The church

was also the center of social activities. The Negro churches had social and fraternal organizations, political organizations, and self-help organizations. These self-help groups were designed to aid blacks in securing land or finding employment.

These black churches were Protestant. Almost all were Baptist. The Baptist organization had no hierarchy of superior officers over the local church. Therefore, in the Baptist church they were free to develop a church to fit their needs. The Methodists had the second largest number of black churches. The Catholic churches continued with integrated membership for a short time. By the 1890s Louisiana Catholics did not welcome black members. Eventually, with their large numbers, black Catholics in Lafayette and other places had their own segregated churches. The Catholic, Episcopal, and Presbyterian churches eventually lost almost all of their black members.

Usually there were no whites involved in the movement that resulted in at least one black church in every plantation community. In some cases white ministers helped freedmen get their churches started.

Whites were eager to have the freedmen out of white churches. As slaves, blacks had been under unquestioned white control. Freedmen were a different matter. Stories of violence between the races added nothing to the comfort of white church-goers who had blacks in segregated seats of their congregations. At the same time, blacks were more than eager to secure their own meeting places.

In order to attract workers, planters granted land for black churches. Blacks ordinarily built their churches and used them as schoolhouses, too. They sometimes built small schools on the church grounds.

Black Leadership. The role of the black church in developing leaders can hardly be overestimated. These leaders were thinkers and planners. They planned for the future. Outstanding leaders arose from all the different groups of blacks. Many of the black leaders were ministers, but deacons and others also became leaders. The roles of these church leaders extended far beyond religion to the uplifting of the race. They were usually educators as well.

John McDonogh, a white man from New Orleans, had freed many of his slaves. He provided funds for schools for free persons of color before the Civil War. Descendants of this important group of educated blacks produced a number of leaders.

Among the black leaders of the Reconstruction period were a few well-educated men. They were mostly from New Orleans. The New Orleans environment stimulated leadership. Some of them had white fathers who had

C. C. Antoine was an important black leader.

sent them to the North or to France to become educated. Now they returned home to take the lead in black civil rights work. Dr. A. P. Dostie, Charles and Joseph B. Roudanez, P. B. S. Pinchback, and C. C. Antoine were among these leaders. Others included Oscar J. Dunn, Francis Dumas, Antoine Dubuclet, P. G. Deslonde, and William G. Brown.

Education. By the mid-1870s it was clear that the federal government was withdrawing from the policy of protecting Negro rights. The black organizations then became even more important. The freed Negroes soon realized that they were going to have to develop their own solutions. Thus, the black community turned inward. They formed their own segregated subculture within the dominant society. Black Louisianians adapted themselves to the second-class citizenship imposed on them by the majority of whites. They turned to education as a ladder on which they could climb.

Education was a prime goal of black people. It had been denied them as slaves. Blacks felt that they could best overcome the oppression of whites through education. They worked hard to establish schools of their own so that they could help each other become educated.

The Union army first brought public education to Louisiana. General Nathaniel Banks set up public schools in New Orleans during military occupation. These schools were primarily to educate the freedmen. However, they were open to whites as well. Many freedmen enrolled in the classes.

The idea of public education was not new to Louisiana. Plans for public education were outlined in both the 1845 and 1852 constitutions. Neither plan was ever put into effect. There was no public education, as we know it, in Louisiana until after the Civil War.

The Freedmen's Bureau was to provide public schools. Northern missionaries and philanthropists helped with these schools. During the 1870s schools were integrated in New Orleans with whites and blacks attending schools together. There were disturbances, and the integrated schools lasted only a few months. The remarkable fact about the first schools was the great enthusiasm with which the blacks greeted the schools. Actually, only a small percentage of blacks in the state attended school during this entire period. Even fewer whites enrolled in the first years of public education.

In 1877, soon after President Rutherford B. Hayes was inaugurated, the Louisiana Legislature set up a dual school system. There were segregated schools for blacks and whites.

Louisiana had not recovered from the great financial losses resulting from the war effort. There was little money to fund schools. When the funds were divided, neither school system had nearly enough. The schools that did exist were of very low quality. New Orleans had the best ones. As the years passed and children from the mass of both black and white people enrolled in public schools, more public money was needed. The black schools received what was left after minimum needs of the growing white schools were met. That amount was very small, and black schools were poor indeed.

Robert's Academy was a private black boarding school.

A fund established by George Peabody helped some Southern schools. From 1867 to 1877 this fund and individual contributions were the main sources of support for white schools.

Negroes knew that the Redeemers would not provide public funds for black education. They planned to provide education for the race themselves. Groups of churches sponsored private academies, which were modeled after the private academies of the planters. The same architecture, goals, and courses were used.

Northern churches and interested citizens sent money, supplies, and missionaries to help the freedmen.

Mr. and Mrs. Holbrook Chamberlain were visitors to New Orleans after the Civil War. Their only child had died, and they needed a change from Boston. The Chamberlains gave funds to found a college in New Orleans that would help educate black leaders. The American Home Mission Society gave financial support. The Chamberlains helped with more funds as the years passed. The name of the college was Leland, named for Mrs. Chamberlain's family. It was founded in 1870. Leland was moved to Baker, Louisiana, in 1923. Leland College educated many leaders who poured out over the state. Its faculty in the early years was all white. They were highly qualified persons from Harvard, Brown, and other great colleges and universities. Leland College continued to serve the black community until it closed after World War II.

New Orleans University was founded the following year by Methodists. Straight University, which later became Dillard, was founded during the same period.

The Redeemers were so busy perfecting their controls over society that they were unaware of the black educational movement going on around them. Negroes made every effort to keep their schools unnoticed by whites for fear of opposition.

Farmers. The farmers had a different philosophy of life from that of the planters. Their lifestyle was simple. They did not value the pretense of aristocracy. Manual work was not beneath them. They were accustomed to providing their own labor force— mainly their large families. This situation had not changed.

Independent farmers, both white and black, spread out over the North Louisiana hills. They felt the damage of the war. Some lost their land when railroads were given the right-of-way to lay tracks. Some farmers had not attended to recording homesteads. There was no record of their homesteads in the courthouses. This neglect resulted in the tragedy of a number of Louisiana small farmers

and plain folk losing their land. This was the land that they had cleared and farmed for years. Most of all they considered these homesteads their homes. Yet, there were no legal records. The railroads received their land.

Much of the North Louisiana population consisted of subsistence farmers. That is, they were self-sufficient people who supplied almost all of their needs from their farms. Most of the farmer's energies were used to grow corn and other grains. He and his family planted a garden and raised barnyard animals. Eggs, milk, corn, and other produce were traded to neighbors or to the merchants in town. In other words, the barter economy of the pioneering days resumed shortly after the war.

The farmer and the planter had one thing in common—cotton. After the Civil War there were several years of such heavy rains that no crops were made. Caterpillars devoured large portions of crops. The Panic of 1873 and the depression that followed added to the problems.

Farmers saw little reason to grow commercial farm crops such as cotton. There was no way to market them. Many changed from commercial farming to subsistence farming. Louisiana farmers did not begin a sizable return to growing cash crops until the problems of finance and transportation were eased.

The farmer had always added to

the small amount of money received from his cotton crop by taking odd jobs. One was to gather pine knots and stack them on the river banks to sell to steamboat captains as fuel for the boats. There were occasional jobs hauling materials for planters or merchants. Some raised range cattle in the woods. A few set up small "wildcat" sawmills to cut timber.

The farmer continued to live simply. He lived off his farm except for a few purchases elsewhere. The Civil War had brought new ideas and new desires into the piney woods. The situation of the war opened up new possibilities. People wanted more. Change was in the air.

After the war the hill farmers, along with artisans and other wage earners, talked of ways to better themselves. They knew the country was not going to remain a frontier forever. More people were coming into the hills. They were clearing land, building homes, and starting farms. The simple life in the new country was changing.

The Civil War liberated the mass of white people from their docile place in the plantation system. Never again would the planter elite monopolize state politics. The war over slavery and the privileges assumed by the ruling class highlighted the situation of small farmers, craftsmen, and small businessmen. They began to explore ways to get their voices heard in

reform. Life on the small farms was no longer as satisfying as it had been. The farmers sought to make changes.

Business and Trade. The operations of business and trade had greatly deteriorated during the war. Many people had placed their savings in Confederate bonds. Now the bonds were worthless. Businesses had sold goods to the Confederacy on credit. Those debts would never be paid. There was little gold money in the state. Confederate paper money had no value. Many businesses were closed. Cotton gins and sugar mills had been destroyed. Sugar production was almost at a standstill. The business owners had nothing to sell. The federal military control and the success of the Union navy's blockade had ruined business.

The movement of goods and products had all but ceased. Poor means of transportation and impassable roads made it difficult to obtain what was needed to rebuild and repair. Also, crops could not be shipped to market. The Mississippi River had been reopened after 1862 when New Orleans was occupied. Some river traffic continued, and New Orleans began to revive. After the war, when the Red and the Arkansas rivers were reopened, there was more traffic. New Orleans remained the main outlet for American cotton and grain being sent abroad. Railroads were gradually rebuilt. New lines were added.

Business for the state was no longer concentrated in New Orleans. Planters tended to do business closer to home. Several merchants away from New Orleans became much more important. This change caused towns to grow. Baton Rouge and Shreveport grew rapidly. One big difference between the antebellum towns and the postbellum towns was the growth of the merchant class. New Orleans factors quickly declined in importance. Many were bankrupt. The disastrous crops of 1866 and 1867 put some out of business. The development of the cotton exchange changed business, too. The commercial class of New Orleans gained with the increasing commercialization of agriculture.

The Panic of 1873 caused another major economic crisis. It brought a halt to economic development of every type in the whole nation. Louisiana suffered a setback in the slow process of regaining economic stability.

All people felt economic hardships. In one way or another the war had disturbed the lives of everyone. Life was extremely hard for many for years afterward. Families sometimes lived on short rations. In time, these families did better, but they still did not do well. The quality of life over the entire state was not high.

The era of Reconstruction was among the unhappiest periods of Louisiana history. The old plantation system had undergone many changes. New lifestyles had developed for merchants, planters, white farmers, and Negroes. By the end of 1877 Louisiana had again found a measure of stability and peace.

En Partie 2 (Studying a Part). 1. Cite the position and problems of the planter class, the freedmen, the freemen, and the small farmers. 2. How were some of the problems solved? 3. Describe sharecropping and tenant farming arrangements. 4. What was the crop-lien system? 5. What was the role of the church? 6. Describe the status of education for both blacks and whites. 7. Who were the black leaders? 8. What was the economic picture in Louisiana during Reconstruction?

Coup d'Main (Completing the Story)

Jambalaya (Putting It All Together)

1. (a) Analyze the problems facing the state after the Civil War. (b) Which problems grew out of the war? (c) Which had their roots in Southern life? (d) Which were common to all parts of the United States?

2. If Lincoln had lived, would there have been conflict between him and Congress over Reconstruction policies? Justify your answer.

3. How did each of these groups view the situation in Louisiana after the war: carpetbaggers, scalawags, Redeemers, freedmen, Radical Republicans?

4. What complications confronted the Democratic legislature in dealing with the freedmen?

5. What caused tension between races and between Louisiana citizens and the federal government?

6. Describe the different attitudes toward national legislation passed and presidential orders issued that affected Louisiana.

7. What struggle occurred for control of the state?

8. Discuss: Congressional Reconstruction was so bitter and humiliating an experience that Southerners found it hard to forgive and even harder to forget.

9. Why were graft and corruption so widespread after the war?

10. Evaluate the Reconstruction period. Prove that it was a tragic era. Give any constructive achievements.

Potpourri (Getting Involved)

1. Write newspaper articles about the activities of (a) the Ku Klux Klan, (b) the Knights of the White Camellia, or (c) the White League. Include editorial comments about the groups.

2. Conduct (a) a Ku Klux Klan meeting or dramatize their activities, (b) a meeting of the legislature under the carpetbaggers, (c) a confrontation between the two governments, or (d) a debate for or against a harsh or lenient plan for Reconstruction.

3. Compare (a) the returning soldier with the freed Negro, (b) the Negro's life before the Civil War with that after the war, or (c) violence during the war with that after the war.

4. Research the Louisiana Lottery. Give arguments for and against the lottery. Report on procedures followed including buying tickets, drawing for the winning tickets, paying the state, advertising, giving to charity, and helping finance elections.

5. Report on the private Negro academies or Negro colleges established during this period.

Gumbo (Bringing It Up-to-Date)

1. Explain the Fourteenth and Fifteenth amendments. Point out implications of the amendments to Louisianians during the time in which they were passed and today.

2. Compare the Civil Rights Move-

ment with the rights of Negroes after the war.

3. Relate Ku Klux Klan activities during Reconstruction to their activities during modern times.

4. Compare voting rights and procedures of this period with those of today. Include the number of registered black voters for each period.

5. Compare education conditions of this period with integration in education of modern times.

6. Relate the Republican party's influence on the Reconstruction period to their influence today.

PART FIVE

Under Bourbon Rule

Louisiana Office of Tourism

CHAPTER 10

LOUISIANA UNDER THE REDEEMER-BOURBONS (1877–1927)

Political Life (1877–1900)

By March 1877 there was no question about the final victory in the struggle for political control. The Redeemers won. At last, after four years of war and twelve years of Reconstruction, leadership in Louisiana was up to the Redeemers. At least, it was almost altogether up to them— but not quite.

The "Understanding" with the North. With the compromise, which gave Republican Rutherford B. Hayes the presidency, there were "understandings" between the Republicans and the Redeemers. Most of these matters were understood by both parties. They were the cautious reminders regarding the freedmen. Much was written down, but some matters were understood above and beyond the written agreements.

The understanding with the Northern officials was that the freedom of the former slaves would not be limited. However much this was written into law, there was no guarantee of the civil rights of freedmen. The understanding between North and South was that political freedom and equality were to be assured all state residents. Equal education was a promise. Such was the compromise. The planters were accustomed to dealing with understandings such as these. The unwritten code of the planters had always had more force in directing the actions of people in Louisiana than those written down in laws. This understanding certainly shaped the course of action of the Redeemers. If the Redeemers had felt completely free of the North, they would have limited the freedom of the blacks more than they did in 1877. Only the fear of provoking Northern interference against their

LSU-Shreveport Archives

Negroes standing in line to register to vote in 1894 in Shreveport.

policies toward blacks kept the Redeemers from taking immediate action.

Action by the Redeemers was delayed in two areas. The Redeemers felt very strongly about both areas—Negro suffrage and Negro education. They could not tolerate Negro suffrage. It was the final blow to the planter outlook on white supremacy. Education for plantation labor would destroy plantations in the future. The insistence on private education for whites had provided planters with a monopoly on the tools of formal education. Now the Redeemers did exert as much power in controlling blacks

as they could without violating the understanding. They did not dare put controls in these two areas immediately. It was nearly two decades later when the Redeemers' final controls were effective against the mass of helpless blacks.

The Status of Freedmen. By 1877 freedmen were voting. Some held political offices. They had the freedom to obtain an education, and they had the right of assembly. That is, they could meet together as they chose. The status of the freedmen was not the same as that of white citizens, however.

Redeemers wanted to return to

controls used before the war for slaves on plantations. Controls were needed to keep cheap labor available and dependable for critical work in the fields.

Redeemers in Triumph. The Redeemers acquired a different look after 1877. "Redemption" was not something in the future. Redemption was accomplished. Rapidly the planter-businessman-Democrat became even more visibly in control of the state than before the war. These men wore the airs of kings. They were called "Bourbons" because of their arrogance. The absolute monarch, Louis XIV, was a Bourbon. The Bourbon kings of Europe were no more assured of their divine right to rule than were these planters. Some linked the planters and Bourbon kings with a saying, "They never learned anything and never forgot anything." Another phrase from a Bourbon king fits the governing group even better. That was the statement of Louis XIV, who said, "I am the state." The Bourbons of Louisiana held the same views except that they believed not in a single ruler, but in the rule of an **elite**, a select few. Their idea was that, by nature, the better educated people with property were meant to govern men with less education and less property. They were the state.

Bourbon Control. The truth was that the Bourbons managed to dominate Louisiana government as if they were kings. Yet, this was within the United States where the people are supposed to rule. Before the war planters had been in control. They were now joined by an increasingly large merchant class. Now they wanted to dominate politics like they did before the war. This is what they meant by "redemption." After losing power through the war and Military Reconstruction, they did not want to lose control again. So, they proceeded to rid the state of all Republicans. They wanted to make sure the Bourbon Democrats would remain in power forever.

Nicholls's Administration. Francis Nicholls was governor of Louisiana. He was a planter, and he shared the attitudes of planters. He was the kind of man who could rule the state for decades. He was an autocrat who believed in white supremacy. Being a politician, he was a little more liberal toward blacks than most fellow planters thought he should be. He was rejected by some planters for that reason. Perhaps the difference was that Nicholls felt times were changing and that some concessions must be made.

Marshal Packard left with the federal troops. Some of Packard's legislators remained in the new Louisiana Legislature. Money from the Louisiana Lottery was used to silence anyone who might cause trouble. Major E. A. Burke, the corrupt Republican who headed the Louisiana Lottery, supported Nicholls. Burke was state treasurer.

A special meeting of the Louisiana Legislature was called in 1877, as soon as President Hayes was inaugurated. A great deal of work was done in reshaping the state government the way the Bourbons wanted it. Government expenses were cut. State services started for the first time during Reconstruction were reduced. The public education system was restyled. A dual system was established—one for whites and another for blacks. Large planters and businessmen received tax reductions. Governor Nicholls complained that "men of large means" did not pay their taxes and that something should be done about it. Nothing was.

The legislature adopted new election laws and destroyed the Returning Board. There was no penalty for falsifying election returns. That provision was helpful to the Bourbons. They saw to it that Republican votes simply did not exist.

Election Controls. The Bourbons set up a system to control elections similar to the one that had existed during Reconstruction. Nonplanter whites grumbled about these high-handed controls. They feared that not only blacks but many whites would be denied the right to vote.

One prospect that quickly proved a reality was the planter control of the Negro vote. Individual planters cast ballots for the sharecroppers on their plantations. Ballots were printed. Voters marked their choices by hand. Planters either supervised or actually marked the ballots for the sharecroppers. A handful of white planters, voting Negroes employed on their plantations, dominated the state.

These Bourbon Democrats called their government "a taxpayers' government." Yet the elite paid little or no taxes. Protest voters from the hills had no chance of outvoting the planters and their black votes. Remaining blacks and nonplanter whites could only watch what was happening.

Louisiana Constitution No. 6: 1879. Governor Nicholls signed a bill passed by the legislature in 1879 to abolish the Louisiana Lottery. Major E. A. Burke, Louisiana political boss and state treasurer, engineered action to destroy Nicholls politically and save the lottery. An order from a

---

PROBLEMS IN 1877

Enormous State Debt

High Taxes

Bad Agricultural Conditions

Little Money

Poor General Business Conditions

federal judge kept the law that would abolish the lottery from going into effect. He issued a temporary restraining order. The lottery company had only begun. Lottery officials produced, in quick order, the calling of a constitutional convention.

Nicholls was out of office with the passage of the new constitution. The convention shortened the terms of office by a year. That vindictive action was taken because Nicholls dared to oppose Burke's lottery.

The 1879 constitution increased the power of the governor. The power of the legislature and local officials was reduced. The capital was moved back to Baton Rouge from New Orleans. Southern University was established. The University of New Orleans was created for blacks. Louisiana State Agricultural and Mechanical College (1873) and Louisiana State University (1860) were merged.

The new constitution, after eight days of debate, included an article to give the Louisiana Lottery Company a charter to last twenty-five years. All of this effort was the work of Major E. A. Burke. Burke had demonstrated just how powerful both he and the lottery were.

Lottery Leadership. Burke owned the New Orleans *Times*. When the New Orleans *Democrat* was going bankrupt, Burke purchased the paper. The *Democrat* was the chief newspaper that opposed the lottery. Burke received

help from the lottery to purchase the paper. He then combined the two newspapers. The newspaper told of the great benefits of the Louisiana Lottery.

Burke was the front man for the lottery. The source of control was Charles Howard who stayed in the background. Howard was the New Orleans agent for the New York syndicate that owned the Louisiana Lottery. Howard became enormously wealthy. He became so rich that he gave the Confederate Memorial Building to New Orleans. He also contributed to the Howard Memorial Library. He was generous with other city enterprises. When he wanted to join the Jockey Club, he was refused. To get even, he bought the race track and turned it into a cemetery. One would have to understand the love of planters and their friends for horse racing to appreciate what a blow this was.

"Kansas Fever." Times were hard, and plans for the new 1879 Constitution disturbed Negroes. They feared that the Redeemers planned to take away their remaining civil rights. Under these conditions, "Kansas fever" affected many Louisiana Negroes. A rumor spread through the state that better opportunities awaited Negroes in Kansas. A Tennessee Negro, Benjamin ("Pap") Singleton, worked to gain support for an exodus of Negroes from the South in 1879.

Henry Adams of Caddo Parish was named as the Louisiana leader of the movement. How many blacks actually left in the mass movement from this state to Kansas is unknown. But many thousands tried. "Kansas landings" remain, like one on Boeuf River near Rayville. It is a sad reminder of the planned exodus to a promised land. Many groups of frustrated Negroes waited at such landings to catch rides on steamboats that passed them by. It was strongly suggested that the failure of the boats to stop was arranged by the planters. Planters were greatly concerned over this movement among their plantation workers. They tried to prevent the freedmen from leaving.

Many of those who made it to Kansas soon returned. They did not find the "heaven on earth" they were seeking. The climate was not to their liking. The people of Kansas did not welcome them as they thought they would. The migrants lacked the skills needed for wheat farming as well.

Bourbon Government. A new governor, Louis Wiltz, was elected at the same time the constitution was ratified. Wiltz was a New Orleans Democrat who had served as chairman of the 1879 constitutional convention.

The lieutenant governor elected was Samuel McEnery, brother of a former governor. When Wiltz died two years later, McEnery became governor. He was elected to the office in 1883. He served as governor from 1881 until 1888. McEnery's chief asset was his willingness to allow Burke, the man running the lottery, to run the state.

During McEnery's governorship the Bourbons ruled the state. A state Democratic convention nominated candidates for office. Delegates were elected according to the population. Due to the large numbers of black sharecroppers on the plantations, the big planters won elections. The planters controlled the votes of their black sharecroppers as long as blacks voted after 1877. The New Orleans ring controlled elections in the city. When members of the ring and the big planters decided on a candidate, that person was going to be elected. The Republican party was gradually being eliminated from the state. The one-party system gave the Bourbons complete control of the government.

Governor Nicholls became governor a second time in 1888. A reform group was responsible for the outcome. The people had become dissatisfied with the Burke-McEnery government running the state. Burke went out of office.

The Lottery Question. The Louisiana Lottery received bets totalling between twenty million and thirty million dollars annually by 1890. Of this gross amount, forty percent was profit.

The 1879 constitution renewed the charter of the lottery company for twenty-five years. There was great concern among lottery officials that those opposing the lottery would destroy it at last. Feverish activity began by 1890 to secure another renewal of the charter.

An election for governor fell in 1892. That year the Louisiana Lottery Company offered the state thirty times as much as it had been paying. That would amount to $1.2 million.

The Anti-Lottery League's efforts to destroy the lottery equalled those of the Louisiana Lottery Company to extend it. The Farmers' Union was persuaded to join hands with the Anti-Lottery League. Out of all this, Anti-Lottery Democrats, or Reform Democrats, nominated Murphy J. Foster of St. Mary Parish for governor. Foster led in efforts to reach the goals of the Bourbons.

There were five political parties in Louisiana in 1892. These were the Anti-Lottery Democrats, the Regular Democrats, the Populists, the Anti-Lottery Republicans, and the Regular (Pro-Lottery) Republicans. Each nominated a full slate of candidates. The contest was so heated that fistfights and even duels erupted. Murphy J. Foster, the Anti-Lottery Democrat, won the race for governor.

The lottery was defeated. The people did not want it even if there would be enough money from it to pay off the state debt. The lottery company moved to Honduras. However, it continued to sell lottery tickets in Louisiana. It took another act of the Louisiana Legislature to prohibit the sale of tickets. In 1894 the legislature finally legally ended the entire lottery business throughout the state. It existed illegally for many more years. For over twenty years it had dominated the government of the state.

E. A. Burke was a gambler. He assembled the largest gambling organization in the United States before the twentieth century. He was also connected with the financial problems of the Cotton Exposition. A total of $1,267,905 was found missing from the funds of the state treasury. Burke was indicted for embezzlement and fraud. He fled from Louisiana to escape prosecution and set up a business in Honduras. He became equally wealthy and powerful in his new location. He was probably equally corrupt.

Foster's Administration. Governor Foster led a movement to take the right to vote from those he termed "the ignorant and unpropertied" in the state. This was mainly an effort to take suffrage from the Negroes. This disfranchisement of freedmen represented the Bourbon response to the outcry of the nonplanter whites. The whites resented the common practice of the Bourbons controlling the black vote.

Lynchings. Between 1882 and 1903, there was a total of 285 lynchings reported in Louisiana. Most of the victims—232—were black. How many lynchings went unreported is unknown, but there were undoubtedly many.

The most famous lynching took place in October 1890 in New Orleans. Police Chief David Hennessey was murdered. Hennessey was investigating the Mafia, which had been in New Orleans since 1877. Twenty-one Italians were arrested for his murder. Nineteen Italians were indicted. Eleven were named principals in the murder. According to the newspapers, at least seven of them were guilty. Six were acquitted. Decisions were not made for three of them. Many people in New Orleans were furious. Hundreds responded to an ad in the newspaper for a vigilante meeting. A mob formed and went to the parish jail. Eleven prisoners were seized. Five of these had not been tried. The mob hanged two and shot the rest. The incident disturbed the Italian government. A formal protest was filed. The United States government made a financial settlement with the families of the Mafia riot victims who were not American citizens. Five years later the United States government paid six thousand dollars to the families of three more Italian lynch victims. They were lynched by a mob on August 8, 1896, at Hahnville.

Violence was a part of the lifestyle of people on the frontier, and Louisiana was still a part of the frontier. Only a handful took part in the beatings, burnings, and lynchings that were carried out. Yet, it was clear that little could, or would, be done to stop those who did.

Services. Very little was done by the government to provide for the health needs of the people. The **asylum for the insane** at Jackson was a disgrace. The mentally ill in New Orleans were locked up in a prison. The disabled people, the blind, the deaf, and the mute occupied an inadequate building in Baton Rouge. After 1880 many parishes established **poor farms** to care for those in financial need. Private citizens or religious organizations took care of some of the unfortunates. **Charity Hospital** in New Orleans provided services for people from all over the state. In 1894 the **Leprosarium** at Carville was opened. In 1921 the Carville institution became the responsibility of the federal government. It is the only place in the continental United States for treatment of Hansen's disease, or leprosy.

Yellow fever did not affect the state during the Civil War. As soon as ships from the tropical countries returned to New Orleans, the deadly fever returned. In 1878 another epidemic swept over the country. New Orleans had nearly four thousand vic-

National Hansen's Disease Center

Indian Camp plantation became the site of the Louisiana State Leprosarium in 1894.

tims. Finally the state set up a system of quarantine. Every vessel was required to anchor down river until all danger of its bringing the disease into the port had passed. After this system began, there were fewer epidemics and fewer victims.

In 1905 New Orleans suffered an unusually severe epidemic of yellow fever. By then it was established that mosquitoes were the carriers of the disease. Great efforts were made to rid the city of mosquitoes. This proved to be the last yellow fever epidemic in New Orleans.

One person who greatly aided the victims of yellow fever in New Orleans was Margaret Haughery. A statue raised to her memory is said to be the first ever raised to honor a woman in this country.

The **convict lease system** of Louisiana was a disgrace. Since before the war, prisoners were leased to private companies. A New Orleans writer, George Washington Cable, protested the brutal practice. About three-fourths of these convicts were Negroes. One company, S. L. James and Associates, had a monopoly on the lease of convicts. People who wanted to lease convicts had to deal with James. James rented convicts to contractors for much more than he had paid for them. Huge profits were made from this business. The courts provided a steady flow of convicts. There were always replacements for the convicts who did not survive the cruel treatment they received. The convict-lease system stayed in existence until W. W. Heard became governor in 1900.

Farmers' Organizations. Life for the small farmer changed radically after the war. The farmers began to meet together to discuss their problems. In 1867 farmers of the United States formed a social organization called the Grange, or the Patrons of Husbandry. By 1874 there were about 10,000 members in Louisiana. The Grange sponsored gatherings, picnics, and retreats to provide more entertainment and social life. Meetings were often held in community lodges.

The Grange recognized the mutual problems of black and white farmers. The first Grange lodge included both races. The farmers' group worked for racial cooperation in agricultural reform. It became a pioneer in its goal of instilling an appreciation of the dignity of the farmer's role. Grange members tried to get lower freight rates on rail and steamboat shipments. Better schools and clean government with honest elections were among their goals. They provided training for leaders who would operate future farm organizations.

The Grange introduced farm co-ops for purchasing supplies and marketing produce. In the 1870s most of the cooperative stores in Louisiana were closed. The economic depression in the midst of the political and social chaos caused them to fail.

The Louisiana farmers felt that the lottery was indirectly responsible for the lack of attention to their problems. If the government had not been involved with the lottery, they believed there would have been more time to handle farmers' problems.

The Grange did not prove to be an effective vehicle for these early reformers. Perhaps it served its purpose in laying the foundation of the reform movement. The Grange died out by the end of Reconstruction. The interest and attention to reform among these people was still alive. There was, however, little if any formal organization of farmers for a decade.

In 1885 J. A. Tetts organized the Louisiana Farmers' Union in Lincoln Parish. By 1887 there were ten thousand members in this state. At that time, the Louisiana organization combined with the Texas Farmers' Alliance. The new organization was the largest national farm organization ever to exist. Its name was the National Farmers' Alliance and Industrial Union, or Southern Alliance. It had over three million members in 1887.

Populists. The Farmers' Union (the Farm Alliance groups) of the 1880s lasted until the 1890s. After the merger of the Farmers' Alliance and the Anti-Lottery League, those who opposed the merger left the group.

In October 1891 the splinter group met in Alexandria. A new direction proved more appealing. This produced the People's party—the Populists. No matter what name it was called, the discontented rural people were bent on reform. The movement had begun in the Midwest and gained national importance. The Populists organized in Winn and other hill country parishes. They bitterly resented the Bourbon Democrats. The list of changes that these reformers wanted was clear. They wanted a government that responded to the people.

The Populists demanded public ownership of railroads. Railroads were being laid across the state after the early 1880s. Crops were shipped by railroad. The wealthy received favored railroad rates. Populists wanted public ownership of utilities as well.

The Populists did not want a handful of party members electing candidates. The people wanted to elect the senators to Congress. At that time they were elected by the State Senate in Baton Rouge. There were also demands, such as a secret ballot, the Populist party was making in other states. (American voters did not vote in secret until 1890.)

Populists wanted a graduated income tax. They wanted a way to put forth legislation. They wanted to be able to recall undesirable officials. They demanded equalization of tax assessments in the state. They also wanted the unlimited production of silver coins.

The hostility against the Bour-

bon Democrats increased. Populists formed a group whose voice was heard among the many people who were nonplanters. There were few Populists in South Louisiana. The party did not have the strength in the state to win an election. The Republicans were in a similar situation. Louisiana sugar planters' need for the protective tariff was the same as the need of Northern manufacturers who voted Republican. For this reason the sugar planters voted the Republican ticket.

The "lily-white" Republicans and Populists formed a "fusion ticket" in 1892. John N. Pharr, a rich sugar planter from the coast, was the candidate of the Fusion party. He came in last in the election. However, this action produced evidence of Populist strength in the state.

The Populists were led by leaders from the hotbed of reformers, Winn Parish, the center of the hill country. Hardy Brian published a newspaper, the Winnfield *Comrade*. With the support of the people of the parish, he expressed the feelings of most of the people of his area about the government.

The Populist party in Louisiana disappeared after the 1896 election. This was true elsewhere over the nation. Only the formal organization of the Populist party was gone, however. The mass of people still shared a hunger for a voice in the government and a redistribution of unequal wealth.

Their desires did not disappear. They would find new expression for their dissent and work toward reform.

The Bourbon Democrats countered the Populist-Republican vote in their own way. They felt that any means were justified to save the state from the Populists and Republicans. The Bourbons had controlled the share-croppers' votes for a long time. There was no way for them to lose an election as long as they did it their way. They felt the heat of mass hostility so warm against them that they resolved not to endure such a risk again. The Bourbons pointed out what they considered a very damaging belief of the Fusionists. The editor of the *Shreveport Evening Judge* was shocked at Populists' proposals. The editor wrote on August 9, 1895, "They even go so far as to say that they are in favor of voting the Negro honestly. . . . Think of this, Louisianians! Are you willing to go this far with them?"

The 1898 Constitution. After the 1896 election, plans were made to elect delegates to write yet another Louisiana constitution. This constitution completed the planters' movement. It was written by Bourbon delegates. There was only one Populist delegate. The constitution was not submitted to the electorate for approval. The 1898 constitution was very much like the 1879 constitution. The major difference was in the restrictions placed on voting.

The Bourbons, however, insisted on provisions to limit the vote. A voter had to own property worth three hundred dollars or had to know how to read. A poll tax of one dollar per year was imposed. A receipt for two-years payment of taxes had to be presented at the polls to qualify to vote. (A day's wages for an able-bodied man was often as little as a dollar a day or even less.) There were no cars or convenient transportation for the people to ride to the polls. For many people courthouses were a day's ride away. They had to stay overnight and return home the next day. The inconvenience and cost of qualifying to vote eliminated many potential voters.

The Louisiana Constitution of 1898 has long since become known for its famous "grandfather clause." Those whose fathers or grandfathers had voted prior to 1867 did not have to meet literacy requirements. The chief purpose of the "grandfather clause" was to eliminate the Negro vote instituted after the Civil War. There was also a body of opinion among Bourbons that too many whites voted. They wanted to eliminate as many propertyless whites as possible.

The Bourbons were not so sure of their power that they totally disregarded the hostility of the Populists. After all, there was always the ghost of the French Revolution to remind them. Continued great excesses in power might bring about the downfall of even the powerful Bourbons. They thought it wise to make some concessions.

The provisions of the 1898 constitution were concessions to the common people. A railroad commission was created. It later became the Public Service Commission. Utilities were included in its jurisdiction. The State Department of Agriculture and Immigration was expanded. A state primary system was planned for the nomination of candidates. The way was paved for school districts to vote bond issues for construction of buildings and maintenance of schools.

"Jim Crow" Laws. "Drawing the color line" was a phrase used to describe separation of blacks and whites. This was the goal of the Bourbons. The dual school system became the first legal action in segregating the two races. Such laws separating blacks and whites came to be known as "Jim Crow" laws. The name came from a comic character in Broadway minstrel shows.

In 1891 Louisiana passed a law requiring separate coaches on railroads for blacks and whites. This law was the first of a series of segregation laws that divided the races in all public places. After trains were segregated, the next step was to furnish separate restrooms at the depots. Such laws included public drinking fountains and eating places.

Segregation laws were passed to ensure that the black and white races were separated in every aspect except the workplace. Laws were passed segregating the races in mental institutions (1902); in streetcars (1902); in saloons (1908); at circuses (1914); and in prisons (1918).

In 1896 the United States Supreme Court gave its decision on the *Plessy v. Ferguson* case. Honère Plessy, a Louisiana black man, had challenged the law requiring separation of the races. The court ruled that "separate but equal" public facilities were constitutional. This decision settled for half a century the legal right of the state to provide segregated schools for blacks and whites.

Political Power. The Republican party remained active in political campaigns until the early 1900s. In 1900 Bourbon Democrat W. W. Heard of Union Parish was elected governor by a large majority. The Republican party was no longer a threat. The one-party system was assured.

The Bourbons now had no party to challenge them. On January 1, 1897, 130,000 blacks were registered to vote. By early 1900 only about 5,000 black voters were registered. Even that number decreased within a few years. Within a few years, too, the number of white registered voters declined to a little more than half of the number in 1897.

Louisiana Office of Tourism

The Tensas Parish Courthouse was built in 1906.

The planters had been casting the ballots for the blacks whom they employed. Black sharecroppers had not been free to vote as they wished. Now that the 1898 constitution kept blacks from voting, the planters no longer had their vote to count. Bourbon power was so secure that they did not need their sharecroppers' votes any longer. (After 1896 no Negroes were elected to the Legislature until 1968.) Louisiana was now a one-party state. It belonged to the Democratic party.

En Partie 1 (Studying a Part). 1. What was the "understanding" with the North? 2. How did the Bourbons control the government? 3. Identify: disfranchisement, Bourbons, "grandfather clause," "Jim Crow" laws, "Kansas Fever," one-party system, Populists, and suffrage. 4. Which two privileges did the Bourbons not want to give the freedmen? 5. How were people disfranchised? 6. (a) How may lynchings took place between 1882 and 1913? (b) How may victims were black? 7. Why did farmers begin to organize after the Civil War? 8. What happened to the Louisiana Lottery?

Industrial and Agricultural Development (1877–1920s)

Sawmill Invasion. At the same time political changes were being made, vast changes were taking place in many other areas. One of the most significant happenings of the time occurred in our forests. With the railroads came Northern investors eager to convert Louisiana's vast forests into lumber. The forests still covered approximately seventy-five percent of the state. For nearly two decades lumbermen came into the state. The lumber industry expanded steadily and rapidly from 1880 to 1900.

In the early 1900s huge mills operated twenty-four hours a day all year. By 1904 Louisiana was leading the South in lumber production with two and one-fourth billion board feet per year. By 1909 the state had reached its peak of over sixteen billion board feet per year. The Great Southern Lumber Company of Bogalusa, established in 1908, had become the larg-

est lumber mill in the world. By 1925 most of the great forests were gone.

Sawmill towns sprang up in the forests almost overnight during this time. Boomtowns—company towns—grew up all over the state. The life of these sawmill towns probably averaged fewer than twenty years. The policy of "cut out and get out" was followed. Many old sawmill towns were completely abandoned. Some survived but were greatly reduced in size. Lake Charles, Winnfield, and Bogalusa survive today. Harvey, Lutcher, Morgan City, Patterson, Plaquemine, and Ponchatoula are old cypress-milling towns which are still in existence. New Orleans and Shreveport also were important cypress-milling centers.

These sawmill towns were built in the center of the timber holdings. They had company-owned houses, churches, and commissaries (company stores). They also had the big mill with its log ponds in which the logs were unloaded from the rail cars.

The hill-country farmers sold the timber off their land, if not the land itself. They themselves became employees of the sawmill. At first, the excitement and the high-ranking urban bosses seemed wonderful. The farmers soon realized that the invaders forever destroyed not only the vast pine forests but also the simple life on the frontier. Long work hours

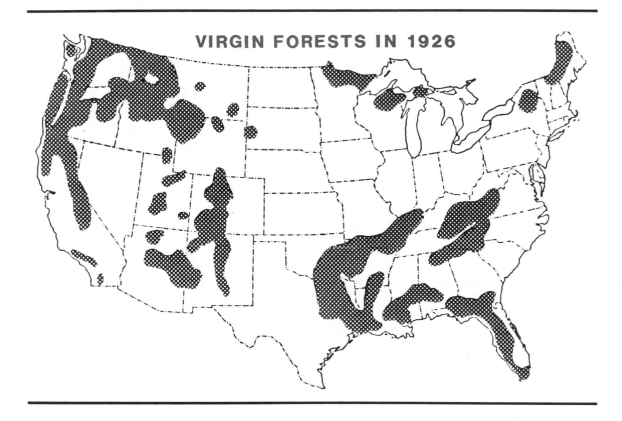

VIRGIN FORESTS IN 1926

left little time for hunting, fishing, or farming. Indeed, wild game had a smaller habitat as the timber was cut. The wages at the sawmill appeared small for the long hours that practically eliminated family life.

Wages ranged from $2.50 a week for the least skilled to $10.00 for the most skilled. Even these wages were often not paid in cash. Instead, the workers got "scrip." Scrip was a certificate of money owed the workers. Sometimes a metal token was used as a money substitute. It was redeemable in making purchases at the company store. Scrip was not acceptable anywhere else.

Reforestation. By the 1900s the state was left with endless acres of cutover land. The priceless timber resources were gone. Many thought that there would never be anything more than the bleak land without trees. Some men thought differently. Outstanding among them was a man named Henry Hardtner of Urania. He believed that Louisiana could have a second crop of trees. Hardtner is now known as the "Father of Forestry in the South."

Hardtner organized the Urania Lumber Company in 1898. He devoted himself to finding ways of making new crops of timber grow. He sought the advice of the United States Forestry Service in 1910 and became a strong supporter of reforestation in the state. He wrote the general conservation laws for Louisiana as a member of the legislature. He helped pass the Reforestation Act of 1910. Under this act landowners could sign an agreement to reforest their lands and be guaranteed a fixed amount of money for as long as forty years.

Not only did Henry Hardtner prove that Louisiana's forests could be rebuilt, but he also proved that forests themselves worked at making a second crop. Largely as a result of his effort, the trees gradually began to grow again.

It is believed that Hardtner's project at Urania was the beginning of the reforestation movement in Louisiana. His project served as an example to other companies. Its fame and influence spread to other states. Yale University sent students to study Hardtner's methods. The contributions by Hardtner and the Urania Lumber Company are still being felt in Louisiana.

Other efforts helped in the conservation of our forests. President Theodore Roosevelt had started an enthusiastic forest conservation movement across the nation. Louisiana's

legislature created its department of forestry in 1904. The public schools were told to teach forestry. Arbor Day was to be set aside for special recognition. These actions and similar legislation brought an increased awareness of the value of the pine forests even then being stripped by out-of-state lumber interests.

Unions. There were many workers from all over the nation who poured into Louisiana with the sawmills. They brought new ideas from these other sections. They brought desires for new goods that could be bought. They wanted more money than had ever been considered essential before. The organization of labor was one of the new ideas. "Union" was a word added to the vocabulary.

Labor unions were organized in the sawmill communities. This was not done without bloodshed. The millowners were supported by considerable public feeling. Most people had never faced the idea that labor had rights. Most during this period felt laborers had no right to question their employers.

Railroads reaching out into the isolated sawmill communities brought newcomers. Ideas spread to Louisiana from California, Kansas, and other states regarding fundamental changes in the social and political life of the country. The nine-hour workday, higher wages, elimination of child labor, nationalization of railroads and utilities, accident and unemployment insurance, survivor's benefits—all these new ideas were causing working people to think of a way to obtain some of the material blessings enjoyed by the more prosperous.

The Socialist Party. Many of the sawmill workers came from the Midwest and California. They introduced local people to the idea of socialism. They distributed literature. "Equal privileges for all; special privileges for none" fit well into local sentiment against Bourbons. People listened intently. Socialism made sense to people chafed by Bourbon rule.

Walter Dietz had migrated to Lake Charles with his family from Iowa. He began work at the roundhouse for the Watkins Railroad that ran through virgin forests to Alexandria. It was his job to wipe off the engines. Later, he graduated to engineer on the train. Still later, he became the bookkeeper for the railroad. He was obsessed with the need for reform. He wanted public ownership of utilities and railroads and other reforms that Populists advocated. He thought that the ten-hour and eleven-hour workdays, six days a week, were criminal. He believed that the business of paying sawmill employees with tokens that had to be spent at the company-owned stores was robbery. Prices were high. Credit was provided only at excessive rates of interest at the stores. Higher wages and shorter

hours were demands to be made. Insurance against accidents at the sawmills was necessary. Child labor had to be abolished. Safety measures must be provided at the mill. Some of the jobs were clearly dangerous. He fervently believed in race and sex equality.

Dietz was angry at the Christian churches. He felt that they should lead in the struggle for reforms. He felt that churches supported the situation as it was. He quit his volunteer work at his church and became a convert to the Socialist party.

Other people joined the cause. Wilbur and Otis Putnam arrived in southwestern Louisiana with their parents in 1888 from North Dakota. Not long after 1900 they too became socialists. They "hoboed" to Girard, Kansas, which turned out the socialist newspaper *Appeal to Reason*.

Some newcomers had been members of the clubs formed after reading Edward Bellamy's book *Looking Backward*. These clubs were formed to bring about reforms also. Bellamy's book predicted the nation's future under socialism in the year 2000. Socialists felt that the society the book pictured was a "wonderful dream come true."

Wilbur Putnam presided at the first gathering of Louisiana Socialists. This was held in New Orleans on September 19, 1903. Leaders of Socialists in New Orleans included Mr.

and Mrs. Alvin Porter, who owned a boardinghouse near Audubon Park. They invited socialists to gather there. A problem arose concerning black members meeting with white ones. Covington Hall, a young man from a plantation near Thibodaux, was a rabid socialist. Nevertheless, with his background in a planter family, he wanted the blacks to meet in separate "cells" from white members. The national Socialist party would not allow this. The Socialist party recognized no difference between the sexes nor among the races.

New Orleans socialists became involved in disputes of organized labor. Covington Hall and others resigned from the New Orleans group. Hall became a fiery leader in the labor war that had erupted between sawmill workers and sawmill owners in western Louisiana. Alexandria became the center of radical movements. Hall published a newspaper designed to stir laboring people to revolt.

No community was more absorbed with the socialist movement than Winn Parish. Eugene Debs visited Winnfield and spoke to an overflowing audience. He also spoke at Southwestern Louisiana Industrial Institute at Lafayette and at various other places. On one circuit, Walter Dietz traveled with him. "Uncle Bob" Smith of Sikes introduced Debs in Winnfield.

Socialism had different expressions in Louisiana. Dietz and Putnam left their churches to work for socialism. In Winn Parish "Uncle Bob" Smith and other Winn Parish socialists were equally hard workers in their Baptist church as well as in the socialist movement.

During the years before World War I a youngster growing up in Winn Parish heard this talk about socialism almost all the time. This boy was Huey P. Long. The gifted youth told all who would listen that he would become governor of Louisiana when he grew up. Long's "Every Man a King" was another way of saying "privileges for all."

Labor Organizations. Violence flared between the sawmill employees and the millowners during the first decade of the new century. The years of labor disturbances in southwestern Louisiana before World War I were known as the "Louisiana Lumber War." In 1910 owners of the largest mills in Louisiana, Arkansas, and Texas met to discuss the organizing of labor. The owners organized into the powerful Southern Lumber Operators' Association. They vowed not to hire anybody who belonged to a union nor anyone who would join one.

The sawmill owners tried to enforce their rule. The laborers felt that they were free people and would join unions if they chose to do so. Laborers called the contract that owners required of them a "yellow dog contract." Any worker who signed one was a "yellow dog."

The group called the Industrial Workers of the World (the "Wobblies") and the Socialist party were closely allied. Often the same leaders appeared in both. The same was true of the Brotherhood of Timber Workers.

When the Southern Lumber Operators' Association declared war on the union, eleven sawmills near DeRidder were closed. Three thousand men lost their jobs.

The union goals included an eight-hour workday, an end to forced trading at company stores, and a $2.50-per-day minimum wage for common laborers.

In a violent affair at a small place called Grabow, near DeRidder, three persons were killed. President A. L. Emerson of the Timberworkers Union was arrested for the murders. Scores of union members were placed in the crowded and filthy basement of the Calcasieu Parish jail at Lake Charles. The Socialists' state secretary, Walter Dietz, converted them all to card-bearing members of the Socialist party.

It was no accident that the Louisiana voters of 1912 gave the Socialist candidate, Eugene Debs, many votes for president of the United States. One out of every fourteen who voted in Louisiana voted for Debs. He received more votes in the state than the Republican Taft. In Winn Parish in 1912 Socialists elected almost the full slate of parish officers. The So-

A sweet gum log on a log wagon in the Calvin area (mid-1920s).

Courtesy of Maud Smith

cialists were a threat to the Democrats' one-party political monopoly.

In the first years of the new twentieth century, the Democratic party dominated Louisiana politics. For nearly three decades the state was run by that party alone. Democrats passed a law with such requirements that only Democrats could be included on the ballot used in primary elections. If a person were not registered as a Democrat, he lost the right to vote in local elections. This change was the "kiss of death" for the Socialist party.

The simmering discontent of laboring people and hill-country farmers burned at white heat. Hostility and disgust had been expressed in the Populist party. It made little difference that the Populist party was gone.

The sawmill owners and planters were exactly alike in their attitudes toward workers. They became allies. The Choctaw Club of New Orleans found both groups to be political friends. Other groups were added. The great oil companies and Union Sulphur Company took the side of management. These groups controlled the government.

Other Industrial Development. Louisiana's industrial development of minerals began in the 1900s. Abundant natural resources discovered throughout the state formed the basis for industry. Salt, sulphur, oil, and natural gas were first produced commercially during this period.

The town of Sulphur in Calcasieu Parish developed around the mining of **sulphur**. The Union Sulphur Company had a near-monopoly in the mining of this valuable resource in the state. Sulphur was discovered long before Dr. Herman Frasch developed a process to commercially produce it.

In 1894 Dr. Frasch watched the first flow of softened sulphur spill into a wooden barrel from a Louisiana salt dome. It was eight years later before the process was considered a commercial success. (The Frasch process has been improved, but the basic idea is still used today for most of the United States sulphur production.)

The Calcasieu Field had produced seventy-five percent of the nation's sulphur supply until 1914. It was exhausted by the early 1920s. During the years 1924–1932, sulphur production was at a standstill in Louisiana.

Salt mining was not successful until 1898. It was being mined on Avery Island. Salt had been obtained on Avery Island long before the Civil War. In 1894 salt was found on Jefferson Island. Production did not begin there until 1923, however.

Louisiana's **petroleum industry** had its beginning in the early 1900s. The unbelievable riches of Spindletop, a tremendously successful oil strike near Beaumont, Texas, had its effect in Louisiana. It caused much clamoring for oil discovery in the state. In 1901, the same year of the Spindletop discovery, the Heywood brothers brought in an oil well six miles from Jennings. During that year seventy-six Louisiana oil companies were formed to drill for oil. In 1902 five producing wells brought forth 548,617 barrels of oil with a total value of $188,985. Two years later, the Mamou, or Evangeline, Field had a total of thirty-three producing wells. On March 28, 1906, the first Caddo Parish oil well to produce in commercial quantities was brought in. The state's first oil refinery was built near Jennings the same year. The following year what was probably the first offshore drilling in the world occurred in Caddo Lake. In 1909 North Louisiana oil wells were linked to Baton Rouge with a pipeline that had its origin in Oklahoma oil fields. Also in that year the Standard Oil Company built a new refinery in Baton Rouge.

By 1916 the oil industry had grown so that Louisiana ranked fifth among the forty-eight states in the production of oil. By 1919 the state had fifteen refineries.

Like the rich lumber resources the petroleum deposits earned profits mostly for Northern corporations. However, jobs became available, and some paid fairly high wages.

The **natural gas industry** really began with the discoveries of oil in the early 1900s. The gas industry developed quickly. The natural gas

pipeline that connected Dixie and Shreveport was laid in 1908. This was the first year that natural gas was used commercially in Louisiana.

One of the largest gas fields ever discovered was the Monroe Gas Field. It was discovered in 1916. Some of the greatest gas production in the world has been in the vicinity of Ouachita Parish. The Haynesville Gas Field started in 1921.

Natural gas had few uses at first. Unless there was a town close to the source, it was not profitable to put down a pipeline to carry the gas. Thus, most of it was flared in the field. This waste has been called one of the worst abuses of natural resources in history.

Other industries were developed from Louisiana's natural resources. Opossum, mink, skunk, raccoon, and muskrat pelts are the raw materials for Louisiana's **fur industry**. Shrimp, oysters, turtles, frogs, and crawfish supply the **seafood industry**. The **Spanish moss** industry developed. The moss was used in upholstered furniture and mattresses.

Many **farm-related industries** increased production. Between 1865 and 1885 the cottonseed oil industry became one of the most important in the state. There were eight factories in New Orleans manufacturing cottonseed oil and its by-products. By 1900 the value of the business was over seven million dollars.

Sulkies were used during the nineteenth and early twentieth centuries.

Postwar Agriculture. The agricultural picture in Louisiana was very bleak during this entire period. This was true for the entire United States between 1865 and 1900. Overproduction contributed to falling prices. The rapid growth of new farmlands, the development of new farm machinery, the use of commercial fertilizers, and improved methods of farming increased production. Prices fell drastically. Cotton sold for sixty-five cents a pound in 1860. In 1895 it sold for five cents. At the same time farmers had to pay high prices for the goods they needed. The value of farmland and equipment fell.

Yet, the Bourbons, with the sharecropper labor, rebuilt the plantation system. Plantations continued to dominate life in Louisiana. Factors were again in business in New Orleans. Planters secured money necessary to produce crops at high interest rates through factors. New York bankers financed New Orleans factors. Some planters received their financing closer to their homes. Again, goods were shipped by water from New Orleans to various points in the state. Warehouses and the hauling business continued. Coopers built wooden barrels to hold molasses, sugar, and other farm products.

Many former aristocratic planters were trying to restore their old places to their pre–Civil War conditions. The small farmers barely managed to provide the essentials for their families. The economy improved little.

For two decades after the Civil War the sugar industry barely survived. It was three decades before the industry recovered to the 1862 level of production. In 1861 the value of sugar planters' property reached nearly two hundred million dollars. By the end of the war the value amounted to about sixteen million. The sugar industry would never again contribute to the prosperity of the state to the extent it had before the war. Sugar planters needed more capital to restore their plantations than did cotton farmers. They did not have the capital. Many sugar plantations changed hands because of capital problems. Other problems slowed recovery. Labor shortages and high wages presented endless problems.

Sharecropping was not used because it did not work well for sugarcane production. Large labor gangs were needed during certain periods of the season. Wages stayed relatively high. Planters were afraid to try to reduce wages for fear of losing their labor force.

The sugarcane workers went on strike during the 1880s. Some of the strikers protested wage cuts. Most wanted higher wages. Strikes were not successful.

About 1885 the Knights of Labor began to organize both black and white canefield workers near Thibodaux. The planters would not deal with the union. In 1886 a strike was begun at the beginning of the sugarcane harvest. The planters would not give in. The strike continued. The strikers would not go back to work. They went to towns instead. Many moved to Thibodaux.

When a light freeze came on November 21, planters realized the best crop since the Civil War might be ruined. One hard freeze could do it. Vigilante committees, with the help of some imported armed men, stopped the strike. On November 22 and 23, 1886, they killed at least thirty Negroes and wounded more than a hundred. The rest of the laborers returned to the fields to harvest the crop.

Before the end of the nineteenth century sugarcane operations had changed. Corporations bought out plantations and built better sugar mills. Sugar-making was taken over by the corporations. Planters sold their cane by the ton. They organized cooperatives. Either the co-ops or the corporations ground the cane. Negroes still formed most of the labor force.

By the time sugar planters re-established their business in the 1890s, another problem arose. The federal bounty, or subsidy, for growing sugarcane was repealed. Some planters went bankrupt.

During the 1880s the famous Louisiana House was built on the riverfront at New Orleans. It could produce six thousand barrels of sugar daily. It employed about eight hundred men.

Cotton continued to be the most important single crop in Louisiana. It was in demand briefly after the Civil War, but prices fell. Cotton farmers struggled. Cotton did not reach the pre-war level of production. There are those who contend that the world demand for cotton reached its peak about the time of the Civil War. During four years of war other areas of the world found that they could grow cotton.

Cotton Exposition. New Orleans hosted a cotton exposition to celebrate the one-hundredth anniversary of the first shipment of cotton from the United States. It was Major Burke's idea to rebuild the economy. The state, the city, and a number of towns and parishes raised about $1,000,000 to finance the event. Major Burke managed to get $1,000,000 from the Democrats in Washington. He had estimated that four million people would attend, and the Exposition would gross $5,000,000. Instead, it grossed much less, and it suffered a net loss of $500,000. It was described as "a collossal white elephant floundering in a mire of stupidity, mismanagement, and corruption." The exhibit was held in Audubon Park in late 1884 and early 1885. Visitors from all over the country flocked to New Orleans for the World's Industrial and Cotton Centennial Exposition. Several times it almost closed because it was so deeply in debt.

The Exposition covered thirty-three acres in Audubon Park. Its building designs made a big impact on architecture. The buildings contained more elevators than existed in all the rest of the world. A pipe organ was the largest in North America. The glass tower of the Horticulture Hall could be seen from twenty miles away. Nothing remained after the Exposition. New Orleans got no new industry and very little commerce from it. It did improve the morale of the people, however.

Boll Weevil. The boll weevil came into this country from Mexico at about the turn of the century. It crossed the Sabine River and headed through Louisiana cotton fields. The new pest invaded the state and made the growing of cotton still more difficult and risky. Entire crops were lost. This time many farmers lost their land. Many were forced to give up farming. The Crop Pest Commission was created to fight the boll weevil.

Rice. During the 1880s Louisiana added a third staple crop—rice. The introduction of this crop to southwestern Louisiana was directly related to the railroad. The Watkins Railroad made a dramatic slash through the western Louisiana wilderness. This railroad was first called the Louisiana Western Railroad. In 1865 it joined the Southern Pacific system. A Kansas banker, Jabez B. Watkins, owned the company. The new railroad ran through forests from Lake Charles to Alexandria. Lake Charles had begun as the site of a large sawmill. Watkins saw the value of attracting migrants into southwestern Louisiana. He promoted the area among Midwest grain growers. They came in large numbers. Seaman A. Knapp, the president of Iowa Agricultural College, was persuaded to come. The name Knapp became famous in Louisiana because of his pioneer work in rice development. Knapp discovered that the hardpan of the Louisiana prairies could be used to hold the water to irrigate rice. Within a few years the grain farmers of the Midwest transformed southwestern Louisiana into the "Rice Capital of the World."

Agricultural Progress. After 1900 Louisiana farm production recovered. Plantations developed in the valleys between North Louisiana hills. Many of these were made by combining small farms. New varieties of sugarcane contributed to increased produc-

A woman hulling rice.

tion. The agricultural experiment station at Kenner helped spread new knowledge about agriculture. Farmers learned scientific methods from government agencies and other groups. Prices of farm products and consumer goods were more in balance than they were before the war. By 1920 Louisiana agriculture had reestablished itself as a force in the American economy.

Transportation. Louisiana's economic development depended on good transportation. Water transportation was extremely important, especially for commercial traffic. Water navigation on the Mississippi was greatly improved by James B. Eads, a famous engineer. The maintenance of a channel at the mouth of the river deep enough for large ships was a big problem. Eads built a system of jetties, or retaining walls, to narrow and deepen the entrance. A wall of willow mattresses, stone, and debris was erected on each side of the proposed channel. By confining the current, the jetties forced the river to cut and maintain its own channel. This work was completed in 1879. Within ten years a depth of thirty-two feet was reached. The swifter current scoured the bed of the river and cleared away the sandbars.

Steamboats finally disappeared from

Mule-drawn and Model T trucks in Minden.

LSU-Shreveport Archives

the rivers and bayous of the state. Trains provided long-distance traveling. Most of the state was rural. Horses and carriages were the chief mode of transportation in local areas. There was no system of state roads. Roads were built by parishes or by towns. Louisiana roads were still mostly muddy trails. There was a growing need for better roads. These had to be secured if the state was to progress.

One road that became famous was Shed Road located in North Louisiana. Its terminal was Shreveport. The road was chartered by Congress and financed by private capital. It was built by the muscles of mules and men. It was the state's first and only all-weather turnpike with a shed overhead. It was designed as an answer to the rainy season when mud was so deep that the roads in Louisiana were impassable by wagon. If the rains came early in the fall, cotton crops grown in the hills of North Louisiana could not reach the Shreveport market until the rains ceased in the spring. Judge John W. Watkins of Minden thought of this shed road as the answer to the problem. Judge Watkins knew that the river soil, if kept dry, would pack hard and make a perfect highway. The Shed Road project was begun in 1874, but it was not completed until 1880. The road was used for more than twelve years. Then the Vicksburg, Shreveport and Pacific Railroad (now the Illinois Central) was

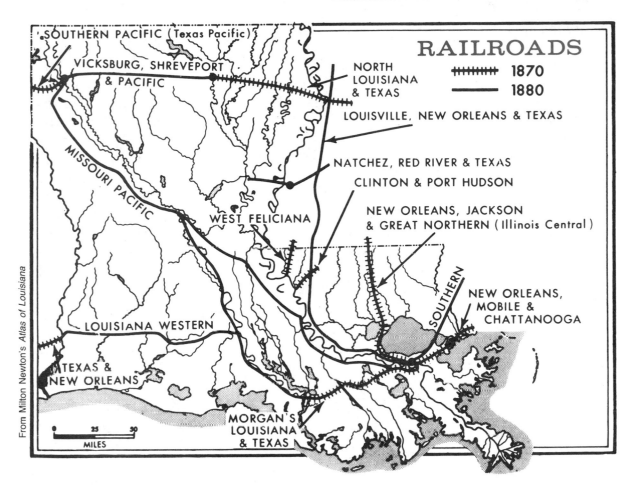

completed. The railroad track paralleled the stagecoach line.

Another famous road in North Louisiana was the Old Wire Road. It stretched from Monroe to Shreveport. The road played a major role in the settlement of the North country uplands. It got its name from the telegraph line it followed.

The stagecoach brought the Old Wire Road to its peak of service in the middle and late 1800s. The stagecoach ride was a rough one. It cost fifteen dollars per passenger. If it rained and the stagecoach bogged down in the clay hills, everybody, including passengers, had to get out of the coach to help push it out of the muck. Sometimes robbers bolted out of the woods in Ouachita Parish to waylay the coach. They robbed the passengers and stole any valuable goods that might be aboard. They even took the team of horses or oxen.

Everyone was left stranded until help came along. Even the legendary Jesse James was reported to have been one of the robbers who operated in this area.

Lagniappe. Outlaws operated during the turmoil that existed after the Civil War. None have generated so many tales as the infamous West Clan. This band of cutthroats robbed travelers on their way to Texas. The Kimbrells were part of this clan. They operated on that part of the Natchez Trace between Montgomery and the little community of Atlanta in Winn Parish.

John A. Murrell, a Methodist minister from Tennessee, became the first leader of the clan. Called "Reverend Devil," he was head of a gang before the Civil War. Their territory then was the neutral strip between Fort Jesup and the Sabine River. West, one of Murrell's men, took over this clan and added other clans after the war.

Don S. Kimbrell and his wife, Mary, were key members of the clan. The Kimbrells were highly respectable people by day. They were active in church and community affairs. He was justice of the peace in Ward 6, Winn Parish. They never robbed local people. At night they were a different kind. The Kimbrells were known as "Aunt Polly" and "Uncle Dan" then. While other clan members waylaid travelers and robbed them on the highway, the Kimbrells had another method. They invited their victims to stay at their home. While the guests slept and least expected anything, Aunt Polly or Uncle Dan slashed their throats with a knife or bashed their heads with an axe. They then took their jewelry, horses, wagon, harness, and anything else they might own. The Kimbrells set up a shop to repair harnesses, saddles, and the other items for sale.

Many stories are told about this clan. One is about hidden gold of the clan that has never been found. Another story concerned deep wells dug a mile apart where they tossed the bodies of their victims. Some of the stories may not be true, however, the wells do exist. At least one of the wells may be seen deep in the woods along the highway where the West Clan operated.

Flood Control. Another big problem for the state during this period was the floods along the Mississippi River. Some levees had been constructed by parish governments before the war. During the Civil War the levees had been entirely neglected. A number of breaks, or crevasses, had occurred. These breaks remained unrepaired year after year. The river

This cart was used for Rural Free Delivery of mail before World War I.

poured freely through them during times of high water. This made it impossible to cultivate large areas of fertile lands. The carpetbag government was supposed to have spent about one million dollars on repairs, but there was little improvement made.

Some federal aid was received in 1879 when the government established the Mississippi River Commission. Under Governor Nicholls a state board of engineers was established. The engineers were to be responsible for the levee work. Little was done due to the lack of funds.

In 1882 a destructive flood drove over a thousand people from their homes. After that flood the federal government helped the state keep the river under control. In 1885 levee districts were created by the Louisiana Legislature. Plans were made to build large systems of levees along the rivers and bayous of the state. Not nearly enough was done. Floods came again in 1912, 1913, and 1916. The first flood control act followed. By then the levee system had been greatly improved, but it was still far from adequate.

In 1927 Louisiana suffered one of the worst floods in its entire history. It was the most disastrous in the history of the Mississippi River Valley up to that time. It covered an area of about twenty-six thousand square miles. It was mainly in North and South-central Louisiana. There were 637,000 driven from their homes. Two hundred fourteen people were killed. Crops were ruined, and hundreds of animals drowned. Property damage amounted to about $236 million. Business was at a standstill. The federal and state governments and the Red Cross came to the aid of the stricken people. After the water receded, it took months to restore the area. The Flood Act of 1928 followed this 1927 disaster. The passage of other federal and state legislation to provide more effective flood controls followed.

En Partie 2 (Studying a Part). 1. Describe the invasion by the sawmill owners. 2. Trace the organization of sawmill workers' unions. 3. Trace the development of the Socialist party. 4. What were some of the goals of the protesting people? 5. Describe the industrial development of this period. 6. What three types of towns developed? 7. What problems did farmers face? 8. Give details about the Cotton Exposition. 9. How did James B. Eads help transportation?

Education

Education was very bad during this period. Some progress was made after 1900. Even then Louisiana's educational system was very poor. In fact, Louisiana's educational system is still suffering from the neglect of education during this time. Louisiana was the only state in which white illiteracy increased between 1880 and 1890. Black illiteracy remained about seventy percent.

After 1877 a dual school system was set up—one for blacks and one for whites. The planters conceded the need for primary schools for blacks. The small plantation schools usually included grades one through three. Some went as high as the sixth or seventh grades. That did not mean the planter class expected to allow the Negroes the right to higher education without a challenge. They would simply find ways to limit opportunities for blacks. Chiefly, the schooling was to be restricted to primary grades. Since Negroes were allowed public schools, such schools had to be provided for the white masses, also. The propertied class had no intention of paying enough taxes to provide public schools of much value.

Not only was there little money, but also neither the public nor their representatives in government were sold on public education. One reason was the stigma that planters had attached to public schools. The rest of the public had largely accepted their view. Planters believed in private schools. At one time persons whose children went to public schools had to sign papers acknowledging that they were paupers. Although this was done before the Civil War, the ugly

Kate Chopin, a famous short-story writer, lived at Cloutierville. She is shown here with her children.

image remained. People unable to afford private schools preferred no schools to paupers' schools or public schools. A a result, only a few people in rural parts of the state received any education at all.

The truth was that these public schools, begun after the war, were public in name only. They were more private than public. School patrons had to furnish the building and the fuel for heating. They bought books and supplies. Patrons supplemented the tax money that paid a teacher for a few weeks or a few months of the school year. Patrons ordinarily extended the school term by paying the teacher's salary for the added time. Teachers bore the expense of institutes or summer college courses. Even school officials were unpaid volunteers who had little time to give.

Generally speaking the schools were of poor quality. The teachers were usually not qualified for the job. Schools were only in session for a few months each year.

In New Orleans, education was more advanced. Free textbooks were first given to the needy in New Orleans in 1898. There was a state compulsory attendance law, but it was not enforced. Therefore, there were many children who attended no schools at all. Those with any means received some education. In New Orleans and elsewhere in South Louisiana there was a tradition of Catholic church schools. A larger portion of the people lived in these areas.

Planters continued to use private education for their children after the Civil War. Their proud claim to "aristocracy" required social distance from the white masses more than ever. Private schools of many types flourished in the 1880s. Numerous private teachers were employed. There was a distinct difference in the planters' private academies after the Civil War. They were forced to be privately financed. Before, public tax money voted by planter legislatures had paid some of the expenses for the "private" academies.

Although whites in rural Louisiana generally ridiculed the efforts of black freedmen to become educated, they did not ignore one fact: a number of blacks were gaining at least some education. Whites would not allow the children of their race to be uneducated if any blacks were being educated. The idea of white supremacy would not survive among educated Negroes. Moreover, the mass of whites felt that they needed education to face the planter class with a feeling of equality. They, too, had a label of inferiority to overcome. Therefore, children of farmers and of other plain folks first entered the public schools in small numbers. This was a mere trickle to the flood that came later, increasing with every new school year.

It is doubtful that the public school system of Louisiana would have continued but for the white masses who poured into public schools. Gradually, the stigma of pre–Civil War days faded. The scant funds provided by tax monies were distributed by parish police juries. The money was never divided equally between the schools for whites and schools for blacks. Black schools received less and less as the whites swelled the size of their public schools.

In 1906 the legislature gave parish school boards the authority to issue bonds for the construction of public schools. The bonds were secured by special taxes voted by people in a given school district. Over two hundred schoolhouses were erected the following year under this arrangement. These were schools for whites with the dual system allowing very little for the Negroes.

Improvements made after 1900 included lengthening the average school term from one month to three or four months a year. All children between seven and fifteen years of age had to attend school at least 140 days a year. This was in accordance with a law passed in 1916. Funds were also provided for libraries. Within several years school libraries increased their holdings from 21,000 volumes to 100,000.

Tax monies granted for public schools increased from $1.5 million in 1904 to $3.5 million in 1908. More students were in school than ever before. In 1907 the State Department of Education set up various departments. The state teachers organized in 1884. T. H. Harris began a long term as State Superintendent of Education in 1908. Many changes took place under Harris so that schools gradually improved.

By the School Act of 1888 parish school boards were authorized to establish central or high schools. By the 1890s all larger cities and towns had opened a public secondary school. High school courses were standardized. By 1900 there were thirty-five white secondary schools. There were no Negro secondary schools. White children from small villages and rural areas often boarded with relatives in order to attend public schools. Black children did the same to attend their church-sponsored schools.

Many of the improvements in education did not come from public funds. The Peabody Fund, after 1910, paid the salary and traveling expenses of an elementary rural school inspector. In 1915 the Rosenwald Fund furnished money for Negro school construction. It also paid the salary and travel expenses of a Negro agent who worked to interest the communities in providing better schools. The Jeanes Fund provided for supervisors for already-established black elementary and secondary schools.

Grambling State University

Charles B. Adams, founder of Grambling State University.

Until after World War II, Louisiana whites would not accept the concept of black high schools. After Booker T. Washington made public his support of vocational training in the 1890s, black schools above the elementary level were called training schools. None was called a high school. By 1919 there were seven parish training schools established.

Several institutions of higher learning developed just before and after the turn of the century. Some were combinations of older schools. Some

changed their names. Others changed their locations. The schools mainly offered basic courses. They did not offer the wide variety of courses offered by modern schools.

En Partie 3 (Studying a Part). 1. What improvements were made in education during this period? 2. What were training schools?

World War I

World War I broke out in Europe in 1914. In 1917, the Red Revolution in Russia brought Lenin and Communists into power. Louisiana people reacted quickly against the state's Socialist party. It is true that some of the old Socialists aligned with the Communists, but this was not true of most of the people who were battling for reforms under the Socialist banner. Angry citizens complained about the work of J. R. Jones of Jonesville, state secretary of the Socialist party. He published a small Socialist paper for Louisiana. Military men were sent to destroy his press and files. The Socialist party could not survive in the years of war.

The Red Scare that followed the war was just as bad. The United States attorney general led in a witch hunt against communists. The Louisiana Socialist party was reduced to not much more than a name.

World War I stirred strong feelings of patriotism in Louisiana. "Uncle Sam Needs You" war posters found plenty of response. Louisiana contributed 80,834 men to the army. Blacks were among those who enlisted in the military service. Louisiana's most distinguished serviceman was Major General John A. LeJeune of Pointe Coupee Parish. He rose to commander of the United States Marines. Many soldiers were trained at Camp Beauregard near Alexandria. Aviators trained at Lake Charles. Several other military camps were established in the state.

An epidemic of influenza spread from Camp Beauregard into the civilian population. Many soldiers and many civilians died. Spinal meningitis, which followed the flu epidemic, claimed more lives.

The home front again was very supportive of the war effort. Local organizations raised money and furnished war supplies. Women made bandages and knitted clothes for the servicemen. Meatless days and wheatless days were observed every week. About $150 million worth of Liberty loan bonds were bought by Louisianians.

World War I songs were sung from New Orleans to every rural school and church in the state. The catchy tunes caught the ears of Louisianians.

This was before radio and decades before television. The songs reflected the spirit of a people who fervently believed in their country. They believed in the rightness of "stopping the kaiser." They believed heartily in themselves as Americans. There was a contagious optimism and a cheerfulness about the old songs such as "Over There." They were whistled, sung, and "banged out" on pianos across the state.

En Partie 4 (Studying a Part). 1. Relate the Socialist party to World War I. 2. How did Louisiana participate in the war? 3. Describe the patriotism displayed by the people during World War I.

Lagniappe. Jazz, someone has said, was not invented. It just happened. A special kind of music that was heard among the blacks of New Orleans was first identified as jazz in the early 1900s. "Satchmo," Louis Armstrong of New Orleans, was well known as "Mr. Jazz." In fact, he received mail addressed "Louis Armstrong, Mr. Jazz, U.S.A."

Louis Armstrong was born July 4, 1900. When he was six years old, he was placed in a home for correction.

It seems that he had accidentally shot off a pistol he found at his home. At the home, he was assigned to play a bugle as the flag was raised over the home in the morning and lowered in the evening. He went on to make history. Armstrong was known and loved around the world.

When Satchmo died July 6, 1971, he was buried in New York. The following Sunday, a memorial service with traditional jazz music was held in New Orleans.

Combining jazz with death is peculiar to New Orleans. The funeral begins with a march to the grave by mourners. A band with muffled drums leads the procession.

Postwar Changes

Social and Political Changes. Automobiles were introduced before World War I. After the war there were more. By the 1920s the Model T was traveling over the muddy or dusty roads of the state. The car made it possible for the farmer and his family to make trips to town more often. Women cut their hair. Skirts became shorter. In 1920 some citizens heard the first presidential election returns to be broadcast over radio. In 1918 the Eighteenth Amendment to the United States Constitution was passed. This amendment prohibited the sale of alcoholic beverages. The Nineteenth Amendment passed the next year. It gave women the right to vote. The first tractors were brought to plantations on trial. They were tried as experiments. These machines could replace men and mules. More tractors and more trucks were brought to plantations and farms. Blacks sought better living conditions. A great wave of black migration to Chicago and other northern cities took place. More Model T Fords and other cars appeared on the scene. Roads in the state were still poor. The state was still rural in character, but Louisiana was changing. It was changing slowly through new machines and new technology.

Reform had been sweeping over the nation since 1900. Socialist Walter Dietz said that both the Democrats and Republicans took over the ideas of the socialists. In 1910 John M. Parker organized the Good Government League. This was meant to get rid of the Choctaws, a political ring in New Orleans. The ring candidate, J. Y. Sanders, had won the race for governor in 1908. The candidate of the Good Government League had won in 1912. The ring had elected their man in 1916. He was Ruffin G. Pleasant. Parker, of the reform league, carried the state in 1920. He was a representative of the planter-urban alliance. This group pledged themselves to subdue the Choctaws.

Parker, known as the "gentleman reformer," made no basic reforms. He did support the building of better roads and led in getting legislation passed to provide more funds for Louisiana State University. It was he who called for the Constitutional Convention of 1921. A new constitution attempted to bring the state laws more in line with the times. The 1913 constitution had not served the state well.

Political Discontent. The Bourbons were politicians. They never represented the majority of the people of Louisiana. They were keenly aware that times were changing. They could not entirely ignore the discontented people they governed. Only a fraction of the people voted. Members of the upper class held office. That was the planter class and New Orleans political leaders. In a free country the common people never forgot the promise of equality and freedom for all men. The Bourbons' claim to aristocracy and a right to govern had never been accepted by the mass of people. The highhanded action of the Bourbons was resented. Even the Bourbons knew that severe discontent existed among the people. It could not be ignored.

An important reason for the feel-

These columns at Cheneyville remain from a historic church built in 1843.

ing that Bourbon government could not last was public education. Most of the whites had had the opportunity for a generation to obtain such public education as Louisiana afforded. The schools were not of highest quality, but, even so, they were creating change. The voting citizens of the state in the 1920s were more educated than their forebears.

The Bourbons were not going to risk another crisis like the Civil War, which had destroyed their fathers' way of living. Therefore, laws were designed without apology to maintain the control which the Bourbons held in 1900 and for twenty-eight years afterwards. They were made strong with as few loopholes as possible. But deeper problems were brewing for the Bourbons. Their time was passing.

En Partie 5 (Studying a Part). 1. How did life change for most Louisianians after World War I? 2. What problem did the Bourbons have to face?

Coup d'Main (Completing the Story)

Jambalaya (Putting It All Together)

1. Which party dominated Louisiana politics completely for the first three decades of the twentieth century?

2. Which class of people were in control?

3. Why did the state become a one-party state?

4. What were the beliefs of the Bourbons?

5. Which new political party formed in the state in the early 1900s?

6. What was happening in each of these areas in the early 1900s: (a) transportation, (b) education, (c) petroleum industry, (d) agriculture, and (e) services for the people?

Potpourri (Getting Involved)

1. Map Work. (a) Show the section of the state flooded in 1927, or (b) show World War I Louisiana camps and other government installations.

2. Research (a) the women's rights movement, including their efforts to obtain the right to vote, or (b) the development of unions in Louisiana.

3. Compare (a) the development of the Populist party or Socialist party in Louisiana with their development in the rest of the United States, (b) life before with life after the inventions of this period, or (c) patriotism during World War I with that during the Vietnam War.

Gumbo (Bringing It Up-to-Date)

1. Compare (a) the 1898 constitution with the 1974 constitution, (b) the Cotton Exposition with the 1984 World's Fair, or (c) the women's voting rights movement with the present women's rights movement.

2. Relate (a) the Louisiana Lottery of the 1800s to present lottery proposals for Louisiana and lottery systems being used today in other states, or (b) the "Jim Crow" laws to current racial problems.

A HAZARD OF TRAVEL

CHAPTER 11

THE REVOLT AGAINST THE BOURBONS (1928–1940)

Huey Pierce Long

From 1928 to 1935 Louisiana's government was dominated by Huey Pierce Long. He has been described as the state's most colorful political figure. He has also been described as a demagogue and as Louisiana's most original and aggressive governor. Long styled himself as "the Kingfish."

Background. Huey's background was not like that of the poor people he represented. He was born in 1893 at Winnfield in Winn Parish. He was seventh in a family of nine children born to Huey Pierce Long, Sr., and Caledonia Tison Long. Huey's parents owned their three-hundred-forty-acre farm. They belonged to a very proud group of people living in the hill country. They had a very different lifestyle from the planters.

Huey's family was unusual in many ways. Six out of the eight children who grew to adulthood attended college. College educations were not common for farm families of that period. The family included, besides Huey, a lawyer, a dentist, a United States representative, a Louisiana governor, and a college teacher with a master's degree from Columbia University.

Huey was brash, ambitious, and highly intelligent. He annoyed adults with his questions and opinions. Huey was a gifted child who presented problems. He did not fit into the small rural school. In fact, he did not graduate from high school. There was a mix-up about graduation over which Huey did not have control.

Huey always found an outlet for his sharp mind and abundant energies. Once he had a chance to sell books. At first he and his friend Harlie Bozeman helped a peddler selling books at the Winn Parish Courthouse. Later they rode the train to sawmill towns nearby and sold more books. The boys' pay for their sales was a selection of books, but that was what they wanted.

Huey decided that he could stop the crowd if he played a banjo and sang. He decided that when he saw a banjo player near the place where he planned to sell his books. The only problem was that he could not play a banjo. He asked the man playing one to sell him his. The man agreed. In the sale Huey made an agreement for the man to teach him to play. Huey learned so quickly that right away he started playing and singing to attract crowds. After that he performed to attract people to buy his books. The amount of his sales surprised everybody. Huey never quit using catchy songs as a selling tool. He always included musicians among his associates. "Every Man a King" was his song that told a lot about his outlook.

From an early age he worked at being a good salesman. He became one of the best. After selling books, Huey sold cooking oil. He continued to develop his skills. He became so good at selling that people could not believe it. At age nineteen he became sales manager for the Faultless Starch Company sales office in Memphis, Tennessee. Years later his selling experience helped him sell his political ideas. It also gave him an understanding of people. It developed his ability to persuade them.

Huey Pierce Long grew up in a hotbed of political discontent—Winn Parish. It is referred to as the "Free State of Winn." The title was probably derived from the rugged individualism of the settlers there. This was the same area that opposed secession before the Civil War. Winn Parish had given little support to the Confederates. Some people still think that Winn Parish seceded from the Confederacy. In the 1890s the Populists were active in Huey's area. By 1901 the Socialist party was in that section.

Hearing his elders talking about political problems was a part of Huey's life. He heard talk about Bourbons. The adults he knew mocked these people who thought that they were better than others. They felt strongly that they themselves were not getting a fair share of opportunities. They talked morning, noon, and night about reforms they thought must be made. They were angry.

Socialism was the subject of much of the talk. The Socialists were very active in Winn Parish. Huey read the pamphlets and newspapers. There were protests about the low wages of the common man. Many other injustices to the working man were cited.

Harlie Bozeman and Huey Long, both bright boys, formed a debate team. They were young students at Winnfield High School. They were invited on at least one occasion to debate against a Socialist speaker from

Alexandria Daily Town Talk

Long with outgoing governor, O. H. Simpson, after Long's inauguration in 1928.

the North. The subject was "Democracy versus Socialism." A crowd of hill country farmers was the audience. "Huey and Harlie were just boys in knee pants. But they held their own. They really won that debate," an old Socialist recalled admiringly.

Huey got much of his education from exchanging ideas with people.

He was also very well read. It was said that Huey possessed almost total recall of his reading. He was supposed to have read a five-hundred-page volume in half an hour. Huey supposedly said, "There may be smarter men in the United States, but they ain't in Louisiana."

When Huey set a goal to succeed in politics, he decided that he needed to prepare. With the encouragement of his brother Julius he became a lawyer. Huey entered Tulane University Law School as a special student. He did not have a high school diploma so he could not attend as a regular student. He attended for less than a year before he passed the bar exam.

Huey began his practice as his brother's partner in Winnfield. They soon parted ways. Then Huey set up a practice for himself. To supplement his income, he sold containers for kerosene. His law practice grew as his cases involving timber companies increased. He moved to Shreveport and developed a very successful practice.

Beginning of Huey's Political Career. Huey's political career began in 1918. He became a candidate for membership on the state Railroad Commission. The commission had been established by the Constitution of 1898. Its purpose was regulating railroads, steamboats, pipelines, telegraph, and telephone companies. The commission had done little up to this time.

Long campaigned with the support and help of his family and the people his family knew. He had a large number of friends in the Third Commission District. Many of these friends were made during his selling days.

He carefully made campaign plans. These included becoming acquainted with those who had run and those who had been elected since the commission started. One method he used was unusual for that time. He conducted a very successful direct-mail campaign. His wife, Rose, mainly took care of that part of the campaign. Huey hit the campaign trail. He spoke to as many as he could on a one-to-one basis. He went to the voters wherever they were. This meant that he went to the backwoods. Some heard a candidate for an important office for the first time. He spoke to crowds. He told them that the commission would be an agent of the people. It would be against big corporations. Huey displayed his posters everywhere. He sold himself so well that he won the election.

Huey started his new job in December 1918. He concentrated on serving the public interest. This meant that he had to represent the people against large corporations. This issue caused him to split with Governor Parker, whom he had supported earlier. Standard Oil Company had managed to get written into law its own version of a bill levying a severance tax on gas, oil, and other natural resources. Long's objections were heard throughout the state. He fought an unsuccessful campaign to put Standard Oil's operations under the control of the commission. Even though he did not win, he gained a lot of publicity. In 1921 Huey became chairman of the commission. It had a new name: the Public Service Commission.

Governor's Election: 1924. By the end of 1922 Long started his campaign for governor. On his thirtieth birthday, in 1923, he filed as a candidate for governor. He used some of the same plans he had used in the commissioner's election. Two of his most effective methods were state-wide circulars and speeches. He even made speeches on the radio.

Huey went directly to the people. He called them by name. He made them feel important. This was the first time that campaigning had been taken to them in their small country towns. He made them feel that he was one of them. He spoke to the farmers about the wealthy. He told them what they wanted to hear.

Huey was at his best on the platform. He was a master at making a political speech. He attacked his opponents in his humorous manner and in plain language. His use of ridicule was one of his striking characteristics. He labeled his political enemies with such names as "Turkey Neck" and "Kinky." The Bourbons had long poked fun at people they considered to be of lower social status. Now they themselves were the objects of biting ridicule and caricature.

Long made it very clear where he stood on most issues. He opposed the concentration of wealth, corporate interests, and banking. He supported the right of labor to organize. In labor disputes, he opposed the use of injunctions. Huey was not racist. In his sense of timing, however, he knew that he must not try to take the mass of people faster toward a more democratic order than they were willing to go. One issue that he treated lightly might have caused him to lose the election. The Ku Klux Klan was active again. It was strong in North Louisiana and southwestern Louisiana. The organization opposed Negroes, Jews, and Catholics. Two opponents strongly opposed the Ku Klux Klan. Long said little about it. Huey finished third in the race. The Klan issue might have made the difference. He received 74,000 votes. Rains had kept many of the poor—the Long supporters—away from the polls.

Governor: 1928. Huey had prepared for the 1928 campaign for governor to gain support where he needed it. He did not support either candidate in the 1924 runoff election. He did support a Catholic, Joseph E. Ransdell, in his successful race for United States senator in 1924. Ransdell probably owed his victory to Huey's support. Long also supported Edwin Broussard against J. Y. Sanders for the United States Senate in 1926. The Protestant Sanders was a former governor. Broussard was a very popular French Catholic from rural South Louisiana. Long actively campaigned for Broussard. Broussard won. Long had gained support for himself in French Catholic South Louisiana.

Long emphasized his carefully planned programs during the 1928 campaign. The programs were tailored to take care of problems that existed in the state. Louisiana had only three hundred miles of paved roads; so he promised more and better roads. There wasn't a bridge over the Mississippi. He promised to remedy this problem. Louisiana had the highest illiteracy rate in the United States. Textbooks were worn out and out-of-date. Huey promised better schools and free textbooks. More care for the blind, deaf, aged, or sick was another of his pledges. New Orleans was promised natural gas.

Huey made the people aware of their needs. He did this in his campaign speech made under the Evangeline Oak at St. Martinville. This speech has been described as the greatest speech he ever made. In the following part of the speech, he demonstrated his ability to appeal to the people.

Where are the schools that you have waited for your children to have that have never come? Where are the roads and the highways that you spent your money to build that are no nearer now than ever before? Where are the institutions to care for the sick

and the disabled? Evangeline wept bitter tears in her disappointment. But they lasted through only one lifetime. Your tears in this country, around this oak, have lasted for generations. Give me a chance to dry the tears of those who still weep here.

Long did not receive a majority in the first primary. However, his impressive showing caused his opponent to withdraw. Since there was no Republican ticket, he was declared the winner.

Huey gave a new feeling of confidence to the mass of people. He was one of them. They identified with the first of their kind to be elected governor of Louisiana. About twenty thousand of his followers traveled to Baton Rouge for his inauguration.

Break from Bourbon Rule. This unusual man seemed destined to break the Bourbon rule. He was never a Socialist, but the cries of the common people were in his ears all of his life. The break from Bourbon rule came in 1928 when Huey was elected governor of Louisiana. Historian Joe Gray Taylor says, "What the Jacksonians, the Radical Republicans, the Populists, and the Socialists had failed to do, Huey Long accomplished." He did more than simply defeat a political party. His election marked the end to the plantation system's hold on the state as far as the government was concerned. Huey put an end to the one-party aristocratic rule that had gripped the state. Aristocrats laid claim to a monopoly of all refinements. Gentlemen, as defined by the Bourbons, were out-of-date in Huey Long's Louisiana. These "gentlemen" had been concerned with preserving their position, status, and wealth. Elitism had no place in Huey's world.

Long flaunted convention. He poked fun. He made jokes about the Bourbons' insistence on formal manners. He knew that the defeated Bourbons were cringing when he was pictured serving "pot likker" in Washington, D.C., or receiving a foreign official while he was clad in red pajamas. He spoke in the language of the backwoodsman. Yet, he was a well-educated man and could speak as correctly as any Bourbon when he chose to do so. He chose to speak in the language of the mass of the state's people. They were not educated. He wanted to identify with the common man. These people in Louisiana understood exactly what Huey Long meant.

The revolt against the Bourbons was not unique to Louisiana. In some measure the same series of events went on all over the South. Bourbon rule was finally rejected along with its notion of an aristocracy. It was a move further toward the equality of man promised by the Founding Fathers of this nation.

Long's Program. As governor, Huey set about putting into action the program he had promised for the public good. He did not have an easy job getting his programs carried out. He had to wheel and deal to win. He managed to get natural gas piped to New Orleans homes and businesses. He managed to get a small bond issue for road and bridge construction. This program became a constitutional amendment. Since good roads were a prime goal, Huey began a program of hardtopping roads. New bridges were built. Louisiana State University was a pet project. A crash program to teach people to read and write was started. Huey started the free school books program. (Only years earlier, Socialist Wilbur Putnam had been arrested for advocating free textbooks.)

Huey had many other programs. A graduated income tax became law. He got the poll tax repealed. Homestead exemptions were made so that most homeowners paid no state or parish taxes on their houses. Charity Hospital in New Orleans received more funds to expand its services to poor people. The Louisiana State University Medical School was started to provide more doctors for the state. Schools received more funding. A new governor's mansion and a new capitol were part of his program.

More care was given the unfortunate people of the state. He adopted a motto, "Share Our Wealth," which might have come directly from the theme of the old Socialists.

Huey Long became noted for his bitter enemies. He made some of his enemies by using a spoils system. He removed political opponents from key jobs and replaced them with his own supporters. He then asked for contributions from his appointees for his political campaign fund. Eventually Huey became heady with power that amounted to almost a dictatorship. He seemed to want power more than anything else. He became ruthless as the job of getting his programs into motion became more difficult. He, like the planters before him, felt that the ends justified the means.

When Long called a special session of the legislature to increase the tax on oil production, his opponents resisted. The president of Standard Oil set up his headquarters in a hotel in Baton Rouge. He directed a program to oppose Long. Lobbyists fought Long's tax. When the anti-Longs showed an increase in strength, some former Long followers joined his opponents.

Impeachment. An attempt to impeach Long followed. Before April 6, 1929, the House of Representatives adopted an article of impeachment. That was the date set for the end of the special session. Later they adopted

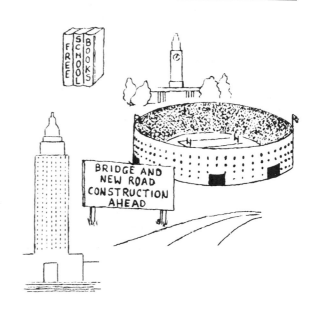

Long increased severance taxes on natural gas and petroleum. His programs included free textbooks for public and private schools. Long built a new state capitol building and modernized the public system of roads. Over fifteen hundred miles of roads were completed, and bridges were constructed over the Mississippi at Baton Rouge and New Orleans. The U.S. government then provided more financial aid for road construction, thus providing jobs for the unemployed. L.S.U. football was another of his pet projects.

six more charges. Long questioned their legality. The Senate rejected Long's argument by one vote. Then before the impeachment trial was to start, fifteen senators signed a very important statement. It said that they would not vote to convict Long under any circumstances. It took two days to get enough legislators to vote Huey's way. Huey said, "I buy 'em [solons] like sacks of potatoes. I used to try persuasion and reason and logic. From now on, I'm a dynamiter. I dynamite 'em out of my way." The remaining members knew that it was pointless to proceed. Long was forever indebted to those fifteen senators. Some feel that the experience brought drastic changes in his behavior. It made him more vicious in his attacks against his opponents.

The Great Depression. The nation was hit by the Great Depression at about the time that Huey Long became governor. The economic crash came in 1929. The creeping slowdown of business added to the despair of the people. The depression in Louisiana was as dreary as elsewhere across the nation. Everyone was affected. Probably the city dwellers suffered from lack of essentials more than the people who lived in rural areas. Most of the people in Louisiana still lived on farms.

Prices of farm products had been dropping since the mid-1920s so that farmers had not shown a profit for some years. When the Depression hit, prices dropped even lower. Cotton sold for as low as five cents per pound.

All farmers—planters, small farmers, large farmers, and sharecroppers—were joined in a desperate situation. Crops could not be sold for enough money to pay for the seed. Much less cash was available for the farmer's family. Yet, most farmers were not used to much cash, so they were able to manage without it. They were able to raise almost all of the food they needed as they had done before the Depression. Through credit at the country stores they were able to buy some of the things they could not produce on the farm. Flour, coffee, and sugar were three items that they desired but could not produce.

In response, the federal government began a program of price supports in 1933. Under this program farmers were required to limit their crop production. In return they were guaranteed a minimum price for their crops. This federal program begun by President Franklin D. Roosevelt provided for subsidies. The government programs gave a new measure of security. Acreages were regulated in an effort to secure higher prices for farm products by making them less plentiful.

The idea of work-relief was introduced to the state. The WPA (Works Progress Administration) included both blue-collar and white-collar jobs. In New Orleans a large number of urban workers were employed on work-relief projects. Many of these agencies had their headquarters in New Orleans. Blue-collar workers were employed to improve roads. Others worked on reforestation and drainage projects. The Historical Records Survey and the Federal Writers' Project were among white-collar projects. Other New Deal programs were the CCC (Civilian Conservation Corps) and the NYA (National Youth Administration), which provided student jobs.

In Huey's autobiography *Every Man a King*, published in 1933, he offered a program to end the Depression. So great was the need for a way out of the Depression that people looked for strong leaders to give direction. Not all were satisfied with Franklin D. Roosevelt. Long gained a big following with his program. This program would redistribute the country's wealth. Every head of a household who did not already have $5,000 would receive that amount. Family personal income was to be limited to $1 million per year, and family fortunes limited to $5 million. The people were ready to listen to a new radical program such as Share Our Wealth.

United States Senator. In 1930 Huey Long defeated Joseph E. Ransdell to become United States Senator Long. Ransdell had been one of his supporters. Long did some clever "politicking" to retain control of the state while he was in Washington. Lieutenant Governor Cyr and Long had become bitter enemies. Cyr said that Huey had vacated the governor's office. Cyr argued that Huey could not hold two offices at the same time. Therefore, Cyr had himself sworn in as governor. Huey had the National Guard block Cyr's entrance when he tried to take office. Then Huey took

steps to disqualify Cyr's actions. With political maneuvering he prevented Cyr from becoming governor. Huey declared Cyr's office vacant. In time the courts supported Long. Huey finally took the oath of office as senator in 1932. Alvin King, the president of the Louisiana Senate, became governor for the short time left in Huey's term.

Long maintained close contact with the state government from Washington. His political machine controlled every aspect of state government. The machine also controlled many of the parish governments.

Huey's Political Ambitions. Senator Huey Long quickly became a national figure. He left the national Democratic party and broke with President Roosevelt. There was talk that Huey wanted to be president of the United States in 1936. He did, in fact, aim for national office. He had even written a book of fantasy in 1935—*My First Days in the White House.*

Most historians agree that Huey Long posed a threat to President Franklin D. Roosevelt. Of course, there were other political figures of the period who were also threats. Some say that it was Long who caused Roosevelt to search for a program like Share Our Wealth to appeal to the people. This turned out to be the first Social Security Act, passed in 1935. No doubt, the Roosevelt ad-

Long's grave, marked by a bronze statue of him, faces the capitol.

ministration was determined to "get Long." Huey knew about the situation and its implications.

Huey's Death. Those opposing Long were as ruthless as he was. His enemies felt very strongly, and he had many enemies. His followers felt that he could do no wrong. People were either intensely for Huey Long or intensely against him. There was no middle ground. Any means used to win this "biggest fight yet" were all right in Huey's mind. Huey must have felt that he was right because he thought he was fighting for the common man. He developed a large following of devoted common people. Voters listened to him so that even Roosevelt feared him. Yet, even people who supported Long repeated, "Power tends to corrupt and absolute power corrupts absolutely." That, many thought, was the story of Huey Long.

There was mounting tension in Louisiana by 1935. There was talk that somebody was going to kill Huey Long. He often acted like a dictator with high-handed methods that offended many. Fear of assassination caused him to shield himself with armed bodyguards.

Senator Long ordered a special session of the legislature in September 1935. One of his goals was to remove Judge Benjamin Pavy from office. Pavy was a very popular anti-Long judge who had held his seat

twenty-eight years. By gerrymandering judicial districts Pavy would have been put out of office. Huey got a call that he was needed at the session. On Sunday night, September 8, 1935, Huey left the House chamber in the capitol.

As Huey walked down the hall, Carl Austin Weiss, Judge Pavy's son-in-law, shot him. Weiss fired one shot at Huey at close range. Long's bodyguards killed Weiss with at least twenty-six bullets.

Huey was taken to Our Lady of the Lake Hospital with a bullet wound in the lower part of his body. Surgery was delayed while two noted New Orleans surgeons made the trip to Baton Rouge. They were said to have had an accident, so they returned to New Orleans. This left Dr. Arthur Vidrine to operate. He was a doctor whom the New Orleans medical establishment had labeled incompetent. Huey disagreed. He had made the country doctor Vidrine head of Charity Hospital over the objections of the New Orleans group. Dr. Vidrine operated, but not in time. Huey died September 10, 1935.

It is not certain what his last words were, but most who were present say that he said, "God, don't let me die. I have so much to do."

Trainloads of sobbing people attended his funeral on the lawn of the capitol he had built. At least 100,000 mourners viewed his coffin. Their grief was genuine. Their reason for mourning him was real. Long had established the white masses as people of dignity, deserving respect. They were people whose voices in government should be and would be heard. Henceforth, the claim of a Bourbon to govern would be a myth of the past. All white people of Louisiana would now walk together at the same level. Minorities, including the state's blacks, had a way to go before achieving equality. The supporters of Huey P. Long loved him for making a move in this direction. Many ordinary white men and women felt that Huey Long was their deliverer from the oppression of the Bourbons. He need have done no more to have their complete devotion.

Others felt that he was a disgrace. For many years after his death the fight would continue. Long and anti-Long factions of the Democratic party would struggle for power.

Following Huey Long's Death

Louisiana Scandals. The Louisiana scandals erupted a few years after Huey Long's death. The scandal-ridden five-year period following his death has been called the Louisiana Hayride. (The name came from a popular song.) In 1939 there was a series of startling federal indictments against some of the leading political figures of the state. The scandals shocked the entire nation and made front pages everywhere. It was referred to as the "most systematic theft upon an American state" to ever take place. Long's followers had all too frequently helped themselves to public monies and properties. Huey had said, "God help 'Loozeeanah' if I die. My rascals will steal the state blind." He had need to worry. There had been too many opportunities for personal profit for the weak men Long left in power. These men had come to terms with the Roosevelt administration. As a result, federal money flowed into the state. By one means or another, much of it was used for the personal gain of some of Long's followers.

Among the most prominent of Huey's "rascals" to be convicted was Governor Richard Leche. Others were Dr. James Monroe Smith, president of Louisiana State University; Seymour Weiss, president of the Roosevelt Hotel in New Orleans; and Monte Hart, a prominent contractor. At least a dozen others were involved. Using the mails to defraud, income tax evasion, and other charges were filed against at least eight men. Seven, including Leche and Smith, went to jail. Four people involved in the scandal committed suicide. Many were discredited. The cost of the scandals has been estimated at $100 million.

Governors: 1932–40. Huey Long was governor officially until January 25, 1932. The president *pro tempore* (for the time) of the Louisiana Senate, Alvin O. King, then became governor briefly. Oscar K. Allen was the next governor elected. Allen was handpicked by Long. He continued Long's programs until his death in 1936. James A. Noe finished his term. In 1936 Richard W. Leche, governor, and Huey's brother, Earl, lieutenant governor, polled more votes than anyone in the state's history, including Huey, up to that time. Leche resigned under pressure in 1939. Earl Long completed his term.

During all these elections there were two big factions: Longs and anti-Longs. North versus South Louisiana, rural versus urban (or New Orleans), and Protestant versus Catholic were other confrontations. The Long forces won in all the elections for governor. All of these people continued the policies started by Huey P. Long, but none could replace him.

Coup d'Main
(Completing the Story)

Jambalaya (Putting It All Together).

1. (a) Who headed the revolt against the Bourbons? (b) What was the difference between Long's philosophy and that of the Bourbons? (c) How were they alike?

2. How did Long reshape Louisiana's political system?

3. Explain the ideology of Share Our Wealth.

4. Trace the personal and political life of Huey Long.

5. What did Long call his autobiography?

6. How did Long maintain control of the state?

7. What kind of government did Long's political machine provide?

8. List Long's contributions to the state. Divide your list into negative and positive contributions.

9. (a) What was the Great Depression? (b) When did it begin? (c) When did it end? (d) Which Louisiana group probably suffered the most from the Depression?

10. Discuss the effect of the Depression on agriculture.

11. What important federal legislation did Long influence?

12. What were the work-relief programs introduced?

13. (a) What was called the Louisiana Hayride? (b) Give details.

Potpourri (Getting Involved).

1. Stage (a) a debate between the Long and Anti-Long factions regarding Huey's chief issues, (b) a political rally typical of the day, (c) a speech

Huey Long-style, presenting your platform, or (d) a debate on Huey Long's merits and demerits.

2. Interview someone who remembers the Depression, or pretend that you lived here at that time. Report on problems, help received from the government, and job opportunities.

3. Compare (a) the political career of Huey with that of his son, Russell, (b) Huey's contributions as governor with those of any other Louisiana governor or with all others, or (c) opinions of Huey Long by noted writers.

4. Interview someone who lived during Huey Long's time. Ask what their feelings were about his programs. Try to discover little-known facts about the man.

5. Report on political machines in Louisiana.

6. Role-play or illustrate campaigning for governor, impeachment proceedings, the assassination, or any other significant event in Huey's life.

7. Examine (a) Joe Gray Taylor's statement: "Huey Long may have been the most remarkable American of the twentieth century," or (b) the statement: "Huey P. Long seemingly left behind him a permanent political organization that entailed radicalism, reaction, and reform."

Gumbo (Bringing It Up-to-Date).

1. Compare (a) the role of the government during the Depression with its role today, or (b) Huey's welfare programs with welfare programs of modern times.

2. Report on Long's political influence during his lifetime, in the 1960s, and in the 1980s.

3. Stage a "Meeting of the Minds" between Huey Long and later governors. Include Edwin Edwards. Discuss how each would have handled the problems of each time.

PART SIX

In Recent Times

Louisiana Office of Tourism

CHAPTER 12

MODERN LOUISIANA
(1941–Present)

World War II marked four years of turmoil that ended with spectacular changes in the world, the United States, and Louisiana. In many ways its legacy was like the Civil War of the century before. "Before World War II" refers to a time that seems separated from the post–World War II period by many more years than those of the war. Louisiana, like the rest of the world, entered an awe-inspiring new era. This war brought even greater changes, perhaps, than had the Civil War.

Louisiana in the 1940s

World War II. Louisianians responded to the call of their country in World War II in many different ways. Many did so by serving in the military, working in factories, and making sacrifices on the home front. The collection of scrap iron and rationing of sugar, tires, and gasoline were a part of life during wartime. So was the use of substitutes for such things as nylon stockings and butter. Such activities as Mardi Gras were cancelled for the duration of the war. More than 325,000 Louisiana men and women volunteered or were drafted into the military ranks. Louisiana became almost an armed camp. Five large military training camps and ten flying fields appeared. Other military and naval establishments mushroomed within the state. Louisiana was the site of maneuvers, or mock battles, to train soldiers for the overseas battles. Many of the nation's great generals were in Louisiana during the war at one time or another because of the state's role in these training exercises. These leaders included General Dwight Eisenhower, who later became president of the United States. General George Patton also came here.

General Claire Chennault of Waterproof led the famous Flying Tigers, a group of daring volunteers who flew against the Japanese. The group was not a part of the United States military establishment when they began their operations. They were former United States military pilots released from military service at their own requests. They were then free to join China in its war against Japan. After the United States entered the war, Chennault and his men joined the United States Army. They continued their fight as United States servicemen.

Louisiana had German and Italian prisoner-of-war camps. Prisoners were used on the plantations to meet the problems caused by labor shortages. They were also used to build levees and to do numerous other jobs. Many Louisianians were prisoners of war in camps in Japan and Germany. Some returned to tell the horrors of their experiences.

Shipyards constructed much-needed seagoing vessels. Andrew Jackson Higgins employed 40,000 workers in his assembly-line production in New Orleans that turned out ships very rapidly. Henry J. Kaiser made national headlines with the astounding speed with which he turned out ships. A merchant ship was built in ten days, a liberty ship in two weeks.

Sam Jones. Sam Jones led the state through almost all of the war years. The lawyer from Lake Charles was elected governor of Louisiana in 1940. He was the first anti-Long governor elected after Huey's death. He was opposed by Huey Long's younger brother, Earl.

The state was divided into the Longs and the anti-Longs. The Long followers dubbed Jones "High Hat Sam." It was for the purpose of linking Jones with the Bourbons, the people that Huey Long displaced in 1928. The Long followers well understood the symbolism. The anti-Longs ridiculed the Longs for their antics. The Longs and their followers clung to their image. In fact, the more the former Bourbons poked fun at the Longs' image, the more fervent Long supporters became. The anti-Longs won. Probably the Louisiana Hayride scandals caused the Longs to lose the election.

Sam Jones's style as governor was completely different from that of Huey Long. Jones led in passage of laws that repealed powers of the government. Changes made by Jones included reducing auto license fees. He created 20 departments to take over the duties of 175 boards and commissions and reduced the expenses of government. Eight thousand people were removed from the state payroll. A **civil service program** for state employees was established. Louisiana's debt was eliminated. Jones left a surplus of fifteen million dollars. However, Jones did continue the welfare services started by Huey Long. Taxes

Oil rigs dot the Gulf just off Louisiana's coast.

were increased some to improve the school hot-lunch program. He also increased old-age pensions.

Jimmie Davis. In 1944 Jimmie Davis of Jackson Parish was elected governor. Davis came from the same North Louisiana hill country from which the Longs came. Indeed, he had a close relationship with many people in Winn Parish. Oddly enough, despite his background, Davis was allied with Sam Jones and the anti-Long forces.

There was little to distinguish his administration. His time as governor was dominated by the war and the postwar adjustment period. Davis's administration left a fifty-million-dollar surplus.

Davis became famous for his country music. He sang the songs of the hill country, including gospel music. He and Charles Mitchell wrote "You Are My Sunshine." He used his hillbilly band on a campaign tour of the state. Davis acted in minor roles in Hollywood movies while he was governor.

Postwar Adjustment. World War II was finally over in 1945. The new world that waited brought dramatic changes in Louisiana life.

In the nineteenth century and for several decades afterwards, most of the population outside New Orleans had made their living from agriculture. Modern machines and technology changed the old farming methods. The armies of laborers used on plantations were no longer needed. Chemicals were used to destroy weeds in the crops. Airplanes spread fertilizers, herbicides, and insecticides.

When war brought new opportunities for employment to blacks, many of them relocated. Many blacks left Louisiana for other states. After the war, more moved to the cities in other states as well as in Louisiana. The state's black population continued to decline.

In 1940 Louisiana's population had been nearly sixty percent rural. By the end of the decade the state's population was forty-nine percent rural.

There were many other adjustments that had to be made when the war was over. Colleges were overcrowded. Returning servicemen used their G.I. benefits and went to college. Many veterans needed work. Wartime factories turned to making peacetime products. Women had entered the work force during the war. After the war they wanted to keep their jobs. Louisiana's industrial development had expanded, and people were moving to the cities.

Earl Long. In 1948 Earl Long became governor of Louisiana. For eight years the "Long machine" had been out of office. Huey's widow and his son Russell campaigned for Earl. So did Gerald K. Smith, Huey's minister.

Earl had the same Populist-Socialist background as his older brother Huey. Earl had organized Huey's first campaign. He was the man who had designed Huey's statewide organization and made it work. Huey Long had possessed a magic when he addressed crowds of people. Earl did not. But Earl had a deep person-to-person appeal that Huey did not have. The Longs—both Huey and Earl—belonged to the mass of people who had taken little part in the government before 1928. Earl, as had his brother, identified with the needs of these Louisiana people. Even his enemies agreed that Earl had a sincere desire to uplift the mass of people. Many were in need of employment, education, and training for jobs. His

campaign slogan was "Service to the People."

Earl, particularly in his last years, followed few rules in his personal lifestyle. He became "Uncle Earl" of his famous "Pea Patch Farm" near Winnfield. He aroused strong anti-Long factions as readily as Huey.

Earl labeled Sam Jones, his opponent, with "do-nothingism." His critics felt that Long tried to do everything for everybody. He expanded welfare programs already in existence and contributed his own. He provided a fifty-dollar monthly pension for the aged. He added fourteen trade schools, two charity hospitals, and bonuses for veterans. He experimented with free hot lunches for all school children. The state had medical programs that were similar to Medicare and Medicaid of today three decades before the rest of the nation. Earl added free ambulance services for charity hospitals and free dental clinics that traveled the state. During his administration large sums of money went for improvement of roads and for road-building.

Earl raised teachers' salaries to a minimum of $2,400 per year. Black teachers, for the first time, received the same salaries as white teachers. There was "a massive step taken to begin equalizing educational opportunities." Other state employees were not as happy. Earl abolished their civil service system everywhere except in New Orleans. (The Long forces did not control New Orleans.)

Earl needed money to carry out campaign promises. A sales tax bill was passed by the legislature. Taxes were placed on beer and cigarettes. In 1948 a two-cents-a-gallon tax was added to gasoline. Oil and gas producers showed their disapproval by wearing black armbands. Gasoline pumps were covered in black. Citizens complained loudly about taxes. For the first time the state's per capita taxes were the highest in the United States. Up to this time the natural resources had borne the tax burden.

Russell Long. When United States Senator John H. Overton died in 1948, two years of his term were left. Overton had been a Long supporter. Anti-Long forces tried to win the vacated seat, but they were unsuccessful. Russell Long, Huey's son, was elected. He served as senator well into the 1980s and became one of the most powerful national political leaders. He became chairman of the Senate Finance Committee and at one time served as Senate Democratic Whip. His powerful influence in Congress has served to the state's advantage.

News Stories of the 1940s. In 1940 the bridge across the Mississippi River at Baton Rouge was completed . . . **Lyle Saxon**, well-known Louisiana author, died in 1946 . . . WDSU-TV in New Orleans brought

television to Louisiana in 1948 . . . That same year the International Trade Mart opened at New Orleans . . . In the late 1940s **Dudley LeBlanc** designed one of the most spectacular promotions to ever sweep the country. He became a millionaire when his patent medicine **Hadacol** made such a hit. Bob Hope was hired to advertise the new product.

Louisiana Hayride. Between 1948 and 1958 a radio show, the "Louisiana Hayride," spawned a number of entertainers. The most famous was Elvis Presley. The "Hayride" provided a stage in Shreveport for unknown talent to perform before a weekly live audience. The listeners to 50,000-watt, clear station KWKH could tune in from as far away as Canada, Australia, and New Zealand. In addition, the "Hayride" was carried by CBS Radio and the Armed Forces Radio Network.

Industrial Development. Louisiana experienced the greatest industrial boom in its history after World War II. Louisiana was now spotlighted as the state most likely to become an industrial complex. Industry was favoring locations here as factory sites that would require less fuel for heating than in the North. The state's location at the mouth of the Mississippi River had always provided special advantages. With a view toward water transportation, the industrialists found much to recommend Louisiana. The state's vast natural resources were a decisive factor.

The backlog of consumer products that had not been available during the war created an enormous market. Marriages delayed because of the war brought many new homes into being. New inventions swelled the variety of consumer products. New industry created thousands of jobs. There was a period of a flourishing economy after the war.

The impact of **petroleum and natural gas** on the industrial development of this state is difficult to comprehend. Since the first oil well was drilled at Jennings in 1901, oil has provided riches for the state. The first natural gas was used commercially in the early 1900s. Since then, refineries and other facilities have become features of the Louisiana landscape. In 1937 the processing of farm products still exceeded industry based on petroleum. However, since World War II, Louisiana's industrial growth has been stimulated chiefly by the petroleum industry. The petroleum industry led in value of products produced. The petroleum and chemical industries made tremendous gains. Between 1935 and 1953 the state's industrial growth increased 100 percent. By 1940 South Louisiana outranked the northern portion of the state as the major petroleum-producing section. In the same year Louisiana oil production had topped the one-million-barrels-per-day mark. By then natural gas had become a vital factor in industry and in homes.

On November 14, 1947, an event of worldwide significance occurred within the Louisiana oil industry. About forty-five miles from Morgan City, in the Gulf of Mexico, the Kerr-McGee Corporation brought in the first commercial oil well out of sight of land. This 900-barrels-per-day well gave birth to the **offshore oil and gas industry**. The impact of the offshore oil industry on the state's economy can hardly be estimated.

Increased demand for sulphur resulted in increased production. Sulphur was being obtained at Jefferson Island, Grand Ecaille, and Garden

The LSU Rural Life Museum includes buildings documenting nineteenth-century plantation life.

The custom of posting death notices, such as this one in St. Martinville in 1938, has faded.

Island Bay. Other mineral production increased as well. Salt continued to provide a major industry.

En Partie 1 (Studying a Part). 1. (a) What did Louisiana contribute to the war effort? (b) What military operations were located here? 2. Identify: Claire Chennault, Earl Long, Jimmie Davis, Lyle Saxon, Russell Long, and Sam Jones. 3. What postwar adjustments had to be made? 4. (a) When did Louisiana experience its greatest industrial boom? (b) Why did it happen?

Louisiana in the 1950s

Industrial Expansion. The 132-mile stretch of Mississippi River banks between New Orleans and Baton Rouge attracted a vast cluster of industries in the 1950s. This stretch was referred to as the "Miracle Strip." It is the location of a variety of industries. Two nationwide surveys done in 1956 showed this strip to be the fastest-growing industrial area in the country.

This was the time of the greatest plant-building and relocation of industry in our history. With it came a complete reshaping of commerce within the country to a north and south axis along the Mississippi River. In the Mississippi River the nation gained a "fourth seacoast." This area is important economically and is of great value during times of war.

In 1954 for the first time in our history, Louisiana became more urban than rural. There were more people living in towns of two thousand or more than in the country. There were 3,800 businesses that could be called manufacturers. The value of their products amounted to over $3 billion. In 1939 the total products manufactured in Louisiana had been valued at $565 million. In the 1950s the largest manufacturing industry in the state was petrochemicals. Food processing was the second largest industry.

Over $98 million poured into the state from its offshore oil leases. Spending rose to keep up with this bounty. A law was passed requiring the votes of two-thirds of elected members of the legislature for the passing of bills to raise taxes or to levy new ones.

New patterns of living appeared rapidly. People moved to industrial areas where the jobs were. Suburbs multiplied. All over Louisiana, as over the rest of the nation, old-time Main Streets were deserted. Businesses created shopping centers on the fringes of the cities. Schools and churches moved from downtown areas. Homes were almost always built away from the hearts of cities and towns. Real estate on Main Streets declined in value. The prices of land on the fringes skyrocketed. Downtown areas were neglected. Chambers of commerce all over the state worked hard to reverse the trend, but there was no use. It was a permanent change. Concerned people worked to beautify and to bring different uses to Main Streets. As a result of this postwar change, Louisiana cities have sprawled out over large areas.

Increasing industry and a swelling population brought problems for the state highways as well. The number of vehicles, including big commercial trucks, increased at a phenomenal rate. The state's highways and bridges were not capable of handling the heavier loads. Gravel roads had to be resurfaced. Two-lane highways had to become four-lane ones. In some places six and eight lanes were required. The modern highway systems—both state and federal—were developed.

Tidelands. Louisiana lost a major lawsuit over the money pouring in from tidelands oil and gas. Millions and millions of dollars worth of mineral rights off Louisiana's coast were involved. The state had sued the federal government for its share of the mineral rights of the submerged lands. In 1950 the decision was in favor of the United States. However, a final solution to the tidelands issue is still pending.

Korean War. There was never any real peace after World War II.

Louisiana Office of Tourism

The new governor's mansion was built in the Louisiana plantation style.

Russia, ally of the United States in the war, became a threat. A "cold war" developed between these two nations. As a result of the cold war, fighting began only a few years after World War II ended. The Korean War started in 1950. It lasted through 1953. This war upset the lives of Louisiana people. It cost the lives of some and left more wounded.

In Korea, Billy Whisner, a native of Shreveport, downed 5½ Communist planes to become an Air Force ace. (The credit for ½ results from sharing a kill with another pilot.) In World War II, he had shot down 15½ German aircraft. He was one of the top-ranking aces of that war. Whisner is one of the few American two-war aces.

PAR. The **Public Affairs Research Council** (called PAR) was founded in 1950. PAR is a private nonprofit research organization. It is devoted to improving Louisiana government. It seeks to correct the state's basic political weaknesses. It does this through making the public aware of the government's shortcomings. It does not take sides with one political viewpoint.

Robert F. Kennon's Administration. Robert F. Kennon became governor in 1952. Kennon had defeated District Judge Carlos Spaht. Kennon promised a businesslike administration. He presented a similar version of the Long welfare program. Spaht was supported by Earl Long. Other candidates were Hale Boggs, Bill Dodd, Jimmy Morrison, and James McLemore. The number of Negroes registering to vote was more than three times that of the 1948 election.

Robert F. Kennon's administration is noted for several accomplishments. These include the reinstatement of state civil service. Permanent registration of voters was authorized. Provision for voting machines in every precinct in the state was made by Kennon. His reforms also included **home rule** for municipalities. He made an effort to remove politics from the operations of four major state departments. These included the departments of highways, welfare, institutions, and wildlife and fisheries. Kennon established boards that were not under the control of the gover-

nor. Kennon's reforms included blasts at **gambling**, both organized and unorganized. The law reached all the way to church bingo games. Smashing of slot machines by the state police was a part of the movement.

Republican Movement. Louisianians voted in large numbers for Dwight Eisenhower in his successful bid to become president of the United States in 1952. This was the beginning of the Republican movement in the state.

No-Fence Law. In 1954 laws were passed banning livestock from major roads. The law provided state money for fencing and enforcement of the law. Today the "no-fence law" is a local option on lesser roads in the state. Livestock may still roam across public roads in a few places. They present a hazard for drivers on the highways.

Labor. In 1954 another major issue was before the Louisiana people. A **right-to-work** law was a threat to union power. The law allows any person to work for an employer without having to join a labor union. Members united to get the right-to-work law repealed. Victor Bussie, president of the AFL-CIO, led the fight to repeal the law. His efforts failed until 1956 when it passed.

A **strike** at the town's big papermill at Elizabeth dragged on for months and months. There was much violence and destruction of property. In time, the mill that had employed a large number of people in the area was forced to close its doors.

The Civil Rights Act of 1957. Congress passed the first civil rights act since Reconstruction. The first civil rights bill passed after the Civil War became the Fourteenth Amendment to the United States Constitution in 1868. Even with these safeguards civil rights had never been respected as law. Nearly one hundred years later, this history-making law was to be enforced. The law marked a milestone in the achievement of this country's ideal of equal rights for all citizens. Louisiana, as one of the states with old plantations, was one of the states most affected. The civil rights issue was such a critical one because of the large proportion of blacks in the population. At the time of the Civil War there were more blacks than whites in Louisiana. In some parts of the state there were more blacks than whites in the 1950s, also. After World War II about one-third of the state's population was black. The civil rights movement changed relations between the races in Louisiana.

School Desegregation. School desegregation had its beginning in 1954. With the *Brown v. Board of Education, Topeka, Kansas* case the United States Supreme Court decided the fate of the state's dual school system. After 1877 the state had one system of schools for whites and one for blacks. In 1896, in the *Plessy v. Ferguson* case, the Supreme Court had ruled that "separate but equal" facilities were legal. Black schools had never been equal to white schools. While waiting for the *Brown v. Board of Education* decision, many school officials produced a flurry of activity. The idea was to upgrade black public schools to make them appear equal. After the 1954 decision the Supreme Court ordered school desegregation. It directed school boards to make a "prompt and reasonable start toward full compliance." The federal government did not enforce the rule in Louisiana for several years.

Education. Lack of education was a handicap in the changing world of the 1950s. In Louisiana formal education had not been valued to the extent that it had been in New England, for instance. Whether to get a formal education had been a personal choice. The type of work done by most Louisianians prior to World War II required skills not learned from books. The demands of industrialization and modern technology made formal training necessary. The lack of a large pool of trained laborers had its effect on continued industrial expansion within the state. Weaknesses of the Louisiana dual school system were evident. The state now faced both integration and

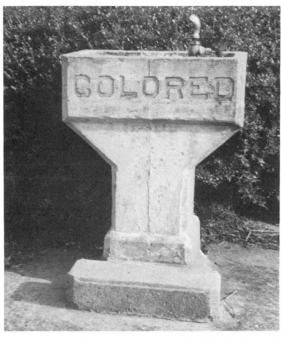

Separate drinking fountains gradually disappeared during the 1960s.

dents. In 1958 Governor Earl Long, in a special session, got a law passed reducing state subsidies for free school lunches. This restricted these lunches to the needy. That same year Louisiana State University at New Orleans opened. The next year a branch of Southern University opened in New Orleans. Louisiana State University at Alexandria was located on the grounds of the state agricultural experiment station. It opened its doors in 1960, also.

Public Welfare. Public welfare became a way of life for many people in the state. The money spent for public welfare in Louisiana during the years after World War II rose to

upgrading of the total school system. Louisiana faced a rethinking of the value of formal education.

Education was one of the major concerns of the state in the 1950s. In 1956 New Orleans schools were the first in Louisiana ordered to desegregate. In 1957 the Russian **Sputnik** was launched and the space program started. The craft was the first man-made satellite to orbit the earth. It led the way in a giant worldwide effort to explore outer space. As a result, Louisiana schools, like others across the nation, were ordered to provide more science courses for stu-

twenty-four percent of the total spent by the state for all purposes. In the 1954–55 fiscal year it amounted to nearly $108 million. About sixty percent of federal funds received by the state went to welfare programs. There were three types of charity hospitals in the state—general, mental, and tuberculosis. Louisiana's welfare programs surpassed all other states.

Earl Long's Third Term. Earl Long won a third term as governor in 1955. It was the first time since colonial days that a governor served three terms. It was the last Long/anti-Long state election held. Race was again the issue. All candidates had declared themselves in favor of segregation.

Long had killed civil service in 1950. He did not attempt to kill it when it was reinstituted by Kennon. Earl proposed tax increases, but they failed to pass. He worked with all his political skill to assist blacks without destroying himself among white voters. At the time he remained faithful to the national Democratic party. Many white voters had become Dixiecrats. The big issue that separated the two parties was race. Dixiecrats fought to keep blacks segregated. Long fought efforts to remove Negroes' names from the rolls in North Louisiana. He made his feelings on the issue clear. Some people felt that it was a confusing change in Earl.

No ordinary individual in any case, Earl's behavior often seemed strange. He suffered some kind of illness during his last years in public office. His illness worsened, but he remained in the political limelight. He embarrassed both Louisiana and himself with some of his antics. At one time he had his picture taken with a pillow case over his head. The picture was seen all over the world. Reporters followed him and recorded his escapades. His term was spent going in and out of hospitals. He was absent from Baton Rouge much of the time. His trips to Texas made headlines. So did a trip to Mexico. Noticeable signs of a change in Earl's behavior indicated the beginning of his personal tragedy.

Two Parties. For the first time since Reconstruction a Republican for president of the United States carried the state in 1956. When Dwight Eisenhower ran for president for his second term, Louisiana voted for him. It was a sign that the two-party system would be revived in Louisiana.

Racial Organizations. The Ku Klux Klan appeared at various places in the state. An old law designed for use against the Klan was revived. This time it was used to try to destroy the National Association for the Advancement of Colored People (NAACP) in the state. The law required that all organizations list their membership with the secretary of state. White Citizens' Council officials spoke before citizens' groups. They organized some groups in Louisiana. Other groups opposing integration were formed.

LSU Football. Louisiana State University grabbed the limelight with its winning football team of 1958. Paul Dietzel, head football coach, created the "Chinese Bandits." This defensive team delighted fans. He called his offensive teams catchy names—the "Go Team" and the "White Team." The "Bayou Bengals," officially the "Tigers," became national champions that year.

Hurricane Audrey. Audrey, the first hurricane of the 1957 hurricane season, blew in from the Gulf of Mexico and hit the Cameron Parish coastal area on June 28, 1957. Be-

tween four and five hundred people lost their lives. Many of them were children. Over $150 million in damages resulted. Many people might have been saved had they understood the language of radio announcers urging them to move to higher ground. Many people thought this meant that they should move to the cheniers in the area. The cheniers were only slightly higher than the surrounding land. After Audrey, specific language was used to make any future warnings clearer. Storm-tracking by the National Weather Service was greatly improved, too.

News Items of the 1950s. In 1951 Angola, the state prison, gained national attention for the state. The convicts there protested the inhu-

The Louisiana State Exhibit Museum at Shreveport is known for its dioramas.

mane treatment they were receiving. It was called the worst prison in the nation.... In 1952 Governor Kennon had penologists help correct the problems at Angola.... In 1955 the two hundredth anniversary of the coming of the Acadians to Louisiana was celebrated. Festivities centered around St. Martinville, the Acadian capital of Louisiana.... About half of the people in Louisiana in 1956 were watching the news on their own television sets.... That same year the legislature created the **State Archives and Records Service**. The purpose of this state agency is to preserve the state's historical documents.... The journal of the Louisiana Historical Society, the *Louisiana Historical Quarterly*, ceased publication in 1958. The journal was begun in 1917. *Louisiana History* replaced it.

En Partie 2 (Studying a Part). 1. What development took place in industry? 2. How did the Civil Rights Act of 1957 affect Louisiana? 3. (a) What had been the attitude toward formal education? (b) What caused a change in attitude toward formal training? 4. What was the status of public welfare? 5. Identify: no-fence law, PAR, Republican movement, right-to-work, and Robert F. Kennon. 6. What was the tidelands issue? 7. What was different about Earl Long's third term?

Louisiana in the 1960s

Earl Long's Death. Earl Long came in third in the race for lieutenant governor in the 1960 election. It was the first time that a Long candidate had failed to make the runoff since Huey's time. In the fall of 1960 Earl ran against incumbent Congressman Harold McSween for the United States House of Representatives from the Eighth District. Long was the nominee of the Democratic party in the second primary. Long's illness became worse with the pressures of the campaign. He was near collapse. Personal problems bedeviled him. Moments after his victory over McSween, Earl Long had a heart attack. He died a few days later in a hospital in Alexandria.

Jimmie Davis's Second Term. Jimmie Davis was elected governor again in 1960. He declared himself to be a segregationist. Integration was the big campaign issue. Ironically, "Peace and Harmony" was his campaign slogan. His four years in office were noted not for peace but for turmoil. School desegregation orders for East Baton Rouge and St. Helena parishes brought unrelieved conflict. Leander Perez, the symbol of Louisiana segregationists from Plaquemines Parish, strode across the state's political stage. His fiery approach to segregation in the parish over which he ruled made national headlines. The debate over state aid to private schools began.

A law was passed requiring the withholding of state income taxes. It was under Jimmie Davis that a new governor's mansion was constructed. Governor Davis's "Sunshine Bridge," built halfway between Baton Rouge and New Orleans, became the subject of much ridicule. Opponents argued that it had no value. Davis argued that it was needed for industrial expansion.

In the midst of financial troubles, threats of war, and desegregation problems, Governor Davis diverted the attention of Louisiana people with his own brand of showmanship. He led his horse Sunshine up the capitol steps and into his office. A Baton Rouge legislator was not amused. He sent Davis a bale of hay. He suggested that there were others, as well as the horse, who needed the hay.

Improvements under Davis included a constitutional amendment. It provided for a legislative auditor. A capital budget law and a law to invest idle funds were both passed under Davis. The first college student loan law was passed during his administration.

Toledo Bend Reservoir. The Toledo Bend Reservoir project was completed in 1960. This was a joint project with Texas. It provides electrical power, navigational facilities, water for industrial uses, and recreational opportunities for thousands. It is the largest man-made reservoir in the eastern two-thirds of the United States.

deLesseps S. Morrison. Mayor deLesseps S. Morrison of New Orleans was an extraordinary reform mayor. He was first elected in 1944. Morrison unseated Robert S. Maestri, who had been mayor from 1936 to 1946. Morrison was mayor of New Orleans four times. He was in office fifteen years. He ran for governor unsuccessfully three times. In 1964 he was killed in an airplane accident in Mexico. Mayor Morrison left behind many civic improvements. He left a new city hall and civic center, a network of expressways and boulevards, a new bridge over the Mississippi, and the Moisant International Airport. These remain as monuments to his administration. Even these accomplishments do not loom so large as his success in securing an amendment to the Louisiana Constitution. It allowed metropolitan New Orleans to operate under a home-rule charter drafted by a citizens' committee.

John J. McKeithen. John McKeithen of Columbia took a stand as a segregationist in the 1964 race for governor. He won the election. A member of the Long political circle, McKeithen surprised Louisiana voters with his reforms. Major reform bills were passed to improve state government. The powers of the governor

Louisiana Office of Tourism

Caspiana House, on the campus of LSU at Shreveport, serves as the Pioneer Heritage Folk Center.

were reduced. One of the changes included reduction in the power of the governor to appoint local officials. In 1966 a bill was passed making it possible for a Louisiana governor to succeed himself. The law on investing idle state funds was made stronger. An amendment dedicating tidelands revenue to pay off state debt and finance capital construction also passed. A code of ethics for government officials was approved. A central list of state employees was compiled. An inventory of public property was begun. Tax disadvantages for industry were removed. An industrial boom followed. McKeithen personally made efforts to attract industry to Louisiana.

McKeithen was reelected governor in 1968. He was the first Louisiana governor to succeed himself in the twentieth century.

Hurricanes. During the 1960s portions of Louisiana were laid waste by three hurricanes. In 1964 Hurricane Hilda took the lives of thirty-two persons in the Lafourche Parish area. It did $100 million in damages to property. Hurricane Betsy, in 1965, claimed fifty-eight lives. The damage amounted to $1.2 billion in Southeast Louisiana. Plaquemines Parish received the brunt of Hurricane Camille in 1969. Nine lives and $322 million worth of property were destroyed.

Desegregation. Congress passed the **Civil Rights Act of 1964**. This time desegregation began in earnest. The years 1960–68 were landmarks in the dying of an era in which blacks were controlled to provide an army of plantation labor. This new law brought many changes for Louisiana. The act provided that "all places serving the public" should be open to all the public "on an equal basis." This included voting booths, public schools, parks, and hotels.

The civil rights movement took many forms in Louisiana. Federal voting registrars were sent to parishes in the state where blacks could not register. The federal government stepped in after Congress passed the Voting Rights Act in 1965. That year Bogalusa was the scene of much racial conflict. Governor McKeithen earned respect for his handling of the tense racial situation there. McKeithen formed a biracial committee to work on current problems. Integration brought lawsuits among school boards and private citizens as well. Many delaying

tactics were tried. There were various plans used to implement the orders of the court. There were even more plans to get around these orders. When the federal open housing law passed in 1968, it became illegal to refuse to rent or sell homes to people because of their race or color. Problems arose. Whites found ways to get around this law.

Federal programs became a dominant part of Louisiana. Many of these brought much-desired federal funds into the state. Desegregation was required for the state to be eligible for federal funds. This proved effective in completing the process of integration.

The Youth Rebellion of the 1960s. The clash of pre–World War II and post–World War II ideas may have been most visible among the youth in the 1960s. Louisiana, like the rest of the nation, suffered through probably the most painful crises of the nation's past. Suddenly, it seemed, all of the old familiar values of the pre-World War II generation were questioned. Many such values were rejected by a rebellious generation of young people. The Vietnam War caused the loudest protest. Yet, the rebellion went much deeper. The right of the United States to draft young men for military duty was challenged. Draft cards were burned. Some young men fled to Canada to escape the draft. Many rejected the value of material possessions. This was shown in clothing. Faded and ragged jeans became so popular that stores could only sell new garments designed to appear old and worn.

In many ways it was a tragic era. The use of alcoholic beverages and drugs brought early deaths and countless lost years of life to many young people in the state. New music, new dance styles, and new literature expressed the chaos, idealism, problems, and tragedy of the youth rebellion. It was a time of questioning of values all over the nation.

Decline in Industry. In 1967 Louisiana was enjoying an industrial boom. The peak was reached in early spring. By fall a downhill trend had started. Labor troubles of every kind developed. New construction was shut down, and the industrial boom fizzled for awhile.

News Items. The 1960s brought a variety of other important developments. The Freeport Sulphur Company completed a large half-mile-long steel island. It rose above the water of the Gulf of Mexico. The company began the **first offshore sulphur production** on April 14, 1960. . . . From 1961 to 1965 the **Civil War Centennial** was celebrated in the state. . . . In 1963, many Louisiana Democrats did not like John F. Kennedy and called for **free presidential electors**. Democratic elec-

No. 46, Hokie Gajan, former LSU star, gains yardage for the New Orleans Saints.

tors would be free to vote for the candidate of their choice. . . . Louisianians again voted **Republican**. This time it was for Barry Goldwater for president. . . . In 1967, Louisiana made national news when *Life* magazine printed a three-part story on **organized crime** in the state. . . . The **New Orleans Saints** became the state's professional football team to the delight of the many football fans. The natives gave cheerful support, even when the Saints won few games. . . . In 1968 Ernest Morial, a black man, was elected to the House of Representatives from Orleans Parish. He was the **first black** since Reconstruction to serve in Louisiana's legislature. . . . In 1964 the **first black undergraduate** enrolled at Louisiana State University. . . . In 1965 **Shirley Ann Grau** won a Pulitzer Prize for *The Keepers of the House.* . . . A **Board of Regents** was created in 1968 as an agency to supervise the state's higher education program. . . . Louisiana had a **Pulitzer Prize** winner in 1967. Jack R. Thornton won in photography . . . . In 1968 Southern University track star **Willie Davenport** was an Olympic gold medal winner. . . . *Louisiana Heritage* magazine was first published in 1968. Its last issue was in 1972. . . . **Terry Bradshaw** of Shreveport was the first draft choice for professional football in 1969. . . . *Acadiana Profile*, a magazine for bilingual Louisiana, was introduced in 1969.

En Partie 3 (Studying a Part). 1. What was the key political issue in the governors' races in the 1960s? 2. How did desegregation affect the state in the 1960s? 3. Describe the youth rebellion. 4. When did the first offshore sulphur production begin? 5. Identify: deLesseps Morrison, Ernest Morial, free presidential electors, John McKeithen, New Orleans Saints, Terry Bradshaw, Toledo Bend Reservoir, and Willie Davenport.

Louisiana in the 1970s

Pete Maravich. In 1970 "Pistol Pete" Maravich played basketball at Louisiana State University. He not only broke college records but also helped make basketball a more popular game in Louisiana.

Edwin Edwards. Edwin Edwards, a native of Avoyelles Parish, became governor in 1972 and again in 1976. Although this Crowley lawyer has an English surname, Edwards has a French background. He speaks French fluently. He spoke of his lowly background during his campaign, but in fact Edwards's family produced several judges in Avoyelles Parish. Edwards's charm matches that of Huey Long. He quickly gained a huge following. He was elected with votes that included those of most blacks and organized labor.

Constitutional Convention. Edwards had made a campaign promise to rewrite the cumbersome 1921 constitution. In 1970 voters had to decide on fifty-three amendments to the constitution. The Constitution of 1921 had become the most often amended of all state constitutions except that of Georgia. It was extremely long with over 225,000 words. Popular opinion favored the writing of a new constitution.

Edwards kept his promise. A constitutional convention convened January 5, 1973. It did not adjourn until a year later on January 19, 1974. The convention was composed of 132 delegates. There were 105 elected by the people from the House of Representatives districts. Twelve were appointed by the governor to represent special interests. Fifteen were appointed by the governor from the public at large. Meetings were open to the public. E. L. ("Bubba") Henry served as chairman of the convention.

The proposed constitution was submitted to the voters and approved. It became effective at midnight December 31, 1974. It was Louisiana's **eleventh constitution**, more than any other state. This one is brief, as constitutions go. It contains 30,000 words.

Superport. A Superport Authority was created during Edwards's administration. This authority planned the construction, maintenance, and operation of Louisiana's Superport. This project was funded entirely by private capital provided by a group of major oil companies, Louisiana Offshore Oil Port (LOOP). The Superport is an offshore oil terminal in the Gulf of Mexico. It loads and unloads oil tankers, thereby relieving them of the need to go inland.

Superdome. In New Orleans in 1975 a hotly debated Louisiana Superdome opened for business. Many Louisiana citizens were annoyed. Others praised its construction. This huge structure has been the site of many sporting events. It is also used for concerts, conventions, trade shows, and other events. Its vast, completely enclosed arena seats 19,678 for basketball. It seats 67,650 for baseball and 81,187 for football. Over 95,000 can be seated in the Superdome when it is used as an auditorium. The dome's major tenants include the New Orleans Saints and Tulane University with its various events. The annual Sugar Bowl events are staged in the dome.

The Superdome was the home of the former New Orleans Jazz, professional basketball team. In the opening year, the Jazz played before 26,500 in the Superdome. This was more than its ordinary seating capacity. It was the largest crowd ever to see a National Basketball Association game in the history of the sport.

The 1976 Bicentennial Celebration. In 1976 the Bicentennial of the Declaration of Independence was celebrated. An office for a bicentennial committee was set up in Baton Rouge. Patriotic programs and events refreshed pride in Jefferson's moving words of the Declaration.

One of the lasting results of the 1976 celebration was a focus on historical preservation. Since 1976 the movement to restore prized buildings has grown rapidly. Many buildings have been placed on the National Register of Historic Places. Historic

Louisiana Office of Tourism

The Superport is located eighteen miles off the Louisiana coast.

districts have been designated. Emphasis on genealogy and respect for the past have grown as by-products of the celebration. Some Louisiana groups dedicated to preservation were very active in the celebration. Local historical groups were organized in many communities. The value of the past has been emphasized.

Women's Rights. After World War II women joined in the movement for equal rights and equal pay for equal work. Southern states of the plantation system, including Louisiana, kept women in a subordinate status. The women's rights movement was hotly resisted. While times were changing, they had not changed enough for the state to ratify the Equal Rights Amendment.

King Tut Exhibition. Increased interest in cultural events was seen with the exhibit of the priceless art and historical objects of King Tut. The Treasures of Tutankhamen were exhibited in New Orleans. Huge crowds waited in lines to view the treasures of this ancient Egyptian king.

Black Artist. Clementine Hunter, one of the world's most famous

Louisiana Office of Tourism

Clementine Hunter painted life as she knew it.

in 1887. Her mother's parents had been slaves. At fifteen she moved to Melrose plantation to work as a field hand. Later she worked as a cook at Melrose. At the time there was a writers' and artists' colony at Melrose. The cook Clementine received encouragement when she suggested that she would like to draw. It was there that she started her painting. Visitors at Melrose admired her work. Her artwork started gaining fame in the 1940s. Her work is displayed in many museums. She has been the

T. Harry Williams, Pulitzer Prize—winning author.

primitive artists, held three of her key exhibits in the 1970s. Her work was shown at La Jolla, California, in 1970. In 1973 her Louisiana Folk Paintings exhibit was presented in New York at the Museum of American Folk Art. From 1978 to 1979, her work was included in the traveling exhibit of the Smithsonian Institute. In 1979 in Huntsville, Alabama, her artwork was included in the Black Artists/South exhibit.

Hunter, a Louisiana native, was born on a plantation near Cloutierville subject of many magazine and news stories.

News Stories of the 1970s. In 1970 **T. Harry Williams** of Louisiana State University won a Pulitzer Prize for his book *Huey Long* . . . . The **Louisiana Educational Television Authority (LETA)** was created by an act of the state legislature in 1971. In that year ninety-five percent of all Louisiana families had television sets . . . . The **Rock Festival of Life** at McCrea in 1971 attracted thousands of youths from all over the nation . . . . In 1972 Senator Allen J.

Ellender died, and J. Bennett Johnston was elected to succeed him . . . . That year eight blacks were elected to the House of Representatives. Louisiana ranked ninth in the nation in the number of **black legislators** . . . . **Ernest J. Gaines**, black novelist from New Roads, won the 1972 Louisiana Literary Award for *The Autobiography of Miss Jane Pittman* . . . . The North-South toll road bill passed in 1974 . . . . The economy of the entire state was affected by the strike of dock workers in New Orleans during this period. When the port closed

The walls of the African House at Melrose plantation are lined with colorful murals depicting plantation life seen through the eyes of Clementine Hunter.

down completely, millions of dollars were lost . . . . The **Independence Bowl** in Shreveport hosted McNeese State University and the University of Tulsa in its first game ever. General Omar Bradley was honored for his contribution to the "spirit of independence" with an award that now bears his name—the Omar Bradley Award . . . . In 1975 the flagship **public television** station began broadcasting in Baton Rouge . . . . In 1975 **Fort Polk** at Leesville became the permanent home of the First Brigade, Fifth Infantry Division (Mechanized). Fort Polk is the largest military installation in Louisiana . . . . In 1976, a **right-to-work bill** was passed . . . . In 1976 Louisiana elected its **first woman state senator**, Virginia Shehee from Shreveport . . . . In 1977 New Orleans elected Ernest Morial as its **first black mayor** . . . . Louisiana passed a **first-use tax** on natural gas in 1978 . . . . In November 1978 Richard Nixon came to Louisiana to visit his old friend **Joe D. Waggoner** . . . . Brian Weber took his case to the Supreme Court. He sued Kaiser Aluminum and the United Steelworkers on reverse-discrimination charges. Weber lost. Private industry was allowed to set up many kinds of affirmative-action employment programs . . . . Louisiana led all states in 1978 in industrial expansion. . . . Dr. Andrew Schally of New Orleans won the **Nobel Prize** in medicine in 1978.

Natural Disasters. Nature took its toll during this decade. In 1971 Hurricane Edith did $15 million in damages when it reached the coastal land east of Cameron. Much more property damage was done when Carmen entered the state through the Atchafalaya Bay in 1974. In 1977 Babe swung through St. Mary, Iberia, and St. Martin parishes. A path of destruction and damage was left behind. Flooding of the Ouachita, Tensas, Black, Red, Atchafalaya, and Mississippi rivers in 1973 caused thousands to leave their homes. Damages amounted to millions. Floods in South Louisiana in 1977 caused much damage.

Desegregation. The struggle over desegregation continued in the 1970s. School system after school system received orders from the federal courts. School officials spent long hours working out plans to satisfy federal requirements. Faculties and student bodies were integrated. The traditional school system of old disappeared. Completely new programs were started in an effort to solve problems generated in the desegregation of schools.

During the course of desegregation and a resulting "white flight," a number of private schools were founded in the state. ("White flight" became a popular description of the various designs of whites to maintain a segregated society in spite of the law.) These were similar to the earlier plantation academies. The expense of maintaining such schools became overwhelming. Many of these private schools were associated with churches. Few of these schools survived.

Busing of schoolchildren became a highly emotional issue linked with school desegregation. From time to time judges would order certain children bused over long distances to achieve "racial balance." Some schools were closed. Others were forced to change their functions to become another type of school. Only one factor remained constant—the courts were in control. Few people were happy with the results of court orders, whatever they were.

En Partie 4 (Studying a Part). 1. (a) Who wrote Louisiana's eleventh constitution? (b) When? (c) When did it become effective? 2. What were some of the permanent benefits of the Bicentennial celebration? 3. What was the status of desegregation in the 1970s? 5. Identify: Clementine Hunter, Edwin Edwards, Ernest Gaines, Pete Maravich, Superdome, Superport, and T. Harry Williams.

Louisiana in the 1980s

David Treen. In 1980 David Treen became the first Republican governor of Louisiana elected since Reconstruction. He made a good record in office. Treen was handicapped by the popular Edwards getting ready to reclaim the governor's chair in 1984. Edwards was often before the public. Too, there was the deep recession that had settled over Louisiana and the rest of the nation in 1981 that continued into 1983. State revenues from the idle oil industry as well as other tax monies had been severely slashed.

Edwards's Reelection. In 1984 Edwin Edwards was reelected by a landslide. He got sixty-four percent of the votes. Edwards was the first man ever elected governor of Louisiana three times. The 1983 race between Edwards and Treen was far more expensive than races in any other state.

Edwards soon put a one-billion-dollar package of new tax bills through the legislature. He contended that the state's revenue from natural resources had dwindled so that heavier taxes were necessary to maintain state services. The new tax package shifted the burden from Louisiana's oil and gas industry to other businesses and individuals. After this tax-raising session, the voters became negative to-

New Orleans's French Quarter is an artists' colony.

ward the governor, the legislature, and state government in general.

Shortly after Edwards took office, a trip to France was made to pay for his campaign debts of $4.4 million. Each person making the trip was to pay $10,000. Many did. Later, slightly reduced rates were used to fill seats that might otherwise have been empty. A total of 617 made the trip.

Within a few months Governor Edwards became the subject of several federal investigations. These brought the number of investigations into the affairs of Edwards to eight. A federal grand jury in New Orleans investigated his connections with nursing homes. Some had received state permits from his administration. In Baton Rouge another investigation involved Edwards and a former natural resources secretary. Their relationship with oil companies under their jurisdiction was the subject of this investigation. Texaco, which once paid Edwards a $50,000 legal fee, also employed Louisiana's secretary of natural resources, William Huls. The company was alleged to have been given some special consideration by Edwards in obtaining drilling rights to a nineteen-thousand-acre offshore oil lease. The cancellation of the contract of an auditing firm was questioned. The firm said that Texaco may have underpaid royalties by as much as $300 million. On February 28, 1985, Governor Edwards was indicted by a federal grand jury on fifty-one counts. Charges included racketeering, conspiracy, mail fraud, and wire fraud. Charges were made against his brother Marion and others. Edwards remained under investigation in the Texaco case.

In less than a year after he started his third term, Edwards suffered the most dramatic shift in popularity in the state's political history. A survey showed that only thirty-seven percent of the voters were pleased with his performance. The polls gave him his lowest rating in his thirty years in public office. A recall petition was started. The necessary number of signatures was not obtained by the deadline set by law.

Multibanking. The legislature approved multibanking in 1984. Multibanking holding companies could form statewide banks. Louisiana banks could now branch into other parishes. Louisiana Bankshares, the state's first of this kind, opened in the mid-1980s. With its huge financial pool, Louisiana Bankshares will be able to make large loans. These loans are necessary to back major construction projects.

Visitors. Louisiana had some interesting visitors in 1984. Freed slaves' descendants came from Buxton, a town in Canada. The town was founded by fifteen blacks freed by a Jackson clergyman. The clergyman, Rev. William King, had inherited the slaves from his father-in-law, John Phares, in 1848. The descendants saw Phares's will in the Clinton Courthouse. King did not believe in slavery. He bought land in Canada so his slaves could be freed without worry. The group settled in a rural area and named it Buxton for an abolitionist.

World's Fair. In 1984 the **Louisiana World Exposition** opened in New Orleans. It ran from May 12 until November 11. The fair opened one hundred years after New Orleans hosted the World's Industrial and Cotton Centennial Exposition. The theme for the 1984 World's Fair was "The World of Rivers—Fresh Water as a Source of Life." The major attractions included an exhibit from the Vatican and Louisiana's own exhibit. The Louisiana Pavilion had a unique boat ride to help carry out the theme, "Louisiana! A Celebration of the Bayou State." The fair was a glowing cultural achievement. Visitors praised the attractions and exhibits.

At the Cabildo an extraordinary exhibit, The Sun King, displayed artifacts that belonged to Louis XIV. Original documents relating to Louisiana history were on display.

Financial troubles plagued the fair from the start. Louisiana World Exposition (LWE), a private company, received loans from the state before the fair opened. A state committee took charge of the firm's finances in July 1984 after LWE was unable to pay the bills.

There was considerable division over Governor Edwards' decision to bail out the World's Fair with state funds. The fair cost Louisiana taxpayers about sixty-five million dollars. Twenty-seven and a half million dollars were in direct loans. Ten million dollars were in guarantees against losses. The rest was for street improvements and other costs. Just five days before closing the fair filed for bankruptcy. The fair was more than one hundred million dollars in debt.

One reason for the financial disaster was the failure to draw the expected eleven million people. Barely seven million attended. The World's Fair was a complete financial failure. It did not generate the economic benefits for the state that were expected.

The FBI ran an undercover sting operation involving LWE. One FBI man acted as a businessman offering money—sometimes in the form of campaign contributions—to obtain World's Fair contracts.

News Stories of the 1980s. The first **Super Derby** was held at Louisiana Downs in Bossier Parish in 1980 . . . . In the 1980 **"Brilab"** investigations, federal agents posed as insurance executives to obtain state contracts from Louisiana officials. The federal agents offered bribes. The planned action resulted in indictments and convictions . . . . In 1980 Louisiana abolished its head-and-master law.

In 1985 Freddie Spencer successfully defended his title of world champion.

Until this time the husband was considered head and master of the household. He had total control of community property.... **Dr. Ralph Waldo Emerson Jones,** Grambling State University's president for forty-one years, died in 1981.... In 1981 a new bridge over the Mississippi River at New Orleans was under construction ... New Orleanian **John Kennedy Toole** in 1981 posthumously won the Pulitzer Prize in literature for *A Confederacy of Dunces.*... Sonya Landry became managing editor of the *Shreveport Sun* in 1982. Her grandfather started this newspaper. It is the **oldest weekly black newspaper** in Louisiana. ... **Hal Sutton**, from Shreveport, was named professional golf's Rookie of the Year. He was top money-winner on the tour in 1983 with earnings in excess of $400,000.... In July of the same year the International **Special Olympics** were held in Baton Rouge. ... Shreveport's **Freddie Spencer** won title after title riding his motorcycle in races all over the world. He became world champion in the 1980s.... **Terry Bradshaw** returned home to Shreveport after he played his last football game in the 1983 professional football season. He had led the Pittsburgh Steelers to victory in four Super Bowl championship games.... A new magazine, *Louisiana Life*, was introduced in 1981. It won the Regional Magazine of the Year award in 1983.... Louisiana's native-born son, author **Truman Capote**, died in the summer of 1984.... Louisiana ranked last among the states in the percentage of students completing regular high school programs according to a 1984 study.... Also in 1983 Louisiana State University received a $125-million donation. This was the largest single donation ever made to an educational institution in the nation. C. B. ("Doc") Pennington donated the entire fund to build and operate a nutrition and preventive medicine research center on the LSU campus.... That same year Barksdale Air Force Base in Bossier City celebrated its fiftieth anniversary. The major installation of the Strategic Air Command was formally dedicated on February 3, 1933.... **Paul Prudhomme**, the internationally famous Cajun chef from New Orleans, represented Louisiana at President Reagan's inaugural festivities ... Louisiana had two members on the United States Olympic gold-medal women's basketball team—**Kim Mulkey** and **Janice Lawrence**. The women had played with the national champion Lady Techsters at Louisiana Tech University in Ruston. Mulkey is from Tickfaw, near Hammond. Lawrence is from out of state.... In 1984 the nation's longest school strike took place in St. John the Baptist Parish.... That same year Commissioner of Agriculture Bob Odom announced that an important economic agreement had been reached with Taiwan. Taiwan agreed to purchase four million bushels of Louisiana soybeans.... In October 1984 the **Wall Street Journal** took a close look at Louisiana's oil industry. In a series of articles the *Journal* painted a poor picture of the state.... In 1984 the legislature passed a child-restraint law requiring that children of certain ages wear safety belts while in moving vehicles.... **Grambling Coach Eddie Robinson** achieved a milestone in his career in 1984. He chalked up his 315th career win in football. Only legendary Bear Bryant won more games.... President Reagan paused before his 1985 inaugural ceremony to ask for a moment of silence in memory of **Gillis Long**. United States Representative Long died January 20.... In 1985 Ruston got a new biological technology research facility. It is the first major facility of its kind to locate in the state.... Most Louisianians were surprised when, in February 1985, **Russell Long** announced his retirement from the Senate.... In July 1985 Lake Charles was designated the port of one navy oiler and two minesweepers.... Louisiana's first nuclear-powered generating plant opened at Taft in 1985.

Making news in the 1980s were terrible accidents. In 1980 the Jefferson Island Salt Dome caved in after being punctured by oil drilling equipment.

Another accident in 1980 threatened the seafood industry. This disaster was a chemical spill in a river in St. Bernard Parish. The crash of Pan American Airlines Flight 759 in Kenner was the second worst commercial aviation disaster in United States history. In 1982 forty-three tank cars carrying toxic chemicals derailed near Livingston. Explosions spread toxic vapors over a wide area. Almost three thousand people were forced to leave their homes.

Current Outlook. Louisiana made an economic leap forward in the 1970s. From 1970 to 1982 Louisiana's advances made history. They even matched Texas. While it lasted, the state outperformed the nation in nearly every category. It almost doubled its own capital and its mining and manufacturing income. Personal income in the state nearly doubled, also.

The spurt was fueled by an oil and gas boom and what amounted to an economic revival in the South. The international oil glut choked off the Louisiana gushers. A national recession, while late in spreading to Louisiana, crushed the state boom. However, Louisiana's oil and gas production was declining even before the glut came. The state has gone from what one legislator called an "embarrassment of riches" to the "rags of poverty."

As Louisiana approaches the year

2000, there is more reason for optimism for the future than ever before. There are many problems. These a resourceful people can tackle. By learning the lessons of the past, an educated public can use that past as a springboard for planning a better tomorrow. The foundation for the better tomorrow is our rich resources—human, natural, and industrial.

En Partie 5 (Studying a Part). 1. Why was the 1984 World's Fair considered a financial failure but a cultural achievement? 2. Identify: Freddie Spencer, Hal Sutton, multibanking, and David Treen. 3. What caused the drop in Edwin Edwards's popularity?

Coup d'Main
(Completing the Story)

Jambalaya (Putting It All Together)

1. Why is World War II considered a significant time in the history of Louisiana as well as the rest of the United States?

2. Describe the civil rights–desegregation movement since World War II.

3. How did new machines and modern technology change life on the plantations?

4. Explain the changing role of blacks since World War II.

5. Cite the changes in the lives of Louisianians brought about by inventions and changing attitudes.

6. Discuss changes in education, agriculture, and industry.

Potpourri (Getting Involved)

1. Show how the following differed: (a) the political issues of each decade: 1940s, 1950s, 1960s, 1970s, and 1980s, (b) the inauguration of all Louisiana governors from 1940 to the present time, or (c) the political careers of Huey Long and Earl Long.

2. Make a diorama showing Louisiana maneuvers during World War II.

3. Conduct research to discover changes that have taken place in any of these areas since World War II: clothing, transportation, art, films, interior design, architecture, advertising, music, entertainment, housing, food, education, and government programs.

4. Show the relationship between each of the following and the civil rights movement: Emancipation Proclamation, Thirteenth Amendment, Fourteenth Amendment, and Fifteenth

Amendment. Also, discuss the Civil Rights Acts of 1957, 1960, and 1964, and the Voting Rights Act of 1965. Summarize steps taken in Louisiana in the field of civil rights.

5. Cite evidence to show that journalists and writers exert an influence on the thinking of people of the state.

6. Interview a veteran of World War II, the Korean War, or the Vietnam War.

Gumbo (Bringing It Up-to-Date)

1. Compare the present attitude of Louisianians toward desegregation with the attitude of Louisianians during Reconstruction.

2. Trace the historical background of some aspect of black-white relations. Compare feelings then with feelings now.

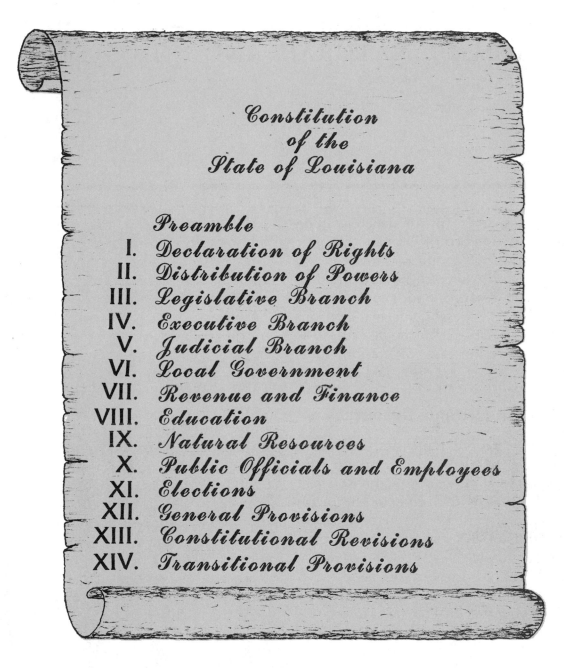

Constitution
of the
State of Louisiana

Preamble
I. Declaration of Rights
II. Distribution of Powers
III. Legislative Branch
IV. Executive Branch
V. Judicial Branch
VI. Local Government
VII. Revenue and Finance
VIII. Education
IX. Natural Resources
X. Public Officials and Employees
XI. Elections
XII. General Provisions
XIII. Constitutional Revisions
XIV. Transitional Provisions

CHAPTER 13

OUR RESOURCES—
HUMAN, NATURAL, AND INDUSTRIAL

Louisiana's future depends upon the full use of our human, natural, and industrial resources. Programs and policies will have to be developed to put our resources to good use. To provide the best Louisiana environment requires skillful management of our soil, water, air, vegetation, minerals, fisheries, wildlife, and industry.

Our Human Resources

The people represent Louisiana's most valuable resource. Louisiana people include those from almost every land around the globe. The great mixture of races and ethnic backgrounds of the state's people is related to its rich history. Someone has said that numbers of peoples of completely different ethnic stock have lived together in Louisiana in relative peace longer than anywhere else in the United States. Whether or not this is true, we do know that the state's people have come from widely different lines of descent. Moreover, a respect for differences has developed among these various groups.

Racial Composition. Before the Europeans came, Louisiana belonged to the Indians alone. The blood of Indians runs through the veins of many of our present-day residents. During the colonial period French, German, Swiss, English, Spanish, African, and Indian people lived here. Italians, Belgians, Bohemians, Hungarians, Irishmen, Orientals, and others have come in waves of settlers to Louisiana. The sawmills brought into the state by Northern investors opened the way for the migration of many people. They came from all sections of the nation and Mexico. They, in turn, were descendants of migrants from many different countries. There has been mixing of these different peoples producing an unending variety of individuals.

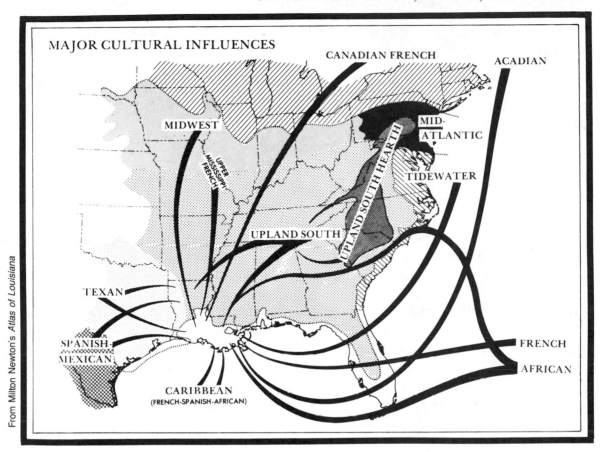

MAJOR CULTURAL INFLUENCES

CANADIAN FRENCH

ACADIAN

MIDWEST

UPPER MISSISSIPPI FRENCH

MID-ATLANTIC

TIDEWATER

UPLAND SOUTH HEARTH

UPLAND SOUTH

TEXAN

SPANISH-MEXICAN

CARIBBEAN
(FRENCH-SPANISH-AFRICAN)

FRENCH

AFRICAN

From Milton Newton's *Atlas of Louisiana*

Life in Louisiana is far richer because of the many cultural groups. Each has added its flavor to the state. Different cultures have exchanged ideas drawn from every corner of the world. This exchange of ideas is referred to as "cultural borrowing."

The daily lives of some of these people continue to reflect the "old country" heritage. Some groups set aside a special celebration to recall their heritage. It is this potpourri of the world's peoples that gives our state a special quality and excitement.

Lagniappe. Louisiana once turned its back on the rich French heritage of the state. Now the state hopes to set an example as a bilingual state. Local French dialects of both blacks and whites have been spoken for a long time. In the 1930s students were forbidden to speak French in schools. Many parents whose native tongue was French refused to pass it on to their children. Now French is being taught in the schools. Lafayette has the only French-English bilingual radio station in the United States. The state-funded Council for the Development of French in Louisiana (CODOFIL) sponsors an exchange program every summer. About three hundred high school and college students spend a summer in France. CODOFIL is the leader in preserving our unique French heritage.

Population. Louisiana ranks as the **nineteenth most populous state** in the country. The state has experienced steady overall growth. According to the 1980 Census there were 4,206,312 people in Louisiana. They are unevenly distributed over the state. Half of the population is in three areas: New Orleans, Baton Rouge, and Shreveport. Lake Charles, Lafayette, Alexandria, and Monroe are the other four major **metropolitan areas**. Two-thirds of the people reside in these seven areas. Some parishes have no large population centers.

Louisiana exceeded the national average in the rate of its population growth from 1980 to 1984. The state's population increased 6.1 percent. The national average was 4.2 percent. More people left Louisiana than moved in during the year that ended July 1, 1984. This was the first time that has happened in more than a decade. In nearly every year the excess of births over deaths was great enough to offset the outward migration. The

population still rose 22,000 from the July 1, 1983, total. The total in 1984 was 4.4 million.

The out-migration pattern has mainly been of poor blacks and college-educated people. There were not enough jobs for them in Louisiana. The blacks started leaving the state in large numbers before World War II. Mechanization caused the mass exodus from the farms. Many blacks are now returning to the state.

Many whites, particularly from rural North Louisiana, migrated to other states during World War II and afterward. Many North Louisianians moved to South Louisiana. As a result a number of northern parishes lost population. In the 1970s the expansion in the oil and gas industry and building booms caused some northern parishes to begin to grow again. All southern parishes gained. South Louisianians have a tendency to "stay at home." Cajuns resist moving elsewhere. The economic situation of the 1980s has resulted in some population loss in South Louisiana. Still, South Louisiana enjoys the advantage of political power because of the greater population in that area.

Louisiana is mostly an **urban state**. The 1980 census showed that Louisiana has a higher percentage of urban people than all Southern states except Texas and Florida. It is still more rural than the United States as a whole. Orleans Parish is the most

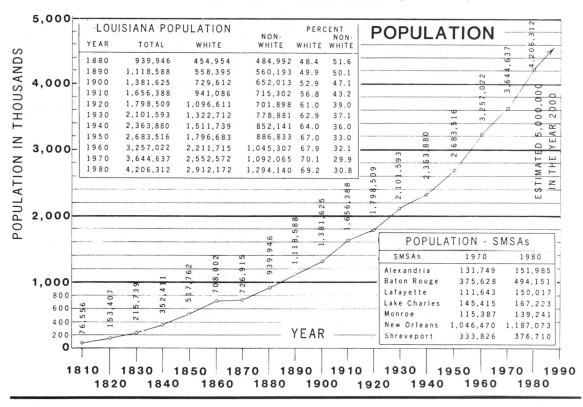

LOUISIANA POPULATION				PERCENT	
YEAR	TOTAL	WHITE	NON-WHITE	WHITE	NON-WHITE
1880	939,946	454,954	484,992	48.4	51.6
1890	1,118,588	558,395	560,193	49.9	50.1
1900	1,381,625	729,612	652,013	52.9	47.1
1910	1,656,388	941,086	715,302	56.8	43.2
1920	1,798,509	1,096,611	701,898	61.0	39.0
1930	2,101,593	1,322,712	778,881	62.9	37.1
1940	2,363,880	1,511,739	852,141	64.0	36.0
1950	2,683,516	1,796,683	886,833	67.0	33.0
1960	3,257,022	2,211,715	1,045,307	67.9	32.1
1970	3,644,637	2,552,572	1,092,065	70.1	29.9
1980	4,206,312	2,912,172	1,294,140	69.2	30.8

POPULATION

POPULATION - SMSAs		
SMSAs	1970	1980
Alexandria	131,749	151,985
Baton Rouge	375,628	494,151
Lafayette	111,643	150,017
Lake Charles	145,415	167,223
Monroe	115,387	139,241
New Orleans	1,046,470	1,187,073
Shreveport	333,826	376,710

urbanized. It is 99.9 percent urban.

The typical citizen lives in the city, but his attitudes are rural. One reason for this situation is the fact that the average person's roots were in the country. The rural attitudes of the people are a very important factor in making all types of decisions for the state.

In 1980, the residents of Louisiana lived on 44,521 square miles of land. This means that the state's **population density** is 94.5 persons per square mile. This figure compares with the national average of 63.9 persons per square mile. Orleans Parish has 2,801.6 persons per square

mile. Residential areas in Caddo, East Baton Rouge, and Jefferson parishes are larger than those in Orleans Parish. New Orleans has many closely-spaced dwellings. Residences in other areas are on more spacious lots. Cameron Parish is our least densely populated parish. It has only 6.6 persons per square mile.

Age of the Population. Louisiana has a young population. The age of the state's population is reflected in the vigor and vitality of the people. Age has much to do with the way money is spent. The state has a much higher percentage of young people compared with other states. The median age is 27.3. This is over 2.5 years less than the national median age. Of the state's total population, 22.5 percent are under the age of five. This is higher than the national average.

Labor Force. Louisiana has a higher ratio of females than the national average. Women have joined the state's labor force in great numbers. The majority of the state's labor force is male. A high percentage is black. The national average of blacks in the labor force is lower. New Orleans has a larger labor force than any other part of the state. The state's work force in 1980 was younger than the national average (27.5 versus 30.1).

Per Capita Income. In 1982 the per capita personal income in the state was slightly over $10,200. This compares with the United States average of $11,685. Per capita income is the average income per person—men, women, and children included. It is used to judge the wealth of a state. The state's per capita income in 1982 represented a gain of almost forty-five percent over 1979 income. Louisiana ranked among the top forty percent of the states in per capita income growth during this period. In 1983 the state ranked thirty-fifth in the nation in per capita income.

En Partie 1 (Studying a Part). 1. How does Louisiana rank in population? 2. What is the population of the state today? 3. What are the seven major metropolitan areas? 4. In which three metropolitan areas does half the population live? 5. Describe migration patterns that exist today. 6. Explain: Louisiana is essentially an urban state, but it is rural in character. 7. Why is the population density important? 8. What does the age of the population determine? 9. Describe our labor force. 10. (a) What is per capita income? (b) How does Louisiana compare with the rest of the United States?

Our Natural Resources and Industrial Development

Louisiana is rich with a wide variety of natural resources. It has been said that these resources would allow the people of the state to live comfortably even if we were isolated from the rest of the world. Almost every section of the state has been industrialized with a natural resource being used as a base.

The state has benefited greatly from mineral resources. Other resources are equally important. Extremely fertile soils are the state's basic resource. The state's farm products, fur industry, livestock and dairying, forests, and the various products from the waters are all important to the economy of the state.

Lagniappe. Soil, water, and vegetation are renewable resources. A renewable resource is one that, after its use, may be restored to its original state of usefulness. This depends upon the natural resource being given proper treatment. Restoration means renewing a renewable resource. A nonrenewable resource is one that no longer exists after it is used by man. It cannot be restored to its former condition or replaced in its original amount. Nonrenewable resources include petroleum, gas, sulphur, and salt.

Agriculture. Almost every kind of farm produce grown in the Western Hemisphere can be produced in the Pelican State. Louisiana has the climate, soil, and rainfall that combine to produce bountiful products from the land. This state occupies an important place in agriculture. The state leads the nation in diversified agriculture. Agriculture dominated the state's economy until recent years. It is still a major part of the economy and society of this state.

Agriculture in Louisiana has been transformed since World War II. Those who lived on farms earlier would be shocked at the sight of today's modern farms. The modern equipment that has changed Louisiana would be hard for them to believe. Perhaps the planter would be the most amazed. He would find no lines of plantation cabins and no small armies of black workers. Indeed, he would find no more plantations. He would find commercial farms. Instead of one-owner operations, he would find that big corporations have now taken over many farm operations.

It took the two decades between World War I and World War II plus another few years to destroy the old plantation system. The plantations were doomed with the introduction of machinery. Tractors were introduced in the 1920s. By World War II they were in wide use. The mechanization of cotton and sugarcane farming was not complete until the 1950s. Cotton pickers and cane cutters completed the cycle. They replaced men in the harvesting of these two crops. Corn pullers, potato diggers, milking machines—the list of farm machines to replace manual labor goes on and on. The modern cotton gin that replaced those of the first half of the twentieth century can gin as much cotton as a number of the small gins of the past. These gins compress the bales into such small packages that a man from the past would stare in wonder at their size.

As machines moved onto the plantations, blacks started leaving in such numbers that few were left. The only ones left on farms were skilled or semiskilled workers. The small farmers have almost disappeared. The share-cropper no longer exists.

The use of airplanes in planting, poisoning, defoliating, and fertilizing was part of the revolution. Machines were not alone responsible for the agricultural revolution. New chemicals were as important in the dramatic changes in farming as the invention of new machines. Effective herbicides, insecticides, and fungicides added to the new agricultural

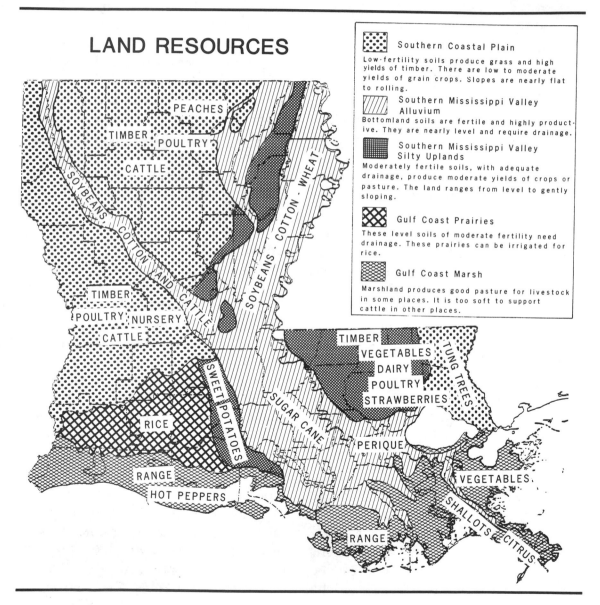

LAND RESOURCES

Southern Coastal Plain
Low-fertility soils produce grass and high yields of timber. There are low to moderate yields of grain crops. Slopes are nearly flat to rolling.

Southern Mississippi Valley Alluvium
Bottomland soils are fertile and highly productive. They are nearly level and require drainage.

Southern Mississippi Valley Silty Uplands
Moderately fertile soils, with adequate drainage, produce moderate yields of crops or pasture. The land ranges from level to gently sloping.

Gulf Coast Prairies
These level soils of moderate fertility need drainage. These prairies can be irrigated for rice.

Gulf Coast Marsh
Marshland produces good pasture for livestock in some places. It is too soft to support cattle in other places.

methods. Weed control by chemicals accounted for a vast reduction in labor.

The improved variety of crops, new fertilizers, new methods of farming, and other factors greatly increased production. Overproduction has caused serious economic problems for agriculture, forcing prices down. Consequently farmers made smaller profits, if any. As a result, government programs to control production were developed. The character of farming has changed as controls have been put into effect. What and how much the farmer plants are often determined by government controls. Government controls are intended to prevent overproduction and thereby result in reasonable market prices by limiting supply.

Many other changes in Louisiana farming have taken place since World War II. The impossible happened. "King Cotton" lost its throne. There has been a swing back to cotton since 1976, but cotton has lost its status. New crops have been introduced. Some crops have decreased in importance. Soybeans have become the big crop on huge commercial farms. Thousands of acres of hardwood trees have been destroyed to make room for soybeans. Corn production has declined. It is no longer a major part of the diet of most of the state's citizens. Corn is no longer needed as feed for farm animals. Rice has moved

to North Louisiana. Crawfish and catfish farms have sprung up everywhere. Wheat became a new crop in the 1980s. It is often used for double cropping. Wheat is planted in the fall on the same land from which soybeans have just been harvested. Small farms of under fifty acres are on the rise.

People from the past would find the lifestyle of modern farmers quite different from their own. Many farmers live in town. Their families go to the farm only on occasional visits, if at all. Some farmers fly their own airplanes with the same ease that farmers and planters of the past drove their pickup trucks. Machines are used for almost all work.

Many of these changes have come about as a result of research. This research is done by the government and private concerns. Louisiana is a leading state in agricultural research. Attempts to apply scientific knowledge to farming have gone on for many years. It began with the creation of the United States Department of Agriculture in 1862. Our land-grant university, Louisiana State University, is the state's center of agricultural research. Much of the research is done at the fourteen agricultural experiment stations scattered throughout the state. Many trained scientists in a number of fields work to produce a better variety of crops, improved farm practices, and better

A cane-cutter at work.

methods of livestock and crop production.

The Louisiana Cooperative Extension Service extends research findings from Louisiana State University throughout the state's population. It passes on helpful information from the United States Department of Agriculture, other farm people, and other researchers as well. Specialists and agents work in each parish. A series of adult education courses, workshops, and short courses are held throughout the year.

A well-planned **promotion** program advertises Louisiana products. A major part of this promotion has taken place at fairs and festivals. These events play an important part in the economic and cultural development of the state. Over the years, these fairs have created interest in the improvements in quality and yield of livestock, sugarcane, cotton, yams, rice, dairy products, and many of our other agricultural products. The annual state fair is held in Shreveport. Parish fairs are held throughout the state. In fact, Louisiana has more fairs and festivals than any other state.

The Louisiana Department of Agriculture sponsors competitions among different groups. Future Farmers of America (FFA), 4-H members, and adults compete in exhibitions. These include displays of livestock, poultry, and the many farm products grown in the state.

Promotion is a vital part of marketing crops. Promotion of Louisiana products has made the state's crops known around the world. In an aggressive foreign marketing program, a foreign trade representative works full-time to sell the state and its products.

Agriculture will continue to be a mainstay in the state's economy. When agriculture prospers, the entire state prospers. It has a multiplier effect on the state's economy. This means that related businesses create jobs and provide income for the state. Such businesses involve storing, shipping, processing, packaging, and merchandising of farm products.

Perhaps the best indication of the present and future condition of agriculture in Louisiana is found in the word coined to describe it—**agribusiness**. Farming has become more and more a way to make a living and less and less a way of life. The farm people in the rural areas have become part of the vast economic system. The differences in life on the farm and in the city have become fewer. The future of agribusiness seems to promise that these differences will continue to disappear.

The future of Louisiana agriculture will be shaped by the world's growing food needs. The need to feed the world and to conserve energy will both influence the farming picture.

Forest Industry. The forests of Louisiana were among the first of the state's natural resources to be developed. Today they produce the raw materials for one of the state's chief industries. Forestry is the largest single land-use industry. Forests occupy nearly forty-seven percent of the state's total land area. The state ranks among the foremost producers of timber in the nation. It ranks high in the nation in the production of pulpwood and southern pine plywood.

This multibillion dollar industry has developed from the cutover lands of the early "cut out and get out" days. After those days lumbering began a steady decline. The native forests had been cut, especially the giant longleaf pines and the cypress. These two varieties make fine lumber, but they grow very slowly. By the early 1930s and the Great Depression, Louisiana lumber production had fallen drastically. Most major sawmills and lumber companies had ceased operating. A carefully planned conservation program was started.

Acres and acres of cutover land, which had seemed useless, were planted. Gradually, the trees began to grow again. It was a slow process to which government agencies and laws greatly contributed. During the 1940–50 period the tree-farm movement began. More than two million acres of forest lands were restored to production by a massive reforestation effort.

The thriving industry it is today has come through dedicated work.

New related industries have developed. The old ones have continued to expand. For many years, Louisiana forests have supported an industry that is a mainstay of the state's economy. All together, the wood industries add billions of dollars to the Louisiana economy each year. Lumber is just one of the products of Louisiana forests. **Poles, matchsticks, pilings, crossties, barrels, plywood, veneer, pulpwood, baskets, handles, paper, crates, charcoal, furniture, fence pickets, golf tees,** and **boat paddles** are all made from Louisiana timber.

LOUISIANA FOREST RESOURCES

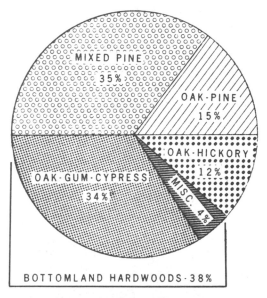

TOTAL·14,526 million acres

Louisiana's forest products feed our sawmills, pulp mills, veneer plants, cooperage plants, and plants treating wood products with chemical preservatives. The naval stores industry and tung-oil manufacturing are money-makers dependent upon Louisiana trees.

Although demands for more and more forest products are expected, the amount of land with forests has declined since 1965. This reduction has been due largely to the destruction of forests for construction of roads, houses, and businesses. There has also been the use of forest lands for farming, particularly for growing soybeans.

Since the recession beginning in 1981, the forest industry has faced setbacks. The high interest rates caused homebuilding to decline. Many plants closed. In the mid-1980s some of these plants returned to production.

Today, Louisiana forests are restored. Trained foresters tend the state's great resource. Laws protect against waste. The business of restocking goes on steadily. The "second forest" replaced the virgin forests. It will be replaced by the "third forest," which is already beginning to evolve. Plans have been made for the third forest to meet expected needs in the year 2000. The third forest is growing on fewer acres with greater production. It has required the united efforts of government, industry, and landowners.

Both the government and private

industry have spent much time and effort to ensure the future supply of timber. Special attention is given to insect and tree disease control. Seedlings are planted where mature trees have been cut. A fire control system of observation towers and lookouts is part of the conservation program. As a result of all these efforts, the basic forest resources of Louisiana will be available to support the many forest industries in the future.

Forest growth potential in the state is as great as that of any other southern state. The contribution of forestry to the economy is expected to vastly increase. The optimism is due to expected development in many areas. New techniques, improved equipment, new products, and more efficient production are in the plans for the future.

Mineral Production. The economy of the entire nation is greatly enhanced by the state's mineral industry. Louisiana ranked second among the states in the value of its mineral production in 1983. Oil and gas production accounts for ninety-six percent of the value of the mineral industry. Louisiana produces nearly one-fourth of the petroleum produced in the United States. More than one-third of the natural gas produced in the United States comes from our state. Each year the state is a leading producer of crude petroleum, natural gas, natural gas liquids, and sulphur.

Louisiana also produces sand and gravel, cement, stone, and clay. The state is the leading producer of salt.

Lagniappe. By state law a tax is levied on all natural resources severed, or taken, from the land for market. This tax is called a **severance tax.** Four-fifths of this tax goes into the state public school fund. One-fifth is returned to the parish in which the oil is produced. About the same division is made of severance taxes that come from the production of natural gas.

The Louisiana **oil** industry has brought untold riches to the state. "Black gold" is a suitable name. The exploring, producing, manufacturing, transporting, and marketing of oil have been a leading source of income and employment. Probably nothing has been more important in changing the face of Louisiana than the discovery and use of petroleum.

Until the 1930s, North Louisiana was the site of most of the state's oil and gas production. In the late 1930s drillers with new equipment and techniques began to develop South Louisiana fields. This was at the same time that World War II was brewing in Europe. By 1940 this section outranked the northern portion of the state in petroleum production. In that year the state oil production topped the one-million-barrels-per-day mark. Offshore drilling started a new phase in 1947. Oil and gas production moved offshore.

By 1954 fifty-nine parishes in the state produced oil or gas, or both. By the following year the number of offshore wells had risen to four hundred. In the next year, 1956, the deepest well in the world at that time was drilled in Plaquemines Parish. The exploration, development, and production of oil and gas continued at a rapid pace. Many improvements have been made in the equipment and processes. Wells are drilled deeper and deeper. Each year drillers have moved into deeper water in the Gulf of Mexico. Wells have been placed beyond the three-mile limit in the waters controlled by the United States.

By 1977 sixty-one parishes had a history of petroleum production. Only East and West Feliciana, St. Helena, and Vernon were not involved. Caddo Parish, Rodessa, Haynesville, and Jennings fields reached the charmed circle in oil production. These exceeded a cumulative production of 100,000,000 barrels. East Baton Rouge and Caddo were two of the most productive parishes.

In the mid-1980s a large portion of the state's petroleum production was offshore. A large share of the world's drilling rigs are in the Gulf of Mexico. Louisiana accounts for at least ninety percent of all offshore production in the United States. About ten thousand miles of pipelines have been laid on the sea floor. These pipelines connect production platforms with onshore refineries and transmission stations.

Offshore drilling greatly changed the petroleum operations in coastal Louisiana. By 1977 more than ten thousand offshore workers each week made their homes on the oil platforms scattered in the Gulf of Mexico. The "citizens" of this "city at sea" work, eat, live, and sleep for a week at a time offshore.

Once a week, on crew-change days, most of the city's population leaves for shore. Another ten thousand commute out to replace them. The largest fleet of privately owned helicopters in the world ferries most of them. Six companies operate more than three hundred helicopters for this purpose. More than a thousand boats and barges do the same thing. All are busy carrying people or equipment and supplies to and from shore bases.

Oil production peaked in 1971, but reserves began to decline. Production in the Gulf began declining in 1972. Oil companies went farther out into deeper waters in search of more oil. Production continued to decline because old fields were becoming exhausted. The start of a new boom began in 1973. The energy crisis exploded and energy prices soared. Suddenly all the oil and gas that in the past had been unprofitable to extract now promised profits. There was increased drilling and a decrease in the number of wells abandoned. One reason for this was improvements in technology. Another was the deregulation of natural gas prices by Congress.

In 1979 the emphasis was on oil shortages. In the mid-1980s in the oil industry the word was *glut*. Oil producers—not consumers—faced a crisis. An oversupply of petroleum products and falling prices threatened their financial and political stability. The upheaval of 1979 had a lasting impact on oil use. It led to greater conservation efforts. It also brought a drive to improve the oil-fueled motors. A worldwide shift to other fuels was made. A stockpiling of oil reserves became a national priority.

Louisiana has enjoyed incredible wealth from its **oil and gas production**. Much of the abundant store of mineral deposits once found within the land area of the state is gone. Geologists are looking for new sources of these deposits. Some consultants believe that there are many barrels of recoverable oil still to be found in Louisiana. They believe that these deposits are in untested rocks atop the state's paleozoic rock formations.

These deposits are neither readily nor cheaply found. Recovering the new oil and gas will be much more costly than average recovery costs. They lie in traps, which are increasingly hard to find. It is predicted that most discoveries will be made at depths much greater than the 9,400-foot average depth of known reserves. Without discovery of more oil and gas, the state's importance in this field will decline.

The United States government set up the Strategic Petroleum Reserve to furnish oil in the event of war or other emergencies. It is also intended for relief in the event of a world oil crisis. This system stores millions of gallons of oil in underground caverns throughout Louisiana and Texas. The petroleum reserve has five sites. Four of them are in the state. They are Bayou Choctaw in Iberville Parish, Weeks Island in Iberia Parish, Sulphur Mines in Calcasieu Parish, and West Hackberry in Cameron Parish.

The future of the oil industry in the state should continue to reinforce the state's economy even though the industry suffered a decline in all areas in the last few years. It has been found that Louisiana has enough oil and gas to carry the state's economy into the next century, if other areas of natural wealth are developed. New techniques should recover more oil from a given area than the typical twenty or thirty percent pumped from wells in the past.

One-third of the nation's **natural gas** supply comes from the state. Louisiana has ranked second to Texas in gas production for many years. The production, processing, and transportation of this gas are vital parts of the state's petroleum industry. About seventy percent of the gas produced in the state is shipped to other parts of the country.

Natural gas usually occurs with oil. However, there are some sections of the state where excellent gas production has been obtained without oil. There are records of discoveries of natural gas in the 1800s. However, the gas industry really began with the discoveries of oil in the early 1900s.

This business did not develop to any extent until the development of industrial uses for the gas. Heating needs could not consume the large amount of natural gas that was available. Improvements in pipe-laying methods reduced the cost so that more and more people were able to use gas for heating. Gas was sent by pipeline to other sections of the United States. Still other uses had to be found before the gas business could grow. As the uses for natural gas expanded, drillers began to seek out deposits.

In LaSalle Parish the Olla Field was discovered in 1940. It brought a big boom to the oil and gas industry. By then natural gas was a vital factor in industry and home use. By 1968 the state was producing one-fourth of the nation's supply of natural gas in its 126 plants.

The natural gas reserves in Louisiana began declining in 1970. Problems have continued to develop so that the future of the natural gas industry cannot be predicted. Awareness of the limits to the supply have caused changes in the industry. Probably more changes will continue to be made. However, this industry should continue to be an important part of our economy for many years.

Louisiana is the saltiest state in the Union. The state's numerous **salt** domes are pillars of pure salt up to a mile in diameter and fifty thousand feet deep.

The history of salt in Louisiana dates back to the salt licks found by early explorers. Records of work at Drake's Salt Lick near Goldonna in Natchitoches Parish date back to 1812. Before the Civil War one of the largest sites was the Bistineau Works near Shreveport. Other locations included Price's Salt Works near Drake's and those at Catahoula Lake, Castor, Friendship, and Negreet Bayou. John Marsh Avery started evaporating brine from Avery Island's salt dome to help the Confederate cause in 1862. In 1889 a new company, International Salt, took over the operation on Avery

Louisiana Office of Tourism

Mining salt in South Louisiana.

Island. This company was joined in salt production by other companies. In 1894 salt was found on Jefferson Island. Production there did not begin until 1923, however.

In modern times the five salt domes strung along the southwest coastline yield the bulk of the state's salt production. A very small percentage of the state's salt reserves has been taken. Salt is still there—perhaps billions of tons. It is likely that there are many salt domes about which we do not know. Drilling for other minerals sometimes discloses new domes.

Louisiana is second to Texas in the production of **sulphur**. The world's largest sulphur producer, Freeport Sulphur Company, operates in the state. The world's largest sulphur warehouse is located at Port Sulphur. The only offshore sulphur operations in existence are located off the coasts of Louisiana. The mining platforms there are the largest steel islands in the Western Hemisphere.

Louisiana has two towns named for their sulphur deposits—Sulphur and Port Sulphur. At Sulphur in Calcasieu Parish in 1867 drillers found sulphur. It was not until Dr. Herman Frasch invented a process to extract sulphur that the commercial industry started.

The Calcasieu Field produced seventy-five percent of the nation's sulphur supply until 1914. It was exhausted by the early 1920s. From 1924 until 1932 sulphur production was at a standstill in Louisiana. In 1928 the Gulf Production Company discovered sulphur in an oil well in Plaquemines Parish. In 1933 the Freeport Sulphur Company began operations in the Plaquemines Parish dome. Freeport's first mine in the

The crawfish boil is a South Louisiana custom.

Louisiana Office of Tourism

state was at Grand Ecaille. Louisiana again ranked second in production when the newly found sulphur was produced.

Sulphur production has slowed down greatly. In the 1970s Louisiana sulphur mines almost ceased to produce. New sources of sulphur must be found. A process has been developed for extracting sulphur from natural gas. Two plants, one at Lake Charles and one at Baton Rouge, are in operation.

The production of sulphur is important in attracting other industries that use sulphur or sulphur compounds. It is likely that growing needs of farms and factories will require greater supplies of sulphur. Demands for sulphur to make fertilizer for growing crops to feed an increasing world population make it urgent to find new sources for sulphur. The search for new sources continues.

Some of the state's mineral resources are not buried deep in the ground. Some are right on the surface or not far below it. **Gravel, sand, silt, clay,** and **shale** are among these deposits. Centuries-old streams brought them to the state.

Most of the gravel, sand, and shells are used in the construction business, but there are other uses. Some of the state's sand of a special quality is used in the manufacture of glass. Gravel and sand are also used in making cement and building roads.

Silt may be made into bricks, tiles, and the like.

There are large **peat** deposits in South Louisiana. Only a few states have nearly as much peat. Peat is mixed with soil to make a potting soil for plants. It is also used to wrap around the roots of plants being sent from one place to another. Peat is easy to dig and load onto barges with draglines.

In this period of concern about energy-producing fuels, Louisiana's **lignite** coal deposits in North Louisiana hill country are being eyed. This inferior grade of coal is not very good as a fuel. Still it may have to do in an energy crunch.

Other Louisiana minerals include **limestone**, which is desirable for road building and soil improvement. **Bentonite** and **gypsum** are two other minerals mined in our state. In addition, tons of **clam** and **oyster shells** are dredged from our waterways and marketed yearly.

Wildlife and Fisheries. Louisiana wildlife provides the raw materials for the **fur-producing** industry. The state has long been the nation's top fur producer. Louisiana produces more furs than Canada. The trees, swamps, and bayous shelter large quantities of **nutria, muskrat, mink, otter, opossum, skunk, red fox, gray fox,** and **raccoon.** The fur industry relies greatly on these and other fur-bearing animals such as the

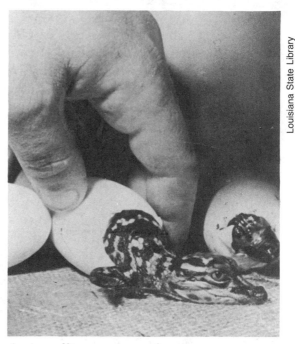

Louisiana State Library

A tiny alligator emerges from its egg.

bobcat, beaver, and **coyote.** The meat of these animals is also used as pet food and as fertilizer.

In 1984 Louisiana's fur business ran into problems. The largest market, Germany, did not have the money to purchase the furs. The depressed market meant lower prices for those sold.

New Orleans has been the shipping center for raw furs since the French first settled Louisiana. The state has never made the finished product. The state is now considering expanding the fur industry to process the skins and make fur coats. If Louisiana produced furs from start to finish, problems such as the one with Germany would not develop.

During the 1950s and 1960s **alligator** hunting was stopped. Their number had dropped drastically. In 1970 the federal government added the alligator to the endangered species list. Carefully controlled authorized hunting seasons began in 1972. The alligator returned to peak levels after a successful wildlife management program. The first statewide hunting season was in 1981. Hunters searched for alligators for the first time in eighteen years. Over 14,600 alligators were taken. Their hides and meat brought over two million dollars. The alligator has again taken its place in commercial production. Louisiana's alligator hides bring top prices in both domestic and foreign markets.

Louisiana's fish and game are in the highest ranks of the state's natural resources. The state leads others in volume of fish and shellfish catch. Louisiana is noted for its freshwater and saltwater fisheries, which make up one of the state's largest industries. The many miles of shoreline and bayous provide an excellent habitat for fish. This feature has enabled the state to take a leading role in this industry. The freshwater and saltwater fishing industries add millions of dollars to the state's economy yearly.

The seafood industry includes the processing of buffalo fish, catfish, bullheads, crawfish, menhaden, crabs, clams, shrimp, oysters, trout, red-fish, flounders, red snappers, and the like. Vast schools of tuna from the Gulf of Mexico yield a product that compares favorably with that from other sections of the country. There are more tuna in Louisiana's estuaries than on the East coast or anywhere else along the Gulf coast. Louisiana **shrimp** are known to world markets for both quality and size. The state ranks among the top three in the nation in shrimp production. **Menhaden** is not a food fish, but it provides fish meal for animal feeds. It is used in making some soaps, paints, lipstick, and linoleum. It is even used in the hardening of steel. Louisiana's oyster industry provides the nation's finest oysters. It is the only state to harvest oysters the year round. The state's **oysters** have a flavor not found in those from other states. Twenty percent of the nation's oyster demand is supplied by Louisiana. Two other contributors to our economy are frogs and turtles.

Industry and Commerce. Louisiana's abundant water supply has contributed greatly to the state's agricultural and industrial growth. Since early times, water has been one of the state's most important resources. Our largest cities and greatest industrial centers are located on or near important bodies of water. New Orleans and Baton Rouge are on the Mississippi. Shreveport and Alexandria are on the Red River. Lake Charles is on the Calcasieu. Monroe is on the Ouachita River. Lafayette's location near the coast has contributed to its status as the state's oil center. Morgan City, on the Gulf coast, is an exit point for people going offshore.

This water-rich state has much to offer industry in the way of transportation. Louisiana has more navigable waterways than any other state in the nation. Four world **ports**, twenty-two inland ports, and a **superport** obtain supplies and move goods to market. Louisiana combines domestic road, rail, and air facilities with five thousand miles of intrastate waterways. These are linked to nineteen thousand miles of the Mississippi River system.

The state's great **port of New Orleans** ranks second in the nation in annual and general cargo and third in the world in the volume of commerce. The port is Louisiana's largest

Baton Rouge is the United States' farthest inland port.

Louisiana Office of Tourism

single industry. It has an estimated annual economic impact on the state in the billions of dollars. It generates many full-time jobs. It is the largest grain (corn, soybean, and wheat) exit port in the world.

Since 1947 the port has operated the Foreign Trade Zone No. 2. Within the zone, products may be stored indefinitely. They may be examined, handled, sorted, graded, combined, relabeled, processed, and packaged. Foreign and domestic goods may be brought into the zone without formal customs entry or without paying duty and excise taxes.

Baton Rouge is one of the largest ports in the nation. It is farther inland than any other port in the United States. The **port of Lake Charles** is the nation's largest rice port. It is the state's third largest port. The fourth largest port is the newest—the **port of Morgan City**.

Chemicals and **chemical products, petroleum** and **petrochemicals, pulp, paper**, and **forest products** are leading Louisiana industries. Manufacturing, with the highest employment in 1984, included businesses related to food and kindred products, chemical and allied products, transportation equipment, furniture and fixtures, paper and allied products, textiles and apparel, and fabricated metal products.

Louisianians are employed in min-

ing, wholesale and retail trade, insurance, real estate, transportation, communication, public utilities, service industries, tourism, forestry, agriculture, fish, shellfish, and game. The wholesale and retail trade industry employs more people than any other employer in the state. These represented a high percentage of Louisiana's private nonfarm wage and salaried employment in 1984.

An important Louisiana industry is ship and boatbuilding. The manufacturing of equipment for these vessels is important as well. Large seagoing vessels are built in New Orleans. Fishing boats and other smaller boats are built at locations scattered throughout the state. Providing repairs and replacements are other big businesses.

In 1974 the Louisiana Film Commission was formed to lure movie dollars to the state. The results have been promising. At least a half dozen movies have been filmed here. More are expected. Production crews spend money for Louisiana services, labor, rentals, catering, hotels, restaurants, and entertainment.

Foreign-based companies represent more than a dozen countries. They are making a wide range of products in the state. Products range from chemicals to fabrics and food products. In fact, about ten percent of the total industrial investment in Louisiana over the past decade has come from foreign sources. In 1978 the state ranked fourth among the states in total foreign investment. *South* magazine identified Louisiana as having the largest investment in the South stemming from foreign industry and manufacturing. The trend is toward increasing outside investment. There is an aggressive effort on the part of the state to attract these investments. International investment will continue to be a noteworthy factor in the state's industrial growth.

En Partie 2 (Studying a Part). 1. List Louisiana's natural resources. 2. Why is Louisiana a good agricultural state? 3. Describe the agricultural revolution. 4. What part have research and promotion played? 5. How much and what have our forests contributed to our economy? 6. List the minerals the state produces commercially. 7. What role has mineral production played in the state's economy? 8. Trace the development of production of each of our minerals. 9. Describe our wildlife and fish resources. 10. What are our industrial centers? 11. What are our major ports? 12. (a) How much foreign investment has been made in Louisiana industry over the past decade? (b) To what have these investments led?

Current Problems

Louisiana's current problems are many and varied. Some are old; some are new. Some are unique to the state. Others are shared by other states. Some are major problems while others are minor. Some have been discussed throughout this text. Others are mentioned for the first time in this chapter. Some have a simple solution. Some require answers which are determined by one's point of view. No one can say for sure that the answers are the right ones.

Among the most pressing current problems are the following:

1. Air quality
2. City concerns
3. Conservation
4. Crime prevention
5. Drug control
6. Economy
7. Education
8. Health and welfare
9. Highways
10. Housing
11. Industrial expansion
12. Land use
13. Litter and waste control
14. Mineral depletion
15. Preservation
16. Prison conditions
17. Quality of government
18. Unemployment
19. Water management

Louisiana Office of Tourism

Weir Fishing. Fishing is a popular sport in Louisiana.

Air Quality. Finding a way to control air **pollution** is a major problem in Louisiana. The Clean Air Act of 1970 was passed to control air quality in the nation. The major sources of pollution exist mostly in urban areas. Regulations aim at controlling emissions in these areas. The Environmental Protection Agency was set up to police air pollution.

Air quality is measured for four types of polluting agents. The amount of haze is measured at thirty-two stations in Louisiana. The results show that most areas of Louisiana have air quality that meets or exceeds the clean-air standards of the Louisiana Air Control Commission.

City Concerns. Louisiana's cities are finding that they are not as popular as they once were. At one time most people wanted to live in the cities. Now many of them want to get out of the cities. This is true all over the country. The move to the suburbs has left downtowns abandoned. Movement away from the downtown to the outlying areas has caused cities to make new plans. Costly urban renewal programs have been started. Problems of housing, lack of parking space, and crowding are some of the problems that cities still face. Clean air and space for playgrounds and parks are other urban concerns. Too much traffic is another.

Many of Louisiana's smaller towns have become "bedroom communities." Residents commute to urban centers for employment. These bedroom communities do not have supporting industries. Therefore, survival of these towns is in question.

Conservation. The conservation of our soil, vegetation, water, air, and minerals is the duty of everyone. Assistance is obtained from groups like the Soil Conservation Service, the Louisiana Cooperative Extension Service, the Agriculture Adjustment Agency, the Louisiana Forestry Commission, the Louisiana Wildlife and Fisheries Commission, and vocational agriculture teachers. Many groups point to different ways to help conserve natural resources. There is debate among these conservationists about the best program to follow.

Some methods used for conserving water and soil have proven successful. Planting grasses and legumes on pasturelands keeps runoff water clean. The plants cause more water to soak into the ground. Their presence makes the remaining water move more slowly on its way to the streams. Levees and low-level water-control structures control water levels and saltwater intrusion. Farm ponds keep rainfall "at home." The state's 14,056,000 acres of forests let the rain down gently to the soil so that it soaks in better. Roots hold the soil in place. Terracing on sloping hillsides holds water in place and keeps it from eroding topsoil. Irrigation water can be managed to conserve it for other uses. Good systems for draining off excess water are helpful. Control of erosion helps prevent pollution of streams. Reservoirs catch the floodwater and release it slowly. The flow is no faster than the stream channel below can handle it. Channels are enlarged or cleaned out to permit floodwaters to get away faster. They provide outlets for farm drainage systems.

Mineral conservation is practiced, also. Oil and gas wells are spaced, and waste in production is prevented. In 1973 Clean Gulf Associates was organized. This group provides the best oil spill containment and clean-up equipment. The equipment is used in several cities along the coast of Louisiana. Since oilfield wastes contain a variety of hazardous materials, many safety precautions are taken.

Nature normally maintains a balance for wildlife. This balance is regulated through food supply, predators, and weather conditions. Modern man has upset this neat order. Highly trained biologists work at maintaining our wildlife resources. Protecting endangered species is one of the concerns of people working at conservation. Laws and law enforcement help conserve our wildlife. Wildlife management areas and refuges play a big part in the conservation program.

The Wildlife and Fisheries Commission has acquired land for wildlife refuges. These lands belong to the citizens. They will be maintained in their natural state for years to come. The state's holdings include a large portion of the Tensas Basin. The Tensas contains one of the last stands of bottomland hardwoods in the Mississippi Valley. The United States Fish and Wildlife Service also owns about five thousand acres in the Tensas area.

The Atchafalaya River Basin is the largest forested wetland complex left in the United States. The Basin, as it is known in South Louisiana, is ranked as one of the nation's most precious natural resources. The 443,000 acres are home to hundreds of species of wildlife and millions of migrating birds. It is one of the greatest sport and commercial fishing areas in the country. The Atchafalaya Basin is a crucial safety valve for the Mississippi's annual spring floods. The Basin is of utmost importance in flood control for the state. It acts as a floodway for the combined flows of the Mississippi and Red rivers. The Basin acts as a giant sponge. It absorbs and transforms impurities, stores reserve supplies of drinking water, and stabilizes groundwater flow.

No one questions the value of the Atchafalaya Basin. Many question whether public ownership or private ownership should control it. The debate has gone on for years. One side wants the land preserved for its wilderness character. This side feels that the duty of preserving the Atchafalaya Basin belongs to the federal government. On the other side are the landowners who want their rights. Plans have been made for the United States to purchase 50,000 acres. Dow Chemical Company donated 54,000 acres, and the state purchased some lands. These lands will comprise the public access areas.

Lagniappe. Caroline Dormon was an independent-minded Louisiana woman before such independence was fashionable. She dreamed of creating a national forest in Louisiana. Largely as a result of her efforts, the broad Kisatchie National Forest today stretches across seven parishes. The national forest covers lands cleared by "cut out and get out" timber harvesting.

Caroline Dormon was born near Saline in Natchitoches Parish at a place called Briarwood. She grew up near the longleaf pine forest of the Kisatchie. Dormon did not slow down even after her hopes for a national forest were realized.

She won world acclaim for her work. Caroline published what are now considered to be classic texts on Louisiana trees, wild flowers, and birds. Her first book was *Arbor Day Program for Louisiana*, published in 1928. She created her own detailed illustrations for the book. She was the first woman elected associate member of the Society of American Foresters. In 1965 Louisiana State University granted an honorary doctorate to Dormon— "noted botanist, botanical illustrator, contributor to horticulture, successful experimenter in hybridizing Louisiana irises and author of archaeological and ethnological studies of the American Indian."

When she died in 1971, she willed Briarwood to the Foundation for the Preservation of the Caroline Dormon Nature Preserve. It is now a 121-acre botanical garden.

Conservation agencies of the federal, state, and local governments are working together to ensure that nature's gifts remain for future generations. Much research has been done and continues to be done on conservation problems. Conservation of our natural resources has become an everyday concern of the state's citizens.

Crime Prevention. More than nine hundred agencies work together to control crime in the state. These agencies and their personnel include the police, courts, corrections, and juvenile branches of the criminal justice system. In recent years Louisiana has ranked high in crimes of murder and manslaughter, aggravated assault, and total violent crimes. The state was also high in the rate of thefts of cars and other vehicles. The crime rate is naturally higher where most people in the state live—the cities.

Drug Control. Alcohol is clearly the most abused drug in Louisiana. The division of hospitals offers help to alcoholics. It also helps people with drug abuses of all kinds. These services are performed at forty-one locations.

Louisiana has the other drug problems common to the entire nation. In addition, Louisiana faces a special situation resulting from its location near the Gulf of Mexico. The state's position on the Gulf makes it a popular point of entry for drug smugglers. Most of these operate from South and

Louisiana Office of Tourism

Avery Island is a bird sanctuary.

Central America or Mexico. Some fly the drugs in under cover of darkness. Others transport drugs in ships.

The smuggling of marijuana labeled "Acapulco Gold" and other drugs has been a recent challenge for Louisiana. The United States Customs Service compares it with the Prohibition days of the 1920s and early 1930s. At that time running rum and whiskey produced quick, but risky, profit. The drug smugglers operate with a mother ship technique, adapted from rum-running days. These mother ships wear a foreign flag. They lurk offshore beyond the twelve-mile limit of United States jurisdiction on the free high seas. The mother ships feed shuttle boats. The shuttle boats have been able to outrun patrol vessels. However, they cannot outrun helicopters.

In early 1985 a swift patrol boat was unveiled that is faster than those known to be in the possession of smugglers. The first of these new boats did not cost the taxpayers a cent. It was paid for with funds obtained from the sale of smuggling vessels captured by United States agents.

Economy. The economic direction of the state is not clear. The state of Louisiana still depends on oil for about one-fourth of its income. The declines in oil and gas in recent years have caused much alarm. Low oil prices affect the state's economy as a whole. For a long time it has been a known fact that if oil and gas were doing well, the economy in general would be doing well. When prices drop, production falls off, and jobs are lost. Each one-dollar drop in the price per barrel of oil costs the state treasury about two million dollars a year in lost income. In 1984 the state budget was based on an average oil price of thirty dollars a barrel. The importance of severance taxes on oil and gas to total state revenue has long been recognized. This severance tax revenue has re-

lieved the taxpaying citizens of the state to a great extent. Louisiana citizens have been jolted into reality. The affluence of the years of the oil and gas boom came to an abrupt end in the 1980s. In 1984 the tax burden was shifted from Louisiana's oil and gas industries to other businesses and individuals.

Financing of Louisiana's government has received much attention since the picture in the oil industry has changed. Louisiana has for many years depended on funds that are no longer available. It is necessary for the state's financial base to be redesigned. The state is concerned about the choice of a replacement for these sources of revenue. Changing the economic base is a pressing problem. There is also a greater need for persons who spend government money to be accountable for their actions.

It is possible that energy will again come to Louisiana's economic aid. Louisiana claims a large share of an offshore oil and gas trust fund. The fund contains billions of dollars. The coastal states and the federal government have quarreled over how to split oil and gas revenues from disputed offshore areas. Those disputed boundary regions are called "8Z" tracts. The escrow account exceeded five billion dollars in 1984. More than two billion dollars is related to Louisiana offshore tracts. Settlement of the offshore oil dispute with the federal government could bring the state a billion dollars or more. Another possible increase in revenues could come with the deregulation of natural gas. In the meantime new sources must be found to keep Louisiana on a sound financial footing.

Education. Education has top priority among concerns for Louisiana. An excellent educational system and economic development go hand in hand. Improving education is a concern that affects the ability of the state to attract industry. Some business investors do not include Louisiana as a possible site for their operations. One reason is that there are not enough educated workers available. The quality of education affects not only our economic development, but also many other aspects of our lives. Public concern has added pressure to secure an excellent educational system.

It will take years to improve the state's educational system. The poor educational background of the twentieth century still casts its shadow across the state. The present movement toward excellence in Louisiana schools has caused every problem to be examined for causes and solutions. Louisiana is one of only ten states that has both a tenure law and lifetime certification, or licensing, to teach. The tenure law makes it difficult to remove incompetent teachers

from the classrooms. At the same time it offers Louisiana teachers some job security from political interference.

Until 1985, Louisiana was the only state that elected both the board of education and its superintendent. This situation set the stage for neither the board nor the superintendent knowing who was actually in charge. Making the state superintendent an appointive position had been debated for years. The 1985 legislature made the position appointive. The State Department of Education makes regulatory decisions. The legislature passes laws about education that do such things as mandating the teaching of a subject. The political overtones in the business of education have added untold problems.

Louisiana faces many more educational problems. Even though the system has withstood the shock waves of desegregation, important revisions must be made. One of the state's continuing problems is illiteracy. In 1984 Louisiana was still at the bottom in the nation in literacy. Inadequate education, as revealed by testing, has caused much concern in all segments of our society. Standardized college admissions examination scores were up slightly in the mid-1980s, but they were still below the national average. Louisiana has the highest high-school dropout rate in the nation. Louisiana schools suffer from shortages of qualified teachers. It is predicted that these shortages will get worse. The state's salary scale for teachers is low compared to the pay scale of other states. Working conditions for teachers need to be improved. The state needs a system for upgrading teacher quality and teacher pay. Another problem is maintaining the large number of institutions of higher learning. Some decisions have to be made about the programs schools of every level offer, the type students who will be served, and the distribution of funds for education. An excellent program must be provided to train students to do more than one job and to adjust to change.

Some steps have been taken to remedy these problems. An educational reform movement is underway. Many new programs have been introduced to raise the level of education for all students. In 1982 the only state-supported high school for the gifted and talented in the United States opened in Natchitoches. In 1985 Governor Edwards called the Louisiana Governor's Conference on Education to try to develop a plan for improvement of the state's educational program.

Health and Welfare. A puzzling health problem in Louisiana is the high risk of cancer in South Louisiana. People of South Louisiana run a greater risk of dying of cancer than those who live in other areas of the nation. In North Louisiana, Caddo and Bossier parishes rank in the top ten percent of lung cancer rates for white males in the nation. Why this is so remains a mystery.

The Louisiana Legislature became alarmed by the cancer problem. A law was passed at the 1983 legislative session. The law requires that the state keep records and issue annual reports on the occurrences of cancer. Studies are being made, and a remedy for this situation is being sought.

State hospitals and institutions provide public health services. Parish health clinics are also available. Lack of funds for these programs has always been a problem.

The problems of the elderly are the same for Louisiana residents as for those across the nation. Regulating and enforcing the rules for the ever-increasing number of nursing homes is a government responsibility. Mandatory retirement for people who remain active is questioned. Inflation has caused social security and other retirement plans to be inadequate. Louisiana is trying in numerous ways to ensure a more secure and dignified old age for its citizens.

Highways. Louisiana has about 54,260 miles of public roadways to maintain. More highways are needed. This need will continue to be far greater than the available funds can accommodate. The greatest problems exist on the rural state system. Lane width, shoulder conditions, and operating speeds have to be dealt with. Road repairs consume a big part of the money assigned for highways in the state. The life of Interstate 20 was predicted to be twenty years. This life expectancy was based on the projected volume of traffic. The volume has been much greater than predicted. This brings up the question of just how long this important highway will last.

The number of fatal accidents on Louisiana's highways is troubling. For several years the state was near the top of national ranking in auto fatalities per year. In 1983 Louisiana dropped to tenth place in this category. Several reasons for the improvement were cited by the state police. One is the tougher drunken-driving laws passed. Another is lowered speed limits. Most important is the strict enforcement of these laws.

The need of a North-South expressway has been felt for many years. Completion of Interstate 49 should meet this need. The new route will bring problems as well. Some small towns will be cut off from the through traffic. The results could mean loss of trade that the traffic now brings.

Housing. The goal of the federal Housing and Community Development Act of 1974 is to provide every family with a decent home and suitable living environment. It is very difficult for the state to meet this goal. Low-cost housing is offered through government programs. Housing is far from adequate in many areas of the state.

Many young people can no longer expect to own their own homes. Other types of housing are being sought because of the tremendous rise in the cost of owning a home. Government controls of mobile home locations and safety standards are met with mixed reactions from the public.

Industrial Expansion. In order to keep Louisiana citizens employed the state must attract job-creating industries. New industry is needed for the economic impact it has on the state. The Louisiana Office of Commerce and Industry tries to attract industry.

The enormous Red River project holds exciting possibilities for industrial expansion. Five lock-and-dam structures designed to make the Red River navigable from the Mississippi to Shreveport are being constructed. The project is expected to be completed in 1993. It will provide a nine-foot-deep and two-hundred-foot-wide navigation channel. It will begin at the Mississippi River sixty-five miles above Baton Rouge. Simmesport, Alexandria, Natchitoches, and Shreveport are expected to take new life with completion of this project.

Land Use. Conflicts have arisen over **land use** in the state. Our most desirable lands are preferred for almost everything. If we are to grow the best crops and have the highest yields, then we must use prime farmland. It is estimated that twelve million acres in Louisiana are considered prime. Many acres of this prime farmland are shifted to other uses every year. Should the land be used for producing minerals or for agriculture? Should the wetlands be reserved for wildlife? Or should oil companies be allowed to drill there and contaminate the environment? Should oil companies be allowed to drill offshore in the Gulf? Forestland or farmland—which shall it be? Should this be decided by law?

Should the wetlands be saved? Louisiana ranks second only to Florida in the amount of wetlands. Louisiana wetlands cover more area than the entire state of Maryland. Part of the problem in preserving these wetlands lies in the matter of identifying them. Wetlands have been described as a transition zone from water to land. The definite line is difficult to draw. Wetlands are most often associated with the Louisiana coast. Yet the northern parts of the state also share in this natural resource.

The value of the wetlands is clear. Not only do wetlands provide habitat for fish and wildlife, but they also serve as protection against floods. They stabilize water tables and reduce pollution.

Louisiana is losing its wetlands through both natural and man-made causes. Erosion is eating away at thousands of acres of marshland. Drainage to allow the use of the land in agriculture, logging activities, and construction of roads take a toll in these wetlands. If the riches of the wetlands are going to remain, there must be careful studies in understanding and preserving this valuable real estate.

Litter and Waste Control. Louisiana has a serious **litter** problem. Few states can match Louisiana's litterers and illegal dumpers of roadside trash. A small percent of the public causes thousands of dollars in needless expenses each year. This is done daily by littering the highways and forests that cover the state. Trash is tossed in ditches. Wrecked cars are dumped on public and private land. Magnificent forestlands are used as a site to dump trash. The marring of the natural beauty of the state is enough to discourage dedicated people who work to preserve the state's beauty. The cleaning and hauling necessary to remove the litter is a heavy financial burden on the state. Many of our citizens are greatly concerned over this needless waste of money that could be used for more worthwhile projects.

In addition, the state must solve the problem of proper disposal of industrial waste, including toxic materials. The problem of storing nuclear waste has created much con-

Louisiana Office of Tourism

Shrimp boats line the banks of a South Louisiana bayou.

cern. The Vacherie salt dome on the Webster-Bienville boundary line near Heflin was considered for possible storage of nuclear waste. The United States Department of Energy did not select the site for the first repository. The Vacherie salt dome is a prime candidate for the nation's second repository site to be built in the 1990s. Many Louisiana citizens are troubled by the idea of nuclear waste storage.

Vandalism also causes many dollars to be spent needlessly. Road signs destroyed by vandals are a tremendous loss to the state. The defacing of property as a form of enjoyment is revolting to most citizens. Countless dollars are spent removing markings on bridges, buildings, and other public property.

Preservation. Interest in historical preservation has been stimulated by the creation of the National Register of Historic Places. Through the National Endowment for the Humanities and the National Endowment for the Arts federal funding has reached into the state for cultural projects. Art exhibits and cultural activities have been included on a parish level. Exciting projects in the arts have brought opportunities for participation to many state residents.

There is more awareness today of "vanishing Louisiana," but more efforts to preserve the past for the future are needed. Louisiana began building its first adequate state archives building in mid-1984. Up until that time the state's valuable archives were not properly cared for and preserved. Much has been destroyed. Thousands of precious documents rotted in an old lumberyard warehouse in Baton Rouge while legislators debated the archives building issue. Louisiana was the only state in the United States without a state archives building.

The four-storied 118,920-square-foot building will have exhibit galleries, a research room, a conservation laboratory, a record center, and some of the finest equipment available for preserving documents and for microfilming.

Prison Conditions. Of course the best solution to problems in prisons would be to find a way to eliminate crime. We know that this will probably never be. Therefore we must provide and maintain our prisons in a way that will make them more suitable for their purpose. Overcrowded conditions exist at city, parish, and state facilities. More buildings are badly needed. More personnel are needed to supervise prison activities to provide as much of a natural environment as possible for the prisoners. More work in rehabilitation must be conducted. New methods of control may be necessary. The answer may not be in "locking up." New and more effective punishments may have to be found.

Louisiana ranks first in the United States in **inmates** per capita. The state courts are sentencing 1,400 more criminals each year than are being released. The number of inmates serving life sentences has increased ninety percent since 1979. The total prison population has increased seventy-five percent during the same period. In 1984 the total prison population was 13,500. Of these 1,497 were serving life terms. The average lifer is a 35.8-year-old black with less than a high school education. It costs $250 per taxpayer each year to operate the state prisons and parish jails in Louisiana.

Quality of Government. Louisiana has suffered throughout its history from the poor image of its government. Unfortunately the state is frequently viewed elsewhere as being highly corrupt and backward. Our government has had its share of flamboyant politicians. Often they have had a flair for dramatic and sometimes outlandish actions. Even so, they have been attractive to voters of the state.

Students of politics believe that this has occurred in Louisiana because of our abundance of oil and gas revenues. These revenues have paid most of the cost of government, so the average citizen has not concerned himself with our government.

Thus, as some political scientists see it, our unique blend of cultural heritage and political economics is largely responsible for our low rating of government performance. Politics has become the great theater of our state. Politicians have become our greatest entertainers.

These political scientists feel that since the burden of taxes has shifted, the views of voters have changed. In other words, when the money for government costs is coming out of the pocket of the taxpayer, he is going to be more concerned about how the money is spent. The modern post—oil boom taxpaying voter is now looking for a more serious, soberminded, businesslike politician. In time these new politicians could change our image.

Good government is important to the efforts to attract industry to the state. It is necessary in building a spirit of cooperation between the governing officers and the citizens. Because of its importance, concerned citizens of Louisiana have taken steps to create a better image for the state. A lasting image such as the state desires can only come with better performance. There is still much work to be done in this direction.

Unemployment. For many years the unemployment rate in Louisiana has been excessive. It has been higher than that of many other states. In 1983 figures for the state climbed to a new post-Depression record. In December 1984, the jobless rate in Louisiana climbed to 10.4 percent. In the same month there were 1,750,200 people employed in the state and 203,700 looking for work. Unemployment was far above the national rate of 7 percent. The state government seeks to develop job opportunities and relieve the high unemployment.

Water Management. Despite an abundant water supply, the state is not immune to water problems. **Water shortages, flood prevention and control, water pollution, saltwater intrusion, drainage,** and **maintenance of channels** are the most critical of these problems.

Water pollution is one of the biggest problems for Louisiana today. Supplies of good quality water

Louisiana Office of Tourism

The Mississippi River at New Orleans.

are necessary to the development of every area of the state. Cities are having a hard time finding sources for a good water supply. Pollution of our waters has become a major concern. This problem has become worse as the population has increased and the state has become more industrialized. Oilfield wastes, industrial wastes, agricultural chemicals, and sanitary landfills are sources of water pollution.

Water pollution is not altogether confined to freshwater bodies. Seawater near the places where streams enter the Gulf of Mexico may become polluted by the contents of the river. As a result oysters grown on shallow sea bottoms near shore may be unfit for human food. Offshore

petroleum production may pollute seawater to the point of killing oysters, shrimp, and many fish in nearby waters. Pollution of coastal waters results largely from oilfield operations. Oil spills relating to offshore drilling are an ever-present problem. Pollution control in our coastal waters is getting more and more attention.

Both the federal and state governments have passed laws to control water pollution. Such control is the problem of our regulatory agencies. Yet it cannot possibly be achieved without the aid of all citizens.

Navigation of the Mississippi and inland rivers poses a challenge. The **maintenance of deep channels** at the mouth of the Mississippi has been a problem since the French settlement. Large ships must be able to enter the river.

The United States Army Corps of Engineers has the duty of enlarging and improving our navigable streams that are our main drainage outlets. The State Department of Public Works is charged by law with the task of providing parishwide drainage outlets. Over six million acres of the state's land have some degree of drainage problems. **Drainage** is really just a small part of flood control.

Flood control problems still plague the state. The Mississippi River has to be controlled by man. Very early in our history it was realized that if the river were not controlled by man-made works, the land would be flooded during periods of high water. Levees were used alone until our modern flood control system was developed.

A flood control system was planned by the United States Army Corps of Engineers. A levee system along both sides of the Mississippi and along the sides of its main tributaries above the Red River was developed. The carrying capacity of the upper Red River was increased. Two great floodways were created. These are the Atchafalaya Basin Floodway and the Morganza Control Structure and Floodway. This was done by running levees alongside the Atchafalaya River. The levees extended from the Mississippi and Red rivers almost to the Gulf near Morgan City. The Atchafalaya was deepened and widened so it could carry a greater load. The amount of water the Mississippi had to carry past Baton Rouge, Donaldsonville, and New Orleans was reduced.

Other measures have been taken to protect the state from floods. The Bonnet Carre Spillway was built at New Orleans. When the spillway is opened, great quantities of water flow through it from the Mississippi to Lake Pontchartrain.

Since 1928 when flood control began, there have been no failures of flood control works. There has been no general overflow of valleys. People of Louisiana have felt more secure. This security has become more permanent as efforts have been continued to safeguard the property and state's citizens from floods.

What would happen if the Old River Control Structure failed? To understand the major problem, it is necessary to know the history of the project. It involves the Atchafalaya River. This river has a unique story. About a century and a half ago a person could jump across it at some points. It was little more than a ditch. Its channel was filled with logs and debris in some places. The stream was a distributary of both the Mississippi and Red rivers. The Atchafalaya River was once connected with the lower channel of the Mississippi. In 1831 Captain Henry Miller Shreve cut off one of the great loops of the Mississippi to form a straight and shorter channel. Old River, a seven-mile long stream, was formed by the Shreve cutoff and connects the Mississippi with the Atchafalaya and Red rivers. The Atchafalaya became swollen with waters from the Mississippi. Eventually it became the major river it is today.

The Atchafalaya flows from a point on the northern boundary of Pointe Coupee Parish to the Gulf. At the coast it flows into Atchafalaya Bay, 170 miles from its beginning. Because of its shorter and steeper grade, Atchafalaya waters are swifter than those of the Mississippi.

In 1950 an important study was

begun because of the threat of the Mississippi to change its channel to flow through the shorter channel of the Atchafalaya to the Gulf. The conclusion drawn by the engineers' study was that this would happen if the Atchafalaya were left alone.

The Mississippi River Commission made a detailed plan to prevent the great river from changing its course. Should this happen, Baton Rouge and New Orleans would be left on dry land. There would be great losses in massive floodways, industrial complexes, and other areas. The Mississippi below Old River would become a saltwater inlet of the sea.

To solve this major problem a project was begun in 1954 and completed in 1963 to dam Old River. The Old River control locks are designed to control the flow of water from the Mississippi through Old River into the Atchafalaya.

Engineers disagree whether the controls will prevent the Mississippi from changing its channel to claim that of the Atchafalaya. Some believe it will. Others think that the powerful Mississippi will do as it pleases when and if it is ready to change courses.

Another water problem is caused by beautiful flowers—**water hyacinths**. These pretty purple flowers completely choke and clog many of the state's waterways. Because they double their number every two weeks,

they present a big obstacle. So far nothing has stopped them. Meanwhile they have cost the state untold millions. Unless a solution is found, they will continue to do so.

En Partie 3 (Studying a Part). 1. Make a chart using these headings: Current Problems; Causes; and Solutions. Fill in the chart with problems in the text and other problems that have arisen. Classify each problem as a Louisiana problem only or as a United States problem, also. 2. Who must take the responsibility for solving these problems?

Outlook. For a prosperous future we must continue to tap Louisiana's vast resources. We must produce more products and services for the increasing demand. The state's future growth appears to be fairly secure even though the question of whether minerals will be available dims the picture. The state's most important resource, its people—with skillful management of soil, water, plants, wildlife, and industry—will provide the best Louisiana environment possible. The people will determine the state's future.

Many years ago John Law described what Louisiana had to offer. In 1952 Hodding Carter wrote in *John Law Wasn't So Wrong*:

But now, 250 years since the French first came, Louisiana is proving that John Law was not as wrong as he thought himself in his heart to be. Out of the river god's cornucopia pours as diverse a wealth as can be found anywhere in all the world. It comes from tropic sea and flowing rivers, from sun-blessed farmlands and forests, from the bowels of the earth, from the ingenious minds and skillful hands of a new industrial surging. Today 350 years after John Law's emigrants cursed his trickery and died, their descendants and sons of the later comers, more than two and one-half million of them, are fashioning a purposeful union of city, town, and countryside whose common denominator is confidence.

Coup d'Main
(Completing the Story)

Jambalaya (Putting It All Together)

1. What might you do to help preserve the beauty of our state?

2. We are running out of certain natural resources. What could our scientists do about the problem? the average citizen? the government?

3. What natural resources must we have for existence?

4. Why are people our greatest resource?

5. Complete a chart with the following headings: Resource; Location or Source; Problems Involved; Practices of Conservation or Restoration; and Current Outlook.

6. Classify each resource as renewable or nonrenewable.

7. What are Louisiana's assets and liabilities at the present?

8. What are wise and unwise practices concerning the state's natural resources that have existed or now exist?

9. Support this statement: Louisiana has changed from a rural, agricultural economy to an urban, industrial economy.

10. How is the state's economy related to our natural resources?

11. Update the current problems discussed in your text. Give any solutions that have been found. Add any other problems now facing the state.

Potpourri (Getting Involved)

1. Cite evidence to support one of these statements: (a) The mass media have reduced the people of the state to a level of mediocrity. (b) The

scientific revolution created a chain reaction that has influenced every aspect of Louisiana life.

2. Compare Louisiana with another state. Compare size, population, landforms, rainfall, vegetation, and major ways of making a living. Include the differences in religion, form of government, language, customs, and career opportunities.

Gumbo (Bringing It Up-to-Date)

1. Create your own ideal Louisiana. Identify all changes that you will have to make in the present state. How could these changes be made?

2. Relate some lessons that can be learned from events in our state's history to a current problem.

3. Conduct a survey to determine whether Louisianians are content with the state of the state. Compare the results with the one done by the Louisiana Committee on the Humanities in 1978.

4. Investigate (a) careers in Louisiana and predict possible future careers in the state, or (b) the migration of people from Vietnam and Mexico.

5. Use the latest available information to summarize the trends in major occupations, distribution of income, leisure-time activities, church membership, school and college enrollment and achievement, and the relationship of the labor force to the total population. What is the significance of these developments?

6. What should be the goals for Louisiana for your generation?

7. Make a list of the state's current problems and your solution for them.

8. Trace the agricultural revolution. Compare Louisiana farming operations of today with those in antebellum days. Compare ownership, management, labor, production, economic value, social life, daily routine, use and sale of goods, and equipment.

9. Record evidences of conservation practices in the state today.

10. Make a record of land use in a given area. Trace the history of land use in that area and government regulations of its use.

11. Interview both blacks and whites to find out their assessments of where the state is, where it is going, and how best to get it there. Draw conclusions. Do blacks have views that are similar to those of the whites? Do the blacks and whites agree?

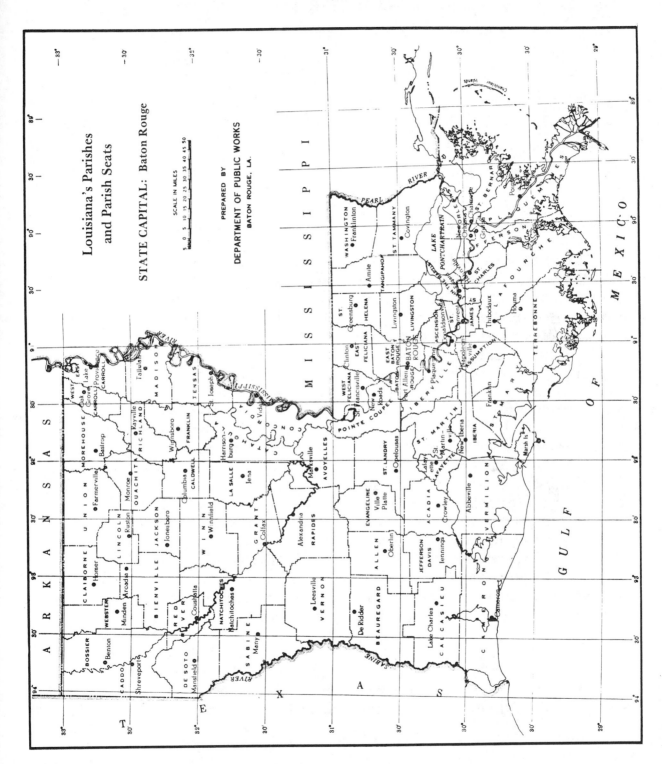

Louisiana's Parishes and Parish Seats

STATE CAPITAL: Baton Rouge

SCALE IN MILES
5 10 15 20 25 30 35 40 45 50

PREPARED BY
DEPARTMENT OF PUBLIC WORKS
BATON ROUGE, LA.

CHAPTER 14

LOUISIANA GOVERNMENT

The government of Louisiana does not differ to any great extent from that of other states. It is different, however, in one important respect. Its judicial system is unique. This results from the fact that Louisiana does not use the common law practice. Common law judgments are made on the basis of the results of previous legal cases. The common law is associated with English custom. Louisiana refers to civil law, or a civil code. Louisiana laws are written laws. The supreme, or final, reference law is the state constitution. All Louisiana's constitutions have safeguarded the basic law evolved through the century of French and Spanish rule. Today's judicial system shows some influence of English common law.

Branches of Government

The Louisiana constitution provides for three branches of government: the **executive,** the **legislative,** and the **judicial.** These same three branches exist in our national, or United States, government. Each branch of the government has its own duties to perform. The executive branch manages the state's business and carries out the laws. The legislative branch enacts laws and sets policy. The judicial branch interprets the laws. The three branches are part of a system of **checks and balances.** This term means that each branch stands watch over the other to prevent any branch from doing anything that it is not authorized by law to do.

Executive Branch. The executive branch has the duty of the administration of our state government. Leadership in pointing directions and forming goals for the state is expected from the executive branch. The governor holds the supreme authority of the state as head of the executive branch. This branch includes other officials and a maximum of twenty departments.

Members of this official group are elected by the people at statewide elections. They serve terms of four years and are paid an annual salary. A candidate for election must be a qualified voter. He must have been a citizen of the state for five years and must be at least twenty-five years old. The attorney general must have practiced law in the state for at least five years before the election.

All state officials except the governor and lieutenant governor appoint first assistants. These executive assistants must possess the same qualifications required of the state officials. Their appointments must be approved by a majority vote of the Senate. If vacancies occur in the offices with less than a year left, first assistants may fill the office. If there is more time left, the vacancy must be filled at the next statewide election.

According to the Louisiana Constitution of 1974 some officials in the executive branch may be appointed by the governor. Approval by two-thirds of the Senate is required. Officers that may be appointed if the legislature approves include the commissioners of agriculture, insurance, and elections. The same two-thirds vote would be needed to combine any of these offices.

Louisiana's **governor** is the chief executive of the state. He manages the state government. He appoints many top officials to state agencies, boards, and commissions. With the advice and consent of the Senate he makes appointments for nonelective offices. The governor serves as a member of the most important boards and commissions. The governor is responsible for preparing and presenting an annual operating budget to the legislature. He is commander in chief of the state militia. In this role he may call out the national guard. The governor alone has the right to grant pardons and paroles, commute sentences, or remit fines. He has the power to grant reprieves for crimes against the state upon recommendations of either the pardon board or the parole board.

Governors propose legislation in messages to the legislature. They take an active part in getting desired legislation passed. The governor may draft bills. He has supportive legislators introduce them. The governor may veto or approve a bill passed by the legislature. The governor does not sign and cannot veto any resolutions of the legislature. It is the governor's privilege to call special sessions of the legislature to consider specific matters.

The governor presides at strictly ceremonial occasions. This includes welcoming celebrities who visit the state. He congratulates Louisiana citizens for outstanding accomplishments

Louisiana Office of Tourism

Louisiana's thirty-four-story capitol is the tallest in the nation.

in various fields. The governor entertains important people who come to the state. Dedicating memorials and monuments is yet another task.

The governor may succeed himself for one term unless he has already served a full term and half of another. He lives in the governor's mansion in Baton Rouge. In addition, he is paid all household, office, and travel expenses.

The lieutenant governor acts for the governor in case of his absence. He also serves as an ex officio member of various boards and commissions. This means that he is a member of certain boards and commissions because he holds his position as lieutenant governor. In case of a vacancy in the office of lieutenant governor a successor is named by the governor. The appointee must be approved by the majority of both houses of the legislature.

The secretary of state is the custodian of the Great Seal. He affixes the seal to all official laws, documents, proclamations, and commissions. He serves as the chief election officer of the state. In this capacity he prepares and certifies the ballots for all elections and announces election returns. His other duties include supervising the publication and distribution of the acts and journals of the legislature and Supreme Court reports. He also administers and preserves the official archives of the state. He maintains and registers trademarks and labels. He issues extradition papers and records and files articles of incorporation.

The treasurer is the keeper of all public monies. He manages the receiving and spending of state funds. He reports annually to the governor and the legislature.

The attorney general is the state's chief legal officer. He is concerned with all legal matters in which the state has an interest. He serves as an advisor. He determines the meaning of Louisiana laws and explains them when called upon. The attorney general supervises lawyers throughout the state. He represents most state agencies as legal counsel. He also represents the state in all criminal cases on appeal.

The commissioner of agriculture advances, protects, and promotes agriculture in the state. Under him are the Department of Agriculture and thirteen agribusiness-related agencies.

The commissioner of insurance supervises the insurance laws of the state—the Louisiana Insurance Code. He serves as ex officio member of the Louisiana Insurance Rating Commission. He examines all insurers doing business in the state. He also approves insurance contracts used in the state.

The superintendent of education heads the Department of Education. It is his duty to carry out the policies of the State Board of Elementary and Secondary Education. It is he who carries out the laws of the state affecting schools under the board's jurisdiction.

The commissioner of elections administers the laws relating to elections. This involves voter registration and the physical arrangements for elections. He is custodian of the voting machines at all times. He purchases voting machines and sees that they are kept in perfect working condition. They must be stored between elections. They are delivered to the many voting precincts throughout the state. Then they are returned to storage after elections.

Legislative Branch. The Louisiana Legislature is composed of two houses: the **Senate** and the **House of Representatives**. There are thirty-nine members in the Senate. The House of Representatives has 105 members.

Lawmaking is the basic function of the legislature. It passes laws on any matter. It proposes amendments to the constitution. These duties are outlined in the constitution. Since it passes the laws, the legislature sets the policies of the state on all important issues. It decides the level of spending for various services of the state. Since this is so, it also sets the level of taxation required to finance these services. The Senate must confirm many of the people nominated by the governor to fill public office. The same is true for the governor's appointees to serve on boards and commissions.

SEPARATION OF POWERS

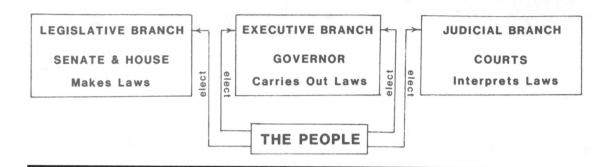

When the legislative sessions are held for voting to confirm or deny appointees, no visitors are allowed. This type of session is called an **executive session** or **closed session**. This means that the sessions are closed to all persons except the members of the Senate and certain necessary Senate personnel. This includes secretaries recording the session. (All public bodies are allowed executive or closed sessions under certain circumstances.)

Representatives and senators must be at least eighteen years old. They must have been a citizen of the state for at least two years. They must be residents of the district from which they are elected for one year before their election to office.

They are elected from single-member districts for four-year terms. Terms begin the second Monday in March. After each census the legislature must reapportion itself on a population basis. Membership in the House is based on the numbers of people being represented. Increases and decreases in population have to be taken into consideration. If the legislature does not reapportion according to changing population figures, any voter may challenge the census. A voter may petition the Supreme Court and demand that this be done. The Supreme Court may then make the reapportionment itself.

Members are paid for each day spent at legislative sessions. They are allowed mileage and monthly expense allowances. They are permitted to hire either a secretary or a legal assistant. They receive a limited amount for furnishings and equipment for their parish offices. They also receive pay to cover rent and utilities for the office.

The legislature is a part-time agency. Unlike the executive and judicial branches, the legislature meets for not more than sixty legislative days during its regular annual session. This begins the third Monday in April. The sixty-day session is held during a period of eighty-five calendar days. The twenty-five extra days included in this span are to allow the legislature a **split session**. The legislature may meet for part of the sixty-day session, take a break, and return home. This is important for the lawmakers. It allows them to return home and talk to the voters they represent. They are able to learn the voters' wishes on certain issues that must be voted on during the last part of the session. It also permits more thorough study of bills being considered.

The legislature may also meet in extra sessions. **Special sessions** or extraordinary sessions of no more than thirty days may be held. The governor or the presiding officers of both houses may call a special session. The presiding officers of the Senate and House are authorized to call these special sessions only by majority votes of each house. Special sessions are limited to subjects listed in the call for the session. Certain procedures must be followed. In the event of a public emergency the governor may call the legislature to convene without prior notice.

Veto sessions of the legislature are held automatically. During these sessions, the legislature considers bills that the governor has vetoed. Veto sessions are held forty days after the end of regular or special sessions. There is one exception. The majority of the members of either house may declare in a written statement that a veto session is not required.

The legislature functions through **standing committees**. There is a standing committee for each major area of concern. Rules of each house fix the number and size of these committees. The committees study a problem and report to their legislative bodies. They include their recommendations for action. The presiding officer of each legislative branch appoints members to the committees. The fate of a bill is often decided by the committee. For this reason there is much competition among legislators to be named to these very influential committees. Usually a senator serves on no more than three committees. A representative serves on no more than two.

Each legislative branch elects its own presiding officer. The president of the senate and the speaker of the house are both very important positions. Both houses elect other officers also. Floor leaders are chosen by the governor to promote legislation he wishes to be passed and to represent

THE COMMITTEE SYSTEM OF THE LEGISLATURE

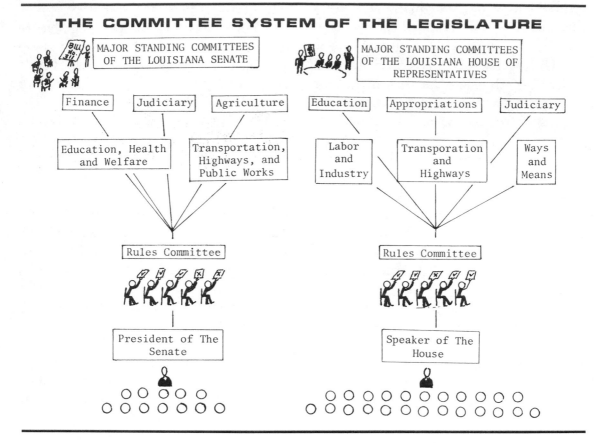

his views.

While in regular session, only legislators may speak before the legislature. Only in joint sessions are visitors occasionally invited to speak. The legislature receives written reports and hears from the governor during joint sessions.

Proceedings of the legislature are carefully recorded. There are two chief records of legislative action. One is the **legislative calendar**. Another is the **legislative journal**. It is published daily during sessions. The journal describes in detail the proceedings of each day but is not a word-for-word account. It omits debates or assignments. The calendar is printed weekly during the regular sessions. It is a record of the title and number of each bill or resolution. It contains the name of the author of each. There is an outline of all legislative action taken from the beginning of the session until the date of the calendar. The official newspaper of the state prints the acts and constitutional amendments. After a session the calendar, acts, and journal are available in bound volumes.

A number of legislative agencies contribute to the work of the lawmakers. The **Legislative Council** was established in 1952 to assist lawmakers with research. The council provides clerical assistance to the legislators in drafting bills and resolutions. The Office of the Legislative Auditor has the important concern of the state's fiscal, or financial, affairs. It studies the budget, revenues, and expenses. It advises the legislature on financial issues. The **Legislative Fiscal Office** and **Legislative Budgetary Control Council** are other important agencies assisting the legislature. The **Louisiana State Law Institute** aids in revising statutes and in amending the constitution.

To be considered for passage each bill or joint resolution must be introduced by a member of the legislature. Each bill must meet the requirements of the United States and Louisiana constitutions. Some bills require a two-thirds vote and some three-fourths to pass. A bill must be delivered to the governor within three days after it passes both houses of the legislature. The governor has ten days after he receives the bill to approve or veto it.

Lobbying is the best known and most commonly used method of trying to influence the legislature. It is a part of the legislative process. There are both professional and volunteer lobbyists. Usually it is the professionals to whom people refer. These people give assistance to legislators because they are able to supply information on issues of particular concern to them. Lobbyists represent one viewpoint—the one they are paid, or volunteer, to represent. Since there are two sides to most issues, there are usually lobbyists representing both sides.

Lobbyists are required to register with the Senate at each session. They are required to reveal whom they represent and who pays them.

Citizens who wish to get their side heard often volunteer as lobbyists on special issues. Such citizen-lobbyists include teacher groups. Some represent art groups and museums. There are people representing many other groups.

Lagniappe. Louisiana is represented in the United States Congress by two senators and eight representatives. The total number of these—ten—is the number of electors Louisiana is allowed for presidential elections. The two senators are elected from the entire state. The state is divided into eight districts to elect representatives.

Judicial Branch. The judicial branch of the government is composed of many courts. Both federal and state judicial systems function in Louisiana. The federal court system deals with violations of the federal constitution and federal statutes. The state system handles violations of the state constitution and state statutes. This discussion is limited to the state system.

Each of these courts falls into a category, or type, of court. The type depends on its function and jurisdiction. Some courts handle misdemeanors. Others handle felonies. Only one, the Supreme Court, is alone in its category. It is the only court of final, or last, appeal in the state judicial system.

There are other types of courts in the state's judicial system. These are courts of appeal, district courts, juvenile and family courts, city and municipal courts, justices of the peace, and miscellaneous courts. The powers of these various courts are defined by the Louisiana Constitution. Each court handles certain types of cases.

Lagniappe. A *felony* is any crime punishable by death or hard labor. The defendant (the accused) is entitled to a trial by jury in felony cases. A *misdemeanor* is any offense other than a felony. Conviction usually carries a maximum penalty of a five-hundred-dollar fine and six months in jail. The defendant in a misdemeanor case is entitled to a trial by a judge alone. *Capital punishment* is the infliction of the death penalty for the commission of certain crimes.

The Supreme Court is headed by the chief justice. He is the member who has served longest on the Supreme Court. The court holds yearly sessions in New Orleans. It hears cases that have been heard in lower courts. These cases are said to have

LOUISIANA CONSTITUTIONS

1812 — HAD 7 BRIEF ARTICLES
1845
1852
1861
1864 — CALLED CIVIL WAR CONSTITUTIONS
1868
1879 — ENDED RECONSTRUCTION
1898 — CONTAINED GRANDFATHER CLAUSE
1913
1921 — CONTAINED OVER 225,000 WORDS REVISED OVER 50 TIMES
1974 — CONTAINS 30,000 WORDS

been "appealed to this higher court." In this way the Supreme Court acts as a court of appeal. It also has a few cases that begin with the Supreme Court itself. Decisions of the Supreme Court are final. They cannot be appealed to any other state court.

Courts of appeal have no authority to try criminal cases. A unanimous agreement by a court of appeal is essential to reverse a judgment of a district court. The court of appeals is often the highest court for civil cases.

District courts are the general trial courts. These have broad jurisdiction. They handle civil, criminal, and probate matters. There are thirty-three judicial districts. Each has its district court. New Orleans has two district courts—one civil and one criminal. The number of parishes included in a district and the number of judges for each vary.

District court judges serve as juvenile court judges in parishes without a separate juvenile court. Juvenile courts handle matters involving children. If the juvenile is fifteen years old or older and is accused of having committed a capital offense, these courts do not handle the case. Juvenile and family courts also handle cases involving action for divorce, separation, annulment, and child custody. Civil cases from juvenile courts are sent to courts of appeal.

Parish and city courts are two other types of courts in Louisiana's judicial system. There are three parish courts in the state. Every parish seat has a city court. Every ward that has over five thousand inhabitants is entitled to a city court. These city courts have authority to handle certain cases.

Mayor's courts and justices of the peace courts handle any violation of municipal ordinances. Justices of the peace courts are located mostly in wards with less than five thousand population. They are "Courts of No Record." No permanent record is kept of the proceedings of these minor courts. In courts of no record the judges may be removed by recall elections.

The Louisiana **attorney general** is the top official in the state's judicial system. **District attorneys** are elected in each judicial court district. Each of these district attorneys is in full charge of every criminal suit started or pending in his district. He determines when, whom, and how he shall prosecute. He also serves as legal advisor to the police jury.

Each parish elects a **clerk of the district court**. The clerk records court proceedings, preserves court records, and performs certain judicial functions when the judge is absent. The clerk of court has other assigned duties also.

The sheriff holds one of the most respected positions in the parish. It is his job to enforce state and parish laws and to collect state and parish taxes. He must also carry out district court rulings.

Constables are elected for each ward in the parish. The constable acts as law enforcement officer for the ward and as officer of the justice of the peace courts.

Marshals are elected officers of city courts. They act as law enforcement officers for a municipality.

Coroners are licensed physicians elected by each parish to hold inquests, order autopsies, and investigate suspicious deaths.

Lagniappe. Did you know that in the late 1800s one of Shreveport's city judges fined lawbreakers bricks instead of money? Then he put prisoners to work laying bricks for Shreveport streets.

Each parish except Orleans has a **jury commission**. It consists of the clerk of court or his deputy and four members appointed by the district judge. The jury commission is responsible for selection of juries for the two kinds of juries in Louisiana. These include **grand juries** and **petit, or trial, juries**. The jury members are selected by drawings from a jury list compiled by the commission.

The **grand jury** is a group of twelve persons who serve for six

THE GOVERNOR'S OPTIONS ON A BILL

He may sign it, and it becomes law.

He may veto it. He shall then return it to the Legislature with his veto message. This has to be done within 12 days after delivery to him if the Legislature is in session. If the Legislature adjourns, he shall return it as provided by law.

He may pocket veto. The bill becomes law if the govenor fails to sign or veto it within 10 days after delivery to him, if the Legislature is in session. It must be returned within 20 days after delivery to him, if the Legislature is not in session.

months. It is their duty to investigate all crimes punishable by death, election frauds, charges against public officials, conditions in private prisons, and other causes for public concern. **Petit, or trial, juries** are divided into those for the trial of civil cases and those for the trial of criminal cases. Petit, or trial, juries hear cases and issue verdicts.

Lagniappe. A Louisianian, Edward Douglass White, served as chief justice of the United States Supreme Court from 1910 to 1921. He was the son of a former governor of the state.

En Partie 1 (Studying a Part). 1. Where is Louisiana's capital? 2. (a) What is Louisiana's supreme law? (b) When was it written? 3. (a) Compare civil with common law. (b) Which does Louisiana use? 4. What are the three branches of our state government? What is the duty of each branch? 5. Explain the system of checks and balances. 6. Who heads the executive branch? 7. List the other executive officials. 8. (a) What are the duties of each of the executive officials? (b) What are the qualifications of each? 9. What is the term of office of members of the executive branch? 10. What are the duties of the legislature? 11. What are the two houses of the legislature? 12. (a) What are the qualifications of members of the legislature? (b) What is their term of office? 13. What is the procedure for passing a bill? 14. What is lobbying? 15. What makes up our judicial system? 16. What is the rank from bottom to top of Louisiana's courts? 17. Which courts handle cases concerning federal constitutional questions? 18. What is the difference between a grand jury and a petit jury?

Finances

Taxes are the major source of the money the state spends. The state also obtains money from licenses, fees, state land leases, oil royalties, and federal funds. Parish revenues are obtained from local taxes, court fines, leases and royalties on parish-owned lands, and state funds. The Louisiana Constitution or statutory law sets limits on parish tax levies, court fines, and parking and license fees. Revenues from some sources are dedicated to specific purposes and to a particular branch of government.

Louisiana has different kinds of taxes. They include sales, severance, income, petroleum products, beverage, tobacco, corporation franchise, property, gasoline, and a number of minor taxes.

Over seventy percent of the state's total expenditures pay for three services. These are education, health and welfare, and highways. These same three services also receive over seventy percent of all federal grants to the state.

The state legislature decides how the state's money is spent. Each fiscal (financial) year, a balanced operating budget for the state must be prepared. The budget must show the estimated funds that will be available. Also, plans for spending these funds must be shown. The state often uses bond sales as a means of borrowing money to meet the major costs that cannot be met out of current state revenues. The state usually issues bonds for permanent improvements. This includes public buildings and state highways. A vote of two-thirds of each house is necessary to authorize bond issues.

En Partie 2 (Studying a Part). 1. What are Louisiana's main sources of money? 2. Who determines how this money will be spent? 3. What are the state's main expenditures?

Lagniappe. Americans in fiscal 1983 paid an average of $1,216 in taxes to state and local governments. In Louisiana the average was $1,051. Each Louisiana resident owed $2,650 as a result of state and local debts. That debt, which did not include interest, was thirty-six percent higher than the national average that year.

Local Government

Local government includes parishes, municipalities, and special districts. Louisiana has three classes of municipalities. They are **villages** (population between 150 and 999), **towns** (population between 1,000 and 4,999), and **cities** (population over 5,000). Parishes and municipalities are allowed to exercise any power and perform any function necessary and proper in the management of their affairs. They have all powers except those prohibited by the Louisiana Constitution or state laws.

Parishes are divided into **wards**. Wards are divided into **precincts**.

The power of local political units to govern themselves is called **home rule**. The voters in a parish determine what form of government shall be used. Voters may decide to change the existing form. This they do by forming a parish charter commission. Ten percent of the voters (or ten thousand—whichever is fewer) petition the parish governing body to form such a commission. The commission has for its goal the study of a new plan of government for the parish. After the plan is presented, voters must decide by majority vote whether they prefer the new form.

Most parishes have the **police jury** form of government. Members of the body are elected for four-year terms. They represent districts in the parish. Police jurors are paid a monthly salary. Some receive travel expenses.

To qualify as a police juror, the citizen must be a registered voter and resident of the district he wishes to represent. If a vacancy occurs, the remaining members of the police jury select a replacement. This individual serves only until an election can be held.

Other parishes have home-rule charters. They are developed and approved by the people in the parish. A home-rule charter is a parish constitution. It usually provides for a legislative and executive branch of parish government. A few parishes, usually the largest metropolitan parishes, use this system. It is a commission form of some type. This form resembles the jury system except the number of individuals serving on the commission is smaller. In some cases each commissioner heads a department of government.

The **municipalities** operate under several different types of charters and forms of government. They have the right to draft and adopt their own charters unless the population is less than 2,500. The **mayor-alderman** type government is the plan these small towns must follow. Almost all of the cities in the state have the **mayor-council** form of government. Some use the **commission** form. The voters elect the officials who have terms of varying lengths. Each commissioner is head of a separate department. The commissioners act as a body to determine policy. Another form is the **council-manager plan**.

The school board administers the local school system. Members are elected for six overlapping terms. The local system is supervised by the state board of education. These systems are organized on a parish basis except for Monroe and Bogalusa. Members of the local school board are elected by the voters according to seats allowed on the basis of population. The board, with approval of the voters, levies property taxes. These taxes support the school system. The board appoints the local superintendent, makes contracts, and issues bonds. The parish school board orders and maintains public school buildings in the parish. It manages school lands. It also approves public school teachers, supervisors, and all other parish school personnel. It carries out the laws pertaining to schools passed by the State Board of Education and such local laws as are made by the parish school board itself. The school board also determines the number of schools. It creates, consolidates, or abolishes school districts. It prepares an annual budget that must be approved by the state school budget committee.

Louisiana has **special districts** created to perform certain services that existing government units are unwilling or unable to administer. The powers of these districts are limited to a specific purpose or purposes. The most common special districts are the drainage, sewerage, road, fire, levee, garbage, and school districts.

En Partie 3 (Studying a Part). 1. What are the units of local government? 2. Who determines the form of government for a parish? 3. What is the police jury? 4. What is home rule? 5. What is the population range of (a) a village, (b) a town, and (c) a city? 6. Who administers the educational system?

Citizens' Participation

Registration and Voting. The Louisiana Constitution provides for the permanent registration of voters. It provides for the secret ballot and for the conduct of all elections.

To register to vote a person must appear before the parish registrar of voters. The registrar of voters is located in the parish seat. The voter must prove his identity. When the registrar secures the needed information, the voter's name is placed on the official list of voters. Only United States service personnel are permitted to register by mail. Failure to vote at least once during a four-year period cancels the registration of a voter. In Orleans Parish the voter is disqualified after only two years of failing to vote.

To be eligible to vote, a person must be at least eighteen years of age. He or she must be a citizen of the United States. The person must be a bona fide resident of the state, parish, municipality, and precinct in which he is registered as a voter. Louisianians are required to live in the state thirty days before they may register. This requirement is the same as the residence requirement for voting in the national presidential elections.

The right to vote is not given to prisoners in penitentiaries. Nor is it given to those declared mentally incompetent. Persons under an order for imprisonment for conviction of a felony or indicted do not have the right to vote. Deserters from military service or persons dishonorably discharged from the service may not vote.

Political Parties. There are requirements by Louisiana law for political parties. Parties nominate slates

Let your vote count for a better Louisiana.

of officers for election through their organizations.

Elections. Louisianians vote between 6:00 A.M. and 8:00 P.M. They vote in primary, general, special, property, and bond elections. Voting machines are provided at polling places in geographical precincts as drawn by ordinance by the parish governing authority.

Commissioners open and close polls. They determine whether voters are qualified. They keep order in the polling places. They maintain and complete election forms. They also record the vote as shown on machines and announce election results in their precincts.

Citizens make a statement at the polls. Their voting reflects their values. Through the years Louisianians have developed a reputation for not taking their part in government seriously. The more the citizens bear the cost of government through taxes the more likely they are to take an active part. They are then likely to make their wishes known. They will then demand efficiency and honesty from the officials they elected. It is up to the people to decide through their votes what Louisiana is and will become.

THE STATE SEAL

En Partie 4 (Studying a Part). 1. What are the qualifications for voting? 2. Who cannot vote? 3. (a) How do you register? (b) How often? (c) Where? 4. When and where do you vote? 5. Why should you vote?

Coup d'Main
(Completing the Story)

Jambalaya (Putting It All Together)

1. What is there about Louisiana's government that sets it apart from that of other states?

2. Define:

    a. Capital Punishment
    b. Checks and Balances
    c. Civil Law
    d. Common Law
    e. Executive Assistants
    f. Executive Branch
    g. Executive Sessions
    h. Felony
    i. Joint Sessions
    j. Judicial Branch
    k. Legislative Branch
    l. Legislative Calendar
    m. Legislative Council
    n. Legislative Journal
    o. Misdemeanor
    p. Municipalities
    q. Political Parties
    r. Polls
    s. Precincts
    t. Registrar
    u. Severance Tax
    v. Special Sessions
    w. Split Sessions
    x. Standing Committee

3. Describe the form of government used in (a) your parish and (b) your village, town, or city.

4. Who are your parish officials?

5. Name Louisiana's United States senators and United States representatives. (b) Which ones represent you? (c) Name the state senators and representatives who represent you.

6. Give your location: (a) state senatorial district, (b) state representative district, (c) United States senatorial district, (d) United States representative district, (e) your ward, (f) your precinct, and (f) your voting station.

7. How many electors does this state have?

Potpourri (Getting Involved)

1. Reenact (a) the Constitutional Convention of 1973, (b) a town meeting in which a proposed law is being debated, (c) a session of the legislature, or (d) the passage of a bill.

2. Compare (a) the government of Louisiana with that of another state or (b) the civil service system with the spoils system.

3. Trace (a) the constitutional changes that have taken place in Louisiana, (b) the forces that have changed Louisiana's political structure throughout its history, (c) steps the government has taken in response to crises that reflect the traditions, customs,

and values of the state, or (d) political pressures that have influenced major decisions made by the state's leaders.

4. Evaluate the role of specific government leaders. Relate the leadership to the progress of the state.

5. Report on the relationship of state, parish, and city governments.

Gumbo (Bringing It Up-to-Date)

1. Report on how and when Louisianians vote.

2. Report on ways that citizens may (a) voice disagreement about our government, (b) communicate with state leaders, and (c) lobby.

3. Study some controversial laws of Louisiana such as forced heirship or blue laws. Report your findings to the class.

4. Investigate salaries and special privileges or benefits of current government officials. Compare these with those of private businesses and those of government officials in other states.

5. Research juvenile law enforcement.

State Symbols

The following have been designated as official state symbols by legislative action:

State flower: magnolia
State bird: brown pelican
State tree: bald cypress
State fossil: petrified palmwood
State gemstone: agate
State insect: honeybee
State dog: Louisiana Catahoula Leopard dog
State crustacean: crawfish
State reptile: alligator
State drink: milk
State fruit: tomato (1986)
           cantaloupe (1987)
State colors: blue, white, and gold
State songs: *Give Me Louisiana,* by Doralice Fontane
        You Are My Sunshine, by Jimmie H. Davis and Charles Mitchell
        Song of Louisiana, by Vashti Robertson Stopher
State march song: *Louisiana My Home Sweet Home,* by Sammie McKenzie, Lou Levoy, and Castro Carazo

APPENDIX

List of Maps

Governors of Louisiana

FRENCH LOUISIANA

Pierre le Moyne, sieur d'Iberville	1699
sieur de Sauvole (died in office)	1699-1701
Jean Baptiste Le Moyne, sieur de Bienville	1701-1713
Antoine de la Mothe Cadillac	1713-1716
Jean Baptiste le Moyne, sieur de Bienville	1716-1717
Jean Michiele Seigneur de Lepinay	1717-1718
Jean Baptiste le Moyne, sieur de Bienville	1718-1724
Pierre Dugue, sieur de Boisbriant	1724-1725
Etienne Périer	1725-1733
Jean Baptiste le Moyne, sieur de Bienville	1733-1743
Pierre François de Rigaud, Marquis de Vaudreuil	1743-1753
Louis Billouart, Chevalier de Kerlerec	1753-1763
Jean Jacques d'Abbadie (died in office)	1763-1765
Charles Philippe Aubry	1765-1769

SPANISH LOUISIANA

Antonio de Ulloa	1766-1768
Don Alejandro O'Reilly	1768-1769
Don Luis de Unzaga	1769-1777
Don Bernardo de Gálvez	1777-1785

Don Estevan Miro 1785-1791
François Luis Hector, Baron de Carondelet 1791-1797
Don Manuel Gayoso de Lemos (died in office) 1797-1799
Don Francisco Bouligny 1799
Sebastian, Marquis de Casa Calvo 1799-1801
Juan Manuel de Salcedo 1801-1803

TRANSITIONAL PERIOD

Pierre Clement de Laussat (November 30-December 20) 1803

TERRITORY OF LOUISIANA

W. C. C. Claiborne 1803-1812

STATE OF LOUISIANA

W. C. C. Claiborne 1812-1816
Jacques Villeré 1816-1820
Thomas Bolling Robertson (resigned) 1820-1824
Henry S. Thibodeaux (succeeded as president of the senate) 1824
Henry Johnson 1824-1828
Pierre Derbigny (died in office) 1828-1829
Armand Beauvais (succeeded as president of the senate)............... 1829-1830
Jacques Dupre 1830-1831
Andre Bienvenu Roman 1831-1835
Edward Douglass White 1835-1839
Andre Bienvenu Roman 1839-1843
Alexandre Mouton 1843-1846
Isaac Johnson 1846-1850
Joseph Walker 1850-1853
Paul O. Hebert 1853-1856
Robert Charles Wickliffe 1856-1860
Thomas Overton Moore 1860-1864
Gen. G. F. Shepley (military governor) 1862-1864
Henry Watkins Allen (under Confederate government).................... 1864-1865
Michael Hahn (under Federal government--resigned) 1864-1865
James Madison Wells (succeeded as president of senate)............... 1865-1867
Benjamin Flanders (under military authority) 1867-1868
Joshua Baker (under military authority) 1868
Henry Clay Warmoth... 1868-1872
P. B. S. Pinchback (lieutenant governor, acting governor) 1872-1873
John McEnery (elected, but ruled out) 1873
William Pitt Kellogg (governor de facto) 1873-1877
Francis T. Nicholls... 1877-1880
Louis Alfred Wiltz (died in office)... 1880-1881
Samuel Douglas McEnery (succeeded as lieutenant governor)........ 1881-1884
Samuel Douglas McEnery 1884-1888

Francis T. Nicholls 1888-1892
Murphy James Foster 1892-1900
William Wright Heard 1900-1904
Newton Crain Blanchard 1904-1908
Jared Young Sanders 1908-1912
Luther Egbert Hall 1912-1916
Ruffin G. Pleasant 1916-1920
John M. Parker 1920-1924
Henry L. Fuqua (died in office) 1924-1926
Oramel H. Simpson (succeeded as lieutenant governor) 1926-1928
Huey P. Long (qualified for U.S. Senator, 1932) 1928-1932
Alvin O. King (succeeded as president of the senate) 1932
Oscar K. Allen (died in office) 1932-1936
James A. Noe (succeeded as lieutenant governor) 1936
Richard W. Leche (resigned) 1936-1939
Earl K. Long (succeeded as lieutenant governor) 1939-1940
Sam H. Jones 1940-1944
Jimmie H. Davis 1944-1948
Earl K. Long 1948-1952
Robert F. Kennon 1952-1956
Earl K. Long 1956-1960
Jimmie H. Davis 1960-1964
John J. McKeithen 1964-1972
Edwin W. Edwards 1972-1980
David Treen 1980-1984
Edwin W. Edwards 1984-

Louisiana Parishes
(Showing date parish created and parish seat)

Acadia (1886) ....Crowley
Allen (1912) ....Oberlin
Ascension (1807) ....Donaldsonville
Assumption (1807) ....Napoleonville
Avoyelles (1807) ....Marksville
Beauregard (1912) ....DeRidder
Bienville (1848) ....Arcadia
Bossier (1843)..............................Benton
Caddo (1838) ....Shreveport
Calcasieu (1840) ....Lake Charles
Caldwell (1838) ....Columbia
Cameron (1870) ....Cameron
Catahoula (1808) ....Harrisonburg

Claiborne (1828)............................Homer
Concordia (1807) ....Vidalia
DeSoto (1843) ....Mansfield
East Baton Rouge (1810) ......Baton Rouge
East Carroll (1877)............Lake Providence
East Feliciana (1824) ....Clinton
Evangeline (1910) ....Ville Platte
Franklin (1843)........................Winnsboro
Grant (1869) ....Colfax
Iberia (1868) ....New Iberia
Iberville (1807) ....Plaquemine
Jackson (1845) ....Jonesboro
Jefferson (1825)..............................Gretna

Jefferson Davis (1912) ....Jennings
Lafayette (1823) ....Lafayette
Lafourche (1807) ....Thibodaux
LaSalle (1908) ....Jena
Lincoln (1873) ....Ruston
Livingston (1832) ....Livingston
Madison (1838)..........................Tallulah
Morehouse (1844) ....Bastrop
Natchitoches (1807) ....Natchitoches
Orleans (1807) ....New Orleans
Ouachita (1807)...............................Monroe
Plaquemines (1807)........Pointe-a-la-Hache
Pointe Coupee (1807) ....New Roads
Rapides (1807) ....Alexandria
Red River (1871) ....Coushatta
Richland (1868) ....Rayville
Sabine (1843) ....Many
St. Bernard (1807) ....Chalmette
St. Charles (1807) ....Hahnville

St. Helena (1810) ....Greensburg
St. James (1807)...........................Convent
St. John the Baptist (1807)...........Edgard
St. Landry (1807) ....Opelousas
St. Martin (1807).............St. Martinville
St. Mary (1811) ....Franklin
St. Tammany (1810) ....Covington
Tangipahoa (1869) ....Amite
Tensas (1843)............................St. Joseph
Terrebonne (1822) ....Houma
Union (1839) ....Farmerville
Vermilion (1844) ....Abbeville
Vernon (1871)...............................Leesville
Washington (1819) ....Franklinton
Webster (1871) ....Minden
West Baton Rouge (1807) ....Port Allen
West Carroll (1877) ....Oak Grove
West Feliciana (1824) ....St. Francisville
Winn (1852) ....Winnfield

Glossary

Acadian. One who came from or a descendant of one who came from Acadia (Nova Scotia) when exiled by the British; an adjective used to describe the culture of the Acadians, such as an Acadian house.

Acadiana. A twenty-two-parish area officially named by an act of the Louisiana Legislature.

Acadian Coast. Land along the Mississippi River north of New Orleans where many of the Acadians settled. It is the center of French Acadians' initial settlements (St. James and Ascension parishes).

Acadian Country. A distinct culture area influenced primarily by the French.

Algiers. A city across the Mississippi River from New Orleans, noted for its shipyard.

Anglo-Saxon. A person of English or Scotch-Irish descent who settled in the New World.

Anglo-Saxon Country. The part of Louisiana not included in Acadiana.

Ark-La-Tex. A circular area including parts of Arkansas, Louisiana, and Texas located near the point where the borders of these three states meet.

Arpent. An old French measure of land, less than an acre, 605 arpents being equivalent to 512 acres; a lineal measure, roughly equal to 192 feet.

Avoyelles Prairie. Relatively high plateau in Avoyelles Parish.

Backland. The land between the frontlands and swamplands.

Backswamp. Flat, wet area in the floodplain beyond the natural levees.

Banquette. A sidewalk.

Bar. A shoal area or area of deposition where material is being deposited from water; a sandbar.

Barataria. Inlet of the Gulf of Mexico on the boundary between Jefferson and Plaquemines parishes; a bay, bayou, and village.

Barrier beach. Beach ridge pushed up against the land.

Barrier island. Beach ridge separated from shore by open water.

Batture. That part of the inner shore of a stream which has been thrown up by the action of the current and which, at certain seasons of the year, may be covered as a whole or in part by the water.

Bayou. A sluggish stream through lowlands; a term used mainly in the lower Mississippi Basin and the Gulf coast region.

Big House. The residence of the planter and his family and the business center of the plantation operation.

Birdfoot delta. A triangular area at the mouth of a river through which several river outlets pass. The outlets fan out in different angles to form a pattern resembling the footprint of a bird.

Blue Laws. Extremely strict laws regulating personal behavior.

Blufflands. Areas of considerable relief generally bordering the alluvial valley.

Bottomlands. Lowlands near stream beds.

Bousillage. A mixture of grass and clay used to fill the spaces between the posts of a French cabin; a French shotgun house.

Brackish. Salty water.

Brake. A wooded swamp; a thicket.

Briquete entre poteaux. Bricks placed between posts of a French cabin.

Cajun. A Louisianian of Acadian descent.

Calinda. An African dance.

Cane River Country. A stretch of land along Cane River Lake, the old channel of Red River.

Capital. Accumulated wealth used to produce additonal wealth.

Channel. The deepest part of a river, harbor, or strait which affords the best passage.

Chenier. Sand ridges covered with growing oaks. **Cheniere.** An -e- is added when used as a place name.

Chert. A type of flint, common in gravel beds of North Louisiana, used by Indians for making tools.

Claypan. A shallow layer of impervious clay underlying the topsoil.

Coastline. A line along the coast following generally the path of the shoreline but not including every irregularity.

Contour plowing. The practice of plowing on a slope along points of equal elevation rather than up and down the slope.

Coureurs de bois. Early French settlers who hunted and trapped alone in the deep forests of North America, often following Indians' ways of life.

Creoles. A white descendant of the French or Spanish settlers in Louisiana during the colonial period. See text page 75.

Crevasse. Point where a river breaks out of its levee.

Crop acreage. Acres of land planted in a crop.

Crop rotation. The practice of changing crop types on a piece of land on a yearly or longer basis so as to restore the soil.

Culture. Learned patterns of thinking and living that have been passed from generation to generation among a people; the characteristic features of a particular group.

Cutoff. A shortening of a river's course caused by water cutting across a loop, or meander, of the river. An ox-bow lake is often formed in this manner.

Cutover land. Land that has been cleared of trees.

Defoliating agent. A chemical used to make leaves drop off plants.

Delta. A deposit of sediment at the mouth of a river where water flow is slower.

Deltaic lakes. See lagoonal lake.

Depression. A period of decreased economic activity.

Distributary. A river branch flowing from the main stream in a directon away from the stream.

Dixiecrat. A member of the State Rights Party which was formed in 1948 in opposition to the civil rights plank in the Democratic platform.

Dogtrot house. One building in two separate parts joined by a covered passageway.

Drought. Prolonged dry weather which affects the earth's surface and prevents the growth of plants.

Elevation. The height above sea level.

Erosion. The wearing away of rocks and soil caused by water, ice, wind and other natural forces.

Estuary. An arm of the sea that extends inland to meet the mouth of a river.

Fais-do-do. "Go to sleep"; a dance of the Acadian country; a country or village dance usually held on Saturday nights.

Farm. An agricultural operation carried on by members of a family and/or hired day labor.

Filé. A powder made from sassafras leaves and used to season food.

First bottom. Permanent swamps.

Five Islands. Jefferson, Weeks, Avery, Belle, and Côte Blanche; salt domes around Vermilion Bay.

Flatwoods. Flat, timbered lands.

Fleur de lis. Lily flower used on the French flag.

Floating land. The top layer of certain marshland or swampland that floats on water beneath it. Because of its instability, floating land quivers when walked upon.

Floodplain. The floor of a valley over which a river spreads sediment when it overflows its banks.

Florida parishes. The parishes in Louisiana that were once a part of Florida.

Frasch process. A process of mining sulphur by pumping superheated water into the sulphur bed which melts and is forced in molten form to the surface.

French Louisiana. Acadiana.

Frontland. Land on the side of the natural levee, sloping away from the river or stream.

Geologic age. The age of natural features of the earth described by reference to past periods of time, always of great length.

German Coast. An area settled by Germans in about 1720. (St. Charles and St. John the Baptist parishes).

Grasslands. Lands where grass is the chief kind of native vegetation.

Great Raft. A great logjam in Red River.

Gris-gris. An object worn as a protective charm against evil, or used for the purpose of inflicting injury; to voodoo, bewitch, or cast a spell over.

Gristmill. A mill that grinds grain, especially corn.

Growing season. The time between the last killing frost in the spring and the first killing frost in the fall; the part of the year with warm enough days and nights for plants to grow.

Gumbo. Dialects of Central Africa, probably Negro; any thick soup in which okra is an ingredient.

Gumbo clay. A sticky, clayey soil found in many low regions of Louisiana, especially in northeast Louisiana.

Gumbo-ya-ya. A get together where people meet just to talk.

Hardpan. A layer of soil made up of clay particles, minerals, and organic matter which clog the pores of the soil and make it water resistant.

Hill Country. Usually refers to North Louisiana uplands.

Impressment. To force into public service, especially the British practice of forcing American seamen to serve in the royal navy.

Indentured servant. A person who is bound by contract as servant of another for a designated time and under specified conditions.

Indigo. Plant first grown in Louisiana under Crozat as a money crop, used for making a blue dye; a deep violet blue.

Isle of Orleans. Not an island. The land that makes up the Isle of Orleans is bounded on its west, southwest, and south by the Mississippi River; on its southeast and east by the Gulf of Mexico; and on its north by Lakes Maurepas, Pontchartrain, Borgne, and the Iberville River (Bayou Manchac). See text page 180.

Jambalaya. A Spanish-Creole dish made with rice and some other important ingredient, such as ham, shrimp, crabmeat, sausage, or chicken.

Jetties. Manmade structures extending into the sea to influence currents and/or protect a harbor; mats placed along levees to protect the levees from washing during periods of high water.

Joie de vivre. Joy of living.

Lafourche. A bayou in South Louisiana known as "the longest street in the world" as there have been homes along the bayou banks for two-hundred years.

Lagoonal lake. Lake formed by wave action beating openings into shorelines, or by sinking of the land. Coastal lakes are formed behind cheniers or natural levees.

Lamb's quarter. A weed.

Landform. The kind of land such as plains, plateaus, hills, and mountains.

Lagniappe. Something thrown in for good measure; something extra.

Laissez les bons temps rouler (lay-zay lay bawn tawn roolay). "Let the good times roll," the motto of many Louisianians.

Les Rapides. Village on Red River, present-day Pineville.

Line settlement. Houses closely spaced along a road.

Livre. Old French money equivalent to twenty cents in American money.

Locks. An enclosure placed in streams with a gate at each end, used to raise or lower boats as they navigate the stream.

Lowlands. Scene of river activity--floodplain, delta, cheniers, and coastal marshes.

Mardi Gras. Fat Tuesday; Shrove Tuesday. The last day before Lent is celebrated in New Orleans. Carnival season is from Twelfth night to Shrove Tuesday.

Marsh. An area of flat treeless plains dotted with shallow lakes and lagoons. It is often flooded.

Marshgrass. Thick grass that grows in marshlands.

Marshland. Grass-covered land of low elevation which is almost always wet and is void of trees.

Meander. A winding or large curve of a river valley; a winding course; to turn and glide to and fro as a river; one of the loops formed by a river as it cuts its course over the earth's surface. This feature is found in old stream beds.

Migratory birds. Birds that move from one region or climate to another. They usually move south in the winter and north in the summer.

Mortar. A strong vessel used to grind up various products such as grain. Indians usually made them of stone or wood.

Mudlumps. Mounds of clay extending above the surface of the water at the mouths of passes of the Mississippi River.

Mulatto. One who has mixed Negro and Caucasian ancestry.

Natural levees. Ridges along main river channels and its distributaries; the natural outlets.

Natural region. An area within which all of the natural elements or qualities are the same.

Naval stores. Products such as turpentine or pitch, originally used to calk the seams of wooden ships.

Navigable. Having features that allow passage of boats or ships.

North Louisiana. Geographically, that part of the state above the 31st parallel. Culturally, North Louisiana is identified as that part of the state in which is found Anglo-Saxon Protestant (WASP) culture. This same culture exists in geographical South Louisiana.

Oxbow. A u-shaped bend in a river; a lake, usually crescent in shape, formed when the meanders of the river were cut off by the action of the stream; also called horseshoe lakes.

Palmetto. Any of various fan palms grown in southern United States.

Peach Country. Area around Ruston.

Perique. A unique, strong-flavored tobacco grown in St. James Parish.

Pestle. Cut and shaped implement used with a mortar to grind grain. Louisiana Indians made them of wood or stone.

Pimple mounds. Small elevated mounds scattered throughout Louisiana. Their origin is unknown.

Pirogue. A type of canoe used in Louisiana. It was originally made of a single log.

Pitch. A resin found in certain evergreen trees; a black, sticky substance found in the distillation of coal tar, wood tar, petroleum, etc. and used for waterproofing, roofing, pavement, etc.

Plantation. A lifestyle involving armies of cheap, abundant labor to raise staple crops. The U. S. census defined a plantation as a farm operation involving a certain number of slaves, usually twenty. This idea is incorrect. From 1870 to 1910, the census did not recognize that there were plantations.

Plantation system. An interlocking system of controls by which southern planters were able to dominate all political, educational, and social institutions.

Planter. The final authority on a plantation which involved not only farming operations but also often included small manufacturing operations and a commisary, or store.

Pleistocene. An epoch in the geologic time scale. It began about 1 million years ago and was marked by glaciation and continental ice sheets.

Pot likker. The juice or stock from greens, usually mustard.

Prairie. Generally, a relatively flat area of tall grasslands in the west-southwest.

Praline. A type of confection made in Louisiana of sugar paste and nut meats.

Raft lakes. Water impounded in parts of the main tributary valleys of Red River, commonly attributed to the Great Raft.

Rapids. Part of a river where water moves swiftly as it descends to a lower level, passing over rocks or other obstructions thereby creating turbulence and sounds usually audible for a considerable distance.

Real. Spanish silver coin valued at ten sols (1 sol = 1 penny); worth approximately twelve and one-half cents and at one time widely used in North American colonies where it was referred to as a "bit".

Recent. The period in geologic time from the end of the last continental glaciation (18,000 years ago) to the present.

Redneck. A term of affection applied generally to members of the North Louisiana cultural group. The name was given to the farmer who sunburned the back of his neck while plowing. In recent times, the term has been given unfavorable meanings which conflict with the original meaning.

Relief. The difference in elevation between the high and low points of a land surface. Relief features are surface outlines of the land, such as plains, mountains, etc.

Rice Country. Rice-producing area of southwest Louisiana. Crowley is the unofficial "Rice Capital."

Ridge. A long and narrow elevation of land or a range of hills or mountains.

Rigolets. The name of the strait that connects Lake Borgne and Lake Pontchartrain.

Rigolet de Bon Dieu. An arm of Red River that extends from a point about two miles below Grand Ecore to Colfax, where it again unites with the Red.

Riverbed. The bottom of a river.

Roux. A basic brown sauce.

Sagamite. Hominy or porridge of coarse corn made by the early Indians of Louisiana.

Salt dome. A place where salt has pushed up through overlaying earth materials into a rounded peak.

Salt islands, or land islands. Elevated domes in the marshy areas of South Louisiana. They were formed by salt plugs being thrust upward.

Sassafras. The dried root bark of a number of related trees of the laurel family, used in medicine and for flavoring.

Sediment. Particles deposited by flowing water, wind, or ice.

Selective cutting. The practice of cutting mature trees and also some young trees when they have grown too thickly.

Silt. Fine clay particles deposited by water.

Shoreline. The line where the water of the Gulf meets the land.

Shotgun house. Type of architecture; characterized by all rooms being arranged in a straight line.

Shrove Tuesday. The Tuesday before Ash Wednesday, a day of penitence and confession immediately preceding Lent.

South Louisiana. Geographically, that part of Louisiana below the 31st parallel. Culturally, South Louisiana is mostly identified with Acadiana. Cultural pockets of a similar nature exist all over the state.

Spillway. Emergency outlet for river waters at floodstage.

Strawberry Country. Area around Hammond.

Sugarcane Country. An eighteen-parish area in the south-central part of the state below the thirty-first parallel.

Swamp, or swampland. Low, wet forested area.

Syndics. Spanish name for justices of the peace.

Tafia. An alcoholic drink made from boiled-down cane juice.

Teche Country. The land along Bayou Teche.

Terrace. A level narrow plain with steep front bordering a river, lake or sea.

Topography. A description of the surface features of a particular region; the configuration of the natural and artificial features of a particular region, including such things as mountains, rivers, cities, etc.

Tributary. River flowing into a main river and contributing water to the largest river.

Truck farm. A farm where many vegetables are raised.

Uplands. Hill lands; hills.

Vacheries. Stock farms.

Versailles. City near Paris, France; site of the magnificent palace which cost 150 million francs; King Louis XV lived lavishly there.

WASPS. White Anglo-Saxon Protestants.

Watershed. A dividing ridge between drainage areas; a region or area drained by a river or lake.

Wattle and daub. A method of building whereby a wattle, or frame, of poles and interwoven twig is covered with mud or plaster.

Weathering. The breaking of rocks into smaller pieces by actions of freezing, heating, and cooling, tramping of animals, or the movement or changing of soil by man.

Wold. A region of older, dense, uplifted material.

Wetlands. Low areas characterized by wetness of soil and abundant rainfall.

Yam Country. Area with Opelousas as the "Yam Capital."

Pronunciation Guide

This guide includes names and other words that may be unfamiliar or difficult to pronounce. You will encounter these words in your study of the text. They are often of French, Indian, or Spanish origin and do not follow the rules for pronouncing English words. Experts in French, Indian, and Spanish were consulted to determine the pronunciations used for this guide. There are other acceptable pronunciations which have not been included. Only the hard-to-pronounce parts of a name are included. Words that can be found in a standard dictionary are excluded. Accented syllables are capitalized. The following phonetic symbols have been used: āge, at, fäther, bē, let, īce, it, gō, not, ôrder, oil, fŏŏt, boot, out, fūme, but, rüle, measure (zh). A schwa (ə) represents the a in <u>about</u>, e as in <u>taken</u>, i as in <u>pencil</u>, o as in <u>lemon</u>, and u as in <u>circus</u>.

Acadia (ə KĀ dē ə)
Acolapissas (ak ə la PI səs)
Adai (Ā dī)
Alejandro (ə lā HÄN drō)
Alexandria (el eg ZAN dri ə)
Algonquin (al GON kwin)
Almonester (al mō NES ter)
Andres (ähn DREZ)
Antoine (ÄHN twähn)
Antonio (an TÔ nē ō)
Arceneaux (ÄR cə nō)
Armesto (ar MES tō)
Arriola (är rē Ō lə)
Arroyo Hondo (är RŌ yō ŌN dō)
Ascension (ə SIN shun)
Assinais (as si NĀ us)
Assumption (ə SUMP shun)
Atakapa (ə TAK ə paw)
Atchafalaya (ə CHAF ə lī ə)

Atlatl (AT əl)
Aubry (Ō bry)
Avery (Ā ver ē)
Avoyelles (ə VOI yelz)

Badine (BÄ dēn)
Balize (bā LĒEZ)
Banquette (ban KET)
Baptiste (bap TĒEST)
Barbé al espagnole (BÄR bā äl es pä NYŌL)
Barbé-Marbois (BÄR bā mär BWÄH)

Bastille (bas TĒL)
Bautista (bə TĒES tə)
Bayou (BY you) (BY yō)
Bayougoula (bə yoo GOO lə)
Beaujeu (BŌ zhə)
Beaujolais (bō jə LÄ)
Beauregard (BŌ rē gärd)
Bernardo (ber NAR dō)
Biche (beesh)
Bienville (bi EN vil)
Biloxi (bi LUK si)
Bistineau (BIS tə nō)
Blanche (blanch)
Blanque (blänk)
Boeuf (bef North Louisiana) (buf South Louisiana)
Bogalusa (bō gə LOO sə)
Boisblanc (BWÄ blän)
Boisbriant (BWÄ brē änt)
Boisrenaud (BWA rə no)
Bonnet Carre (BON nāy käh RĀY)
Boré (bō RĀ)
Borgne (born)
Bossier (BŌ zher)
Boucheries (BOO shə rē)
Boulaye (BOO lā)
Bouligny (boo lēg NĒ)
Bourbons (BUR bəns)
Bousillage (boo zē YÄZH)
Briquet entre poteaux (BRI ket ähn trə po TŌ)
Broutin (brū TAN)

Bute (būt)

Cabildo (käh BĒL dō)
Caddi (KAH dī)
Caddo (KAD ō)
Cadillac, la Mothe (kä DĒ yak, lə MŌT) (kad ə lak)
Ca Ira (sä ē RÄ)
Cajun (KĀ jun)
Calcasieu (KAL kə shoo)
Calvo, Casa (KÄL vō, KÄ sə)
Capuchins (KAP ə chin)
Caresse (kə RES)
Carmelite (KÄR mel īt)
Carondelet, Hector (kä rôn dē LÄ, ector)
Castillo (kas TĒ yō)
Catahoula (kat ə HOO lə)
Cavalier (ka və LYĒR)
Chaise (shāz)
Chalmette (shal MET)
Chandeleur (shahn deh LOOER)
Charendon (sha reen DON)
Chateauguy (shə tō GĒ)
Chauvin (shō VAN)
Chawasha (chə WASH ə)
Cheniers (shə NEER)
Chennault (shə NÔLT)
Chepart (shā PAR)
Chevalier (shev ə LYĒR)
Chicot (SHĒ kō)
Chitimacha (chit ə MÄCH ə)

Choctaw-Apache (CHOK taw ə PACH ē)

Chopin (shō PAN)

Choupique (SHOO pik)

Claiborne (KLĀ bern)

Cloutierville (KLOO shay vil)

Cochons de lait (KŌ shon dā lā)

Cochrane (COCK rain)

Cocodrie (kō kō DRĒ)

Code Noir (kōd nwär)

Coiron (KWÄ ron)

Colfax (KÄHL fax)

Collet (CŌ lā)

Concordia (kon KŌR di ə)

Cortés (kar TAYZ)

Cosme (cos)

Côte (coat)

Coup d' main (coo duh MĀNG)

Coureurs de bois (ku RĀER də bwä)

Courtableau (korh TÄHB lə)

Courtbouillon (KOO bē yon)

Courir (koo RIR)

Coushatta (kə SHAT ə)

Creole (KRĒ ōl)

Crozat (krō ZÄH)

Cyr (sēr)

D'Abbadie (dah bə DĒ)

Dagobert (dag ə BER)

Dakin (DAY kin)

D'Artaguette, Diron (dar ta GET dē RON)

Dauphin (daw FIN)

De Lesseps (del ES seps) (DAY lə seps)

De Muy (dā MOO ē)

Denis (dee KNĒĒ)

Derbigny (der BĒN yē)

De Russy (deh RUSS see)

Des Allemands (dayz äl lə MAHN) (DEZ AL monds)

Desdunes, Rodolphe (DES dūn, ru DOLF)

Deslonde (des LON dē)

Destrehan (d'ess TREE ähn)

Detour des Anglais (dā toor dā ÄYN glā)

De Vaca, Alvar Cabeza (dāy VÄH cäh, ÄHL var käh BĀ sä)

Docantes (dō CAHN tes)

Dormon (DOR mən)

Dostie (DOS tee)

Douay, Anastase (doo Ā, äh nähz TAH sē)

Doucet (doo SĀ)

Doustoni (dust Ē ōn ē)

Driskill (dris KILL)

Dubuclet (du BUK lā)

Dugedomona (DUG də mon əh)

Dulac (DU lak)

Dumas (DU məs)

Du Pratz, Le Page (du PRĀ, le pazh)

Du Ru (dew rew)

Eads (ēdz)

Ecaille (EH kīy) (Ē kîy)

Encalada (ehn kə LA də)

En partie (en par TĒ)

Estevan (es TĀY vähn)

Etienne (Ā tē en)

Evangeline (i VAN jə lən)

Fais-do-dos (fā dō DŌ)

Farril (FAH ril)

Farrar (fə RAR)

Feliciana (fə lish i AN ə)

Felicie (fā LĒ sə)

Ferriday (FAIR ə day)

Filé (fee LAY)

Filhoil (fīl HOIL) (fi YŌL)

Filles a la cassette (fē yē ə lə kə SET)

Fontainebleau (fôn TÄHN blew)

Fortier (fore SHĀY)

Foucault (fou KŌ)

François (frähn SWAH)

Frasch (frash)

Gabriel (GĀ bre əl)

Gallier (GALL ē ā)

Gálvez (gäl VÄZ)

Garcitas (gar SĒ təs)

Gayarre (gäh yə RĀ)

Gayoso (gäh YŌ sō)

Genêt (jə NĀ)

Godchaux (GOD shaw)

Goldonna (GOL don ə)

Gonzales (gōn ZÄ les)

Grau (grow)

Griffes (grief)

Gris-gris (grē grē)

Guachoya (WÄ CHOI yəh)

Hardtner (HART ner)

Haughery (HAW er i)

Helena (HEL e nə)

Hernando (er NÄN dō)

Hidalgo (ē DAL gō)

Historique (hi STOR rēk)

Houma (HOO mə) (HŌ mə)

Iberia (ī BĒR i ə)

Iberville (IB er vil)

Ildefonso (il dā FON sō)

Isleños (is LĀ nyos)

Istrouma (is TROO mə)

Iti shumo (i TI hū mə)

Jacques (zhak)

Jambalaya (JAM bə lä yə)

Jean (jhon)

Jena (JEN ə)

Jesuit (JEZ ū it)

Jesup (JES up)

Joie de vivre (zwah duh VĒV rə)

Joliet (JŌ li ā)

José (hō ZAY)

Joutel (shew TEL)

Juan (hwan) (wahn)

Juchereau (JOO cher rō)
Julien (ju li EN)

Kadohadacho (KAD ō hə dä choh)
Karankawas (ka RAN ka wä)
Kerlerec, Billouart (kair LÄ rek, bē loo WAR)
Kisatchie (kə SACH i)
Koasati (kō ə SÄ tē)
Koroa (KÔ rä wä)

La (lah)
Labadieville (la ba DE vil)
Lafayette (lä fä YET) (la fi ET)
Lafourche (lə FOORSH)
Lafreniere (lä frä NYAIR)
Lagniappe (lan YAP)
La Salle, René (lə SÄL, rē NÄ) (lə SAL)
Las Casas (lahs KAH sahs)
La Tour, Le Blond (lah TOOR, luh BLON)
Laussat, Clement (lō SÄ, KLA mahn)
Laveau (lah VŌ)
Le Blanc (leh blawn)
Leche (lesh)
Leclerc (leh CLAIR)
Lecompte or Lecomte (lə COUNT)
Le Jeune (lē JŪN)
Lemos (LAY mōhs)
Le Moyne (leh MWAHN)
Leonidas (lē ON ə dəs)
Lepinay, (LÄ pē nä)
Linares (lē NAH rēs)
Livres (LĒ ver)
Llulla, Pepe (YU yah, PAY pay)
Lopez (lō PEZ)
Los Adaes (lohs Ä dīze)
Louaillier (LOU el yē)
Louis (LOO i)
Louisiana (loo zee ANN ə)

Louisiane (loo zee AHN) (loo ē zi AN)
Louisianians (loo zee ANN i əns)
L'Ouverture, Toussaint (loo ver TUR, too SAN)
Luis (LOO ēes) (loo I)

McCrea (mak KRĀ)
McDonogh (mak DON ō)
McEnery (mak EN er i)
McIlhenney (mak el HANE nē)
McKeithen (mə KITH ən)
Macon (MĀ kon)
Maestri (MĀ stre)
Maison de Charite (MA zon deh CHAR it tee)
Malbanchia (MAL banch i ə)
Mañana (mon YAH nə)
Manchac (MAN shak)
Mandela (mähn DĀY lä)
Manuela (man ū ELL ə)
Marigny (mä re NYĒ)
Marquette (mär KET)
Marquis (mär KĒ)
Marseillaise (mär se YĀZ)
Mason, Balthasar (MA sone, BAL thə sar)
Matagorda (MAT ə gôr də)
Maurepas (mōr ē PÄ)
Maxent (mak SÄN) (max SON)
Mendoza (men DŌ sä)
Meso (MES ō)
Metairie (MET ə rē)
Michiele (mi SHEL)
Miguel (mi GEHL)
Milhet (mēl Ā)
Miro (MĒ rō)
Mlle., Mademoiselle (mad ə mə ZEL)
Moisant (MOI sänt)
Mongoulacha (mon goo LA chə)

Moniteur (MAHN ih toor)
Montaigne (MŌ tan)
Montpensier (MŌ peen sē yä)
Morales (MŌ räl is)
Morganza (mor GAN zä)
Morial (MŌ rē al)
Moscoso (mōs KŌ sō)
Mouton (moo TON)
Mugulasha (MOO goo ləh shə)
Muskhogean (musk HŌ gən)

Narváez, Pánfilo (när VÄ eth, pan FĒ lō)
Nashitosh (NAK i tosh)
Nasoni (nə SON i)
Natasi (na TÄ si)
Natchezan (NACH ez ən)
Natchitoches (NAK i tosh)
Navarro (nä VÄR rō)
Navatsoho (nan ə SŌ hō)
Negreet (nē GRĒT)
Newellton (NEW el ton)
Nicholls (NIK ulz)
Nisone (nə son Ē)
Nissohone (nə son Ē)
Nouvelle (nō VEHL) (noo VEHL)
Noyan (nwä YÄN)
Nuestra Pilar (noo EH strah pē LAHR)
Nuñez, Vicente (NOON yez, vē SIN tə)

Okelousas (ok e LOO sə)
Opelousas (op ə LOO səs)
Ordonnateur (or don nat TEUR)
Orleans (OR lē ənz) (ÔR lee uhnz)
Ortiz (ôr TĒZ)
Ouachita (WASH i taw)

Paleo (PĀ lē ō)
Panmure (pahn MUHR)
Pascagoula (pas cə goo lə)

Pauger (pō ZHĀ)
Pavy (PAV i)
Pénicaut (PEN i kō)
Perez, Leander (pə REZ, lē AN der)
Périer (PĀ ri ā)
Perique (pe RĔK)
Petit (pā TĒ)
Phares (FAIR is)
Pharr (far)
Philippe (fē LĒP)
Pierre (pē AIR)
Piñeda, Alonzo Alvarez (pē NYĀ dä, ä LŌN sō ÄL vä räs)
Pirogue (pē RŌ) (PĒ rōgue)
Pizarro (pē ZÄR ō)
Place d' Armes (plas duh ÄRM)
Plaquemine (PLAK ə min) (PLAK min)
Plaza de Armas (PLAH thā deh ÄR mähs)
Pleistocene (PLIS tō cēne)
Plessy, Honoré (PLES sē, ôn ə RĀ)
Pointe Coupee (kōō PĀ) (kōō PĒ)
Ponchatoula (pôn chə TOO lə)
Pontalba (pôn TÄHL bə)
Pontchartrain (pôn chär TRAIN)
Potpourri (pō poo RĒ)
Potsherd (POT shurd)
Poulet (pōōl Ā)
Poydras (poi DRÄS)
Presbytere (PREZ bə tere)
Prien (PRĒ ən)
Primot (PRĒ mō)
Prudhomme (PRŌŌ dôhm)

Quadroons (quad ROONS)

Quinapissa (ki nə PI sə)
Ramirez (rah MĒER ez)
Ramon or Ramone (rah MÔN)
Rapides (rap PĒDZ)
Real (rā ÄHL)
Rigolet Bon Dieu (RIG o lēē bon dew)
Rigolets (RIG uh lēēz) (ROW gully)
Rillieux (RILL lou)
Rio de las Palmas (RĒ ō dä lähs PÄHL mähs)
Robeline (RŌ bə lēn)
Rodriguez (rō DRĒ gez)
Roman (RŌ man)
Rost (räst)
Roudanez (rō DAN ez)
Russy (RUS sē)

Sabine (sə BĒN) (sab BĒN)
Salcedo (säl THĀY dō)
Salvador (sähl və DÔR)
Sanchez (sähn CHEZ)
Santiago (sähn tē Ä gō)
Santo Domingo (sähn tō də MING ō)
Sauve (sōv)
Sauvole (sō VŌL)
Sebastian (sāy BÄS tē ən)
Sedella (sā DA yä)
Seigneur (SĒN yēr)
Señora (sān YOR ä)
Señorita (sān yō RI tä)
Serenos (sāy RĀY nyōs)
Serigny (SÁ rē NYĒ)
Sieur (syur)
Siouan (SUE ən)
Soacatino (SŌ cə tin ō)
Soule (sōō LÄ)

Talapouchas (tal ə PUSH)
Taliaferro (TÔL ē vēr)

Tangipahoa (tan ji pə HŌ)
Tchefuncte (che FUNK tə)
Tchoupitoulas (chop i TOO ləs)
Teche (tesh)
Te Deum (tə DĒ əm)
Tejas (TĀY häs)
Tensas (TEN saw)
Terre (tahr)
Terrebonne (TER bon) (TER ruh bôn)
Thibodaux (TIB ə dō)
Toltec (TŌL tek)
Toma de Posesion (TŌ mä day po ze si ŌN)
Tremoulet (TRĒ mou lay)
Tunica (TŪ ni kə)

Ulloa (ōōl YŌ ə)
Unzaga (ōōn ZÄH gäh)
Utrecht (YŌŌ trekt)

Vacherie (va shə RĒ)
Vaudreuil, Rigaud (vō DRĀY, RĒ gō)
Versailles (ver SĪY)
Vieux Carré (vyōō kä RAY)
Villeré (vēl ā RĀ) (vēl är Ā)
Viva el Rey (VĒ vä el RA)

Washa (WASH əw)
Washita (WASH ə taw)
Weiss (wīce)
Wietzel (WĪT səl)
Wiltz (wilts)

Xacatin (hah sē NĀ)
Xavier (ZĀ vi er)

Y (ēē)
Yatasi (YÄT ə si)
You, Dominique (yoo, dô mē NĒK)
Yazoo (YÄZ ü)

INDEX

Book design by Jim Calhoun
Cover art and design by Karen H. Foval
Composed by E.T. Lowe Company
in Garamond type
Printed by Kingsport Press
on 50-pound Arcata Opaque book paper
Smyth sewn and bound by
Kingsport Press in
Appleton Ascot, with
printed four-color process cover